The History of
Speech Communication:
The Emergence of a Discipline,
1914-1945

by
Herman Cohen

Speech Communication Association
Annandale, Virginia

Speech Communication Association
5105 Backlick Road, Building #E
Annandale VA 22003
703-750-0533 Fax 703-914-9471

ISBN: 0-944811-14-0

#30797014

■ ACKNOWLEDGMENTS

I hereby acknowledge my indebtedness to my colleague Gerald Phillips for pointing me in the direction of this study, and for providing encouragement during the years it was being researched and written. I am grateful to Dennis Gouran for providing an environment in which this work could be accomplished, and for his scrupulous reading of portions of the manuscript. I owe a great debt to Rita Munchinski for assuring that facilities, equipment and staff support were always available. I would still be struggling with this volume were it not for the computer salvation provided by Annette Keller. Her skill in formatting and reformatting saved me from what seemed an impossible task. Bonnie Schaedel is thanked for her service as computer mentor in the early stages of the book.

I am grateful to the national office of the Speech Communication Association, especially to James Gaudino for his welcoming acceptance of this book. Carolyn Cooke and Ann Messersmith have my gratitude for shepherding the work through the various stages of publication from typescript to final product.

I am pleased that all or part of this book was read and reviewed by Robert Avery and Malcolm Sillars, both at the University of Utah, and by Samuel Edelman at California State University at Chico. I am appreciative of the time, knowledge and wisdom supplied in conversations and interviews with Samuel Becker, of the University of Iowa, William Burch Jr., of Yale University, Dennis Gouran and Gerald Phillips of Penn State University, Franklin Haiman of Northwestern University, Robert Jeffrey of the University of Texas at Austin, Dale Leathers, of the University of Georgia, and Malcolm Sillars and Richard Rieke at the University of Utah.

The assistance provided by graduate students was invaluable. Maureen Montgomery, my research assistant, was at my physical and intellectual side almost from the time I started to write. She provided materials, searched the library, secured journals, suggested procedures and served as critic in residence. The index to this book is substantially the work of Enrico Pucci. I am indebted to graduate students in seminars who were subjected to the reading of numerous drafts of these chapters: Their comments and criticisms were extremely helpful.

Finally, I express my gratitude to my wife Marlee for her willingness to listen and for her supportive care and concern.

■ CONTENTS

■ FOREWORD

I first learned of Professor Cohen's intention to write the volume that follows some years ago while serving on the Research Board of the Speech Communication Association. At that time, my reaction was that such an undertaking would be of considerable value, but that it would also require a substantial investment of time, personal energy and sustained commitment. Completion of the project has convinced me that both of my initial perceptions were accurate. The document that emerged represents a significant contribution to our understanding of the origin and evolution of an academic discipline and carries the stamp of a distinguished scholar whose vision and dedication in bringing the work to fruition will enlarge the perspective of all who consult it.

Upon entering the profession in 1968, I was struck by what appeared to be an identity crisis among representatives of the field--and which to some extent continues to this day. Do we have a subject matter of our own? Is orality the defining characteristic of the discipline? Is the study of communication most profitably viewed as an art or a science? What is the scope of subject matter appropriate to inquiry? These questions were being discussed—often quite contentiously, if not acrimoniously.

Being concerned with identity is not a bad thing. More problematic in the search for identity, have been the quality of the dialogue and the manner in which it all too frequently has been conducted. What appeared to be lacking among many of the more outspoken participants in the "identity" debate at the time I entered the field was much sense of perspective. To a novitiate, a history such as the one Professor Cohen has produced, would have been most helpful. It would have perhaps been even more helpful to those involved in disputes by better informing the judgments and pronouncements toward which many of them were inclined.

As uninformed as some of the controversies and disputants of the late 1960s and early 1970s were, debate at least reflected an effort to explore the merits of competing positions on issues. My perception is that in the 1990s, while some of the same kinds of issues persist, the reflective posture of those who take positions on them has eroded. I am not sure that most of the participants are even interested in debate. They are more inclined to identify with certain schools of thought and proponents of them on grounds that are largely irrelevant to the merits of ideas. Excessive emphasis on the instrumental value of higher education in the last quarter of the current century has promoted a tendency to endorse or identify with those points of view that appear to have the greatest prospects for one's personal and professional gain. In light of such motives, arguments relating to what the discipline is, is becoming, and should be are not advanced, but merely echoed.

Professor Cohen's excursion through the early history of the discipline and his sustained effort to call our attention to what was intellectually at stake in its emergence can do much to provide a context for renewed and more meaningful examination of matters that influence inquiry, what we teach, and how we view ourselves both now and in the future. To that end, this book is an important addition to the scholarly literature of our field.

Dennis S. Gouran
The Pennsylvania State University

■ INTRODUCTION

This book was motivated by a realization that the field that has evolved into the discipline of Speech Communication is lacking not only a formal history but any real historical sense. In contrast to almost every other academic field, we seem ignorant (sometimes blissfully) of how the discipline reached its present stage. The names of scholars and teachers who were important in the development of the discipline have been forgotten. It sometimes seems that figures in Speech Communication have a shelf life of less than a generation.

The lack of historical consciousness has had serious consequences for the profession. To borrow a term from anthropology, we are a deracinated people who are unaware of our roots. Like deracinated peoples we periodically reinvent our histories, and each time they are different. Our lack of awareness of our past has allowed us to raise questions and engage in disputes which are really part of our heritage. Our ignorance has allowed us to engage in colloquies and disputes, without understanding that the same matters were the subjects of discussions years earlier. For example, with almost monotonous frequency, discussions, sometimes acrimonious, take place between social scientists and rhetoricians. Almost never do they know that there is a deep context for such discussions. They do not know that these questions were raised in the first year of the life of the speech association and that a spirited debate took place among Everett Hunt, Charles Woolbert, James Winans and others as early as 1915.

Speech Communication is, admittedly, a derivative discipline. Yet many present day members of the profession have no clear idea of what disciplines we have drawn on and with what consequences. Many graduate students and faculty, for example, are ignorant of the fact that the contemporary Speech Communication discipline came into being by seceding from its then parent discipline- English. In my own experience I have found that hardly anyone in the discipline is aware that, for almost a century the rhetorical tradition was preserved in literary studies in Departments of English. In this volume I demonstrate that while elocution was the dominant oral form, rhetoric became the concern, and even the property, of English departments. Even a cursory examination of rhetoric and composition textbooks of the late nineteenth and early twentieth centuries will support my assertion.

The story of the founding of the discipline is likewise murky, if not obscured. There is no comprehensive understanding of why the National Association of the Academic Teachers of Public Speaking came into a being, or that speech, or Oral English, as it was designated at the time, was a fairly standard component of the English curriculum. Indeed the association was founded by seventeen dissenting members of the National Council of Teachers of English at an N.C.T.E. convention.

We may want to invent heroic or intellectual causes which brought about a new discipline. The actual history is less dramatic, however. The new profession, by the testimony of its founders, came into being, primarily, to escape the domination of English departments, where the teachers of Oral English occupied a place below the teachers of Literature and English Composition. Only seventeen members of the N.C.T.E. were sufficiently venturesome to form a new association.

Since this study focuses on research in the new profession, it is important that we provide some background for the problems and difficulties, as well as the outcomes of research. From its very beginning, the new profession was ambivalent about research. Woolbert had been told by the administration at the University of Illinois that there would be no Department of Public Speaking at Illinois unless faculty members held doctorates and unless they conducted research. Winans, in a memorable metaphor, told the members of the association that "research is the way into the sheepfold." Thus, research was seen not as the path to answer scholarly questions, but, rather as the path to academic respectability. But what kind of research? How do we do research? These questions were difficult to answer since the members had no research tradition at all. They were, after all, teachers of Public Speaking. In contrast, then, to most academic disciplines, Speech Communication began as a performance field which now had to find a research function. The far more common pattern was that of the field engaged in research making practical applications of its research findings.

Since the new profession had no theoretical or methodological foundation for research, the leaders of the profession urged that teachers talk to and observe workers in other fields. Perhaps there they would find hints as to how they could carry on their research work. Thus, from its very inception the discipline was derivative in theorizing and conceptualizing about its work. In the early days of the profession, little research was produced. Much more space in *The Quarterly Journal* was devoted to pedagogical experience sharing, opinion giving and mutual reenforcement articles. The derivative nature of research has continued, in varying degrees, to the present day.

When I set out, more than a decade ago, to study the history of the Speech Communication discipline, I thought it possible to write a history of all aspects of the discipline from the founding of The National Association of Academic Teachers of Public Speaking to the present. I was soon aware that a complete history would require more than one volume. I saw that my focus, for this volume, needed to be narrowed. Rather than offering an abbreviated narrative, I decided to limit this work to the formative years before World War II. There are good reasons for this choice. The early years of Speech Communication are the least understood, and the most misunderstood, of all the historical periods in the history of the profession. In the years from 1915 through 1945, the foundations of the discipline were laid, and, for good or ill, many persistent characteristics of the discipline were established. Many of the intra-disciplinary quarrels of later years were first aired in these years.

Not all divisions of the profession, in the early years, are examined in this work. The reason for my decision has to do with the later history of the discipline. In its early development, Speech Communication was a much broader field than it now is. Almost as soon as the National Association came into being it became a welcoming host to all the oral arts. Although the title "Public Speaking" was retained for a long time, the profession was much more diverse than the title would indicate. The "orphans" gathered under the Public Speaking umbrella included fields which did not have academic homes and were largely regarded as extra-curricular activities, such as Theatre and Debate. Many of the survivors of Elocutionism also joined the cause, under the new name of Expression or Oral Reading. Persons interested in voice and diction, anatomy, physiology, phonetics, dialects and speech defects were welcomed. Indeed they were among the most prolific early contributors to *The Quarterly Journal*. When radio broadcasting began to develop, it also became part of the discipline.

In time, these protected children grew large enough and strong enough to leave home. They formed their own associations such as The American Speech and Hearing Association and the American Theater Association. To be sure vestiges of these fields remain in the Speech Communication Association and in the journals, but their main research is contained within their own organizations. Although the influence of these divisions was not altogether negligible, I decided to restrict my examination to the those divisions of the profession which remain part of the discipline. This decision was made not only because of space limitations but to provide a sharper focus for this volume. I am hopeful that a second volume dealing with the post 1945 period will allow for as detailed treatment as is contained in this volume.

The reader must remember that the period we cover was quite different from our own. The present Speech Communication Association came into being in the midst of the First World War, and my examination concludes at the end of the Second World War. The social and political climate of those days may not be readily understandable today. For most of this period we found an intense patriotism, especially during the war years. The patriotism was often accompanied by statements of praise for democracy. Articles and books were motivated by the perception that speech was an inherent characteristic of democracy. The profession viewed the teaching of speech as a means of providing students with the tools of democracy. The commitment to speech in the interest of a democratic society was most marked in the late 1930s and 1940s, when the totalitarian states of Europe, who suppressed speech, seemed antithetical to American ideology. Speech teachers, together, with the population in general, sensed a threat to "The American Way of Life."

Ironically these were years where racism and bigotry were seemingly accepted, and even biased material was published in the journals of the association. In the body of this book I cite examples from writers such as Smith, Sheffield and Johnson. A few additional examples would not be out of place as means of illustrating the spirit of the times. In a article titled "Analysis of a Debate on Evolution," Ina Perego of Rockford, Illinois High School included the following gratuitous sentence.

> *Upon the appearance of the Jewish presiding officer and the speakers of the evening, the applause became enthusiastic. (24)*

From our point of view, we are curious as to why Ms. Perego felt it necessary to identify the chairman by his religion. What difference did it make?

A much less trivial example was that of C.M. Wise, then a well known speech scientist at Louisiana State University, in a 1933 article titled "Negro Dialect." I take the liberty of quoting Professor Wise at some length.

> *Male Negroes hear white speech very little, indeed, except from the overseers, who, through enforced continual association with field or industrial workers, often grow to speak considerably like Negroes themselves. The result is not so much an improvement of the lower class speech in respect to pronunciation as a borrowing of high sounding words after the well known Negro fashion. The improvement by this time might have been much greater if the Negroes had been in the least degree literate...they might have realized that there was such a thing as a speech problem and become sensitized to their own speech and that of white people. But the average Southern Negro is entirely unconscious of his variant speech and does not know that improving it would improve his social standing——up to a point where his pigmentation would effectually block further advancement.*

There is the added fact that a very large majority of Southern Negroes have always, both before the war and after, been quite content in their subordinate positions, conditioned to them from childhood. They have no idea of how affairs could be different. Now that Negroes are becoming slightly educated, some of the principles just explained will gradually cease to operate.

. . . In infancy nearly every white person is cared for by a Negro servant and he first learns to talk partly from her. The social scorn which he will later feel for Negroes is not yet operative . . . . (527-528)

In the 1990s we find it difficult to imagine how such a distinguished humanist as Hoyt Hudson, of Princeton University, the editor of *The Quarterly Journal*, could bring himself to accept such racially biased material. Perhaps the racism of pre-war America was so pervasive as to be unconscious. In the body of the text, I refer to a study by Alma Johnson, in 1939, in which she simply assumed that there was a "Negro problem," and that the problem was only a Southern problem. (See Chapter 9, p. 42.) I also cite an essay by W. Palmer Smith in which he argued for the suppression of the use of their native languages by immigrants. He urged his students to help instill "American values" in their families by teaching them to use English instead of their original languages. (See Chapter 3, p. 2-3.) Almost all the authors of this period, including women authors, made almost exclusive use of the masculine third person pronoun. If one did not know the usage of the time, one could assume from these publications that all students and all readers were male. Now and then, students were referred to as "boys" and "girls." At the University of Texas separate courses in Public Speaking were offered for men and women students.

Another important movement of the era covered in this volume was "Social Adjustment" and its corollary "Mental Hygiene." Because of the influence of John Dewey and his popularizers, many members of the profession saw the speech classroom as not so much a place for improvement in communication as an arena for the remodeling or "adjustment" of personality. The Dewey motto of "adjusting the child to society and society to the child" was seen as a mandate to adjust the personalities of the students. It was assumed that most of us were maladjusted. The popularity of Freudian psychology also played an important role and a number of writers stipulated that speech teachers must be trained in psychiatry, and even psychoanalysis. Thus, this work is, in part at least, an intellectual as well as a professional history. The ideas of a profession at a certain time in history must be understood in the context of the social, political, psychological and philosophical ideas then current.

Although my work is more detailed and comprehensive than work done earlier, I would not want to leave the impression that the history of the discipline has not been previously touched. The most complete work to this time is the 1954 publication *A History of Speech Education in America*, edited by Karl Wallace (Wallace, 1954). That praiseworthy work is a series of essays by a variety of writers rather than a unified historical treatment. Also, as the title indicates, its focus tends to be pedagogical. Other works have been useful, if fragmentary or anecdotal. Theodore Windt has written an admirable brief biography of Everett Hunt (1989). Loren Reid has written briefly, but charmingly, of his reminiscences as an early member of the speech profession (1990). Herbert Wichelns' brief history of the early years of the Eastern Communication Association is insightful (1959). The Speech Communication Association published a short history of the association on occasion of its 75th anniversary (Jeffrey, 1990).

The materials for this work were derived from a number of sources. I relied on more than 40 years of experience as teacher, researcher and departmental administrator to provide me with insight and analytical perception. I also made use of my experience as an editor and association officer, especially the presidency of the Speech Communication Association. Most of all I relied on the written record of the profession. I scanned the national journals of the profession from 1915 through 1945. I also read as widely as possible in the books which might bear on the history of the profession. Since an uncommonly high proportion of contributions in the discipline are found in textbooks, I paid particular attention to them.

I am hopeful that this volume will provide an integrative prospect of Speech Communication. I am also hopeful that a second volume will give us a clearer perspective about the later years of the discipline. In a second volume I hope I will be able to analyze the divisions of Speech Communication which did not exist in 1945, or were only at an embryonic stage in their development, such as Interpersonal Communication Organizational Communication, Communication Theory, Health Communication and Gender Communication.

■ 1
THE ELOCUTIONISTS

The development of Elocution as a field of study was an outgrowth of work carried on in Europe, particularly in Britain and France. The movement itself grew out of laudable scientific objectives of eighteenth century investigations. Perhaps the most notable of the investigators was Thomas Sheridan, the Irish teacher of voice and action. In keeping with the precepts of his time, Sheridan and others set out to codify the rules of delivery. Acting on the common assumption of their time that rules and laws for human behavior were as discoverable as rules and laws for nature in general, the investigators set out to observe and record the ways in which humans expressed their emotions. Scrupulous care was taken to examine the physical movements, gestures, postures, and vocal characteristics of people as they expressed varying states of feeling. When the observations had been made, it would then be possible to prescribe exactly, physically and vocally, how each emotion should be portrayed. One of the original motivations for the study of Elocution was for the assistance of actors. In a short time, however, Elocution found its greatest application in oral reading and, to a smaller extent, in public speaking. Elocution was an art which devoted its total attention to the classical canon of "pronunciato." Sheridan defined delivery broadly and gave Elocution the character it would have for well over a century.

> *A just delivery consists in a distinct articulation of words, pronounced in proper terms, suitably varied to the sense, and the emotions of the mind; with due observations of accent; of emphasis in its several gradations; of rests or pauses of the voice, in proper place and well measured degrees of time; and the whole accompanied with expressive looks, and significant gesture. (1)*

Sheridan's work was accompanied and followed by a large number of works on Elocution. Some of them were "scientific" based on observation and categorization; others were "manuals" designed for use by speakers, actors and readers. All of the books contained elaborate taxonomies. As the century progressed towards its end, and in the early days of the nineteenth century, the work became more elaborate and more detailed. Sheridan's principal work, "*A Course of Lectures on Elocution*," contained 262 pages. When Gilbert Austin published his *Chironomia: or Rhetorical Treatise on Delivery* in 1806, it was a volume of over 600 pages, "comprehending many precepts, both ancient and modern, for the proper regulation of the voice, the countenance and gesture. Together with an investigation of gesture, and a new method for the notation thereof; illustrated by many figures" (title page), Austin felt that the teachers and writers of rhetoric had neglected the canon of "pronunciato," and he was determined to rectify their errors.

> *Although the ancient writers have left various and complete systems of rhetoric, as far as relates to the four first divisions, viz. invention, disposition, elocution, (that is the choice of language), and memory; and although modern writers have expounded, and detailed, and added to all these precepts, insomuch that in every language abundant instructions can be obtained in all that relates to these **four** divisions by every man who studies public speaking; and although within the British Islands, in all these divisions, the public speakers have arrived at distinguished excellence; yet it is a fact, that we do not possess from the ancients, nor yet from the labours of our countrymen, any sufficiently detailed and precise precepts for the **fifth** division of the art of rhetoric, namely, **rhetorical delivery**, called by the ancients **actio and pronunciato.** (ix)*

The work of Sheridan and Austin became popular in Britain, as did the writing of a number of their contemporaries, such as Joshua Steele (*Prosodia Rationalis*, 1775) and John Walker (*The Elements of Elocution*, 1781). All of these works, which were to have a decisive influence in America, dealt, more or less, with the same topics covered by Austin—the voice, the countenance, gesture and notations of gesture, position, motion and elevations of the feet, the lower limbs, the arms, the hands, the head, the eyes, the shoulders and the body.

The popularity of the Elocutionists caused a shift in emphasis about oral communication. Numerous manuals were published, some designed for use in the schools, and others for use in the home. The increased concentration on delivery resulted in less attention being paid to the substance of rhetoric. Now the other four canons were neglected as emphasis was given to "pronunciato."

The developments in Britain quickly spread to the United States. Although few rhetorical works had been produced in America, the popularity of elocution prompted the publication of numerous elocution books. As in Britain, they were produced to meet the demands of a diverse market. Some were to be used in the schools but, in time, elocution became more popular for its use in the home, in social and church groups. Books were written to meet that demand. These books not only contained many illustrations with very specific instructions as to how to express a wide range of emotions, they also contained generous offerings of poetry, prose and drama for the use of readers. By the middle of the nineteenth century, Elocution books were in abundance and almost every middle class home contained at least one such volume. The books were often adapted to very specific audiences; some contained material included for children who had just begun to read; others were designed to be read by young people and adults. The selections in the books included many of the "classics" of literature; many of them contained "morally uplifting" selections advocating chastity, temperance and religion. Most of the books also contained physical and breathing exercises, as well as vocal exercises.

The perspective of the American texts was not only derived from the British elocutionists of the previous century, it was also strongly influenced by the thought of Francoise Delsarte, a French teacher of acting, whose writings were deeply imbedded in a mystical Catholic philosophy. In keeping with the Romantic spirit of the times, Elocution assumed the characteristics of a philosophy and a way of life as well as a science. *The Delsarte System of Oratory* proved to be one of the intellectual foundations of American Elocution well into the twentieth century. The character of Delsarte's approach was demonstrated in the preface to *The Delsarte System*.

> *Orators, you are called to the ministry of speech. You have fixed your choice upon the pulpit, the bar, the tribune or the stage. You will become one day, preacher,*

advocate, lecturer or actor; in short you desire to embrace the orator's career. I
applaud your design. You will enter upon the noblest and most glorious of vocations.
Eloquence holds the first rank among the arts. While we award praise and glory to
great musicians and painters, to great masters of sculpture and architecture, the
prize of honor is decreed to great orators.

Who can define the omnipotence of speech? With a few brief words God called the
universe from nothingness; speech falling from the lips of the apostles has changed
the face of the earth. The current of opinion follows the prestige of speech, and today,
as ever eloquence is universal queen. . . .Then virtue and the glory of God should be
the one end of the orator, of the good man. A true artist never denies God. . . . one
cannot treat of eloquence without entering the domain of the highest philosophy.

What, in fact, is oratorical art? It is the means of expressing the phenomena of the
soul by the play of the organs. It is the sum total of rules and laws resulting from the
reciprocal action of mind and body. . . . And thus having become an orator, a man of
principle, who knows how to speak well, he will aid in the triumph of religion,justice
and virtue. (1887, xxiii-xxix)

Delsarte's work was complex and so involved in taxonomy that it is not possible to
summarize the totality of his thought. Nevertheless, we can indicate something of the
flavor of the work. Delsarte's opinion was that, prior to his time, oratory had not really
been taught because it was not grounded in the laws discovered and promulgated by
Delsarte.

Let us note an incontestable fact. The science of the Art of Oratory has not yet
been taught. Hitherto genius alone and not science, has made great orators. Horace,
Quintilian and Cicero among the ancients, and numerous modern writers have
treated of oratory as an art. We admire their writings, but this is not science; here we
seek in vain the fundamental laws whence their teaching proceed. There is no science
without principles which give a reason for its facts. (3)

The premise that Elocution was based on a set of scientific laws and facts was very
influential with American teachers of elocution, particularly later in the nineteenth
century. They also adopted much of Delsarte's complicated classification system and
his perspective concerning the connection of mind and body. The vocabulary was also
taken almost directly from Delsarte. Delsarte's classifications, his conceptions and his
theories are all but unintelligible to the modern student, when they do not seem
ludicrous. The academic elocutionists relied heavily on the Delsartian Scientific Mys-
ticism.

An inspection of Delsarte's work shows it be replete with diagrams, charts and
drawings, illustrating and demonstrating his theories. The theories were based on
Delsarte's notion of a human organism consisting of three states: the eccentric, the
concentric and the normal.

In the sensitive state, [eccentric], the soul lives outside itself; it has relations with
the exterior world. In the intellectual state, the soul turns back on itself, and the
organism obeys this movement. Then ensues a contraction in all the agents of the
organism. This is the concentric state. In the moral or mystic state, the soul,
enraptured with God enjoys perfect tranquility and blessedness. All breathes peace,
quietude, serenity. This is the normal state—the most perfect, elevated and sublime
expression of which the organism is capable. (72)

Delsarte then proceeded to apply this mystic classification scheme to the most minute aspects of delivery. Almost no consideration was given to any others aspects of speech; Delsarte devoted three pages to what he called, "The Oratorical Value of Speech," in which he assigned an inferior role to the substance of oratory. He wrote that

> *[it] lies not in speech, but in inflection and gesture. . . The role of speech, although subordinate, is not only important but necessary. . . Speech has nothing to do with sentiment. . . but a discourse is not all sentiment; there is a place for reason, for demonstration, and upon this ground gesture has nothing to do;. . . "(1887, 128-129)*

Even with his disregard for speech, the emphasis given to voice and gesture was significant. In a work of some 160 pages, Delsarte devoted only about a fourth of the space to voice; the bulk of the book was a detailed treatment of gesture. It is in "Part Second—Gesture" that Delsarte connected his "triune" nature of man with expression. He devoted separate chapters to the head, including the eyes and the eyebrows, and the torso and the limbs, including the fore-arm, the elbow, the wrist and the hand. He classified all visible parts of the body as "concentric," "eccentric" and "normal" and assigned traits of personality to them. For example, he even discussed the relationship between the eye and the eyebrow. "The normal brow and the eccentric eye indicate stupor," is only one of many examples of the connections Delsarte made. For each of the parts of the body Delsarte included a chart and a page of drawings, which he called "Criterion." Under the "Criterion of the Hand," for example, he included nine drawings, among them the "eccentric-concentric" hand, which was "convulsive," the "normal-normal," which denoted "abandon" and the "concentric-normal," which communicated "prostration." In the "Criterion of the Legs," "eccentric-normal" (seventh attitude) represented intoxication. Delsarte ended his work in the same mystical spirit with which it began.

> *Honor then to the fine arts! Glory to eloquence! Praise to the good man who knows how to speak well! Blessed be the great orator! Like our tutelary angel, he will show us the path that conducts or leads back to God. (165)*

We have given our attention to Delsarte, not because he is relevant to the present field of Speech Communication, but because he so influenced the teaching of elocution in American schools and colleges. Even the American home and everyday life were affected, sometimes indirectly, by the teachings of Francoise Delsarte. An examination of some of the most popular elocution texts will serve to demonstrate not only the influence of Delsarte, but also something of the character of the materials being taught to students in American colleges. S.S. Hamill, late Professor of Rhetoric, English Literature and Elocution at Illinois Wesleyan University and the State University of Missouri, published his *The Science of Elocution* in 1882. Although Hamill did not directly acknowledge the influence of Delsarte, he, at some length, discussed "positions of the feet," "position of body," "positions of arms in repose," "position of arms in gesture," "positions of hand" and "the eye and countenance."

Hamill offered a most complex classification system in the 170 pages which he devoted to his discussion of voice. For our purpose, we need not spell out Hammill's complete taxonomy. It is sufficient to note that he devised combinations about voice which are not unlike those that Delsarte fashioned for gesture. Thus we find that "pure," "orotund," "aspirate," "pectoral" and "guttural" tones may all be combined with "effusive" and "explosive" forms.

Of more interest, however, than Hamill's discussion of voice is his "philosophic" statement about elocution as a science.

> *That Elocution is a science, that there are certain established principles observed by all good speakers and violated by all bad ones, none will deny who have carefully investigated the subject. To understand and to practically illustrate these principles should be the prominent object of the student of Elocution. . . . When Elocution shall be studied in our colleges and universities as a science, its principles known and practiced, then, and not until then, will good speaking be the rule, and not, as now, the rare exception. (7-8)*

Moses True Brown, Principal of the Boston School of Oratory, and Professor of Oratory at Tufts College, made an even stronger "scientific" statement than Hamill's and recognized the influence of Delsarte in his *The Synthetic Philosophy of Expression*, published in 1886.

The study of Human Expression has for centuries attracted either the curious or critical attention of one or more of the great minds of each succeeding age. But it is only within the last half of the present century that this important subject has presented such a unity of classified knowledge as to make good its claim to be ranked among the recognized sciences.

> *In conclusion, he [the author] may be permitted, in justice to his intent, to say that he has made an honest and sincere effort to present a consistent and logical body of truth, which he hopes may hold an humble place as a philosophy in the literature of human expression. . . In hopes that if he has been unable to evolve such an orderly procedure of logical statement as may merit the title of philosophy, his effort may stimulate other and better thinkers to a broader unfolding of the Science of Expressive Man. (iii-viii)*

Inscribed on the cover of Brown's book were the names Darwin, Mantegazza and Delsarte. Delsarte we know from our earlier discussion; Darwin is, of course, a recognized historical figure; Mantegazza was Paolo Mantegazza (1831-1910), an Italian physician and anthropologist. In the preface to *The Synthetic Philosophy*, Brown indicated the reasons for his indebtedness to these three figures.

> *. . . to the researches of two great philosophic minds, Darwin and Mategazza, we owe the substance of that body of truth which forms the present Philosophy of Human Expression, and with equal confidence we may assert that to Francoise Delsarte we owe the practical application of philosophic methods to the speech arts,—Reading, Oratory, and Dramatic Expression. (iii)*

Darwin's contribution, wrote Brown, was found in his *The Expression of the Emotions in Man and Animals*, "a treasury of exhaustive research and thorough analysis." Mantegazza is recognized as, "a Florentine scientist who has literally made the globe his quarry in search for human expression." His most important contributions, according to Brown, are found in *La Physionme et l'expression des Sentiments*. "It presents the most critical and exact analysis of the human body and each of the expressive organs . . . suggestive of the widest and most searching methods of modern science" (iv). Brown acknowledged weaknesses in the work of Delsarte, "The knowledge left by Delsarte is fragmentary, and often obscure, and incoherent. And yet the extracts from his manuscripts, . . . show that a strong intellect and a stronger psychological insight were at work. . . striving to solve the problems of human expression. . . He [Brown] has largely adopted the nomenclature of Delsarte. He has not hesitated, however, to criticize the dicta of the great teacher whenever he has found what he considers error or unsound statement"(v, vii).

In spite of his professed "scientific" approach to the study of expression, Brown presented a perspective, modeled on Delsarte, and only slightly less mystical.

> *There are two subsistences of whose reality man is conscious, and whose recorded phenomena, and deductions there from, make the sum of that knowledge which he calls science.*
>
> *These subsistences are (1) Matter; and (2) Spirit, Mind, or Soul. . . . There are two words, everywhere spoken, when man would cover with a name his concept of the aggregate of Matter and the aggregate of Mind. These words are the Universe and God. The Universe is matter in form, occupying Space, existing in Time, held by law. God is Spirit; and is sustaining Cause, animating Centre, and pervading Soul of the Universe. (2)*

From this abstract beginning Brown developed what he termed . . . "a single principle The Law of Correspondence." His explanation is complex and convoluted to the modern student. Brown's Law of Correspondence was divided into nine laws of gesture, derived from Delsarte, Brown spoke of a three-fold division of the body, which corresponded to a three-fold division of the "Psychic."

> I. *The vital nature predominates in the Limbs, and is manifested through their activities.*
>
> II. *The Emotive nature is manifested through gesture and Form of the Torso.*
>
> III. *The Mental nature manifests itself through gesture and form of the head. (43-44)*

Brown offered nearly as many charts and diagrams as Delsarte, but without the drawings. Indeed much of his material was drawn directly from or adapted from Delsarte. As with Delsarte, and in contrast to Hamill, Brown devoted only one chapter of 17 to voice or what he called, "articulate speech." The bulk of the work was devoted to the application of the "laws" to expression and he even accepted the precepts of phrenology.

> *A convex or rounded forehead indicates an undeveloped mind. The prominence of the forehead in form of a horizontal ridge, immediately above the eyebrows, indicates aptitude for long-continued Mental labor. (230)*

Interestingly, the Brown book, in contrast to almost all the other Elocution texts, contained no exercises or drills for the students. One may conjecture that Brown's students learned about Elocution, rather than doing Elocution. On the other hand, Brown may have assumed that the instructors would provide the exercises.

Perhaps the most popular Elocution text in the United States was, *Practical Elements of Elocution* by Robert I. Fulton, Dean of the School of Oratory of the Ohio Wesleyan University and Professor of Elocution and Oratory in the Ohio State University; and Thomas C. Trueblood, Professor of Elocution and Oratory at The University of Michigan. In the third edition, published in 1893, Fulton and Trueblood began with "scientific" assumptions similar to those of Hamill and Brown, and they used the same language to describe the states of the human being.

> *We have found valuable truths which must have a common basis and should meet on common ground. While this volume is a recall to the old truths. . . it presents them in the newer garb and more recent philosophy of Mantegazza and Delsarte.*

> *The student of today is not satisfied with the mere statement of facts; he seeks the underlying principles or laws governing a world of facts. We have endeavored not only to trace each element back to nature. . . but to show its response, in expression, to man's Mental, Emotional, and Vital natures. So far as we know, there has no published attempt to harmonize all the vocal Elements of Dr. Rush's Philosophy with the triune theory of Delsarte. (v-vi)*

The Dr. Rush to whom the authors referred was Dr. James Rush, (1786-1839), a Philadelphia physician who wrote, *The Philosophy of the Human Voice*, which was used by nineteenth century teachers of Elocution as one of the important scientific bases for their teaching.

Fulton and Trueblood began their book with a "philosophical" introduction "which treated such topics as relation of science to art," and the relation of Elocution to "kindred subjects." In writing of Elocution as science and art, the authors offered their conception and definition of Elocution.

> *It is not an exact science but a liberal one through which the highest excellence in the art is attained. . . It is the **purpose of Elocution** to develop individuality, to correct bad habits of speech and gesture, and to make the body a fit instrument to serve the mind and soul. (1)*

Following a discussion of "man's triune nature," derived from Delsarte, Fulton and Trueblood undertook a fairly detailed discussion of the anatomy and physiology of speech, with numerous anatomical drawings and charts of English phonetics, largely derived from Rush. The material on "the elements of vocal expression," was even more complex than that found in the Brown and Hamill texts. The classification system was not much different, but it was accompanied by a large number of diagrams which contained very specific notation schemes, some of which resembled musical scores, while others required the student to assimilate very elaborate notation systems. Part III, "the elements of action," occupied less space than the treatment of voice but was very specific and abundantly illustrated. The authors also specified correlations between action, emotions and traits of character. One example of Fulton and Trueblood's perspective may be seen in their explication of *"First Position Right."*

> *In this Position the right foot is placed about one-half its length in advance of the heel of the left, so that a straight line projected through and parallel with the right foot must strike the heel of the left. The feet are at angle of about 75° with each other. The right foot is at an angle of about 37°, left at about 38°. with the line FF projected in front of the body; the little swaying movements of the body may cause this line to vary about 15°, as indicated by the short arc in Fig. 24, without changing the position of the feet. . . The significance of the First Position Right is that of mentality, self-poised and under control. It is used in **narration, description, didactic thought, and in the gentle emotions**,— in short whenever the speaker is in a normal Mental state, and not swayed by strong emotion or passion; hence our classification of this position as **Mental**. (388-389).*

Fulton and Trueblood even presented a chart which indicated the relationship between the lips and emotional, vital and mental states.

Lips closely shut	*= firmness*
Lips completely apart	*= astonishment*
Lips slightly apart, corners of mouth depressed	*= grief*

Lips slightly apart, corners of mouth raised   = *joy*

Lips completely apart, corners of mouth depressed   = *horror*

Lips completely apart, corners of mouth raised   = *hilarity*

Lips closely shut, corners of mouth depressed   = *discontent*

Lips closely shut, corners of mouth raised   = *approval (371)*

Fulton and Trueblood recognized that discourse was not entirely a matter of presentation by including an appendix on "Truth, Personality and Art in Oratory," written by James W. Bashford, President of the Ohio Weleyan University. Bashford's discussion, covering some 30 pages, was a combination of some of the precepts of traditional rhetoric and the "spiritual" philosophy of the elocutionists, with none of the specific applications, diagrams and exercises presented by Fulton and Trueblood. This point of view was exemplified in Bashford's definition of "eloquence."

> **Eloquence** in its literal meaning is **the speaking out of that which is within one**. . . .*Eloquence is the **art of spiritual reproduction**, rather than of spiritual transportation. It is measured by the success of the speaker in making his thought and feeling and will become incarnate in other lives. (Fulton and Trueblood, 1893, 421)*

Curiously, Bashford's definition is actually closer to some of the psychologically oriented rhetorical writings of the late Twentieth Century than it is to the work of nineteenth and early twentieth century teachers of rhetoric and composition. So far as can be determined, Bashford's conception of rhetoric seemed to have no influence on his contemporaries. Bashford began the appendix with three questions which might well have been drawn from a Public Speaking text of the 1990s. The questions dealt with *"personal fitness* for the task," *"What am I to speak about?"* and *"relating to the audience and occasion."* "Inasmuch, therefore, as we have found the three elements entering into oratory, let us call them by more abstract but inclusive terms, *Personality, Truth, and Art"* (421-423).

In the Introduction to the appendix, Bashford sought to demonstrate the prevalence of his perspective by citing the works of Aristotle, Quintilian, Whately, Herbert Spencer and Phillip Brooks. His first chapter on "Art" was largely concerned with adaptation. He defined art as *". . . The ideal expression of thought, sentiment, or purpose to be conveyed to others"* (431). Bashford began Chapter II, "Art," by emphasizing that Rhetoric and Elocution are subordinate to the search for truth.

> *While recognizing the value of Rhetoric and Elocution, we must admit that they are only **a means to an end**. The aim of public speech is to influence hearers through the truth presented to them. . . For the sake of his hearers and for his own reputation, the speaker must be even more interested in finding the truth than in persuading the audience to accept the view he holds. (440).*

Chapter III was devoted to a four page discussion of "Personality." Bashford made use of a classical conception of

> *ethos. . . only as Truth becomes incarnate in **character**, and art reveals this lofty **personality** to the audience, does eloquence reach its end, and the convictions of the speaker become the purposes of his hearers. . . . We advocate the development of the loftiest **character**, not simply because it is demanded by ideal considerations, but because it is essential to the highest success of the public speaker. (447)*

Thus Bashford presented brief explications of *pathos*, *logos* and *ethos*, without ever mentioning those terms. For the benefit of the students, Fulton Trueblood included a 14 page outline of text, in addition to the table of contents.

A sign of things to come was found in the advertisements inserted by the publisher, Ginn and Company, under the rubric of "Announcements." Among the advertised texts were Fulton and Trueblood's *British and American Eloquence*, a volume dealing with the lives and orations of famous speakers; *Essentials of Public Speaking*, by the same authors; *Extempore Speaking* and *Masterpieces of Modern Oratory* by Edwin Dubois Shurter, Associate Professor of Public Speaking at the University of Texas.

The presence of the Shurter collection of speeches suggests to us part of the reason for the popularity of Elocution in the late nineteenth and early twentieth centuries. To understand the importance of Elocution in American life, we must revisit those earlier days and examine some aspects of social and technological life. Present-day Americans may have some difficulty envisioning those earlier days. We must imagine a world virtually without mediated sound or images. A world without movies, radio, television and phonographs was a world without constant sound and pictures; diversions were not available as they are today. Entertainment was largely self-made. If music was wanted, nineteenth century persons had to create it for themselves. Piano playing was regarded as a requisite for the well-bred young woman and local bands and orchestras were common. Touring theatre companies occasionally visited communities but much theatre was locally produced. Literary societies and reading groups were found in cities, towns and villages across the country. Speeches were special occasions; the Chatauqua and Redpath speakers bureaus provided the setting for speakers. Speakers as diverse as Ralph Waldo Emerson, Mark Twain and William Jennings Bryan toured the country presenting speeches and readings. The American tours of Charles Dickens and Oscar Wilde have been written about extensively.

In this scene an important means of entertainment was the presentation of readings from literature. The need to perform this art proficiently made training in Elocution popular with ordinary men and women and books were produced which would give them explicit instructions to make proper presentations. The books also contained extensive selections from prose, poetry and drama for the student's use. The teacher of Elocution was almost as much a part of the cultural scene as was the piano teacher. Elocution lessons were offered as part of the school curriculum as well as by private teachers, and in churches and youth groups. Elocution was an art for all ages and stages of life, and books were written for general and specific audiences, with instructions and literary selections obviously intended for diverse readers and speakers.

An examination of selections found in these books helps to give us a picture of the levels of literacy of the period. The works to be read and mastered by school children were much beyond our present expectations. For example, in *The Webster-Franklin Sixth Reader and Speaker* by George S. Hilliard and Homer B. Sprague, published in 1878, the students were given 115 "Lessons in Prose" and 114 "Lessons in Poetry." The selections included excerpts from Shakespeare, Dickens, Scott, Irving, Hawthorne, Webster, Emerson and Longfellow, among others. The preface to the book was indicative of the nature of instruction in Elocution in the schools.

> *"The Sixth Reader" is . . . intended for use in high schools, and the most*
> *advanced classes in our public grammar and private schools. While the main object*
> *in its compilation has been to teach the art of good reading, both by furnishing a*
> *choice variety of selections best adapted for practice and reading exercises, and by the*
> *preparation of the most complete and thorough rhetorical instructions on the part of*

its authors and compilers, it has been their design to give this work somewhat more of an elocutionary character. . . . (v)

Elocution was seen as a means of personality improvement by a number of writers. Mrs. J. W. Shoemaker, Principal of the National School of Oratory in her *Advanced Elocution* made her statement clearly.

> *Truly it may be said that this is the Renaissance period in the history of Elocution, and the outlook is hopeful and encouraging. It is evident that teachers, however their methods may differ, are today centralizing about this objective point—the enlargement and elevation of human personality through the proper cultivation of the power of expression. . . it [the book] is a synthesization of the inheritance of the past and the wealth of thought of the present, the latter crystallized from such writers and philosophers as Austin, Rush, Darwin, Delsarte, Engel, Brown and others. (3)*

Thus the same influences which were present in the college level texts were also found in the more elementary books used in the schools. Shoemaker's book contains 280 pages of text and about 100 pages of selections. The selections were classified as narrative and descriptive, characterization and dialect, tender and pathetic, didactic and moral, reverent and religious, national and patriotic, dramatic, declamatory and forensic, colloquial, mirthful and miscellaneous. In the advertisements inserted by the publishers, are listed *Shoemaker's Best Selections for Reading and Recitation*, numbers 1-27 and *Best Things from Best Authors*, volumes 1-9.

Grace A. Burt of Erasmus Hall High School in Brooklyn in *The Art of Expression*, published in 1907, divided her book into Part I "The Art of Expression" and Part II "Recitations for Public Use," which occupied twice the space of Part I. A British work, popular in the United States was *The Reciter's Treasury of Verse with an Introduction to the Art of Speaking*, compiled and edited in 1904 by Ernest Pertwee, Professor of Elocution in the City of London School. Pertwee's introduction to speaking was 70 pages in length, but the selections cover about 800 pages. Although the book was printed in Edinburgh it included at the end "Additional American Recitations" for readers in this country. *Steps to Oratory* by F. Townsend Southwick, Principal of the New York School Of Expression, published in 1900, is about evenly divided between instruction and selections.

Charles Wesley Emerson, President of Emerson College of Oratory, Boston (now Emerson College) was the author of a number of slim books, issued in multi-volume format. Among them were *The Sixteen Perfective Laws of Art Applied to Oratory* (1892), published in four volumes of about 100 pages each and *Evolution of Expression* (1902), also in four thin volumes. In spite of the pretentiousness of their titles, the volumes contained only a few pages of text with the rest of the work being devoted to wide ranging selections. In his brief statements Emerson adhered to views presented by the university elocutionists.

> *It is hoped that the brief explanatory text introducing each chapter may aid teacher and pupil to avoid arbitrary standards and haphazard efforts, substituting in their place psychological law. Growth in expression is not a matter of chance; the teacher who understands nature's laws and rests upon them, setting no limits to the potentialities of his pupil, waits not in vain for results. (1905. Vol. I, 7)*

The awareness of the increasing importance of Psychology was also seen in Southwick's somewhat misnamed *Steps to Oratory* in which he wrote, "The criticism has been justly made that the so-called old elocution did not take account of fundamental psychological processes" (3).

Another indicator of the social climate, vis a vis speech, was the popularity of collections of speeches. These volumes, often published in elaborate, richly bound, multi-volume editions were sold in book stores, by mail through magazine advertisements, and even door to door. One of the most popular sets, judging from its recent availability in second-hand bookstores, was *Modern Eloquence*, published in nine volumes in 1900. Three volumes each were devoted to after dinner speeches, lectures and occasional addresses; the collection was almost 4000 page in length. The prestige of the work is shown in the listing of the "Committee of Selection," which included among others Edward Everett Hale; George McLean, Professor of English Literature at Princeton; Lorenzo Sears, Professor of English Literature at Brown; and Champ Clark, the renowned congressman from Missouri. The volumes contained an abundance of photoengravings of prominent orators. It is worth noting the presence of professors of English on the selection committee. They were the preservers, then, of the rhetorical tradition. (See Chapter 2.) The florid and romantic character of the era is reflected in the introduction to the collection, written by Lorenzo Sears.

> *True eloquence is irresistible. It charms by its images of beauty, it enforces an argument by its vehement simplicity. Orators whose speeches are "full of sound and fury signifying nothing," only prevail where truth is not understood, for knowledge and simplicity are the foundations of all true eloquence. Eloquence abounds in beautiful and natural images, sublime but simple conceptions, in passionate but plain words. Burning words appeal to the emotions, as well as to the intellect; they stir the soul and touch the heart. Eloquence, according to the definition of Lyman Beecher, is "logic on fire." (xiii)*

A less expensive but more extensive set of orations was edited by William Jennings Bryan in 1906. In *The World's Famous Orations*, Bryan reprinted, in chronological order, the great speeches from ancient Greece to his own time. Each period in history was allotted one of 10 pocket-sized volumes. In the preface Bryan noted that he had consulted with the British Prime Minister, Campbell-Bannerman; two former Prime Ministers, Balfour and Roseberry; Churchill; Asquith and Bryce (vii-viii). Bryan, one of the most eloquent orators of his time, offered, in the introduction, a brief guide to the appreciation of rhetoric, much of which is extracted from traditional rhetoric. He presented a view of oratory much closer to the classical writers than to the Elocutionists.

> *The age of oratory has not passed; nor will it pass. The press, instead of displacing the orator, has given him a larger audience and enabled him to do a more extended work. As long as there are human rights to be defended; as long as there are great interests to be guarded; as long as the welfare of nations is a matter for discussion, so long will public speaking have its place. There have been many definitions of eloquence. Daniel Webster has declared that it consists in the man, in the subject, and in the occasion. No one can question the truth of his statement. Without the man, the subject and the occasion are valueless, but it is equally true that without a great subject and a proper occasion, a man speaks without effect. The speaker, moreover, is eloquent in proportion as he knows what he is talking about and means what he says. In other words, knowledge and earnestness are two of the most important requisites of successful speaking. (x-xi)*

The Bryan and Reed collections were only two examples of this extremely popular genre. The fact that they were issued in multi-volume sets and that many were published in leather-bound editions with many illustrations, suggests that the collections were intended for the libraries of bourgeois homes. In addition to general collections of speeches, collections of sermons were also popular. Blair's sermons, for example, although they were first published in the late eighteenth century, remained popular through much of the nineteenth century.

CONCLUSION

The Elocutionary Movement, although it had its inception in Britain, and was refined and romanticized in France, became the dominant mode of teaching speech in the United States in the nineteenth and early twentieth centuries. Elocution saw itself as a "science" and promulgated "laws," which were to be observed by teachers and pupils. The laws themselves were extracted from a mystical "philosophy," much of it the product of the thought of Francoise Delsarte. Movements and vocal tones were assigned relationships to various emotions. Elocution became deeply imbedded in the culture of the time. In a literary-oral society Elocution became an important form of entertainment and, even, of literary improvement since the students read from the great works of British and American literature, as well as trivial and maudlin selections. Almost all of the books for younger readers contained extensive selections from literature. The emphasis in the Elocutionary Movement, however, was placed entirely on the reading of literature, and none on the preparation and presentation of original speeches. The only canon of the ancient five to be treated was *pronunciato*. Nevertheless, the public speech was an important event in most communities and attracted attention which is difficult for a modern student to understand. Collections of speeches were widely published and were very popular.

Meanwhile the rhetorical tradition of speech was being kept alive in the newly formed English departments and in some theological seminaries. The preservation of the tradition is the subject of the next chapter.

■ 2

THE TRADITION IS PRESERVED

While Elocution was the dominant means of teaching oral expression in American colleges and universities, the study of rhetoric and related matters had not disappeared from the curriculum. Much of the belletristic material that had been part of the rhetoric courses was now maintained and expanded in the recently established departments of English. Many of the new English departments found themselves in a situation they had not encountered before. As a result of increased enrollment after the Civil War, a need for basic instruction in speaking and writing English became apparent. Faculty members at American colleges and universities were now engaged in an activity unknown to their European contemporaries—teaching college students to write and speak their native tongues. In part, this situation was due to the proliferation of colleges and universities in the United States. Private or religiously supported institutions were common here, and denominations built their colleges as they moved west. By the early nineteenth century, colleges were much more common and much less selective than in Europe. As a British traveler remarked, "What a magnificent country. France has four universities; England has two; and Ohio has 37." Clearly, many of the American students were different from students in European universities, or even in the elite American universities, where students were expected to be proficient in writing and speaking their own languages.

An additional factor which affected the teaching of English was a result of the enactment of the Morrill Act of 1863. That legislation changed the demography of American higher education by providing for the establishment of institutions now known as Land Grant Colleges. The intention of the legislation was not to develop colleges that resembled the elite universities of the East or even long established state universities such as Virginia and North Carolina. The function of the new institutions may still be seen in the few schools that continue to exist as A and M (Agricultural and Mechanical), A and T (Agricultural and Technical), A and I (Agricultural and Industrial).

These new students could, in no way, be called university students. They did not resemble European university students; nor were they like the students of the established American universities. It soon became clear that they were not really fluent in English. Thus the faculties found it necessary to establish courses which, at that time, were unique to American higher education. Thus, out of this need, courses in English composition were developed. As James A. Berlin has pointed out in "Writing Instruction in Nineteenth-Century American Colleges" the prevalent curriculum had been derived from eighteenth century British rhetorics or from their American adapters (1984).

The new academic settings, resulting from the turn to mass education, created new challenges for colleges. The texts, widely used during the early part of the century, were not suitable for the new academic clientele. No longer could faculties be confident that their pupils could master the works then in use. . . such as Blair's *Lectures on Rhetoric and Belles Letters*. Campbell's *Philosophy of Rhetoric*, Adam's *Lecture on Rhetoric and Oratory* and Whately's *Elements of Rhetoric*. Nor were the appropriate texts found among the works by American adaptors and imitators, including Quackenbos' *Course in Composition and Rhetoric*, Jamieson's *Grammar of Rhetoric* and the books by Abraham Mills which were truncated versions of the British classics, in which Mills often inserted extraneous material from other authors. The books, however, always gave Mills the credit of authorship. James Boyd, another American adaptor, prepared an edition of Kames' *Elements of Criticism*. The chapter on "Standard of Taste," however, contains this head note.

> *The following chapter is taken from one of Dr. Blair's lectures, being far superior to the one of Lord Kames, which is here omitted. (480)*

No matter how adapted and abridged these texts were, they lacked the ability to respond to the needs of the new students; the books were didactic, and in some cases, theoretical and did not include specific instruction and exercises to assist the students in learning to write, speak and read their own language. Because of the inadequacies of their earlier education many of the sons of farmers and mechanics found the existing course material over their heads. The new students required more specific and applied instruction than had heretofore been offered.

Understandably, the new situation called for new instructional materials. After the Civil War the need was met by a very large number of textbooks representing a new genre. . . the English Composition book. Although the genre was new, it, nevertheless, was strongly influenced by the eighteenth century rhetorical tradition. Much of the theory underlying the instruction was derived from the works of Campbell, Blair, Whately and other earlier writers. In keeping with the tradition of belles lettres, no clear distinction was made in the new texts between modes of discourse. Although the primary emphasis was on writing, oral discourse was certainly not ignored and such rhetorical concerns as argumentation and persuasion were directly addressed. Not surprisingly, many of the new texts were produced by professors at Eastern universities, where the preservation of the rhetorical tradition was strongest. Thus the teachers at elite institutions became the teachers of students at inland colleges.

While departments of Elocution and schools and colleges of Oratory were dealing almost entirely with oral expression, departments of English had become responsible for teaching the rhetorical aspects of communication. The Elocutionists gave very little, if any, attention to the substantive aspects of communication. Their major concern was with delivery. Some critics said that the elocutionists were specialists in, "graceful gestures and pear shaped tones." The only canon of ancient rhetoric to which they paid attention was "pronunciatio." The treatment of the canons of "inventio," "dispositio," "elocutio" and even "memoria" were willingly granted to the teachers of English Composition. The teachers of composition became specialists in the new departments of English and were responsible for teaching their students to write and to speak. In due course, many departments instituted separate Oral English sections and the National Council of Teachers of English established an Oral English Division as an integral part of the discipline. In time, the professors of English not only produced English Composition textbooks, they also wrote more specialized texts, particularly those dealing with argumentation and with the general field of Oratory.

Examinations of some of the leading texts of the period give us a clearer picture of the nature and content of the works; especially we can see how the oral and rhetorical aspects of composition were treated. In 1908 William Trufant Foster, Professor of English and Argumentation at Bowdoin College published *Argumentation and Debating*. Much of the book would seem familiar to fairly recent students of the subject. He discussed propositions, analysis, the brief, evidence, argument, examples and refutation. Of special interest is his treatment of style in Chapter 11, "Arousing the Emotions: Persuasion" in Chapter 12 and "Debating" in Chapter 13.

The material on style was not altogether different from the standard English Composition texts of the time, except that more attention was given specifically to oral style and almost all of the examples of effective argumentative language were taken from speeches, some even from student debates.

Chapter 12 was an indication of the attention given to traditional rhetorical principles. Foster began that chapter with a quotation from Cicero; he then went on to make a distinction between conviction and persuasion, which mirrored the ancient and the eighteenth and nineteenth century rhetoricians.

> *Conviction addresses the understanding; it aims to establish belief on rational grounds. But so strong are the influence of inherited opinions, the pressure of the crowd, personal desires and feelings, that action is not often based on purely rational motives. . . . The volition must be secured through arousing the emotions. This the work of persuasion. (262)*

Foster then explicated the sources of persuasion, which reside in "I. The Man; II. The Subject; III. The Occasion." The ancient canon of "ethos" was restated and only slightly modified by Foster.

> *The attributes of the man himself which are most effective in Persuasion are Sincerity, Earnestness, Simplicity, Fairness, Self-Control, Sense of Humor, Sympathy, and Personal Magnetism. (266)*

In his discussion of the sources of persuasion, Foster devoted far more attention to "the man" than to "the subject" or "the occasion." His list and his explanations seem to be derived from the writings of eighteenth century rhetoricians, especially Hugh Blair. The attributes Foster chooses are, however, less numerous than those of Blair. When Foster talked about the subject, he did not devote much attention to the elements of "inventio" discussed by the ancient theorists. Such treatment was unnecessary because he had dealt with argument and evidence, in great detail, in earlier chapters. Rather he emphasized the relation between the speaker, the audience, and the subject in a twentieth century restatement of the Aristotletian triangle. A similar theme was followed in the discussion of the occasion.

Foster devoted Chapter 13 to "Debating" in which he offered detailed instructions about the conduct of debates and in which he treated delivery. In the discussion of gesture he presented a not very subtle attack on elocution.

> *In debating, no gestures are necessary. If any come in response to the thought or feeling of a man as he speaks, and if these appear natural to the audience, so much the better, even though they are not labelled and depicted in books on gesture. So many fantastic tricks have been performed in the name of elocution that audiences are quick to detect and ridicule anything which does not seem to be spontaneous. (Foster, 1908, 320)*

In the chapter on debate, Foster issued a warning about the evil of debating against the students' convictions. He understood, with Aristotle, the need to understand both sides of a proposition but he surely did not favor speaking on both sides.

> . . . we urge students to refuse—even for the sake of practice, even for supposed honor of a beloved institution—to speak against their convictions. . . .This lack of sincerity and earnestness on the part of the speakers is due not only to the lifeless practices of elocution, but as well to the almost universal custom of ignoring the interests and beliefs of the individual speakers. (326)

To strengthen the pedagogical function of his book, Foster offered more than 150 pages of Appendix in which he presented the students with practical materials. Included in the Appendix were exercises based on each chapter, specimen analyses, specimen briefs, and instructions to judges. He concluded with a list of 275 propositions beginning with "The term of office of the President of the United States should be six years," and ending with, "The Rhodes scholarships for the United States will accomplish the objectives of the founder" (486).

Foster was of course, only one of a number of examples of the maintenance of the rhetorical tradition in English textbooks in the pre-speech period. (It is interesting that, in his later years, Foster was a co-author with Lew Sarrett of a popular public speaking text.) Foster's book, which was revised in 1917, was a textbook for students of argumentation and debate, a field with a strong oral component. The interest in rhetoric and orality was hardly limited to that genre, however. Most of the standard composition texts included rhetoric, and in some cases speech, in their treatment of composition. Indeed "rhetoric" was often contained in the titles of these works. *Hart's Composition and Rhetoric,* written originally by John S. Hart in 1870 and revised by James Morgan Hart in 1897, is a particularly good example of the inclusive approach to the teaching of the management of discourse. The elder Hart was a member of the faculty at the State Normal School at Trenton, New Jersey; the younger Hart was Professor of English Philology and Rhetoric at Cornell. At the outset they offered a definition of rhetoric.

> *1. Rhetoric is the art which treats of discourse. 2. By discourse is meant any expression of thought by means of language. 3. Discourse may be either oral or written.*
>
> *Note 1. The Greek phrase the 'rhetoric art' meant the art of the 'rhetor or public speaker. Inasmuch as public speaking among the Greeks, and later among the Romans, was usually argumentative, the adjective 'rhetoric' used as a noun, designated the art of argumentative discourse, persuasion. It has this meaning in Aristotle's well-known treatise, and in Whately's "Elements of Rhetoric," based directly on Aristotle, but commonly in time the term Rhetoric has been so extended in meaning as to include everything connected with composition in all its forms.*
>
> *Note 2. In treating of discourse, we divide the subject into two parts: that which considers the arrangement of the matter or thought to be expressed; and that which considers the manner and details of expression. The former of these is treated under the head of Invention, the latter under the head of Style. (1)*

As part of Chapter VIII Hart presented a brief section on "discourse" in which he discussed orations, addresses, lectures, speeches, and the "general principles of constructing discourse." All of Chapter XI is devoted to "Oratory and Debate." Although the treatment consumed only twelve pages, it was clearly derived from classical rhetoric, including the taxonomy of deliberative, forensic and epidemic oratory. In the development of the text, Hart frequently cited the works of Blair, Campbell and Whatley as well as Aristotle, Cicero and Quintilian, mostly in the section on style, which is quite dependent on eighteenth century writers, particularly Blair. In his treatment of style, Hart used the classification of style as possessing "purity," "propriety," and "precision." This taxonomy was identical with that used by Blair.

One of the more widely used textbooks of the Nineteenth century was *The Principles of Rhetoric* by Adam Sherman Hill, Boylston Professor of Rhetoric and Oratory at Harvard, published in 1878 and revised and enlarged in 1895. (By this time "rhetoric" had come to be understood as being synonymous with composition and Hill's title was an historical artifact, since oratory was no longer taught by the Boylston Professor. The chair, first occupied by John Quincy Adams, was entirely dedicated to the teaching of English.) In the preface to the 1878 edition Hill defined rhetoric in a distinctly classical way.

> *Logic simply teaches the right use of reason, and may be practiced by the solitary inhabitant of a desert island; but Rhetoric, being the art of communication by language, implies the presence, in fact or imagination, of at least two person, the speaker or the writer, and the person spoken or written to. Aristotle makes the very essence of Rhetoric to lie in the distinct recognition of a hearer. Hence, its rules are not absolute like those of logic, but relative to the character and circumstances of the person or persons addressed. . . Being the art of communication by language, Rhetoric applies to any subject-matter that can be treated in words, but has no subject-matter peculiar to itself. (v-vi)*

In keeping with the belletristic tradition of the eighteenth century, Hill did not draw a distinct line between oral and written discourse. In the pattern of writers such as Blair and Adam Smith, he viewed much of rhetoric as being equally applicable to speaking and writing,

> *Part I of this treatise discusses and illustrates the general principles which apply to written or spoken discourse of every kind. Part II deals with those principles which apply exclusively or especially, to. . . kinds of prose writing which seem to require separate treatment. (vi)*

Interestingly, Hill reserved his treatment of argument and persuasion, Part II. We detect traces of eighteenth century faculty psychology as Hill differentiated between exposition, argument and persuasion.

> *Argument, like exposition, addresses the understanding; but there is an important difference between the two. Exposition achieves its purpose if it makes the persons addressed understand what is said, argument achieves its purpose if it makes them believe that what is maintained is true. . . . (327)*

> *Argument, if understood to mean merely the process of convincing, seldom occurs by itself; it is usually combined with PERSUASION, which includes all those processes that make the persons addressed willing to be convinced or ready to carry conviction into action. Unlike argument, persuasion is addressed not so much to the intellect as to the feelings. (386)*

Given Hill's conception of persuasion, we should not be surprised to find that almost all of his illustrations were drawn from speeches, rather than from written prose. Hill quoted copiously from most of the earlier standard rhetorical texts, including Aristotle, Cicero, Quintilian, Bacon, Blair, Campbell, Whately, and DeQuincy.

George Pierce Baker, Professor of English at Harvard, and Henry Barrett Huntington, Assistant Professor of English at Brown, had been students of Adam Sherman Hill at Harvard. In 1895 (revised 1905) they published *The Principles of Argumentation*, which they dedicated to Hill. The first four chapters of the work, dealing with argumentation, analysis, evidence and brief-drawing, resembled Foster's book. The most interesting part of the book is found in Chapter V, which is devoted to "presentation." To the authors, presentation did not mean delivery. In a chapter of a bit over 100 pages Baker and Huntington really offered a small text on rhetoric, under the headings of 1. "Persuasion" and 2. "The Rhetoric of Argument." In those sections the students learned about arrangement and style, as well as the elements of persuasion. In the treatment of persuasion Baker and Huntington devoted about 40 pages to that topic. The section on persuasion connected the elements in the rhetorical situation and showed their relationship to each other. In concluding their discussion, the authors indicated the value they gave to rhetoric.

> *Persuasion may, then arise from the subject itself, the relation to it of speaker or audience, the relation of speaker to audience, and from pure excitation. . .It is not enough. . .to know how to analyze a case, select and value one's evidence, and choose one's means of persuasion: One must also be able so to clothe thought and feelings in words as to get from one's audience just the desired response. . . this essential part of argumentation, the rhetoric of argument, is often neglected by even careful students. (340-341)*

In addition to exercises at the end of each chapter, Baker, and Huntington presented an appendix of almost 250 pages (so long as to require its own table of contents). The appendix contained a variety of materials to assist students in developing their argumentative skills, including examples of argumentative speeches, specimens of matters discussed in the body of the text, and an assortment of exercises. Not surprisingly, the only traditional authority cited was Whately.

John Franklin Genung, Professor of English at Amherst, was one of the most prolific writers of composition textbooks. His *The Practical Elements of Rhetoric*, published in 1886 was his best known textbook and one which clearly showed the influence of traditional rhetoric, beginning with Genung's definition of rhetoric, which included spoken as well as written discourse.

> *Definition of Rhetoric. . ..Rhetoric is the art of adapting discourse in harmony with its subject and occasion, to the requirements of a reader or hearer. The word discourse, as it will be used in this treatise, is a general term denoting any coherent literary production, whether spoken or written. Rhetoric as Adaptation. . . Literary discourse, properly considered, does not exist for itself alone; it is not a soliloquy, but a determinant address to readers or hearers, seeking to impart to them some information or thought, with accompaniment, as occasion requires, of emotion or impulse. Hence, whatever is thus imparted must strive after such order and expression as is best fitted to have its proper power on men; consulting their capacities and susceptibilities. This idea of adaptation is the best modern representative of the original aim of the art. Having at first to deal only with hearers, rhetoric began as the art of oratory, that is, or convincing and persuading by speech; now, however, when the art of printing has greatly broadened its field of action, it must fit itself to readers as well. (1)*

Genung, like many of his contemporaries, divided the province of rhetoric into style and invention.

> *The principles of rhetoric therefore group themselves naturally around two main*

> *topics: style, which deals with the expression of discourse, and invention, which*
> *deals with the thought. (7)*

In Part II "Invention," Genung devoted Chapters VII and VIII to "Invention dealing with Truths: Argumentation" and "Invention dealing with Practical Issues: Persuasion." Genung wished it be clearly understood that argumentation belonged to the province of rhetoric and not to logic.

> *Reasoning as a science belongs to logic rather than rhetoric; we are here*
> *concerned merely with reasoning as it appears in literature, that is, reasoning*
> *contemplating readers and hearers, and adapting itself as an art to their capacities*
> *and requirements. It is to this rhetorical art that we give the distinctive name*
> *argumentation. (407)*

Genung, in agreement with the thought of his time, accepted the distinction between conviction and persuasion. He saw persuasion as almost an exclusively oral mode of discourse ". . .the form that persuasion takes in literature, being almost altogether oral address, is oratory." . . . It is the type which, for success, calls for the largest resources, being an address to the whole man—Intellect and feeling, culminating in an appeal to the will and therefore utilizing most fully the highest powers of the rhetorical art (469-70). Persuasion differed from argumentation not only in its purpose but also in the faculties which were addressed.

> *Argument can demonstrate with all clearness what were good to do; it can convince*
> *the intellect that the truth of a question is here or there; but when it comes to the*
> *actual doing, argument alone supplies no impulse. To awaken feeling and interest,*
> *and so inspire the will to embody the truth in action. To impart this impulse is the*
> *business of persuasion. (447)*

In a continuing recognition of faculty psychology, Genung stipulated that, in order to attain, "The Speaker's Achievement of his Object," the student must address three human faculties: "the Intellect," "the Feelings," and of "The Speaker's Alliance with his Audience," in which he treated of, "Personal Character," and "Sagacity and Tact" (449-455). Of the traditional rhetorical writers, only Whately was cited with any frequency. When Genung wrote about "The Speaker's Achievement of his Object" he was very specifically a faculty psychologist.

> *Now, in order to achieve such an object, the speaker must enlist the whole man on*
> *his side; must make him at once see, feel, and will the truth. In discussing, therefore,*
> *the procedures necessary to this end, we must take up each side of human nature in*
> *turn, and consider what manner of address is most naturally adapted to it. (456)*

Genung, therefore, devoted separate sections of the chapter to "Address to the Intellect," "Address to the Feelings," and "Address to the Will." He stipulated that appeals to feelings must take into consideration the nature of the audience.

> *In addressing the feelings the speaker has to consult wisely the taste and culture of*
> *the persons addressed. Uneducated people are more easily swayed by pathos and*
> *humor; but at the same time more palpable and striking, more coarse-grained means,*
> *have to be used. . . Educated people, on the other hand, act more from judgment than*
> *from sympathy, and hence are less susceptible to emotional appeals; but when they*
> *are moved, it is likelier to be by a pathetic **touch**, or by some stroke on the subtler*
> *chords of human nature, than by a broad joke or a display of tears. (460-461)*

The "Address to the Will" is also adaptive and is dependent on the orator's use of motive appeals.

> *Hence the proposed action must be so placed before them as to coincide with their own desires and interests; not by itself but through certain intermediate active principles called **motives**. It is the skillful appeal to motives that the orator has the secret influence with his audience. For motives are the universally recognized springs of moral action, the causes of which the deeds are the effect. (464)*

When Genung came to write about oratory proper, he reenunciated the classical divisions of speeches as modified in the eighteenth century. He stipulated that all "oratoric discourses" are of two classes; *Determinate Oratory*, "oratory that contemplates direct and immediate action as its result" and *Demonstrative Oratory*, "that class of orations wherein no defined end is directly proposed." Under the heading of Determinate Oratory he placed "Oratory of the law, or forensic oratory. . . , Oratory of legislative assemblies or parliamentary oratory, . . . and Oratory of the pulpit, or sacred oratory . . . Demonstrative oratory was really Genung's version of epideictic oratory. . . . wherein. . . the demands of of persuasion are presented in a general impulsion toward noble, patriotic, and honorable sentiments, and toward a large and worthy life" (472-473). In 1895 Genung published a shorter text, *Outlines of Rhetoric*, which devoted less attention to traditional rhetoric and was more nearly a text in written composition.

One of the textbooks which did not come from a professor at an elite Eastern University was *The Essentials of Argumentation* by Elias J. MacEwan, published in 1899. Neither the publisher, D. C. Heath, nor the author indicated MacEwan's institutional affiliation. In the preface, however, MacEwan wrote that, "No apology is offered for the appearance of this book. It is an outgrowth of a dozen years' experience with classes in one of the leading Agricultural Colleges of the country" (iii). One senses, in MacEwan's description of his students, the differences between his college and the more traditional literary oriented older Eastern institutions.

> *In a school having but a single course of instruction for the first two years, and differing the last two years in only a few technical subjects, a school essentially scientific, the time for literary work was necessarily limited. That kind of literary training, therefore, had to be provided which was most helpful to those who, in spite of limited preparation, must go out to be leaders of their class. They had not time to study all the niceties of literary expression. They could, at best, master only the elementary principles of rhetoric, and make themselves familiar, in a general way, with the ordinary forms of prose composition. (iii)*

Although MacEwan may have had reservations about his students, his treatment of argumentation does not differ substantially from that of Foster or Baker and Huntington. In Chapter III, in the section on persuasion, the author drew from traditional rhetorical sources. He accepts, as did his contemporaries, the division between conviction and persuasion.

> *In matters involving abstract truths, in mathematics, pure science, and in mere matters of historical fact, the work of argumentation is complete when proofs have been so presented as to induce the desired belief in those addressed. Such truths have little or nothing to with human conduct. They are addressed to the intellect and their effect as only intellectual. In discussing matters involving the direction of human conduct, it is not usually sufficient to convince the understanding. Men accept a truth, and ignore it in their actions, or they act inconsistently with it, or even in defiance of it. To direct the conduct of those addressed, the speaker or writer must so*

> *appeal to their emotions, so arouse feeling, as to induce a willingness to carry*
> *conviction into action. This is called Persuasion, and in argument upon human*
> *affairs is almost invariably combined with conviction. (214)*

In the section dealing with persuasion, MacEwan treated "ethos," which he called "personal appeal." His rhetorical emphasis was shown when he wrote of the necessity of an audience in persuasion.

> *Persuasion was formerly confined, as it is now for the most part, to oral address.*
> *It presupposes an auditor or audience. The orator has before him those whom he is to*
> *persuade. He feels their pulse, reads their faces, endures their hisses or is inspired by*
> *their applause. While he is preparing his speech in advance, all this must be present*
> *to him; and even he who would persuade through the editorial column or the*
> *magazine article, must in imagination have before him the class addressed, and seem*
> *to look them in the eye, command their attention, work on their feelings, and use the*
> *expedients of one actually before them. (219)*

Even though he was dealing with both oral and written composition, MacEwan placed great stress on "ethos" which he also referred to as "value of character."

> *Nothing but the sterling qualities of manhood will give a speaker success in*
> *moving his audience through his own personality. Fervor must be sincere, sentiment*
> *genuine, eloquence spontaneous. . .He must be known as a man of industry as well*
> *as of sound judgement. . .The speaker must be known as honest, sincere, fair and*
> *frank;. . .Evident common sense and a modest friendly manner in a speaker will do*
> *much toward making an audience trust his revelation of himself or the management*
> *of his material. . .To have influence, the speaker must be known as a man of ability.*
> *(242)*

MacEwan paid as much attention to "pathos" as to "ethos." In his case, however, he had a more modern psychological approach than some of his contemporaries. MacEwan wrote of the "motives" which the speaker might use in attaining persuasion, and he discusses "classes of motives," "appeal to the highest motive," "low appeal" and "alliance with those addressed" among other topics.

> *The most common means of persuasion consists in placing before an audience*
> *some motive for action. . .In every case the speaker must know to what emotion he*
> *may successfully appeal, or what motive he may present. These motives are so*
> *numerous and diverse that to understand them is no easy matter. . . Other things*
> *being equal, it is best to offer the highest motive which will be effective. Men are*
> *induced. . .by various appeals to the brotherhood of man, to sympathy for those*
> *benefited, to a hope of reward, to mere vanity. . .A motive is more likely to be effective*
> *if it is in accord with the habitual state of mind of the audience. . .Alliance with those*
> *addressed is absolutely necessary so to move them as to stir their activities. (234-241)*

As was not uncommon late in the nineteenth century, MacEwan's text included an appendix of more than 125 pages. In the appendix were found texts of speeches by Webster, Brutus, Marc Antony, Burke, and Huxley, outlines and briefs of those speeches, a glossary of over 200 "Propositions for Argument or Debate" beginning with, "Self-made men are the strongest men," and ending with "The practice of appointing literary men to diplomatic positions is a wise one." In the book itself, MacEwan cited Aristotle, Cicero, Quintilian, Bacon and Whately. It is interesting to note that the book contained an advertisement for the publisher under the heading of "Higher English." Included is O'Connor's *Rhetoric and Oratory*.

As an example of a late nineteenth century textbook MacEwan showed that, at that time, rhetoric and oratory were evidently considered to be a part of "literary studies" and that no clear line was drawn between written and oral discourse.

The conviction-persuasion dualism was the starting point for J. H. Gardiner, a former Assistant Professor of English at Harvard, in *The Making of Argument*, published in 1913. Gardiner felt that this distinction must be understood before the students undertook the study of argument.

> *This active purpose of making other people take your view of the case in hand, then, is the distinguished essence of argument. To accomplish this purpose you have two tools or weapons, or perhaps one should say two sides to the same weapon, "conviction" and "persuasion." In an argument you aim in the first to make clear to your audience that your view of the case is the truer or sounder,. . .and in most arguments you aim also to touch the practical and moral feelings of your readers . . . It would be a waste of breath to convince a man that the rascals ought to be turned out, if he will not on election day take the trouble to go out and vote; unless you have effectively stirred his feelings as well as convinced his reason you have gained nothing. In the latter case your argument would be almost wholly persuasive, in the former almost wholly a matter of convincing. . .These two sides of argument correspond to the two great faculties of the human mind, thought and feeling, and to the two ways in which, under the guidance of thought and feeling, man reacts to his experience. (2-3)*

Although Gardiner designated the consumer of argument as, "the reader," his views seemed to be derived from the traditional precepts of rhetorical theory. His concerns were not much different from those of Blair or Whately. He accepted the conviction-persuasion dualism, and his writing was informed by faculty psychology, although he gave it a slightly modern psychological veneer. In the final chapter of his book Gardiner gave his "readers" specific instruction about debating.

Gardiner dealt with "pathos" and "ethos" in Chapter V, "The Argument Written Out." In section 55 he wrote of the "The Power of Persuading," and he tied persuasion closely to the emotions of the audience.

> *Finally, we have to consider the question of how an argument can be made persuasive probably the most difficult subject in the range of rhetoric on which to give practical advice. The key to the whole matter lies in remembering that we are here dealing with feelings and that feelings are irrational and are the product of personal experience. (190-191)*

In sections 56 and 57 of Chapter V, Gardiner wrote of "The Practical Interests of the Audience," and "The Appeal to Moral Interest." In section 58, he summarized his perspective on persuasion.

> *Finally, we have to consider the appeal to the emotions, which is the distinguishing essence of eloquence,. . . This appeal is through the appeal to principles and associations which are close to the heart of the audience . . . Morality, so far as it is a coercive force in human conduct, is emotional; our moral standards lie beyond and above reason in that larger part of our nature that knows through feeling and intuition. (200)*

Gardiner treated "ethos" in section 59 under the heading of "Fairness and Sincerity." He, essentially, reiterated the traditional rhetorical message about ethical proof, except for his reference to "readers."

> *In the long run, however, nothing makes an argument appeal more to readers than air of fairness and sincerity. If it is evident in an argument of fact that you are seeking to establish the truth, or in argument of policy that your single aim is the greatest good of all concerned, your audience will listen with great favor. (208)*

(Note that Gardiner now had the "readers" listening.)

In spite of his ambivalence about "readers" and "listeners," Gardiner actually devoted four pages in Chapter V to "Voice and Position." In contrast to a number of his contemporaries, Gardiner advocated that his readers study with teachers of elocution or singing. Finally, however, he took a position not unlike that of Richard Whately's advocacy of "natural delivery."

> *What you are or should be aiming at is habit—the instinctive, spontaneous execution of rules which you have forgotten. When the habit is established you can let all these questions of voice, of attitude, of gesture, drop from your mind, and give your whole attention to the ideas you are developing, and the language in which you shall clothe them. (228-229)*

Gardiner's textbook furnished evidence that as late as 1913, only one year before the establishment of the National Association of Academic Teachers of Public Speaking and the founding of the present-day field of Speech Communication, teachers of English were devoting their attention to topics which became standard elements in speech curricula. These teachers of English were concerned with the entire domain of human communication and were willing to consider oratory and rhetoric as components of "literature." Indeed, Gardiner's ambivalence about "readers" and listeners" was indicative of how broad and how rhetorical was the discipline of English. The time-binding between generations of writers on argumentation is shown by the dedications and acknowledgements in their text books. Baker and Huntington dedicated their work to Adam Sherman Hill, and Gardiner and Foster gratefully acknowledged the influence of George Pierce Baker.

A later composition text, and one which more closely resembled the later texts, was *The New Composition and Rhetoric* by Fred Newton Scott, Professor of Rhetoric in the University of Michigan, and Joseph Villiers Denny, Professor of English in Ohio State University. Nevertheless, in their 1911 edition, the authors were explicitly rhetorical in their preface, in which speaking, as well as writing, was considered as a component of composition.

> *Composition is regarded as a social act, and the student is therefore constantly led to think of himself as writing or speaking for a specific audience. Thus not mere expression but communication as well is made the business of composition. (iii)*

(The use of the term "expression" may have been a pejorative reference since that term was often used in the titles of elocution texts.) The use of the term "communication" in Scott and Denney was one of the earliest appearances we have been able to find of the term in a rhetorical context. The Scott and Denney text showed its derivation from eighteenth century writers of the School of Belles Lettres in its emphasis on criticism as well as composition. "The aim is to keep the students' powers of construction and criticism in proper adjustment" (iii). The objective of the book was reminiscent of Blair's lectures, published more than 125 years earlier.

In the preface of their text Scott and Denney made obvious their inclusion of oral discourse, particularly in argumentation.

*Especial attention is paid to oral argument, and explicit instructions are given for
the conduct of debates, both formal and informal. (iv)*

Indeed, the authors devoted more than 60 pages to their treatment of argument. In
contrast to most writers of the period, Scott and Denney did not draw a clear distinction
between argumentation and persuasion: their definition seemed to encompass both
genres and to anticipate later writings in speech communication, notably from Charles
Woolbert, who held that the "conviction-persuasion dualism" did not exist in real life.

*By argumentation a person tries to convince others that they ought to believe or act
as he wishes them to believe or act. (Scott and Denney, 1911, 353)*

The interest in rhetoric and oral discourse was not, by any means, restricted to
writers of English Composition textbooks. For example, Ralph Curtis Ringwalt, Professor of English at Columbia, published *Modern American Oratory* in 1898. The work
consisted of seven examples of American speech-making under the traditional headings of deliberative, forensic and demonstrative oratory, with the addition of the
standard eighteenth century category of pulpit oratory. Perhaps it was a sign of the
times that Ringwalt chose to reprint four examples of demonstrative oratory and only
one each of the other genres. The speeches were preceded by almost 90 pages of
prefatory material which Ringwalt called "The Theory Of Oratory." It is this section
which is of interest to us. The author in his discussion reviewed the historical definitions of oratory, which he found synonymous with rhetoric, from Aristotle to John
Quincy Adams. Finally, he settled on a definition of his own which was consonant with
other definitions of the time.

*. . .Oratory is largely contingent on the character and condition of the minds of
the hearers, and for this reason no absolute standards for it can reasonably be laid
down. . . . No oration can be judged finally from any other aspect than that of a
hearer. Oratory (the true object of which is to produce an effect at the time of
delivery) is composed of two elements, matter and manner; and for the purposes of
ultimate criticism these two are inseparably connected. (6)*

The section dealing with the theory of oratory was a summary of classical and
eighteenth century rhetorical theory designed to provide students with criteria for the
criticism of orations, but also as a guide for students in their own speech making. The
work seemed to be both a later day condensed version of Blair's lectures and a
precursor of Thonnsen and Baird's *Speech Criticism*. Ringwalt provided a bibliography
which consists of "Treatises," including all the major works in rhetorical theory,
"Histories" and "Collections of Speeches."

The inclusion of rhetoric and oral discourse as components of English was illustrated by the advertisements inserted in Ringawalt's book. Under the heading of
"For the Study of English," the publisher, Henry Holt and Co., listed Baker's *Specimens
of Argumentation-Six Speeches*, Wagner's *Modern Political Oration*, as well as Ringwalt's
book. Under the heading *Specimens of Prose Composition*, we find Baker's *Argumenta-
tion-Modern*. In "The Pamphlet Library," is listed a pamphlet version of Wagner's book.

In 1879 William Mathews published *Oratory and Orators*, which went through at
least twelve editions. This work was an oratorical compendium. In the space of some
450 pages and fourteen chapters, Mathews covered such topics as the history of oratory,
the qualifications of the orator, the tests of eloquence, political, forensic, and pulpit
oratory, and a plea for oratorical culture.

In his work Mathews cited most of the traditional rhetorical sources, both classical and modern. His conception of oratory was, as he acknowledges, drawn from Campbell.

> It [eloquence] is, as Dr. Campbell has properly defined it, "the art by which a discourse is adapted to its end;" and therefore it is impossible to say of any discourse, abstractly considered, whether or not it is eloquent, any more than we can pronounce on the wholesomeness of a medicine without knowing for whom it is intended. While there are certain qualities which all discourses have in common, yet there are others which must vary with the varying capacities, degrees of intelligence, tastes, and affections of those who are addresses. The style of oratory that is fitted to kindle the enthusiasm of Frenchmen, would often provoke only the merriment of Englishmen. (212)

During his career Mathews also produced other communication-related books, such as *The Great Conversers, Wit and Humor* and *Words: Their Use and Abuse.*

Austin Phelps, Bartlett Professor of Sacred Rhetoric at Andover Theological Seminary, produced a volume titled *English Style in Public Discourse* in 1883. Perhaps because Phelp's book was drawn from his lectures to future clergymen, he, together with other writers, did not distinguish explicitly between writing and speaking or between readers and listeners. Phelps presented a revealing portrait of college graduates of the time.

> I have endeavored to meet what I have found to be the actual state of culture, on the subject of my instructions, among theological students, the large majority of whom have been graduates of American colleges. The chief features of that culture have been a limited knowledge of English literature, a more limited acquaintance with the philosophy of language, a still more partial familiarity with the English pulpit, and rather crude opinions, with some degree of indifference on the whole subject of the style of the pulpit. (iv)

When Phelps delineated the qualities of style, he drew on the triumvirate of British rhetoric—Blair, Campbell, and Whately. He wrote that, "Four distinct things lie at the basis of these qualities. These are thought, language, the speaker, and the hearer" (6). Out of the relation of thought to language grow Purity and Precision, two of the three prime characteristics explicated by Blair. (Phelps omitted propriety.) The relation of thought and language to the speaker or writer produces Individuality.

> It is that quality by which the speaker diffuses himself through his style; not merely that by which he lives and breathes within and throughout its every variation and sinuosity of expression. It is that which Buffon had in mind when he said, "Style is the man himself," and which others have meant by saying that "style is character." (6)

Although it was more romantically embellished, Phelp's view of Individuality resembled Blair's definition of style, "It is not easy to give a precise idea of what is meant by style. The best definition I can give of it is the peculiar manner which a man expresses his conceptions by means of language. It is different from mere language or words" (101-102).

The relation of "thought and language and the speaker to the hearer". . . produces three qualities of a good style. They are perspicuity, energy, and elegance. Perspicuity expresses the clearness of thought to the perceptions of the hearer. Energy expresses the force of thought to the sensibilities of the hearer. Elegance expresses the beauty of thought to the taste of the hearer (7). These were, of course, terms used widely by the

British writers and were almost identical to the classification of Richard Whatley, who wrote in Chapters I, II, and III of Part III of *Elements of Rhetoric*, "Of Perspicuity of Style," "Of Energy, or Vivacity of Style," and "Of Elegance or Beauty of Style" (167, 178, 213).

Although Phelps book was limited to the treatment of the canon of "elocution," the work was clearly in the rhetorical tradition. It drew upon the ancient writers as well as more modern theorists. In the advertisements inserted by the publisher Scribner, other works by Phelps are listed, including *Men and Books; or, Studies in Homiletics*, and *My Portfolio: A Collection of Essays*.

Another religiously based work published during this period was *A System of Christian Rhetoric* by George Winfred Hervey. Hervey sought in this book to create a synthesis of rhetoric based on scripture and that derived from traditional rhetorical sources. We are not concerned with the religious aspects of the work, but we should note the continuing rhetorical influence. In Book I, which he called "Inspiration in Preaching," Hervey displayed his reliance on faculty psychology when he wrote of "Partial Inspiration: its Effect on the Will," in Chapter I, "Sub-inspiration in its Actions on the Intellect" in Chapter II, and "Inspiration as Affecting Style and Delivery" in Chapter III. In Book II, which Hervey titled "Of Invention," he dealt with such matters as "Of Political Subjects," "Topics or Loci Communes," and "Adaptation." These categories are clearly restatements of traditional rhetoric. In Book III, "Style," Hervey used a taxonomy which was almost identical with that of Whately. Hervey classified style as possessing perspicuity, energy and gracefulness (271). Hervey was also the author of a quaintly titled volume, *The Rhetoric of Conversation, or, Bridles and Spurs for the Management of the Tongue*, which I have been unable to locate.

The works we have discussed were written at a time when Elocution was flourishing, and many of the authors did not hide their opinions, usually disdainful, of that "science." Hervey was both critical and eloquent in his description of Elocution.

> *Elocution is theoretically a part of rhetoric, but practically it is now regarded by many as an independent art or science, demanding its own professors, text-books, and classes. This is all very well. But in order to an [sic] enlightened progress, elocution must ever remember that it is still a part of rhetoric, and that although the two may be prudently separated, yet they are never immersible. Words are deep-rooting, and they who occupy themselves chiefly with whatever appears above ground, with leaves, flowers, and fruits of vocables, run the hazard of forgetting the seeds whence they sprang, and what kind of soil and culture is the most friendly to their growth and fecundity. But, it may be said, is not the mere answer in this matter; all that we now ask is that elocution do not come imagine that rhetoric is part of itself, and so the handmaid be heir to the mistress. (524)*

Foster was more blunt and direct in his condemnation of Elocution. He wrote later than Hervey, at a time only six years before the formation of the discipline of "Public Speaking," and at a time when the status and respectability of Elocution were being questioned at many colleges and universities. Nevertheless, Foster found it necessary to offer his critique.

> *There seem to be abundant reasons why the old style "elocution" has been largely superseded in American colleges and schools by courses in argumentative writing and speaking. There is little place for special teachers of elocution. To maintain such teachers is to place the emphasis precisely where it does not belong. All training in spoken discourse—however its name may shift with the winds and tides of popular disapproval—should be subordinate to training in thinking. It should be the means to the end of clear and direct expression of the pupil's own thoughts. Training in*

*public speaking should be conducted by teachers who aim **first** to produce sound thinkers, **second** to train these thinkers in the clear, correct, straightforward, and effective expression of their own thoughts. (vi)*

Mathews was more ambivalent in his comments concerning Elocution. Although he condemned the excesses of Elocution, he nonetheless, in his chapter "A Plea for Oratorical Culture," criticized colleges for neglecting the teaching of expression.

> *We admit that an over-minute system of technical rules—especially if one is enslaved to them—may and almost always will, have the effect which has been complained of. The great fault of such systems is that they attempt to establish mathematical rules for utterance, when they are as much out of place here as they would be in a treatise on dancing. A proper system of oratory or elocution is not a system of artificial rules, but simply a digest of the methods adopted and practiced by all the great orators who have ever lived. (418, 421)*

Earlier in the chapter, however, Mathews made a case against the deficiencies of the teaching of elocution.

> *Not a year passes but we see hundreds of young men turned out of our colleges whose failure in public life is assured in advance, because they have acquired and probably will acquire no mastery of the arts of expression. . . Skill in oratory is identified with intellectual shallowness . . . . A leading New York journal stated a year or two ago, that it knew of a college, the speaking of its students at one of its commencements ought to have been felt by its officers as a burning disgrace, whose trustees, nevertheless, rejected the application of a teacher of reputation and experience to give gratuitous instruction in that branch of education—For what reason do you think, candid reader? Not because they questioned the competency of the teacher, but because they "didn't believe in teaching of elocution at all!" (409-410)*

CONCLUSION

During the later part of the nineteenth century and the early part of the twentieth century the rhetorical tradition was kept alive in the newly established Departments of English in American colleges and universities. The departments, in a changing academic atmosphere, undertook the responsibility of teaching their students to communicate in English. Although most of the work in the new departments gave primary emphasis to instruction in writing, the courses in English Composition did not slight instruction in speaking. Some departments even created Oral English sections. At the same time the departments undertook responsibility for instruction in belletristic rhetoric, with special emphasis given to Blair, Campbell, Whately and the classical theorists.

The text-books written to meet the new demand were reflective of the situation in American colleges. Although first priority was given to writing instruction, most of the new books integrated a good deal of modern and classical rhetoric. Indeed many of them were written with a rhetorical perspective and included "rhetoric" in their titles.

Most of the text-books paid at least passing attention to oral discourse, and many of them devoted substantial space to speech. In keeping with the tradition from which they sprang, the Composition texts made no clear distinction between writing and speaking. When they stipulated the objectives of their work, the authors, almost always, spoke of improvement in both modes of discourse. The Composition books, which presumably were reflective of the instructing offered, treated the classical proof of "logos," "ethos" and pathos." They treated all of the canons of ancient rhetoric although most attention was given to "logos," "elocutio" and "dispositio." The authors, by and large, adhered to the faculty psychology influenced rhetorics of the eighteenth century and their conception of rhetoric was remarkably similar to those of Blair and Campbell. In their treatment of style, the writers relied on classifications developed by Blair and Campbell and refined by Whately. Overall, however, these were, in no way, theoretical works; they were books designed specifically to meet a demand and they had as their objective the training of not completely literate students in the effective use of their language.

We can classify most of the texts of this period into two categories—those which treated English Composition as a subject concerning written and oral discourse in general and those which were devoted to the more specific application to argumentative discourse. The argumentation texts were closer to being speech texts and when the schism between oral and written communication occurred, argumentation was a sub-field which the new discipline sought to acquire.

The teachers of elocution were not well treated in the writings of the professors of composition. They saw themselves as being concerned with the substance of communication—with logical thinking, clear use of language, cogent organization and purposeful discourse. They saw the elocutionists not only as superficial and trivial but as perverters of rhetoric who stressed all that was offensive to rational discourse.

In all of these texts we find an awareness of the triangularity of rhetoric as propounded by Aristotle. The relations among the subject, the "rhetor" and the audience was made clear. The idea that rhetoric was intended for particular audiences at particular times and places was stated explicitly. As part of the concern with audience the authors were careful to distinguish between conviction and persuasion, a distinction which, by then had become traditional in rhetorical theory.

Thus in the period immediately preceding the foundation of the field of speech, the traditional precepts of rhetoric were nurtured and preserved by departments of English. They helped set the stage for and they provided some of the material for their new rival.

■ 3

THE NEW PROFESSION

The first organization of teachers of public speaking preceded the establishment of a national association by four years. The regional association, now known as the Eastern Communication Association, was founded as the Eastern Public Speaking Conference in 1910. Herbert Wichelns of Cornell University has detailed the history of the founding in *A History of the Speech Association of the Eastern States* (1959). As Wichelns told the story, Paul Pearson of Swarthmore College was the originator of the association. In the spring of 1910 he invited the teachers of Public Speaking in the colleges in Pennsylvania, Maryland, New Jersey, Delaware, the District of Columbia, and southern New York to attend a conference at Swarthmore. He was strongly supported in his efforts by James Winans of Cornell and Wilbur Jones Kay of Washington and Jefferson College. The conference was held at Swarthmore on April 15 and 16, 1910 and was attended by fifteen teachers in addition to Pearson, Winans and Kay. The colleges and universities represented included many of the most prestigious in the East, including University of Pennsylvania, Princeton, Pittsburgh, Johns Hopkins, Haverford, Bucknell, Princeton Theological Seminary and Vassar (Wichelns, 1). It is interesting to note how few of the institutions represented now have active speech programs.

According to Wichelns, based on later letters from Winans, Pearson's action was prompted by a number of motives.

> Probably all three [Pearson, Kay and Winans] felt the need of professional men to know their fellow workers and talk shop. Imitation may have had something to do with it; other departments had national and regional associations. Loneliness may have been an influence; those were the days of small colleges with but one or two faculty members representing speech. Dissatisfaction with the waning elocutionary mode of thought of the National Speech Arts Association may also have been a factor. (1)

In spite of the founders intentions, the influence of the elocutionists was still present. Wichelns quoted from a letter written in 1958 by John H. Frizzell of the Pennsylvania State College that ". . . the elocutionists and expessionists 'ganged up on us to give us a bad time.'" (2)

The second annual meeting of the conference was held at the College of the City of New York. At that meeting the members appointed a committee to "urge the cause of a college entrance requirement in oral English." The members also authorized the publication of a journal. Thus the *Public Speaking Review* came into being as the first publication of a speech association. The *Review* had a life of twenty-eight issues over a period of three and a half years and it began with 83 subscribers. Typically the *Review* "was a pamphlet of thirty-two pages. . . Eight issues a year appeared." (Wichelns, 3).

The editorial policy as outlined in the first issue gives us an idea of the concerns of public speaking teachers early in their history.

> *The departments of the* Review *will be declamation, oratory, extemporaneous speaking, argumentation, acting drama, reading in schools, book reviews, criticisms of speakers and news items. (Wichelns, 3)*

The editorial policy of the *Review* was certainly not that of an organization dedicated to research. Moreover, it indicates that the term "Public Speaking" was applied to a much broader conception of oral communication than the name would suggest.

Although the *Review* was sponsored by a regional association, it attracted contributions from teachers in other parts of the country, notably in the Middle West. Wichelns wrote that of the seventeen men who founded the National Association, eleven had been contributors to the Review. (3)

The *Review* was even less of a refereed or research journal than its successor, the *Quarterly Journal of Public Speaking*. Wichelns reprinted a letter from Winans written in 1934.

> *When Pearson saw he must really send copy to the printer, he sent appeals to members of the board. . . And some of us would sit down and scratch off whatever we could think of, or adapt out of lecture notes. I doubt if ten per cent of the stuff we sent in was carefully prepared; and I doubt if there were any rejected manuscripts. . . . Nevertheless, some good things can be found in the old* Review. *(Wichelns, 4)*

Although the Eastern Public Speaking Conference continued after the founding of the National Association of Teachers of Public Speaking, and as the Eastern Communication Association has continued to this day, it no longer has in its membership many of the elite institutions which joined the conference in 1910. After 1914 the leading profession became the National Association of Academic Teachers of Public Speaking, which had a national rather than a regional focus. Nevertheless, the Eastern Conference set the pattern for the establishment of a national association.

The formal establishment of a national association of teachers of public speaking did not occur in a revolutionary setting. Rather the founding of the organization that was eventually to become the Speech Communication Association was marked by ambiguity and a measure of parliamentary uncertainty.

In the very first issue of *The Quarterly Journal of Public Speaking* James O'Neill of the University of Wisconsin, the first president of The National Association of Academic Teachers of Public Speaking, summarized the circumstances leading to the establishment of what came to be called "The National Association." O'Neill recognized that the teaching of public speaking was widespread at both the secondary and collegiate levels and that, indeed, a number of separate departments of Public Speaking were already in existence. Thus a new discipline was not being founded; rather, for the first time, the teachers of the discipline were being brought together in a national organization. Nor was the new association the sole representative of teachers of the oral arts: the Eastern Public Speaking Conference had been in existence since 1910, met regularly and was already a cohesive force for teachers at some of the country's most distinguished institutions. In addition, The National Association of Elocutionists, now renamed The National Speech Arts Association, was an active representative of teachers of Elocution. The primary identification of teachers of speech, however, was with The National Council of Teachers of English. The N.C.T.E. contained in its organizational structure a section devoted to Oral English. Indeed it was at the 1914 convention of the N.C.T.E. in Chicago that the plans for the formation of the new association were made.

O'Neill in his 1915 report, "The National Association," spoke of the increasing presence of the teaching of public speaking.

> *For a number of years departments of public speaking, under various titles, have been growing in size usefulness, and academic dignity. . . Today the various courses covered by the general heading "Public Speaking" are offered in a majority of the leading colleges and universities in America, in well organized, independent departments. The number of such departments is rapidly growing. Many normal schools, the leading private schools, and most of the large high schools have a definite part of their curricula in the hands of special teachers of public speaking. (1915, 51)*

The actual conditions concerning the teaching of public speaking were discussed in the same issue of the journal by Clarence E. Lyon of the University of South Dakota in "The English-Public Speaking Situation." The title of Lyon's article indicated to the 1915 readers as well as contemporary readers that the relationships between Departments of English and the field of Public Speaking were ambiguous. In the introduction to his article, Lyon admitted his own bias.

> *The question of proper organization of departments of Public Speaking in relation to departments of English ought to be of vital interest to every teacher of public speaking. The difficulties and problems inherent in the situation are manifold. The problem demands our best thought for its correct solution. For my own part, I have been long convinced that the remedy for present ills in department organization is to be found in a clear-cut division of the two departments. (44)*

Lyon undertook to determine the status of Public Speaking through the use of a questionnaire. He surveyed "forty-five institutions, thirty-five of them state universities." He found that, in the thirty-six universities which responded, in twenty three cases "the two departments are now separate." "Two [universities] being without speaking of any kind." Lyon was impressed by the almost unanimous views, of institutions without separate departments.

> *Now, the most striking thing about the situation is that in eleven out of the thirteen cases where they are not separated, those in authority (professionally) believe in the resolution favoring complete separation. And the two dissenting opinions are from professors of English. (45)*

In addition to determining whether English and Public Speaking were taught in separate departments, Lyon also asked two additional questions.

> *Do you employ teachers who teach public speaking only? (Eighteen of twenty-seven institutions answered in the affirmative.) Do you concur in the resolution passed by the Public Speaking Conference of the New England and North Atlantic States to the effect that, "The departments of Public Speaking in American colleges should be organized entirely separate from the departments of English ?" (Twenty-four of twenty-six institutions answered in the affirmative.) (46)*

It is clear from the context of the Lyon article that considerable departmental autonomy existed before the move to establish a national association and that sentiment for separation had been expressed through the resolution of the New England and North Atlantic Conference, which had been adopted in 1913.

Given the setting described by Lyon, O'Neill's narrative of the founding of the association becomes more intelligible since the means whereby the new association came into being were quite complex and involved considerable political and parliamentary maneuvering.

As O'Neill told the story, the first steps occurred almost accidentally at the 1913 meeting of the N.C.T.E.

> *At that time a large number of teachers of public speaking happened to attend the meetings of the National Council of Teachers of English in Chicago. At a largely accidental and wholly informal gathering held at that time, the whole situation was discussed at length. It was decided to send out a questionnaire in order to find out how the teachers of the country felt in regard to departmental organization in their respective institutions, and in regard to a national association of teachers of public speaking. (1915, 52).*

At the 1914 meeting of the N.C.T.E. the results of the questionnaire were reported by C.D. Hardy of Northwestern University at the meeting of the Public-Speaking Section of the N.C.T.E. The response was overwhelmingly in favor of forming a separate association. Of the 116 replies received, 113 favored the formation of a national association. The result, however was not as clear cut as it might seem. The respondents were not at all unanimous about the affiliation of the new association.

> *An opportunity was given for the expression of a preference as to whether such a national association should be an independent organization or a section of the Council of English Teachers, National Speech Arts Association [the former National Elocution Association], or National Education Association. Those voting expressed preferences as follows: Independent, 41; Council of English Teachers, 41; National Speech Arts Association, 10; National Education Association, 16; miscellaneous, 5. (1915, 52-53)*

Since it was evident that the choice was between an independent association and affiliation with the N.C.T.E., a second vote was requested from those who had not voted in favor of those choices. When those votes were computed together with the existing votes for independent status or N.C.T.E. affiliation, the result was still inconclusive. The new total was 57 for independence, 56 for N.C.T.E., and three miscellaneous. (1915, 53)

At the 1914 meeting of the Public-Speaking Section a motion was made that a National Association of Teachers of Public Speaking be organized, "To meet independently of but simultaneously with the National Council of Teachers of English." After considerable debate the motion was tabled by a vote of 18 to 16.

> *On Saturday morning, November 28, 1914, a group of teachers of public speaking met and again discussed the wisdom of organizing a national association . . . . Since a majority of public-speaking teachers are already carrying on their work independently of other departments, and expressed a desire for an independent national association, it was voted unanimously to organize The National Association of Teachers of Public Speaking, for the purpose of promoting research work and more effective teaching. (1915, 54-55)*

Thus the new association was in fact founded by a dissident group of 17 members of the N.C.T.E, a much smaller number than 116 respondents to Hardy's questionnaire or the 45 institutions which answered Lyon's questionnaire. The founding group were later designated as the "Seventeen Who Made History" by Andrew Weaver in 1959. They were:

> I.M. Cochrane................................*Carleton College*
> *Loren Gates*....................................*Miami University*
> *J.S. Gaylord* ....*Winona Normal*
> *H.B. Gisalson* ....*University of Minnesota*
> *H.B. Gough*...................................*DePauw University*
> *Binney Gunnison* ....*Lombard College*
> *C.D. Hardy*....................................*Northwestern University*
> *J.L. Lardner*...................................*Northwestern University*
> *G.N. Merry*....................................*University of Iowa*
> *J.M. O'Neill*..................................*University of Wisconsin*
> *J.M. Phelps* ....*University of Illinois*
> *F.M. Rarig* ....*University of Minnesota*
> *L.R. Sarett* ....*University of Illinois*
> *B.C. Wye*..*University of Cincinnati*
> *J.A. Winans* ....*Cornell University*
> *I.L. Winter* ....*Harvard University*
> *C.H Woolbert*................................*University of Illinois. (195-199)*

O'Neill was elected the President of the new association and Winans was chosen as the Vice-President. An Executive Committee, consisting of the officers and Rarig, who was Chairman of the Public-Speaking Section of the N.C.T.E., was appointed. A Publication Committee was established, but it was voted that the Executive Committee serve as the Publication Committee. An indication that the separation from English was not complete was shown by the appointment of a Committee on Relations with National Council of Teachers of English. Rarig and Winans served as the only members of the committee.

At the first meeting criteria for membership were drawn up.

A.   *Any teacher engaged in giving regular academic courses in separate and independent departments of Public Speaking in universities, colleges, normal schools, or secondary schools in the United States.*

B.   *Any teacher giving such courses in universities, colleges, and normal schools in any department other than the department of Public Speaking.*

C.   *Any member of a secondary school faculty whose work is primarily or exclusively in public speaking, regardless of departmental organization.*

D.   *Any person not included in A, B, or C whose application for membership shall be favorably acted upon by the membership committee. (O'Neill, 1915, 55-56)*

The first convention of the association was set for November, 1915 in Chicago. The dues for membership were "$2.00 per year, plus $1.00 registration for the first year."

After dealing with the report of what had transpired in Chicago in 1914, O'Neill turned to an exposition of the future goals of the National Association of Academic Teachers of Public Speaking. Significantly, the first goal as stated by O'Neill was the encouragement of research.

> *First, we wish to promote and encourage research work in various parts of the field of public speaking; we wish to encourage and assist individuals and committees*

who will undertake by scientific investigation to discover the true answer to certain problems. . . . Our second main purpose is to publish The Quarterly Journal. *Through this periodical we hope to distribute to all the profession the results of research investigation. . . . In short we propose a national organ owned and controlled by the public- speaking teachers of the whole country, of a character that will stand comparison with the professional journals of our colleagues in other departments. We expect* The Quarterly Journal *to serve the teachers of public speaking as other journals serve teachers in other fields. . . . Here we will have at once a means of communication between ourselves and the gathering together of much of that tangible part of the products of our labor by which the profession as a profession will largely be judged by others. In the third place the National Association wishes to assist in every possible way the organization and activity of local or sectional associations and conferences. (55)*

In the statement of the final goal of the National Association, O'Neill reflected the ambivalence felt toward the N.C.T.E. and the reluctance to make a clean break with the discipline of English.

Finally, it may be well to state, what we trust would be taken for granted anyway, that in this moment there is no desire for seclusion and aloofness. . . . Of course we propose at all times and all ways to co-operate cordially with English teachers as individual co-workers and in professional associations, especially the National Council of Teachers of English. We realize that in many ways our interests coincide. We wish to promote helpful relations in every possible way. To this end we have decided to hold our annual convention at the same time and place as that chosen by the National Council of Teachers of English—Chicago, on the week end following Thanksgiving. This will enable many teachers interested in both departments to attend meetings of both associations. (56-58)

The O'Neill narrative calls for observation and analysis since it contains statement of conditions which affected the new association in its formative years and which presaged some of the later developments of the profession.

We should note, first of all, that the establishment of the new association was far from revolutionary. The surveys undertaken by Lyon and Hardy clearly indicated that much, if not most, institutions had already established autonomous Departments of Public Speaking. The surveys also showed that most teachers of Public Speaking desired to have an association of their own. Nevertheless, those teachers of Public Speaking gathered at the 1914 meeting of the N.C.T.E. were ambivalent about whether they wished to form an entirely independent association or whether they wished to retain their affiliation with the N.C.T.E. In the two votes which were taken, the results were a virtual tie between the choices. A motion to create an independent association was tabled in a vote which was also almost a tie. The association came into being because seventeen dissidents chose to break off from the main group and, in a separate meeting, establish the National Association of Academic Teachers of Public Speaking.

We have no records of the attendance at the 1914 meeting; therefore we are unable to say what proportion of those in attendance were represented by "The Seventeen Who Dared." Since 34 persons voted on the motion to table, we might assume that they were about half of the Public Speaking teachers at the meeting. We know who the founders were; we find no records of the teachers who were excluded from the critical meeting. It would be interesting to discover how those who favored affiliation with the N.C.T.E. perceived the new organization as being different from the already existing Public-Speaking Section of that organization.

The institutional memberships of the founders were also significant. Only two of the original members were from colleges or universities outside the Middle West. Nine of the fifteen members from the Middle West represented universities which are now members of "The Big Ten," the universities which, to this day, have been leaders of the profession. The New England and North Atlantic Public Speaking conference was represented only by members from Cornell and Harvard, and there were no representatives from the South or the West. The demography of the founders might be explained on several grounds. Most obviously, in the days before air transportation, the location of the meeting in Chicago, a site more central to Middle Western members, might have explained their predominance. On the other hand, the institutions in the Middle West might have been those most strongly in favor of an independent association. Whatever the case, the institutions which founded the association were the same institutions which continued to dominate the profession for the next 75 years. Thus the N.A.A.T.P.S. was founded in a "rump session" by a group of seventeen Middle Western, predominantly Anglo-Saxon males.

We have referred in the previous paragraph to the initials of the new organization. The name given to the organization was not only ponderous, it was also highly limited and qualified. One might have expected that the group would choose such a name as the National Council of Teachers of Public Speaking, parallel to their parent association, or perhaps they might have selected a simpler name such as the National Public Speaking Association. Neither O'Neill nor others explained why the name was chosen, but we might speculate about the reason. We note that the field of membership was limited to "Academic Teachers of Public Speaking." A reasonable guess is that both the terms "academic" and "public speaking" were included to differentiate the organization from the Elocutionists and private speech teachers. By 1914 Elocution had fallen into disfavor in American colleges and universities. Leff and Procario describe the situation:

> In the early 20th century, academics had come to regard elocution as a cosmetic technique totally devoid of substance. In American universities, increasingly devoted to scientific research, elocution could survive, if at all, as a pariah. The founders of academic speech, then had to declare their autonomy from English, but do so in a way that avoided the odium attached to elocution. (4)

The criteria for membership also seem rigorous in regard to the elocutionists since membership is restricted to teachers "engaged in giving regular academic courses in . . . public speaking." From the beginning then the association was conceived as a society limited to *academics* who were *teachers* of *public speaking*. Later in this chapter we will discuss how this name came to be misleading since its scope was, by no means, limited to public speaking. As we shall also see "Public Speaking " was subject to various interpretations.

The association's attitude toward the discipline of English, and specifically toward the N.C.T.E., was reminiscent of the child who ran away from home but, nevertheless, wanted to retain the respect of his parents. The break from the parent group was clothed in ambiguity and was not really a clean break, let alone a revolution. The chairman of the Public-Speaking Section of the N.C.T.E. was one of the founding members, and a place on the Executive Committee was reserved for the N.C.T.E. chairman. In addition a liaison was stipulated between the N.A.A.T.P.S and the N.C.T.E. In the National Association's statement of goals it was careful not only not to offend the N.C.T.E., it was explicit in its intention to retain a close relationship because "We realize that in many ways our interests coincide." Indeed the Association decided to hold its meetings simultaneously with the N.C.T.E. In fact in its early years it adjourned its meetings so that members could attend the sessions of the Public Speaking Section of the N.C.T.E. We have no records to indicate how many members of the National Association retained their membership in the parent organization.

The first stated goal of the National Association was "to promote and encourage research work in various fields of public speaking." In order to understand the continuing importance of this statement, it is necessary to place it in a historical context. We have noted that the majority of the institutions represented by the original members were Middle Western state universities. By the second decade of the twentieth century these institutions, although many of them were also land grant colleges, had already begun to regard themselves as research universities. The Big Ten universities together with many other large state universities had been affected by changes in American higher education which had begun in the last part of the nineteenth century.

During that time a number of new private universities had been established with lavish endowments by the new class of immensely wealthy American tycoons. Among those universities were the University of Chicago endowed by the Rockefellers; Stanford University, which was established through wealth made in the railroads; Duke University through the benefit of tobacco money; Cornell University, Johns Hopkins University, and Rice University. All of these universities were based on what came to be called "The Johns Hopkins Model." Johns Hopkins, and then the other institutions, sought to establish centers of learning which were different from the existing prestigious Ivy League universities.

The model chosen by Johns Hopkins was that of the German universities of the nineteenth century which regarded themselves as "learning universities" rather than "teaching universities." The German universities perceived their central mission to be the creation of knowledge rather than its dissemination.

The new American universities seized upon the German pattern and deemed that research would be the most significant characteristic of institutions of higher education. By the second decade of the twentieth century the leading American state universities had largely accepted the Germanic conception of a university and had placed high value on research. Not only were universities to be judged by the quality and quantity of their research; the same criteria also applied to departments and disciplines. Thus if the new discipline was to be accepted in the modern university, it had to establish itself as a discipline capable of undertaking and carrying out research.

The Association, however, faced a fundamental problem in meeting its objective; members of the profession had done no research, and it is not at all clear that they knew what research was or how to conduct it. To meet this shortcoming a Research Committee was established as component of the original organization and free-ranging discussion took place in an effort to determine how teachers of public speaking could become researchers. Almost immediately it became clear to the members that they had no research tradition at all and that they must quickly define for themselves what kind of research was appropriate and how they should undertake their work. As the Research Committee recognized in the first issue of *The Quarterly Journal*, the discipline, because of its history, was not really prepared to undertake research. To this point the teachers of public speaking were no more than teachers of public speaking. In contrast to most of the disciplines in the humanities and the social sciences, public speaking had begun as a "performance field" with little or no theoretical background and it was now seeking the means to become a research field. In this respect the new profession more closely resembled the arts than the humanities and the social sciences. In its first report, "Research in Public Speaking," the Research Committee indicated its awareness of the situation and also presaged the derivative development of the discipline.

> *Some academic subjects have arisen as pure sciences and later been applied to the practical problems of life. Public speaking has come by the other road, having been at first a practical or semi-practical subject and then aspiring to become more like a pure science. . . . One advantage accrues its late tendency to orient in research problems, which is that considerable research work has already been done in the borders of its territory by several of the natural sciences, such as physiology, psychology, and sociology. Some benefits are sure to arise also from the scholarly work which has been done in literature and language. (Research Committee, 1915, 25)*

Besides its recognition of public speaking's research shortcomings, the statement of the Research Committee was interesting in its interpretation of research as "pure science." The classification of such fields as psychology and sociology as "pure sciences" is also worthy of our attention. The view that knowledge about research derived from other fields could shape research about public speaking was one that would be persistent for years to come. In a later report from the Research Committee, "Making a Start Toward Research Work," the Research Committee was more explicit about the need to be dependent on the research methodologies of other disciplines.

> *One of the very first requirements is to catch the spirit of scholarly inquiry. This may be done by talking with men who have done research work in some field which is not too remote from the field of public speaking. Such men are inspired with the spirit of investigation and are glad to try to inspire others with the same kind of feelings and ambitions. To get acquainted with with such a worker is often the surest and easiest way to catch the spirit of research. Such an introduction to the work of scholars may lead one to devote himself to similar work for the rest of his life. . . One very suggestive way of learning to think in a searching manner in any new field is by analogy, that is, by taking some type-study in which has proved successful in a neighboring subject, and by adapting the material in the new field point by point to the outline used in the type-study. This analogical treatment is most valuable when the new field is most like the in which the problem has been worked in a type-form. . . Many teachers of public speaking could easily take courses in the departments of physiology, psychology, sociology or literature which would give them a working knowledge of a technique of inquiry which they could adapt to their own field without great difficulty. (Research Committee, 1915a, 194-195)*

These statements from the Research Committee are cited at some length because they are indicative of early problems in the profession, some of which were persistent through much of the history of the association. One can easily discern that the founding of the association was not based on research interests different from those of the parent profession of English. Rather it appears that the founders had no clear idea of what sort of research they should pursue, or, for that matter, exactly what constituted research. They did understand, however, that to exist in an academic environment it was absolutely essential that they conduct research. In the very first issue of *The Quarterly*, J. A. Winans of Cornell, in his article "The Need for Research," made precisely that point.

> *. . . I hold that by the scholarship which is the product of research the standing of our work in the academic world will be improved. It will make us orthodox. Research is the standard way into the sheepfold. (1915, 17)*

The solution to the problem, as seen by early advocates of research, was to emulate the work of those already respected in the academic world. Since, apparently, the founders did not understand how research was to be conducted, they, from the very beginning, consciously or not, saw public speaking research as derivative. Models were to be found outside the profession. Since they were also lacking any theoretical base, they were immediately attracted to the question of how to do research rather than what should be researched. They hoped that observation and consultation with other disciplines would provide them with methodological competence. The derivative nature of much of the research, as well as the reliance on methodological borrowings, became a distinguishing characteristic of early, and some later, Speech Communication research.

So intense was the research motivation that the editor of *The Quarterly* made an offer to researchers which could not be refused. Any researcher was all but guaranteed publication with the highest priority.

> *The Executive Committee of the National Association wishes to do everything possible to aid in the work undertaken by the Committee on Research. In order to encourage workers and to distribute to the profession the results of the work done, we have adopted this policy. We will give in the pages of* The Quarterly Journal *the right of way over all other materials to articles giving the results of research which come to us through the chairman of the Committee on Research. We will give practically unlimited space to such articles and will save space for articles promised to us in advance. If you are working on a research problem, register with the Committee on Research stating on what date you will be ready to publish results. The committee on Research will then assist you in every way possible and will notify the Executive Committee of the probable date of of the forthcoming article for publication. We will not only save space for your article, but will avoid publishing articles of a similar nature on the same subject until yours has appeared. ("The Quarterly Journal and Research", 1915, 84)*

The potential researchers were not completely innocent about research, however. The Research Committee and Winans, in articles in *The Quarterly Journal*, suggested possible topics for research. Present-day members of the Speech Communication profession may find the topics naive but the committee and Winans were reflecting their perception of questions which needed answering and problems which needed to be solved. Winans in "The Need for Research" suggested fairly broad areas of investigation rather than specific research topics.

> *What is worth doing? Suppose we take the matter of voice training. How little we actually know about that!. . . The relation of logic to belief, of attention to belief, of emotion to belief—there is plenty of material ready to be adapted to our use on these questions. Persuasion, a tremendous study in human nature, needs much work. . . . The whole psychology of persuasion needs labor. . . . Many have used the speeches of Brutus and Antony to illustrate persuasion. A Master's thesis might well be written on them, reviewing the literature touching upon them and considering their psychology. . . . The whole topic of "suggestion" bristles with hints for us. . . . Novelty, familiarity, and interest might form a subject for intensive study. Studies in crowds, and in the means of influencing society are pertinent when we take the broader view, and these are waiting for those grounded in history, psychology and social science. . . . Men of literary attainment will find many studies awaiting them in the literature of oratory. If it be worthwhile to study the influences which form a writer, why not the influences which form a Webster?. . . We shall not for some time*

*be driven to to the painful emendation of the text of Demosthenes or to studying the
influence of Quintilian on Patrick Henry. We ought not to be led into dry-as dust
studies, and I do not fear that we shall be. We are too constantly confronted by the
practical nature of our work. Our difficulty will be in getting into a sufficiently
scientific frame of mind. (1915, 20-23)*

Winans was aware, as he was outlining his suggestions, that the new profession
would, of necessity, be dependent on established disciplines. He saw this process as
adaptive rather than dependent or derivative.

*Much work has been done in these fields which is immediately available to us,
provided we learn how to adapt it. For some time, probably, while we are learning
the use of our tools, our work should be adaptation. Then we shall be able to take up
many problems that others will not touch. (1915, 20-21)*

In his article, Winans envisioned research in public speaking as being guided by
"science"and the search for truth and facts. He was certainly aware of the deficiencies
in public speaking research and he displayed a defensiveness about the profession,
which was not unknown in later days.

*We have lacked scholarship. We complain of prejudice and unjust discrimination,
and we have grounds; but we had best face the truth. In the long run men pass for
what they are. We have lacked scientific foundation for our special work. . . . I have
no great humility before teachers in other lines. Toward them we bristle with
defiance. But that is just the trouble- we do bristle. We are not yet able to take
ourselves for granted. We shall feel better and do better when we can. . . we shall not
only stand better when we have more scholarship: when we have the better
understanding of fundamentals and training in the methods which test and
determine truth. . . I look forward to a good time coming when our work will have
the recognition we crave for it: and that will come as a matter of course when we
have established a body of established knowledge. (1915, 17-23)*

The report of the Research Committee in the same issue of *The Quarterly Journal* was
more specific and considerably more detailed than Winan's article. It was, however,
written in very much the same spirit as Winan's work. The committee also seemed to
be governed by the need to be respected and accepted by the generality of the academic
world. They too saw the hope of academic salvation in the "adaptation" of the work
of others. The awareness of the research naivete of the profession is evident in their
statement.

*It [public speaking] now aspires to become a scholarly subject with a body of
verified knowledge and a professional tradition and ethics. . . . It seeks admission to
the society of the elect in scientific work and it is willing to undergo any reasonable
initiation. Knowing that at present the countersign of the society of scholars is
"research," it proposes to fit itself for and engage in research work. ("Research in
Public Speaking," 1915, 24)*

Although the Research Committee recognized the new profession's lack of research
experience and knowledge, and their dependence on other disciplines, we must
acknowledge their desire to engage in research and to recognize the realities of the
academic environment in 1915. The new association must be credited with the foresight
of creating such a committee at the very inception of the profession. They also
recognized the formidable task before them in moving a field toward research when
it previously had been a field almost entirely devoted to instruction in performance.

In spite of these limitations the Research Committee set out to specify what preparation was needed to engage in research and the possible areas in which research might be done. They specified "... an outline of some of the subjects and problems with which students who are preparing for research work in public speaking must become thoroughly familiar before they begin their technical investigations." The main headings of the outline were:

I.   *The structure and function of experience, especially of those experiences which are most valuable for a liberal education...*

II. *The processes involved in studying and learning and the order in which they function...*

III. *The methods of teaching and learning...*

IV. *Methods of studying a book...*

V.   *Interrelations between public speaking and literature, reading and composition...*

VI. *The structure, functions, and development of audiences.... ("Research in Public Speaking," 1915, 25-26)*

The Research Committee felt, "That there is a real need of a bibliography of books on public speaking and kindred subjects can hardly be doubted." The "classification of titles" suggested by the committee gave a clear picture of how the discipline was perceived at its outset and presented us with a taxonomy which may be compared with perceptions of divisions in the 1990s.

1. *Elocution and expression.*
2. *Public speaking and oratory.*
3. *Debate and discussion.*
4. *Expressive reading and reciting.*
5. *Reading and literature.*
6. *Teaching each of the foregoing subjects.*
7. *Physiology and psychology.*
    (1) Of tone production and phonetics.
    (2) Of gesture and pantomime.
    (3) Of spoken language.
    (4) Of written language.
8. *Psychology of social groups.*
9. *Sociology of communication.*
10. *History of each of the foregoing subjects.("Research in Public Speaking," 1915, 28)*

So far as we can discover, no such bibliography was ever published by the association. It would have been interesting to learn which titles the committee might have included. More significant by far, however, is the view of the profession, from the perspective of 1915, that is revealed by the divisions. We do not exaggerate when we say that this is a most remarkable statement in that it is a harbinger of a world yet to be and presages developments which were not to occur for many years. The subjects included in the list indicate a much broader range of interest than the name "public speaking" would suggest. Members of the Research Committee were far-seeing in their inclusion of such categories as "psychology of social groups" and "sociology of communication." These were subjects which had until this time never been included in the domain of public speaking. In fact, in spite of the noble intentions and farsightedness of the committee, many years would pass before these topics were, generally approached by speech researchers. Nevertheless, the list indicates an unexpected broadness of vision of the founders. One is also struck by the use of the term "communication" in the list of topics. This usage did not become common in the profession until the post World War II period.

Another unexpected entry in the list is the inclusion of "debate and discussion." Although numerous textbooks in debate and argumentation had been published before 1915, and articles on the subject beginning with the first issue of *The Quarterly Journal*, discussion was a subject whose serious consideration was not to appear for a number of years. (See Chapter 9.)

Psychology had already begun to influence public speaking by this time. Texts such as Phillips' *Effective Speech* (1908) and Winan's *Public Speaking* (1915) drew heavily on the work of the psychologists of the time , particularly the ideas of James, Lange and Titchener. This orientation was shown by the detailed treatment given to psychology in the taxonomy. Particularly interesting is the inclusion of "psychology of social groups." Except for the work of Mary Yost (1918), the consideration of the group as an element in the study of public speaking was to be delayed for a number of years. It is noteworthy also that the committee linked psychology with physiology and that its domain was extended beyond public speaking *per se* to phonetics and gesture.

An interest in language was manifest in the taxonomy well before it assumed any real importance in the profession. Interestingly, the report did not limit itself to the psychology of spoken language; it also included written language. The linguistic bases for the study of communication were established early, and the founders were concerned with more than "orality." It must be said, however, that this orientation remained dormant until it was awakened externally later in the century.

The committee recognized the importance of historical knowledge of communication in its proposed bibliography by recommending that the "history of each of the foregoing subjects" be studied. This recommendation was carried out only partially. Much attention was given to historical studies in rhetoric and public address in the early years of the profession, but little consideration was given to more general histories of specific components of the new profession or to more general histories of the development of the discipline. In the mid-life of the association and in later years a few historical works were published, notably *History of Speech Education in America* (Wallace, 1954), Windt's biography of Everett Hunt (1990), and Reid's reminiscent history (1990).

The Research Committee seemed conscious of the importance of teaching when it urged that the bibliography include "teaching each of the foregoing subjects." The committee had, in effect, opened the path for pedagogical research. The early issues of *The Quarterly Journal* were replete with articles dealing with pedagogy. That concentration has continued and was reenforced with the establishment of *The Speech Teacher*, later *Communication Education*, in 1952. Although the committee did not sense a conflict between teaching and research, disputes about their relative importance erupted in the journal almost immediately. Later in this chapter we will discuss the debates involving Charles Woolbert and Everett Hunt on the teaching/research question.

The proposed bibliography did not make a clean break with the elocutionary past since it included "elocution and expression" and "expressive reading and reciting" in its list of topics. "Reading and literature" seemed to anticipate the development of oral interpretation as a division of the discipline.

We have devoted considerable space to the discussion of a brief list of topics to be included in a bibliography. We have paid close attention to this section of the report not only because it revealed the 1915 perceptions of public speaking but also because it was an indicator of what the future of the profession might be. Over time the discipline actually came to bear resemblances to this early classification scheme although the resemblances, in most cases, were not apparent for years. The vision of the founders called for a discipline broader and more inclusive than the title "public speaking" would connote. Moreover, the importance of the social sciences was, even then, visible to the founders. Psychology and sociology are mentioned three times in the list of topics and we find only one reference to literature and one to history. It is worth noting that, in its classification, the committee saw the need to research the pedagogy of "performance" areas and to investigate the histories of the more theoretical aspects of the field.

The "topics and problems. . . suitable for scientific study" were not as far seeing and visionary as the categories of the proposed bibliography. Perhaps constrained by their inexperience and limited knowledge, the Research Committee could do no more than propose what now seems to us vague and simplistic questions for investigation. The following is a partial list of suggested research topics.

I.   *A study of the voice. . .*

II.   *A study of gesture. . .*

III. *An analysis of the processes.*
      1. Of speaking to an audience.
      2. Of listening in an audience.
      3. Of preparing an address.

IV.   *A scientific study of the relations between the processes.*
      1. Of speaking and listening.
      2. Of preparing an address and delivering it.

V.   *An experimental investigation to determine what processes are most valuable in the preparation and delivery of addresses in order to secure certain definite results in the audience.*

VI.   *A genetic study of the development of the processes used in public speaking.*

VII. *A study of the more or less unconscious give-and-take between the speaker and the audience.*

VIII. *An interpretative study in the light of modern methods of great orations and orators of the past.*

IX.   *A first-hand study of the methods and techniques of living orators.*

X.   *A study of the history of public speaking and methods of teaching it. ("Research in Public Speaking," 1915, 29-30.)*

In spite of the apparent naiveté of the Research Committee, they understood that research could not be undertaken *de nova*. They realized that preliminary preparation was needed before research work could be done.

> *The field of public speaking is rich in problems suitable for research of a high order. It is for the most part an undeveloped field. One who proposes to do research work in this field needs a general preparation in certain fundamental problems as well as a technical training in special methods and problems to be investigated. Such*

a general preparation would include certain problems derived from physiology,
pedagogy, and sociology. . . . ("Research in Public Speaking," 1915, 28-29)

It is, of course, apparent that the training required to do research was derived from external disciplines and not from public speaking itself. These suggestions spoke to the dependent and derivative nature of a newly established field with no research tradition. Even as the field matured its research continued to be dependent on and responsive to the work done in other disciplines.

"For those whose preparation has included a thorough training in the technique of research work" the committee suggested more specific problems to be investigated.

1. *To determine the effects in the audience of having the speaker stand at different distances from his audience and to determine the best distance.*
2. *To determine the size (real or partly real and partly imaginary) of the audience which makes the utterance most effective.*
3. *To determine the effects in the audience of using one's usual voice and of using an assumed voice.*
4. *To determine the effects on the audience of increasing or decreasing:*
   a) The number of Latin words.
   b) The amount of predication.
   c) The number of figures of speech.
   d) The number of certain kinds of words such as abstract or concrete terms.
   e) The length of the sentences.
   f) The use of analogies.
5. *To determine the effects in the audience of the speaker's using kinds of images, ideas, thoughts and purposes.*
6. *To determine the effects in the audience of directness, repetition, emphasis, clearness, etc.*
7. *To determine the amount and kind of bodily movement which is most valuable in order to secure certain results in the audience and to secure the best growth in the speaker.*
8. *To vary the methods of teaching and to note the corresponding results in the students. ("Research in Public Speaking," 1915, 30)*

These topics have been reproduced rather fully because they illustrate with clarity the self-conceptions held by the National Association at its founding and the ways in which they conceived that research would be conducted. Almost all of the proposed topics are framed in empirical, if not scientific, terms. One of the key words in most of the topics is "determine," indicating that definite conclusions would result from the investigations. Another significant term used in the list is "effect;" The committee apparently foresaw that research would result in specific outcomes. Not surprisingly, much of the early research in the field could be characterized as effects research.

Almost all of the topics suggested that some kind of experiment needed to be conducted to "determine effects," and they were all practical experiments designed to seek specific answers to specific questions and problems, with the expectation in mind that the experiments would result in improved performance and teaching. The topics were, however, so vaguely and broadly framed that the present-day reader has difficulty deciding exactly what the committee had in mind. Although most of the suggested topics required mastery of some experimental methodology, the committee made no suggestions about how these studies might be conducted. They were, of course, aware of their methodological deficiencies and had recommended that other disciplines provide the methodological models for the new profession. Many of the topics now strike us with their innocence and they are not really "research" questions. We must remember, however, that with no background in research, the committee was doing its very best. Their lack of knowledge of, and apparent lack of interest in, theory may explain the very practical nature of the suggested topics. Perhaps the committee was seeking to avoid the "dry as dust" studies condemned by Winans who thought, such studies would not be done because of "the practical nature of our work".

An interesting note concerning research was found in an editorial in the first issue of *The Quarterly Journal*. The editorial reported that "In February, 1915 the National Council of Teachers of English announced through the *English Journal* that a committee on speech training was then being formed."

> *The purposes of the committee, according to official announcements, are in brief as follows: (1) to act as an agent through which may be made a careful and scientific study of the use of the mother tongue; (2) to discover the most common causes of defects in the American speaking voice; (3) to be the means of co-ordinating and giving publicity to the teaching of experts regarding the most efficient methods of improving the voice, especially the voice of children; awaken and educate public opinion in these important matters. ("Two Important Committees," 1915, 74)*

The Association did not see the establishment of the N.C.T.E. committee as being competitive. Rather they welcomed the action of the parent organization.

> *This should be a good thing for both committees rather than a hindrance to either. There is much to be done in this hitherto neglected field, and it is encouraging to note that the value of thorough work is being recognized by men outside the departments of Public Speaking. Any real accomplishment on the part of either committee, whether in scholarly research or in giving effective publicity to the results of such research, will be applauded by everyone interested in American education.* The Quarterly Journal *looks for hearty co-operation between these committees, and bespeaks for both the cordial support of all of its readers. ("Two Important Committees," 1915, 74-75)*

The association's acceptance of the N.C.T.E. committee may have been indicative of the new profession's continuing dependence on the older organization. Throughout a substantial portion of its early history the association had an ambivalent relationship with the discipline of English. In any case they accepted the event with no critical comment.

The N.C.T.E. committee was, in fact, not so much cooperative with the National Association as it was reactionary, in the sense that its mandate was to concern itself with the very matters that had caused elocution to fall into disrepute. Its focus was almost entirely on voice improvement, not on the improvement of oral discourse. The concern of the N.C.T.E. may well have signified the conception which English had of Public Speaking and may point to the reasons for the separation of 1914. The performance aspects of oral communication seemed to belong to the domain of speech while the substantive rhetorical matters remained the province of English; they would continue to write the rhetoric textbooks and teach the rhetoric courses. (See Chapter 2.) The research they proposed to undertake was quite different from that envisioned by the association.

The pronouncements from Winans and the Research Committee were, by no means, universally accepted. In the very next issue of *The Quarterly Journal* Everett Lee Hunt, then of Huron College, raised doubts about the orientation of the profession and questioned whether research had any role to play in the discipline of public speaking, in his article, "The Scientific Spirit in Public Speaking," he conceived of public speaking as a field dedicated to educating young public speakers rather than to scientific investigation. Hunt was careful in his article to differentiate between scholarship and research. Scholarship was a necessity for all teachers of public speaking; scientific research was something else.

> *The man who can attempt to fill a chair of public speaking without being constantly led by his intellectual curiosity into a multitude of scholarly pursuits is not worthy of a position on a college and university faculty. A teacher of public speaking must inevitably hold for himself as high an ideal of scholarship as is held by any member of any profession. But that is a very different matter from holding before an association of public speaking teachers the ideal of research as a means of traveling the orthodox way into the sheepfold. (Hunt, 185)*

Hunt had noticed the submissive metaphor used by Winans when he said of research, "It will make us orthodox. Research is the standard way into the sheepfold." Hunt did not feel that the new profession should regard its members as sheep nor did he respect orthodoxy for its own sake.

> *I am not a radical of the type which opposes orthodoxy merely because it is orthodoxy. If I were sure that we belonged in the fold, or that we should be happy after we were safely within, I should be among the first to follow a shepherd. Again, I do not protest against the "research" ideal because of a desire to be "artistic" or to pose as a dilettante. But I do protest as emphatically as possible against the worship of scientific research as the **summum bonum** in our profession. (1915, 185-186)*

Hunt envisioned public speaking as teaching field rather than a research field. He meant no disrespect for science, but he saw its function as the search for and the creation of knowledge, useful or not. Public speaking, on the other hand, did not seek for knowledge. It was, rather, a practical field and a creative field-not a scientific field.

> *I have only praise for the true scientific spirit when it is acting in its own field. But it is not in any sense the chief purpose of chairs of public speaking to annex realms of undiscovered knowledge. . . . The function of teachers is to produce public speakers, ridiculous as that idea may be to seem to university scholars. (1915, 186)*

The young Hunt, then age 25, writing from the sanctity of a small undergraduate college in South Dakota might have been content had public speaking continued as a discipline primarily concerned with performance and with teaching, but his vision was not consonant with the vision, held by the Research Committee and by Winans, that without research competence the new profession would not be welcomed into the community of university scholars. Hunt, in fact, depicted public speaking as being closer to the arts than to the sciences, and he thought that the creativity of public speaking set it aside from most other courses.

> *The distinctive mark of the work in public speaking is that it is creative. Whether a student is giving forth a message of his own, combining facts in an argument, or interpreting a lyric poem, he must give full play to a vigorous creative imagination. Nine tenths of the college curriculum is absolutely non-creative. . . . How few students have any knowledge of the working of what I may term the creative mood. How laborious a process original thinking is to them until they become awakened to its joys. How unbalanced is a curriculum which constantly centers the student's mind upon material impersonal objects instead of encouraging a free expression of his own individuality. It is because of this distinctive creative element, this unique*

feature in college work, that effort expended upon courses in public speaking seems so worth while. (1915, 187-188)

From his 1915 perspective Hunt apparently saw the academic world as a dichotomy between science and creativity. Although he mentioned the study of literature, he made no reference to humanities or social sciences, which were already fairly highly developed by that time. He also seemed to associate "research" solely with science and he did not seem to be aware of other modes of research.

It was Hunt's opinion that the public speaking profession would distinguish itself through the quality of its students rather than through its research.

> *Professors are learning the joy of active life in the full tide of human events. As a result of this union the time is not far distant when the teachers of public speaking will be known by their fruits. It is the results of their instruction that will win recognition for them, not their methods. When among the alumni of any institution there is a large number of men who feel their intellectual interests have been broadened, their self-confidence and power increased, by the contact with instructors in oratory and debate, then the general recognition of the chair of public speaking will be inevitable. (1915, 192-193)*

Hunt saw research as specialization and felt that the teacher of public speaking could not compete with specialists. Public speaking, for Hunt, was an integrative field.

> *The one faculty which marks the successful teacher in oratory and debate is a certain expertness in association. It is his judgment in combining factors, and not his mastery of one, that brings results. No teacher of public speaking can hope to preserve a proper balance in his work and excel the psychologist in his research, the sociologist in his knowledge of reform, the rhetorician in his mastery of style, the historian in his certainty of all the events that preceded the gunpowder plot. Yet when he enters these fields under the banner of science he inevitably invites critical comparison. (Hunt, 1915, 190)*

One is fascinated by Hunt's assertions that public speaking could not be competitive with precisely the disciplines it later came to depend on.

In the conclusion to his article Hunt gave token recognition to the importance of graduate study, but he held firmly to his conception of public speaking.

> *I hope universities like Cornell and Harvard will soon offer graduate work in public speaking. I should be among the first to take advantage of such an opportunity. But may we as a profession never accept scholarship in lieu of spontaneity. May we never substitute imitation for originality. May we never exalt learning above sincerity, academic recognition above service, or logic above life. (1915, 193)*

In light of Hunt's later career his youthful opinions are interesting since he went from Huron College to Cornell University, a research directed institution, and later he moved to Swarthmore College, an elite Liberal Arts college, where he served many years as Dean. Later in his career Hunt was a productive "researcher," especially in his work on Plato and classical rhetoric. Perhaps, given his definition, he did not consider his work to be research. Hunt was not allowed to attack research without an energetic rejoinder. In the very same number of *The Quarterly Journal* Winans replied in an editorial titled "Should We Worry."

For a fuller description of Hunt's later career see T.O.Windt's *Rhetoric as a Human Adventure: A Short Biography of Everett Hunt.* (1990)

Winans, a 43 year old full professor at Cornell, refuted the 25 year old Hunt with no trace of condescension. Winans gently accused Hunt of not understanding the difference between scholasticism and research. It was really scholasticism which was the object of Hunt's displeasure, not authentic scholarship. Winans agreed that scholasticism should be shunned. "We all know the thing he is fearing and we all dislike it." (1915a 197). Besides, Winans felt that Hunt was attacking a non-existent problem since ". . . we have no research to mention, and it has not grown up to school age, and when it does it need not fall into the 'worship of scholastic research as the *summum bonum* of our profession'". (1915a, 197.) Winans went on to make the point that teaching and research were closely related to each other.

> It is not, of course, the "chief purpose of a chair of public speaking to annex new realms of undiscovered knowledge"; but is the business of any teacher to know what he teaches is true. And to be a progressive teacher, an inspiring teacher, if you will, he must be growing in knowledge. . . . After all what is research ? Are we in terror of a word ? Research is simply a determined effort, by sound methods, to find out the truth about any subject. It does not stop with guesses and speculation, it does not accept traditions at face value or jump at conclusions; but it puts all to the test of investigation. Do we know all we ought to know? Are we not unduly depending on guesses and untested theories and traditions? (1915a, 199, 201)

Winans was also quick to respond to Hunt's claim that the teacher of public speaking must be a generalist rather than a specialist and to the assertion that the public speaking teacher could not surpass, in knowledge, professors in other disciplines.

> Yet specialization is already coming. It is bound to come in large departments. One man does specialize in voice work and it is a subject large enough for a large man. Another specializes in debating, etc. This does not mean that each knows nothing of other branches and is not capable of teaching them, but that he is best in one branch. It is a mistake to suppose that the teacher of public speaking who endeavors to conduct research will be expected to "excel the psychologist in his research." The psychologist is not expected to excel the physiologist in his own field, but only to be well grounded in physiology, able to consult intelligently with the physiologist and to apply to psychological problems the fruit of his work. So the teacher who would apply psychology to public speaking needs such training in psychology that he will not blunder in the application. (1915a, 200)

Winans admitted that he had perhaps overemphasized the importance of being accepted into the "sheepfold," but, nonetheless, he still maintained that acceptance would improve the quality of teaching.

> I accept the implied criticism that in my former article I put too much stress upon the possibility of securing a better position in the college world. But that is an effective and proper motive, especially since, as I urged before, a better position will put us in a frame of mind conducive to good teaching. (1915a, 200)

Finally, in the conclusion of his editorial, Winans prophesied about the inevitability of research.

> I am academic enough to have faith in the worth and inspiration of knowledge. The real question is, have we the courage to seek it? Or perhaps for us of middle age the question is, are we willing to risk the possible embarrassment of a new generation wiser than ourselves? Well it is coming anyhow. (1915a, 201)

The 1915 exchange between Hunt and Winans was merely the opening skirmish in a battle which was to go on for a considerable time and in which Charles Henry Woolbert would soon be engaged. Nonetheless, we can already see the shadows of issues which would be argued almost to the present. The question of whether the new profession should regard itself as a teaching or research field was raised. Although the younger Hunt chose to regard research as an unsuitable activity for teachers of public speaking, the more mature Winans, while defending the importance of research, perceived that research and teaching had an almost symbiotic connection and the one need not diminish the other. The issue of the proper domain of public speaking was also raised in the exchange. Hunt displayed a variety of anti-scienticism, which although it did not completely denigrate science, regarded its concerns and methods as being entirely inappropriate for public speaking. Winans displayed a rather naive respect for "truth," but he did not appear to be wedded to science as the sole methodology for acquiring knowledge.

The relationship to other disciplines was pursued further in Hunt's article and in Winan's response than in the earlier statement by the Research Committee. Hunt held to an integrative position in which the teacher of public speaking used the classroom as a center for creativity in which the student learned to discourse on almost any significant topic. Winans, on the other hand, thought it was the duty of the academic to learn as much from other disciplines as would allow him to conduct his research. Thus the continuing discussion of whether speech should be an independent or dependent discipline was begun and would continue throughout the history of the profession. In time the Winans position came to represent orthodoxy in the discipline.

We cannot be certain how influential the Hunt-Winans debate was with the membership of the National Association. At any rate, at the 1915 meeting of the association, the first for the new profession, only two papers dealt with research, and they were phrased in most general terms. Smiley Blanton, of the University of Wisconsin, presented a paper on "Research Problems in Voice and Speech"; J.S. Gaylord's presentation was titled "Research Problems in the Science of Speech Making." Considering the professional immaturity of the association, perhaps greater definition and specificity should not have been expected since the association was still seeking to arrive at a definition of research and was only capable, at that time, of speaking of generalized "research problems."

That first meeting of the association was held at the Congress Hotel in Chicago at the same time that the N.C.T.E. was meeting at the Auditorium Hotel. *The Quarterly Journal* noted that:

> These two hotels are so joined that anyone can pass from one to the other without going out of doors; so that those interested in the meetings of both organizations will find it convenient to go from meetings of one to those of the other as if the two conventions were in the same hotel. For all practical purposes they will be under the same roof. There will be no meeting of the National Association while the Public Speaking Section of the English Council is in session. (Forum, 1915, 308)

This seemingly routine announcement was indicative of the ambivalent relationship between the National Association and the English Council and of the association's unwillingness to separate completely from the parent organization; they even went so far as not to meet at the same time that the Public Speaking Section of N.C.T.E. met.

The program of the Public Speaking Section of N.C.T.E. paid no attention to research. It consisted of presentations on "Oral Composition in the High School," "Practical Applications of Oral Expression in High Schools," and "The Preparation in

Expression of the High School Teacher of English", the last presentation was by Thomas C. Trueblood who was, of course, the leading figure in Elocution but who would also become an active member of the National Association (Forum, 1915, 310-311).

In 1916 *The Quarterly Journal* reprinted the presidential address of J.M. O'Neill at the 1915 convention. In that speech O'Neill discussed some of the questions earlier raised or implied in the pages of the 1915 journal. He came down solidly on the side of Winans and the Research Committee about the value of scholarship.

> *Professional freedom means an intensification of interest and study in this field. It means specialization which alone can make deep and adequate searches for truth. There is evident already an awakening that means better scholarship, more scientific research, better teaching in the field. It means the passing of the day of guesses and thumb-rules. All this is coming because the **opportunity** for its encouragement and expression exists now as it has never existed before. (1916, 54)*

O'Neill had reservations about how the research of the new profession was to be carried on. Among his caveats were the questions of derivative materials and the motives for research.

> *Now, I am far from saying that we should not draw on the findings of others. I am insisting only that as a profession we must insist on an honest crediting of all our borrowings. . . . We ought to go and take what we may require, but we must insist on a more accurate documentation than can be afforded by an exchange of winks. . . . What attitude are we to respect and encourage on the part of a person who makes an important discovery or perfects an improved method ? Is such a one to give the benefits of this to the profession for the good of education, or is he to keep it a well guarded secret in order to profit by using himself for good fees paid by those who need it ? (1916, 61)*

O'Neill also had his eye on the future of research as he expressed his concern about the public speaking teachers of the future,

> *The work and achievement of the next generation will largely conditioned by the atmosphere in which we train our students today. . . . Are they to be teachers or time servers?. . . Are they to be scholars and investigators who are contributing to human knowledge by a patient searching and testing or contributing to genuine education by a thorough instruction of the great mass of students, or are they to be an unreasoning and unquestioning light brigade of thumb-rule practitioners. (1916, 62)*

The issues raised by O'Neill are still with us. The position he took regarding the connections of teaching and research are currently prevalent. The professional acknowledgement of the research of others has certainly been respected. His hopes for future researchers was not fulfilled in "the next generation," but in time researchers came to resemble the O'Neill portrayal. His concerns about the exploitation of research proved to be groundless as the profession conformed to general academic norms.

Immediately following O'Neill's article appeared an article by Charles H. Woolbert, of the University of Illinois, in which he undertook to make a case for "The Organizations of Department of Speech Science in Universities." We must take notice of the limitations imposed by Woolbert in the very title of the article. To Woolbert the discipline was no longer "Public Speaking;" it was now "Speech Science." Throughout his fairly brief career Woolbert held to a scientific rather than a humanistic perspective concerning the new profession. This orientation would become even stronger after he completed his Ph.D. in Psychology at Harvard in 1918. The title of the essay also indicated that Woolbert's concern was with research universities, not with under-graduate colleges and he made that point explicitly in his article.

> As the following case is made out strictly with the needs and requirements of universities in mind (I am ready enough to agree that colleges are not governed by the same conditions and do not feel the same needs). The question revised again should read: Should speech studies **in universities** no longer be kept within the jurisdiction of the department of English? (1916, 65)

Woolbert saw the need to distinguish between the new profession and its parent in order to justify disciplinary autonomy and departmental separation. He declared that English and speech science were "two lines of study, because *they are essentially different disciplines*." Woolbert construed the new field as being limited to orality. "English is given up specifically to thought that is written, speech science to thought that is spoken." The emphasis on orality, which was in fact rather rigorously observed by the profession in years to come, imposed limitations on the field for at least three decades as it concerned itself, in all of its branches, almost entirely with oral discourse. A reorientation of the field was necessary before the discipline began to deal with non-oral communication.

Another important distinction noted by Woolbert was the time orientation in which each of the disciplines operated. "English is concerned with the past more than with the present, while speech science must occupy itself more with the present than with the past." This distinction led Woolbert to depict English as a field in which the professor was "immured in his library, surrounded by his books." Moreover, the English teacher's life, said Woolbert, was passive and contemplative.

> Give him his choice and he chooses the library and the notebook. In other words, if he is asked to to choose between the two activities, first, teaching students an art to be used in the present, and, secondly investigating the literature of the past, he will choose the latter. . . . But the man who is rightly trained to teach speech science finds his greatest inspiration in giving the world something for the present, in helping men and women to make speeches, to interpret literature, and to present the drama for the profit and delight of others. (1916, 66)

The disjunction described by Woolbert was curious given his propensity for science and research. His description, in fact, depicts English as a field characterized by scholarship while "speech science" seems to be concerned with teaching and practical application.

Perhaps the most serious charge Woolbert brought against English departments was that they did not practice science.

> It is only by a stretch of the term that English can claim sanctuary as a science; or else the effort to make the subject qualify as a science entails an almost rigid and hard limitation of the field of its activities. . . . Speech, on the other hand, claims as its ancestry disciplines that are of the elect among the sciences: physics, physiology, anatomy, psychology. Wherein it impinges upon the field of English, it touches where English as a science confesses to be least strongly academic: rhetoric, composition, the art of effective presentation. (1916, 66)

Woolbert's statement raises a number of questions. Much more than Winans, Woolbert held a strong presupposition about science. Apparently the value of a discipline was to be judged by its adherence to scientific standards. Thus English, because it failed to measure up to those standards, was not among the "elect." We have no evidence that, in this stage of its history, English regarded itself as a science nor that it had any aspirations to be a science. Woolbert's claim about the ancestry was undocumented, if not dubious; certainly the disciplines cited did not acknowledge their parenthood. One wonders what the reaction of members of the N.C.T.E. was to Woolbert's description, especially his colleagues in the English Department at the University of Illinois. In contrast to the conciliatory speech of O'Neill, Woolbert was almost hostile to English.

> . . . a professor of speech science is out of place in a department of English. No matter how well trained he may be for the work or how well liked by his colleagues personally, still he is in the wrong pew and cannot escape embarrassment and intolerable restrictions. Clearly he can contribute nothing to the councils of the department. . . . Even worse, he cannot sympathize with his colleagues' point of view. (1916, 68)

Woolbert, having made his case against departments of English, went on to specify what should constitute a department of speech science. In spite of his concentration on science, he presented a scheme which continued to see the new discipline as one oriented primarily to performance. Under the heading "The Scope of Speech Science as an Academic Study" he presented the following ten main divisions, with considerable elaboration, in outline form.

1. *Phonology*
2. *The Technique of Expression*
3. *The Psychology of Expression*
4. *Application of Laws of Expression*
5. *The Acting Drama*
6. *Extempore Speaking*
7. *Argumentation and Debate*
8. *Persuasion*
9. *The Pedagogy of Oral Expression*
10. *The Aesthetics of Speaking, Interpreting, and Acting (1916, 70-71)*

Although Woolbert's scheme was really directed to performance courses, he did specify such "scientific" sub-topics as: the physiology of the voice; the physics of sound; phonetics; the relation of the receiving mind to the expressing mind; memory, perception, imagination and ideation in speech; and the psychology of crowds, public movements, reforms and revolution.

The typology advocated by Woolbert and the content of the early issues of *The Quarterly Journal* demonstrated that the conception held of "public speaking" was different from our present conception of the term. Woolbert seemed to conceive of public speaking as a umbrella discipline for all the oral arts. His scheme included sub-categories that today we designate as Theatre, Oral Interpretation, Speech Science, History of Public Address, and the Psychology of Communication. Woolbert's conception of the field, remarkably, bears resemblance to the contemporary discipline. Woolbert's proposal actually was close to that enunciated earlier by the Research Committee.

In his article Woolbert also specified which topics should be assigned to the undergraduate, undergraduate and graduate, and to the graduate curricula. For the the most part, the more strictly performance courses were assigned to the undergraduates and the more theoretical courses to graduate students. He also suggested topics for research, some of which were not altogether different from those proposed in 1915 by the Research Committee.

1. *The Reaction of Hearers and Spectators in Differing Modes of Oral Presentation*
2. *The Relation of Oral Expression to Belief and Acceptance*
3. *The Speech Methods and Practices of Various Historical Times, Races, and Peoples*
4. *The Psychology and Logic of Evidence as Employed in Different Fields: Law, Politics, the Church, Science, Commerce, and Education*
5. *Standardization of Vocal and Expressional Theories*
6. *Studies in the History of Expression, Public Speaking, Play-Producing, and Acting*
7. *The Literature of Oratory, Debate, the Drama, Pageants, and Pantomimes*
8. *Investigations into the Traditions, Ideals, and Aesthetic Standards in the Allied Arts of Oral Expression*
9. *The Relation of Expressional Methods to the Acoustics and Arrangements of Public Halls*
10. *Physiology and Hygiene of the Voice*
11. *Abnormal Mentality and Speech*
12. *The Relation of the Voice and the Emotions (1916, 74)*

In order to show how speech science was both independent and interdependent, Woolbert constructed a diagram to illustrate the relationships. He said:

> *Let the central circle represent the field of speech science and arts, and the smaller circles those disciplines that touch upon it and contribute to it. . . . It is obvious that there is a large field of study and investigation within the large circle, the greater part of which is not provided for by the present departmental divisions of the university curricula. (1916, 72)*

In the large and the smaller circles Woolbert sought to relate specific disciplines to specific aspects of "speech science and arts." The following chart indicates how Woolbert perceived the relationships.

DISCIPLINE	DIVISION OF SPEECH SCIENCE
Education	*Speech Material*
Sociology	*Social Adjustments and Human Behavior*
Political Economy	*Speech Material*
Political Science	*Speech Material*
Law	*Evidence*
History	*The Literature of Public Address*
	Speech Material
	Social Adjustment and Human Behavior
English	*The Literature of Public Address*
	Rhetoric
	Criticism
Physics	*The Physics of Sound*
Physiology & Anatomy	*Use of Vocal Apparatus*
	Hygiene
Psychology	*Thought-Processes*
Philosophy	*Aesthetics*

The sub-divisions of speech science and arts which were independent of other disciplines were the following:

Stage Craft
Stage Art
Speech Art
Persuasion
Debating
Argumentation
Expression
Elocution
Rhetoric
Phonology (1916, 72)

The Woolbert taxonomy was significant in the history of the discipline because it predicted in general form, but not in specific detail, much of the form that Speech Communication would assume over the years. Woolbert described a discipline which was dependent on other disciplines for its theoretical foundations. The subject matters which he regarded as indigenous to speech were the applied and performance aspects of the discipline. From the outset Woolbert conceived of the new science as a derivative or perhaps a synthetic discipline. Whether it could truly be regarded as synthetic would depend on the discipline's ability to integrate the materials drawn from outside into a unitary discipline with distinctive focus and with autonomy which would free it from excessive theoretical and methodological dependence.

The Woolbert essay was important because it was written by a person important in the first decades of the profession, one of the first persons in the field to hold a Ph.D. and the person most responsible for the introduction of a scientific (or social-scientific) perspective.

The first announcement of a graduate program in public speaking was contained in the "Forum" of the 1916 *Quarterly Journal*. The Master's degree in Public Speaking had "been approved by the graduate committee and adopted at the University of Wisconsin." Interestingly, at this very early stage, the program was divided into two options, one of which was destined to become the main body of Speech Communication; the other which eventually developed into Communication Disorders. The requirements for the options were stipulated as follows:

A. *For those specializing in Oratory, Argumentation, Debate, Composition of Public Speeches, etc:*

1. *Public Speaking 118a, 118b, Teacher's Problems* . . . . (4)
2. *Public Speaking 205, Seminar in Rhetoric and Oratory* (4)
3. *English 156, Literary Criticism* . . . . (2)
4. *Philosophy 108, Psychology of the Emotions* . . . . . . (2)
5. *Philosophy 213, Advanced Logic* . . . . (2)
6. *Law Course in Pleading or Evidence* . . . . (4)
7. *Electives* . . . . (6)

B. *For those specializing in Voice-Training, Reading, Correction of Speech Disorders, etc.:*

1. *Public Speaking 118a, 118b, Teacher's Problems* . . . . (4)
2. *Public Speaking 201, Seminar in Voice and Speech* . . . (4)
3. *Physiology 106* . . . . (3)
4. *Philosophy 108, Psychology of the Emotions* . . . . . . (2)

> 5. *Philosophy 107, Abnormal Psychology* . . . . (2)
> 6. *Philosophy 210, Psychological Seminar* . . . . (2)
> 7. *Electives* . . . . (7)
> *("A Master's Degree In Public Speaking," 1916, 95)*

The electives in the new master's program were to be chosen "from graduate courses in Public Speaking, English, Psychology, Education, or those in Drama or Oratory in foreign languages."

The graduate program at Wisconsin was noteworthy because it construed "public speaking" in a broad sense and it offered a two track program stressing both the humanistic and scientific aspects of oral communication. The program may be said to have contained the seeds of its own partial destruction since the matters stressed in the second option laid the foundations for the establishment of a another new discipline—communication disorders—which in time grew to be larger than the parent discipline. In addition the program was based on derivations from other disciplines. Granted that the curriculum in Public Speaking was in the first stages of development; nevertheless, it is obvious that the new master's students would take most of their course work outside the field.

In the same year, 1916, Alice W. MacLeod, of the University of Montana, undertook to survey "Majors and Credits in Public Speaking." She reported that, "The Universities of Michigan, Wisconsin, Cornell, and Ohio Wesleyan gave . . . the A.M. degree. The Syracuse University Graduate School allows sixteen hours credit to count toward the A.M. and Ph.D. degrees." (150-151)

The debate concerning research and the direction of the discipline was renewed later in 1916 in a back-to-back pair of articles by Hunt and Woolbert. Perhaps these articles represent as clearly as any others the initial schism in the profession. In his article Hunt undertook to respond to earlier criticism and to clarify his position. Hunt asserted that the position of the discipline of Public Speaking was different in the reasons for its establishment as compared to other disciplines.

> *. . . instead of being the outgrowth of the desire of men in long-established positions to come together with the sole object of mutual inspiration, the National Association is, partially, at least, the product of a desire to establish independent positions through organization. The National Association of Academic Teachers of Public Speaking therefore. . . bears a closer resemblance to a labor union than to an academy of arts and letters. (1916, 253)*

Hunt's comparison with labor unions may not have been apt, but he had made a point which was perceptive and which may be valid even today. The new profession, he maintained, was established not so much because of intellectual differentiation from a parent discipline as it was for a desire for autonomy and independence from English. The schism between Philosophy and Psychology, for example, was based on genuine conceptual and theoretical differences. The fact that at the moment of its establishment the National Association was uncertain about its own focus and unclear about the nature of its research placed it in the risky position of becoming a politically independent but intellectually derivative field.

The danger which Hunt saw in the ideas of Winans, Woolbert and others was that, in keeping with the trends of the times, an attempt was being made to transform the field not only into a science but a specialized science. Hunt felt that the criteria being applied were invalid.

> *By what strange fate are teachers of oratory, teachers of a discipline that was the*

crown of Greek and Roman education, now humbly attempting to creep back into
our educational system under the guise of a new science discovered by a process of
specialization! The truth is we specialize in speech science because others have
specialized. (1916, 255)

But, said Hunt, Public Speaking cannot be a specialized field because it is, by its
very nature, a general field.

All of the sciences have staked out claims. Most of them have done it by
discovering new territory. Their possession of permanent abiding places and
consequent rise to power and influence have led them to demand that every
intellectual activity have a home of its own. If Public Speaking cannot give its street
and number it is suspected of staying out nights. To be homeless and a wanderer has
its disadvantages, but Public Speaking would never be able to stay home if it had
one. (1916, 255)

Hunt thus highlighted a question which is present even today—if the discipline is
to be an authentic academic specialty what is its distinctive mark which differentiates
it from other disciplines? Instead, Hunt asserted, the strength of the new discipline was
based on its general nature. The teachers of Public Speaking, if they are specialists, are
"General Specialists." Hunt saw in Public Speaking a resemblance to Aristotle's
conception of rhetoric as a "tool of common knowledge." By its very nature Public
Speaking could not be confined to a particular subject.

I wish to submit three assertions for consideration in determining some of the
ideals of the association. First, neither speech science nor speech art can be confined
to a particular field of knowledge. Second, any general acceptance of the idea that
speech science or speech art possesses a distinctive and individual field for
specialization will prevent the instruction in Public Speaking from reaching its
highest effectiveness. Third, the Professor of Public Speaking in a college finds his
greatest work in stimulating, as a means to effective expression, a wide range of
general reading and a keen interest in contemporary thought and action. In other
words, the Public Speaking Professor must be a specialist in versatility. (1916,
255-256)

Hunt saw in both Woolbert's scheme for departments of "Speech Science" and the
University of Wisconsin's new graduate curriculum a plan for a profession which
sought to draw its strength by derivation from other fields. He saw a discipline which
would never become a science because it would combine knowledge from other
disciplines rather than creating its own knowledge. Of the Woolbert article and the
Wisconsin plan he wrote:

His (Woolbert's) article is conclusive proof that he does not regard speech science
as an addition to the realm of the known. The article instead of telling of the
discovery of a new science, is a plea for the unity which exists among many long
recognized factors. (1916, 257)

Instead of seeking to relate the new discipline to already existing disciplines, Hunt
contended, the association needed to emphasize those factors which were distinctive
to Public Speaking and the role of the discipline as a synthesizer and applier of
knowledge.

The more we sacrifice to academic recognition, the more we attempt to imitate
other departments in our organization, the more we will emphasize our points of

similarity and minimize the points of difference. For a real development of our work,
it is the points of difference that need to be emphasized. (1916, 258)

Hunt's plans for the profession were actually more grandiose than any scheme proposed by the Research Committee, Winans or Woolbert. He visualized Public Speaking as the grand synthesizer of all the liberal arts, if not all human knowledge.

The Public Speaking department is to serve as a clearing house of ideas. The
instructor should inspire in his students a vital interest in the affairs of the world, in
politics, sociology, economics, literature and art. . . Such a possibility may not bring
immediate academic recognition. It may take some time for specialists of a certain
type to admit the worth of a profession different from their own. But since there is a
real need in our colleges for such chairs of general culture, since the value of our
work is indisputable, teachers of such a type may face the future with confidence.
(1916, 262-263)

Hunt's case for the generalist was well argued, but we realize now how futile an enterprise he was advocating. Although he disdained "academic recognition," that was precisely what was needed at that point. If Public Speaking were to be accepted into the academic community, it could hardly make its case as a "bridge discipline" or an inter-disciplinary field. Nevertheless, one must credit Hunt for his strong adherence to a humanistic perspective of the new profession and for his perception that Public Speaking must make its own distinctive mark rather than seeking to flourish as a discipline dependent on other disciplines.

Immediately following Hunt's article in the 1916 *Quarterly Journal*, Woolbert was given an opportunity for a rejoinder. Under the title "A Problem in Pragmatism" he specified how fundamental were the differences between him and Hunt. So much at variance were the two men that Woolbert said, "Mr. Hunt and I differ so widely as to fundamentals that it cannot be said we are arguing. We are merely stating personal preferences." Woolbert was quick to delineate the premises of his approach to the work of the field, and in so doing, made a clear statement of his scientific point of view as contrasted to Hunt's humanistic view.

I stand for a search for the facts; the facts of how speaking is done; of what its
various effects are under specified conditions; how these facts can be made into laws
and principles; and how other people may can best be taught to apply them. The facts
we use are too often guesses; our methods too purely personal; we need to get
together on some commonly acceptable basis. The only one I know of comes from
scientifically conducted investigation and research. Hence I stand for research; also I
deem it impossible to do successful teaching without laws and principles; I do not
believe that the necessary courses can be taught except as they are organized under a
unified interest in a separate and independent department; and I know thoroughly
well that our universities are not going to make way for a discipline that cannot
furnish the facts, the laws and the unified interest. (1916, 264-265)

Woolbert, probably correctly, argued that he and Hunt represented dissimilar historical and intellectual conceptions and different academic settings. The emergence of the German modeled research university, of which Illinois was by 1916 an example, served to explain the divergences of their orientation to the new profession. To some extent the differences were dependent on the respective situations of Hunt and Woolbert but they were also representative of two conceptions of the academic enterprise which reflected views of the academy which were strikingly unlike. In contrast to

Hunt's humanism, Woolbert presented a picture of what he saw as the new world of higher education.

> Mr. Hunt and I are of different epochs and countries. He is of romantic golden age, I of a common ignoble now. He is from Greece, I am from Germany(!). . . He cries out for the glory that was Greece and the grandeur that was Rome; I am surrounded by libraries and card catalogues. . . . Another way of making clear the fundamental personal differences between us is to point out that I am studying a problem in administration for a university, while Mr. Hunt is fairly and frankly concerned in the problem as it applies to a college. . . . My circumstances compel me to accept the universities definition of a professor as "one who finds and teaches truth." We inmates of the universities simply are not permitted to overlook the concept "find." (1916, 265)

Woolbert had drawn a clear line between himself and Hunt. Yet his scientific pronouncements may have been as rigid as Hunt's generalized humanism. Woolbert presented a portrait of a university governed by the search for "truths," yet he did not tell his readers exactly what meaning he gave to "truth" or how the "truths" of Public Speaking were like or unlike the "truths" of chemistry, or even of psychology. He also seemed to equate research and the "finding of truth" with the collection of "facts," in the search for laws and principles. Woolbert's views seem to be driven by a model derived from the natural sciences although he did concede that his definition of science was not that which Hunt understood.

> I suspect that I am merely encountering one more person who doesn't like the name "speech science." One man I know almost had a convulsion over it. He immediately wanted me to prove that that I could see a science like Chemistry of (sic) Physics or Biology. . . . I think he felt better when I made it clear to him that the "science" I see is synonymous with the disciplines known under the names "political science," "household science," "library science," "military science," "sanitary science.". . . For what is a science? I will quote one characteristic definition: "A science consists of a large body of observed facts which are related to one another and are arranged under general laws." (1916a, 267)

From today's perspective Woolbert's statement, reenforced by a quotation from Titchener's *A Textbook of Psychology*, is confusing. To exemplify a "hard" definition of science he cited disciplines which titled themselves sciences but which hardly conform to his definition. If Public Speaking were to model itself on "household science," it certainly would place itself in a different position than if it modelled itself on the the more conventional scientific disciplines.

The relationship of Public Speaking to other disciplines was another matter on which Woolbert thought that Hunt was misinformed. Woolbert maintained that the new field could rely upon and yet not be dependent on other disciplines.

> He (Hunt) cannot see that I was merely showing that no one discipline could swallow us up, that we had as much use for some of their laws as they have, and that some of them have no other function with us than to supply us with raw materials. (1916a, 271)

Woolbert was adamant that the teacher of Public Speaking could not be solely, or largely, responsible for the general education of students. That task must fall to the specialist—not to the "general specialist."

> To provide enough teachers to be general specialists would be to set up a whole

*monastery in our midst. It would require about fifty on the speech staff at the
University of Illinois to do a really first-class job of the general specialist business.
We still have to trust to the economist and the historian and the teacher of literature
to do most of the head filling. Then we teach how to unload—how mind you. We are
a machine for unloading much more than loading. I fear there is to be no return to
the good old days of Mark Hopkins and the general utility college teacher. The tide is
moving the other way. . . . And some of us have just enough faith in facts, laws, and
method to believe that therein is the way of salvation and now is the accepted time.
(1916a, 273)*

The problem of definition of the new discipline was reflected in the question of
proper nomenclature. Although "Public Speaking" was the name designated in the
name of the National Association, an editorial in 1916 indicated that the profession as
a whole had not agreed on a name for the new departments.

*There is hardly a book written or reviewed or reference made to any of our work
but demands a special explanation as to what is meant by the term "public
speaking." The great majority of our departments in the United States are today
called Departments of Public Speaking. There are a few Departments of Oratory, a
few of Expression, one of Oral English, one of Speech, and one or two of Elocution.
. . . It must be perfectly plain to anyone who has had to deal with professional
matters among widely scattered universities, and to a certain extent to each student
or teacher in this field, that misunderstandings, confusion, and sometimes
embarrassment results from this babble of titles. It seems to us that this question of
department names ought to be seriously considered in the immediate future, and
something like uniformity hit upon. . . . This would be an excellent topic for
discussion at the Annual Conference. . . . In order to help out the general situation,
the Quarterly invites a competition for the October number, and solicits entries in a
department-naming contest. . . . Send in your choice at an early convenience.
("Wanted an Accurate Title," 1916, 294-295)*

This seemingly trivial discussion was of importance in the history of the discipline.
It indicated that the National Association was unsure of its own central focus and
apparently was not certain that Public Speaking was the most appropriate label for its
activities. Such questioning was completely understandable since the writings of
Winans and Woolbert, the articles in *The Quarterly Journal*, and the graduate program
at Wisconsin amply demonstrated that the discipline's concerns extended well beyond
Public Speaking to include subjects as diverse as Theatre and Voice Disorders. In many
ways, the discipline was on its way to becoming an "umbrella" discipline for all the
oral arts.

Moreover, the problem has proved to be persistent. From 1916 to the present,
discussion has continued concerning appropriate titles for the discipline, professional
associations, journals in the discipline, and names of departments. The last name
change for the association was in 1970 to Speech Communication, and that was
controversial. Since then many suggestions have been made to rename the association
and the discipline. Only recently a majority of the voting members of the Speech
Communication Association elected to adopt "communication" as the correct name
for the association, but the required two thirds vote was not achieved. The variety in
names of departments is much greater than in 1916. The inability of the association
and the discipline to agree, over time, concerning proper nomenclature is indicative
now, as it was in 1916 that the disciplines still lacks consensual agreement about the
focus, the limitations and the specifications of the discipline. A glance at the current

SCA directory's list of departments is a clear indication that there is no agreement, let alone unanimity, in the names chosen for departments.

In the same issue Winans announced that that the 1916 convention would again be held in the same city and at the same hotel, the Hotel Astor in New York, as the English Council. The connection between the new profession and the parent discipline continued to be maintained as Winans put it:

> . . . *We wished to work in harmony with the English Council, and we learned from the leaders of the Council that they would be pleased to have us meet at the same time and place. (1916b, 293)*

Thus, in spite of Woolbert's depreciation of English, the association's attitude towards English continued to be ambivalent. Winans' stance seemingly supported Hunt's assertion that the National Association had come into being more for autonomy than from genuinely different intellectual conceptions. Indeed the division was not between an established established organization and its rebellious offspring. In 1916 the N.C.T.E. itself was only six years old.

The same section of *The Quarterly Journal* reported the 1916 meetings of the New England Public Speaking Conference and the Eastern Public Speaking Conference. In neither of the meetings were any papers presented which could be designated as research. Almost all of the presentations dealt with pedagogical and applied concerns. A large proportion of the papers were devoted to voice training. The rubric "Public Speaking" was no more appropriate for the Eastern Conference than for the National Association since a separate division of the program was devoted to Drama. It is interesting from our present perspective that most of the institutions represented at the two meetings are no longer significant in the Speech Communication discipline. Among those colleges and universities were: Harvard, Bowdoin, Dartmouth, Amherst, Brown, Colgate, Princeton, Johns Hopkins, Swarthmore and Yale. An interesting sidelight to the Eastern Conference was that, "After the conference adjourned the members joined a crowd of Princeton citizens and listened to several short addresses. Among the speakers were President Wilson and Governor FIelder" (The Eastern Public Speaking Conference, 1916, 300-303).

Later in 1916 in a further announcement concerning the second annual convention, the significance of the Hunt-Woolbert dispute was clear.

> *Everett Lee Hunt of Huron College is expected to come from South Dakota to discuss further his theory of "the General Specialist" and to go into more detail than he did in the July Quarterly in regard to how to carry out his idea. And having Hunt, we shall need Woolbert to talk to us of the Specialized Specialist: and he has been given the task of making research more tangible to us. It is up to Woolbert to atone for the envy he is causing us by entering on two years of study into the psychology of public speaking at Harvard, to come out of the laboratory frequently and tell us how it goes. ("The New York Meeting," 1916, 415-416)*

As promised, at the 1916 convention of the association Woolbert made a presentation in which he clarified and expanded his views on the importance of research, which was published in the 1917 *Quarterly Journal* under the title "Suggestions as to Methods in Research." Interestingly, in spite of his earlier pronouncements, Woolbert now presented himself as naive in research, and he suggested that he would be better prepared to discuss research in a year's time. He was, of course referring to the time he was about to spend at Harvard gaining his Ph.D. in Psychology.

Perhaps in an attempt to come to better terms with the Hunts of the world, Woolbert began his essay with a lengthy discussion in which he drew a clear line between teaching and research. He, in fact, titled the section, "Research Not for All Teachers."

> *The only sure notion that has come to me in the last few months is that research is not for everybody. . . . All of us who have observed the lines of cleavage on universities faculties between teachers and investigators, have been compelled to see that not everybody is fitted to research; just as not everybody is fitted to teach. In the main we are a teaching branch of the educational tree, and we shall always remain so. . . . It is for this reason that I do not share the fears of some of the brethren that this movement for research is to rob us of our distinctive character and to draw us away after false gods. (1917, 12)*

No matter how this statement struck the readers of 1917, it now strikes us as an unusual position. Woolbert seemed to be moving away from his earlier orthodox stand on research, and he acknowledged that research was not the universal responsibility of the profession. The distinction he created between teachers and researchers seems to us rigid and arbitrary. In the early history of the discipline such a position may not have been startling, however. The National Association was, after all, composed almost entirely of teachers who had almost no knowledge of, let alone interest in research. At the same time, Woolbert was hardly charitable to those who would not do research. The categories he described were hardly exemplars of academic excellence.

> *There are many types of teachers who will not be interested in research. Anyone who has a closed system of teaching expression, debate, or speech composition will have no interest in it. . . . Moreover, it is not for those who look upon speech arts and practices as merely a matter of incidental training. If you honestly believe that the whole end of and aim of instruction in matters of speaking and reading is merely clearing up the defects of other curriculums, then you have no need for research and no interest in it. Or again, if you are so constituted that you can not face a pile of statistics or a welter of figures and reports, then it will be unwise for you to give up what you are doing and try the new game. . . . A man who is teaching sixteen or twenty or thirty hours a week is not going to have much effort to put to research . . . I worked on that kind of a job once. . . . Then too, it is not for those teachers of English who side with the notion that there can be no such thing as research in rhetoric. Rhetoric and speech matters have so much in common, with a common ancestry and much of a common aim, that if one is not meat for research, in all probability neither is the other. Obviously also, research is not for the man or woman whose real vocation is Chataqua work or preaching or playing the political game, and to whom teaching is only an avocation. . . . And lastly, research will make little appeal to those who are content to rest all decisions upon our old friend, common sense. . . . Some will wonder why in the world we should worry about any other kind of truth than that of plain, everyday sense. Research is surely not for them. (1917, 13-14)*

After Woolbert had taken care of his "Rouges Gallery" of speech teachers, he then devoted himself to pointing out that certain kinds of research did not require a laboratory. Under the heading of "Research of a Non-laboratory Nature," Woolbert suggested that speech teachers could follow the model of other new disciplines.

> *One of the first tasks of research is to find out something about our method. That it can be done, is suggested by the success of other disciplines; say education. Educational research is now working out a method that probably will stand the test*

of scientific validity. So with business administration and sociology and others.
Speech problems can do the same. (1917, 15)

Woolbert's recommendations are interesting in retrospect. He, along with Winans and the Research Committee, sought to find the methodological bases for the new discipline in the work of other disciplines. There seemed to be little or no thought given to what methodology might be specifically suited for the study of "speech problems" or to how the profession could generate its own methods. Woolbert, probably unconsciously, really advocated a derivative discipline, at least so far as methodology was concerned.

Woolbert cited education, sociology and business administration as examples of other newly emerging disciplines. As we view those disciplines from the perspective of 75 years, we recognize that all of them have achieved greater centrality in the academic world than speech communication. Perhaps those disciplines were more successful in developing their own rather than derivative research methodologies. Although Woolbert cited the new disciplines under the heading of non-laboratory research, they are today among the disciplines which make the most extensive use of laboratory and experimental methodologies.

Since no determination had been made concerning the central content of the new discipline, Woolbert advocated that the non-laboratory researchers take advantage of the training and education they had acquired in other fields. Of course, the new researchers would also borrow the research approaches from those fields.

Those who have specialized in literature can find some exceedingly interesting problems in the literature of speech. The method that is used in the department of English can easily be employed by anyone with a bent in that direction. . . . Critical studies of the literature of the occasional speech, debate, political campaigns, the pulpit, and the drama are possible and fruitful. Especially in the field of acting, stage production, and the acted drama, we have an unexcelled chance for new studies. I resent it when I see the this work preempted by the philologist and the literary critic—the English scholar. . . . The teacher trained in history can also find profitable work. Undoubtedly most of us swallow texts on history of oratory in a purely uncritical mood. How do we know from present literature that what we accept as facts are such?. . . . The economist can study the relation of economic conditions to the use or disuse of the public forum, the effect of factory and modern industrial systems on oratory and public meetings, the difference in speech conditions in the crowded city as against the country district. . . . Personally, if I were trained in political science, and disposed to investigate, I could get great fun out of investigating the relation of campaign oratory to various political campaigns. Among our members we have not a few legal luminaries. What fun it would be to attend trials and court sessions of various kinds to make systematic study of the conditions of the effects of speech at the bar and before the bench. For the preacher also there are golden fields ripe to the harvest. As a sample of some of the sheaves that the preacher could bring in, let him take the trail of the great and only Billy Sunday during one of his campaigns, analyze his methods, his manner of handling a crowd, his dependence on preliminary organization as a matter of tuning his auditors. (1917, 15-17)

Woolbert undoubtedly did not realize the kinds of problems he might be causing as a result of his suggestions. Essentially he was asking the non-laboratory researchers to turn to their previous specializations and not to seek to find methods of investigation uniquely suited to the questions and problems of their new profession. To greater or lesser degrees during the history of the discipline, research in speech has been characterized by the derivativeness advocated by Woolbert.

We must note, however, that Woolbert was not far off the mark in hypothesizing about the kinds of studies which might be undertaken. Many of the proposals he made, vague though they were, were incorporated in the early research in the field, and some of them continue to be carried out to the present day.

Disappointingly, when Woolbert turned to his specialty which he titled Laboratory Experimentation he did no more than describe the work he was doing for his dissertation at Harvard. In fact, he was able to offer little guidance as to methodology or theory because the work was still in its very early stages.

> *Thus far the work has been of the most rudimentary character, and the results are not yet. (sic) What we are doing is trying to find out how to begin. We are experimenting with methods in hope of finding what our method is. (1917, 18)*

The search for method in Woolbert's experiment was laudable, but it showed the lack of definable and specific methodologies suited to communications research. The work which was explained was simplistic and would probably strike present day researchers as extremely naive. We should not rush to condemn Woolbert, however; after all he was carrying out his research in the esteemed Department of Psychology at Harvard. Perhaps, from this example, we learn as much about the state of research in psychology as in speech. The lack of precision in research is indicated by the global title Woolbert gave to his project: "Conditions and Effects of Speech."

When Woolbert came to discuss "Some Suggestions for Experiments" we are struck by the naivete of his conceptions, although there is no doubt that all of the suggestions were "behavioral." He makes fourteen suggestions some of which are:

> *(1) Should a speaker place his weight on one foot or divide it between two feet?*
>
> *(2) Should a speaker restrain gesture or give way to it?*
>
> *(3) Does a speaker impair his efficiency by reading from a manuscript?*
>
> *(4) Does the size of the room affect impressiveness, and how?*
>
> *(5) What is the relation between the speaker's rate of delivery and the distance of the audience?*
>
> *(7) What are the effects upon the speaker's rate or impressiveness when he sits, leans on the desk, stands in a group with his hearers, reads with with his audience behind his back or to one side, stands behind a desk or without a desk or prop?*
>
> *(8) What are the effects of all these situations when the speaker delivers extempore speeches, or recites from memory?*
>
> *(11) Under what circumstances is monopitch endurable? When is a wide variety of pitch most acceptable? When is the minor cadence appropriate? (1917, 20-21)*

The reader cannot fail to notice that all of Woolbert's suggestions, including those which we did not cite, were studies of one or another aspect of delivery. One is tempted to believe that his exalted view of science was really pretty narrowly confined both in his research at Harvard and in his proposals. He did not think of other areas in which laboratory experimentation might be used. We are not surprised to find that when Woolbert published his textbook *The Fundamentals of Speech* three years later that he subtitled it: *A Behavioristic Study Of The Underlying Principles Of Speaking And Reading:*

A Text Book of Delivery (1920). We should stress, however, that his writing later was, by no means, confined to delivery. As we shall see later, he wrote at some length concerning the persuasion-conviction dichotomy.

Woolbert concluded not by arguing for research for research's sake. Rather he made a practical statement that the modern educational system demanded research and the speech teachers must comply.

> *No research; no favor in in the eyes of educators. We occupy a delightful position among disciplines, but the test of its permanence is our willingness to do in Rome what all good Romans do. We may long and sigh and pine; but presidents and deans are not moved that way, sad to relate. They are becoming pretty stony-hearted toward all who conclude not to make serious and persistent efforts to increase the kingdom of knowledge. I get just as peevish over some aspects of this as anybody possibly could; but we face a stern fact, and I for one am ambitious to see the profession make the best of the situation and play the game according to the rules; this year's copy. Only thus, I firmly believe, shall we know the truth; and the truth once found, will in very deed make us free. (Woolbert, 1917, 26)*

We must conclude, after assimilating Woolbert's disquisition, that the message he presented was distinctly mixed. He excluded a significant portion of the profession from the ranks of researchers; he stipulated an arbitrary and unnecessary distinction between research and teaching; his conception of research problems was simplistic and largely limited to the study of speech performance; and he argued for research not for its innate and essential value but because research would allow us, in Winan's words, to enter "the sheepfold." He also conceived of research in speech, particularly the "non-laboratory" variety, as dependent on other disciplines for methodologies. Nonetheless, Woolbert's essay was an early systematic rationale for research and he laid the groundwork for extensive and serious consideration of the problem. The sub-text of his argument was that the acquisition of knowledge was an important end in itself.

At the 1916 convention of the Association, Hunt did present his defense of the "general specialist" and it was duly printed in the 1917 *Quarterly Journal* under the title "Academic Public Speaking." The audience and readers may have been disappointed, however, that the clash between Hunt and Woolbert did not really develop since Hunt did not directly attack the importance of research. Rather he devoted most of his essay to pointing out how the public speaking curriculum at Huron College helped to provide broadly based general education for the students. Early in the essay he was more explicit about how the foundation of Public Speaking was liberal rather then technical. He began his discussion with four presuppositions.

(1) *We are teaching public speaking for the purpose of producing public speakers.*

(2) *We are teaching public speaking not as part of a professional course. . . but as an avowedly liberal course of instruction.*

(3) *We are teaching college or university students a small proportion of whom enter school with any active intellectual interests. . . .*

(4) *in spite of our liberal pretensions we are teaching in a period when specialization has proceeded to such an extent that many teachers are interested in little beyond their own subjects. (1917, 29)*

In his essay Hunt again stressed the role of public speaking departments as integrators of general knowledge. He wrote that the responsibility of the department was:

> *. . . to act as sort of associative department to establish relations between the closed compartments of knowledge that make up a college course, and thereby to create, for want of a better term, I have called an interesting mind. . . . My charge against the technical expert is not that his methods and facts are not valuable and necessary, but that he tends to overlook the whole question of arousing intellectual curiosity. . . 1917, 31)*

One cannot doubt that Hunt intended that he and his students be generally educated nor that he wanted them to be well read.

> *Periodical reading is usually the first thing I emphasize and insist on. I hold them to account for a knowledge of the* Atlantic, The North American Review, *the* Nation. *the* New Republic, Literary Digest *and* Current Opinion . . .

> *I cannot do less than to read regularly in addition to the periodicals named the* Yale Review, *the* Unpopular Review, *a couple of the educational magazines, the* Scientific Monthly, Drama, Poet Lore, International Journal of Ethics, *a couple of art magazines, (the* Seven Arts *seems promising,) the* Hibbert Journal, *and of course, the* Century, Harpers, Scribners *and the* Independent. *(1917, 32)*

At the end of the article Hunt briefly dealt with the problem of research. He wrote that Woolbert's ". . . definition of a professor [as] 'one who finds and teaches truth'. . . seems to me to be almost a stroke of genius." (1917, 34). He felt, however, that research was only one of many paths to truth. Hunt seemingly did not accept Woolbert's position that truth must be scientific truth.

Quite apart from research, the status of the profession in 1917, in at least one part of the country, was revealed in a survey of "Public Speaking in New England Colleges," by Bromley Smith of Bucknell University. In contrast to the 1990s, most of the elite New England institutions offered courses in speech and some of the curricula were extensive. Among the institutions in which speech courses were taught were: Bates (seven courses), Dartmouth (six courses), Amherst (four courses), Harvard (seven courses), Massachusetts Institute of Technology (two courses), Mount Holyoke (five courses), Radcliffe (two courses), Smith (eight courses), Brown (three courses), and at Yale (65-67). Thus early in its history the new profession exhibited considerable strength in the leading Eastern institutions. It is a cause of concern and curiosity to the present Speech Communication profession as to why and how those programs were displaced so that today the discipline occupies an insignificant or non-existent position in the elite Eastern colleges and universities.

By 1917 signs began to appear that the bonds between the association and the N.C.T.E. were beginning to weaken. In an editorial in *The Quarterly Journal* we read:

> *The question came up at the last meeting as to whether it is worthwhile to continue meeting simultaneously with the National Council of Teachers of English. It was felt by some that there has been so little interchange between the two organizations at the last two conventions that it is hardly worthwhile to sacrifice other considerations for this, although there was not the slightest objection to such an arrangement in itself. . . . President Lardner would, therefore, like to have sent either to him or to* The Quarterly *before the first of March, the opinions of as many members of the Association as wish to aid in deciding these matters. ("The Time And Place For The Annual Convention," 1917, 80-81)*

Although the break with the English profession was not complete and abrupt, after

1917 the relations were distinctly more distant and the teachers of public speaking no longer felt as strongly their alliance to their parent discipline.

In the meantime *The Quarterly Journal* was having problems in its role as the research outlet for the Association.

> . . . *we have suggested that with the financial security of* The Quarterly *assured, we may now devote our attention much more exclusively to the problem of improving* The Quarterly. . . . *We are not complaining of the literary support we have received, nor are we ashamed of the appearance that* The Quarterly *has made; but we are far from satisfied. . . . In the first place, we want more material submitted-more material on hand all the time. We have always had enough copy for* The Quarterly, *but in some instances barely enough.* (Improving The Quarterly, *1917, 82-83*)

The editorial made a number of suggestions as to how *The Quarterly* might be improved.

> *First, plan to work up during the coming year at least one main article on some problems of the field in which you are interested. . . . In the second place, see to it that all happenings of professional interest known to you. . . be reported in full to* The Quarterly. *In the third place, please report articles of interest which you discover in other journals.* (Improving The Quarterly, *1917, 84*)

The plaintive plea of the editorial was indicative that the Association had not yet found its voice and was uncertain of its direction. The fact that the journal needed to ask that articles be submitted was evidence that research was not a central concern of the membership. Submission of an article was almost an assurance that it would be published. In fact, the editorial specified how publication would take place.

> . . . *start on it now; pick out the subject; consult some member of the Board of Editors in regard to the proper month for publication, length of article, sources of information available, or other points on which we can be of assistance to you.* (Improving The Quarterly, *1917, 84*)

Although relations between the N.C.T.E. and the Association were not as close as they had been, the English Council had not lost interest in speech. Another 1917 editorial carried a report of the establishment of the National Speech League by the N.C.T.E. *The Quarterly Journal* welcomed the new league.

> *An editorial in the December issue of the English Journal announces that the committee on American Speech have undertaken to organize a National Speech League, the members of which for the most part shall be outside of the teaching profession. . . . Such signs of important and potential activity outside of the circles of professional teachers of speech is most encouraging, and seemingly cannot fail to have far-reaching and beneficial effect. It means that the public at large in the future is going to be aroused and instructed concerning the need for thorough, intelligent, effective work in speech. . . . We trust that all readers of* The Quarterly *will lend in every possible way their hearty support and assistance to the new National Speech League, to the Committee on American Speech and all other sincere organizations which are working improvement in the public and private speech of this country.* (The National Speech League, *1917, 84*)

The magnanimity and generosity of the Association was impressive. At the same time, however, we may be curious as to why the Association did not undertake the kind of project envisioned by the N.C.T.E. Since the Association was the only one representing speech, sponsorship by teachers of public speaking rather than teachers of English seemed reasonable and logical. Such an innovative action might have contributed to the legitimacy of the new profession. This oversight was particularly evident in the acceptance by the teachers of speech of a key provision of the Council statement.

> . . . it will have its own peculiar mission, namely, that of pointing the way to better training in speech in the schools, particularly at first in the elementary schools. In this connection, it can continue to perform a valuable service in urging teachers of English to study phonetics and train their voices. . . (The National Speech League, 1917, 85)

The abdication of the responsibility to provide and encourage speech training in the schools seems to have been an error. Had the National Association made such a suggestion the importance of the discipline in elementary and secondary education might have been strengthened. The Association also apparently did not object to the N.C.T.E.'s plan to improve the competencies of English teachers rather than introducing teachers of speech to oversee speech improvement. This episode was not the last in which the speech profession allowed other disciplines to take the initiative which should have been taken by speech.

In April of 1917 The Quarterly Journal published a most important and historically neglected article. In a 15 page article, titled "Argument from the Point of View of Sociology," Mary Yost of Vassar College presented a perspective which might have served to re-orient, at least partially, the research direction of the new profession. As we have indicated earlier in this chapter, Mary Yost was probably the first member of the profession to earn a Ph.D. Although she does not say so explicitly, the article was apparently drawn from the dissertation in Sociology which she had recently completed at the University of Michigan. Although her remarks were directed specifically to argumentation, they had clear scholarly implications for research in public speaking. Before the subject was approached by Woolbert, Yost set out to question, and perhaps to destroy, the traditional distinction between conviction and persuasion.

> This explanation of the terms conviction and persuasion was formulated when the when the belief held sway that the mind was divided roughly into three compartments, the reason, the emotions, the will—roughly the assumptions of the old faculty psychology. Today, however, the leading psychologists have found these assumptions inadequate to explain the phenomena of the mind. A conception of the mind as an organic unit performing a particular function—reasoning, feeling, willing—as may be demanded by the situation the individual is meeting has taken the place of the more rigid, formal idea. (111)

The central point of Yost's argument was that argumentation theory, for which one can just as easily read rhetorical or speech theory, had, up to her time, been logic-based. The time has come, said Yost, to consider another base—that of sociology.

> All of the usual text-books—the good and the poor alike—approach the subject of argument from the point-of- view of logic. This is not surprising since the principles of argument were first given scientific expression by Aristotle in terms of logic, and the Aristotelian tradition in all rhetorical matters has been little questioned by modern rhetoricians. . . . The new point-of-view I chose from which to study argumentation was one suggested by sociology. (112-113)

The shift from logic to sociology meant that the focus of communication was now not on the logic of the argument. The new focus was now centered on . . . "communication between members of a social group, a society in the sociological meaning of the term." Yost's sociological approach was fundamentally concerned with the characteristics of social groups, which, in most cases, constituted audiences, and the response of those groups to arguments. She specified three "problems" which were involved in a sociological approach.

> First there is the search for the social characteristics of the typical social group in which argument arises, which will distinguish it, as a species is differentiated from its genus, from social groups in which any act of discourse may arise; second the search for characteristic effects which argument as an act of communication has on both members of the social group, speaker as well as audience; and third, the search for characteristic stages in the process of the act of communication by which these effects are produced. (113)

In delineating how argument may be looked at from a sociological perspective, Yost presented a surprisingly modern conception of the communication situation. She postulated a situation which called forth argumentation. Her explanation bears some interesting resemblances to Lloyd Bitzer's "rhetorical situation" enunciated more than 50 years later.

> If argument is an act of communication between members of a social group, there must be something in the situation of the group which calls forth argument rather than some other act of communication. Now purposive communication takes place in any social group in response to some need of the group. Moreover, it is the member who initiates the act of communication who is aware most vividly of of the need and is most desirous of meeting it. It is, therefore, the view of the group situation as the writer or speaker of an argument sees it which we are concerned with here, his conception of the need of a group. (114)

Yost, for the purposes of her essay, confined herself to the discussion of argument. Yet it is immediately clear that her perspective was equally applicable to any mode of discourse. Her premise that discourse arose out of particular needs in particular social situations was one which had not previously been enunciated and, furthermore, would not be revived for many years to come. She, in fact, provided us with one of the very earliest models of human communication. It is worth noting that she used the term "communication" more often than "argumentation." Whether knowingly or not, Yost had opened a new way of examining communication, and in so doing had offered what amounted to a new research paradigm.

Yost shifted her attention from the question of how communication arises in response to a situation to how the elements in the communicative situation are influential in the outcome of the argument.

> . . . what are the characteristics of the social situation in which we find the outcome of argument? Argument arises, as we have seen, when the normal working of the social group has been interrupted, checked in a certain way. When argument is successful, we find the social group again able to develop through the cooperative efforts of audience and speaker in a direction in harmony with the speaker's initial conception of the needs of the group. The situation has undergone a certain change, the relations between the members of the group, as we have found them to be when the argument was started, have shifted. (Yost, 1917, 115)

Not only did Yost offer a new perspective for the study of communication, she also shifted the focus of investigation so that the "group" became a significant factor in communication. To be sure, audiences had previously been considered, even as "groups," as, for example, in George Campbell's discussion of "men in general" and "men in particular." But Yost's treatment encompassed far more than the examination of motives and characteristics. She looked at the audience as a "social group" placed in a particular setting at a particular time, and she carefully examined the factors which influenced the relations and interactions between speakers and groups. One might even speculate that Yost laid the groundwork for research and teaching in group communication. Sadly, such an effect seemed not to happen. When the discipline turned to "group discussion" a few years later the conceptual base was altogether different from Yost's. The social-psychological orientation of Yost was not considered; instead close attention was paid to the more logic based idea of "Reflective Thinking" derived from the work of John Dewey.

Yost delineated a relationship between speaker and audience that brought about a "sense of self," which caused the speaker and audience to identify with each other.

> *Not only, then, is there a characteristic change in the content of experience for both speaker and audience but there is a change also in the sense-of self audience and speaker are feeling. On the part of the audience there seems to be a more active awareness-of-self than is found as the result of every act of discourse, but the awareness is less tense at the end of the argument than it was at the beginning. On the other hand, the speaker's sense-of self is not only greater in degree than the audience's, both at the beginning and at the end of an argument, but also the tenseness and aggressiveness have increased not decreased. The combination of these effects on speaker and audience produces a social situation where the two can think, feel, and act in harmony with one another. (116)*

In order to attain the identification between speaker and audience which Yost postulated, the speaker had to speak in terms of the audience's interests. To accomplish this goal required not so much reasoning as an association between speaker and audience. She drew on associational psychology to make her point.

> *The speaker can win only if he is able to translate his ideas in terms of the audience's experiences and interests so that the associations aroused by his argument are more vivid and compelling than those which came to the consciousness of the audience first. . . . What we may call the formalities of reasoning are very little in evidence. The problem, as we have said, resolves itself into ascertaining how one set of associations can get and hold the attention when a set connected with opposing ideas already has possession of the field. (118)*

Surprisingly, in spite of the modernity of her perceptions, Yost connected her analysis to traditional rhetorical theory, in this case to Plato. But, she felt that Platonic theories of discourse had only a moral basis to explain this view of communication. Yost hoped to show that her interpretation was consonant with Platonic ideas. More important, however, was her perception that argument (read rhetoric) is an act of communication not an act of logic. The explication of this idea requires considerable quotation, but it is necessary to make it clear.

> *One of the most significant movements in the rhetorical history of the last twenty years has been the reappearance of Plato's idea of discourse and its warm advocacy by the best modern rhetoricians. . . The advocate of the Platonic idea today, however, is rather at a loss for a basis other than what might be called the moral one, on which*

to explain this organic theory of discourse. I believe the assumption concerning the nature of any social group in which communication takes place, which it was necessary to make in order to explain the phenomena of the social activity of the group which give rise to argument gives such a basis. . . . Not only does the theory of argument when discussed from the point of view of sociology indicate the social basis for the Platonic theory of discourse, but it points also to the importance of the functional aspect of argument when formulated from the point-of view of logic. Indeed, when argument is considered primarily as an act of communication, the formal aspect not only seems of much less significance than it did under the traditional theory, but it appears much less fixed and rigid than the usual treatment would lead us to believe. If the narrative of the murder of a man is given by the lawyer with the purpose of winning the jury from a belief in the prisoner's innocence to a belief in his guilt, is not this narrative an argument since the speaker designs it to fulfill the function of argument? (120-121)

Seventy five years have passed since Mary Yost published "Argument from Point-Of-View of Sociology" and yet it is a disturbingly modern essay. In her article Yost broke with the traditional logic-based model of communication to postulate a theory of communication based on the findings of contemporary sociology and psychology. Although she wrote specifically of argument, it is clear that she presented a theory applicable to almost any communication situation. The fact that she saw argument as centered in communication and not in logic was a conception entirely new to teachers of public speaking. Yost's focusing on the social group and its role in communication also presented a new perspective as did her analysis of the relation of the speaker and the audience. Yost's concentration on social groups and their characteristics also represented a new theoretical approach to communication research which would not be seen in the profession until much later in its history.

Although we have devoted much space to the explication of a single article by a single author, we are left with some disturbing question. If Yost's work was as prescient and forward looking as we claim, why it did it have hardly any discernible influence? Why is her work all but unknown today? Why did the new profession chose to follow the "harder" experimental psychological approach of Woolbert rather than the "softer" sociological approach of Yost?

Perhaps part of the answer to our question may be found in the fact that Mary Yost was a one act performer. Significant though it was, her essay was never followed up by other scholarship. *The Index to Journals in Communication* lists only one additional publication by Yost, "Training Four Minute Men at Vassar," a brief descriptive piece on wartime speaking at Vassar. (1919, 246-253) In contrast, articles on the psychological foundations of the discipline continued to flow from the fertile brain and active fingers of Charles Woolbert. Woolbert himself was certainly aware of Yost's work since he cited her in his article "Conviction and Persuasion: Some Considerations of Theory" in the very next issue of *The Quarterly Journal.* (1917a, 249-264)

Without seeking to denigrate the intellectual stature of the new profession we might, nevertheless, speculate that Yost's fairly abstract and theoretical presentation was less immediately intelligible to them than Woolbert's more specific and concrete articles. Even though the speech teachers were relatively unsophisticated, the world of psychology was more familiar to them than was the world of sociology.

We must also not discount the possible influence of sexism on the reception of Yost's research. In 1917 Mary Yost could be granted a Ph.D. at the University of Michigan; she could publish articles in journals; she could teach at Vassar College; but she was not even allowed to vote. It is perfectly possible that less attention was paid to Yost's work simply because she was a woman. In any case, Mary Yost was not heard of again in writing although she did occupy a seat on the Executive Committee of the Association.

Mary Yost may simply be a name in history now and her potential contributions may have largely been forgotten. Nevertheless, the question must be asked, "How might the profession have been different (perhaps even better) if her sociological model had been adopted in addition to the psychological model of Woolbert? Would the discipline be less governed by the ideology of the laboratory, experimentation and replicability? Sociology, like all other disciplines, had, and still has, shortcomings but it might have given a different, less rigid perspective to research. If the profession was to be derivative, might not sociology have allowed the field to be more flexible? Possibly, assuming Yost's point of view might have allowed for greater adaptation and less outright dependence on other disciplines.

In the very next issue of *The Quarterly Journal* Woolbert responded to Yost in his article "Conviction and Persuasion: Some Considerations of Theory," in which he presented a psychological, rather than a sociological, basis for investigating persuasive discourse. At the outset of his essay he recognized Yost's contribution, but he indicated he had a different perspective from which to view the age-old persuasion-conviction dualism.

> *New impetus has been given to the subject by the discussion of Miss Yost "Argument from the Point of View of Sociology". . . . Basing her conclusions upon the data of sociology she contends that the partition of public address into persuasion and argument is meaningless and antiquated. As a further contribution to the subject and as support to Miss Yost's attitude, I offer here some citations and conclusions from modern psychology. (1917a, 249)*

Before Woolbert began his discussion of the psychological perspective he found it necessary to present yet another attack on rhetoric, not only for its position on the dualism, but also because of its general non-scientific orientation.

> *Relying upon rhetoric and composition, we have, as it turns out, built upon shifting sands. Rhetoric as a science has been too much of the study, if not of the arm chair; too many of the conclusions of the rhetoricians, lacking strict empirical basis, are merely verbal shufflings, and not valid solutions of problems. An excellent illustration of the reliance on words and pure abstractions of the study-chair is to be found in the customary explanation as to why persuasion and conviction and persuasion should be looked upon as two different things rather than as one. (1917a, 249)*

In the next issue of *The Quarterly Journal*, Hunt would respond to some of the matters raised by Yost and Woolbert but he did not address matters which are now apparent in Woolbert's appraisal of rhetoric. Woolbert insisted on evaluating rhetoric as a science at a time when rhetoric made no such claim, at least not as Woolbert understood science. He strongly implied that a discipline was not really respectable unless it could find its place among the sciences. The sub-text of the statement was that disciplines which have no "strict empirical basis" are not useful and that, in the case of rhetoric, its conceptions were "merely verbal shufflings." The attack on rhetoric was not as significant as Woolbert's perspective which regarded empirical knowledge as the only reliable and useful knowledge. We find in Woolbert's statement an almost positivistic posture toward research. Although his views were only the prelude to a detailed discussion of persuasion and conviction, it anticipated the numerous conflicts between "empiricists" and "rhetoricians" which would mark the history of the profession. Questions concerning "correct" methodological and conceptual approaches to the study of human communication began almost with the founding of the profession and have continued to this day, resulting in a discipline which is oriented both to the humanities and to the social sciences.

After citing numerous writers on argumentation and public speaking and pointing out the errors of their ways, Woolbert found that the problems of the persuasion-conviction dualism could only be solved by relying on the research of psychologists.

> Let me say plainly here, what I have already indicated, that I see no hope for a solution from rhetoricians and lexicographers. Belief, argument, persuasion, reasoning—nothing other than ways of influencing the mind; mental processes can be described and explained only in terms of psychology; the solution of the difficulty, accordingly, is to be found in psychology alone. (1917, 253)

While acknowledging that Woolbert directed his remarks to the specific question of the dualism, we must also recognize that his statement had serious research implications, then and in the future. The unitary position of Woolbert is striking. In discussing a topic as basic to public speaking as persuasion he took the categorical stance that explanations and descriptions could be stated "only in terms of psychology." Woolbert, in essence, found psychology to be the only useful research model. In spite of his ritual nod to Mary Yost, he saw no role for any other discipline as research model for the new profession. So much for sociology since it did not fit Woolbert's unitary system. His unwavering reliance upon psychology further strengthened the derivative nature of the discipline and placed psychology in the position of the pre-eminent guiding discipline in the future development of significant "social science" research.

The fact that Woolbert was, at the time of this article, a Ph.D. student at Harvard undoubtedly influenced his perspective, and he continued to hold largely to the same position for the rest of his life. Mary Yost had already completed her Ph.D. in sociology, but her words had a negligible effect as compared to Woolbert's.

Not only did Woolbert depend on psychology for his theoretical foundations, he depended on, even for his own time, the "hardest" varieties of psychology, those that were based in physiology with a strong behavioral perspective. His conception of psychology was one of a science with irrefutable laws. This point of view was revealed when he encountered the argument of rhetoricians and in which he argued that no meaningful distinction could be drawn between the "physical" and the "mental."

> But some will say, "That is well enough for psychology; yet in practical matters of speech there is a clear-cut division adequately described by the accepted meanings of the words conviction and persuasion; why then needlessly squeeze the two into one?" The question is a good one and must be met; it carries with it a strong presumption that cannot be ignored. My first reply is this; once we submit our problems to the court of psychology, we must abide by the decisions and laws of evidence enforced in that court. I fear we shall have only a sorry patchwork if we solve one problem by psychology and another, vitally interwoven with it, by a combination of rhetoric, dictionary meanings, and everyday usage. The psychologist cannot make any distinction between "physical" action and "mental" action; to him it is one and the same thing. Mind and body are two aspects of the same entity; all action is both of the mind and of the body; (1917a, 255)

Woolbert postulated that speech was centrally concerned with response and that any kind of response, whether physical or mental, really was action. As we shall see later, the idea of stimulus and response came to play an important role in Woolbert's intellectual conceptions.

> *Therefore, in all matters of human experience, whatever events can be brought under the term response must be conceived as also belonging to the term action; any classification that denies this must thereby ignore the nature of mind, and can only be a loose and meaningless manipulation of words. (1917a, 257)*

Woolbert laid at least part of the blame for misunderstanding at the feet of the rhetoricians because they had failed to focus on the response rather than on outside observations.

> *. . . the error of the conviction-persuasion, emotion- intellect, thought-action duality is found in the fact that we discuss this issue, not in terms of what the observer perceives him doing. What we have been talking about for ages in our rhetorical theory is not what the actor does, but what a spectator can detect by eye and ear. (1917a, 258)*

Woolbert sought to find a connection between his stimulus-response perspective and Yost's concentration on social groups. He postulated that the effectiveness of a communication situation is determined by the response of the social group.

> *. . . following the cue of Miss Yost. . . a speech or an argument always implies a social situation. . . . The social situation in speech-making and in listening as an auditor is felt most acutely when an observer can detect by eye and ear that the speaker has hit home, that he has moved his hearers. (1917a, 261)*

Woolbert, in fact, distorted Yost's position by seeking to incorporate her social group model into his stimulus response model. Yost's emphasis in her communication model was actually on the speaker and the way he controls the communicative situation. Yost's concern was not so much on securing response as on reaching agreement in the social group.

In concluding his lengthy treatise, Woolbert summarized the major points of his argument.

> *(1) As a matter of theory of public address and appeal, all dualistic attitudes separating response into action and non-action are untenable and misleading. (2) The dichotomy into perceived movement and movement not perceived, to which the rhetorical theory of tradition is committed, is restricted in its application. . . . (3) The whole theory of argumentation, conviction, persuasion, the rhetoric of public address, must be rewritten to fit the facts of mind as accepted today; which will be tantamount to restating them in terms of stimulus-response, object-subject, and environment-attitude. (1917a, 264)*

In enunciating what amounted to a credo, Woolbert demanded nothing less than the reorientation of the profession. Had his views prevailed, it is likely that the sub-fields of rhetorical theory and criticism would not exist in their present forms in the Speech Communication discipline, since Woolbert had decreed that the only dependable method for studying persuasive communication had to be based on the laws of contemporary psychology. The discipline of English has, in recent years, revived its interest in rhetoric; if Woolbert had been completely persuasive in his statements we might today find rhetoric completely under the jurisdiction of departments of English.

The implications of Woolbert's position, as articulated in this article, are decidedly mixed. He, assuredly, deserves credit for seeking to integrate the theories and methods of science, particularly psychology, into the research approaches of the new discipline. After all the ambiguous statements of Winans and the Research Committee, Woolbert provided a specific research paradigm and a explicit point of view toward the study of communication. What may be referred to as the "social science" or "empirical" traditions in the discipline certainly had their first clear enunciation in the writings of Woolbert. A large portion of the present day discipline should, without doubt, be indebted to him. At the same time we must be aware of the possible harm done by Woolbert's position. Although he denied a dichotomy between persuasion and conviction, he was responsible for creating a dichotomy in the profession. Woolbert arrayed himself, and his supporters, against almost all of traditional rhetoric. In contrast to Yost, who saw communication as the achievement of mutual agreement, Woolbert placed himself in an "all or nothing" posture vis-a-vis the traditions of rhetoric. Positivistic, scientific psychology was, for Woolbert, the only means of studying human communication. For him, there was no middle ground. Psychology was correct and all other approaches to communication were in error. We cannot say that disputes between "empiricists" and "rhetoricians" would not have occurred without Woolbert, but he certainly was the instigator of the conflict.

Although Woolbert sought to place the study of speech on a firm scientific footing, we may, nonetheless, question the wisdom of his exclusive reliance on one variety of psychology. Possibly the scope of the discipline might have been broader had methodologies from more flexible social sciences, such as anthropology and sociology, been available. The problem with Woolbert's dependence on behavioral psychology is not with psychology in itself; rather the concern is with excessive derivation from one field and the shaping of Speech Communication as a derivative discipline.

It did not take long for Everett Hunt to respond to his adversary. In the very next issue of *The Quarterly Journal*, he offered his views under the title "An Adventure in Philosophy." Although Hunt was polite to both Woolbert and Yost, he strongly disagreed with their presuppositions and with their applications. In spite of Woolbert's characterization of rhetoric as "verbal shufflings," Hunt found that Woolbert was himself trapped in terminology.

> *Using a term of William James's I would accuse all who place emphasis on terminology—a terminology hoary with age, or a terminology in the latest and most "approved terms of stimulus—response, object-subject, or environment attitude"— of "vicious intellectualism." (1917b, 301)*

Hunt also accused Woolbert of imposing intellectual unity where it did not exist.

> *This attempt to find "terms in which you can state the unity so there will be no omissions" is so typical of the monistic mind that I cannot refrain from quoting from William James ". . . . Everyone is nevertheless prone to claim that his conclusions are the only logical ones and that they are necessities of universal reason, they being all the while, at bottom accidents more or less of personal vision which had far better be avowed as such." Not only does the attempt to compel teachers of Public Speaking to borrow their terms from psychology seem to be an example of this "personal vision," but the attempt to determine which particular psychological terms shall be used seems to exaggerate the importance of terminology and to make again the mistake of assuming that certain ideas are inherently "fundamental." (1917b, 301)*

Hunt's response to Woolbert contained a certain amount of irony. In the above quotation, and in other places in the article, he offered numerous quotations from William James and John Dewey, important figures in the psychology of the period, albeit not precisely of Woolbert's stripe. Hunt used the writings of the Pragmatists to refute Woolbert. More importantly, however, he attacked Woolbert, and to a lesser extent Yost, from a humanistic perspective, grounded in philosophy, which was more open and less arbitrary than the psychology of Woolbert. Hunt concluded his adventure with a summary that did more to refute monism and behaviorism than to advance any other approaches to the study of speech.

> *Again I repeat that these remarks are not attacks upon Miss Yost and Professor Woolbert. Their service is of incalculable value. But now that the teachers of public speaking are awakening to the joy or to the stern fact that they must become scholars, the science of speech, if such there be, will be formed largely by analogies from other fields. In this process of building up a new content, I have only these suggestions to offer:*
>
> *(1) No new science can rightfully claim to be fundamental in shaping the concepts of public speaking.*
>
> *(2) No one formula can be discovered which will express the whole process.*
>
> *(3) Distinctions and definitions are by their very nature little more than half truths, and their inadequacies can never be remedied by new terminology. (1917b, 302-303)*

Hunt's vision of how the profession should conduct its investigations, although lacking in specificity, was more open to multiple influences than either Woolbert's or Yost's. Instead of a discipline almost entirely dependent on one outside discipline, Hunt envisioned a discipline with the ability to synthesize and analogize from a number of disciplines. He also expressed serious reservations that a single model would be sufficient. In some ways, Hunt and Woolbert were characteristic not only of two views of the academic world, they also seemed to represent two different eras. Hunt was of the philosophic world of the late nineteenth century, and he drew on the literary and philosophical figures of the time. Woolbert was very much a child of the twentieth century with his emphasis on science, laws and a governing ideology. Oddly, Woolbert, more than Hunt, resembled the elocutionists with their belief in infallible "laws" of human behavior.

The exchange between Woolbert and Hunt came to a formal close in Woolbert's 1918 article, "The Place of Logic in a System of Persuasion." Woolbert did not emulate Hunt's graceful statements of good will. In this article, which was really an extension of his article on considerations of theory, he chose to attack Hunt directly and without mercy, not in the body of the article but in the footnotes. He found nothing redeeming in Hunt's position and said so explicitly.

> *The criticism offered by Mr. E.L. Hunt on this use of a single term to cover all activities of both body and mind fails to dislodge me from my position. . . . Mr. Hunt then assumes to refute my conclusion that they are all one by naively referring to these processes as if they must be different; yet he does this without taking the slightest pains to challenge my reasons for thinking them to be one—the testimony of psychologists quoted in liberal measure and unequivocal—in import. He should first have refuted the psychologists; only then could he logically assume that he could speak of "theorizing" and "thinking" as if they were in a different category from "action." Until he actually overthrows the psychologists—not merely sneers at them—he is in no logical position to make such conclusions as the one quoted above. (1918, 19-20)*

Woolbert's attack on Hunt was not merely unmerciful; Woolbert either misunderstood or misconstrued Hunt's position. He was not so much arguing against the specifics of Woolbert's theories as he was inveighing against an academic approach which placed all its academic eggs in one research basket and which was intolerant of other approaches.

Woolbert made use of his newly acquired knowledge of Freudian psychology to launch a psychoanalytic attack on Hunt in a section of the article where he described fallacies.

> . . . all fallacies in reasoning reveal attempts to supplant a wish which we are ashamed of by one which we think will be more socially acceptable.Every fallacy that is given a name in the textbook can be shown to be the out-cropping of a suppressed wish. Fallacies are the unwitting disclosures of hidden wishes. (1918, 37)

Woolbert provided documentation for his forthcoming psychological assault on Hunt.

> For the vast ethical significance of the suppressed wish in our lives, see Holt "The Freudian Wish," cit. supra; [Holt, whose work on Freud was published in 1915, was Woolbert's dissertation advisor at Harvard] also see the works of Sigmund Freud and of his followers. For a clear understanding of mechanism of the sub-conscious in our lives, especially in its relation to logic and speech, see Bernard Hart, "The Psychology of Insanity," particularly of what he says of "rationalization." (Woolbert, 1918, 37)

With his theoretical foundation firmly in place, Woolbert then initiated his psychological attack on Hunt.

> The strictures made by Mr. E.L. Hunt in the October Quarterly Journal on my article concerning certain theoretical considerations of Conviction and Persuasion in The Journal for July make an interesting study in the escaped wish. Mr Hunt ridicules psychology, denies the validity of science, and then makes philosophy look nonsensical and ridiculous. Is it a very wild guess to suspect that Mr. Hunt is doing his best to vent a troublesome wish to shine in one or all of these fields? . . . We can be grateful to Mr. Hunt for the illustration he has furnished us for our point. How many people would see any difficulty in deciding what hidden wish has cropped out in this sparkling array of bad logic offered in a cause of exceedingly doubtful credit to its upholders. (1918, 37)

Seldom has such a personal attack appeared in the pages of *The Quarterly Journal*. One can perhaps understand Woolbert's irritation with Hunt's opposite position, and one can appreciate how deeply Woolbert felt that Hunt was absolutely wrong; but these factors do not explain the personal contempt expressed by Woolbert or the psychological explanation for Hunt's writings. One can speculate that Woolbert held to his position so firmly that he was unable to conceal his disdain for Hunt's ignorance. It is also possible that Hunt's position simply goaded Woolbert to anger. In any case, Woolbert's remote psychoanalysis of Hunt's personality hardly seemed warranted. Although Woolbert continued with his pronouncements on persuasion, this exchange was the last time that he and Hunt confronted each other in print. Perhaps it is a mark of Hunt's forbearance that he chose not to respond. On the other hand, Woolbert's technical philosophical case may have been beyond Hunt's expertise.

Quite apart from the disagreement between Woolbert and Hunt, the logic and persuasion article represented the first mention of Freudian psychology that we have been able to identify in the writings of teachers of public speaking. Woolbert's article contained a number of allusions to Freud, but he relied most on Freud in a portion titled, "The Motive Power of Inference." Woolbert argued, contrary to traditional logic, that inferences were psychological rather than logical. Indeed, inferences were, as Woolbert interpreted Freud, explained by the theory of the wish.

> *Whence do . . . inferences arise? For the making of new judgments we must find a driving force. We find it [a driving force] the motor attitude of the organism, the set, the determination, the bent, which actuates it at any one time.This is a matter of nervous organization. However, we can speak of this in terms that fit more clearly into our every-day usages; for there is a concept to express it that is so comprehensive, so illuminating, that we can use it with great profit. I refer to what Freud calls the Wish. Everything we do is the result of a wish, either hidden from sight in the subjective promise or in words objectively in the open. . . it is the wish that motivates inference and judgment. Inferences are hardly made out of blue sky; they are forced upon us. Every inference arises because we are pleased to make it; we believe because we want to; we respond in a given way because that is the way we are heading. So to speak of levels of inference is also to speak of levels of openness in wishing. (1918, 36)*

Although Woolbert titled his essay "The Place of Logic in a System of Persuasion," logic was, in fact, made subordinate to psychology in his system. In his summary Woolbert indicated that much of what had been regarded as logical processes was actually psychological mechanisms.

(1) *Inferences, judgments, logical connections are made in nuero-muscular patterns.*

(2) *Most of them are made below the level of consciousness.*

(3) *In speech, on the behavior level of words, these inferences are to be tested by the well-known laws of logic.*

(4) *There are three levels of social exposure on which inferences are made: (a) hidden, (b) semi-open, and (c) open.*

(5) *Each level has its own formula for practice and use: (a) the rules of Rhetoric, (b) the laws of Testimony together with advice as to Prestige, and (c) Logic.*

(6) *All inferences are made as the result of wishes and all fallacies are the result of escape of suppressed wishes, thus inducing inconsistencies between words used and attitudes held. (1918, 39)*

One is struck by the categorical nature of Woolbert's assertions. When he spoke of "all inferences" and "all fallacies," he allowed no room for exceptions. Persuasion, for Woolbert, could no longer be regarded in the schemes of contemporary textbooks; rather it had to be examined on the basis of the most recent psychological findings. In the section which he titled "Corollaries," Woolbert illustrated this new relationship. The following are among the most interesting examples of the dominant role played by psychological knowledge:

(a) *There is such a thing as "the will to believe;" it is a clear manifestation of hidden inferences.*

(b) *We assume to believe one thing and then proceed to do its opposite, what has been called "irrational conduct;" because the hidden, unspoken, and often unconfessed inference is stronger than the verbal one.*

(e)   *A speaker may win by personal graces and by his reputation in spite of defective*
       logic; because in the minds of the audience the hidden inferences he instigates
       are paramount.

(h)   *The speaker is more than a mouth-piece of truth, he is a maker of it; because he*
       induces the the inner logic which is the most powerful of all.

(j)   *Men will flagrantly and wantonly pin their faith to open fallacies that any*
       critical mind can see must be easily detected; for the reason that some hidden
       wish blinds them to the absurdity of breach of rules of open talk. (1918, 38-39)

Whether Woolbert was correct in his analysis in light of theories of persuasion of the 1990s is really not a matter for our consideration; obviously time has passed him by and thought has advanced beyond that of 1918. The matter that does deserve consideration is Woolbert's influence, particularly in this essay. In discussing the place of logic he, for the first time, provided a foundation for the study of persuasion, indeed for all communication, which is deeply rooted in psychology. Following the example of Woolbert's writings, the discipline was able to make use of psychological models and theories to discover methods for teaching and research. Increasingly, over the years, various psychological conceptions have been used to inform our understanding of persuasion in particular, and human communication in general. Although the overall effect of this influence may have been beneficial, one may, nonetheless, question whether Woolbert, at the outset, and the discipline, over time, have not been overly dependent on a single discipline to provide a theoretical and methodological base.

Woolbert did not cite any specific works by Freud; he cited an article by Holt on Freud and he referred to "the work of Sigmund Freud and his followers." We cannot say with any degree of certainty how deep was his knowledge of Freudian psychology. Nevertheless, Woolbert must be credited with the introduction of a psychoanalytic perspective to the study of communication, misinformed though he may have been. Although no direct connection is claimed, it is interesting to note the use made of Freudian psychology by the advocates of "mental hygiene" a decade later. (See Chapter 6.) Charles Henry Woolbert's name may not be widely known to present day members of the discipline, but, without question, he must be regarded as the founder of an important and durable conception of what the new discipline should be, what its central concerns should be, and how its research should be conducted. Disputes between "humanists" and "scientists" have arisen from time to time in the history of the discipline; the grounds of the disagreement, however, were established in the confrontations between Woolbert and Hunt.

In spite of the pages written by Yost, Woolbert and others and the later more sophisticated treatment of persuasion, the persuasion-conviction dualism still seems to remain with us. Current textbooks and syllabi continue to distinguish between "speeches to inform" and "speeches to persuade." Indeed, very recently I was asked to judge the state final contest in "informative speaking."

Woolbert's work was the most significant early psychological influence on the profession, but it was by no means the earliest. The publication of *Effective Speaking* by Arthur Edward Phillips in 1908 and of *Public Speaking* in 1915 by James Albert Winans were works indebted to psychology before Woolbert began to write his essays. Phillips and Winans were readers of psychology while Woolbert was a professional psychologist. Woolbert was quite aware of the work of Phillips and Winans and quotes both of them in his articles.

E.A. Phillips was, in fact, a teacher of elocution. He was in 1908 Director of the

Department of Public Speaking of a Lutheran seminary and Principal of the Phillips School of Oratory, both in Chicago. Phillips said that the writing of his book grew out of a practical problem.

> *About fifteen years ago, when I first began to teach the Art of Expression, I found a constant demand for instruction in Public Speaking. The student would ask, "Can you give me some definite steps which, if followed, would lead to confidence and power when I seek to persuade or convince? Are there any laws and rules that would be direct, practical helps?". . . . True, there were many isolated aids, but nothing like a well-ordered practical system was to found. In fact, there was more than half truth in the couplet: "All a rhetorician's rules teach him but to name his tools." (5)*

Phillips related that he had restudied,". . . among others the work of Aristotle, Quintilian, Cicero, Whatley, Campbell, Blair, Hill, Genung, Bautain Kames" (6). (Note that Phillips acknowledged nineteenth century writers in rhetoric and composition as well as the traditional rhetoricians.) He was, however, ". . . led to the conclusion that little that was new had been added to Aristotle" (6). He also perused "Analysis of Master Speeches"and "Study of Contemporary Speaking" and concluded that neither offered an answer to the problem. Finally he turned to "Psychological Research." There the pathway to effective speaking was clear.

> *Further, I carried the study into the field of Psychology. What are the laws of impression, if any? Could Psychology say why one thing would likely to be remembered, why another thing would not? Why one statement would sway an audience, why another would not? How far did the latest psychic discoveries furnish reliable conclusions in respect to different methods in argumentation, in choice of material, in expression? (7)*

In the first chapter of his book Phillips found that the most important reason for ineffective speaking was the lack of knowledge of the psychological laws which govern oral discourse.

> *The main reason for this state of things is a failure to realize that effective speaking is an art, an art founded upon the science of psychology . . . . The truly effective speakers never have enthroned blind impulse as their god. They have controlled and directed it with the judgment born of a careful study of the laws governing action and belief. They recognized that entrenched error, prejudice, self-interest, conceit, doubt, fear, desire, ignorance, are barriers to conviction, and that these barriers could only be broken down or overcome by the application of certain principles of psychology. . . . When this course is followed by the average speaker; when the man who has something to say will devote time and thought to the application of the psychological principles by which this "something to say" becomes effective, there will be a more rapid spread of the truth. (14-16)*

The principles of psychology were utilized, for the most part, in Chapters III, IV and V. In those chapters Phillips dealt with "The Principles of Reference to Experience," "Reference to Experience and the General Ends" and "Action and Impelling Motives." Reference to Experience he defined as, "coming into the listener's life," and he offered fairly simple guidelines as to how to accomplish the goal.

> *The more the speaker brings his ideas within the vivid experience of the listener, the more likely will he attain his end, and obversely: The less the speaker brings his ideas within the vivid experience of the listener, the less likely he will attain his*

end. . . . An experience will be vivid in the degree that it is originally intense, recent, frequent in recurrence and frequently recollected. (33, 35)

In Chapter V Phillips turned to the relation of action and impelling motives. To a modern day reader Phillips' treatment may seem somewhat primitive, but he was one of the very first speech teachers to write of motives, although they had been discussed by some of the writers of rhetoric and composition textbooks. (See Chapter 2.) Phillips definition of motives was:

Impelling motives may be defined as man's spiritual, intellectual, moral and material wants. For working purposes, they may be given the following classification: Self-Preservation, Property, Power, Reputation, Affections, Sentiments, Tastes. (48)

Phillips saw the impelling motives in opposition to what he called "the restraining motives," although he did not specify what the restraining motives were, or how they were to be overcome. That was the lesson taught by psychology.

If, then, we are seeking Action so frequently, and if further, Action is the result of the superiority of the Impelling Motives over the restraining motives (as Psychology teaches), it is plain that the more we bring these Impelling Motives to bear upon a given audience or person, the more likely we will attain our End. (62)

In contrast to the writings of Yost and Woolbert, Phillips continued to support the idea of the Conviction-Persuasion Dualism. At least in his discussion of the "general ends" of speaking, he differentiated between "belief" and "action."

Belief is acceptance. The speaker is not content that the listener shall see or feel. The subject matter must come into his mind as reality—truth . . . Action is doing. It is never passive. The end of the speaker can be denoted as Action, therefore, when his dominant desire is to have the listener act—to be, to go, to give, to bring, to join, to do. (20, 22)

Since Phillips did not refer to specific psychologists or their writings, we cannot know from whence he derived his psychological ideas. Apparently he had read the work of psychologists of the time since his book was a simplified version of ideas current in the early years of the twentieth century.

We must be aware that the task undertaken by Phillips was much different from that carried out by Yost and Woolbert. They sought to reorient the discipline and to provide a rationale for the use of psychological and sociological theories and methodologies in research and teaching. Phillips had no such objective in mind. He was merely seeking to apply the findings of psychology in a fairly simple public speaking textbook. His work was in no way theoretical. Winans' *Public Speaking* is in many ways a different kind of book than Phillips'. The text had a curious history. First, it was a booklet published in 1911 as *Notes on Public Speaking,* and it was intended for Winans' own classroom use. In 1915 it was published by a local Ithaca publisher, the Sewell Publishing Company (1915b, v). In 1917 *Public Speaking* was published and nationally distributed by the Century Company. In contrast to Phillips, Winans was scrupulous in acknowledging his indebtedness to psychologists and the readers, even the undergraduate students, had no difficulty determining the source of Winan's ideas. Ironically, Winans devoted a good deal of space to delivery while Phillips, the elocutionist, in his book, deliberately said not a word about delivery.

It will be observed that this volume does not discuss effectiveness in respect to

Delivery. Voice, Action, and Expression have been treated in the author's work, "The Tone System," and will be discussed further in volumes to follow. (9)

In the introduction to his book Winans indicated his indebtedness to his former teachers of Psychology. The text itself contained numerous references to psychologists. The most frequent citations were to William James, but there were many references to Titchener, Thorndyke, Dewey, Royce and others.

The first psychological idea to which Winans addressed himself had to do with attention, which he thought was absolutely central to public speaking. In fact, four of the sixteen chapters were devoted to attention. He spelled out the importance of attention in Chapter III, "Principles of Attention."

> *In the first place, it is evident that the aim of a speaker is to hold the attention of his audience. Secondly,. . . one of the grand essentials of good speaking is "thinking at the instant of delivery." And, thirdly, as in all studies, we need power of attention in the preparation of speeches. Throughout this subject, then, we shall need knowledge of the principles of attention. (1915b, 63)*

Winans cited a private letter written to him by Professor Titchener and then concluded.

> *What the speaker needs then, is such preparation that his ideas will command his attention, and awaken him to energetic thinking and earnestness. (Winans, 1915b, 64)*

The chapter on "Principles of Attention" was followed by one devoted to "The Speaker's Attention to His Topic." In a later chapter Winans considered "Attention of the Audience Interest." All of the chapters dealing with attention were very carefully documented to the writings of psychologists who furnished the material on which Winans relied. He was most dependent in those three chapters to James, but he also cited the work of Titchener, Pillsbury, Royce, Dewey as well as many less well-known psychologists of the period. Interestingly, from Phillips he derived the idea of impelling motives. Winans' treatment of attention was not entirely dependent on the work of psychologists; he also cited many of the composition texts of the time. Earlier we discussed the contributions of many of the writers of the texts which he quoted and we indicated their interest in persuasion. (See Chapter 2.) Among the more prominent writers on rhetoric and composition mentioned were Gardiner, Hill, Ringwalt, Genung, Phelps, and Baker. The chapter on "Principles of Attention" was, in fact, a 25 page summary of current research on attention. Only when he treated "The Speakers Attention to his Topic," and "Attention of the Audience-Interest" did Winans apply those principles to public speaking.

Winans also made use of the work of psychologists in his chapter on "Emotion." The material in that chapter was drawn almost entirely from the writings of William James. At the outset of the chapter Winans sought to eliminate the bias often associated with emotion.

> *One often meets a prejudice against the very words feeling and motion. . . . This prejudice is often really against excessive emotion. . . . Emotion is a constant factor in our mental states, unless we reach absolute indifference. To be without emotion, indeed, is to be without interest, without happiness, as well as without sorrow, without desires good or bad. Even our reasons are usually emotions. (1915b, 108)*

Winans also drew on the older psychological idea of association as he traced the association between words and emotions. He was also clear that the associations were a product of culture.

> *We may say that the feeling which is aroused by a word or an idea depends greatly upon the association one's mind has for it; upon what has been attached to it by observation, study and experience. Home, flag, and mother are examples of words notably strong in emotional associations and therefore tending to arouse vivid imagery and strong feeling. . . . That individuals differ greatly in their associations for even the commonest words—a fact the speaker must bear in mind —is brought home to us by the story of the street gamin who was asked his idea of home. He replied: "A big dry-goods box with plenty of rags in winter.". . . To the youth who has lived the ordinarily protected life, the idea of justice has little emotional significance. . . . But suppose he has suffered injustice, or is of a people that has suffered injustice:. . . I have in mind students from Porto Rico and the Philippines who believed their countries wronged by the United States. (1915b, 114)*

Much of the chapter dealing with audience attention was devoted to audience analysis and adaptation. In order to make a satisfactory adaptation, Winans felt that the speaker must keep in mind the purpose of the speech. Winans classification system resembled the nineteenth century taxonomy of the ends of discourse; yet it was based on psychology, and it was close to that of Phillips, whose influence Winans openly acknowledged. Those ends were:

1. *To interest*
2. *To make clear*
3. *To induce belief*
4. *To influence conduct. (1915b, 179)*

It will be noted that Winans continued to distinguish between conviction and persuasion to the extent that he specified separate purposes for inducing belief and influencing conduct. "In many instances belief must be won before action can be secured." Yet when Winans came to discuss belief specifically, he combined it with persuasion in a chapter titled "Persuasion and Belief" which followed the chapter on "Influencing Conduct." In order to achieve this synthesis, it was necessary for Winans to draw a very fine line of distinction.

> *The term [persuasion] is broad enough to include conviction, but we shall for convenience use the latter term to designate the process of "bringing anyone to recognize the truth of what he has not before accepted." (Whatley, Elements of Rhetoric, 1915b, 249)*

Winans upheld what has continued to be a practice in much communication pedagogy. He acknowledged that conviction and persuasion were really inseparable but, "for convenience" he treated them as if they were separate entities. In order to deal with the distinction, Winans first treated "Persuasion When Active Opposition is Lacking" before he turned to "Persuasion and Belief." In the chapter on belief he sought to create a linkage between persuasion and conviction.

> *Our primary study in this chapter is how to win belief, either as an end in itself, or as a preliminary to action; and on investigation we find we are facing the familiar problem of securing exclusive attention. "The most compendious possible formula perhaps," says James, "would be that our belief and attention are the same fact. . . ." (James, Psychology, 1915b, 300)*

Winans seemed to anticipate Yost's interest in groups, although in a much simplified form. We must, of course, remember that Winans was writing for undergraduate students—not for his peers. Nevertheless, Winans did not seem to possess Yost's sociological knowledge and his conception of groups was quite naive compared to her well ordered treatment of social groups. The following indicates Winan's view:

> *Differences in Groups. No one is likely to overlook the fact that a group of farmers may be interested in topics very dull to laboring men, and that both farmers and laborers may be interested in themes which will not touch a body of artists;. . . The obvious means of safety is to know your audience, its interests, its information and its habits of thought. (1915b, 183)*

As can easily be seen, Winans' concern with groups was almost entirely with audience adaptation while Yost was concerned with the social group and the ways in which it influenced the communicative situation.

Although the Phillips and Winans books were written as beginning texts, they nonetheless exerted a significant early influence. Yost and Woolbert were aware of their existence and cited them in their own work and Winans relied on Phillips. They represented the first serious attempts to introduce the principles of psychology to speech pedagogy. A reading of Winans' text leaves the reader with the impression that in addition to a course in public speaking the students were also introduced to a course in the principles of psychology. Almost all of the chapters in the book are replete with citations from and references to contemporary psychological works. One suspects that since he was not so narrowly focused that Winans had a broader knowledge of psychology than Woolbert.

The early writings of Phillips and Winans combined with the prolific output of Woolbert may have insured the dominant influence of psychology on the new profession. At the same time, they may have minimized the possibility of influence from other social sciences. Thus Mary Yost's single, though significant, article may have been destined, ultimately to be of little consequence.

EPILOGUE

At the 1927 convention of the National Association James M. O'Neill, by then a distinguished elder in the discipline, presented an address in which he looked back at the history of the association, and in which he assessed the present state of the profession. His presentation was published in *The Quarterly Journal* in 1928 under the title "After Thirteen Years." In the article O'Neill presented a brief narrative of the founding of the association, and he reported on an informal survey he had made of founders of the association concerning the reasons the new discipline came into being. Most of the responses dealt with structural and strategic problems rather than intellectual problems. Some of the responses were:

> *. . . we needed an independent organization through which we could unify the university and college teachers of speech, and through which we could improve the scholastic standing of speech education in our colleges and universities. (Lardner, Northwestern)*

> *According to my recollection the purposes. . . were the following:*

1. *The separation of Speech as a profession and as an academic subject from English.*
2. *The establishment of Speech in colleges and universities as a separate and worthy academic subject.*
3. *The development of a body of knowledge worthy of such an academic subject through encouragement of research in the scientific phases of the field.*
4. *The establishment and publishing of a journal. . . (Rarig, Minnesota.)*

. . . First, we were indisposed to be in our respective institutions the tail of the English Department, wagged at will, sat upon from time to time, and held remote from the nourishment end of the creature. Secondly, a growing professional consciousness, a finer professional unity. . . . (Sarett, Illinois)

It was the hope, I believe. . . that it would greatly stimulate research work, promote more effective teaching. . . . (Cochran, Carleton)

To be free from the domination of the English Council; To have more time for programs and discussions; To further research work in our field; To win recognition in educational institutions as a department of study, teaching; and research; (Gaylord, McCormick Theological Seminary.)

. . . to see what we could do to make Speech separate from English. The only thing a speech man could find by way of a gathering of his profession was in a section of the English Council. . . . The split-off was brought off by college teachers. These found little to satisfy their needs in the meetings of the English Council. (Woolbert, then at Iowa, 1928, 247-250)

Finally, O'Neill offered his own recollections of the motivation for the founding of the National Association.

We organized the National Association for the promotion of research and better teaching in speech. True, most of us at the time called what we were doing public speaking, but already in many places this has become an inaccurate label. The broader conception of the whole field of human speech was even at that time taking shape in our professional thinking. (O'Neill, 1928, 251-252)

Twenty seven years after the O'Neill article, Andrew Weaver of the University of Wisconsin, an early member but not one of the founders, offered a tribute to "Seventeen who Made History." By 1955 only Phelps, Rarig, Merry and O'Neill were still alive. Forty years after the founding of the National Association, Weaver reviewed the subsequent careers of the founders, and he concluded with an eloquent eulogy.

The history of mankind bears eloquent testimony to the fact that a mere handful of men who are obedient to a great vision can shake the world. So it was with the seventeen. They were men of foresight and courage. They established a beach-head on a bleak and barren coast, and they held it and expanded it under the guns of the enemy. They were not of those who shrink back; they had what it took! (199)

CONCLUSION

Although problems of the orientation of the discipline have been occasionally raised throughout its history, the framework for the present field had been outlined by 1918. It would be a discipline which encompassed all of the oral arts, in effect an umbrella discipline. It was also to be a kind of superordinate nurturing discipline since it assumed responsibilty for sub-disciplines which remained in the association until they sensed that they had achieved sufficient maturity to venture forth as independent disciplines. Theater and Communication Disorders are representative of fields which, early in their lives, were components of the present day discipline of Speech Communication.

The dependence on outside disciplines to provide research models for the new discipline was clearly visible in the first years of its development. The lack of knowledge about research compelled the association to turn to disciplines which had developed research methodologies. The naiveté about research impeded the discipline in finding its own approaches to research and in developing its own theoretical foundations. Early scholars, such as Winans, Yost and Woolbert displayed ingenuity in formulating ways in which the perspectives of the social sciences could be brought to bear on the study of human communication. At the same time, their dependence on sociology and psychology impeded the growth of research orientations uniquely suited to the new discipline. Such dependence guaranteed Public Speaking's continuing existence as a derivative field. The work of early scholars ensured that a scientific perspective would be present in the history of the discipline.

The dispute initiated by Hunt and Woolbert provided the basis for intermittent disagreement within the field of Speech Communication. The differing orientations of writers who saw the discipline as a branch of the humanities and those who envisioned it as a division of the social sciences has remained with us to this day. One could divide the profession into Hunts and Woolberts. At various points in history the two schools partially resolved their differences; at other times they have diverged widely. The Hunt-Woolbert debate also brought into focus the question of whether the primary mission of the discipline was to teach about speech or to teach students to speak. Hunt saw the speech classroom as locus for general education through speech; he disdained excessive specialization. Woolbert, on the other hand, visualized a world in which research was carried on to discover "laws" and "truths" about speech.

Part of the early confusion of the profession certainly arose out of the conditions of its founding. Neither the Eastern Public Speaking Conference of 1910, nor the National Association Of Academic Teachers of Public Speaking were motivated by intellectually impelled causes. Rather the organizations came into being in order to share information and impressions among members; to fulfill their desire for autonomy; and to escape the domination of departments of English. Thus the new profession lacked the strong motivation to research which characterized disciplines which had diverged from their parent disciplines because of intellectual and conceptual differences. The profession was, of course, incompletely developed by 1918. It would, as it developed, extend its interest to new sub-fields as soon as research identified them. Other additions were the result of changes in the technological, academic and cultural environments. Pedagogical and research interest in such areas as group communication, interpersonal communication, organizational communication, and mass communications were developments of the future. However, the initial concerns with public speaking and persuasion have remained as central issues in the profession.

4

THE PROFESSION DIVERSIFIES

The present day profession of speech communication began as a reactive organization, more concerned with separating itself from English and establishing its autonomy than with defining its intellectual mission. In its early years it faced the problem not only of determining how it would fit itself into the academic world of the early twentieth century but also of defining the boundaries of the new discipline. Although the founders of the profession had assigned the title "Public Speaking" to the discipline it soon became clear that the scope of the profession was much broader than its title. An examination of early numbers of *The Quarterly Journal of Speech* reveals that under the rubric of "Public Speaking" such enterprises as rhetoric, speech science, theatre, debate, oral interpretation, group discussion and pedagogy were included. Apparently, all oral activities could be subsumed under one title. The new profession seemed to become an umbrella for almost all the oral arts.

PUBLIC SPEAKING

Well before the establishment of the national association the field of public speaking was hardly unknown. We know from Lyons' survey and other sources that courses in the subject were fairly widely offered, sometimes in separate departments and, at other times under the auspices of English departments. (See Chapter 2.) Often the courses sponsored by English were known as Oral English. No subject, of course, even in those days, could be taught without appropriate text books. As we earlier indicated some instruction in speaking was contained in the rhetoric/composition texts of the late nineteenth and early twentieth centuries. But by the first decade of the present century, text books and more popular guides to public speaking were produced. We have earlier mentioned the works by Phillips and Winans, and we will return to them in the course of this discussion.

One of the earliest works was of the popular genre. Brander Matthews, Professor of Dramatic Literature at Columbia University, whose present reputation is as a dramatic critic, published Notes on Speech-Making. This slender volume was actually a reprinting of two articles Matthews had written for the *Cosmopolitan Magazine* and for the *Century*, to which were appended material from other authors, including Lyman Abbott. In our time we may believe that we are in the midst of a dramatic communication technology transition to electronic media. In Matthew's time the technological concern was, as it had been for some time, that the printing press had supplanted oratory.

> *There are those who hold that the invention of printing sounded the knell of the noble art of oratory, and that he is little better than foolish who seeks now to*

influence others by the human voice, the range of which cannot but be strictly limited, when he can have at his command a megaphone like the modern newspaper, the range of which is immense and indeterminate. . . . Because a man reach a million in a newspaper, there is no reason why he should not also reach a thousand with a speech. The printed word is wide-spread, no doubt, but indirect, unimpressive, while the spoken word is direct, personal, almost hypnotic in its force. Furthermore, as it happens often, the very best way to arouse the reverberation of the press is to say what you have to say in a speech which the newspapers must needs report. (13-15)

Matthews believed that, in the nature/art question, ". . . speaking is an art like reading and writing; and that like them it does not come by nature." (21) In the space of fewer than 100 pages, Matthews managed to cover speech preparation, organization, the importance of content, indoor and outdoor delivery, and some final advice from Lyman Abbott. Although written by a respected member of the academic community, Matthew's little book was intended for a general audience rather than as a textbook for high school or college students. Nevertheless, it was indicative of the importance given to public speaking at the beginning of the twentieth century. In 1903 Edward Dubois Shurter, Associate Professor of Oratory at the University of Texas published *Public Speaking: A Treatise on Delivery.* Although the subtitle was essentially correct, Shurter provided a six page introduction and a ten page chapter which dealt with matters other than delivery. Shurter agreed with Matthews that the printed word would never replace the spoken word.

True, newspapers and magazines have in some ways affected the requirements for the public speaker, but they have by no means supplanted him and they never will. The proof of the assertion lies not alone in the peculiar social and political demands under a republican form of government, but is inherent in human nature itself. If men are moved by the printed word, must they not be aroused still more by the spoken word? If the author can convince through the lifeless type, how much more effectively can men's sensibilities be touched through the directness and earnestness of the living man! (1903, 1)

One wonders how Matthews and Shurter might have reacted to the electronic media of our own time.

Although the bulk of Shurter's book was devoted to delivery, he was at pains to make clear that he was not an old fashioned elocutionist.

This position doubtless represents the reaction from the mechanical, artificial, "elocutionist" methods, but like most reactions, the truth probably lies midway. It is better, of course, to have mind action and a rough mechanism, than a finished method and no motive power; but it does not follow that some attention should not be paid to the voice and body as agents of expression. In short, public speaking is an art and it does not come by chance. To acquire this art requires work — conscientious, systematic, continuous preparation and practice. Like any other study, we get out of it what we put in. (1903, 6)

Both the introduction and Chapter I of *Public Speaking* gave evidence of Shurter's knowledge of rhetoric since he cited Whately as well as Cicero and Plato. We will discover how extensive was Shurter's knowledge of rhetoric when we discuss his Rhetoric of Oratory later in this chapter.

The mythology of our profession credits James Winans with the introduction of the concept of public speaking as "expanded conversation." (1915, 17-26) Winans, writing at a time of rapid expansion, undoubtedly popularized the idea, but he was certainly not the first writer to express it. Certainly similar ideas had been promulgated by Blair and Whately, among others. In Winans' own time, the idea was expressed earlier by Shurter, although in a somewhat truncated form.

> . . . the criteria of the best public speaking are those of the best conversation—not the most showy or noisy, but the best, from the standpoint of effectiveness. In the conveyance and lodgement of thought, what constitutes effectiveness in conversation? Among other things, a good conversationalist must possess the qualities of clearness, directness, simplicity, vivacity, spontaneity, and sincerity. Hence these same qualities must be effective in public speech. (1903, 7)

Considering his interest in delivery, Shurter's own conception of public speaking was surprisingly modern, but, at the same time, reminiscent of the rhetorical writers of the eighteenth and nineteenth centuries. He was also careful to distinguish between public speaking and elocution.

> What is public speaking? It is speaking to a collection of individuals. Its purposes are to convey thought, to mold opinion, and to awaken feeling. Any one or all of these purposes may be present in a given address, but in any case there is thought to be conveyed, whether in the form of exposition, argument, or appeal. Public speaking, then, as the term is used in this book, is speaking in public with the purpose of convincing and persuading, and not for entertainment simply, which is usually the purpose in reciting, dramatic reading, or acting. . . . Eliminate at the outset, the extraneous or fanciful ideas often connected with the art of speaking in public. A pleasing, musical voice is an added charm, but not indispensable. Grace is desirable, but a fine carriage or pretty gestures do not carry a cause or win a verdict. (1903, 7-8)

Winans has also been given credit for asserting that the speaker must have "Full realization of your words as you utter them" (1915, 28). As was the case with public speaking as expanded conversation, Shurter also seemed to have anticipated Winans.

> Public speaking, then, being the communication of thought, it follows that you must have something to say; and a clear and vivid concept of this something to say must be present to the mind at the moment of its utterance. (1903, 9)

In Chapter I Shurter used an address of Henry Grady's as an oratorical example to which he appended a list of questions and exercises. Some of those items were indicative of Shurter's rhetorical consciousness.

> 1. Who is the author or speaker? Under what circumstances was the selection first written or spoken?. . .

> 3. Can you see the thought-movement from beginning to end? Is the line of thought logical and consecutive. . . .

> 7. Analyze the language in order to call up the associated ideas. What associated ideas present themselves to your mind. . . ?

> 8. Analyze the selection to find its emotion. Note the varied and changing emotions. (1903, 14-15)

To be sure, Shurter's questions were advanced for a public speaking text, but, at the same time, they resembled material in the composition/rhetoric texts of the period. Indeed, the possibility of Shurter's connection to English composition and oral English is indicated in his use of the conventions of written English. In a section which he called

"Processes in the Preparation of an Address for Delivery," he included, "The Theme of the Address," "Paragraphs," "Sentences," and "Words." (1903, 10-11) Although he devoted only 16 pages to the substance of public speaking, we should remember E.D. Shurter as a teacher who presented significant aspects of public speaking earlier than the profession itself.

Another example of the mixture of elocution and rhetoric was provided in 1906 by Grenville Kleiser, "Formerly Instructor in Elocution Yale Divinity School, Yale University. Now Instructor in Elocution, The Jewish Theological Seminary of America and Other Institutions." Kleiser's textbook *How to Speak in Public* went through at least eight editions. In the book Kleiser devoted 184 pages to the treatment of delivery, 31 pages to instruction in public speaking, and 214 pages to "Selections for Practice." Kleiser's work was not as advanced as Shurter's, but it, nonetheless, was indicative of the perspective in the years before the formal founding of the profession.

Under the head of "Previous Preparation," Kleiser listed physical, mental and moral preparation. Under the physical classification he included health, elocution and appearance. (185-187) The necessary mental attributes were:

1. *General Knowledge.*
2. *Memory.*
3. *Rhetoric.*
4. *Originality.*
5. *Imagination.*
6. *Personal Magnetism.*
7. *Logical Instincts.*
8. *Figures of Oratory. (187-192)*

The continuing influence of English was apparent in Kleiser's understanding of rhetoric. He restricted the term entirely to writing. He found support in classical rhetoric. "Cicero says that writing is the best and and most excellent modeler and teacher of oratory." (188)

Perhaps because of his affiliation with religious institutions, Kleiser wrote of moral preparation. In actuality it was his statement on ethos. It was to be expected that he would begin his list of moral qualifications with religion.

1. *Religion. A truly successful orator must be a religious man—that is one of Godward bearing. This will put upon his utterance the unmistakable stamp of honesty and sincerity, so that men will instinctively believe in him. The remaining moral attributes were:*
2. *Character.*
3. *Sympathy.*
4. *Fearlessness.*
5. *Self-renunciation.*
6. *Perseverance and Industry.*
7. *Strong Opinions and Convictions. (193-195)*

The rest of Kleiser's brief treatment of public speaking was routine. He discussed speech preparation and divisions of the speech. He then added an additional four perfunctory pages on delivery, which dealt with the immediate speaking situation (196-215).

Curiously, one of the first serious books dealing with public speaking was not written by a public speaking teacher at all. Walter Dill Scott, Associate Professor of Education and Psychology at Northwestern University, intended The Psychology of

Public Speaking for professional psychologists rather than students of public speaking. He did, however, dedicate his book to Robert Cumnock, founder of the Cumnock School of Oratory, which later became the School of Speech at Northwestern. We must keep in mind the fact that Scott's textbook was written two years before Phillips *Effective Speaking* and nine years before Winan's *Public Speaking*. It is, of course, impossible to attribute any direct influence of Scott on either Phillips or Winans. What is interesting, and significant, is that the connection between public speaking and psychology was made by at least one psychologist before the relationship was perceived by teachers of public speaking. Not only did the new discipline derive conceptions from psychology, it allowed another discipline to make the first application of its research to public speaking. Scott saw an inevitable connection between psychology and public speaking.

> *The public speaker's task is to influence the human mind. Psychology is a systematic study of this same mind. It is absurd to suppose that psychology could have nothing of benefit for the public speaker. The connection between psychology and public speaking is so direct that psychology as a science will be extended by a careful study of the action of the mind as manifested in public speeches, in their delivery and in their influence upon audiences. At the same time, every public speaker should be benefited by systematizing his knowledge upon the subject of the human mind, for his success depends upon his ability to deal with the same human mind. (11-12)*

Scott also claimed to be the first psychologist to write about the connection between that field and public speaking.

> *The author of this work does not pose as great speaker, but as one who has an abiding interest in public speaking, and who has learned more by his failures than by his successes. Whatever of psychology is of greatest value to the public speaker will be regarded as appropriate to the series. There is, to the author's knowledge no published work under this title, and indeed no psychology published for the special use of public speakers. This fact will necessitate a re-writing of many facts of psychology and at the same time will call for new applications and fuller presentations of many of the truths which in other forms would have no special value to the public speaker. (11)*

An examination of the contents of The Psychology of *Public Speaking* brings into question the originality of the early writers on public speaking who were influenced by psychology. At a remove of over eighty years it is, of course, difficult to demonstrate causality. What we do know, however, is that many of the topics addressed by Phillips, Winans and Woolbert were previously treated by Scott. Winans, for example, is usually credited with the introduction of the James-Lange theory of emotions into public speaking. In actual fact Winans' treatment of the theory came nine years after Scott's writing on James-Lange. Moreover, Winans deals with the matter in a manner remarkably similar to Scott's. It is, of course possible that Scott and Winans were both close readers of William James. The table of contents of Scott's book was indicative of the orientation he brought to the subject. In spite of the hope he had earlier expressed he, in contrast to the public speaking textbooks, offered no specific advice or instruction to the students of public speaking.

The concentration on emotions, attention, suggestion, and crowd psychology were paralleled in Winan's later work. The real credit that should be given to Winans is that he was able to make applications of these psychological principles in a performance oriented public speaking course. We do know that Winans knew of Scott since he cited him three times in *Public Speaking*. The references, were to *The Psychology of Public Speaking* and two other Scott works, *Influencing Men in Business* and *The Theory of Advertising*.

Scott spoke of his "abiding interest in public speaking." His interest was by no means shallow. His knowledge of oral discourse seemed somewhat broader than the public speaking teachers' knowledge of psychology. Scott used almost no foot notes, but in his bibliography he listed: George Pierce Baker, Moses True Brown, Cicero, Cumnock, Delsarte, Demosthenes, Mantegazza, Quintilian, Ringwalt, Rush, and Shoemaker. This is a remarkable list since it includes the traditional elocutionists as well as the writers in Composition/Rhetoric and the classical rhetoricians.

It is interesting to note that Scott perceived psychology to be an understood and misunderstood discipline; he exhibited a defense similar to those shown by members of the speech profession. He recounted the experience of returning to his rural home town where the reaction to the news that he was teaching psychology as: "What under heaven is that?", "What in earth is that?", "What yer teachin' that tomfoolery fer?" Psychology, although it may have begun from a position similar to that of Speech, obviously moved much more quickly to a position of respectability; within a decade Psychology had become the dominant social science. By 1918 Woolbert perceived Psychology to be a controlling epistemology.

Although Scott wrote only one book on public speaking, he had a distinguished career as a psychologist and educator. He was later a professor of applied psychology at the Carnegie Institute of Technology; he then served nineteen years as President of Northwestern. He published a number of other works, mostly dealing with personnel and business psychology. One of his books, *The Theory of Advertising*, was republished as recently as 1985. Scott lived until 1955 and was the subject of two biographies, one written four years before his death, the other 13 years after his death. Both Jacobson and Lynch refer to Scott as a "pioneer," in one case "in psychology and education," (Jacobson, 1951); in the other "in personnel management." (Lynch, 1968)

Jacobson offered clarifications for Scott's interest in public speaking.

> . . . *Walter registered for the usual freshman courses—Greek, Latin, mathematics and elocution. . . . How did Scott happen come to be concerned with the problem*

> *[public speaking] in the middle of the first decade of the twentieth century? The reason was a practical one. Just before then he had emerged as a national figure. He spoke before large gatherings of business and professional men and women. . . . He undertook to point out and explain to advertising men how advertisements might be made much more effective. He thought and talked in terms of getting the maximum message-conveying impact across by means of printed words and accompanying pictorial illustrations. It was only natural that he should become conscious of a similar study of the spoken word. . . . As a student Scott had taken a course in public speaking under Professor Cumnock and the experience had left a lasting impression. The fact that he called Cumnock an artist tells us much not only about Cumnock but also about Scott's attitude toward public speaking. (25, 76-77)*

It is impossible, of course, more than 85 years, later to explain why Scott's work was almost entirely ignored by the new profession and by its successors. Before the discipline of public speaking was established, Scott had laid the psychological foundation for psychological research in human communication. It is curious, and perhaps indicative, of the lack of historical consciousness of the profession, that although Jacobson went to some pains to explicate the psychological dimension of Psychology of Public Speaking, no work in Speech Communication has been devoted to his contributions.

In Chapter 3 we gave considerable attention to *Effective Speaking* by Arthur Edward Phillips, and its early use of the psychology of the time. Those psychological ideas were brought to bear on a remarkably complete treatment of public speaking, for its time. Phillips premised his book with a statement of what he called the "general ends."

> *. . . We may conclude that the general ends of speech are five. The speaker wishes the listener to see—Clearness, or to feel—Impressiveness, or to accept Belief, or to do—Action, or to enjoy—Entertainment. Whatever may be the topic, the end in view will be found under one or a combination of these heads. (18-19)*

Phillips statement of the general ends is interesting in several ways. It is based on similar conceptions to those of theorists of the eighteenth century who, in turn based their conceptions on faculty psychology. Although Phillips did not direct the ends to specific human faculties, his ends, a term also used in the eighteenth century, were stated in terms of audience response. It is interesting to compare Phillips' classification with that of George Campbell in 1776 in his *Philosophy of Rhetoric*.

> *The word eloquence, in its greatest latitude, denotes "that art or talent by which the discourse is adapted to its end." All the ends of speaking are reducible to four; every speech being intended to enlighten the understanding, to please the imagination, to move the passions, or to influence the will. (23)*

The general ends controlled the development of Phillips' text. Further, he posited his perspective on the importance of experience, particularly that of the audience. Experience,then, was the key to adapting speech to listeners.

> *Reference to experience as here used, means reference to the known. The known is that which the listener has seen, heard, read, felt, believed or done, and which still exists in his consciousness—his stock of knowledge. It embraces all those thoughts, feelings and happenings which to him are real. Reference to Experience, then, means coming into the listener's life. (28)*

From a pedagogical perspective, the structure of *Effective Speaking* is interesting. Perhaps because of the influence of psychology, Phillips presented the more psychologically based and theoretical material before he came to specific and applied material. After the discussion of general ends and experience, he turned to the explication of action and motives, interestingness, forms of support, and the central idea. After devoting nineteen chapters to these matters he spoke of organization, style, speech preparation, and the after-dinner speech. All of these discussions were firmly anchored to the centrality of experience. A statement, made by Phillips in the chapter on style, is representative of the connection.

> *That material is best which comes most vividly into the experience of the audience in the briefest time. (181)*

Phillips' contributions to the study of public speaking are important not only because of their psychological foundations but because he had provided a coherent treatment of the subject before members of the new profession had turned their hands to the writing of textbooks.

Although Winans and Phillips are justly given credit for introducing psychology to public speaking, other teachers were toiling in the same field, although with less sophistication. An example was *Practical Lessons in Public Speaking*, which was privately printed in 1910 by Arthur MacMurray, of Kansas State University (now the University of Kansas.) MacMurray's slim volume, which may have been intended for his own students, was not unlike many textbooks which followed it. It treated such routine matters as: speech preparation, subject choice, organization and delivery. More important, historically, was MacMurray's use of fairly simplistic psychological principles. In his very first chapter, for example, he states that, "The speaker must always cause his audience to feel he is master of the situation." (12)

> *He also wrote of the necessity ". . . for the speaker to infuse warmth and power of personality into his speaking." (30-31); "The speaker must learn to arouse in himself emotional responsiveness." (30-31); "To back up one's mental energy by appropriate physical energy." (39); and "Enthusiasm as an element in Public Speaking as well as in character can be developed." (51)*

MacMurray gave no indication of the sources of his psychological notions. His 95 page book does not even contain an index.

One of the early and important members of the Eastern Public Speaking Conference was Irvah Lester Winter of Harvard University, who then was actually identified as an Associate Professor of Public Speaking. He published *Public Speaking: Principles and Practices* in 1912 with revised editions in 1915 and 1917. Winter's work was, in its own way, fascinating; in form, and to some extent in substance, it resembled some of the Elocution texts of the time. In a book of over 400 pages, Winter devoted only 56 pages to "A Discussion of Principles." The remainder of the volume was given over to selections exemplifying the principles. An excerpt from the Table of Contents of the revised edition gives us an idea of how much Winter remained influenced by Elocutionism:

PART ONE

A DISCUSSION OF PRINCIPLES

TECHNICAL TRAINING
  Establishing the Tone
  Vocal Flexibility
  The Formation of Words
  Making the Point

Indicating Values and Relations
Expressing the Feeling
Showing the Picture
Expression by Action

PLATFORM PRACTICE
   The Formal Address
   The Public Lecture
   The Informal Discussion
   Argumentative Speech
   The After-Dinner Speech
   The Occasional Poem
   The Making of the Speech (xi)

By using the term "Platform Practice," Winter did not offer exercises for the students to perform; rather he intended that term to cover the settings and circumstances in which speeches were given.

In an advertisement contained in Winter's book the publisher, MacMillan, drew attention to such works as Shurter's *The Rhetoric of Oratory*, Harding's *Select Orations Illustrating American Political History*, Lane Cooper's *Theories of Style*, and Laycock and Scales *Argumentation and Debate*.

Our discussion should certainly include an example of the texts used in classes in Oral English. One of the best and most popular was *Oral Composition* by Cornelia Carhart Ward of Hunter College High School. Ward was convinced that Oral English was part of the English curriculum and not a separate course, let alone a separate discipline.

> *This book is an attempt not only to place oral composition where it belongs in the curriculum, but to reconcile the supposed differences, to bridge the supposed gap between oral and written expression. The pupils must be made to realize that talking, though often more effective than writing, is, on the one hand, just as easy, but, on the other hand, needs as much thought and preparation as writing. Most pupils write better than they speak. Should they not have a chance to equalize their effort? (vi)*

Ward's book was actually a melange of English Composition and Public Speaking, with more emphasis on composition. Reasonably enough she began with an introduction titled "Why We Should Know how to Speak" in which she discussed the power of speech and the important place it plays in our lives (3-20). After a chapter on speech preparation, which was not essentially different from writing preparation, Ward explicated "Expression as Conditioned by Thought" from a literary rather than speech orientation. The sub-divisions were the paragraph, the sentence and use of words. (62-124) A chapter dealing exclusively with delivery then followed. (1915, 125-160) Part IV of Ward's book was not really Oral English as much as it was English Composition. Under the heading "Kinds of Writing and Speaking," she dealt with the standard English genres of narration, description, exposition, and argumentation. (163-197)

The text book often thought of as the first modern public speaking text was *Public Speaking* by James Albert Winans of Cornell. We have earlier discussed Winans' role in the research debate and the discussions concerning the role of psychology in the new discipline. (See Chapter 3.) Although Winans' contribution may not have been as original as they once seemed, and although his work may have been quite derivative, we cannot doubt the influence of the textbook and the presentation of an alternate way of looking at public speaking.

In Chapter 3 we discussed the influence of psychology on Winans and the ways in which his work served to re-orient the profession's view of itself and of public speaking. Now we shall examine Winans' more general approach to public speaking. In spite of Winans' present reputation, his book retained some of the tradition of giving extensive treatment to delivery. Of the sixteen chapters of the text no fewer than five are devoted to delivery. Of course Winans' perspective toward delivery did not even resemble those of the elocutionists. He had no use for "graceful gestures and pear shaped tones." Rather his orientation was directed to the development of a mode of delivery which was based on the conception of public speaking as an extension of conversation. Indeed he titled his Chapter I "The Problem of Delivery-Conversing with an Audience." Although Shurter gave attention to the phenomenon of public speaking as an extension of conversation, his treatment was quite brief. It was left to Winans to give the subject the explication it deserved. The key to Winans' development of the idea was that conversational speaking and public speaking were not in opposition to each other, but rather that they were points on a continuum and that a clear line between them could not be drawn.

> *When does the talker or converser become a speech-maker? When ten persons gather? Fifty? Or is it when he gets on the cart? is there any real change in the nature or spirit of the act? Is it not essentially the same throughout, a conversation adapted as the talker proceeds to the growing number of his hearers? There may be a change of course, if he becomes self-conscious; but assuming that interest in the story or argument remains the dominant emotion, there is no essential change in his speaking. (1915, 17)*

Winans felt that the important characteristics of conversational delivery could be simply stated.

> *To summarize, then, your delivery will have the desired conversational quality when you retain upon the platform these elements of the mental state of live conversation: 1. Full realization of content of your words as you utter them, and 2. A lively sense of communication. When the first element is lacking, we may characterize the delivery as absent-minded; when the second is lacking, we may describe the delivery as soliloquizing not communicative, or indirect. (1915, 28)*

When he treated delivery proper, Winans devoted four chapters to the subject—gesture, platform manners, voice training, and study and delivery of selections. Winan's work on delivery is unimportant except that, in spite of his attempt to provide a psychological basis for delivery, he provided specific instructions and exercises, which might well have been drawn from a contemporary elocution text. One wonders whether Winans' students might not have found some dissonance between his earlier treatment of public speaking as conversation and his specific material on delivery.

The contributions for which Winans deserves credit were his use of the psychological research of his time to provide a theoretical base for the teaching of public speaking. It certainly was curious that the most complete application of psychology to public speaking should occur in a textbook for under graduates. In Chapter 3, in the context of the influence of psychology, we have discussed Winans' treatment of attention, emotion and persuasion.

The structure of Public Speaking seems anti-climactic to today's reader. After Winans covered the topics we have mentioned, he finally came to the material we might expect to find in the early chapters of a textbook. The final three chapters are given over to selecting the subject, finding material, and "extemporaneous or written—plans and outlines."

The textbooks published before or at the time of the establishment of the National Association reflected the distinct threads of Elocution, Oral English and Public Speaking which we will trace in this chapter. Much of the writing in the early years of *The Quarterly Journal* represented an effort, not altogether successful, to arrive at some agreement about the definition of public speaking and how it should be taught. One of the chief functions of *The Quarterly Journal* was that of sharing fundamental information about public speaking with the members of the profession. The new association had little specific, or general, knowledge of what was actually taking place in the profession. Thus the early pages of the journal were to a considerable extent devoted to a form of group maintenance in which members shared information on "how we do it at our place." These sorts of articles were, at first, devoted to general discussions such as "Oral English in the High School" (Lyman, 241-259), "College Courses in Public Speaking" (Trueblood, 260-265), "Speech Training in Public High Schools" (Dawson, 1-8), "Oral English in the High School" (Dowd, 1-11) and "A Special Course in Oral Expression for High Schools." (Herring 140-152)

By 1917 the focus of the sharing articles had shifted to descriptions of speech programs at specific institutions. Some of the articles were concerned with curricula while others concentrated on particular courses. These articles included "Public Speaking I at Cornell University" (Winans, 1917, 153-162), "The Foundation Course in Public Speaking at the University of Texas" (Duffey, 163-171), "The Beginning Course in Oratory at the University of Michigan" (Hollister, 172-177), "The Department of Speech at Grinell" (Ryan, 203-209), "Course I in Public Speaking at Washington and Jefferson College" (Kay, 240-248), "Spoken English II at Smith College." (Williams, 229-234) In addition to the descriptive articles of programs at specific institutions, a group of prescriptive essays were published in which the authors made recommendations as to how specific courses should be conducted. These articles included: "A Beginning Course in Public Speaking for Colleges and Universities" (Houghton, 150-159), "Coaching Debates" (Wells, 170-183), "A Fundamental Course in Speech Training" (Forncrook, 271-289) and "How to Begin Speech Correction in the Public Schools." (Swift, 239-245)

The proliferation of articles of this sort was completely understandable. At the same time that Hunt, Woolbert and Winans were disputing the problems of research most of the membership of the association were more concerned with the problems of pedagogy. They were, after all, teachers, as the name of their association indicated. Almost none of them had carried on research, and we can conjecture that their interest in research was low. They were, however, all teachers, and the articles allowed teachers to share useful information about teaching with each other and to offer mutual encouragement. More than seventy years later we might find it difficult to understand the insecurity of a new profession in which there were few if any accepted standards as to what courses in public speaking should be. The sharing of information about the ways in which courses were taught at other institutions must have provided members not only with helpful hints but also with a greater sense of confidence about their teaching. These articles must surely have served to maintain and increase the sense of professional identity and cohesion so necessary for the new profession.

To give ourselves some perspective and to allow us to see how persistent are the questions raised early in the history of the profession, it is enlightening to examine a few of the early articles to understand how the teaching of speech was seen at the outset of the profession. A reading of the early articles demonstrates that, in many ways, the profession was finding its way, and that it had not yet completely defined its individual identity. The boundaries between Public Speaking and English, and between Public Speaking and Elocution were not entirely clear.

The very first pedagogical article in *The Quarterly* dealt not with Public Speaking but with the older and more traditional concept of Oral English. In his essay "Oral English in the High School" R.L Lyman of the University of Chicago treated speech as an integral element in the English curriculum and not as discrete entity. In fact Lyman viewed speech as essential in teaching English. "I assert that emphasis on oral composition is one of the means, perhaps the best means, of teaching English as a tool." (243) Lyman was careful to define what he meant by the term "oral composition."

> *When we use this term we have in mind those classes which are wholly or in part substituting oral for written expression of the pupil's own thoughts. (245)*

Thus the 1915 classroom, as described by Lyman, was really an integrated setting for instruction in both written and oral composition. In fact, Lyman described an experiment conducted by the Illinois Teachers Association.

> *In brief the procedure was as follows: The committee drew up a program for one semester of oral work. . . . One of these sections was to be called a "writing section," in which no oral work was to be done; the other a "combination section," in which two-thirds of the themes were to be oral and one-third written. (Lyman, 1915, 246)*

It is worth noting that Lyman does not speak of speeches, rather his references are to "oral themes." An inspection of some of the details of the program will give us some idea of how much work was involved in such a course and how literary, rather than rhetorical, was its orientation.

1. *Two and one-half days were to be given to oral work for eighteen weeks.*
2. *In this time each pupil was to present in class seventeen oral themes.*
4. *Eight of these themes were to be worked over into written themes. . . .*
5. *Seven periods of the semester were spent in drilling upon spelling, punctuation and grammar.*
8. *Some of the themes were worked up by groups of four or five, the class voting which group, had done the best work. The time was evenly divided between description, narration and exposition. (246)*

The experiment, according to Lyman, was a success. The committee reported that, "The themes, written by the combination sections average better better in thought and in rhetorical and grammatical structure. . . " (247). The teachers reported that the "improvement in speech is very marked."

Historically the results of the experiment, laudable though they may have been, are not as important as the underlying presumptions concerning Oral English. It is clear from Lyman's description that the course he envisioned was, in fact, one which dealt with the oral aspects of English Composition rather than Public Speaking. The standard literary genres of description, narration and exposition were employed rather than genres of speech. The speeches themselves were referred to as themes. One is reminded of Brigance's later statement that a speech is not "an essay on its hind legs." Lyman argued that the separation of Speech from English was unwise since they were both part of the same entity. He made his point by attacking a text book.

> *A certain textbook, entitled* Oral English in the Secondary Schools, *is a splendid example of all that a high-school text ought not to be. In the first place, it*

makes the mistake, which I urge you never to make, of treating reading and speaking
as one and the same thing. Again it makes the mistake of separating interpretation
from the literature class, and separating oral work from the composition class.
Interpretation is a part of the literature; oral expression is a part of composition.
However wise it may be to keep the public speaking department in a college separate
from the English (there is a radical difference of opinion here), I submit that in the
high school there ought to be no such separation. (252)

Lyman understood that the teachers of the Oral English classes were not technically equipped to deal with delivery or what he called "the formal elements of speaking." After offering a few perfunctory suggestions, he said, "My final suggestion upon these technical matters is: Don't bother about them." (255) Indeed Lyman was insistent that form, written or oral, be minimized and that the emphasis of the course should be on content.

Let us turn finally to a few considerations more important than matters of
elocution. . . bring into your classrooms situations that arouse the desire of the
pupils to express opinions. . . . Do not begin with a learned discussion on your part
of the formalities and formidableness of oral work. Get the members of the class to
talking freely and spontaneously from their seats, or from the standing position at
their places, about matters of interest. Let this go on for some time, your suggestions
about form in speaking being so far merely incidental. Your suggestions should
always have the need of the audience as the point of departure. . . This is the teaching
that bridges the gap between the oral work to which the pupil has been accustomed
and the more formal work into which he is being introduced. (255-256). . . the
speaking aspects of oral work are of secondary importance. The thought, the
contribution, its effective arrangement, it composition is the great desideratum. (258)

Lyman's essay, though it was clearly of another day, was an illuminating description of how instruction in speaking was conceived of by supporters in English departments of courses in Oral English. Undoubtedly, the content of the courses was oral, but they were essentially courses in English not Speech. One could speculate that the perspective enunciated by advocates of Oral English may have contributed to the perceived need of the members of the new profession to distance themselves from departments of English. In some ways Lyman's plan of a "combination course" seemed to anticipate the Communication Skills movement of some thirty years later in which students in both schools and colleges were taught speaking and writing in an integrated setting.

We cannot predict what course the development of the profession would have followed had the curriculum in Oral English become the standard mode of instruction. It is at least possible that oral work might have occupied more time in the high school English course, and thus more secondary students might have been exposed to some speech training. On the other hand, it is more likely that speech would have been seen as an adjunct to the English course and that instruction would be governed by the conventions of English. Certainly the development of the new profession with its different orientation and agenda would have been inhibited.

In the same issue of *The Quarterly Journal* Thomas C. Trueblood of the University of Michigan, the grand old man of Elocution, published "College Courses in Public Speaking," which he had read at the 1915 convention of National Speech Arts Association, (formerly the National Elocution Association). Apparently by this time in their history the Elocutionists, perhaps to gain respectability, were willing to give attention to Public Speaking as well as Elocution. Trueblood, however, was hardly willing to consider Elocution to be subordinate to Public Speaking, quite the reverse.

A thorough study of the principles of elocution should be the basis of all college courses in public speaking. This means a knowledge of the physiology of the vocal and breathing organs, of control of the breath, and the placing of the tone; a knowledge of the essentials of good articulation and pronunciation, and much practice in difficult sounds and words; an understanding of the laws of emphasis in its application in the reading aloud of well-selected passages of literature; a careful study of the elements of quality, force, pitch and time and their application in the delivery of well-chosen selections from the poets and the orators; a study of the elements of gesture, and the practice of exercises best fitted to give grace in attitude, bearing, and movements of the body in expression. (260)

This passage (which may well be a contender for the longest sentence in the history of the journal) clearly showed the contrast between the perspectives of the supporters of Oral English and the Elocutionists. Where Lyman's advice about delivery had been, "don't bother much," Trueblood advocated thorough preparation in elocution as a prerequisite for courses in public speaking. Indeed Trueblood proposed that the course in elocution "... should occupy at least three hours of class work per week during one semester, or, if possible, for a full year" (260). After the completion of the work in elocution, the student would be given the privilege of:

... proceed[ing] along two lines of work—the interpretative and the self-expressional, the main purpose of the one being to give proper expression to the best thought of the great authors; of the other, to give the best expression to one's own thoughts. (260)

Under the title of public speaking Trueblood was, in fact, making the case for Elocution and Oral Interpretation more than for public speaking. Understandably, it was difficult for the Elocutionists to surrender their interests. When he came to discuss the public speaking curriculum, Trueblood presented a scheme consisting of five courses: Public Speaking, Study of Great Orators, Argumentation and Debate, Advanced Public Speaking, and Debating and Oratorical Contests. In the unit on great orators Trueblood proposed that after the lectures on the orators had been concluded, five speeches on each orator be presented. He used Lord Chatham as an example.

1. *The Oration*
    (1) Length, twenty minutes.
    (2) Subject, a eulogy on Chatham, a carefully prepared and committed speech.
2. *The Topical Speech*
    (1) Length, seven minutes.
    (2) Subject, Chatham's work as premier or some other topic relating to his life-work. The speech should be carefully outlined and given extempore.
3. *The Brief*
    (1) Length, seven minutes.
    (2) Subject, an outline of one of Chatham's speeches. . . . The speech should be extempore as far as words are concerned.
4. *The Discussion*
    (1) Time, seven minutes.
    (2) Subject, Chatham's Oratory. A critical estimate of his methods and sources of power. . . . This speech may be largely extempore in form.
5. *The Declamation*
    (1) Time, seven minutes.

> *(2) Subject, a selection from one of Chatham's orations. The student should search for the passage of eloquence which appeals most strongly to him, commit and deliver it with as much moral earnestness as he can command. (263)*

In the public speaking course the students were required to make "at least eight speeches, each about seven or eight minutes in length." After the first month of the course in Argumentation, when a text book was studied, the work consisted of classroom debates and briefing. The course in Advanced Public Speaking had as its purpose "to give each of ten or twelve picked students opportunity to present a public address of forty-five minutes on some subject of public interest." The debating and oratorical contests were the "culmination or topping off of the classroom work. . . . These contests are a great source of power to students as well as honor to themselves and to the college they represent." (265)

The Trueblood curriculum is of historical interest because it was the first formal proposal in *The Quarterly Journal* for college courses in public speaking. Coming, as it did, from an elocutionist, it is a somewhat surprising document. To be sure, the courses are all, to one degree or other, performance courses, but they are much more than courses in elocution; they even include elements of what later would become rhetorical criticism. The emphasis on argumentation and debate seems to be a carry over from the courses earlier offered in the English curricula and later taken over by the newly formed departments of public speaking. Clearly, they were not the courses in Oral English described by Lyman. Trueblood, however, hardly represented the conversion of elocutionists to public speaking. At the 1915 convention of the National Speech Arts Association no one except Trueblood showed the slightest interest in public speaking when the convention program of the N.S.A.A. was reported in *The Quarterly Journal*.

Meanwhile at least one collegiate institution was practicing something akin to Lyman's proposal. "The Forum" in 1915 reported:

> *The class in public speaking at the Fort Hays, Kansas, Normal School is credited to the department of English and is conducted by two teachers simultaneously. Both teachers meet the class. The professor of public speaking and pageantry instructs in delivery, etc. The professor of English and head of the department looks after the composition and structure of the efforts. It is really a combination of the college rhetoric course and the regular public speaking course. ("Forum," 1915, 322)*

The arrangement at Fort Hays Normal may well have been an example of some of the factors which impelled the teachers of public speaking to rid themselves of English department domination. The professor of public speaking was really the elocutionist, concerned with the "how" of speech while the professor of English was responsible for the "what"—the mastery of matter rather than form. Many members of the association felt that English departments had placed them in distinctly subordinate positions.

In a 1916 article Charles A. Dawson of Niagara Falls High School wrote on "Speech Training in Public High Schools." His article is interesting because he saw speech training as more than public speaking. As one might expect, Dawson specified that the objectives of a speech course should include:

> *Preparation for connected presentation of matter to an audience; that is for effective "speech," technically so called . . . . "Preparation for oral reading, with or without the book."*

But the first objective listed by Dawson was: "Preparation for good conversation and informal discussion, for rapid formulation and brief, telling expression of ideas of matters of immediate interest" (2).

Although the article was fairly orthodox, it was significant because Dawson included in the high school course material which seemed to anticipate later instruction in group and interpersonal communication.

The relation between the new discipline and English was spelled out in James O'Neill's 1915 Presidential Address when he expressed both cordiality and hostility; cordiality toward departments of English; hostility, or at least wariness, toward some supporters of Oral English.

> *In rejoicing in the new freedom and power which we now have as an organized profession, and which we as individuals now have as a rule in our department work, I trust there is no trace of antagonism to, bitterness toward or disrespect for our foster-mother, the English Department. . . . And of course I do not mean that this freedom is dependent upon or must be made use of in, an offensive warfare with English Departments. . . . we ought to give particular support and sympathy to our colleagues working in English departments. From the very nature of the case the work of the two departments must be interrelated and sympathetically adjusted at many points. This is evident from work now being done in classrooms by some English teachers, and from the activity planned by the newly organized Committee on American Speech of the National Council of Teachers of English. All of this as it should be, and I feel confident that this association and the members of it are ready to work with English teachers and English teachers' organizations for the common good of education. (O'Neill, 1916, 54-55)*

In spite of the warmth professed by O'Neill he warned the members against, ". . . one type of English teacher who is a distinct menace. . . " O'Neill did not have in mind the ". . . English teacher who ignorantly opposes serious oral work in any form. . . ." The danger, said O'Neill, came, ironically, from the friends of speech in English departments, the supporters of Oral English.

> *The type of English teacher toward whom we must individually and collectively be on our guard is found among those teachers who profess a deep interest in public speaking in all its phases, who perhaps say that it is the coming thing, a great discovery, a wonderful labor-saving device. Their technical training is so woefully deficient that they have an entirely erroneous conception of what constitutes thorough or even intelligent instruction in any of the phases of public speaking, and they are likely to do as much harm as good when they attempt to give any instruction or advice in this field. (56)*

The connection between Oral English and public speaking was also discussed by John C. French of Johns Hopkins University. French referred to the course offered at his institution as "spoken English." Even in that course, elocution had not yet completely departed.

> *The first few weeks of the year are devoted to a rapid survey of the principles of expression, and the last few weeks to practice in extemporaneous speaking. (167-168)*

The rest of the year was devoted to the "occasional speech" under which French included such settings as addresses of welcome, inauguration ceremonies, introductions of speakers, and appeals for volunteers. These speeches were differentiated from what French termed as "routine or professional" speeches such as lectures, sermons or lawyers' arguments. French justified such assignments on the grounds of practicality.

"They bear a definite relationship to practical needs as any work done in college, and even the careless student is ready to see 'the use of it.' " (168)

French concluded his essay by reference to the goals of work in both writing and speech.

> . . . *We ought to be able to say of every graduate of a college that he can write a lucid and correct exposition and can make, before a moderately large audience, a self-possessed and fitting speech. (170)*

Incidentally, French, 52 years before Lloyd Bitzer, used the same terminology as Bitzer.

> *But the occasional speech is non-professional, and the exigencies that demand it are incidental and sometimes unexpected. These exigencies are numerous and varied. (168)*

The persistence of the influence of elocution in speech pedagogy was illustrated by J.S. Gaylord of Winona Normal School. Gaylord, in contrast to the more traditional elocutionists, emphasized gesture as symbol.

> . . . *Expression has a symbolic function. It tends to use its various forms as figures of speech and to suggest its meanings by analogy. This function is closely related to that of conventional language. It is a question whether any important progress could be made by the use of natural language only. (192)*

Gaylord seemed to have some latent awareness of physical action as later described in the more recently developed field of non-verbal communication.

One of the first detailed reports about a curriculum at a specific institution was offered by Mrs. Mary H. Dowd of Manchester, New Hampshire, High School. Dowd described how Oral English was taught in her high school. Although we may regard bi-lingualism as a recent problem, Dowd, and presumably other high school teachers, dealt with it in a perhaps more diverse form than we do now.

> . . . *The problem of teaching high school pupils to speak intelligently, not to say eloquently or even fluently the English tongue is beset with difficulties other than reasonably to be blamed upon the ever-increasing proportion of pupils who hear no English spoken in the home. We have about eleven hundred pupils. A cosmopolitan lot they are as they gather in the assembly hall on opening day; a fair proportion of native-born Americans, French, Germans, Italians, Greeks, Poles, Russians, Syrians, Belgians, a Chinese or two. . . . (1, 3)*

The task of teaching Oral English to these heterogeneous students must have been formidable indeed. In such an environment it might well have been impractical to undertake a conventional course in public speaking.

The objectives of the Oral English classes were considerably broader than we would expect a course in public speaking, or even English Composition, to be. Indeed, Dowd wrote as if Oral English were a means to achieving desirable social goals.

> . . . *We may, I think, reasonably hope to do four things: 1st, to interest these young people in themselves, and in one another, as they are related to the two worlds—the one in which they move, the other which revolves around them; 2nd, to start the play of intellectual imagination; 3rd, to foster a desire for things excellent and of good repute; 4th, to develop strong, direct personalities, animated by high purpose and willingness to take pains. If, in these impressionable years, we can help pupils to acquire these powers, we shall at the same time, I believe, also help them to*

*such correct expression, of clear forceful delivery, as are not only marks of culture
but assets in any practical business in life. (3)*

In spite of the abstract character of her prose, Dowd seemed to anticipate the later
interest in the public speaking classroom as an arena for social adjustment and
personality change. (See Chapter 5.) She also dealt, although differently from Smith,
with the problems of students who were not native speakers of English.

Surprisingly, Manchester High offered four years of Oral English and the topics
covered almost all aspects of oral communication. Conversation, anecdotes and jokes,
dramatized telephone conversations, and "retail (sic) a well-known story for an
imaginary listener, as a five year old child, a blind man, a prim old lady. . . " were, for
example, covered in the first year. The first year course made use of peer rather than
teacher criticism and the examples given seemed to reenforce the doubts of O'Neill
concerning the qualifications of some teachers of Oral English who emphasized form
at the expense of substance.

> *Each pupil appears formally before the class four times, and is each time subjected
> to the criticism not of his teachers but of his peers, who are usually far less tolerant
> than the teacher of ers and ands; of illiterate verb and pronoun forms; of voices that
> "can't be heard back here";. . . . (4)*

In the second year course the connection with the English curriculum became
stronger.

> *Heretofore, attention to vocabulary and sentence form has been incidental, but
> now criticism is based on the principles being taught in composition hour, where the
> sentence is the unit of study. . . . (4)*

Dowd spelled out the four year program in great detail. It is not necessary for us to
examine it carefully except to note that the courses were distinctly Oral English courses
rather than courses in public speaking. Dowd, for example, invariably referred to "oral
themes." Her article demonstrated however, that it may not have been easy for the
members of the new profession to break cleanly with their English heritage. The
publication of articles such as Dowd's may also have been consonant with O'Neill's
desire to maintain cordial relations with the "foster-mother." There was also the
possibility that a clear boundary between Oral English and public speaking had not
been drawn in the minds of the members of the National Association.

One of the earliest descriptions of a specific collegiate public speaking program (as
distinct from Oral English and Elocution courses) was that at Huron College. Everett
Hunt explained that freshman at Huron were required to take a one semester two hour
course. In keeping with Hunt's educational views, the freshman course was more
concerned with the general education of the students than with the mastery of the
techniques of public speaking.

> *I try to conduct the course in such a way that the freshmen will come to know the
> joy of living with ideas. . . . I have found it most profitable to confine my own
> remarks largely to the subject matter of the speech. . . . It is necessary, of course, to
> keep technical points in mind; but one can so cover them that these points will never
> seem to be ends in themselves. . . . And if, at the end of the semester, the students
> have in a measure conquered their nervousness and self-consciousness, and if I
> occasionally see them reading good books and magazines just for the pleasure of it, I
> feel the course has justified itself. (1917, 31-32)*

In the second semester of the freshman year an elective course in the interpretation of literature was offered at Huron. As in the case of the public speaking course, the interpretation course seemed to be directed to the cultivation of the minds of the students.

> . . . I begin by emphasizing the joy of good talk. Conversation is presented as having all the possibilities of an art. . . . Then I have an excellent opportunity to emphasize the identity of the laws of speech and writing. . . the whole aim being to persuade the class that poetry is to be loved and is worthy of serious study. Then I give a few lectures on elementary principles of esthetics and we discuss the various arts in their relation to each other. (1917, 33)

In the sophomore year students could elect a three hour course in Forms of Public Address. The course seemed, in actuality, to be a course in argumentation. This course, as well as the freshman courses, was seen by Hunt as much an exercise in mind-broadening as in argument per se.

> It seems well, when winning can be lost sight of, to indulge occasionally in opinionative, interminable sorts of questions, in order to awaken the mind to the joys of and dangers of paradox. . . the Great Man Theory of History, Art and morals, Inheritance of acquired characteristics, etc. . . It has been my experience that a teacher who knows only the formal side of debate loses the respect of the students. . . . In these class discussions I always regard the acquiring of any new intellectual interest as of equal importance with improvement in formal argumentation. (1917, 34)

In the junior year Hunt offered a course in Tennyson and Browning and a course in modern drama in the senior year. The program at Huron could be hardly described as a public speaking curriculum. In spite of the departure of the National Association from English, Hunt's offerings continued to draw on the parent discipline as well as on a general humanistic tradition.

At the 1916 convention of the National Association, James Lawrence Lardner of Northwestern University gave a speech which was reprinted the next year in *The Quarterly Journal*. Lardner reported on the course he offered which was an interesting melange of theory, practice and criticism. It was, however, clearly a course in public speaking. Lardner described the purpose of the course as being directed to the "practical problem of teaching students to influence an audience" (Lardner, 1917, 48). Lardner stressed the importance of practical training in public speaking, while not ignoring the more informational aspects.

> If we limit, our speech-training to give the information about speech-making, in my judgment we omit one of the great purposes of our work—training for skill. (Lardner, 1917, 49)

Lardner's course was as concerned with developing the students' critical and analytical sense as well as their performance skills. Presumably, the students would learn how to influence audiences by analyzing speeches to determine whether the speaker was effective in adapting to an audience, and if not why not. He cited examples of a dull United States senator who visited Northwestern and Woodrow Wilson's "speech-making tour of the West to talk preparedness."

The speech assignments were closely tied to adaptation to specific audiences.

> It meant something definite for me to say to Mr. A "Write a speech to get money from the audience of the First Methodist Episcopal Church of Evanston for the slum sufferers of Chicago," and to Mr. B. "Write a speech to secure funds for the same

people from an audience in a small rural church one hundred and fifty miles south of Chicago." (Lardner, 1917, 54-55)

Lardner also required that his students present speeches "before an audience composed of students from other classes in the Department." The speeches were then evaluated by the new audience.

The model Lardner chose for a public speaking course was quite different from Hunt's model and altogether different from the courses in Oral English. These examples illustrate the diverse views held about public speaking courses at the very outset of the profession.

The diversity of the situation was brought out in a paper by Bromley Smith of Bucknell University read before a 1916 meeting of New England Public Speaking Conference and printed in *The Quarterly Journal* in 1917. Smith's examination was limited to the colleges and universities of New England but his report made clear how heterogeneous the situation was. Smith himself embodied some of the professional confusion. Although he used "public speaking" in the title of his paper, in the text he often referred to "the pedagogy of spoken English."

Illustrative of the diversity was the fact that even in an area as small as New England no agreement could be secured on so fundamental a matter as the name of the discipline, and thus of the departments. Smith said:

> *Thus we find eleven different titles for the departments in which instruction is given in some part at least of the field of reading and speaking. (57)*

So early in the history of the discipline the most common departmental name was English. Among the other titles were: Public Speaking, Oratory, Spoken English, Rhetoric and Composition, and Science and Art of Expression. The situation in regard to the names of courses was even more confusing.

> *. . . We are in danger of being submerged by the variety of courses offered. . . . All told, Public Speaking appears under twenty-three titles. Swinging over to the interpretative phase of spoken English, we find a bewildering variety of attractive courses. . . . New England educators, in their attempts to describe the courses which use the speaking voice, have forty-five expressions. (58-59)*

After citing similar variations in data about credits, requirements and electives, and course content, Smith was led to a painful conclusion.

> *With these facts before us it ought not be impertinent to assert that in New England as a whole there is no pedagogic basis for the teaching of Public Speaking or of Interpretation. The college authorities apparently have not made up their minds in which departments the courses belong, they do not agree as to what courses should be offered, they are at sea as to who should take the the subject, they do not know how much time should be given to it, they do not comprehend whether it is taught properly, and they have no way to determine whether the instructors are qualified to teach. (61)*

But, according to Smith, all was not lost. The solutions to these problems were in the hands of the profession itself.

> *At first sight one would be inclined to say that a subject so chaotic in its pedagogy ought to be driven from the educational world. But another glance will reveal that the fact that the world is tremendously interested in the human voice, Everywhere people are conversing, addressing audiences, reading literature and*

> *interpreting dramas. . . . We are therefore led irresistibly to the conclusion that the*
> *teaching of such a subject as Public Speaking and Interpretation should be placed on*
> *a sound pedagogic basis and qualified teachers should be provided. (61)*

But the real problem, said Smith, was that the profession was not prepared to undertake the necessary improvement.

> *Let us acknowledge frankly that as the profession stands today we cannot supply*
> *enough qualified teachers. Most of us have not had the technical training required.*
> *Many of us have been drafted or have drifted into the work. Some have had the*
> *training given in schools of elocution, others have been good debaters while in*
> *college, a few have swung from written composition in argument and theme writing*
> *to oral composition as a means of relief from the drudgery of pencil correction. (62)*

Smith's description of the condition of the discipline in 1917 is instructive. We have a picture of a profession not really prepared to begin its work. The faculties were not well educated and no disciplinary agreement had been reached concerning even such basic matters as the names of departments and the content of courses.

Another problem mentioned by Smith was that supporting courses were not available in the colleges and universities of 1917. In no other departments were matters related to speech discussed.

> *One could find numerous courses in written composition, but few or none in oral*
> *composition. There would be offered a course in the "Lives, Characters, and Times of*
> *Men of Letters, English and American," but none in the "Lives, Characters, and*
> *Times of Orators, English and American." A student could devote hours to*
> *"Johnson and His Circle," but not a minute to "Burke and His Circle." Three hours*
> *a week with "Eighteenth Century Periodicals," but not a second to "Eighteenth*
> *Century Orations." A half year could be spent on "Bacon" but no attention was*
> *given to "Chatham." "The Drama in England from 1642 to 1900" looked enticing,*
> *but what about "Public Utterances in England from 1642 to 1900?" One could*
> *listen to lectures about "Emerson" for weeks but never to lectures on "Webster."*
> *(62-63)*

The conditions described by Smith had serious implications for the future of the discipline. At this time the teachers of public speaking had only performance courses to offer when they entered Winans' "sheepfold." Theoretical critical and conceptual courses available to other emerging disciplines had not been developed by the speech people. They could continue to teach skills courses, or they could borrow materials from other disciplines. The problems were similar to those faced by those persons who sought to find appropriate research methodologies. (See Chapter 3.) Even as Smith deplored the lack of existence of courses dealing with speech, he used analogies from other fields, most notably from English. Apparently the models for a substantive curriculum would be found not within public speaking itself but in related fields.

Smith did not tell his readers the specific ways in which the problem could be remedied but, in general terms he recognized that the solution had to come from within the profession.

> *Here then is a vast untrodden field, one that touches a dozen phases of thought.*
> *By making this investigation it will be possible to give the spoken word a literature*
> *as formidable as that of many other branches of learning. It is for us to create this*
> *literature. By doing so we may become the teachers of the coming generations. (1917,*
> *63)*

Over time the "literature" of speech was developed, although whether it was "as formidable as many other branches of literature" is open to question. To be sure, courses in specific periods and genres were introduced in the years to come, as were courses in theory and criticism. The analogy with English, used by Smith and others, proved to be incomplete, however. Work in English departments, whether composition or literature, was firmly grounded in a literary tradition. Canonical texts and authors had been agreed upon and students were expected to be familiar with them. Although such courses as "The History and Criticism Of American Public Address"or "British Oratory" were offered, often at the graduate level, the rhetorical texts never achieved the status that the literary texts did in English. Students in Speech, for example, were never expected to know the works of Lincoln in the way that students of English were expected to know the works of Shakespeare. Smith may well have been right in his definition of the status of the profession, but it seems that his proposals never came to complete fruition.

Smith, however, in keeping with the spirit of a new profession, finally expressed optimism about the future,

> It [the profession] finds today a renaissance in all phases of the spoken word. Slowly but surely the educational world is orienting itself toward the disciplinary values of speech. If we had at times thought the task insuperable, we now feel that there is a way, a sure and safe one, though we may have missed it. (64)

Although the National Association had, in part, been established to counter the dubious reputation of Elocution, the elocutionists did not surrender. In fact, many of them became members of the association and, as in the case of Trueblood and others, presented their views in the pages of the Quarterly Journal and argued for the retention of some variant of elocution in the curriculum. As we indicated earlier, even some of the strongest supporters of public speaking envisioned a two fold division of the discipline into public speaking and interpretation. One of the most interesting of this genre of articles was "The Educational Value of Expression. (Although "expression" had earlier been used as a synonym for elocution, by 1917 it had come to be the accepted euphemism and "elocution" was seldom heard in respected academic circles.) Interestingly, Charles M. Newcomb of Ohio Wesleyan University tried to weave together the old strands of elocution with fibers of the advanced psychological and philosophical thought of the time, although his views were decidedly closer to William James than to Delsarte. Indeed the underlying presupposition of Newcomb's essay was grounded in American Pragmatism.

> One of the distinctive notes in the philosophy of today, however, is the thesis that there is no such thing as "absolute truth" but that a thing is true only when its use is considered, that knowledge is never an end in itself; but always a means to an end, and that thinking is only a servant in the interests of the practical means of life. (70)

Before making his case for expression, Newcomb admitted the low regard in which it had been held in college and universities of his time.

> We all recognize the fact that in academic circles expressional work has never been accredited with much educational value. In too many instances a distinctly cold reception has been given the presumptuous individual who dared assert that it had any educational value. (69)

Newcomb made the connection between elocution and the new philosophy by playing semantic games with the term "expression."

> *The mind is not a static affair to be filled with knowledge and the law of mental growth is not a process of receiving but a self-projection through doing—in short, self-expression. . . . Why do we require a pupil to recite? Partly for the sake of the teacher that he may know how well the pupil has prepared the lesson, but more for the sake of the pupil, for expressing the thought he makes his own. A "well stocked mind" is valuable only because it gives the possessor potentiality for expression. Money has no use except to be spent, when it expresses itself in terms of buying value. So also knowledge is valueless except that it may be expressed to others. (73)*

Newcomb sought to make a case for the philosophical justification for expression, but the case was made for expression in general rather than the specific case for elocution. He attempted to link reflective thinking to declamation by presenting it as a variety of problem solving.

> *We have heard much discussion concerning the value of declamations. Is it not true that when the speeches of great orators are given by young students, the speaker must re-create in his own mind in some degree the thought and emotion which fired the master mind when the utterance was first given to the world? (77)*

From our present perspective Newcomb's essay contained a fascinating anachronism. He cited "Dean Parker of Chicago" concerning "Types of Learning." One of them was "associating symbols and meanings." This association, which, has become basic to our understanding of human communication was simply dismissed by Newcomb. "With the second type (associating symbols and meanings), we are not so much concerned. . . ." He did find value in Parker's remaining types.

> *1. Acquiring motor skill. 3. Acquiring skill in reflective thinking.*
> *4. Acquiring habits of enjoyment. 5. Acquiring skill in expression. (75-76)*

Newcomb's case for the philosophical and psychological justification for the study of expression may have done nothing more than display that he had read James, Dewey and Perry, but that did not prevent him from making a grandiose statement about the importance of the subject.

> *Viewed in the light of the new psychology, expressional work is no longer to be considered as a wandering planet in the outer rim of academic space, but is rather the central sun of the whole solar system of education. (79)*

Bertha Forbes Herring of Nicholas Senn High School, Chicago also came to the defense of expression. In her case, however, she dwelt on the incompetence of teachers of Oral English to deal with the interpretative aspects of speech.

> *Oral English, as the subject is usually understood by the average teacher of English, seems to be confined to the problems involved in oral composition, to the exclusion of other important factors making up the broader subject of effective self-expression. As a result of the efforts of the National Council of Teachers of English and similar organizations, English teachers are being urged to undertake the teaching of reading, voice culture and the technique of speech. If the English teacher must teach reading, let her confine herself to that phase of the subject, and not undertake to teach the the special technique of speech and voice training. (140)*

Although the preponderance of Herring's long article was devoted to rather detailed descriptions of her teaching techniques in her expression classes, she did mention that she was also responsible for courses in story-telling, public speaking and play reading. Senn High also sponsored "a debating club, a dramatic club, and we are evolving a general literary club" (151). Herring's description was not very important in itself, but it was important as an indication of the three-way struggle being waged, in polite terms, between the Expressionists, who sought to maintain the desirable elements in Elocution; the proponents of Oral English who were unwilling to surrender a specialty that had been their possession; and the new profession which was attempting to define itself in a new set of circumstances. Fortunately, after a time, the situation sorted itself out. Oral English, for the most part, disappeared from the English curriculum, apparently because of diminished interest. Elocution and Expression became transformed into Oral Interpretation, a direction in which they were already headed. Oral Interpretation remains a constituent of the discipline to this day.

It is, we think, unnecessary to proliferate the descriptions of speech programs at various institutions. To draw our discussion to a close, however, it is enlightening to examine, briefly, two disparate programs: those at Cornell University and at the University of Texas. These and other descriptions of programs were written at the request of the editor in order to provide and to share information. The material from Cornell was supplied by Winans who presented a picture of a practical course.

> *The aim of the course is practical public speaking. We put into it, whatever we find best adapted, under the conditions, to training students for the effective presentation of their own ideas. At the same time we believe we make this purpose serve the broader purposes of education. (1917, 154)*

And speak they did. In the first term of sixteen weeks the students made eight presentations, including one oral reading. In the second term six speeches and readings were expected of the students.

In keeping with his desire for a "practical" course, Winans disagreed with French and Lardner concerning the value of the "occasional" speech.

> *It may be noticed that we have no occasional addresses required. We find that the make-believe situation does not encourage the sort of speaking we seek. We are rather inclining to speeches with special problems involved. . . . These are always to be delivered to the actual audience, not to an imaginary audience. (1917, 162)*

The foundation course offered at the University of Texas was altogether different from that given at Cornell. Duffey justified sexual separation on the grounds of geography and tradition. Separate sections and altered content were offered to women students.

> *Owing to conditions somewhat peculiar to this University and to the South, the courses in public speaking are not given to mixed classes. There is no prohibition against men and women registering for the same course, but in actual practice the women students, so far as public speaking is concerned, are instructed in separate classes. . . . This is primarily a training course for teachers. . . . The fall term's work in this course corresponds to the foundation course later described, except that the practice work consists in oral reading rather than public speaking. For the purpose of this article, then, the foundation course in public speaking. . . is offered to men students and intended primarily for freshmen. (163)*

Although the Texas course was called "public speaking," it hardly meets a present definition. It was, in fact a slightly modified course in Elocution. Duffey's description of the first lectures give us a clear idea about the orientation of the course.

> *The first lecture treats of four separate misapprehensions, namely: "that an orator*

*is born not made"; "that training makes a person artificial"; "that giving a man
enough practice, he does not need technique"; and lastly, "that a man should be
natural and earnest, but there is no need of training to acquire these qualities." (164)*

Topics covered in the rest of the course included: change of pitch, inflection,
emphasis, natural power, pause, silence, imagination, memory, will, spontaneity,
abandon, and emotions and passions. " Exercise in harmonic gymnastics were now
given, the awkward and the slovenly especially were given attention" (Duffey, 1917,
164-167).

What was called public speaking consisted of various kinds of exercises, none of
which required any real creativity, Those that came closest to public speaking were
assignments in which the students gave declamations of famous speeches; and in
which they made presentations of the ideas of great speeches, but in their own words.

Duffey apparently could not resist an attack on the proponents of Oral English.

> *We find that the prejudice of teachers, both in the university and in the high
> school against the traditional "elocutionary" training dies hard. The average teacher
> of English, for example, is wont to think that learning to speak means the mastery of
> grammar and rhetoric, and that all else is worse than useless. Thus students
> naturally have wrong ideas as to what training in public speaking really involves.
> (164)*

These descriptions of courses were undoubtedly of interest and of value to members
of the profession and teachers were able to get a sense of how public speaking was
taught at a range of institutions. Perhaps some of the descriptions and advice were
helpful in developing and improving courses. *The Quarterly Journal*, in effect, became
a kind of grab bag out of which one could take whatever was useful.

The diversity of material taught under the rubric of public speaking must have been
confusing, especially to inexperienced teachers. Many of them must have been puzzled
by the conflicting approaches of the advocates of Oral English, Public Speaking and
expression.

The lack of a clear definition of public speaking indicated the profession's inability
to define itself. At this early point in its development it had proclaimed itself as The
National Association of Academic Teachers of Public Speaking, yet it had conflicting,
if not confusing, perceptions about what Public Speaking was or ought to be. In spite
of the revolt against Oral English and the repudiation of Elocution, both of those fields
not only remained alive, their contributions were welcomed, or at least published, in
the pages of *The Quarterly Journal*. In addition, as we shall soon see, the title of the
profession was extended to cover a number of oral activities, some of which could be
designated as Public Speaking only under a definition of wide latitude.

The vagueness in defining public speaking, or the developing field in general, was
not easily clarified. The continuing disputes within the discipline concerning name of
associations and titles of journals was indicative of the lack of agreement about the
central focus of the discipline. After almost 75 years, consensus has not been reached
about the content of the "basic course" which was the most discussed aspect of the
discipline in the early days of the profession.

RHETORIC

Although the study of rhetoric has become central to teaching, study and research
in the modern discipline of speech communication, it was not given even semi-serious
consideration in the first years of the profession. Only in relatively more recent times
has rhetoric occupied much of the time of scholars in the discipline. The reasons for

the early lack of interest are not hard to find. We earlier pointed out that the rhetorical tradition had been preserved by the discipline of English. Indeed many early authors, including Hunt and Woolbert, had unquestioningly, assigned rhetoric to the older discipline. Woolbert, in particular, was quite sharp in his condemnation of rhetoric when he charged that it had no basis in science. (See Chapter 3.) Since the profession, even its outlines of research possibilities, was largely concerned with public speaking as a oral performance field, rhetoric was left to English and regarded as a component of English Composition. In fact, the title "rhetoric" was retained in a number of English departments and course titles. It was the good fortune of the new profession that, after some time, English became less interested in rhetoric, leaving it more available to the teachers and researchers in speech.

Ironically, as we near the close of this century, the interest of English and other fields in rhetorical studies has undergone very rapid growth, resulting in a condition where rhetorical studies are hardly the sole possession of speech communication. In fact, speech communication, for the most part, has never developed its own rhetorical theories and conceptions and has, paradoxically, relied on its "foster-parents" to provide them. Thus a contemporary examination of rhetorical theory and criticism reveals derivations from a number of literary figures including Kenneth Burke, Richard Weaver, Wayne Booth, and a number of European writers.

The members of the new profession were not entirely uninformed about rhetoric. Many of them, after all, were members of English departments where rhetoric was being taught in composition courses and where conversations with colleagues were likely. More important, however, was the academic environment in which the public speaking teachers had been nurtured. Almost all of the members of the association were really children of the nineteenth century. Most of them had studied at colleges and universities in the later decades of the nineteenth or the very early days of the twentieth century when the curricula were rigid and classical. Thus we may safely assume that the members of the profession had studied Greek and Latin and were not altogether unfamiliar with Classical writers, including Plato, Aristotle and Cicero. We should not be surprised to find that some of the earliest excursions in rhetoric were explications of Greek and Roman rhetorical texts.

The first serious work dealing with rhetoric was published in 1909 by Edwin Du Bois Shurter, whose work in public speaking we discussed earlier in this chapter. His book, *The Rhetoric of Oratory* went through at least two additional printings in 1909 and 1911. By 1911 Shurter's department's name had been changed from "Oratory" to "Public Speaking." This largely overlooked volume deserves consideration, if for no other reason than that it was so far ahead of its time. Shurter published *The Rhetoric of Oratory* at a time when the interest of teachers of public speaking hardly extended to rhetoric. Shurter's work was also different from the composition/rhetoric texts of the period since his attention was directed exclusively to oratory and he was unconcerned with writing. Shurter wrote that his book was ". . . intended primarily as a text-book for school and college students" (1911, v). It is difficult to determine who those students were since the book gave no specific instruction in speech-making, except in the final chapter on "The Writing of an Oration." We know of no courses in rhetorical theory or criticism in Public Speaking Departments at that time, although, to be sure, courses in Criticism were common in English departments.

What Shurter offered the students of 1909 was a survey of the history of rhetoric. The main headings of the table of contents reveals how the work was developed.

What is oratory?

Kinds of oratory
The divisions of the oration
Style in oral discourse
The making of an orator: general preparation
The writing of an oration (ix-x)

Each of the sections was developed through references to and quotations from writers such as Aristotle, Cicero, Quintilian, Blair and J.Q. Adams, and quotations and examples from orators, both classical and modern. As the students read through the book they, along the way, acquired an incomplete but serviceable history of rhetoric and oratory.

Shurter's definition of rhetoric testified to the fact that the term, in his time, had come to be connected to writing.

> *Rhetoric is the science which treats of discourse. Discourse is any communication of thoughts by words either oral or written. Rhetoric originally applied to the oral form only; it treated of discourse which was composed for public speaking. The term "rhetoric," indeed is derived from the Greek **rhetorike**, the art of speaking. (1-2)*

Actually Shurter was less flexible in his conception than were his contemporaries such as Genung and Hill and others who had no difficulty incorporating oral discourse in their definition of rhetoric.

In the space of five pages, Shurter provided his readers with a ". . . most cursory review of the history of oratory" spanning the time from ancient Greece to the American Civil War. In his discussion of the history of oratory, Shurter saw a connection between oratory and freedom. His view was very much like that of eighteenth century Scottish writers, notably Hugh Blair, Adam Smith and David Hume. Most specifically he and the Scottish writers saw a close connection in Athens and Rome. Shurter wrote:

> *We should expect oratory and the struggle for liberty, in its various forms, to go hand in hand. And the most cursory review of the history of oratory (which is all that the scope of this treatise will permit) shows this to be true. . . . The liberty of the Athenians which made their public actions dependent upon their own will, and their will susceptible of influence in the popular assemblies, naturally resulted in the study and practice of the art of public address. . . . Grecian eloquence perished with the death of Grecian liberty. . . . It was not until the period of the Gracchi in the second century B.C., that classical Roman oratory began. This was the period of a struggle for a larger degree of liberty for the plebeians as opposed to the aristocracy. And just as there was a decline in Grecian oratory after Demosthenes, so, with the departure of freedom and the reign of the dictator in the age succeeding Cicero, there was a similar falling off in Roman oratory. (9-11)*

So similar was Shurter's language to that of Blair that one may suspect that the Lectures on *Rhetoric and Belles Lettres* were clearly in his head if not at his elbow. Shurter did recognize his dependence on Jebb's *The Attic Orators*. In classifying the types of rhetoric Shurter was able to combine the classifications of the classical, eighteenth century and contemporary writers. To the traditional division into deliberative, forensic and demonstrative oratory, he added, as did the eighteenth century writers, pulpit oratory. Under the heading of demonstrative he included a number of sub-divisions which reflected the oratorical conditions of his own time. They were:

The Eulogy
The Commemorative Address
The After-dinner Speech
The Political Speech
The Platform Address. (35-54)

We have no means of knowing why Shurter included the political speech and the political address as varieties of demonstrative rhetoric when they seemed to be sub-divisions of deliberative rhetoric. Perhaps he restricted himself unnecessarily to the Aristotle's criteria of deliberative oratory.

Shurter treated oratorical organization rather traditionally, but his treatment of style is more interesting. Shurter accepted the eighteenth century notion that style was integrally related to the individual speaker. He, however, expanded his conception to include an element which he had previously considered in his discussion of delivery in Public Speaking.

We may therefore lay this down as a basic principle: The best oratorical
style for a given individual is that of his best conversation. (96)

As might be expected at that time in history, Shurter was careful to distinguish oral from written style.The rhetoric of oratory requires a style of its own. The speaker must so present his ideas as to attract and hold the attention of the hearers; he must arouse their feelings to accord with his own; he must make his style of presentation tell in persuading them of his own ideas and beliefs. . . To be sure, the ideal oratorical style, as has previously been observed, results in a discourse that both speaks well and reads well, but this result is not always—or necessarily attained. (97, 98)

The most novel aspect of Shurter's discussion of style as his integration of style with the conviction/persuasion dichotomy. He apparently was willing to accept the dichotomy only as a pedagogical device because as he wrote ". . . although in actual practice appeals to reason and feeling are inseparable." Clearly, the unitary view of conviction and persuasion, as enunciated later by Woolbert and others, was current a decade earlier, although in truncated form. (See Chapter 3.) In violating the in- separability of conviction and persuasion, Shurter reverted to an eighteenth century distinction based on faculty psychology. He described conviction as . . . "ideas ad- dressed primarily to the understanding" and persuasion as ". . . appeals to their feelings" (98, 106). He was also very close to eighteenth century writers in his belief in the dominance of reason, but the importance of emotion.

All men are more or less emotional, but most men are not moved to action unless
appeals to their feelings are fundamentally reasonable. . . . The first aim of the orator,
then, must always be to secure conviction. . . . To convince a hearer that your
reasoning is sound is one thing, but to induce him to to adopt your reasoning as a
rule of conduct,—to sacrifice his personal and selfish interests, to act contrary to a
previously formed habit or opinion, to vote for a certain man or measure, to
contribute toward a given cause,—this is quite another thing which it is the function
of persuasion to accomplish. (106)

Under the heading of conviction Shurter discussed the following elements of style: clearness, sequence, unity, and emphasis. His treatment of the stylistic elements of persuasion was quite different from that of conviction. He devoted a significant portion of that section to a discussion of motive appeals. Only after that discussion did he turn to persuasive oratorical style. Under the heading of "Distinctive Qualities of Style in Persuasion," Shurter enumerated the qualities of persuasive style.

> *Let us now attempt to point out more specifically the distinctive qualities that characterize the oratorical style. These qualities may be classified as follows: (1) concreteness, (2) figurative language, (3) analogy and antithesis, (4) direct discourse, (5) suspense and climax, (6) euphony and cadence, (7) seriousness and dignity, (8) energy, variety, and movement, and (9) iteration. (114)*

Shurter's chapter on "The Making of an Orator—General Preparation" was, as the title suggests, concerned with speech preparation. Fundamentally, however, it was Shurter's own statement concerning ethos. In order to accomplish what he saw as the goal of his chapter, Shurter presented a three part division.

> *There are three fundamental factors that constitute the orator: what he is, what he knows, and his power of using himself and his knowledge. The first constituent is comprehended under what Cicero calls the character of the orator, the second under what Quintilian calls his education, and the third involves the processes of composition and delivery. Elaborating a little on these three factors, we may say that that the orator (1) must be a man of convictions; (2) he must be a man of wide sympathies and keen sensibilities; (3) he must know things; (4) he must know men; (5) he must be a man of wide reading; (6) he needs a large and usable vocabulary; (7) he needs to acquire the habit of gathering speech material; (8) he should practice committing his thoughts to writing; and (9) he should practice expressing his thoughts orally. (167)*

Though Shurter's book is undoubtedly a dated specimen of the teaching of rhetoric, it, nonetheless, deserves more attention than it has hitherto been given. Before the profession had turned seriously to the exploration of rhetoric, Shurter offered an examination of the historical development of rhetoric as well as a discussion of the major features of what later came to be called "rhetorical theory." Perhaps Shurter was ahead of his time and the teachers of public speaking may not have been ready for his work. Shurter himself was probably known in the new, small profession. Between 1915 and 1922 he contributed three articles to *The Quarterly Journal*, although only one was concerned with rhetoric, and we will discuss it later in this chapter.

The first articles dealing with rhetorical matters were published in the October 1916 issue of *The Quarterly Journal*. One "The Style of Wendell Phillips" by J.H. Doyle Ph.D., Superintendent of Schools, Independence, Iowa was a mixture of rhetorical criticism and linguistic analysis. (All holders of doctoral degrees were scrupulously identified in the early issues of the journal.) Doyle made no references in his articles to any rhetoricians; his criteria were apparently self-generated. The central thesis of his essay was that Wendell Phillips was an orator of pertinent facts (1916, 331-339).

The second article was quite different from Doyle's. Lousene G. Rousseau, of Western State Normal School, Kalamazoo, Michigan in her article, "The Rhetorical Principles of Cicero and Adams," made the first genuinely rhetorical contribution to *The Quarterly Journal*. Moreover it represented for its time a more than superficial historical understanding of rhetorical theory. As we might expect at the beginning of the profession, Rosseau's analysis was distinguished more by breadth than depth. In the space of thirteen pages she undertook the task of providing her readers with summaries of both Cicero's and John Quincy Adams' rhetorical theories. It was clear that Rosseau had read and understood the works of Cicero and Adams, although she cited only the 1909 printing of the Watson edition of *Cicero on Oratory and Orators*, which contained *De Oratore and Brutus*. The comparisons she made were quite appropriate, but the necessity of comparison forced her into a taxonomy which told the readers less about the theorists than if she had written separate articles. Nevertheless, the members of the association were at least introduced to rhetorical writers whose works may not have been familiar to them (397-409). Rousseau's essay was the first of many articles dealing with Classical Rhetorical Theory which would be published in the ensuing decades, although, in time Classical Theory would become less popular.

The first serious attempt to define rhetoric came from Hoyt Hudson of Cornell University in 1923. Hudson was aware of the ambiguity, even confusion which surrounded the term. He, of course, knew that, in his own time, rhetoric had come to be almost synonymous with composition.

> *We are more familiar with the word "rhetoric" in the titles of textbooks on writing, of which many published within the past two or three decades have been named "Composition and Rhetoric;" though I am tempted to believe that if you asked some of the authors of these books to tell you which pages were composition and which were rhetoric, they would be at a loss. Some books named "Rhetoric" alone strikingly resemble others named "Composition and Rhetoric" or still others named "Composition" alone. (1923, 168)*

In order to clarify the meaning and function of rhetoric, Hudson took his readers back to Aristotle, whom he regarded as the most important figure in the history of rhetoric. "Wherever we approach the subject of rhetoric, or the subject of oratory or eloquence, we do not go far without meeting finger posts that point us to the work of Aristotle (1923, 168-169). Hudson supported his position with citations from earlier writers, including Henry Peacham and Hugh Blair.

Hudson, by and large, accepted Aristotle's definition of rhetoric and thus based his analysis on the assumption that rhetoric was concerned with persuasive discourse and that it was a useful art. He recognized that Aristotle ". . . makes the rhetorician a sort of diagnostician and leaves it to others to be the practitioners; . . . " but he was also aware that:

> *In practice, however, and in any study of the subject, this distinction can hardly be maintained, since the person who determines the available means of persuasion in regard to a given subject must also be in, most cases, the one to apply those means in persuasive speech and writing. (1923, 170)*

As the preceding citation suggested, and as he pointed out earlier in his essay, Hudson accepted that the ancient conception, which identified rhetoric with oral persuasion, was no longer valid and that its meaning had shifted to written discourse.

> *We recognize that in ancient times persuasion was carried out almost entirely by the spoken word. We know the great place held by public speaking, at least in their democratic phases. . . .Yet in spite of our habit of thinking of writing and speaking as separate processes, the practice of persuasion is essentially one, in that the same principles apply everywhere in the field. A writer on public speaking would hesitate to call his work "Rhetoric," because the word is usually applied to written discourse. But less than a hundred years ago the case was exactly reversed. Bishop Whately. . . gives as another reason against the title "Rhetoric" that "it is rather the more commonly employed with reference to public speaking alone." (1923, 171)*

Hudson's statement concerning rhetoric's functioning in both oral and written discourse was not brought into practice for some years to come. All the early writings in rhetorical criticism dealt exclusively with oratory as did the articles on rhetorical theory. Hudson's Cornell colleague Herbert Wichelns, in his landmark essay of 1925, "The Literary Criticism of Oratory" gave no attention whatsoever to non-oratorical rhetoric. Hudson's view was, in fact, closer to those of the the writers of Rhetoric and Composition text books, many of whom extended the meaning of the term "rhetoric" to encompass both oral and written discourse.

Hudson took his readers on a lightning tour of the history of rhetoric. In the space of a few pages Hudson mentioned Aristotle, Isocrates, Cicero, Quintilian, St. Augustine, Melancthon, Erasmus, Coxe, Wilson, Bacon, Hobbes, Adam Smith, John Quincy Adams, Whately and Bain.

When Hudson turned to a discussion of the analysis of rhetoric, he restricted himself to oral discourse. In that section he offered an early guide to rhetorical criticism, although his treatment was neither as detailed nor as systematic as Wichelns. In partial anticipation of Wichelns' work, Hudson, partly by implication, distinguished between the tasks of the rhetorical and literary critics.

> *It should be noted, however, that the student of rhetoric investigates eloquence not for its graces and ornaments, and not for its effect upon him as he reads it;. . . The student of rhetoric looks upon each oration as an effort in persuasion; he must learn what he can of the audience to which it was addressed; he takes note of the appeals that are made, with reference to the motives that are touched, the motions that are aroused. He must know the character and reputation of the speaker at the time the speech was made. . . . It is true that we must also take into account matters of style and ornament and delivery; but these too are to be estimated with reference to their persuasive effect. (1923, 174)*

The questions raised earlier by Woolbert and others concerning the relation of public speaking to other disciplines was now raised by Hudson about rhetoric's place in the academic world. He adopted an Aristotelian perspective in which rhetorical principles were applied almost as "tools of common knowledge" and he likened the task of the rhetorician to that of the architect who must know something about engineering, painting, sculpture, surveying and landscape gardening.

> *Some question is sure to arise concerning the relation of rhetoric, in our sense, to other fields of study. It is undeniable that rhetoric draws on other fields with considerable disregard for the airtight partitions sometimes put up between college departments. A student of architecture, whose aim is to learn to design buildings, cannot study that subject alone. . . . The case with the rhetorician is analogous. He must learn much from the psychologist, especially with regard to the subjects of attention and emotion. From the social psychologist he draws what knowledge he can of the crowd-mind and the formation of public opinion. . . .Yet the rhetorician does not necessarily become an expert in those fields. He attempts to learn the authorities and sources of information in each and to develop a method which he can apply to specific problems as they arise. He learns, in any given situation, what questions to ask—and to answer. (1923, 176-177)*

One could interpret Hudson's statement as the manifesto of dilettantes who knew just enough to get by. On the other hand, one could see a description not of an independent discipline but of an over-arching interdisciplinary field. Interestingly, in recent years rhetoric has come more and more to be an interdisciplinary field to which a variety of disciplines contribute and is not the sole possession of any single discipline, not even speech communication.

Since the term rhetoric was associated with English departments, Hudson felt compelled to explicate why it was necessary for rhetoric to exist on its own. In effect Hudson was saying "let English be English."

> *If the department of English absorbs, in addition, the work on rhetoric, at least it should do so with the complete knowledge of the breadth and importance of it, and aware of the distinction between rhetoric and other forms of literature. So far as English is the study of language, philology, it is not very closely related to rhetoric; so far as it is a study of literature it deals with a fine art; whereas we have seen that rhetoric is to be classed with the useful arts. . . .The writer in pure literature has his eye on the subject;. . . his task is expression; his form and style are organic with his subject. The writer of rhetorical discourse has his eye upon the audience and the occasion; his task is persuasion; his form and style are organic with the occasion. . . . (1923, 177)*

Hudson even had a plan in mind as to how to divide instruction in various genre between the departments of English and departments of Speech.

> *. . . might it not be possible to put all study of exposition and argumentation into a course or group of courses together with other work in rhetoric and public speaking; while the teaching of narration and description, or of such literary forms as the short story, the familiar essay and the play might be kept in closer relationship to the courses in literature and in distinction to the forms of writing and speaking as a useful art. (1923, 178)*

Hudson's proposal was really radical and prescient. Although he did not explicitly say so, he envisioned a department concerned with suasory discourse, whether written and oral. His notion seemed to anticipate the growth of Communication Skills and Rhetoric programs of the post World War II years, in which practical writing and speaking were taught in one curriculum. Hudson's classification also suggested that he perceived a distinction used later as the difference between "the literature of imagination" and "the literature of reality."

Hudson ended his essay with optimistic hopes for the future of rhetoric.

> *. . . We have a rather definite body of theory and practice, with an honorable history and an excellent academic pedigree. . . . the significance of persuasive discourse is continually being enhanced. Surely it would be a mistake to overlook this significance, and in proportioning our emphasis I do not see how we can give any but a central position to rhetorical study. (1923, 180)*

In contrast to the Wichelns essay, which we will discuss in the next chapter, Hudson's essay has been neglected. To be sure it was not as copiously developed as Wichelns' essay, but it was the first serious treatment of rhetoric in the pages of *The Quarterly Journal*, it provided the initiates in the profession with a solid conception of rhetoric and it opened the path for further exploration of rhetorical theory and criticism.

Hudson, by now at Swarthmore, narrowed the scope of his investigations into the nature of rhetoric in 1924 when he published his essay "Rhetoric and Poetry." In this work Hudson was not so much concerned with the general relationship of rhetoric and literature as with the specific relationship of rhetoric and poetry. He began his discussion with appropriate quotations from James Russell Lowell and John Stuart Mill. Lowell had written of the "distinction 'twixt singing and preaching" and Mill had written the apothegm, "Eloquence is to be heard, poetry to be overheard."

The quotations came into play as Hudson explicated the differences between public and private discourse and the nature of the rhetorical and poetical audiences.

> *We have, then, on the one hand rhetoric, of which the most typical example is the persuasive public address; on the other hand poetry, represented in its purest form, perhaps by the personal lyric. . . . The rhetorician stands at the opposite pole. He composes his discourse with his eye upon his audience and occasion. . . . The man of rhetoric must test himself at every step by such questions as, "What will this mean to them?" "Will they be ready for this step?" and "How can this be illustrated so as to show its connections with their interests?". . . Moreover the rhetorician wants to do something with his audience—and usually something quite specific. (1924, 144-145)*

Poetry's objectives and connections with the audience were quite different, said Hudson.

> *The poet, as Wordworth reminds us, keeps his eye not on the audience or the occasion, but on his subject: his subject fills his mind and engrosses the imagination, so that he is compelled by excess of admiration or other emotion to tell of it; compelled though no one hear or read his utterance. (1924, 145)*

Rhetoric and poetry also differentiate themselves from each other as media of expression and impression.

> *Poetry is for the sake of expression; the impression on others is incidental. Rhetoric is for the sake of impression; the expression is secondary. (1924, 146)*

The distinction drawn by Hudson, and others, between "impression" and "expression" eventually entered the mainstream of speech communication, but in an altogether different form. Largely under the influence of the new sub-field of interpersonal communication, writers began to refer to "rhetorical" and "expressive" communication, or sometimes, simply to "communication" and "expression."

Hunt conceded that, in many instances, neither rhetoric nor poetry are absolutely pure forms. He used, as did Boyle, whom we discuss later, A.A. Jack's work on Byron as poetic rhetorician (or rhetorical poet). But, often, the poet makes use of imitative rhetoric within his writings. Hunt illustrated this point with allusions to Shakespeare and Milton.

> *We recognize that in poetry in its broad sense, especially in dramatic and narrative poetry, there are a great many occasions when the poet must picture a character as trying to produce an effect by speech. On such occasions the character will use rhetoric, and for the time being the poet is writing persuasive discourse. Familiar examples drawn from English literature are the speech of Mark Antony in Shakespeare's* Julius Caesar *and the speeches of the fallen angels in Books I and II of* Paradise Lost. *Yet we should not say that in these cases the poet is any less a poet, even for the moment he is working in rhetoric. He is producing what we properly may call imitative rhetoric. (1924, 147)*

Yet, said Hudson, many poetic genres make direct use of rhetoric, but the use made by the poet is different from the use made by the rhetorician because of differences in audiences.

> *The poet's work in this species is designed for an audience as surely as is the orator's. And in greater or less measure, the same holds true for other of the species of poetry—for narrative, for the ode, certainly for didactic and satirical pieces. Yet*

there are differences plainly discernible between the poet's audience and the orator's,
and between the poet's relation to his audience and the orator's to his. The poet
thinks of a more general and vaguely defined audience than the orator. The poet may
even think of all mankind of the present and the future as his audience . . . .
(Hudson, 1924, 148)

In his treatment of rhetoric and poetry Hudson seemed to anticipate issues raised by Wichelns in 1925 and by Scanlan in 1936, concerning the connections between rhetoric and other forms of discourse, which we will soon discuss. The early interest in the connections between rhetoric and literature was almost predictable since writers such as Hunt, Hudson and Wichelns were so obviously well versed in the literary theory of their own time. Literary criticism was in a stage of exuberant growth and development while rhetorical criticism was seeking to define itself. The obvious model and analogy for rhetoric was literature, especially since so many of the members of the national association had formerly been members of English departments.

Ironically, after discoursing on rhetoric, Hudson spent the most productive years of his career as Professor of English at Princeton. While there, he produced a number of works, almost all of them literary, including: Poetry of the English Renaissance in 1929; an edition of Erasmus' *In Praise of Folly* in 1941; and two post-humous works *Educating Liberally* in 1945, and *The Epigram in the English Renaissance.*

■ 5
MENTAL HYGIENE, PSYCHOLOGY AND PERSONALITY

Speech, like other academic fields, has not been immune from the influence of the social and intellectual climate of the time. In an earlier chapter we discussed the effects of "science" on the development of the Elocutionary Movement. We have also examined the role played by Psychology in the early years of the establishment of the profession. In the years following the First World War, and well into the Second World War, the field of Speech was aware of and sought to integrate contemporary thought into its teaching and research. Much of the application to teaching dealt with the question of the objectives of teaching Speech and what kind of operations should take place in the class room.

The nineteen-twenties was a time of great intellectual ferment. A number of intellectual historians, in fact, feel that the Twentieth Century actually began after World War I. That period was characterized by far reaching changes in morality, the graphic arts, the theatre, music, architecture, and design. Most significant for our interests, however, were the thoughts of psychologists, philosophers, educators and social thinkers. Among the most prominent influences were those of the new psychology, principally that of Sigmund Freud; and the new theories of social adjustment, particularly those of John Dewey. Those works were assimilated by a number of members of the relatively new Speech profession, and their influence was seen in the pages of *The Quarterly Journal of Speech*, and other journals.

From the late 20s to the early 40s, a serious attempt was made to integrate these orientations, not only in the teaching of Speech but also in the ways in which members of the profession should look at the ends and means of human communication.

One of the key terms of this period in American history was "mental hygiene." Although the term may now strike us as being quaint, in its time "mental hygiene" was a concept which was not only widely accepted by professionals, it was also an idea which enjoyed popular reception. Although we may now have an image of scrub brushes applied to the brain, it was an idea which was taken very seriously indeed. The term may have disappeared from our vocabularies, but some of the underlying beliefs are still with us. Put simply, the assumption of "mental hygiene" was that, through proper management, we could insure our mental health as we insured our physical health. The responsibility for maintaining mental health, however, was not limited to the ministrations of physicians. Rather, many elements of society were involved in the search for mental health. The schools and the family bore special responsibility for insuring that we had healthy minds as well as healthy bodies.

Some members of the Speech profession, influenced by Freud's psychoanalytic ideas and Dewey's ideas of "the well adjusted personality," saw the application of the ideas in at least two ways. They reasoned that most speech problems were, in fact, personality problems and could not be effectively addressed without understanding and altering the students' personalities. They also envisioned the speech classroom as a laboratory for personality improvement. One of the earliest proponents of this point of view was Bryng Bryngelson of the University of Minnesota, who made his case in the pages of *The Quarterly Journal of Speech* in 1928.

> *Admitting speech to be the the important social instrument that it is, we recognize that those who are incapable of using it effectively—i.e. "speech defectives"—will naturally reveal a great deal of poor mental hygiene; in the first place, those who are denied a normal speech outlet because of an organic or structural disorder find themselves faced with a serious problem of social adjustment; and in the second place, those who are socially maladjusted by causes other than organic or structural disorder manifest this maladjustment in their defect of voice in speech. It is with this second class of speech defectives that I am concerned. . . . these functional speech defectives show inadequate adjustments on the part of the human organism to their social environment. Their disorder is merely a symptom of a lack of good social adjustment, or an indication of a social morbidity in the realm of the emotional, the affective, and the conative life. (1928, 208)*

The situation did not seem easily remediable to Bryngelson. He felt that speech teachers were as much part of the problem as were the students. In a quasi-Freudian statement he suggested that the teachers recognize their own personality shortcomings, because not until the teachers' problems had been analyzed and solved would the teachers be able to deal with the social adjustment of the students.

> *. . . Mental hygiene has been difficult because it necessarily begins with the study of self, and that is the hardest thing to study. Teachers have not enjoyed even the discussion of complexes, inhibitions, etc., in other maladjusted personalities because they themselves were experiencing similar problems and they resented the implied analysis of their own difficulties. (1928, 209)*

Bryngelson advocated a procedure which seemed to resemble both group and individual therapy. "The members of the class learn to understand not only their own behavior, but also that of their classmates, when participating in a speech situation" (1928, 210).

Several case studies were described by Bryngelson, including one in which the criticisms of fellow students, at the end of the term, were—Harry you are much more worthwhile as your real self, as we see you now." " You are getting a hold of your speech problem. We see very little trace of that bold front." " You talked more sincerely and directly today. Your humor is real wit—before you were always trying to be funny" (1928, 216).

So strong was the interest in psychology that in 1928 *The Quarterly Journal of Speech* published a series of articles on the relation of Behaviorism, Gestalt and Speech. In February of that year W.M. Parrish of the University of Pittsburgh presented "Implications of Gestalt Psychology." Parrish was attacked in June by Giles Wilkeson Gray of the University of Iowa in an article titled "Gestalt, Behavior and Speech." Another article with the same title as Gray's was published in the November issue. The content of the articles is no longer significant, but they do demonstrate the concern in the profession for the application of psychological theories to the teaching of Speech.

Interestingly, the primary applications, as seen by Parrish and Ogden, were to Drama and Oral Interpretation.

One of the strongest statements in support of Mental Hygiene was written by Wayne L. Morse of the University of Minnesota. (Later Morse was a United States Senator from Oregon and one of the earliest opponents of the Viet Nam War.) In "The Mental-Hygiene Approach in a Beginning Speech Course," Morse denied that the objective of a Speech course was to teach Speech.

> *I do not believe that the primary function of the speech teacher is to train students to deliver presentable speeches—such a function is merely incidental to a course in the Fundamentals of Speech. I would say that the primary educational value to be found in a beginning course in speech is the development of behavioral habits which will enable the student to adjust himself more satisfactorily to his social environment. (543)*

In making his argument Morse relied largely on Watsonian Behavioral Psychology and he made numerous references to books and articles in Psychiatry and Clinical Psychology. From our present perspective it is impossible to know how much Morse was influenced by his senior colleague Bryngelson, but he was even more firm in his position that the Speech classroom was the ideal locus for personality improvement.

> *I feel that the speech class offers the best laboratory for the investigation, dissection, and analysis of personality traits that exist in our educational system. It is the best, and in most high schools and colleges, the only division of the curriculum which provides the student with the opportunity to analyze his own behavior in relation to his fellows, and to subject his behavior to the lay-criticism of his fellow students and to the professional criticism of his teacher. (544)*

In much the same vein as Bryngelson, Morse set high psychological standards for the Speech teacher and insisted that the teacher be mentally healthy before he sets out to deal with the personalities of the students.

> *I do not mean to imply that the teacher of speech should be a professional psychiatrist or mental hygienist, but I do mean to contend that it is essential that speech teachers who are dealing so intimately with the personality problems of the students in the beginning speech course should have an extensive psychiatric, psychological, and child-guidance training. . . . A thorough training in psychiatry, psychology, mental hygiene, and child guidance is more essential for the teacher of a beginning course in speech than a knowledge of the great orators—although the latter is no handicap. Another essential in the mental-hygiene approach to speech is that the teacher, himself, must be a well adjusted individual. He must have analyzed his own personality problems before he can help students overcome their emotional disturbances. . . .There are too many examples of teachers of speech who lack normally adjusted personalities. As a result, it is impossible for them to win the confidence of their students,. . . (548, 549, 550-551)*

In part, Morse's advocacy of the mental-hygiene approach was shaped by his opposition to Elocutionism, which was still present in many college classrooms.

> *The so-called elocutionary method, which is so prevalent in most of our private Speech Schools and in far too many colleges and universities, accomplishes little in developing in the students the ability to adjust themselves satisfactorily to their environment. . . . Emotional butchery as practiced by many speech teachers is*

slaughtering too many personalities that might be helped if more teachers of speech
understood the fundamentals of mental hygiene. (547, 552)

As early as 1929 psychological tests were given to students in Speech courses, and attempts were made to find correlations between personality factors and oral proficiency. Franklin H. Knower of the University of Minnesota reported the results of his testing in "Psychological Tests in Public Speaking." Knower administered a battery of tests consisting of the National Intelligence Test, the Inglis Test of Vocabulary, the Tressman Test of English Composition, the Moss Test of Social Intelligence, the Laird Test of Emotional Stability, and the Allport and Allport Test of Aggressiveness. Sadly the findings of the complex study were inconclusive. The only conclusion Knower was able to reach was restricted to the five students with the highest scores on the tests and the five students with the lowest scores, and that conclusion was no more than a speculation.

> *. . . Of the poorer group we may be relatively sure that no matter what his*
> *determining ambition, the chances of his success in any occupation of a social nature*
> *are extremely slight. On the other hand, a student who scores high on four or five*
> *tests of a series such as this may be fairly certain of success in a type of social work*
> *such as that involving the test of public speaking. (1929, 221)*

Knower felt that his study was flawed by the unwillingness of students to give frank answers. When honest answers were given ". . . some of the responses were very helpful. In one case a young chap who is nervous, easily confused, and tends to stutter, had at the age of four years been stolen by gypsies and been so badly scared that he did not talk for four days. Undoubtedly this was a significant cause for his speech difficulty at present" (220).

In 1930 Edward Z. Rowell, of the University of California, who is now known primarily as a rhetorician, explicated the importance of the new psychological knowledge and the significance of "adjustment."

> *But we have not until the last two decades, realized how completely speech*
> *mirrors and "spells out" a personality. Today the concept of adjustment throws a*
> *flood of light on the baffling mental impediments of speech over which some pious*
> *men have prayed. Good speaking often reduces itself to good mental hygiene;. . . .*
> *(65)*

Bryngelson in 1933 in an article titled "The Re-education of Speech Failures" described in graphic detail how personality was transformed in the Speech classroom.

> *This was done by having each student appear before a mirror. Standing there*
> *looking analytically and self consciously at the red hair, the big nose, the big feet, or*
> *so on, he would talk about the difference, describe it in detail, and get thoroughly*
> *familiar with that characteristic so long neglected. The members of the class all*
> *participated in the discussion, calling attention to the difference as well as remarking*
> *about the more normal parts of their persons. Nicknames befitting the differences*
> *were adopted, or if the sensitivity was about a name, that name was sounded in drill*
> *fashion at each day's session. (1933, 231)*

Bryngelson returned to this concern a year later when he published "Clinical Aids in the Fundamentals Course."

> *. . . It is a waste of both time and energy to attempt voice and diction training*
> *with a student who is hypersensitive to big feet, a large nose, red hair, or protruding*

> *teeth, and so on. In the classroom he may respond to voice training in spite of his*
> *blushes and shyness, but you can be assured that the effects of this training will*
> *disappear at the conclusion of the course unless you have first helped him with his*
> *attitude toward his club-feet, freckled face, glass eye or obesity. . . . This student*
> *needs special training in speech under the heading of objective mental hygiene.*
> *(1934, 538)*

Thus, from Bryngelson's perspective, the role of the speech teacher and the Clinical Psychologist were almost indistinguishable. ". . . The clinician is very close to the speech teacher" (1934, 538). Bryngelson's interest in speech and personality was life-long. As late as 1964, he wrote *Personality Development Through Speech.*

E.C. Mabie of the University of Iowa in his discussion of "Speech Training and Individual Needs" cited the results of personality tests given to Speech students.

> *That there is a relation between speech handicaps and personality maladjustments*
> *must be implied from these facts: of the students who need instruction in the clinic,*
> *24.5% made meaningful scores on the Thurstone Personality Schedule; of the*
> *students who have handicaps of voice and articulation, 15.1% made high scores on*
> *the Thurstone Personality Schedule; of the students who are average or mediocre*
> *performers, 10.3% made high scores. Among the superior performers, only 8.5%*
> *were designated by the Thurstone Personality Schedule as emotionally maladjusted.*
> *(345-346)*

The fact that Mabie was a teacher of Theater is an indication of how pervasive was the influence of those members of the profession whose views had been strongly affected by the Behaviorism of Watson and by the goal of adjustment as stipulated by Dewey. In his article Mabie even sought to find relationships between speech competence and environmental factors. He traced the relationships of proficiency to residence in farms, small towns and cities; the occupation of parents; and church activity among other measures. Unsurprisingly, the best speakers were students from cities; with parents in professions; and who were regular church goers (350).

Elwood Murray of the University of Denver who, in time, became one of the leading proponents of personal development through speech, published "Speech Training as a Mental Hygiene Method" in 1934. Murray actually went further than his predecessors in advocating that the Speech classroom function as a therapeutic setting.

> *From the standpoint of the therapy of mental hygiene, or mental health, speech*
> *training has two very great values: first, it affords means and opportunities for*
> *changing the faulty habits of thinking and feelings and attitudes which underlie*
> *maladjustment; and second, it aids the student to obtain the all necessary objective*
> *and critical view of himself. (1934, 40)*

Murray made the case that all forms of speech training can, if properly managed, contribute to the improved mental health of students. Specifically, he demonstrated the value of debate and argumentation, acting and oral interpretation. In his discussion of acting, Murray advocated a procedure which seems to anticipate "role playing."

> *. . . He should be given a part that will compel him to develop attitudes and traits*
> *in which he is now deficient and which he most needs to develop for the sake of his*
> *adjustment. For instance, the individual subjected to marked feelings of inferiority*
> *should be given the spotlight of a lead part. The too submissive person should be*
> *given an aggressive and dominant part, while the over-aggressive and bombastic*
> *person may well find himself required to develop more submissive and subdued traits*

for the part to which he has been assigned. The impulsive and unstable individual may benefit from a part that requires him to be dignified and deliberate. (1934, 43)

Murray cautioned that criticism by the instructor had the potential for great improvement or great damage. "Speech is a directly personal affair. A person's speech characteristics are so tied up with his most intimate ways of thinking, his attitudes and complexes, that the utmost of caution in criticism is demanded. The difficulty increases according to the type and degree of maladjustment of the speaker" (44). Murray, together with other writers urged the use of a variety of standardized psychological tests. If only one test was to be used, Murray suggested ". . . the Bernrueter Personality Inventory, which permits a rating on emotional stability, self-sufficiency, introversion-extroversion, and dominance-submission all in the same test. . ." (1934, 46).

In his 1935 article, "Mental Adjustments for the Release of Creative Power in Speech Situations," Murray took a somewhat broader view of the function of the speech classroom. Nevertheless, he argued that personality was the chief source of speech creativity.

The purpose now is to suggest what appears to be a few of the necessary conditions in the personality of the speaker which may underlie creative speech behavior. Indeed it is a problem of personality. For speech is a personality trait. To improve speech ineffectiveness, to refine it in any manner, if that change is a genuine one, involves a further growth and differentiation, a greater refinement of personality. (1935, 499)

Murray's name will occur frequently in our description of the mental hygiene movement. In 1937 he devoted an entire book, *The Speech Personality*, to the subject, hoping that a textbook would provide teachers and students with methodologies for dealing with personality improvement in the class room. In the first chapter of the book Murray restated, even more explicitly, the rationale for using the Speech course as therapy.

. . . Speech training in itself may serve as excellent personality therapy. It comes as near dealing with the personality of the student as a subject possibly can. In achieving the skills necessary for artistic presentation of a literary interpretation, play, speaking choir, or speech, the student must work with himself analytically and impersonally. He must look at himself as he is, if he is to acquire the necessary refinements. In thus learning more about himself, he is enabled to maintain a truer perspective of himself and his relation with others. (1937, 9)

In his book Murray addressed the students directly and told them that "speech training should be specific to individual needs." He regretted there is not yet available ". . . a device such as a speech quotient which would serve as a measure of the speech personality as the intelligence test does for mental ability" (1937, 29).

So great was Murray's reliance on standardized psychological tests that, in spite of the absence of a "speech quotient," he, nonetheless, recommended that a battery of tests be administered including:

1. *The speech history of the individual.*
2. *Mental hygiene and personality examinations.*
3. *Hearing tests.*
4. *Intelligence examinations.*
5. *Tests of silent reading rate and comprehension.*
6. *Speaking and reading survey (1937, 29).*

Murray admitted that only the last test bore directly on speech performance. Nevertheless, he argued that "these measuring instruments may be very valuable to use in obtaining a more complete picture of the inner conditions underlying many kinds of speaking, and consequently in helping the instructor in being more specific in his suggestions (1937, 29).

Only about one-half of Murray's 500 page book was devoted to text. The remainder consisted of an Appendix which included, among other items, Personality Improvement Sheets for almost all the varieties of communication. In Appendix I—A, Speech Case History, the student was asked to, "List events which you consider were speech failures and discouragements during the elementary grades." In Appendix I—B, Personality Improvement Sheet For Impromptu Talk, the student was told to, "Trace and explain the history of any of the unpleasant feelings or memories aroused" (1937, 274, 280). In one of the very earliest treatments, of what later came to be known as "interpersonal communication," Murray included Appendix 1—F, Personality Improvement Sheet For Informal Conversational And Conference Situations, (An Analysis of Some of Your Social Skills). Murray said that he included this sheet , ". . . to help you eliminate egocentricity (the chief hindrance to adequate social relations) and foster mental objectivity as the basis for enhancing your skills in everyday social and business living" (1937, 347).

Virginia Claire MacGregor of Stanford University joined the mental health discussion in 1934 with her article, "Personal Development in Beginning Speech Training." She saw the purpose of a speech course as going well beyond the development of oral proficiency.

> *Its object reaches below mere mechanics or external manifestations and concerns itself with the individual made manifest. It is directed to the personal development of that individual, not as a speaker alone, but as a human being. It seeks, further, to awaken him to a realization of the necessity for such development if he is to become the effective, well-rounded personality of which he is capable. (1934, 50)*

MacGregor saw, not public speaking, but oral interpretation as the favored vehicle for revealing personality traits and remedying them. "There is no surer means of discovering individual peculiar habits of thought, emotional attitudes, dullness of imagination, self-depreciation, or egotism than an exciting class in oral reading" (50). Later in the article she suggested how the teacher and student might work together to improve personality through oral reading. "Together they analyze his difficulties and set themselves to the job of making positive those qualities of personality which have hitherto been hidden, submerged, or negative." Many students "find themselves through a bit of prose or poetry, the reading of which demands the projection and amplification of latent qualities of strength and vigor" (55). The connection between speech and psychology was shown by Murray in 1934 in his review of Harold Laswell's *Psychopathology of Politics*, which had been published four years earlier.

> *This book is of more than ordinary interest to students of speech in two ways: it suggests the sort of early environmental factors that may cause an individual to develop into an orator and politician, and it enables a view of the deeper seated factors determining the political behavior of individuals and audiences. . . . Some orators (p. 188) are of an intimate, sympathetic pleading type, and resemble the attempts made by some males to overcome the shyness of the female. Other orators fit into the feared yet revered father-pattern. . . . Some might object to the markedly lop-sided Freudian view and terminology which the author employs. Nevertheless,*

we believe the book to be extremely provocative of thought in our work. (1934a, 134-135)

By now, interest in personality and speech was strong enough that in 1935 Murray edited a group of three articles on the subject in *Speech Monographs*. Aria Daniel Hunter of La Junta, Colorado High School compared the speech performances of introverted and extroverted speakers. She concluded, among other findings, that extroverts were more variable in their speech skills and that extroverts spoke longer and used more irrelevant words than introverts (52-53). James A. Tracy of Fort Collins, Colorado High School studied personality differences between actors and public speakers and found that public speakers were more intelligent, less neurotic, more extroverted, and more dominant than the actors (55-56).

Glenn E. Moore, of the Ilif Theological Seminary, asked whether training in Speech Fundamentals resulted in personality changes. He concluded that a majority of his 61 subjects improved in self-sufficiency, introversion, neurosis and dominance (58). In 1936 Murray undertook an experimental study to validate his theories. He studied 125 students at the University of Denver to determine the relationship between personality factors and proficiency in public speaking. He administered the Benrueter Personality Index and a case history which,

> . . . inquired into detail concerning the language and speech background of the speaker's family, the sort of speech training, experiences,and influences undergone by him from infancy and childhood to his present report, and an inquiry into the sort of experiences significant to his present poise, emotional control, and his adjustment to social situations generally. (1936, 97)

The most significant of Murray's findings were:

> The better speakers are extraordinarily high in self-sufficiency and dominance; they tend to be extroverts, many of them markedly so. The poor speakers are just the opposite. . . . The better speakers came from localities and families of the high cultural and social status, they had generally received definite speech training,. . . they usually had marked social advantages,. . . . The better speakers had the advantages of a more adequate medical care. . . . The least effective speakers tended generally to register very definite evidences of maladjustment in their responses on the personality inventory. . . attitude and habits of thinking and feeling which indicated a markedly inferior mental hygiene and outlook on life in general. The concept of Adler that recognition and approval is the main determining factor in the development of the personality (individual psychology) appears especially applicable to speech behavior. (Murray, 1936a, 99-108)

W. Arthur Cable of the University of Arizona in his discussion of "Speech Education Tomorrow," assigned to speech the responsibility for educating the whole human being, including the emotions. "To speech education it is peculiarly given to cultivate the entire man: the intellectual, the emotional, the social and the physical" (1934, 395).

So wide-spread was the interest in personality development that it found specific application at the high school level in "Personality Development Through Debating," by J. Edmund Mayer of Topeka High School. Mayer said that there were nine, "personality traits that may be developed in a debater: self-control, sportsmanship, judgment, co-operation, initiative, courage, tact, honesty and leadership" (1936, 609-610).

Bryng Bryngelson re-entered the discussion with his 1936 article "Speech Hygiene." In the article he made the case that the speech course must have as its objective the improvement of adjustment in the world outside the classroom.

> *The goal in fundamentals courses should extend to adequate speech adjustments outside the classroom. If our work be thorough, it is not enough to see adequate changes effective in class. Society today is suffering as a result of inadequately adjusted personalities at war with each other's inferiority feelings. (1936, 612)*

Immediately following Bryngelson's article in the 1936 *Quarterly Journal of Speech*, we find an article by Robert West of the University of Wisconsin titled, "Speech Training as a Preventive of Neurosis." West accepted the sexual orientation of Freud and sought to show that sexual urges may be sublimated in the speech class. First, however, West dealt with the sexual meaning of speech.

> *One scholar, looking at the origin of language, notes certain positions of the tongue that are suggestive of the phallus. . . . Again another scholar, a physician, thinks of certain disorders of speech as reverberations of unwholesome repressions of of sex impulses. . . According to this view, stuttering is a sort of oral masturbation. . . . Still another authority in the field says that speech is frequently motivated not by a desire for communication, as such, but by an urge to attract the opposite sex. . . . It is the purpose of the present writer to question that interpretation of the phenomena of speech. (614-615)*

West suggested that two other drives are as basic as sex, and that they might be used in the Speech classroom as a sublimation or a sex-substitute. These drives are "the desire for attention and the desire for new experiences." West hypothesized that the desire for attention is stronger in infant development than is sexual desire even after the baby is "weaned from the ministrations of adults who wait on him." Then, says West, he "falls in love" and he is "again into a situation in which he is the recipient of undivided attention." West asserted that the drive for new experiences begins at birth and expands as we grow into maturity. Included among the new experiences are new sexual experiences. Marriage, said West, may satisfy the sexual drive but the drive for new experience remains unquenched.

> *Now if his behavior is sexually motivated, and if he is happily mated, in the biological sense, he will look no farther. But such is not the case. In spite of his ideals of fair play, he flirts, he courts, he seduces. Why ? To satisfy a sexual drive ? No, that could be satisfied under the same roof where he satisfies his desire for food. But he wants new experiences. Thus may be explained a great deal of adultery, bigamy, rape and homosexuality. (616)*

How then do we address the problems of people driven by the desire for attention and new experiences? West stated that the problem might be alleviated in the Speech classroom.

> *Thus I propose that the way to solve the problem of the girl who is said to be "over-sexed" is to find some activity for her that gets her attention and gives her new thrills. But perhaps the most fertile field for all the sublimation of these desires is speech. Because of the very nature of the act, speech is attention getting. . . . But best of all, speech is the means of acquiring new experiences. Not only the thrill of acquiring new skills, but the thrill of going new places and doing new things. . . . Speech is good mental hygiene. It is a prophylaxis against neurosis. It is an amulet, a phylactery, a charm to protect the wayfarer along the journey of life against the two great dangers on the road we travel, loneliness and boredom. (619)*

By 1937 enough work had been undertaken on the connection between psychology and Speech that William E. Utterback of Oberlin College was able to present in 14 pages, "An Appraisal of Psychological Research in Speech." All in all, Utterback was not sanguine about what had been accomplished.

> *The story of our psychological research during the past twenty years is not one of impressive accomplishment. In large part it is a story of misdirected effort. . . .This venture has largely been a waste of time and effort. . . . Experimental work in the psychology of speech is a fruitful field. It is a field, however, that can be cultivated only by those who have had rigorous training in experimental method. (1937, 181-182)*

By 1937 the application of these doctrines was being advocated for the students in the lower grades. Horace G. Rahskopf of the University of Washington wrote in "Principles of the Speech Curriculum":

> *. . . we should seek to integrate all aspects and uses of speech in the maturing life of the child. These aspects and uses can be summarized briefly as follows: Mental hygiene—desirable social attitudes, concentration and orderly thought processes, poise and emotional balance, co-ordination of thinking with speaking. . . . (453)*

Edna Dorothy Baxter of the University of Denver wrote of specific applications of using Speech as a therapeutic methodology for disturbed children in "A Child Guidance Clinic Through Speech." Speech is seen by Baxter as a modality for dealing with children's problems, rather than an end in itself.

> *The first purpose of the Child Guidance Clinic through Speech is to help correct negative behavior patterns and attitudes. . . . The first purpose is two-fold: it seeks to ascertain the undesirable responses that a child makes to life situations and the causes that motivate these responses; and it seeks to apply corrective training through speech vehicles. . . . The second purpose of the clinic is to prepare children to solve their future problems by teaching them objective attitudes in emotional control. . . . The third purpose of the clinic is speech correction and development. It is usually true that the child who is having speech difficulties is also having social difficulties. (627)*

Baxter cited specific behaviors which could be treated through speech. They included: friendliness, co-operativeness, cheerfulness, sarcasm, boisterousness, tidiness, dependability and courage. She also placed strong emphasis on the "adjustment" of the clinician.

> *Any maladjusted clinician, who is not objective in her own thinking, might cause great harm while working in a clinic. None of us are truly objective, but a self-centered, maladjusted clinician has no place in a clinic. (Baxter, 1937, 635).*

This clinical view of the relationship between Speech and Guidance was expressed in 1938 by Donald Nylen of the Seattle Public Schools. Nylen saw similarities between the objectives and methodologies of Speech and Guidance.

> *In both speech work and guidance, the individual is seen as a whole personality. Due consideration is given to the relationship of his physical, emotional, and intellectual aspects. . . . Speech is an important expression of self. As such it is closely related to physical and emotional conditions. The development of expression, therefore, the emotional and intellectual attitudes, the making of gestures, the formulation of words are important keys to the growth of personality. She [the Speech teacher] must be psychologically trained, prepared to handle problems of*

personality disorder which may be indicated through difficulties in expression. (604, 605, 609)

In 1938 Knower published a long and complex article "A Study of Speech Adjustment and Attitudes." Knower regretted that so little attention had been paid to personality as a factor in speech proficiency. "The present study was undertaken with the hope of adding to our understanding of the process of speaking through the application of techniques developed by the students of the psychology of personality to this problem." (1938, 130). Knower administered a number of measures including a 266 item Speech Attitude Scale, a 100 item Speech Experience Inventory, and a 78 item S. C. Scale, involving ". . .the formulation of a negative judgment about the practice of certain characteristics or forms of speech." Knower's article concluded with fifteen findings, most of them having to do with the validation of the instruments. He did, however, find some differences between good and poor speakers in their attitudes about speaking.

> *Speech attitudes . . . vary with such factors as sex, high school and college populations, the demonstration of specific speech problems, as well as proficiency in speech arts, socio-economic status, energy level, knowledge, emotional stability, and sociality. There is a marked relationship between speech attitude and speech experience,. . . .The study suggests that characteristics of the speaker as a personality may have a vital influence on his speech performance. It is possible to apply techniques of the student of the psychology of personality to the study of this problem. (1938, 202-203)*

M. Reid White of the State College of Washington sought to apply theories of personality to the casting of characters in high school plays in his article "Psychological and Physiological Types in High School Plays" White undertook the analysis of six frequently performed plays in order to determine which personality types should be cast in the roles. White made use of a mixture of psychological, medical and endocrinological sources to arrive at his personality classification. So reliant was he on his sources that his taxonomy began to resemble that of the Elocutionists. Specifically, he cited the work of Kretchmer, "Jung's extrovert and introvert psychological types, Kahn's clinico-descriptive classification, the Yin and Yang philosophy. . ." (661). White's categories included: physical types such as "Pyknik—short stocky, square, thick-set;" motility, including "Hyperkinetic—active, alert;" temperament, including, "Post-pituatary—Fair, fat, and forty;" motivation, including, "Focalization—singleness of purpose;" Yin and Yang (extremely feminine versus extremely masculine); clinico-descriptive, including, "Hyperthymic—eternally gay and busy" (White, 1939, 663).

Regrettably, White did not give the reader even a clue as to how he identified the personality of the characters in the plays or how the teacher could recognize personality types or how to develop them in student actors. Nevertheless, he left that responsibility to the teacher. ". . . a player should be cast as to physical type, and then create the outstanding characteristics of motility, temperament, motivation, Yinness and Yangness, and psychopathic tendencies" (665). Elwood Murray rejoined the discussion of speech and personality in 1940. This time, however, in his "Speech Standards and Social Integration," he widened the focus of his perspective. No longer did he limit his attention to "the well-adjusted person." Now he was also concerned with the ways in which we improve our social relations through the use of speech. That said Murray is the "true function" of speech.

Speech should serve as a social integrator; as the tools which enable attention to be obtained, comprehending and understanding to result, experience to be shared in the meeting of minds. . . . (1940, 75)

Murray's premise concerning the function of speech caused him to adopt another iconoclastic posture. This time he argued that communication is not the central objective of speech. In another anticipation of interpersonal communication he asserts that a new form of speech is central to the teaching of speech.

The conventional view is that speech is communication and is to be evaluated in the light of its effectiveness in communication, or the exchange of ideas. This view is scarcely adequate when the resistances, biases and distortions under which persons accept ideas are considered. . . . The speech teacher certainly has a responsibility for the use of speech tools far beyond mechanical or phonetic, grammatical and rhetorical proficiency in communication. . . . If speech is to serve human relations and social integration, the common everyday conversation in the ordinary living of the student must be the chief emphasis of speech teaching and the speech teacher. . . . Invariably the speech tools will be found contributing to whatever degree of maladjustment that exists;. . . One of the speech teacher's chief methods will be that of a technician in human relations, a helper towards insight, understanding and mental objectivity. (1940, 76-77)

Murray seemed willing to have the Speech profession assume the much broader responsibilities required by his orientation.

To some persons the enlarged scope of the work implied will appear to be placing all the woes of the mankind on the speech teacher's shoulders. To others the enlarged scope of and responsibilities will be a challenge for more significant service in the field of education which such an enlarged view of speech permits. (1940, 80)

Forrest Rose of the State Teachers College, Cape Girardeau, Missouri, performed an experiment, in 1940 to determine the effect of speech classes on personality change. He paired 291 students enrolled in speech classes, in nine colleges and universities, with 291 students who were not taking and had not taken any speech courses. He administered the Bernreuter Personality Inventory to his subjects in both pre-test and post-test situations with the objective of determining whether taking a Speech course was related to changes in "neurosis, self-sufficiency, dominance-submission and sociability." Rose found no significant differences between the student groups in his pre-test, but he did discover differences in the post-test.

Speech training results in a greater decrease in neurotic tendency and a greater increase in dominance. . . .With regard to self-sufficiency and sociability,. . . the results are inconclusive. (195)

In the same year Ernest Henrikson of Iowa State Teachers College examined, "The Relation Among Knowing a Person, Liking a Person, and Judging Him as a Speaker." His subjects were 81 students at the University of Montana and 98 at Iowa State Teachers College. He concluded that, "The better known speakers are judged to be somewhat better speakers," and "The better liked students are judged to be better speakers" (23). The study was brief and Henrikson did not suggest what its implications might be.

A more sophisticated study of the relation of speech and personality was begun in 1936 by Howard Gilkinson of the University of Minnesota and Franklin H. Knower of the University of Iowa. It was published in 1940 as " Individual Differences Among Students of Speech as Revealed by Psychological Tests—I." Gilkinson and Knower administered The Bell Adjustment Inventory to 200 men students and 200 women students in Speech classes at the University of Minnesota with a view to ascertaining personality differences between effective and ineffective speakers. The Bell Inventory was designed to measure "Home Adjustment, Health Adjustment, Social Adjustment and Emotional Adjustment." Although their findings were highly qualified, Gilkinson and Knower concluded that effective speakers were significantly higher in Social Adjustment than the ineffective speakers. The findings for the other categories were less conclusive (1940, 255). The Gikinson and Knower study was not especially sig- nificant because of its findings. Rather, it was an early attempt to deal with the correlation of speech and personality through the use of experimental methodology.

Personality tests were also used by Alfred L. Golden of Duquesne University in a study seeking to determine whether the personality traits of drama school students were different from other students. Golden administered a variety of personality measures to 80 drama students at Dusquene University and the Carnegie Institute of Technology. He concluded, using the Allport-Vernon Scale of Values, ". . . that Drama School students have a greater Aesthetic Interest and less Theoretical and Economic Interests than the comparison group of non-drama students." On the Neymann- Kohlstedt Diagnostic Test for Introversion- Extroversion, ". . . it may be said then that the Drama School students tend more towards extroversion than the Non-Drama group and that this tendency is a reliable one." Golden also administered his own Drama School Questionnaire and found other differences.

> The results obtained on the Drama school Questionnaire show a statistically reliable connection between Drama School students and unfortunate family encounters, that Drama School students admit to the charge of "exhibitionists"and "queer ducks" applied to them, and in general that Drama School students possess attitudes in direct contrast to that of the Non-Drama School control group. . . . It would appear that there was justification in ascribing atypical personalities to the Drama School students. Behavior, . . . at the very least may be described as different from comparison groups. . . .The writer wishes to venture the opinion that despite the indication that Drama School students possess extraordinary personalities, in all likeliehood the unusual conduct and attitudes of Drama School students are largely affectations resulting from the peculiar socio-economic factors prevailing in their chosen occupation. (Golden, 1940, 574-575)

In 1941 yet another experiment was reported by Clyde W. Dow of Massachusetts State College. He tested students in classes in Public Speaking and Literary Interpreta- tion to determine whether ability was related to intelligence. Dow acknowledged the work of Murray and others in their studies of aspects of personality, but he felt that intelligence had been neglected. Dow concluded that ability in public speaking and intelligence were unrelated; public speaking skill seemed more closely related to personality than to intelligence. He did find a statistically significant relationship between proficiency in Literary Interpretation and intelligence (114). Since Dow as- signed the proficiency rating himself, and since his subjects were all college students, supposedly of at least average intelligence, Dow's results were, even then, open to question.

In a very specific application of speech to personality improvement Harold A. Dressel of the University of Michigan proposed that the "platform interview" be used as a pedagogical device to increase the students' dominance and to reduce their submissiveness (382-385).

Although the goal of "adjustment," widely mentioned in the personality articles was, at least in part, derived from the philosophy of John Dewey, writers had relied more on psychologists than on Dewey. In 1941, however, Earl Emery Fleischman of the College of the City of New York offered in his essay, "Speech and Progressive Education," a perspective derived directly from Dewey. Together with earlier writers, Fleischmann believed that, "Speech is not merely a tool which we employ when we want to talk with one another." He gave speech the leading role in adjusting people to the world in which they live. Echoing the Dewey dictum that the purpose of education is, "to adjust society to the child and the child to society," Fleischmann stated that speech, "At its core is concerned with human relations and the attitudes and behavior of the individual which affect his measure of success or failure as a human being in a social world" (512). Preceding from the point of view of "reflective thinking," Fleischman assigned a central responsibility to Speech.

> *Speech is the mastery of those skills which make for a more perfect social adjustment in all the human relations of the individual. It is a mastery of a technique of oral communication by means of which he can reach an understanding through the efficacy of language of what goes on in the minds of other people. It is an exercise of control over impulses largely emotional in character, which lead to behavior that creates difficulties for the individual rather than promoting the ends which he wishes to attain. Straight thinking, the exercise of common sense intelligent initiative, pose and self-control are indispensable (513).*

Fleischman felt that the goal of a Speech program was "the development of mature personality, well-rounded, well-informed, alert, responsive, with a sensitivity to, and regard for, others. He then listed the attributes of a "mature personality."

> *1. The ability to think straight, to view things realistically as they are, not as they might be or as we might wish them to be; 2. Freedom from narrow prejudices, rigidities, resistances, which prevent open-mindedness; 3. Freedom from sentimentality, the indulgence in fantasies and other self-protection escape devices; 4. Freedom from infantile behavior designed to attract attention, win sympathy, or to accomplish objects by indirection rather than by honest efforts; 5. Cooperation, imagination, sympathy, insight, understanding; 6. Skill in dealing with the perversities of other people, avoiding clashes, getting around them for the accomplishment of your own objects. (513-514)*

Fleischman was in agreement with earlier writers that,

> *Many speech teachers disavow this responsibility for personality training, either regarding it as of little importance, or relegating it to some other educational department, or leaving it for the individual to work out for himself. (514-515)*

As in the earlier articles, Fleischman imposed a weighty responsibility on the teacher.

> *The speech teacher does not have to be a psychiatrist. After all he is dealing with the normal behavior of normal people—insofar as any of us are normal. . . . No teacher is qualified to teach speech who does not know something of the workings of the human mind and the sway of impulse and emotion in the life of the individual. For the speech teacher is dealing with the mind and the nervous system—the whole personality. . . . (515)*

Fleischman lamented that the speech teachers of his generation had not been exposed to Progressive Education.

> We who teach speech, if we are honest with ourselves, perhaps look back on our own lives with some regret because we did not have the opportunities in our formative years of being subjected to such a course of speech education. Many of the problems that have confronted us since, I am sure, could have been met much more efficiently with the saving of I know not how much waste of energy and with much better success than we did. We might even be better all-round individuals, but for this lack of formal training. (516)

A simple calculation shows that the speech students of 1941 are at least in their late sixties. One looks at the characteristics of that aging generation and seeks in vain for the kinds of changes envisioned by Fleischman and the other writers who saw the speech class room as the setting for profound personality modification.

Clyde Dow, who had earlier sought to find a relationship between speaking and intelligence, in 1941 undertook a study to determine "The Personality Traits of Effective Public Speakers." Dow's subjects were 153 speech students at three Massachusetts colleges to whom he administered a variety of personality measurements. After all his effort, he found only one significant relationship.

> The trait we have called ascendance (the quality in some other studies called dominance) bears a very important relation to ability in public speaking. This trait characterized to a reliable degree (according to the correlations) the good speakers, and the opposite, submission, appeared in poorer speakers. This is the one personality trait . . . that seems to be sufficiently important to influence speaking ability. (531)

In 1941 a physician, Paul Moses of San Francisco, joined the adjustment discussion in his essay "Social Adjustment and the Voice." Moses divided the characters of human beings into the "schizoid" and the "cycloid," without defining those terms. He did, however, offer descriptions of the character types.

> We can describe the schizoid character as unsociable, without a sense of humor, often sensitive, timid, difficult to guide. The cycloid character is friendly, sociable, good humored, often quiet and of a gentle mood. To each type belongs a special voice. . . The persistent falsetto voice is a decidedly schizoid symptom. These men do not lack sociability because of their high voice, but a high voice is a clue to their lack of adaptability and adjustment. (534)

Moses postulated that personality and adjustment were detectable. He spoke, for example, of the disguised voice used by doctors, teachers and military officers and which is in contrast with actual character. ". . . but genuine paternal love reveals a natural voice content by chest register and does not need an artificial lowering"(535). Moses advocated that voice training be provided before instruction in public speaking because "voice hygiene" would lead to improved personal adjustment.

> We try to help by teaching "public speaking." We think a young student clumsy in his way of expressing himself will get an easier adjustment if he learns public speaking. . . If we really want to facilitate social adjustment, then we must change our educational program and teach voice before speech, and give our teachers voice training before they start teaching. (536)

A rather slight article which did not find agreement with Moses' hypotheses was published in 1942. Paul J. Fay and Warren C. Middleton of Depauw University sought to determine whether listeners could ". . . judge introversion, as measured by the Bernreuter Personality Inventory, from the transcribed voices of several speakers." After the completion of their experiment they concluded that ". . . introversion can be judged from the transcribed voice with an accuracy approximating chance expectation" (228). In fairness to Moses it is necessary to point out that he believed that those not trained in voice might not be able to recognize a personality deficient in adjustment.

The principles of Psychodrama, as presented in the work of Jacob Moreno, were examined by John L. Hamilton of the University of Minnesota in 1943 to assess their possible application to the teaching of speech. Hamilton, in his article, "The Psychodrama and its Implications in Speech Adjustment," speculated that exercises in Psychodrama might lead to better speech adjustment in the classroom. Other than anecdotal evidence, however, Hamilton cited only one study and that conducted by Beth Rudolph at the University of Denver. She administered the Bernreuter test to 95 Fundamentals of Speech students and then cast the students "in parts that were directly opposite of normal temperament. . . . Over eighty per cent of the students felt that they had benefited by playing the roles" (66). This obviously subjective essay contributed little to knowledge, but it was evidence of continuing interest in the quest for adjustment.

In 1943 Bryngelson published "Applying Hygienic Principles to Speech Problems." For those students " whose audience consciousness was abnormal," Bryngelson advocated professional help.

> *I suggest that with the help of a psychotherapist, or anyone trained in the uprooting of inferiority feelings, that they may work out their own salvation as speakers. Irrational ideas, morbid fears, erroneous conceptions about self and society often lie in the background, and must be interpreted, understood, and evaluated before these individuals can expect speech freedom before a group. (352-353)*

For Speech students "possessing marked physical differences," Bryngelson argued for the confrontational therapy he had been advocating for more than a decade.

> *We convince them that there is no further use in continuing to conceal the defect, or in using psychological crutches to make it seem less conspicuous. We tell them that the best way to rid themselves of their sensitivity is to expend it by observing it dispassionately in mirrors, by analyzing it carefully, and by talking of it. (1943, 353)*

In spite of Bryngelson's Draconian recommendations, we must be aware that he was not speaking of students with severe physical handicaps. Rather he was addressing the problems of students with, "bowlegs," "large noses," and "prominent teeth."

In the same year, Bryngelson's colleague, Howard Gilkinson, studied the causes of social fears among college Speech students. He found, "That the fearful speakers showed a more marked trend. . . toward generalized low self-evaluation. . .", and, "that a generalized low sense of inferiority frequently operates as a primary cause of the emotional disturbance of a speaker in facing an audience" (83).

By 1945 enough study of personality and its relation to speech had been completed that Murray was able to publish a 19 page article in Speech Monographs summarizing the research done since 1928. After surveying 17 years work, Murray concluded that:

> *Speech development and personality development seem to be closely related, ... The same unbalances . . . which affect personality development adversely tend also to affect speech behavior adversely. Speech training which neglects shifts in the culture*

and changes in the environment appear to interfere with the development of mature speech behavior. (1945, 27)

After 1945 few, if any, articles dealing with personality improvement through Speech were published. The explanations for this abrupt diminishment are not totally clear, but we can speculate that the profession became so concerned with the war effort that these psychological matters were abandoned, at least for the duration. After the end of World War II, a younger group of scholars began to replace those who had been writing about adjustment for almost twenty years. In the post-war years in the Social Science Revolution scholars in Speech turned to other varieties of Psychology as support for their research.

6

ETHICS, FREEDOM AND DEMOCRACY

From almost the very founding of The National Association of Academic Teachers of Public Speaking concerns were voiced about what the goals of Public Speaking courses should be. From the first issue of *The Quarterly Journal of Public Speaking* questions were raised, not only about the content of the courses, but about the fundamental objectives of instruction in Public Speaking. We have earlier discussed the dispute between Hunt, Woolbert, Winans and others concerning the question of whether the new discipline should be oriented toward the sciences or the humanities. (See Chapter 3.) Perhaps the most numerous of the early articles were examples of "mutual reenforcement" in which authors disclosed, "how we do it at our place," and in which the results of surveys were given.

At the same time that procedural matters and disciplinary orientation were pondered, a number of articles were published which dealt with the ethical and moral responsibility of the teacher of Public Speaking to students. Although these articles were written from a different perspective from those on personality improvement, they too had as their objective the personal improvement of Speech students, but in this case from the point of view of morals and ethics. These writers were determined that students emerge from Speech classes as more honest people and as more responsible citizens.

The first significant essay on the moral component of Speech was directed as an attack on German academics in the First World War. In 1918 J.P Ryan of Grinnell College attacked German scholars. He accused German educators of failing to fulfill their obligation of "serving the Truth." Whatever the accomplishments of German scholarship, they could not be forgiven "the terrible prostitution of that scholarship in its efforts to justify barbarism and to condone military atrocities." Ryan felt it important that American academics exercise the responsibility and ethics which the Germans had forsaken (1-2). Ryan's indignation at the Germans is understandable in the context of the war but one now wonders about his service to the Truth in light of what we now know about the power of the propaganda efforts of the Allies.

The patriotic spirit of the war was reflected as late as 1921, when W. Palmer Smith of Boy's High School in Brooklyn published "Americanization through Speech in Our High Schools." Smith's America, particularly in Brooklyn, was a land of immigrants, and Speech was the route to making them "Americans."

> *English speech is probably the factor which has stood the most rigid tests, for it has been found that a foreigner's interest in learning to speak English and the use he makes of his acquirements in the language of America are self-manifestive indices of his attitude toward and his progress in Americanization. These developments put*

oral English and the teaching of the subject in a new light. . . . In fact, English, and particularly spoken English, is so essential for our political and social development that it is being more and more recognized as the key to participation in American life. Our neighbors of other nationalities and their children become good American citizens in direct proportion to the degree which they identify with American ideals. (370)

We might, understandably, be curious as to how after 70 years Smith might view the accomplishments of other nationalities in New York where the Kochs, the Cuomos, the Badillos, the Gulianis, and the Dinkins, not the Smiths, are the political and social leaders. Smith ended his essay with a strong patriotic, and perhaps chauvinistic, appeal.

We can never estimate the extent of the work we may be accomplishing when we help a pupil overcome his inherited linguistic habits, substitute for them English speech habits, and at the same time inspire him with some appreciation of his duties and privileges as an American citizen. That pupil may teach his own father and mother to speak English, he may be an example to his younger brothers and sisters, he may exert his influence over a group of companions and become a nucleus for better citizenship;. . . (374)

One is tempted to ask what position Smith might take, if he were still with us, in the current controversy about whether English should be declared the official language of the United States.

In the same year, in an article concerned with "Speech Education for Secondary Schools," William R. Connor, principal of the Longwood High School of Commerce in Cleveland, referred briefly to the role of the Speech class in promoting citizenship.

The teacher of speech, as a teacher of public speaking and debating, then seems to have a duty in education for citizenship, which in itself, is probably of more significant than all the other services she can perform. (113)

In 1922 Warren Choate Shaw of Knox College published one of the first articles dealing specifically with the question of ethics of the new profession. Shaw's ethical concerns were ostensibly directed against the practices of coaches; but in his article "The Crime Against Public Speaking" Shaw's indictment had application to the more general subject of how Speech should be taught. Although Shaw explicated his charges in some detail, he specified his concerns early in his essay.

If any act or practice that we tolerate or practice in our profession destroys our educational standards; leads us to neglect the overwhelming majority of our students; impairs our efficiency as academic teachers; promotes, through us, fraudulent advertising; forces us as academic teachers to stake our future and our reputation and our future on a mere gambler's chance; deprives us all of proper academic recognition; and prevents young men and women of the highest type from enlisting in our profession as their life work; then I say such an act constitutes a crime that I intend to point out to you today. (138)

A three way dispute about the responsibilities of the teacher of Speech was generated in the pages of *The Quarterly Journal of Speech Education* in 1922 and 1923. In 1922 Everett Lee Hunt of Cornell University had published an essay titled "Adding Substance to Form in Public Speaking." Hunt's article was followed by "The Problem of Speech Content" by W. P. Sanford of Ohio State University. In 1923 James M. O'Neill of the University of Wisconsin undertook a lengthy refutation of the Hunt and Sanford articles. The subject under discussion concerned the duty of the teacher of speech to be responsible for the content of student speeches. In his essay Hunt had proposed that, " First, a course in public should include as source material, a group of essays or addresses which treat a limited number of fundamental subjects upon which any liberally educated man should be able to speak intelligently and effectively in public (1922, 257). Hunt's proposal grew out of what he perceived as a genuine need." Teachers are besieged with students who lack ideas for the composition of speeches, and have little notion of where to seek them. The instructor's suggestions seem to fall on barren ground. . . . The problem of content, therefore, should be recognized and dealt with as an integral part of public speaking (1922, 256).

We may be puzzled that an apparently innocent suggestion of a collection of readings in a public speaking course should generate enough excitement to prompt O'Neill to respond to Hunt and Sanford in a 27 page essay. The discussion, however, struck at the central question of the integrity of the course and whether the instructor was obligated to provide the materials of the course or whether the instructor's responsibility was to assist the student in the management of material. In an ethical frame the age-old question of "what to say" as opposed to "how to say it" had again emerged. In his lengthy refutation O'Neill argued that the instructor who emphasized content over form was not only abdicating her responsibility to teach Speech; she was also moving into areas which are beyond the concern of the public speaking course.

> . . . the subject matter of the student's speeches is not the proper "content" for a course in public speaking. . . . The proper immediate purpose of a course in public speaking is to give the student knowledge of, and proficiency in, public speaking. . . . The function of a course in public speaking is not to provide the student with the whole of a liberal education, but to enable him to gain one important part of a liberal (and liberating) education, viz. the ability to express well, orally, in public, whatever he may have to express. And that is no mean function. . . . An instructor in public speaking, however, should be content to pull his oar in the boat of liberal education, but he should hardly try to pull all of the oars. (1923, 29, 31, 33).

O'Neill maintained that the content of Speech was found in the subject itself rather in outside fields.

> I would earnestly recommend that the teacher and the student in public speaking who are thirsting after content, instead of "centering their attention" upon such matters as taxation and tariff, pursue a course of reading and discussion in the content of this particular historical line. It is one of the most interesting and significant in the whole history of education. I recommend a complete course from Aristotle, Cicero and Quintilian, down to date. . . . In this historical line can be found ample content for courses of sufficient academic responsibility to sit at the head of the table with the wisest and best in any university curriculum in America. (1923, 48)

Thus, in the discussion of responsibility in the classroom O'Neill advocated a standard course of the future—the history of rhetorical theory.

Hunt was not to be silenced, however. In the same issue of the same journal as O'Neill's article Hunt wrote of "Knowledge and Skill." Without any reference to O'Neill he again defended the importance of knowledge vs. skill in terms which are not much different from the present-day dispute concerning education vs. training. Writing in the manner of a person who, later in his life, was to be dean of a prestigious liberal arts college—Swarthmore, Hunt argued for the preeminence of knowledge over skill, but with the understanding that skill is, nonetheless, necessary for the speech teacher.

> *It is not our skills that are feared by the defenders of scholarship. It is skill unillumined by knowledge of a liberal character. It is skill imparted by men so untouched by love of ideas that they are willing to substitute skill for ideas. When a teacher of public speaking is made to feel that he lacks academic weight because he is overmuch concerned with skill, that is only the kindest way of putting the case to him.*

The emphasis on the teaching of skills has led, Hunt said, to the diffusion of effort among teachers who are required to deal with every course in the curriculum and are thus prevented from being scholars.

> *But when a teacher of elementary courses in oral expression and extempore speaking also has elementary courses in dramatic art, and then hastens to meet some elementary debaters, and then must conduct a spasm of training for a declamation contest. . . what has such a man to do with scholarship?. . . The teacher of argumentation and debate who will eagerly investigate the field of logic and rhetoric, who can speak upon the great debates with the background of a student of history or politics has no time for staging plays or coaching declamation contests. (1923, 74-75)*

Some 70 years later the question of generalists and specialists is still with us, although not to the same degree as in Hunt's day, and the question is not presented as a part of our professional ethical responsibility.

The question of the ethics of inter-collegiate forensics was also raised early in the history of the new association. In 1923 William Hawley Davis of Bowdoin College wrote the following communication to The Forum in *The Quarterly Journal of Speech Education*. The letter under inspection is dated 1912, but in view of Davis' reference to "a letter recently received," one is led to suspect a misprint and that the date was really 1922.

WHAT IS DEBATING FOR ?

Dear Editor:

Is it not time to inquire through your columns as to who are or what is responsible among us for the the situation indicated by the following letter recently received here?

******* January 16, 1912*

Bowdoin Debating Council.
Bowdoin College.
Brunswick, Me.

Dear Sir:

We are writing you at this time concerning the subject of the League of Nations, which we understand that you have debated it and was successful with it. As we are to debate it this year as champion debaters here in our college we thought you to be the best source of information to get the real dope on the subject, as we understand that you are the leading debate college in the United States. We will be glad to get the speeches that you had on the subject if you have a copy of them on hand, and also any other information that you may be able to give us. We are not asking you to give us this, but we want to buy it or borrow it if you don't want to sell it and we will return it within the next few weeks.   Thanking you for your kindness, and prompt reply, we beg to remain very truly yours.

*******   *Champion Debaters*

Respectfully yours
WM. HAWLEY DAVIS

Bowdoin College, January 30, 1923. (195)

The ethics of forensics came under attack again in 1923 in an editorial titled, "The Coach versus the Professor," presumably written by Charles Woolbert. This time the targets were those persons responsible for hiring speech teachers and their preferences for winning coaches rather than effective teachers and administrators. The writer cites three cases in which colleges have appointed winning coaches when they could have chosen teachers well grounded in the discipline or teachers whose contracts have not been renewed because, in one case:

> *He has not had the success in contests enjoyed by some of his predecessors and by his opponents. He is frankly told that he is not to be reappointed because he has not brought enough debate and oratorical victories to the college—this by a committee of the faculty on appointments; not by the president alone. The college wants a coach first and a professor second, if at all. (1923, 284-285)*

Woolbert used these examples not only to decry the ethical problem, but also to lament for the future of the discipline.

> *The disturbing element in the present evidence is the frankness of presidents and faculty committees. It would seem that they are by no means yet "sold on" speech education for the whole college. What is worse, the man on the grounds who ought to be interesting them in speech education, finds his hands tied and his tongue stopped; he is either too much bedeviled into giving every last ounce of his time and strength for victories, or by his voluntary devotion to contests he stands committed to the superiority of sporting event over academic discipline. (1923, 285)*

Sara Huntsman of the University of California, in her article, "Public Speaking as a Means in Education," stipulated that the overriding goal of a public speaking course is to assist the student in thinking clearly. She extended the concept to include concern and care for the welfare of others.

> *To think clearly means to relate oneself to life in such a way as to use one's faculties toward the enrichment and fulfillment of life. He serves life best who lives life best and only through the happy and harmonious development of all of his faculties can man relate himself intelligently to the world in which his neighbor lives; and the work and worship by which his neighbor lives, are as vital to him as his own. (10)*

In the " Forum" in 1925 under the heading " Intellectual Parasites," Albert Keiser of Augustana College wrote of the immoral trade of "speeches for all occasions," by commercial firms. Keiser was particularly disturbed by speeches which were offered for sale to preachers and politicians.

> *The conscience of the preacher customers is adroitly lulled to sleep by the following argument drawn from the sacred book itself; "Don't worry about originality. Christ never claimed it. He says 'The words that I speak are not mine, but His that sent me.' The Holy Ghost did not claim it, for it is written, 'He shall*

not speak of himself, but whatsoever He shall hear, that shall he speak.' " The only
thing forgotten by the publisher is the fact that the Son as well as the Holy Ghost
indicate the source of their utterances, while the disciple receives his speech "on a
good grade of plain white paper 8 1/2 inches by 11 inches with no marker of any kind
to indicate that is not the work of the purchaser.". . . It is true, $10 are charged by
one house for every thousand words. . . .This rate, however, does not pertain to
politics, where the firm is posted on all sides of the questions at all times, and can
write cheaper. It is even claimed that "many of the best political speeches delivered
during the past several years were written in this office." (63-64)

Everett Hunt, in 1930, in an editorial title, "Pipe Courses," raised a question still with us when he, in an ethical context, examined the problem of speech courses being less difficult than others in the curriculum. Hunt contended that the unwillingness to "hold our standards high" has caused public speaking to be regarded as "pipe," or easy courses. Hunt placed the responsibility for the situation on the student who, "expects to do less work in his speech course than he expects to do in biology, chemistry, or mathematics." He placed the major responsibility for this defect on the speech teacher.

Too often, the timid instructor compromises with his conscience and lowers his
standards to the level of student expectations and demands. He is slow to assert his
right to his full and just share of the student's preparation time. . . . We should
believe and insist that the facts of human speech are inherently just as significant
and valuable as any other facts which the student is expected to learn. . . . The point
is that one sure way to gain academic respect is to be academically respectable. If we
hold our standards high, we shall find that students of right sort will react to the
challenge of the difficult as long as it is, at the same time, the worthwhile. (1930,
353-354)

Later in 1930 William Schrier, of the University of North Dakota addressed the "perennial" problem of "Ethics in Persuasion." Schrier attacked what he designated as "false persuasion." "We know that that the human race is far from perfect, that some speakers are unscrupulous, and that many auditors are susceptible to low motives." Schrier's article is not important because of its originality but because he raised the question of ethical persuasion. Among other questions, the author asks, "Can we not as teachers develop a professional Code of Ethics which will aid in detecting right from wrong?. . . There is no separate standard of ethics for public speakers; each case of persuasion must be judged in the light of the particular instance and according to the prevailing standard of ethics of the community or of the individual" (476-477). Schrier concludes on an optimistic note. "But when we realize the tremendous power of speech for good or evil, I do feel the wonder is, not that speech has been abused so much, but that it has been abused no more" (486).

One of the strongest statements concerning ethics and social responsibility was published by Angelo Pellegrini of the University of Washington in 1934. In an essay titled "Public Speaking and Social Obligations" Pellegrini spelled out the ethical responsibility of the teacher of public speaking and the commitment to truth required of both teacher and student. He stated his premise at the outset of the article.

Men must learn before it is too late that the road to individual security and
self-realization does not lie over the bodies of those who are too weak or unwilling to
resist the attack of the strong, but that it lies rather along happy firesides made gay

> *by the human gesture of the outstretched hand to those in need and despair.*
> *(346-347)*

What does such a broad ethical statement have do with public speaking? Pellegrini asserted that the case for public speaking has been in economic terms when its real justification has been social. The result of the economic emphasis has been the exploitation of others and placing greater value on individual aggrandizement rather than on the fulfillment of obligations to society as a whole.

> *Everywhere you are reminded that in order to succeed you must be able to "put yourself across," to sell your goods, your personality, your schemes, your virtues, your vices, and in every bargain your soul. Therefore take public speaking. Throw in a little applied psychology. Learn to stand on your own two feet and sell lots in the Mid-atlantic. Study your audience. Discover its infirmities and plow through. Be rugged. Be firm and unyielding. This an age of competition. If you don't sell your community listerine (sic) tooth paste, someone else will sell it pepsodent.(sic). Learn public speaking and you have in your hands an instrument of power. It will eventually make you a soap factory executive. And the next step is a seat in Congress. . . . On both sides are the catchwords of babbitry. Speech training prepares one for leadership and service to one's community. It prepares one for the duties of citizenship. But when these phrases of starched respectability are torn open, there is frequently exposed a heart rotten with greed:—serve, the better to exploit; lead the more effectively to conquer; be a good citizen in order to be the spoilmaster of a municipal administration. (1934, 346-347)*

Pellegrini was clear that this situation must not be allowed to continue.

> *If public speaking is to maintain its position on the college curriculum, it must refuse to serve such unsocial ends. It must cease to be an instrument for exploitation and become an instrument for social regeneration. It must no longer serve purely personal ends; it must devote itself to the realization of our social needs. . . . What principles must be kept constantly before the student in the classroom? There are, I believe, four which, when actively recognized, will affect profoundly the teaching of public speaking. First, the value of public speaking that is intellectual and social rather than economic and personal; second, in a speech there must be the twin virtues of honesty and appeal to reason; third, the content of the speech must be held to an inflexibly high standard; and fourth, demagoguery must be actively hated. . . . I mean here exactly what I say. The student should be taught not only to avoid charlatanism and demagoguery in his own speaking, but to combat it in others wherever found. The instructor must inspire in the student an active hatred for the oracular stupidities of the charlatan, a hatred so intense and so full-blooded that when the occasion presents itself the student will have the moral courage to rise on his feet and challenge them with the zeal and fervor known only to the heart of youth. (348, 350)*

Pellegrini, in a dramatic fashion, had restated the arguments about substance and form, as carried on earlier by Hunt and O'Neill. He also dealt with public speaking in a way which changed the rules of the game, as Bryngelson, Morse, Murray and others had sought to do. Pellegrini placed almost all his emphasis not only on the substance of public speaking but on substance as the only significant element of discourse. Further, the teaching of public speaking, in Pellegrini's view, had as its goal not the improvement of speaking skills but rather the moral transformation of the students. As Bryngelson et. al. had sought to use the public speaking classroom as the locus for the improvement of personality and mental hygiene, Pellegrini saw the classroom as the arena for the inculcation of ethical responsibility. Moreover, the public speaking student in Pellegrini's classroom would be as concerned with the detection of charlatanism as with the development of her rhetorical responsibility.

Pellegrini's position is interesting beyond its apparent statement. He was a teacher of Public Speaking with no formal training in Speech. His perspective, he said, was the result of his experience with a gifted high school debate coach. In his autobiography, *An Immigrant's Quest: American Dream*, he described his route in and out of public speaking at the University of Washington.

> For the next fifteen years I was on the faculty of the speech department at the University; and in 1936, in collaboration with a colleague, I published a college textbook: Argumentation and Public Discussion, which the philosopher John Dewey graced with an introduction. In 1945, now with a doctorate in English, I left the speech department and joined the English faculty. Since I had no formal academic training in speech, I am indebted to debate, particularly as taught by Bess Evans, for the course of my career. (51)

Even by today's standards one detects a certain "radical" tone in Pellegrini's essay; it is of passing interest to note that, by the author's admission, he was then a member of the Communist Party.

> I joined the Communist Party in the early thirties. . . . I chose the Communists rather than the socialists for personal and not ideological reasons. (155)

Pellegrini's association with the party was not the answer to his social concerns. "I need not give a detailed account of my membership in the Communist party. It was brief. The activities it entailed were unpleasant and, so it seemed to me, irrelevant to the challenge posed by the depression." (173).

In addition to the argumentation textbook and textbooks in English Composition, Pellegrini later in his life wrote two books dealing with food: *The Unprejudiced Palate* in 1962 and *The Food Lover's Garden* in 1970.

W. Arthur Cable of the University of Arizona in his 1935 discussion of "Speech in the Educational System," showed the "contribution which speech makes" to the "seven cardinal principles of education." Among those principles Cable includes "Good Citizenship" and " Ethical Character." Training in Speech, said Cable, will help produce "an informed citizenship dedicated to the common good" and "a fine spiritual character that is trusted and admired." Cable, although he was not as eloquent or polemic as Pellegrini, agreed there were ethical aspects to be considered in the teaching of Speech (517-518).

In the November 1935 "Forum" of *The Quarterly Journal of Speech*, H.A. Wichelns of Cornell University in an essay titled "Speech and the Educational Scene: Notes on the Future," projected his view of Speech Education in 1945. He felt that the new decade would require citizens prepared to function in a democratic state and that Speech Education could play an important role ten years hence.

> Society will demand, with increased force, that education produce men and women fit for the responsibilities of a centralized democracy; fit to work and vote in groups, fit to exercise an intelligent public's remote control over affairs. The expansion of function granted the social studies is the curricular expression of this need. What does it suggest about the field of speech-instruction? It suggests that the connection now existing between the teaching of English and the teaching of speech will find a parallel in the new connection between the teaching of social subjects and

*that of speech. . . . The demand for indoctrination, and the outcry against it, is
sufficiently heard even now: the conservatives see Red and impose oaths of
allegiance; the radicals hold that education should prepare the next generation to
remake the world. Between these forces the teacher and director of forensics must
steer his course. He will be best helped if in the next few years we can re-think and
re-state the rationale of discussion in the educational system of a democracy.
(559-560)*

Quite apart from Wichelns' concern with ethics and citizenship, it is significant to
note his prescience in sensing the strengthened connection with the social sciences
which, in fact, developed after 1945. Equally important was his perception about the
increasing importance of discussion. One also notes his description of the left-right
conflict of post-war America.

In 1938 Donald C. Bryant of Washington University seemed to tire of the discussion
of whether Speech courses should effect changes in personality and citizenship.

*By now, can't we simply assume at last that the good "speech personality," the
preservation of democratic institutions, the facilitation of admirable human relations
(or something just a little short of them) is our objective? Can't we postpone for a
while further formulation of goals, and revive our knowledge of means of achieving
them? (247)*

Statements like Bryant's were common then and are still common today. The view
is frequently expressed that we should cease being so introspective and that we should
get on with our work.

In spite of Bryant's complaint the profession continued to be concerned with the
question of the role of the Speech teacher in maintaining democracy. Some members
of the Speech profession and many public figures, felt that democracy was threatened
and that efforts needed to be made to preserve it. In a 1938 report on "Contemporary
Speeches," Winfield DeWitt Bennett of George Washington University noted that many
of the commencement speakers at colleges and universities in 1937 had emphasized
the danger to democracy. Among other speakers concerned about democratic government, cited by Bennett were Walter Lippmann, Chief Justice Charles Evans Hughes,
Dorothy Thompson and Nicholas Murray Butler, president of Columbia University. At
Brown University Chief Justice Hughes had said, "Our first duty is to preserve these
freedoms of learning, of speech, of press, of conscience, and to be alert to the slightest
attempt to impair them" (538-541).

A. Craig Baird of the State University of Iowa addressed the question of the role of
speech instruction in a democratic society in 1938 in his essay "The Educational
Philosophy of the Teacher of Speech." Baird depicted the teaching of speech as having
social rather than practical goals.

*The cardinal aims of education to secure individual success and power are
obsolete unless we read social meaning into these terms. The development of skills,
habits, ideals, knowledge, attitudes, are not, we agree, the end. Rather they are the
means to assimilate each learner into the local and universal community. . . . The
pressure groups are constantly at our elbow. Intense nationalism and limited
freedom of speech probably have a high negative correlation. As the tide of
propaganda rises, so does the pressure increase. We must move with greater and
greater dexterity to escape disaster. . . . Let us experiment socially in speech; but let
us assure ourselves that every forum shall speak and vote free from the pressure of
whatever party happens to be in power in Washington. . . . Among these*

well-meaning but highly propagandistic groups we stand—The teachers of public speaking. In this confusion we are after all timid souls. We too are patriots. But we are not partisans. Our function is to see that the participants in debate and discussion assemble knowledge, present the varied points of view. We assume that the best democracy results from free discussion. Certainly the doctrinaire schools and indoctrination process offer no hope for healthy-minded America. (549-551)

Baird's concern about the connections of speech and democracy is perhaps a stronger statement than those of Wichelns and Pellegrini. The writers of this period showed a stronger consciousness about the role of speech in a democratic society than the authors we read in today's journals. The attention given to ethical and democratic considerations by the authors of the 1930s is nowhere to be found in present-day journals and textbooks. Baird's essay also rejoins the earlier argument between Hunt and O'Neill about substance versus form. Baird in a more developed argument than Hunt's proposes that students "assemble knowledge," not to find subjects for class room speeches, but in order to insure the continuation of a free and open democratic society. Perhaps the loss of such essays with strong moral and ethical strength is part of the price that the field of Speech Communication has paid in its desire to consider Journals as outlets for research. Only occasionally and in much abbreviated form are similar concerns aired in the pages of Spectra.

Robert Allison of Teachers College, Columbia University, saw the teaching of group discussion as an "instrument of democracy." He, like other writers of the time, was much concerned with the threat to democracy of totalitarianism.

> *Lastly there remains one valuable adjunct that looms more and more important in the light of the ever growing tendency toward dictatorship and minority rule. By this I mean the use of group thinking and discussion as the instrument of democracy. (1939, 120)*

Allison supported his point of view with a quotation from a 1924 book *The Why and How of Group Discussion* by Harrison Elliott.

> *It assumes the right of rank and file of folks to think and decide for themselves . . . . In a discussion it is assumed that the group has a right to come to it own opinion even though it may disagree with that of the leader. . . . Group thinking and propaganda are in direct opposition to each other. (1939, 120)*

To appreciate fully the perspective of writers such as Wichelns, Baird and Allison one must mentally reconstruct the social and political atmosphere of the late 1930s. Not only was the nation still suffering the effects of the Great Depression but also the country was subject to both Anti-Facist and Anti-Communist propaganda. The power of Stalin in the Soviet Union, Hitler in Germany and Mussolini in Italy placed the future of democracy in doubt. In addition, America itself saw the possibility of radical change in government as enunciated by spokesmen such as Huey Long, Father Charles Coughlin and Dr. Francis Townsend. By this time Italy had invaded and occupied Ethiopia; Germany had taken back the Rhineland and the Saarland and had annexed Austria and had occupied all of Czechoslovakia; Japan had invaded and occupied much of China. The fear of war was quite palpable, and the future of the United States seemed uncertain. Essays in *The Quarterly Journal of Speech* reflected the national unease in a way which has not since been duplicated. It is to the credit of the profession that it manifested such a strong social conscience about its own activity.

The heightened political sensitivity was demonstrated in an essay in" The Forum" by John Dolman of the University of Pennsylvania. In response to a speech by the actor

Burgess Meredith to the National Association, Dolman issued an attack on Communism and the Congress of Industrial Organizations (CIO) in 1938. Meredith had, in his speech, asked the support of the association " for certain pending legislation looking to the subsidization of the theatre by the Federal Government. Dolman's response went well beyond the immediate question to a clearly political point of view.

> . . . in my judgment the unionization of the theatre—necessary and well intentioned as it was in its inception—has become the worst enemy of the theatre; and particularly when I say that the proposed subsidization of a the theatre by a left wing government at the behest of its heaviest contributor, the CIO, is the most sinister development in the history of the American theatre, and if successful will mean the end of a free theatre in America. . . If Mr. Meredith imagines that the CIO favors government patronage of the theatre because of its love of art for art's sake, he must be very credulous indeed! The CIO is engaged in a desperate struggle for political power, and it favors government patronage of the theatre because that is the way to government control of the theatre; and the theatre—as the Federal Theatre Project has so ably demonstrated—can be far more concerned with social ferment and propaganda than with art.

Dolman then said, "I have been reading a good deal of Communist literature of late." On the basis of his reading Dolman presents his seven point summary of Communist Party plans. The link to the CIO and the theatre is established through points 4, 5 and 7.

> 4. Unionization should be centralized as far as possible, with the ultimate objective of one big union, or labor party. 5. Since the AFL, with its craft unions, is not conducive to that end, Communists are urged to support the CIO as a more effective instrument for large scale organization. 7. Finally, Communists must seek to gain control of every possible instrument for the manipulation of public opinion;. . . .They must encourage music, painting, sculpture, and the theatre, and must make these the vehicles of revolutionary ideas; for it is only through a gradual change in the ideology of the people that the Revolution can be safely brought about.

In a statement reminiscent of the 1950s, Dolman characterizes Burgess Meredith as a naive dupe of the Communists. " I do not accuse Mr. Meredith of being a Communist or the willing instrument of Communists. Actors are not sinister people, and I doubt whether he has any conception of the implication behind the movement he is advocating" (324-328).

In 1939 Arleigh B. Williamson of New York University in an essay titled " Social Standards in Public Speaking Instruction," deplored some of the deleterious effects of democracy on education and, at the same time, urged upon the teachers of public speaking the highest standards of social responsibility. Although, on balance, democratization of higher education was a good thing, Williamson, nonetheless, perceived some social disadvantages.

> This democratization has resulted in some decidedly desirable changes, making possible a growth in freedom of expression of teachers, in social and political tolerance, and in search for an expression of truth, less limited by religious doctrine or dogma, or by the limitations set by privileged groups . . . . Accompanying any movement of democratization is to be found a levelling of values, or what have been considered values in the past. Thus in contemporary education, there would seem to be a threat at some of the ethical standards which dominated earlier education: high

standards of personal honor, truthfulness, general integrity, a willingness to
sacrifice something of self-interest in the interest of society. (372)

In a statement, which in our time, might be regarded as unduly ethnocentric, Williamson attributed some of the decline in standards to the changed composition of college faculties and administrations.

Perhaps a cause for some decline in these standards in present-day education is
that of a democratic infusion into college teaching and administration of men and
women from a lower economic and social life than their predecessors, with perhaps,
in many instances, more limited cultural background and lower ethical standards.
(373)

Nevertheless, Williamson insisted that the teachers of Public Speaking meet the highest standards of morality and citizenship. In much the same tenor as Pellegrini, Williamson sought speech teachers dedicated to social improvement rather than personal aggrandizement.

Those chosen should be persons of integrity, irreproachable in honesty: men and
women willing to forego something of self-interest in the interests of others and
society at large. . . . Public speaking instruction has not merely to do with drills in
composition and in vocal and bodily procedures, but in the development of the whole
man, mind, character, and bodily habits. . . . No one should be encouraged to speak
publicly who is not a thinker schooled in habits of reflection and investigation. No
one should be encouraged to speak publicly who seeks of society only advantage for
himself. . . . Any education which would seem to have as its slogan "Training in
techniques which will prevent a sucker from getting a break," or "Training in
techniques of friendliness that will enable you to get the better of the other fellow,"
simply fall without the pale of true education. (375-376)

Williamson, very much aware of the character of his time, saw a world in moral crisis.

What have we already in this world of dictators? Treaties of nations become
scraps of paper when people regard personal contracts as something to be violated.
The broken pledge of faith in a nation becomes easily possible when no man's word is
sacred, when individual promises are put aside upon the slightest expediency. Weak
nations are easily gobbled up by a government whose citizens have acquired the
habit of filching the other fellow's purse through sharp business practices. Farcical
trials and government oppression of minority groups become easily possible to those
who have lost a sense of justice. (374-375)

In 1939 J. Jeffery Auer of Oberlin College, justified the teaching of group discussion because of its democratic importance. "We must recognize free public discussion as the most potent force in a democracy, as perhaps the only form of force which distinguishes democracy from dictatorship" (536).

William Utterback of The College of the City of New York saw the use of force in public discussion not only as a threat to democracy but to truth as well.

Public discussion appeals to truth as the guide to political action—or so we have
supposed. . . .That we possess a body of truth which can be employed as the basis of
political decision and that it is employed in unfettered public discussion is a part of
the democratic philosophy of government. . . .That type of discussion which appeals
to truth, and which for the sake of convenience we may call public debate, is heard

less and less frequently in the legislative hall and public forum. It is no longer the principal method of public decision, even in democratic countries, and has been abandoned entirely in Italy and Germany. (1)

Utterback's concern went beyond the political sphere to the implications for teachers of Speech.

This appeal to force in public discussion cannot but disturb the teacher of public speech. It challenges his fundamental philosophy, and the challenge is not one he can safely ignore. If our predominant form of public discussion acknowledges no allegiance to truth, appeals to force as the arbiter of political controversy, and repudiates reason in the solution of public problems, the teacher of speech apparently must either abandon his ethical principles or withdraw into an academic utopia. (2)

The Presidential Address of Allen H. Monroe of Purdue University, given at the 1940 meeting of the National Association of Teachers of Speech, was reprinted in abstracted form in the April, 1941 issue of *The Quarterly Journal of Speech*, under the title of " Speech in the World Today." The essay is entirely devoted to the importance of free and democratic speech in a world in crisis. Monroe's message was one of reality and hope.

And so I say today, black as the picture is, speech can still ring free. Even in regimented Germany, Pastor Niemoller has the courage to say, "Not you Herr Hitler, but God is my Fuhrer." And Winston Churchill knows that free men will support him even though he promises them nothing but "blood and tears and sweat." I think it is our peculiar responsibility, as teachers of speech, to maintain the courage of these great spokesmen. I think it is our duty throughout the country to denounce the doctrine of silence and fear and to preach the duty of fearless utterance. . . . and it is our solemn obligation when we speak that we insist upon responsibility for reflective thought and careful investigation in order that our speech may be sound and substantial as well as free. . . . Nor should we forget that speech in the world today is not alone a matter of public utterance. An operating democracy demands clear and thoughtful speech on the farm, in the factory and government. . . . And what of speech tomorrow? If the black days become blacker and speech throughout the world is fettered as it is in so much of Europe by public chains, we shall be sad; but we must not be dismayed—for speech always has broken and always will break through these chains to speak the challenge of men's souls. And when, once more, peace and freedom come again, then honest speech will speak louder in justice's name—for we shall have seen again what happens when men's tongues are tied and only power is left to rule. (172-173)

Monroe's essay is quoted at length not only for its eloquence, but also because it vividly exemplifies the strong commitment of spokespersons for the profession to democratic values and to responsible communication. The essay was significant also because of Monroe's acute perception of the connection of speech and democracy in the troubling times of Facist victories and threatened freedom. Only rarely in the 50 years since Monroe's address have presidents of the SCA concerned themselves with these fundamental issues in their presidential addresses. Although the nation has passed through crises since 1941, they have hardly been mentioned in our professional discourse. An exception was the presidential address of the author of this volume.

I ask that we, as teachers of communication, at all levels, understand that a free and open communicative climate is essential for free dissemination and exchange of ideas and for the open discussion of public questions. Our students must understand

*that their freedom to speak is influenced by the atmosphere in which they live. . . .
We must always know what the conditions are that lead to greater or lesser
communicative freedom. When those conditions change, for better or for worse, we
as a profession have the obligation to make those changes known. We must not be
reluctant to criticize persons, institutions or bureaucracies which restrict the
openness of communication. (6-7)*

J.M. O'Neill of Brooklyn College, who by 1941 had become one of "the grand old
men" of the profession, wrote on "Professional Maturity" on the occasion of the 25th
anniversary of the association. In his examination of the maturation of the profession,
O'Neill saw an indivisible connection between freedom, democracy and the teaching
of speech.

*The life which free men live together in a free society functions at its best, does its
most important work, finds its supreme test, its highest opportunity, and its greatest
achievement, in human speech, when men talk to their fellow men.
Democracy—freedom of the individual, the community, or the nation— can exist if
men speak freely and effectively with other men. The complete and adequate training
of men and women to function fully and properly through speech in a free society
should be the aim and essence of education. . . . If we are to demonstrate our
professional maturity in the world today, we must do everything in our power to see
to it that all the educational forces of this country, in so far as we have influence,
shall insist upon the development of the power and the preservation of the
opportunity to speak fully and freely whatever things men have to speak to their
fellow men. . . . We can plan realistically for the future only on the assumption that
democracy will survive. I am not remotely interested in the plans for teachers of
speech or in other plans for education, if democracy is not to survive the present
conflict. I do not think we should educate the slaves of future dictators. (179)*

The political sensitivity of the association was shown in 1940 by the fact that Elbert
D. Thomas, Senator from Utah, addressed the national meeting on the subject of
national defense. In his speech, Thomas delineated his understanding of the relationship of speech to democracy.

*. . . the use of speech and communication by our American democracy is in direct
contrast to the use which is made of this power by the totalitarian powers. We, in
our democracy, use speech and communication to educate our people, to build up in
our citizens an intelligent understanding of our democratic institutions. . . .The
democratic use of speech in America does not result in a hatred of other peoples or of
minorities among our own. (294)*

Not only were the views of a United States Senator printed in *The Quarterly Journal
of Speech*, the journal also reprinted a talk given by Eleanor Roosevelt (In those days
identified as Mrs. Franklin D. Roosevelt). Mrs. Roosevelt contrasted the use of speech
in a democracy not with Facism but with Communism.

*I go to a great many meetings of young people and I am impressed more and more
by one fact: The youngsters trained by the Communists always can say what they
have been taught to say and they put it over all the other youngsters because they
not only say it clearly but they repeat it, and they repeat it and they repeat it (369).*

Mrs. Roosevelt thought that the ability to speak in favor of democracy had to be
developed gradually.

I believe it would be a very valuable thing if we would urge upon schools and colleges that first they train youngsters in talking about the things they are interested in in their daily lives, and that then they train them to express what they feel later on about the meaning of democracy to them, the meaning of this country to them, what they know about the conditions, what they want to see done. (370)

By 1942 the United States was a participant in the war and the association had appointed W. Hayes Yeager of American University as Chairman, War Committee. That year he published a one page statement under the title " Our Contribution to the War." In addition to the expected patriotic rhetoric and notation of the contribution of association members to the direction of the Speakers' Section of the Office of Civilian Defense and the Speaker' Bureau of the Navy Department, Yeager drew a connection between speech and the preservation of "The American Way of Life." "Can there be any more important use of free speech than in the interest of our country and our homes?"

In an analysis of Hitler's oratory, F.W. Lambertson of Iowa State Teachers College in his conclusion drew a comparison between the use of speech in totalitarian and democratic societies.

In a democracy one of our greatest dangers is that the average citizen shall not think. If he is controlled by his prejudices and urged on by the lunatic fringe of the populace and by the demagogue, we are in a bad way. Co-operative problem-solving is the hope of our nation, not the dogmatic utterances of a dictator. Therefore, to the extent that any speaker robs his listeners of their critical faculties, he is undermining the foundation stones of democracy—critical and discriminative thinking. (130-131)

In an editorial in 1942 the Editor of the *QJS*, W. Norwood Brigance of Wabash College again stressed the significance of speech in the war effort and in the maintenance of democracy.

In "the mind's eternal heaven" some believed, even six months ago, that America could live in isolation and that Japan was a broken down military power. By the same visionary mania some may believe that in the crisis of a great nation its people will not turn to speech—formal public speech—for voicing it triumph or sorrow, and for making steadfast its purpose. (242)

It is interesting in view of Brigance's statement, that as late as 1961, a year after his death, his text book, *Speech: its Techniques and Disciplines in a Free Society*, was still being published.

Not only was Public Speaking related to the war effort and democracy, the contribution of theatre was also recorded in 1942 by Lee Norvelle of Indiana University. He was particularly concerned with "this tremendous program of drama in the camps performed by soldiers for soldiers" where the "emphasis [is] placed upon the democratic way of life and the recurring thought that it is for these principles the men are fighting" (271). Norvelle, much like other writers, forsaw difficult days ahead, but he also offered hope through the power of the theatre .

This high tribute paid to the role that drama plays in our lives renews our faith in its essential qualities and its imperishable nature—an assurance which will mean much to us in the dark months ahead in which we shall be forced to exist on the rind and pits of the bitter fruit of war. (271)

The patriotic/democratic theme was carried forward by John D. Hansen, of Nebraska State Teachers College, Kearney, Nebraska. In his essay "Speech in a Nation at War," Hansen took note of the changes which would have to take place in the teaching of speech and then concluded with an explication of the responsibilities of speech teachers in a nation where democracy is seen to be under threat.

> We have only to compare our situation with that of the dictator nations to realize our responsibility in maintaining freedom of speech and discussion. In those countries people do not think openly whereas in America we may thresh out our problems and determine policies according to their merit. It is our duty as teachers of speech to obtain and impart information not readily gained by the general public through the daily news, to keep critical issues continually before them, and to ensure a sturdy morale by protecting people from the warping effects of misinformation and propaganda. (273-274)

Almost 50 years later the statements of Hansen, Brigance, Norvelle, and others may strike us as excessively patriotic and perhaps a bit naive, but we cannot question the unswerving commitment to democracy held by members of the speech profession in the years preceding and during World War II.

By 1943 *The Quarterly Journal of Speech* was devoting a separate section to "The Nation at War." The first article in that section was written by Everett Hunt, who had moved from Cornell to Swarthmore. He was more moderate in tone in his essay "The Rhetorical Mood of World War II" than some of his contemporaries. Hunt wrote of the rhetoric of a more somber, more self-interested and less jingoistic nation.

> The rhetoric of a holy war is out for the present. We want to survive, and we believe in the American way of life, but we do not seriously hope to spread it rapidly among all our allies, to say nothing of our enemies, and many have reservations and questionings about the perfection of the American way. . . . The jingoistic rhetoric of exuberant boasting is out. We have long respected the strength and skill of the Germans and we cannot successfully pour contempt upon an enemy who has inflicted such defeats upon us as we have suffered from the Japanese. . . . In this war, then, many of the traditional sources of rhetoric in the grand style are out: boasting, heroism, the hills of home, a holy cause, joy in the destruction of the enemy, and, in a softened civilization, even the sweetness of dying for the fatherland. (1943, 3-4)

In the same section of the *QJS* Alfred Westfall of Colorado State College displayed a somewhat less jaded patriotism than Hunt and saw a close connection between the teaching of speech and the preservation of American values and freedom of speech in his article "What Speech Teachers May Do To Help Win The War."

> Freedom of speech is the basis of democracy and independence. It is the foundation of individual self-respect. Given freedom of speech, the other freedoms follow or can be achieved. . . . It is easy to understand why leaders of the democracies listed freedom of speech first. . . . In order to preserve this freedom of speech among its citizens, the democratic way of life requires a wide and generous training in the art of self-expression. . . . The man who surrenders his freedom of speech or allows it to deteriorate through disuse, may be enslaved as truly as the one whose rights are taken from him by force. By teaching the youth of America to exercise and perfect this freedom, the speech teacher is helping to win the war and preserve this democratic way of life for which we have pledged our fortunes, our lives, and our sacred honor. (1943, 5-6)

James N. Holm of Kent State University saw in the war effort a need to reemphasize the ethical criteria enunciated by Pellegrini. In his essay "A War-Time Approach to Public Speaking" Holm asserted that the critical times called for a higher order of public speaking than had previously been taught and for adherence to standards which demanded the teaching of more responsible rhetoric.

> *Are we still teaching public speaking in the way we did during the lush days of prosperity, or in the manner with which met our classes during the educational rush of the depression era? Does the course in public speaking tend to be a course in glorified personal salesmanship, in "selling the idea," high-powered persuasive methods divorced from the ethics of persuasion. . . . Trivial speech subjects, frequently tolerated by the instructor, should be definitely discouraged—topics such as "Saturday in our dormitory," "Tipping should be abolished," and "My high school teachers." Further, there should be a reawakened interest upon that which Aristotle chose to call ethical proof. . . . To any democratic system there must be provided a voice for the minority, a voice for the reformer. These are the voices of the advocate, demanding justice, improvement and reform. For the courts, for the pulpit, for the soapbox we must train speakers in ethical persuasion. (10-12)*

Evelyn Konigsberg of Richmond Hill High School in New York and four other New York high school teachers examined how the war made the teaching of public discussion vital. They also specified methods of instruction to be used in the classroom; and they even suggested a list of topics for public discussion under the headings of "The Civilian and the War," "Latin America," "Problems of the Far East," "Russsia and Current Problems," and "Intercultural Relations." For each of the categories the authors provided "Sources of Information: Patriotic Justification for Teaching Discussion in War Time."

> *Public discussion is the cornerstone of democracy. . . . Especially in time of war, when people are assailed by doubts,. . . are the public schools charged with the responsibility of providing a means whereby people may learn how to discuss mutual problems;. . . Teachers of speech have a special responsibility in this matter, that of training the youth of America, through courses in public discussion, to become familiar with the forms and methods of group thinking, and of engaging them in group consideration of topics now of vital importance to national defense, and on problems with which the American people will probably be concerned for some time to come. (13)*

The *QJS* in 1943 even devoted attention to "Radio War Programs." Kenneth G. Bartlett of Syracuse University concluded his summary by linking radio programs to the teaching of speech and the war effort. The speech teacher, according to Bartlett, had a special role to play.

> *. . . Speech teachers with their contacts with the public and with students could provide a valuable wartime service by pointing up and publicizing worth-while programs. . . .This may not be easy, but in the long run would pay dividends by giving direction and greater meaning to our war effort. (Bartlett, 1943, 103)*

In the February 1943 issue of the *QJS* under the heading of "Our contribution to the War" the War Committee recommended cooperation with the Office of War Information and outlined services the association was prepared to offer the government in the prosecution of the war effort. A number of articles on such topics as "The Status of Speech Defectives in the Military Service," (Johnson, 1943), " War Responsibilities of the Speech Correctionist (Carhart, 1943), "Speech Training of Army and Navy Officers"

(Mallory, 1943), "Public Speaking in the Army Training Program "(Held and Held, 1943), and "Speech Curricula and Activities in Wartime" (Knower, 1943) were published. They were, however, largely reportorial and did not deal with the themes of free speech and democracy. Earl W. Wiley of Ohio State University did return to the themes in his article "The Rhetoric of the American Democracy." Wiley based his argument for democratic speech, in contrast to totalitarian speech, in history and philosophy, carrying his precedents as far back as the Sophists.

> *Rhetorically, the totalitarian is an arch Sophist. . . .The task of speech education in a despotism is as simple as yelling Heil Hitler! in the Reichstag. . . . But free society is another matter. There, instead of totalitarianism, is the individual unrestrained. . . . Democratic utterance originates at the point in rhetoric where, on a basis of reason, the man relaxes his egoism in deference to public purposes. Rhetorically, democracy is a form of action that seeks to keep a balance between the rights of the individual, the rights of the group, and the ideology of the state. . . .The bias of freedom exerted by the speaker is governed by community purpose; it is a fluid and ever-shifting bias geared to the events of the hour. (157-163)*

Emery W. Balduf, formerly head of the school and college section of the Office of War Information, published an article on "How Departments of Speech Can Cooperate with Government in the War Effort." Much of the article was devoted to specific suggestions, but Balduf began with a tribute to the importance of speech in the war and with praise for the teaching of speech.

> *. . . We must still concede that if there is to be a workable two-way flow of ideas and opinions, if there is to be a real meeting of minds, we must employ the arts of speech and discussion in face-to-face situations. . . .Teachers of speech, therefore, should by no means be on the defensive in war-time. This war, more than any previous one, is dependent upon communication. (271)*

It must be emphasized that the tributes to free speech and democracy were far outnumbered by articles dealing with less ideological and more mundane aspects of the war. A number of articles appeared on subjects such as "Radio Classes in the High-School Wartime Program," "Educational Broadcasting in Wartime," "Educational Broadcasting after the War," and "Speaking In College Military Units."

In December of 1943 the National Association of Teachers of Speech held a War Problems Conference. The conference was addressed by Lennox Gray, Head of the Department of the Teaching of English and Foreign Languages in Teachers College, Columbia University. In his address, "Toward Better Communication in 1944 and After," Gray stressed the importance of communication not only in supporting democracy during the war but in the post-war years as well.

> *. . . Communication is the basis of all human community—the basic factor in all education, in all human relations, in all national union, in world federation. Democracy, we are coming to see, depends on democratic communication. (132)*

The president of The National Association of Teachers of Speech, Robert West of the University of Wisconsin, also addressed the 1943 War Problems Conference. In his speech, "The Prospect for Speech Education," West focused on the ethical standards to which the speech profession must be held in the post-war years. The most important responsibility, said West, must be the care with which students are selected and evaluated. Apparently, in his world after the war, not all students would be allowed to master the skills of public speaking because of the ways in which they might use their acquired competence. West cited Hitler's high regard for public speaking and his awareness of its power. Thus speech teachers must be on their guard that no future Hitlers are the products of speech education.

> Our leadership will fail if we neglect our responsibility and if consequently some future Hitler can arise and say, "I got my training in public speaking at Wisconsin, or Michigan, or Cornell, or Wabash." And when such an American Hitler is destroyed, his alma mater will share tragically in his destruction and will inherit from him the odium of public disapproval. (146)

Although West desired to hold students to ethical and moral standards as high as those of Pellegrini, his perspective was considerably more elitist. While Pellegrini, ten years earlier, sought to develop ethical character through instruction, West sought to insure ethical character through selection. Only those students who met West's criteria of cooperation, selflessness, emotional stability, open-mindedness and honesty should be admitted to instruction in speech. West apparently did not recognize the un-democratic character of his proposal and even used a religious comparison to argue his case.

> Believing, therefore, in the effectiveness of our teaching of speech techniques, I seriously propose that we all attempt to pick our disciples as did Jesus of Nazareth. We must not, of course, use as a basis of selection the criteria of religious creed, ethnic background, or political philosophy. I propose that, instead, we consider the following standards, encouraging all students who qualify under these heads, and discouraging in every legal way all who fall short. (145)

West apparently believed in the omnipotence of speech teachers to be able to make judgments about the ethical characters of their students. In spite of the difficulty in making such appraisals, West, nonetheless, felt they must be made.

> Some may fear that it may be difficult to appraise these qualities that I have mentioned. . . .True! But that should not prevent us from making the attempt to apply our criteria. . . . The teacher of Public Speaking, moreover, by the nature of the activity in which the student is engaging is in a peculiarly fine position to size up the students in the qualities desired. Most of us, I am sure, are already applying these tests and are encouraging the students who possess them. What I am encouraging is a more drastic discouragement, or even rejection of those who lack them. (146)

West ended his address with a mild tribute to free speech and democracy and expressed his confidence for the long term, but he also expressed his concern for the short term.

> Mind you I have no fear for the ultimate triumph of truth over error under a system in which any one and everyone is permitted his say. My fear is for those whose life span happens to fall within the period when error is temporarily master of the field. I believe the time has come when teachers of speech can help in making the fight a fair one so that truth will prevail more frequently and the millennium will come the sooner. (146)

The reader, almost a half century after West's address, is left with a sense of puzzlement. Not only did West argue for a system of public speaking instruction contrary to the very nature of American democracy; in his espousal of elitist selectivity and character tests, he also empowered the simple teacher of public speaking to make ethical and moral judgments which are beyond the power of any human being. In addition, West's criteria were so broad and so vague that one was given no specific guidance about how to recognize the virtues and defects of human character. Would Hitler have been identified as a villain had he been a student in an American public speaking class?

One is also bemused by the thought of what might have become of the discipline of speech communication had West's scheme been put into operation. If instead of multiple sections of Public Speaking courses designed for the mass of students, the discipline had restricted itself to teaching only students who were paragons of virtue, what would have happened to speech departments as agents of general education? Would graduate programs have developed and prospered without a solid under-graduate base? What kind of scholar-teachers would have been attracted to programs such as those proposed by West?

Kenneth G. Hance of the University of Michigan undertook to describe "Public Address in a Nation at War." Although his essay was largely descriptive of the large amount of speaking and public discussion taking place in the United States of 1944, Hance understood that such widespread communication could take place only in a democracy where free speech was not only encouraged but required.

> . . . It is significant that such speechmaking is permitted in a nation at war (here is "democracy at work"). Second, it is significant that "all of us" are talking—not a few actual or self-styled leaders or a body of propagandists. (164)

Mrs. Hugh Butler of the Junior College of the Georgetown Visitation Convent complained of the ineffectiveness of government rhetoric in the prosecution of the war. She presented a multitude of examples where government spokespersons had not communicated with their audiences and she pleaded for improvement in speeches.

> As the end of the war draws near, cannot someone who knows the importance of effective speaking on the American people somehow get access to these public officials who are telling us how to gain a durable peace and put their thoughts in words that people can understand? (269)

Although by 1945, as the war was coming to its conclusion, articles stressing the relation of democracy and speech were becoming far less numerous, Paul D. Bagwell of Michigan State College included effective speaking as one of the objectives of the new Department of Written and Spoken English just established at Michigan State University. "An appreciation of the role that speaking and writing play in a democracy." (84)

Andrew Thomas Weaver of the University of Wisconsin in his essay, "The Challenge of the Crisis," addressed the questions of freedom of speech and the social responsibility of speakers. In assessing the future of speech education Weaver said.

> There is, finally, the high function of preparing boys and girls for citizenship in a democracy. It is not enough that a man should bring his latent capacities to full flower, earn his bread and butter efficiently, and live happily with his fellows. He must carry the obligations of civic living. . . . It is not our proper function as teachers to increase the amount of speech; rather, it is to raise the quality. We are charged with a special responsibility to see that freedom of speech is used wisely. (130, 131)

John J. De Boer, Chairman of the Department of Education at Roosevelt College and a former president of The National Council of Teachers of English, presented the case for "English in a 'Communications' Program." In his articulation of the goals shared by English and other disciplines, De Boer emphasized the importance of democracy in communication instruction.

> *English shares pre-eminently with all other areas the task of making young people articulate, their speech and writing intelligible, their reading and listening intelligent, their sympathies broad, their devotion to the democratic process strong and deep. (291)*

After 1945 and the end of the war the newly named Speech Association of America seemed to lose interest in the matters that had greatly concerned members during the conflict. Essentially no references to the relation of speech education to ethics, democracy were found in *The Quarterly Journal of Speech* although Robinson and Keltner in their article in 1946 on "Suggested Units in Discussion and Debate for Secondary Schools," did mention as one of their objectives "To develop an understanding of the place of debate and discussion in a democracy" (385). Although the concern had largely disappeared from the scholarly literature, the textbooks of the period in public speaking, discussion, debate and argumentation still stressed the importance of democracy and ethics in the speech curriculum.

CONCLUSION

Although this chapter has dealt with the emphasis on the relation between speech and ethics and democracy, we must emphasize that concern with these matters was by no means dominant in the the first three decades of the national association. Much of the material of that early period was concerned with what we might call "group maintaince" articles, dealing with "how we do it at our school." Many other articles were purely pedagogical or descriptive reports of various programs. To be sure we did find occasional articles which might accurately be described as "research," but they were far in the minority.

As we look back at the writings on ethics and democracy, we are struck by how different they were from the material to be found in present day journals. One is struck by the high moral tone of the profession and the importance that was attached to the responsibility of insuring that the teaching of speech measured up to scrupulous standards. Perhaps those years were a more naive and less "scholarly" time. Nevertheless, one must admit to warm nostalgic feelings for the idealism of early writers. Some of us may even regret that not even in the pages of Communication Education are such issues raised today.

7

RHETORICAL CRITICISM

As articles on rhetoric appeared in *The Quarterly Journal* they diverged into two separate categories, which continue to exist to this day—rhetorical criticism which sought to develop standards of critical judgment or to make judgments concerning particular oratorical works, and rhetorical theory which sought to describe and define the nature of rhetoric, often from a historical perspective. We will first turn our attention to rhetorical criticism.

The second article which might be labelled Rhetorical Criticism chose Wendell Phillips as its subject and dealt with Phillips' style. H.B. Gisalson of the University of Minnesota in his 1917 essay "Elements of Objectivity in Wendell Phillips" justified the attention given to Phillips, but he never really explained why Phillips was important.

It is not strange that the first article to be published on oratorical criticism in *The Quarterly Journal* should deal with the oratory of Wendell Phillip (See Chapter 4). Neither is it strange that the second article on that subject should treat certain aspects of the oratory of the same man. "Of all American orators, Wendell Phillips is likely to have the most interest for students of public speaking," Gisalson wrote (125). The elements of objectivity in Gisalson's title were, in actuality, stylistic devices, in effect, continuing the approach of Doyle (see Chapter 4). Gisalson counted the metaphors, similes, analogies and anecdotes in twelve of Phillips' orations. Although, perhaps for the first time, Gisalson used the term "oratorical criticism," neither he nor most of the members of the association had a clear idea of what oratorical criticism was or how one went about doing it. They knew of few precedents or models which they could follow. Thus it was not surprising that the earliest excursions in criticism concentrated on the most visible and identifiable aspects of discourse, such as style.

Indeed the third article in which an author undertook to do criticism also centered its attention on style. In 1919 Charles F. Lindsley of the University of Minnesota devoted 22 pages to a detailed study of "George William Curtis: A Study in the Style of Oral Discourse." Lindsley's work, like that of earlier critics, displayed ancestral persistence. These fugitives from English departments, in their search for research topics and methods, turned to stylistic analyses of oral discourse; perhaps because they had seen such critiques undertaken in parent departments. Lindsley gave consideration to Curtis' diction, concreteness, sentences (including a table showing the use of short declarative, loose, periodic, interrogative and balanced sentences), rhythm, figures of speech (including a statistical table showing the use of twenty varieties of figures of speech in ten speeches), and minor images. Rather than depending on rhetoricians for the methods of criticism, Lindsley relied primarily on Herbert

Spencer's essay "The Philosophy of Style." Indeed his article is a formulaic application of Spencer to Curtis' oratory (79-100).

Not until 1920, did the next article of rhetorical criticism appear. The author again was Lindley; this time he applied literary stylistic standards to three orations of "Henry Woodfin Grady, Orator." Writers attempting criticism were apparently unaware of rhetorical writings of the past. Lindsley relied entirely on the work of literary critics.

Not until 1925 did we see the reemergence of rhetorical criticism. In that year Robert Hannah of Cornell and Marvin Bauer of Iowa State College published articles quite different from those of earlier years. Both of these articles were analyses which were audience centered. Hannah wrote on "Burke's Audience" and Bauer on "The Influence of Lincoln's Audience on his Speeches." Both of these articles were significantly more rhetorical than those of Lindsley or Doyle. Where the earlier writers had used the literary canons of style as their model, Bauer's article was imbedded in the material of history, although all of his sources were secondary. He did not exploit the work of any rhetorical theorists, but he did demonstrate that the ideas in Lincoln's speeches were consistent with the belief of his audiences.

> A study of this period leads me to believe that this audience of his—the Republican Party—had a great influence in shaping the beliefs expressed in Lincoln's speeches; a much greater influence on his ideas than he exerted on those of his audience. These ideas were Lincoln's own ideas to be sure; but they were the belief of the times, as far as this particular group of people were concerned. Lincoln merely expressed the ideas that were in the air; he did not as a speaker create them. He accepted the beliefs of his group and in his speeches gave back to the group its own thoughts. (1925 227)

Hannah's essay dealt with the paradoxical nature of Burke's rhetoric. Burke was regarded as one of the most eloquent and effective British orators, yet many of his parliamentary speeches had no discernible effect on his immediate audiences. Hannah's thesis was that, in many cases, Burke spoke not to the House of Commons but to a larger audience, the British nation.

> The audience ignored the speaker we are told. May not the situation have been reversed? May not the orator have ignored his hearers? May not the speaker have had a wider vision?. . . May it not have been the Burke's definite purpose to sacrifice the plaudits of the House and to direct his rhetoric to the people of England and beyond?. . . And when he turned from the ignorant and bigoted House to the people of England, he exercised such power as neither Fox nor Sheridan ever had. With this understanding of his abilities as a speaker and of the audience which he addressed himself, we may well class Edmund Burke with the effective speakers of all time. (1925 147, 150)

Hannah relied largely on historical evidence to make his case and he said nothing about the content of any of Burke's speeches. His essay was as much a work of history as of rhetoric, although he did cite Aristotle concerning audiences ". . . who are unable to comprehend a number of arguments in a single view or to follow out a long chain of reasoning" (1925 147 quoted from *Aristotle's Rhetoric*, trans. Weldon).

In these essays we see a shift from an emphasis on the canon of style to the canon of invention. The later critics seemed aware of history as a discipline which provided guidance for rhetorical studies. Regardless of any direct influence Bauer or Hannah may have had, we know that the historical model came to be influential, and even dominant, in the years to come. In fact in our own times critics who adhered to the

Bauer model were derogated as "historians." In recent years we have witnessed serious disagreement between the descendants of these early historical critics and those who drew a sharp distinction between "rhetorical criticism" and "rhetorical history."

By far the most important publication in the field of rhetorical criticism in its early years also appeared in 1925. That year *Studies in Rhetoric and Public Speaking in Honor of James Albert Winans*, edited by Alexander Drummond, was published. In that festschrift, issued in a limited edition of 400 copies, was contained an essay which is, today, regarded as a landmark in rhetorical criticism, Herbert A. Wichelns' "The Literary Criticism of Oratory." After the attempts made to base criticism of rhetoric on the study of style derived from English and on historical studies, Wichelns set out to provide criteria by which the researcher could undertake to analyze and judge oral discourse. Wichelns' contributions to rhetorical criticism are undoubtedly valuable; yet, at the same time, his essay restricted our perspectives about criticism and may have functioned as a barrier to the advancement of rhetorical research.

It is interesting that Wichelns used the term "literary criticism" in the title of his lengthy essay, although late in the work he did use the term "rhetorical criticism." The scholars of the 1920s were, apparently, still sufficiently under the influence of English that an analogic terminology seemed desirable. In fact the bulk of Wichelns' essay is devoted to a survey of criticism of oratory by literary critics. He limited his discussion:

> . . . in the main to Burke and a few nineteenth-century figures—Webster,
> Lincoln, Gladstone, Bright, Cobden,—and to the verdict these found in the surveys
> of literary history, in critical essays, in histories of oratory and in biographies. . . .
> The chief aim is to know how critics have spoken of orators. (181)

Although criticism of oratory had been undertaken, it was not abundant and Wichelns sought to explain the deficiencies and the reasons why oratory should be seriously studied.

> We have not much serious criticism of oratory. The reasons are patent. Oratory is
> intimately associated with statecraft; it is bound up with the things of the moment;
> its occasions, its terms, its background can be understood only by the careful student
> of history. Again the publication of orations as pamphlets leaves us free to regard
> any speech merely as an essay, as a literary effort. . . .Yet the conditions of democracy
> necessitate both the making of speeches and the study of the art. (182)

Wichelns, in this statement, set some of the standards which would be observed for sometime to come. He did not so much, at this point in the essay, link rhetorical criticism to literary criticism as he did to the study of history. Later as enunciated by Thonnsen and Baird and others, Wichelns position became one of the topics of criticism under the rubric of "Reconstructing the Social Setting."

After his survey of critics, whom he divided into "literary critics" and "rhetorical critics," Wichelns undertook to define and delineate the criticism of rhetoric by establishing the manner in which it was distinguished from the criticism of literature. One of the most significant differences, said Wichelns, concerned the difference between permanence and effect. Of the literary critics he wrote:

> They are all, in various ways, interpreters of the permanent and universal values
> they find in the works of which they treat. (209)

The objective of rhetorical criticism was quite different, however.

> If we turn to rhetorical criticism as we found it exemplified in the previous
> section, we find that its point of view is patently single. It is not concerned with

permanence, nor yet with beauty. it is concerned with effect. It regards a speech as a
communication to a specific audience, and it holds its business to be the analysis and
appreciation of the orators methods of imparting his ideas to his hearers. (209)

Wichelns' position is not difficult to understand. After all the profession was faced with a task which it had previously not undertaken, and it was required to find its own approaches to criticizing rhetorical discourse. The kind of criticism with which the members of the new profession were familiar was, of course, literary criticism. Many of them had spent part of their careers in English departments and had some acquaintance with literary criticism. (Wichelns, in this essay, displayed extensive knowledge of nineteenth and early twentieth century criticism.)

Wichelns went on to specify further differences between literary criticism and rhetorical criticism.

Rhetorical criticism is necessarily analytical. The scheme of a rhetorical study
includes the element of a speaker's personality as a conditioning factor; it includes
also the public character of the man—not what he was but what he was thought to
be. It requires a description of the speaker's audience, and of the leading ideas with
which he plied his hearers—his topics, the motives to which he appealed, the nature
of the proofs he offered. . . . Nor can rhetorical criticism omit the speaker's mode of
arrangement and his mode of expression, nor his habit of preparation and his
manner of delivery from the platform; though the last two are perhaps less
significant. "Style" —in the sense which corresponds to diction and sentence
movement—must receive attention but only one among many means that secure for
the speaker ready access to the minds of his auditors. Finally the effect of discourse
on its immediate hearers is not to be ignored, either in the testimony of witnesses,
nor in the record of events. And throughout such a study one must conceive of the
public man as influencing the men of his own times by the power of his discourse.

What is the relation of rhetorical criticism, so understood, to literary criticism?
The latter is at once broader and more limited than rhetorical criticism. It is broader
because of its concern with permanent values: because it takes no account of special
purpose nor of immediate effect; because it views a literary work as the voice of the
human spirit addressing itself to the to men of all age and times; because the critic
speaks as the spectator of all time and existence. (212-213)

In his essay, Wichelns, for the first time and in a systematic manner laid out a methodology for the criticism of oratory which, for some time, became the standard approach to rhetorical criticism. Later this method would come to be known as Neo-Aristotelian criticism. Although one may infer the work of Aristotle in Wichelns' essay, it is derived as much from Cicero as from Aristotle. What Wichelns had proposed was a model in which the criteria drawn from traditional rhetorical theory would be applied to the analysis and appreciation of oratorical discourse. Wichelns had proposed a critical scheme based on the Ciceronian canons as well as the Aristotelian proofs. In addition he had introduced historical factors such as social and historical setting of a speech and authentification of the text. Oddly enough Wichelns seemed unaware of, or he ignored, the rhetorical contributions made between the Classical Era and his own time. We find no mention of the grand triumvirate of the eighteenth and nineteenth centuries—Blair, Campbell and Whately, although he copiously cited Saintsbury, Morely, Roseberry, Gosse, Hazlitt, Trevelyan and Baldwin among other nineteenth and early twentieth century critics.

No credit should be taken away from Wichelns' vital contribution to the study of rhetorical discourse. At the same time, however, we must recognize that he imposed on rhetoric some constraints which, although understandable in their own time, resulted in some important limitations on rhetorical criticism. Wichelns, as did the rest of the profession, perceived his activity to be limited to oral discourse. In effect Winans assigned the study of written discourse to literature and oral discourse to rhetoric— even though, in most cases oral rhetoric had to be examined in written form. Wichelns did not make allowance for written discourse which was rhetorical in its intent. Certainly in 1925 there was good reason to distinguish the work of the new profession from the parent discipline and to assign writing to English and speaking to Speech in order to create a clear distinction between the disciplines. The result, however, of the limitation was that for years to come written, and other symbolic forms of rhetoric, were ignored in the writings of speech teachers. The profession gave itself permission to include "non-oratorical" forms of rhetoric in the post-war years when literary critics such as Kenneth Burke and others brought "literature" into the purview of rhetoric.

The dichotomy between rhetoric and literature, as stipulated by Wichelns, created an artificial distinction. By basing his essay on the contrast between the two fields, Wichelns may have created the perception that there was no relationship between the two modes of criticism, when in fact, as we now recognize, much of what had been defined as literature was certainly amenable to rhetorical analysis. Perhaps this point was later made most cogently by Wayne Booth in his *The Rhetoric of Fiction* (1961).

Another of the stipulations which limited the scope of rhetorical criticism was Wichelns' emphasis on "effect" in rhetorical criticism. Concentrating so strongly on the effect of rhetorical discourse resulted in a focus which was external and which gave insufficient attention to how a particular piece of rhetoric worked rather than on its immediate or delayed effect. As scholars discovered, determination of effect was both difficult and conjectural, as the historians, on whose work much rhetorical criticism was modelled, could have told them.

The importance of reconstructing the setting of a speech and understanding the character of the speaker often resulted in work which was at least as much history or biography as rhetorical criticism. From a more distant perspective one could represent this early criticism as inferior history, biography or political science. Because Wichelns had posited his essay on an analogy with literary criticism, his conception, and of writers to follow, was that an analysis would be made of one speaker, thus not recognizing the role of rhetoric in social and political movements.

Undoubtedly Wichelns' essay provided a convenient taxonomy for the new scholars of rhetoric. Although it may not have been Wichelns' intention, much of the research based on his writing produced a formulaic, and even predictable, kind of scholarship written to a particular recipe. It has been said that some of the early criticism told us more about Aristotle than about the speaker.

We really do not know how widely read Wichelns' essay was in its own time since it had originally been published in an edition of only 400 copies. Later it was reprinted in other works and it was often referred to.

Although Wichelns' essay was the most enduring in the Winans festschrift, it was not the only contribution to rhetorical theory and criticism. Robert Hannah, whose article on Burke had appeared in *The Quarterly Journal* the same year, presented an essay on "Francis Bacon, the Political Orator." The volume actually contained more works on rhetorical theory than criticism, and we will discuss them later in this chapter.

Hannah's essay on Bacon was as not as narrowly historical as his Burke article, but it did not quite meet his colleague Wichelns' standards. About a third of the essay was given over to setting the historical and biographical scene. The remainder of the piece discussed the political nature of Bacon's oratory; the subjects of his orations; his oratorical style; and a lengthy section on delivery, derived entirely from secondary sources. Nevertheless, the essay was far more historical than rhetorical since the entire analysis was imbedded in a strong historical context. We must, of course, keep in mind the fact that Wichelns and Hannah had set different tasks for themselves; Wichelns sought to find a theoretical and critical basis for judging oratory while Hannah's work was concerned solely with the applied criticism of oratory.

It would seem that not much attention was paid to Wichelns' critical prescriptions since no articles dealing with criticism appeared in *The Quarterly Journal* for another two years. In 1927 Marvin Bauer again wrote on Lincoln, this time dealing with "Persuasive Methods in the Lincoln-Douglas Debates"(1927, 29-39).

In that same year two articles appeared which deviated, at least in part, from Wichelns' pronouncements. These articles were as much concerned with written as oral rhetoric. Desmond Powell of New York University wrote a misleadingly titled article "Byron's Oratory" in which he remarked briefly on the two speeches which Byron had given in Parliament. What Powell said about the speeches was general and impressionistic. The balance of the article was devoted to the notion that Byron's poetry was actually more rhetorical than poetic in its intention and its effect. To support his thesis, Powell relied on Adolphus Jack's essay on Byron in his *Poetry and Prose* and Hoyt Hudson's 1925 essay, "The Field of Rhetoric." Powell cited Jack's statement that, "Poetry is a record of feeling; oratory is an appeal, based of course on emotional experience, but meant to excite feeling." Powell's essay was, at the same time, indicative of the continuing influence of literary studies on rhetoric and a wilingness to consider non-oratorical works as proper objects for rhetorical study (424-432).

In 1927 V.E. Simrell of Dartmouth College chose to examine the work of H.L. Mencken in his article "H.L. Mencken the Rhetorician." Simrell's task was not so much to criticize Mencken's rhetoric as to establish that his writings were, in fact, rhetorical. To accomplish his objective Simrell relied entirely on Aristotle as the provider of criteria.

> One might catalog the rhetorical precepts of Aristotle and record under each examples of Mencken's practice;. . . When I cite Aristotle, it is not for such a purpose, but rather to show that, despite Mencken's frequent condemnation of rhetorical artifice, his methods are precisely those which rhetoric has comprehended since the art was first authoritatively formulated. (399)

In turn Simrell sought to demonstrate that Mencken made use of enthymemes, all the modes of proof and metaphor. In the end, however, Simrell found Mencken's rhetoric to be deficient.

> Aristotle explains that ". . . it belongs to the same faculty of mind to recognize both truth and the semblance of truth." But the explanation does not remedy the deplorable fact that the most able rhetorician in American criticism largely dissipates his power by haphazard amalgamation of truth and semblance of truth, facts, probabilities, and wild assertions, by his inconsistency of persuasive purpose. (410)

Simrell's judgment was, of course, contrary to his stated purpose of showing that Mencken's art was rhetorical. Simrell's essay, even by the standards of its day, would be regarded as superficial and impressionistic, but it was the first attempt by writers in *The Quarterly Journal* to deal with contemporary rather than historical discourse. In 1927 Mencken was at the height of his prominence and his pronouncements were subjects of controversy and dispute.

Gladys Murphy Graham also studied a contemporary figure who was a subject of controversy. In "Concerning the Speech Power of Woodrow Wilson" she undertook to demonstrate that, in spite of the disagreement about Wilson the man, one could not doubt the power of his speech. In 1927 she wrote:

> *The important fact is that Woodrow Wilson has been seen primarily at one extreme or the other, as idol or demagogue. . . . While everything else is in dispute, it is unanimously granted that Woodrow Wilson did possess power in speech. The value of the thing possessed, its permanence, the inherent excellence of any of its elements—these are all matters of question. But even his bitterest enemies grant the simple fact of power. . . .The fact remains: as no one else in generations, Wilson caught—and for a time held —the ear of humanity. He not only used speech widely, he used it with power over widely varying audiences and for an extended period. (1927, 412, 416)*

In her essay, Graham, after completing her discussion of the controversy concerning Wilson, went on to explain Wilson's speech power by examining his literary style, his logical form and his belief and conviction. As much of Graham's article was devoted to Wilson's biography and to recent history as to the criticism of Wilson's oratory. She did not cite any examples of Wilsonian rhetoric although she quoted at length from contradictory evaluations from the same author, writing about Wilson in 1912 and 1920. Graham's essay did not make obvious use of the work of any scholar of rhetoric.

Compared to articles on pedagogy, argumentation and debate, theater, speech science, and even rhetorical theory, the scholarly interest in criticism was slow in its development in the 1920s and 1930s. The next rhetorical criticism did not appear until 1929, when Edwin Paget of Syracuse University undertook yet another examination of Wilson's rhetoric in "Woodrow Wilson: International Rhetorician" (15-24). Wilson was also studied twice in 1930 by Dayton McKean of Princeton University who had easy access to the Wilson papers in the Princeton University Library. McKean concentrated largely on material taken directly from Wilson manuscripts and university histories. Little attention was given to analysis of Wilsonian rhetoric. In the early years of *The Quarterly Journal* Wilson proved to be one of the most popular subjects for critics, surpassed only by Lincoln (1930, 176-184, 1930a, 458-463). Slowly, but very slowly, the number of articles increased during the 1930s. Often as much as a year would pass between articles on rhetorical criticism. Jonathan Swift, Abraham Lincoln, Henry Ward Beecher, Ralph Waldo Emerson, Harry Emerson Fosdick, Wendell Phillips, John Bright and Edmund Burke were among the speakers studied from 1930 through 1935. During that time there were only two articles whose focus was broader than simply the study of one orator. Gladys Murphy Graham wrote on "The House of Lords Debates the Naval Treaty" (414-420) and Earl W. Wiley contributed "A Footnote on the Lincoln-Douglas Debates" (216-224).

Not only did Wicheln's work fail to produce much rhetorical criticism, it also failed to excite much interest in the question of how to do criticism. For more than a decade, members of the profession failed to give further thought to describing criticism or to suggesting how it should be done. One should not be surprised to find that none of the articles in the early years were based on any kind of theory of rhetoric.

In 1933 William Norwood Brigance of Wabash College about whom we will hear later in this volume, sought to chart the direction of research in the field after almost twenty years of exisrence. Since Brigance was a rhetorical critic, he restricted his attention to research in rhetoric. In his essay "Whither Research" Brigance sought the origins of the discipline's interest in criticism, surveyed the early work in rhetorical criticism, defined the present status of the enterprise, and indicated the direction of future research. Brigance recognized that, in its early stages, the profession had almost no choice but to follow the model of English, the parent profession. He compared progress in research in speech to that in English.

> I have summarized this aspect of the trend of criticism and research in our allied field of English because it is a forerunner of our trend in rhetoric and oratory. It was natural, even inevitable, that we should follow the same general route. We have done so with almost painstaking exactness. . . . It seems to me that this type of research represents a transitional stage through which research in English literature and rhetoric must pass. English literature seems definitely passed through it and gone to higher levels. They were nearly forty years in the wilderness. Admitting that we too must go through it, I do not think it should take us forty years. (1933, 555)

Although he did not say so specifically, the "higher levels" to which Brigance alluded was undoubtedly the growth of literary criticism, which was rapidly developing and gaining status in the 1920s and 30s. As we shall see, in a few years Everett Hunt would deal with this matter more thoroughly than Brigance. It remained clear just how dependent the new profession was on English as a source of subjects and methodological approaches.

At the same time, however, Brigance was clear that rhetoric had been too dependent on literature and that although they were related to each other they differed in essential respects. In agreement with Hudson and Wichelns, Brigance saw the emphasis on effect in rhetoric as an important differentiation.

> Next, I think we should agree that oratorical literature is a special form, quite distinct from poetry, essays, drama and other forms of prose literature, with which it is often confused by biographers and literary critics. The tools of rhetoric may indeed be the same as those of literature, but the atmosphere and purpose are different. The literary artist writes with his eye on the subject. . . . He is concerned with permanence and beauty. But the statesman who must dominate a crisis, or the advocate who must mold the mind of a court or jury, has no time to polish plaudits for posterity. He is concerned with immediate and deadly effect. . . . To apply the literary tests of permanence and beauty to rhetorical literature borders on the fantastic if not the grotesque. (1933, 556, 557)

Brigance's ambivalence toward literature is understandable. On one hand, he perceived similarities between literary and rhetorical criticism; on the other hand, he detected great differences in their approaches to the analysis of literary and rhetorical texts. So strong was the need to differentiate between the two fields, that Brigance and others took positions which were more extreme than they needed to be. The controlling ideology that rhetoric was not permanent, that it was completely dissimilar from literature, and that it was solely concerned with effect, imposed limitations on the scope of criticism which persisted for almost two decades.

The failure of literary criticism to deal adequately with rhetoric suggested to Brigance that an alternate methodology was called for. Instead of grounding our work in literature, said Brigance, it could be based in history.

> These facts suggest one direction, at least, in which our scholarship ought to move next, namely to undertake a combined historical and critical study of orators and oratorical literature, and to produce thereby a body of oratorical studies and criticisms worthy of the orators and oratory which induced it. . . . I emphasize the need of combining these techniques for two reasons. First, they are inseparably

interwoven in speech making. The speakers is using the tools of rhetoric indeed, but using them to meet a crisis, to fuse public opinion on issues not only historical in origin, but rooted in immediate historical settings. One cannot study the literature without studying the historical foundation upon which it rests. Second,. . . our techniques from the the rhetorical side have been well developed, but fail generally on the historical side. . . . We must, if we expect recognition of our scholarship, go to the records themselves. . . . We must bring the past before our eyes as though it were the living present. (1933, 557-559)

Brigance listed and explained what ". . . factors should be included" in the histori-cal/rhetorical approach.

(1) *A study of the historical causes behind the issues discussed. . .*

(2) *. . . study of the immediate speaking situation. . .*

(3) *. . . a critical study of the speaker's style. First, the choice of topics and the nature of proofs. . .*

(4) *. . . a study of the speaker's habits of preparation, his voice, his manner of delivery, and especially of his personality, mental habits, attainments and shortcomings.*

(5) *Finally, it will involve a study of the speaker's effect on the audience. (1935, 559-560)*

Brigance, together, with the majority of the critics of the period, fashioned a methodology of rhetorical criticism in many respects indistinguishable from historical methodology. Brigance advocated a critical scheme which, as he acknowledged, was as much rhetorical history as rhetorical criticism.

In 1935 Everett Hunt by then at Swarthmore responded to Wichelns, not in a formal article but in a printed version of a paper given at the Eastern Public Speaking Conference, which was published in the "Forum" section of *The Quarterly Journal*. In his essay Hunt made the point that the line between rhetoric and literature was not as sharp as Wichelns had made it out to be. He began by conceding that, in spite of Wichelns' essay, the profession had produced little criticism.

> *In view of the small amount of criticism, either literary or rhetorical, which has been published by teachers of speech, the attempt to distinguish between rhetorical and literary criticism may seem somewhat academic. (1935, 565)*

Hunt asserted that the relationship of . . . "rhetoric to literary criticism is long and complicated" (1935, 565). The clear-cut distinction made by Wichelns and Hudson was not representative of what had actually occurred.

> *Plato attacked both rhetoric and poetry, and Aristotle, in replying to Plato showed a clear comprehension of the likenesses and differences of rhetoric and poetic. It may be remarked in passing that the best statements of the function of oratory and poetry, of rhetoric and criticism have usually been made in the course of replying to the constant and repeated attacks that have been made on both. (1935, 565)*

Perhaps, said Hunt, the only meaningful distinction that could be made was one proposed by Professor George Reynolds of the University of Colorado.

> *In our present welter of critical confusion, he suggests, perhaps the only critical*

distinction which can really stand is the distinction between literature meant for the solitary reader, and literature for an audience. (1935, 565)

Thus Hunt, together with Reynolds, asserted that the real difference was between public and private discourse and that literature could exist in either sphere. In fact, said Hunt contemporary criticism was bringing rhetorical and literary criticism closer together.

> *But in contemporary criticism, the neo-humanists, with their ethical preconceptions, have plunged criticism into rhetoric again, and even the scientific and pseudo-scientific psychological critics, with their studies of poetic attitude, tone and intention are bringing rhetoric back into the field again. Rhetoric and criticism, in spite of protesting friends and relatives, seem to be affinities. (1935, 566)*

Hunt was remarkably prescient in this essay. He perceived that literary criticism was undergoing important changes and, intentionally or not, its focus was becoming more rhetorical. Decades before the rest of the profession, Hunt not only detected the direction in which literary criticism was going, he also recognized that departments of English would reinvigorate their interest in rhetoric. This time, however, their scholarly intersect would be different. Instead of treating rhetoric as part of English Composition, it was now beginning to be seen as a mechanism for the improved analysis of texts. Many literary critics now saw the distinction between literary and rhetorical criticism as meaningless. Since only Hunt, and a very few rhetorical scholars seemed aware of these significant critical shifts, the profession seemed content to drowse on with its existing, underdeveloped critical ideas. The interest in rhetoric shown by literary critics presaged an important development, only partly to the benefit of the Speech profession. Beginning in the 1940s, and continuing to the present, it became apparent that the really interesting and innovative work in rhetoric was being done by literary, not speech scholars. The works of such writers as Kenneth Burke, I.A. Richards, Wayne Booth, Richard McKeon and Richard Weaver, among others, furnished the theoretical bases for much rhetorical criticism. In fact, a case can be made that literary, not rhetorical critics were primarily responsible for bringing about the shift away from Neo-Aristotelian criticism.

Hunt was fresh from the meeting of the Modern Language Association. There the dominant controversy was between history and criticism. The literary scholars were engaged in a dispute which would not emerge in the speech profession for almost a half century. Each of the adversaries had different ends in mind.

> *The historians, say the critics, ignore values: they ignore values when reading literature which has value, and they study enthusiastically thousands of printed pages which are devoid of any values which can possibly interest the literary critic. But Professor Schlesinger states baldly that historians will never get on with their work until they have thrown off the domination of the critics. Professor Howard Mumford Jones, in his recent essay on Literary Scholarship says pointedly that it is not the primary business of scholarship to produce criticism. The scholar takes a particular period in which certain writers were thought important, and reconstructs the pattern of the mental life of the period without any reference to any present or future interest. (1935, 566)*

Scholars in rhetoric had not drawn the kind of dividing line as that drawn in literature. Until the recent past, history and criticism were seen as integrated aspects of one critical process. History was often seen as a prerequisite for doing criticism. In his essay Hunt mentioned that the National Association of Teachers of Speech had established a "Committee on Research in History and Literary Criticism" under the chairmanship of W. Norwood Brigance of Wabash College. We do not know why "literary criticism" was included in the committee's name since, according to Hunt, "The committee has made careful plans for the publication of a volume of 'rhetorical' studies of American orators. . ." (1935, 565). The envisioned volume was actually published in two volumes in 1943 with the title *History and Criticism of American Public Address*. An additional volume was published in 1955, edited by Marie Hochmuth. Thus rhetorical history and rhetorical criticism were seen as a single entity eight years after Hunt had perceived the difference between them. The linkage between history and criticism was to continue for decades before the literary dispute of the 1920s became the rhetorical dispute of the 1970s and 1980s.

Hunt felt that literary history had more to contribute to the study of rhetoric than did literary criticism. Further, the student of rhetoric was in a position to make contributions to the study of the history of literature.

> *Historical scholars who profess to have no eye on the present, who work independently of contemporary values and interests, are emphasizing the importance of the study of documents which critics would dismiss as outworn rhetoric or oratory. In freeing themselves from considerations of the present, they inquire how opinions of any period came to be what they are. Rhetorical effectiveness, which they so often disdain in their own writing, becomes the subject of their historical analysis. The outworn orator acquires a new importance and if teachers of speech do not analyze him, the literary historians will. For this analysis, however the rhetorician has the indispensable equipment, an equipment which the historian must acquire if his work is to be adequate. In the quarrel between criticism and history, then, the historian becomes the ally of the rhetorical critic in showing the importance of neglected rhetorical subject matter. (1935, 566-567)*

Although history may have been the more important field for rhetoric, said Hunt, criticism had its contribution to make.

> *But, in another way the critic, too, is an ally. If he disdains forgotten orators as the subjects of study, he draws much more heavily upon rhetoric in the practice of his own criticism. . . .Those critics, disdainful of persuasive discourse which does not happen to interest them, become themselves writers of persuasive discourse, and thus excellent subjects of rhetorical analysis. (1935, 567)*

We know now that literary historians did not acquire "the indispensable equipment" which Hunt maintained they "must acquire if his work is to be adequate." To be sure, some literary criticism, in time, was oriented toward rhetorical analysis, but we have no evidence that they relied on speech teachers for their equipment. Rather they themselves proved more adept at devising theories of rhetorical criticism than their speech colleagues. In fact the literary critics provided much of the theoretical foundation for rhetorical criticism.

In the end, said Hunt, we must not reject totally the critics or the historians.

> *If, then, in resentment of the fact that some literary critics do not see literary values in the orators we study, we should decry all values and call ourselves scientific historians, we limit ourselves needlessly. It must be admitted of, course, that the study of American orators has suffered more from the attempt to judge without adequate historical knowledge than it has from any dry-as-dust historian. Our chief immediate need is for historical research. (1935, 568)*

Hunt was hopeful that the development of rhetorical scholarship would not only be strengthened but that it would increase interests in American oratory.

> *The training of scholars in our own field is beginning to bear fruit when the trends in history, criticism, social psychology, and national self-consciousness makes a study of American orators of wider interest than the professional business of thesis writing and teacher training. (1935, 568)*

Hopeful though he was, Hunt's vision of the future did not come to pass. Neither the concentration on American oratory nor the use of the methodology of rhetorical criticism were widely adopted by the disciplines cited by Hunt.

Hunt's essay, one which is no longer much read, was indicative of the continuing close connection between rhetorical and literary criticism. Considering Hunt's earlier humanistic and literary statements, we should not be surprised at his use of literary criticism as both a model and analogy for rhetorical criticism. The taxonomy he created was obviously drawn from the latest doctrines in literary criticism. In spite of all of his perception and insight, Hunt advocated dependence on, if not derivation from, literary criticism.

In his essay Hunt referred to Brigance's recent book, *Jeremiah Sullivan Black: A Defender of the Constitution and the Ten Commandments*. This work, an expansion of Brigance's doctoral dissertation at the University of Iowa, was accurately described by Hunt as ". . . a critical biography of an orator, Jeremiah Sullivan Black, by a teacher of speech, in which the methods of rhetorical criticism begin to emerge with some distinctness" (1935, 565). The work was, first of all, a biography. Brigance justified his study partially on rhetorical and partially on historical grounds.

> *Under his startling eloquence the Supreme Court overthrew trial by military commissions in the North at the close of the Civil War; drew the teeth from an Enforcement Act of the Thirteenth Amendment; and sawed off literally and bodily the ominous provisions of the first section of the Fourteenth Amendment, allowing us today to live under the boon of that amputation. "It is useless to deny it," said a Judge of that Court, "Judge Black is the most magnificent orator at the American bar." (1934, vii)*

Without detracting from the book's quality, which was considerable, we can note that history, not rhetoric, dominated it. In a volume of 34 chapters, only Chapter 30, "The Forensic Orator," was predominately devoted to Black's rhetoric. In the space of fifteen pages, Brigance summarized the salient features of Sullivan's oratory. Even then, Brigance relied quite heavily on historical data, including testimony from contemporary observers of Black. We must not, however, undervalue Brigance's work. It was, so far as we can determine, the first scholarly work of criticism written by a member of the young speech profession. In the book Brigance showed his ability to make use of historical sources and methods and to deal with complex issues of historical, political and constitutional interpretation. Brigance and the profession must have been pleased that the work of one of their members was treated as serious scholarship and published by a prestigious university press.

The next year, 1936, Bower Aly of the University of Missouri extended the conception of rhetoric beyond that of conventional oral and written discourse in his essay, "The Scientist's Debt to Rhetoric." Aly sought to make the point that the investigative methods of scientists are essentially rhetorical.

> *The scientist employs no peculiar system; he uses no process of reasoning not known of old to the rhetorician. . . . So far as inferences are concerned, the so-called*

scientific method is, however, no more the method of science than it is the method of rhetoric. (1936, 585)

Aly perceived rhetoric as being based on language and by no means restricted to intentionally persuasive discourse. His conception of rhetoric applied to written as well as oral communication.

Rhetoric is not the frothy effervescence added to a sea of words. Rhetoric is not style, merely, nor attitude. Rhetoric ought to properly be considered as a much richer concept than any of these. Rhetoric goes down into the very bony structure of language and is a part of it. Rhetoric should be considered in its traditional sense in relation to human action, thought and conduct. If rhetoric be considered as the effective use of language, and if we bear in mind the scientist's clear dependence on language, then the scientist's debt to rhetoric, as well as his dependence on language will be clearly understood.

The rhetoric of the scientist is not, of course, bound by any narrow limitations. The academic may be unable to see the effective rhetoric in simple exposition. He may not fully comprehend the persuasive power of simple words. Many a rhetorician, nevertheless, will have much to learn from such a scientist as Huxley or Spencer or Darwin concerning the effective use of language (1936, 590).

Aly's essay, though its focus was not primarily on criticism, opened new paths for rhetorical criticism. Since the *Rhetoric* of Aristotle, clear lines had been drawn between science and rhetoric and between expository and persuasive discourse. Aristotle was quite specific about the conditions under which rhetoric should be used in scientific discourse.

Even if our speaker had the most accurate scientific information, still there are persons whom he could not readily persuade with scientific arguments. True instruction, by the method of logic, is here impossible; the speaker must frame his proofs and arguments with the help of common knowledge and accepted opinions. (Aristotle, ed. Cooper, 1932, 6)

From Aly's perspective, the field of investigation for the critic was now broader than it had been. No longer was the student of rhetoric to be limited solely to the study of persuasion and, more importantly, with the understanding that scientific discourse was as rhetorical as any other form of discourse, the scientists' use of language became an appropriate subject for rhetorical investigation. Unfortunately, Aly's essay became yet another instance of "a path not taken." Many years would pass before the profession came to recognize that there was, in fact, a rhetoric of science, and when that recognition came, Aly's essay was never referred to. Indeed, much of the awareness of the ways in which science is rhetorical was enunciated by the scientists themselves.

Ross Scanlan of the College of the City of New York further broadened the field of rhetorical criticism in his 1936 essay "Rhetoric and the Drama." By 1936 many of the scholars were well acquainted with Aristotelian rhetoric and were able to use his work as the foundation for the examination of rhetorical texts. Scanlan made use of Aristotle's *Rhetoric* to argue that dramatic texts could also be rhetorical. Scanlan offered several definitional reasons why dramatic literature had not come under the purview of rhetoric.

Many critics and theorists have discussed the right or wisdom of a dramatist who uses his art as a medium of persuasive communication; but none has sought to test the persuasive capabilities of the drama by reference to rhetorical theory.This neglect

arises mainly from limitations in the prevalent conceptions of rhetoric, Examination
of a wide variety of definitions, ancient and modern reveals the following tendencies:
(1) restriction of rhetoric to one form of composition, the public address; (2)
restriction of rhetoric to non-metrical composition; (3) restriction of rhetoric to
problems of style;. . . (7) restriction of rhetoric to certain classes of subjects.
(635-636)

In his depiction of the rhetorical nature of drama, Scanlan relied on Aristotle's statements about persuasion and probability. These factors, he maintained, were as prevalent in drama as in oratory.

> *Aristotle's treatise thus warrants a conception of rhetoric much broader than*
> *those I have mentioned: rhetoric is an art, the function of which is persuasion, the*
> *technical methods of which are comprehended by three terms—ethical representation,*
> *argument, emotional appeal—and the medium of which is language. Persuasion*
> *implies any qualitative or quantitative change in opinion or action effected by these*
> *methods. . . According to this description, rhetoric may extend to forms of*
> *composition other than public address; if the aim is persuasion it may apply to*
> *metrical as well as non-metrical compositions; it deals with much more than*
> *problems of style;. . . nor is it limited to a particular class of subjects. Only a*
> *conception like this, freed from the limitations outlined above, can suggest the full*
> *application of rhetoric to the drama. (636)*

Scanlan asserted that both rhetoric and the drama dealt not with "truth" but, what he termed "a satisfactory appearance of probability." Drama posed a special problem for the critic, however, in that its persuasion was both internal and external—internal because of the persuasion effected among the characters and external because of the persuasion directed to the audience. But, just as the dramatist may represent the agents of his play seeking to persuade each other, so he may employ them to effect some kind of persuasion with his audience, thus giving a larger more external scope to the operation of rhetorical principles and methods in the drama (637).

Scanlan was returning to a modification of a conception of rhetoric prevalent in the late eighteenth and early nineteenth centuries. The belletristic rhetoricians, such as Blair and Rollin, had included the drama as well as poetry among the objects recommended for rhetorical study. Scanlan's essay is yet another example of an idea which engendered little or no interest or follow through. In spite of Scanlan's insight, the drama was largely ignored as the object of rhetorical criticism until after 1945. Only after literary critics such as Burke and Weaver began to examine various literary forms rhetorically, did rhetorical scholars in speech turn part of their attention to the drama. Scholars in speech faced a problem, however, which did not occur among literary critics. The new profession had embraced theatre as part of the new discipline necessitating a division of labor between persons in speech and those in theatre. Rhetoricians undertaking criticism of dramas might have been accused of doing dramatic criticism. Of course, that kind of dichotomy was completely artificial. Nevertheless, Scanlan's and the profession's failure to follow up with rhetorical criticisms of the drama must be regarded as another example of a missed opportunity in the profession.

In 1937 in an essay titled "Some Problems of Scope and Method in Rhetorical Scholarship," Donald C. Bryant, then of the New York State College for Teachers at Albany, brought rhetorical criticism into an alliance with history. His emphasis, however, was different from that of Brigance in that he saw rhetorical history as being very closely affiliated with literary history. He also discussed the question, raised in 1935 by Brigance concerning the relationship between history and criticism.

> *First we must answer those apostles of the contemporaneous who would have us adapt and interpret and criticize poems and plays, speeches and pamphlets, for today in terms of today, and leave off digging into the far corners and obscure recesses of the past for information about the authors of these works. . . . Ultimately, of course, the justification of scholarship will be its use in enabling the voices of the past to be heard effectively in the present. . . . Literature is definitely impoverished without literary history. (1937, 183)*

Bryant was dealing with a problem which has been present in literary criticism since the 1920s—whether criticism should be exclusively concerned with the text itself or whether historical background and biographical data are necessary for an understanding of the text. These views have been expressed under a number of rubrics; including, New Criticism, Deconstruction and Reader Response. In rhetorical criticism, however, the issue was not central until the 1970s.

As strong as the argument might have been for literary history, said Bryant, history was even more vital for rhetoric.

> *The case for rhetorical history is even stronger. Rhetorical criticism must depend entirely on historical knowledge for its effectiveness, because in the first place, rhetorical history, as compared with literary history, is concerned with a lesser proportion of those men whose voices, unassisted, continue still to be heard. (183)*

Bryant thus joined those who followed Wichelns' position that rhetoric was inherently less permanent than literature. The ephemeral character assigned to rhetoric was bound to make it seem less significant than literature, which was "for the ages." It is worth noting that, over his long career, among Bryant's most important contributions were his studies of the rhetoric of Edmund Burke, one of the most permanent of all orators.

Bryant also asserted that the focus of rhetorical criticism was different from that of literary criticism in that literature dealt with esthetic reactions while rhetoric was primarily concerned with the interactions in the rhetorical situation.

> *For several years now, we have had in the writings on our subject a plain statement of the legal separation, if not the divorce, of literary and rhetorical criticism. Rhetorical criticism, we understand, is concerned only secondarily with permanent esthetic canons. It gains its value from its primary concern with considerations of audience-speaker-occasion—of background, surroundings, contemporary effectiveness. . . . Hence it is that rhetorical criticism, unless it be criticism of current speeches, cannot do without without rhetorical history, and full and accurate history at that. (184)*

But accepting the importance of history is not enough, said Bryant; we must decide what kind of history is appropriate for rhetorical criticism. Historians, literary, and otherwise, were engaged in disputes concerning ". . . the problem of individual point of view versus the social" (185). In raising the issue drawn from history, Bryant was anticipating that, by the 1940s and 50s, some venturesome rhetorical souls would explore the rhetoric of historic movements rather than the rhetoric of a single great orator. Bryant sought to transfer the argument about literary history and criticism to rhetorical history and criticism.

> *By our preoccupation with great figures, it is said that we convey the false impression that the past is made of great men and that anything we can find about them justifies the search. . . .Therefore, they [the literary historians] argue the*

emphasis of literary history is to be shifted from figures to society. . . . Literary
history, they say, like political and social history, and the history of public address
like both of them are to be studied in the light of more socially significant
conceptions than great figures, personal gossip and chronology. (185)

In the end, Bryant was unwilling to accept the doctrine of the new literary historians; he argued that social history, especially when applied to public address, would not provide all the knowledge necessary to do rhetorical criticism.

That the interesting facts of human biography can be ignored, even in a picture of
the great society, I am unable to believe. . . . For most of us, forces are symbolized by
men. The danger comes when we forge the facts of symbolism. As Professor Grierson
says, "Poems are not written by influences or movements or sources, but come from
the living hearts of men." And the same fact, it seems to me must continue to be held
true of specimens of public address as well. (1937, 188)

Bryant's essay was indicative of the importance that many rhetorical critics attached to the use of history and historical methodology. To outside observers, on one hand, it must have seemed as if rhetorical criticism were a branch of history, but a very specialized one. On the other hand, historians might have seen rhetorical criticism simply as a field derived from and dependent upon History. These remarks from the young Donald C. Bryant were characteristic of his long and distinguished career. Through his appointments at Albany, Washington University at Saint Louis, and the University of Iowa, his devotion to history was consistent, especially in his studies of Burke.

In 1941 the second scholarly book in rhetorical criticism was published, *The Rhetoric of Alexander Hamilton*, by Bower Aly (Aly, 1941). As was the case with Brigance, Aly's study was also published by a prestigious university press, in this case Columbia University Press. Aly's book, however, although it was also strongly oriented toward history, paid more specific attention to Hamilton's rhetoric than Brigance did to Black's rhetoric. It is a symptom of a kind of professional amnesia that the work of Brigance and Aly is largely unknown or ignored, although their studies represented highly significant progress in critical scholarship.

The next important contributions to the theory of criticism, as contrasted to the practice of criticism, came in 1943. At that time, in commemoration of the publication of *A History and Criticism of American Public Address*,

. . . the Executive Council [of the National Association] in December 1942,
authorized a second research assignment to be undertaken under the auspices of the
association, this time in state and regional public address under the chairmanship of
Bower Aly. The Journal, therefore, presents three articles in this issue—this one,
and those following by Professors Baird and Aly—concerning the possible direction,
methods, and available materials for the new undertaking.—Ed. (300)

In the first of the three articles, "What Direction Should Future Research in American Public Address Take," Dallas Dickey of Louisiana State University undertook the prescriptive task of delineating not only the future direction of research, but of some of the methods as well. In beginning his essay, Dickey chose the historians as the analogy and model for rhetorical critics, and offered a comparison of the rhetoricians' and historians' work.

We may be about where the historians were forty years ago. We now have a
substantial number of scholars dedicated to the study of American public address

and more will join our ranks in the years to come. . . since we have stated clearly that the importance of a speaker is measured by his effectiveness and influence, not by his eloquence. In saying that we may be about where historians were forty years ago, we are yet studying what may be called the more obvious speakers. (301)

After making his comparison with history, Dickey remained firmly anchored to a historical approach to criticism. Unfortunately, he said virtually nothing about how historical methodology might be used in the improvement of rhetorical criticism. Instead, his emphasis on future research was directed to neglected orators whose rhetoric had not been studied to that time. Finally, his challenge to the profession was that they become not better critics but more skilled historians.

We shall expect our scholars to be more than amateur historians, for they must handle and evaluate the forces of social and political history and they must be able to do so with professional competency. (304)

Dickey's essay viewed from the perspective of our time must be reckoned to be a disappointment, considering the prestige which the National Association attached to this set of articles. Although Dickey warned against "amateur historians," that was what he advocated. The most important preparation for rhetorical criticism was not critical acuity but historical knowledge. As Hunt had earlier cautioned, speech teachers could not expect to equal historians in their competence, and if they did, they would become historians and no longer speech teachers.

A. Craig Baird of the State University of Iowa wrote of "Opportunities for Research in State and Regional Public Speaking." Although a substantial portion of Baird's essay was similar to Dickey's in its concern about subjects for research, he did address the question of the validity of rhetorical criticism, and he provided an essential historical context.

At the inception of the movement, both the originality and method of such graduate studies were challenged by graduate deans and by members of speech faculties. Did such studies have validity comparable to those developed in laboratories? Did those who used the rhetorical approach tend to abandon objectivity in favor of subjective essays? Must the product be pure history and nothing more? Were such studies best done by following the normative-survey, the historical, the literary, or some combination of the historical-literary methods?

The last mentioned methodology prevailed. The critic of speeches and speakers became a historian and a rhetorician. But he remained also a speech specialist. Wichelns pointed the way to such a balanced approach (305).

In his essay Baird pointed to a problem encountered by the critics who undertook to study the rhetoric of a region rather than that of a single speaker. Baird imposed on them responsibilities beyond rhetoric. They were expected to be proficient social historians and biographers.

The treatment of a region has usually meant a description, not simply of its outstanding men and women, but of the total culture of a neighborhood in its influence on the speaking activities. Research in the speaking of a locality, then, means that we must become social historians as well as biographers, that we must enter into the whole environment. . . . To qualify as a social historian becomes a formidable job. Easier it is to isolate a single speaker than to immerse him in the surrounding current of speaking and thinking. (307)

Baird moved rhetorical criticism even closer to history than Dickey had. At the same time, however, at least by implication, he widened the scope of criticism so that it could deal with examinations of rhetorical movements rather than the study of a "single speaker." So attached were Baird and other critics to the importance of history that Baird regarded a lack of command of historical methodology as a serious problem to be overcome.

> *In applying this most difficult technique, combining as it does, the historical and rhetorical methods, we have, or soon will have, a certain measure of perspective or philosophical judgment. (Although it is still true that many graduate students and teachers have turned out studies in this field that show only partial command of the historical techniques.)(307)*

Since these essays were written in the midst of World War II, and since the discipline allied itself closely to the conception of the role of speech in a democratic society, (see Chapter 6) one should not be surprised to find that Baird also saw a connection between rhetorical criticism and democracy.

> *The war has all but stilled this research, but it has not stilled the spirit of research. In the past score of years a vigorous coterie of interested scholars has emerged. When the opportunity returns, they will continue to produce, and through their work our democratic civilization will be more fully understood. (308)*

The third of the 1943 essays was "The History of American Public Address as a Research Field" by Bower Aly. Aly noted that the history of speechmaking in America was a neglected field since scholars in other disciplines had paid only marginal attention to public address. Fortunately, that defect was being remedied by the growing interest in rhetorical studies.

> *The professors of literature have ordinarily given only passing notice to speeches, and frequently they have assumed erroneously that speechmaking is merely a branch of literature. Historians have used the texts of speeches as source material for general and specific histories, but they have not attempted a systematic account of the history of speechmaking. Biographers have sometimes made random excursions into eloquence in the lives of great Americans, but their primary purpose has generally been the dignifying of their subject rather than the study of speechmaking. Accordingly, the history of speechmaking in America has yet to be written. Fortunately, the growing interest in the subject comes at a time when rhetorical studies are receiving increase emphasis in American universities and colleges. (308)*

Aly departed, to a considerable extent, from the received knowledge of rhetorical criticism by shifting the focus from the study of the speechmaking of great orators to an authentic historical treatment of American Public Address. In order to expedite that goal Aly listed and commented upon several historical/rhetorical areas which merited investigation. Among them were;

> *Speechmaking and Institutions.*
> *Regional Studies.*
> *Period Studies.*

Movements.
Occasions.
Customs and Manners.
Speechmaking: War and Peace.
The Non-Orators.
Speechmaking as an Institution.
Institutions Devoted to Speechmaking.
Speeches of Events.
Speechmaking and Education.
Speechmaking and Immigration.
Unusual Instances.
American Rhetorical Theory.
Lines of Argument.
Speakers as Leaders.
Biographical Studies.
Races.
Topics.
Age Groups.
Sex.
Humor.
Oratory and the Other Arts.
Rhetorical History and Intellectual History.
Analytic Studies.
Sources.
Iconography.
Critical Essays.
Textual Studies. (310)

It is not important that we comment on each topic in Aly's shopping list. What is important is that we note that Aly suggested numerous areas of investigation which could move the field from the focus that E.C. Mabie referred to, in conversation, as the "study of old dead orators." Obviously, not all of Aly's suggestions were of equal value, but they did display his insight as to what the mature field of rhetorical criticism could become. Understandably, since Aly's concern was with the history of American Public Address, much of what he proposed would require, as did Dickey's and Baird's essays, that copious use be made of historical methodologies.

The publication of the two volumes of *A History and Criticism of American Public Address* symbolized an important advance for the profession and the association. A prestigious commercial press, McGraw Hill, had agreed to publish a serious scholarly anthology under the auspices of the National Association of Teachers of Speech. Only in the case of the festschrift for James Winans in 1925 had a major publisher presented a scholarly work in Speech. The work which Brigance edited included some of the perspectives presented by Dickey, Baird and Aly. As the title indicated, the studies were at least as concerned with rhetorical history as with rhetorical criticism. The volumes began with a section titled "The Historical Background of American Public Address" consisting of five essays, covering some 200 pages, which were devoted to "The Colonial Period"; "The Early National Period, 1788-1860."; "The Later National Period,

1860-1930."; "Woman's Introduction to the American Platform"; and "The Teaching of Rhetoric in the United States during the Classical Period of Education" (1943, 3-212). The fact that Brigance and his distinguished editorial board elected to begin the volumes with history rather than criticism gave testimony to the power then attached to History as a powerful research tool.* In fact, the writers seemed to be carrying out the strictures of Brigance a decade earlier, when he urged rhetoricians to become more skilled in historical methodology.

The remainder of the two volumes was faithful to Bryant's biographical conception of rhetorical criticism. Under the headings of Religion, Reform, Law, General Culture, Education, Labor, and Statecraft, the rhetoric of 28 American orators was analyzed. More than 700 pages were devoted to that task. Most of the notables of American oratory were included; Lincoln was deemed important enough to merit two essays. In the preface to the work Brigance justified the lack of uniformity in the studies.

> In the critical studies, as in the historical studies, the reader will find a wide diversity in the patterns of treatment. To those who would prefer that one standardized pattern of rhetorical criticism be followed, we answer that it would have been neither possible, nor, in our opinion, desirable. It would not have been possible because the best scholars are not all adherents of the same philosophy of criticism. Some prefer the pure Aristotelian pattern. Some prefer their Aristotelianism diluted. Others abjure it altogether. Among such vigorous dissenters no collation would have been possible. Nor do we think it would have been desirable. Uniformity in so large a number of studies would inevitably have led to sterility. (x)

In fact, from the perspective of the present, the studies were not as diverse as Brigance thought they were. They were all single orator studies; no attention was paid to the rhetoric of social or political movements. They were also more or less Aristotelian essays and they were all historically and biographically oriented. The first study on Jonathan Edwards by Orville A. Hitchcock of the University of Akron was exemplary of the work. He began with a brief justification for his study; he then dealt with "The Speaking Situation," "Training" and finally "The Sermons." Under the last heading he treated "Ideas," "Organization," "Types of Proof," "Style," "Effect" and inferences about delivery (Hitchcock in Brigance, 1943, 213-237). Perhaps the most frequently cited work in these studies was Parrington's "Main Currents in American Thought, an important American social and intellectual history" (1930).

Brigance, in the preface, felt that it was still necessary to distinguish between rhetorical and literary criticism, and to stress again the importance of effects. By now, however, he was willing to acknowledge that some rhetoric may have had more than transient excellence.

> Historically, the distinction between the criticism of poetry and public address has often been confused, poetry at times being defended by giving it the practical usefulness of public address, and public address at times being viewed by the absolute standard of a timeless world, with critics trying to measure it in terms of permanence and aesthetic excellence. Neither of these standards has been accepted in this work. That public address may have permanence and aesthetic excellence is not denied, nor is it ignored; but final judgment here is based on effect instead of beauty, on influence instead of appeal to the imagination. (viii)

Brigance's position, which was the orthodoxy of the day, drew a rigid, probably too rigid, a line between rhetoric and poetic. Some time would elapse before the profession

---

* The editorial board consisted of A. Craig Baird, State University of Iowa; Lionel Crocker, Denison University; C.C. Cunningham, Northwestern University; Dallas C. Dickey, Louisiana State University; Louis M. Eich, University of Michigan; Henry L. Ewbank, University of Wisconsin; Frank M. Rarig, University of Minnesota, Grafton P. Tanquary, University of Southern California; Lester Thonssen, College of the City of New York; Herbert A. Wichelns, Cornell University; and W. Hayes Yeager, George Washington University.

in general would come to recognize that poetry might, in fact, be rhetorical, even intentionally rhetorical. After 30 years of existence the speech profession was still trying, at the same time, to distance itself from its parent discipline and yet to use literary criticism as a point of departure in research.

In 1944 Loren Reid of the University of Missouri surveyed progress in criticism to that time and he outlined problems facing the critic in "The Perils of Rhetorical Criticism." Reid cited the Winans festschrift of 1925, the publication of *A History and Criticism of American Public Address of 1943* and The Dickey, Baird and Aly essays of the same year. By 1944 more than fifty doctorates had been awarded by eight universities.**

Reid began his article by stipulating what rhetorical criticism was not. The standards, although negatively stated, were helpful in distinguishing what the rhetorical critic did as compared to other scholars.

> 1. ***Rhetorical criticism is not simply a discussion of the speaker's ideas****. . . . Although the reader needs to know what the speaker said, he really seeks a critical judgment about the ideas of the speech. The critic should study not alone the result of invention, but the inventive process. . . .*

> 2. ***Rhetorical criticism is not simply a narrative of the circumstances under which a speech is delivered****. . . . This kind of setting in which to place a speech might better be conceived of as "rhetorical" rather than an "historical" background. . . .Why was Churchill invited to speak? What was his prestige at the time? What information did he have about the American national temper?. . .*

> 3. ***Rhetorical criticism is not simply a classification or tabulation of rhetorical devices.***

> 4. ***Rhetorical criticism is not primarily an excursion into other fields of learning****. . . . The critic is easily tempted to abandon criticism and instead to produce treatises upon, politics, religion, historical movements, military strategy and what not. . . . It is easy to move from rhetoric into another field. (417-418)*

Reid's cautions were anchored in a historical orientation toward criticism, but he had moved criticism from its status as a branch of history, which earlier writers had described. He was also careful to warn that rhetorical criticism had its own work to do and that it must avoid giving greater emphasis to related matters than to rhetoric. As Hunt and others had warned earlier, the rhetorician had to be a first rate rhetorician and not a second rate something else. Reid pointed to the strong possibility that the critic might produce ". . . something that is not criticism at all"(418).

When it came to choosing a speaker to study, Reid advised the critic to choose an eminent speaker and one, "safely dead and buried."

> *Conservative scholarly opinion generally supports the advice to pick a big man. The sources of material about him are richer. . . . Conservative scholarly opinion also advises that the big man be safely dead and buried, the principal reason being the prime necessity of critical perspective. . . . Recently some dwellers in the lunatic fringe have begun to question the scholarly prohibition upon contemporary speakers. . . (419)*

Reid certainly used the right term—"conservative"—in describing choices available to scholars. His insistence on restricting rhetorical criticism to the study of great dead orators undoubtedly restricted the scope of investigation and may well have given

---

** ** The eight universities were Columbia, Cornell, Iowa, Louisiana State, Michigan, Northwestern, Southern California and Wisconsin. (Six of these institutions continue to offer a Ph.D.; Cornell and Columbia have eliminated their doctoral programs.) The number of graduate programs has, of course increased dramatically since 1938. Because the field is now so so diffuse, it is difficult to derive a specific number.

rhetoric the appearance of stultification. To be fair to Reid, we must recognize that he did suggest that critics should, "Study the everyday speaking of some region."

By 1944 Reid was able to raise some questions about the absolute validity and applicability of Aristotelian categories, although he did not suggest alternative categories.

> *Aristotelian rhetoric cannot be made to cover every aspect of all types of speaking. Some modern treatises are more helpful. . . . As these developments lead the critic away from Aristotle at many points, it is folly to think that the Rhetoric is the only book on the shelf. (421)*

The centrality of effect in criticism was continued in Reid's essay. "Eventually the critic makes a judgment about the effectiveness of a speech" (420). In the conclusion of his essay, Reid portrayed rhetorical criticism as a demanding enterprise.

> *The critic must know what is commonly called rhetoric, but to know rhetoric is not enough. He must know historical methods, but to know historical methods is not enough. He must have infinite patience in search for details,. . . . He must have the imagination to recreate moments long past in time. And he must take to heart his primary and inescapable responsibility as a critic; to interpret, to appraise, to evaluate. (422)*

During the late 1930s and 40s the number of rhetorical criticisms, published in the association's journals, grew somewhat. Almost all of the articles were historically based, and Aristotelian in their analysis. With a few exceptions, the articles were single orator studies. Among the exceptions were two articles published in 1937 which appeared to be preliminary studies for their essays in *A History and Criticism of American Public Address*. George V. Bohman of Dartmouth's "Political Oratory in Pre-Revolutionary America," Bohman (243-251), and "Pioneer Women Orators of America," by Doris G. Yoakam of Northern Illinois State Teachers College (251-259). Other departures were Lois Buswell's "Oratory Of the Dakota Indians" (323-327), "The Speech of the Frontier" (Dale 353-363) and "Congressional Debating" (Fitzpatrick, 251-255). In spite of the breadth of their subjects, these essays were brief and quite superficial. Among the orators who were the subjects of criticism were: Abraham Lincoln (Wiley, 1934, 1-15; 1935, 305-322; 1938 615-621), Edmund Burke (Bryant, 1934, 241-254), John C. Calhoun (Oliver, 1936, 413-429), Samuel Gompers (Hayworth, 578-584), Daniel Webster (Oliver, 1937, 13-32), Henry Clay (Oliver, 1937, 409-426), Franklin D. Roosevelt (King, 439-444), Charles James Fox (Reid, 1938, 17-26), Stephen A. Douglas (Anderson, 75-93) and Phillip Brooks (Hochmuth, 227-236). In 1938 Hugo Hellman of Marquette University and Brigance published brief historically evaluative articles under the titles: "The Greatest American Oratory" (Hellman, 1938, 36-39) and "The Twenty Eight Foremost American Orators" (Brigance, 1938, 376-380).

CONCLUSION

Rhetorical criticism in the early years of the profession was not a topic of consuming interest. The number of articles which offered critiques of rhetoricians, and those which discussed theories or methodologies of criticism were very small compared to more popular subjects such as public speaking, debate, theater, oral interpretation and voice culture. Rhetorical criticism did not have the same kind of applicability as other topics. The new profession was, after all, a profession of practitioners seeking practical answers to practical questions.

The influence of English, the parent discipline, was apparent in the earliest work in rhetorical criticism. Many of those studies were really analyses of oral style based on criteria of literary scholars. At the same time, some emerging scholarship sought to define what rhetoric and rhetorical criticism were. Understandably, the definitions, initially, were drawn as distinctions from literature. If public speaking was to have a legitimate field of research, it had to create some distance between itself and English.

Essays by Hudson and Wichelns, to this day, stand as landmarks in the history of criticism. The work of these two Cornellians established principles of criticism which were to endure for more than two generations and which were later to be attacked by a new group of critics. The differentiation between literature and rhetoric was based on what scholars saw as the contrasting character of the two fields. Rhetoric, they argued, dealt with the immediate rhetorical situation; a particular audience, in a particular place, at a particular time. Rhetoric, they said, was not primarily concerned with permanence or beauty; it was concerned with effect. Rhetoric was also construed as entirely oral. All of these characteristics imposed restraints on rhetorical criticism and narrowed its scope.

In the 1930s and 40s rhetorical criticism underwent a change in its orientation. Beginning with Brigance's work in 1933, and Hunt's in 1935, rhetorical critics began to see the closest analog to their research, not in literature but in history, although Hunt did draw a parallel with the disagreement in literature concerning literary criticism and literary history. So strong was the historical emphasis that scholars were urged to become proficient in historical methodology.

Almost all of the published rhetorical criticism in this period was more or less Aristotelian in its analysis of rhetoric. The typical criticism offered a description of the historical setting, a biographical sketch, the application of Aristotle's and Cicero's proofs and canons to the discourse under study. For the most part, rhetorical criticism dealt with the "great, dead orator." Few studies seemed interested in social or political movements or in the rhetoric of less than prominent persons.

By 1945 articles on rhetorical criticism, although they were far from the most frequently published, had attained the highest scholarly status in the profession. Two important collections of essays had been published and the rhetorical critics were regarded as the intellectual leaders of the profession. Nonetheless, rhetorical criticism had developed through dependence on two sister disciplines—History and English, which provided the necessary analytical mechanisms.

8

RHETORICAL THEORY

The interest in rhetorical theory among the members of the new profession was, in the early years, greater than in rhetorical criticism. Although we have no definitive explanation for this emphasis, we may speculate about the reasons. As we mentioned earlier, the public speaking teachers of the early twentieth century were mostly products of nineteenth century classical educations in which they had been exposed at least to some Latin and Greek and perhaps had some familiarity with the classical rhetorical writers. Also, since almost all the early contributions to rhetorical theory were historical, the task the theorists faced was not as formidable as that of the critics. It was easier to summarize Greek and Roman texts than to determine how one went about criticizing a rhetorical text. The early writers were, in no sense, creating rhetorical theories; they were going back to the ancients and presenting classical rhetorical theories to the public speaking world. Now and then, as their rhetorical knowledge expanded, the early writers on theory ventured outside the confines of classical rhetoric to explore texts of later periods. Initially most of the attention of the writers was devoted to Greek rhetoric, although as we have noted, one of the earliest articles, by Rosseau, dealt in part with Cicero.

Oddly, the first work on ancient writers by Bromley Smith of Bucknell University dealt neither with Plato nor Aristotle but with Protagoras. (Smith would make a minor career of examining works of lesser known Greek writers.) In "The Father of Debate: Protagoras of Abdera," Smith undertook a twenty page treatment of Protagoras. In explicating Protagoras as rhetorician he drew not only on Protagoras' own work but on Plato's *Protagoras* and on Aristophanes' satiric references to him and to Socrates in *The Clouds*.

Smith argued that Protagoras was the forerunner of later Greek and Roman writers, and that many of the ideas in their works had earlier been anticipated by Protagoras. Smith claims, by citing Diogenes Laertes, that Protagoras was the first rhetorician to deal with topics, and, as the title stated, with debate.

> No mean speaker himself, Protagoras was primarily a teacher of the art of speaking. When Diogenes Laertes says he was the first person who employed regular discussions on set subjects, he referred to what the ancients called topics or commonplaces. . . . Again, when Diogenes says that Protagoras was the first who instituted contests of argument, he referred to the practice of debate on questions akin to to those met in real life or possibly in imaginary questions. (1918, 198)

Smith defended Protagoras against the attack by Socrates in Plato's *Protagoras*, and he claimed that Protagoras, through his instruction in speech, produced exemplary citizens.

> *While he was with his pupils, he, like all good teachers, trained not only their minds but their characters. . . . He professed also "to make men good citizens." (Plato, Prot, 319). To make men good for home and state is certainly a high ideal, no matter what opinion the Platonic Socrates might have of it. In preparing the future citizens he drew pabulum from the fields of philosophy and religion, philology and gymnastics, ethics, economics and politics. When the young orators had absorbed the information which he poured out, they were then trained to arrange their thoughts and deliver them aloud. (1918, 199)*

The bulk of Smith's essay was devoted to defending Protagoras and other Sophists against the charge of immorality because of their advocacy that the rhetor must be able to argue both sides of a case. The Sophists were accused of "making the worse appear to be the better cause." After surveying the writings of Greek and Roman writers on the matter, Smith concluded that, under no conditions, did Protagoras support the defense of evil.

> *Even Plato who was scathing in his denunciation of sophists and rhetoric always represents Protagoras as choosing the higher standard of ethics. (Protagoras as a whole) Obviously, then he who would teach his pupils to become good citizens would not encourage them to defend bad causes, though he might direct them to support weak causes. The deeper one goes into the argument for developing both sides of a question the more convinced he will become that justice may be obtained only by a full hearing. (1918, 209)*

Perhaps the best known of Protagoras' statements is that "Man is the measure of all things." Smith recognized that such a remark caused Protagoras to be accused of agnosticism, if not atheism. Smith, however, saw the statement as supportive of Protagoras' pedagogical aims in teaching public speaking.

> *Looking at the saying, however, in another light we can see merely the pedagogical principle of a teacher of speaking. He would certainly say to his pupils that an orator employs this maxim when he attempts to persuade an audience. The orator must believe in a case: what is true to him is true: what is good to him is good. He may err, but he acts on the norm that individual opinion is of the highest moral worth. (1918, 214)*

Smith's Protagorean essay was the first in a parade of articles on Greek and Roman subjects which would appear in the next decade. We have no way of knowing what the reaction of readers might have been to Smith's explication of ancient texts. In 1918 it stood in marked contrast to the applied articles which were the norm in *The Quarterly Journal*. Certainly, at this early point in history, Smith's easy erudition and his facile command of Greek and Latin were impressive. After Smith's essay Protagoras was ignored by the profession for years. We should note that as time went on fewer and fewer authors showed Smith's mastery of classical languages and texts. Increasingly the articles were based on English translations, rather than the original texts.

Smith made his second contribution to the history of Greek rhetoric in 1920 with his article "Prodicus of Ceos: the Sire of Synonymy." This time he dealt with an ancient rhetorician who must have been truly unknown to many of the readers of *The Quarterly Journal*. Prodicus (464-399 B.C.) was a teacher of rhetoric who was mentioned by Plato in the Protagoras. Prodicus' most important contribution to the history of rhetoric was his emphasis on the precise meaning of words. He also gives credit to Prodicus for his ". . . attempt to develop good morality in the pupils" (Smith, 1920, 63).

Everett Hunt, also in 1920, published the first article dealing with the dialogues of Plato. We do not know how proficient Hunt was in Greek and Latin. We do know, however, that his Platonic explication relied entirely on translations. Present day undergraduates in a rhetorical theory course might find Hunt's treatise on the *Phaedrus* useful. It offered an adequate and well written summary of the dialogues. Hunt, made the point, which was repeated in later writings in the profession that Aristotle's *Rhetoric* was actually an expansion of the *Phaedrus*, regardless of Plato's views toward rhetoric as expressed in other dialogues.

> *The references of his [Aristotle's] master Plato to rhetoric and rhetoricians are, for the most part, so contemptuous that it would not seem to have been a Platonic stimulus which produced the Rhetoric. But in the Phaedrus, while he keeps his earlier attitude toward the existing rhetoric, he does admit that there might be a genuine and useful rhetorical art, and he goes so far as to throw out suggestions which appear as fully developed ideas in Aristotle's Rhetoric. . . The three books of Aristotle's Rhetoric are virtually an expanded Phaedrus. He accepts the view that the speaker must first acquaint himself with human nature and he agrees with Plato in condemning as unscientific the Arts of Rhetoric which were so numerous at this time. (1920, 33, 39)*

In addition to his discussion of the *Phaedrus*, Hunt undertook a description not only of the *Phaedrus* and other dialogues but of the political and social scene in Athens and of the status of rhetoric in the city state. Looking at the totality of Plato's work, said Hunt, we must conclude that Plato's influence on rhetoric was far more deleterious than beneficial.

> *Plato in his earlier years despised both rhetoric and rhetoricians. . . . Later he came to see some possibility in rhetoric, and he outlined a theory of it in the Phaedrus. . . . As a standard for judging his contemporaries it is clear that its use results in a very unfair account. . . . His account of the rhetoricians is prejudiced by several other factors. Plato was not a typical Greek in politics or religion. He had little sympathy with the Athenian state and judged nothing in it by its own standards. The unfavorable connotation of the terms sophist and rhetorician as applied to his contemporaries is largely due to the literary power with which he expressed his prejudices. For a complete understanding of the Greek study of and love for rhetoric, we must seek other sources. (1920, 53)*

Hunt's essay on Plato was very much in the spirit of humanism which he had expressed in earlier articles. It was gracefully written and demonstrated that he had read and understood the Platonic dialogues, at least in translation. Undoubtedly members of the profession learned from his exploration of Plato. Hunt's work could hardly be considered original scholarship since his arguments were almost entirely derived from or supported by secondary sources. Considering the state of research in 1920, however, Hunt's work was superior to almost all the previous articles in *The Quarterly Journal*.

Bromley Smith presented his third lesson in the history of Greek rhetoric in 1921 when he published "Corax and Probability." Although the names of Corax and Tisias were often mentioned together as founders of the art of rhetoric, as they are to this day, Smith made it clear that Corax was the authentic founder since Tisias was his pupil. Since almost none of Corax's work was extant, Smith had to gather the information available from Greeks and Romans who knew of his writings. On that basis, Smith was able, through his inferences, to describe the contributions of Corax. Smith claimed that Corax was the first to defined rhetoric as "the art of persuasion." Smith asserted that "the definition indicates that at a very early date men had discovered the value of pleasant, agreeable, delightful Speech" (1921, 18). Corax's second contribution was that he ". . . named the parts of discourse," although there was some dispute about the names of the parts and exactly how many parts there were. The most important contribution of Corax, however, was his conception of rhetorical probability.

> . . . it may be seen that the Sicilian had given to speakers and writers of all ages a permanent principle, a practical method of handling the affairs of life. It was nothing new to any man, for he had used it every day, but Corax had the honor to be the first to set it down in a book. . . . Corax then was only applying common sense when he wrote about probability. He knew that when men were at loggerheads absolute truth could seldom be found; but that probability of cases decided the issue. (1921, 23, 25)

In his essay in which the subject, ostensibly, was Corax, Smith went well beyond the title to write a short history of the conception of probability. Among the philosophers whose writings he examined were: Locke, Cicero, Diogenes, Sextus Empiricus, Pascal, Hume and Voltaire. He also cited Shakespeare and Blackstone. At the conclusion of his essay Smith lamented that probability had been neglected by rhetoricians.

> Having now reached the end of our tether it would not be out of place to tie the frayed ends of this discussion. In what way could this better be done than by uniting Corax' definition of rhetoric to his principle of probability? Rhetoric is the art of persuasion. Persuasion to be attained by presenting matter with such a likeliness to truth that it will be accepted and if necessary acted upon. Could any pedagogical principle be sounder? Yet strangely enough the principle has well nigh been forgotten. No modern texts on rhetoric mention it,. . . . Primarily they seem to agree that persuasion is largely emotional. Likewise they agree that conviction deals with the understanding. Rules are given to hammer these wedges into the mind. Yet the greatest rhetorical principle which might act as a sledge is hardly mentioned. The writers on rhetoric have apparently forgotten Corax' probability. (1921, 41-42)

Smith's dense exploration of Corax and probability might have been somewhat difficult for some of the members of the association to follow; but for those who stayed with his thirty page disquisition, there was much to be learned; not only about Corax but, more importantly, about the centrality of probability to the study of rhetoric. Smith might well have been an exemplar for other scholars to follow. He not only displayed his mastery of ancient rhetorical texts, he also showed his knowledge of the history of philosophy and connected the work of philosophers to rhetoric through their concern with probability. In time other writers would also explore some of the relationships with Philosophy.

The February 1921 *Quarterly Journal* reported the appointment of the Research Committee at the 1920 convention. It is interesting to note that among its fourteen members Hunt was responsible for Classical Rhetoric; none of the other appointees had any concern with rhetorical theory or rhetorical criticism. An indication of the association's apparent relative lack of interest in rhetoric was shown by the appointment of separate persons to represent "Voice Science," "Speech Disorders" and "Applied Phonetics" as well as separate representatives for "Community Theatre"and "Theory of Play Production" (The Research Committee, 1921, 78-79). When the Research Committee submitted its report later that year neither rhetorical theory nor rhetorical criticism were included among their divisions of the discipline, which were:

1. *Speech Correction*
2. *Theory of Expression*
3. *Speech Composition*
4. *History of Oratory*
5. *Dialects*
6. *Reading and Dramatic Production*
7. *Methods (Merry, 1921, 103-104.)*

In 1921 E.L. Hunt was given five pages in which to review Dobson's *The Greek Orators*. With that amount of space available to him Hunt could treat matters not directly germane to the review of Dobson's book. By this time Hunt was not yet ready to relent in his battle with science and his defense of rhetoric as a humanistic study.

> *The scientific spirit has been accused of destroying values. It esteems everything on the earth, under the earth, and in the heavens above as worthy of study. . . . For this the classicists have condemned it. The classicists would be selective. Their theory of values is embodied in their curriculum, in what they present to us as that knowledge which is of most worth. (1921, 181)*

Hunt acknowledged a deficiency among rhetorical scholars—their ignorance of the classical languages, a deficiency which has continued to the present.

> *We can comprehend the scorn of the classicists when they condemn our dependence upon translations. Perhaps we should remain in outer darkness until our Greek is perfected. But we have the evolutionary fever. We want to understand the origin and development of public address. (1921, 182)*

Hunt's acknowledgment could be interpreted as a rationalization. If "we want to understand the origin and development of public address," why didn't we become as adept at Greek and Latin as the classicists? The "evolutionary fever" of which Hunt spoke hardly evolved since the articles on classical rhetoric published in speech journals almost always relied on translations for decades to come. The profession has produced few Bromley Smiths, Otto Dieters or James J. Murphys.

The continuing dispute between rhetoric and philosophy was recognized by Hunt and he thought it should be of particular interest to the profession for its present use.

> *In the relations of these teachers to each other, in their methods of training, in the quarrels between rhetoric and philosophy we may find analogies for practically every question that concerns departments of public speaking today. . . . A thorough study of this ancient feud between philosophy and rhetoric will throw much light on the present academic status of public speaking. (1921, 183)*

In contrast to the views of scientists such as Woolbert, Hunt advocated a continuation of the ancient connection between public speaking and rhetoric. Not for him the evolution of "truths'" and "laws" about public speaking. Hunt regretted that the profession failed to recognize the connection as he did.

> *Our use of the term rhetoric has been narrowed in modern education. How narrow it is may be made clear by the realization that practically the whole movement in the teaching of public speaking is unassociated with it. But the common elements in the present trends in English Composition and Public Speaking*

*point to a restoration of the classical conception of rhetoric. . . Our resources will be
infinitely broader than those of the classical rhetorician, but their statement of the
problem is still valid. And if from them we can learn to see our problems clearly, we
may hope to solve them more intelligently. (184-185)*

Hunt's allegiance to the humanities and the classics caused him to present a view
of rhetoric which was firmly anchored in Classical Rhetorical Theory. Although he did
not change his basic orientation, he did, over time, modify his position. His 1935
contribution to the "Forum" on criticism showed an awareness of the value of the
application of modern literary theories to rhetoric. In any case, Hunt and others, in
their search for theories of rhetoric, settled on the doctrines of the ancients and
continued for some time to use them as the basic sources for the discipline's conception
of rhetoric.

In the report of the 1921 meeting of the Eastern Public Speaking Conference only
one presentation on rhetoric was mentioned, Hoyt Hudson's "Can We Modernize the
Theory of Invention," which would appear in *The Quarterly Journal* in the next issue.
We do not know how Hudson's presentation was received, but we note the secretary's
minutes in which it is reported that, "It being evident that weariness and not discussion
was in the air, the meeting adjourned at 9:30" (J.D. Jr. 1921, 277).

In his article Hudson did not so much modernize the theory of invention as he
sought to revive the classical conception of invention and to apply it to the rhetorical
world of the 1920s. In developing his argument Hudson took his readers on a quick
tour of the history of the idea of invention with stops at Aristotle, Cicero, Quintilian,
Bacon, Lawson, John Quincy Adams, Henry Seidel Canby and Charles Sears Baldwin.
In all his examples Hudson's stress was on the classical use of topoi. He advocated a
return to to topical invention, especially for pedagogical purposes.

*As to how far we can embody the classical theory of invention in our teaching of
argument and speech-making, that is a question which I am attempting to open
rather than close. If the theory is sound, I suppose whatever we have done to
stimulate efficient inventive thinking has been in accord with it. But perhaps more
conscious and scientific applications of it will be possible. Perhaps we can make our
study of speech models more topical and less critical, so that such study will give
more aid than it has to the student constructing speeches of his own; classical
invention should suggest a technique for accomplishing this. (1921, 333)*

The use of topics in invention, wrote Hudson, is by no means confined to rhetoric.
After citing the application of topics in painting, drama and poetry, he wrote:

*I have touched upon these other fields in order to suggest that in rhetorical
invention as practiced in ancient times there was the recognition of a method that is
fundamental to all inventive thinking. (1921, 331-332)*

Hudson's disquisition on invention, like much of the writing in rhetorical theory of
the time, presented very little that was really new. Rather he fashioned a historical
survey and synthesis of classical theories of invention. Since the material was unknown
to most of the profession he did add to their knowledge, if not to knowledge in general.

Bromley Smith added yet another chapter to his history of Greek rhetoric with the
publication of "Gorgias: A Study of Oratorical Style" in 1921. The title of his article was
somewhat misleading since only a small portion dealt with Gorgias' style. The rest was
concerned with Gorgias' rhetorical pedagogy. Smith, in fact, referred to him as "a great
teacher." By an examination of the teaching of rhetoric in Gorgias' time, Smith constructed an analogy with the pedagogy of the early twentieth century.

> . . . *Gorgias aimed at "fine speaking", evepeia, rather than "correct" speaking,"*
> *orthoepeia,. . . . It will be seen from this circumstance that the very early in the*
> *history of rhetoric a division in method was made, a division which has continued to*
> *this day. On the one hand are the teachers of elocution, so called, who teach*
> *declamation and acting, claiming that these subjects arefundamental, that they lead*
> *to original oratory and debating. . . On the other hand are the teachers of public*
> *speaking, who, avoiding as much as possible declamation, strive to make speakers*
> *through the medium of debates, extemporaneous addresses and original orations.*
> *(1921a, 339).   Smith maintained that Gorgias' epistemology had hitherto*
> *unexplored connections with rhetoric. He spoke of the "few fragments" of Gorgias'*
> *writing that have survived.*

> *What little remains has been amply treated by writers on philosophy; but the*
> *relation of philosophy to rhetoric has somehow been passed over. As his peculiar view*
> *of the stability of human knowledge, set forth in his work "On Nature and*
> *Not-Being," is of importance to every teacher of rhetoric, I will attempt to show its*
> *bearing on argumentation. Gorgias argued 1. That nothing exists. 2. That if*
> *anything really exists , it cannot be known to man. 3. That if he could know it, he*
> *could not communicate the knowledge to others. Examine these principles in reverse*
> *order. We first perceive that communication implies a medium, generally words; but*
> *the same words convey different meanings to different people. . . . Because they did*
> *not know the truth, nor were able to communicate it if they did, the final conclusion*
> *reached by Gorgias was that no truth exists. Wherefore, if no truth exists, nor can be*
> *known, nor can be communicated, every man becomes a law unto himself. By this*
> *circuitous route Gorgias reached the same goal as Protagoras. . . that because "man*
> *was the measure of all things," each man was judge of the truth as it seemed to*
> *him. . . . To live in such a world they, as rhetoricians, taught the art of persuasion,*
> *the basis of which was probability. (1921a, 343-344)*

The work of Smith, together with that of Hudson and Hunt, provided the profession with a starting point for the development of rhetorical theories. The knowledge of classical sources by these scholars made for an important contribution. In time other authors and other periods would be integrated in the study of rhetorical theory, but the theorists tended to be used derivatively rather than integratively.

Smith's article on Gorgias may tell us something indirectly about the readers of *The Quarterly Journal*. In contrast to his earlier contributions, this time Smith did not use Greek script in his citations; instead he transliterated them into Latin script, perhaps so that his readers could read, if not understand them.

In the same year in which this small rhetorical flurry occurred, President Alexander Drummond of the National Association sent a questionnaire to the membership ". . . seeking information as to what topics members of the Association would like to see discussed in *The Quarterly Journal* and the meetings of the National Association" (Drummond, 1921, 389-390). Sixty one topics were suggested for discussion at association meetings and 58 for publication in the journal. Of the 119 suggested topics not a single topic was remotely connected to rhetoric. We can safely conclude that, in spite of the work of Smith and his compatriots, rhetoric was not yet a high demand subject among the members of the association.

A more general approach to the history of Greek rhetoric was undertaken in 1922 by Paul Shorey of the University of Chicago in his article "What Teachers of Speech May Learn From the Theory and Practice of the Greeks." More than half of Shorey's essay was devoted to a rapid survey of the history of Greek oratory, after which he turned to the theory and pedagogy of Athenian rhetoric. Shorey, a Professor of Classics at Chicago and the author of five books about ancient Athens, was slightly patronizing in his article—actually a paper originally presented at the 1921 convention of the National Association of Teachers of Speech.

Shorey began his discussion with the intermittent relationship between rhetoric and philosophy, and he concentrated his attention initially on the Platonic dialogues.

> Throughout these centuries the higher education, the high-school and education so to speak, of the Greek or Roman gentleman centered in the study either of rhetoric or of philosophy, or, more rarely, of both in combination. The link between these two competing systems of education was the treatment of the theory of rhetoric by the philosophers.This began with Plato, or with the sophists whom Plato satirized. Platos's dialogues on rhetoric, the Gorgias and Phaedrus, either as wholes or in extracts, were always read or lectured on in the rhetorical as well as the philosophic schools. (1922, 115-116)

Shorey must have perceived his audience to be relatively ignorant about Greek rhetoric, or perhaps they really were ignorant. He presented a characterization of the Gorgias which most present day undergraduate students of rhetoric would already have mastered.

> The Gorgias is a bitter assault upon the rhetoric of the politician, the lawyer, and the professional teacher from the point of view of the absolute, philosophical, and ethical ideal. Gorgias accepts the definition of rhetoric as the art of persuasion,. . . Socrates denies that rhetoric is an art or science at all. It is only a trick of flattery, ... The persuasion that it effects, is opinion not knowledge. . . . The questions thus started were debated throughout antiquity and are still, under other forms, discussed today. (1922, 116)

Shorey saw implications from the ancient debate for the teaching of rhetoric in his own time.

> . . . Our own teaching of rhetoric is too much concerned with the success of the speaker and too little with the edification of the audience. It is more interested in the "psychology" of "putting it over" and "getting it across" than in the training in the habits of logical analysis and suspense of judgment that would enable an audience to resist such hypnotization. Yet the greatest service which high school and college education could render to America would be, not to multiply the number of fluent, plausible, and self-confident speakers but to create in every audience a resisting minority that cannot be stampeded by plausible sophistry and emotional volubility. (1922, 116-117)

One wonders now if Shorey's listeners and readers recognized how patronizing and critical he was of their own discipline which, at least inferentially, he depicted as an enterprise much closer to Sophistry than to Platonism. Apparently he regarded the rhetorical instruction of the 1920s as pedagogy which emphasized fluency at the expense of knowledge, and he was convinced that the education of the listener was more important than the training of the rhetor.

In his treatment of the Phaedrus, Shorey seemed unconvinced of Plato's complete sincerity when he specified his ideal rhetoric.

> But he himself [Plato], somewhat scornfully, outlines a program for a rhetoric of the future which if based on psychology and dialectic might be an art or science. Such a rhetoric would analyze and classify ideas, on the one hand, and types of mind

and temperament on the other. It would proceed; such and such a mind is accessible and easily persuaded by such and such arguments for such and such reasons. That would be a teachable theory and science of rhetoric. (1922 116-117)

Shorey only partially accepted the idea enunciated by Hunt and others that Aristotle's *Rhetoric* was an expansion of Plato's *Phaedrus*. Rather he saw the work as being somewhat ambivalent in its reliance on Plato.

Though Aristotle rarely neglects an opportunity to contradict his old teacher, he evidently wrote with a card-catalogue of Plato's notable passages on his desk. The main body of the Rhetoric, *the first two books, is a working out of Plato's idea that if rhetoric is to be more than a rule of thumb it must be a combination of logic and ethical psychology. (1922, 118)*

Shorey believed that Aristotle's system of classification of topics, proofs and rhetorical types was his most important contribution. In making his point Shorey was again condescending to his readers.

Observing for twenty or thirty years the philosophic, the forensic, the political debates of fourth-century Athens, Aristotle could not be happy till he had reduced this immense chaotic experience to order and found a fit pigeon-hole and label for every type of argument and oratorical device that he had collected. . . Even to understand his classification requires close attention and some historical knowledge of Athenian life and politics. . . . Nevertheless, it is the most original and stimulating part of the Rhetoric. (119)

Shorey claimed that the *Rhetoric* ". . . had other sources than Aristotle's card-catalogue of Plato." He also relied on the work of the Sophists and, "The chief influence here, besides Plato, was Isocrates." (1922, 120)

The idea of the connection between Athenian democracy and the flourishing of eloquence, which was stated as early as the eighteenth century, most notably by Hume and Blair, was restated by Shorey. By now, the idea should not have been totally new to the readers of *The Quarterly Journal* since it had been touched on previously by Hunt. Shorey, however, extended the thesis to Rome and modern states.

True political eloquence is the child of liberty, as the history of British, American, French, and German oratory would suffice to show. It can flourish only where the votes of parliaments and people determine the destinies of states. After the death of Cicero Greek and Roman critics both recognized this truth, which the Greeks could not have been expected clearly to forsee at the death of Demosthenes. (1922, 122)

In spite of the title which Shorey gave to his essay, he did not confine his interest to the Greeks. He also, at somewhat lesser length, discussed Roman rhetoric as well. Presumably Shorey included the Roman rhetoricians whom he regarded as lineal descendants of the Greeks since they had acquired much of their rhetorical knowledge from Athens. Not surprisingly, most of his attention was given to Cicero. He assigned to Cicero the role of bearer of culture to the modern world through his philosophical and rhetorical works.

Nonetheless Cicero remains, in Matthew Arnold's words, the first man of letters of the ancient world, or to phrase it more ambitiously, he is the central figure in the history of European culture. In addition to all his original achievements in oratory and statesmanship, it is he who mainly transmitted to the Middle Ages, the Renascence, and the Eighteenth Century the knowledge of what constituted

> *Graeco-Roman culture for 1000 years—the philosophy in his philosophical works, the rhetoric in his De Oratore, his Brutus, or history of Roman oratory, his Orator, or ideal of the perfect orator. . . The De Oratore is the best of these compositions. For here Cicero can speak out of a richer personal experience than any Greek theorist. (1922, 128-129.)*

To Shorey, Cicero seemed more important as a figure in Greek rhetoric than the Greeks themselves.

> *. . . There can be no doubt that Cicero had a life-long familiarity with the principles of Greek rhetorical theory. . . . Cicero contrives to insinuate a sensible and readable account of the main body of Greek rhetorical doctrine in which the technicalities are rapidly and sometimes contemptuously summarized while the interesting ideas or practically helpful suggestions are brought into the foreground. (1922, 129)*

Shorey's praise of Cicero was certainly merited; at the same time, however, he perceived that Cicero, as well as Quintilian, was not so much an original thinker as a synthesizer, interpreter and transmitter of Greek rhetorical culture. Since there were significant political, social, as well as rhetorical differences between Aristotle's Athens and Cicero's Rome, one may ask whether Shorey followed his own admonition that readers of rhetorical theory needed, ". . . some historical knowledge." Certainly, in Shorey's time, as well as our own, many scholars felt that Cicero made substantial contributions to rhetoric which were more than mere syntheses and derivations from Greek theory.

Finally Shorey asked whether his discussion has made any contribution to the teaching of speech. His reply was ambivalent.

> *But have I answered the question, what is there in it for you as students and practical teachers of the "art of speech"?. . . Somewhere in this vast body of ancient rhetorical literature you will find at least a hint of every useful idea that that modern study of the subject has suggested. . . . It is not easy in the present temper of the world to prove to anybody who is not already convinced, the necessity of the value of anything that used to be called culture, of any knowledge of the past, or for that matter of any study of theory, except perhaps engineering. And animal spirits, vivacity, fluency, magnetism and a good voice will make a very effective popular orator of a man who has never heard a philosopher or opened a book of rhetoric and literary criticism. (130)*

One does not know whether Shorey's audience should have been pleased by his answer. At best he appeared to regard speech as a practical application of ancient rhetorical theory. At the same time he remained convinced that Sophistry rather than Platonism was characteristic of the rhetoric of his time.

Shorey's remarks seemed to signify that "The world changeth not." His statements of despair about the lack of culture in "the present temper of the world" and the emphasis on "practical knowledge" in the l920s could have been uttered in our own time. His opposition to modernism was not much different from remarks sometimes made in the l990s, if one disregards the "flappers." "I should feel baffled and helpless in face of the uncompromising and implacable modernism that cares for only those things whereof the memory of a flapper runneth not to the contrary" (1922, 131).

In a 1923 article titled "Speech," Winans referred to an exchange of correspondence with Shorey, as a consequence of Shorey's presentation. He sought Shorey's advice concerning the name of the profession.

A good deal was made at the Chicago meeting referred to of the fact that Dr. Paul Shorey, in a paper immediately preceding mine, used the term speech several times. It seemed to me that Dr. Shorey did no more than adopt courteously the word of his hosts. I noted that once he used the word speech, hesitated as if not satisfied, and then added "and rhetoric." But since the opinion of this distinguished language scholar seemed important, I ventured to write Dr. Shorey putting the situation in which we find ourselves, with our varied interests, as fairly as I could . . . . He replied, "Your own letter seems to cover the grounds of your questions completely, but since you desire my opinion I will give it. My first impression was that the title 'Professor of Speech' or 'Department of Speech' was both a little ambiguous and little quaint. And I think I intended quotation marks in my voice as I used it." (1923, 228)

The extended course in the history of Greek rhetorical theory was continued in 1922 by Russell H. Wagner of Davidson College when he published "The Rhetorical Theory of Isocrates." Wagner, interestingly, began his discussion of Isocrates by acknowledging Isocrates' defects, which were remedied by Aristotle, but, at the same time, detecting Isocrates' influence on Aristotle.

Undoubtedly the lack of a definitely stated theory in Isocrates' school provoked the writing of the Rhetoric *by Aristotle. The failure of Isocrates to consider "invention" gave rise to the first and second books; but the third . . . adopted a very conciliatory attitude toward Isocrates and followed his theories closely. (1922, 324)*

Wagner also contrasted the point of view of Isocrates with that of Plato, without, however, an explanation of the conflict between Socrates and the Sophists, or of the reasons for Plato's disapproval of rhetoric and its connection to democracy.

The two ideals of Plato and Isocrates were of course diametrically opposite. Political science and rhetoric were considered almost one and the same by Isocrates; an antecedent for oratory by Plato. (1922, 325)

Considering how uninformed the members of the profession were, we might wonder how much of Wagner's description was understood. After the Plato-Isocrates comparison Wagner devoted little space to an exploration of Isocrates' rhetorical theory, in spite of the implications of the title of the essay. For the balance of the article he wrote about the curriculum of the school of Isocrates, his theories of education, and his influence on Cicero.

Wagner, by now at Iowa State College, continued to introduce members of the new profession to the ancient rhetoricians. In 1925, in *The Quarterly Journal of Speech Education*, he shifted his focus from Greece to Rome. In his essay " A Rhetorician's Son: His Advice to Public Speakers" he devoted his attention to an explication of the work of Lucius Annaeus Seneca, in Wagner's words, the son of "of a celebrated rhetor" Seneca the Elder. As Wagner himself conceded, Seneca the Elder

. . . ."was, in fact, not a teacher of rhetoric, but an oratorical enthusiast. He attended all exhibitions of oratory, at the bar and the forum. . . The elder Seneca, in fact is chiefly renowned for his 'Controversiae' and 'Suasoriae'—declamations and orations delivered in the rhetorical schools of the times. These prefaced by remarks on Roman oratory, were for centuries, texts in Roman and Medieval schools. . . " (207)

Seneca the Younger was, of course, a distinguished Roman essayist and tragedian.

Wagner derived a kind of rhetorical theory for Seneca by extracting relevant portions from his essays and epistles. But, so far as Wagner was concerned, Seneca never indicated any indebtedness to his rhetor father. Wagner praised Seneca's work for its relevance to the twentieth century.

> *The comments of one as wise and clear-sighted as Seneca may prove admirable texts for today. Here is a virgin source of classical rhetoric, an unbiased yet thoroughly equipped authority; here is counsel especially suited to our day because the advice is not for the professional speaker, but for him who will need public speaking in his chosen pursuit or in the performance of his duties as a citizen for such students as we have in our classes today. (1925, 209)*

The presentation of Seneca's scattered ideas hardly constituted a systematic rhetorical theory, but Wagner did present a reasonably coherent picture of the more important rhetorically relevant points in Seneca's writings. Seneca was, in fact, somewhat distrustful of eloquence. Wagner was correct when he stated that, "In the unending battle between rhetoric and philosophy, Seneca resolutely ranged himself besides the latter's purple banner" (1925, 209). He cited statements by Seneca, in support of philosophy, such as the following from Epistle XIV and XX:

> *One must therefore take refuge in philosophy;. . . For speech-making at the bar, or any other pursuit that claims the people's attention, wins enemies for a man; but philosophy is peaceful and minds her own business. . . . Far different is the purpose of those who are speech-making and trying to win the approbation of a throng of hearers, far different than that of those who allure the ears of young men and idlers by many sided or fluent argumentation; philosophy teaches to act, not to speak; it exacts of every man that he should live according to his own standards,. . . . This, I say, is the highest duty and the highest proof of wisdom that deed and word should be in accord. (1925, 209)*

Wagner, consciously or not, continued to illustrate Seneca's stance which was, at least, skeptical of the rhetorical practices of his own time. He was clear that ideas were more important than "mere words"; that conversation was more beneficial than lectures; that the delivery of "Speech that dealt with the truth should be unadorned and plain." In contrast to these views, Wagner explained that Seneca extolled the power of emotion over reason and that he approved of the orator's pretending to feel rather than actually feeling emotions (1925, 210-214)

In the conclusion to his essay Wagner correctly depicted Seneca's position and correctly ascribed it, in part, to the lowered rhetorical standards of the time.

> *In appraising the value of Seneca's rhetorical theory, we must not forget that he, like Tacitus, was contemptuous of an art which was in a debased state at the time. The fragmentary and grudging nature of his advice to orators must be interpreted with an eye to the over-emphasis on the exhibitory features of the rhetoric of his day and the absence of the incentives which made public speaking in its best sense all but impossible. (1925, 218)*

Yet, though Wagner recognized the "fragmentary and grudging nature" of Seneca's contribution, he nevertheless ended by asserting his value to the speakers and teachers of 1925.

> *Seneca, the rhetorician's son, even though he casts but a side long glance at his father's art, has a fresh and vivid message to the teacher and the speaker of today. (1925, 218)*

It is difficult for the reader of the 1990s to understand how Wagner came to his conclusion that Seneca's message was "fresh and vivid" for speakers and teachers, unless he wanted them to understand the dangers of rhetorical excess. One is curious as to why Wagner chose the younger Seneca as the subject of his essay when the work of Seneca the Elder was available to him and was more rhetorically significant. But Wagner was not alone in unusual choices; Bromley Smith, among others, had written on fairly obscure figures in the history of rhetoric, such as Prodicus.

The state of the profession's interest in rhetoric was indicated in the report of the 1922 convention of the Association. No meetings concerned with rhetoric were scheduled, although meetings were scheduled for High School, Normal School, College and University, Public speaking, Speech Disorders and Dramatic Reading and Production sections. Rhetoric was not, apparently, seen to be sufficiently significant or distinctive to merit its own section or to be consistently presented on national programs, despite the articles which were beginning to appear in *The Quarterly Journal*. The sole exception to this tendency at the 1923 meeting was a paper presented in the Public Speaking section by Charles Fritz of Otterbein College titled "Research in the History of Oratory: Its Place in a Department of Public Speaking" ("Minutes," 1923, 97-100).

Some interest in classical rhetorical theory was indicated in 1923 when E.L. Hunt was given a total of two and a half pages in which to review Volumes III and IV of the Butler translation of *Quintilian's Institutes* and Ameringer's *A Study in Greek Rhetoric*. In the space allowed him he could no more than devote three paragraphs to each of the works, to note the contents of the Quintilian translation and to recognize the value of Ameringer's study of the influence of Greek rhetorical theory on early Christian preaching (1923, 19-21). An indication that rhetoric had not yet been fully integrated in the discipline was found in a 1923 article by A.M. Drummond of Cornell. In "Graduate Work in Public Speaking," Drummond gave advice to:

> . . . those already in the profession who find themselves unable to work for degrees in our field, even during the summer sessions, but who wish to do something for themselves and the standing of their departments and the profession. Many of these colleagues are located where they may take graduate work in other departments: work which may be as fruitful and sound as any work for a degree in public speaking or speech education—in rhetoric, language, psychology, pedagogy, English literature and criticism, and other related sciences and arts. (1923, 137)

Drummond argued for the basic importance of rhetoric in the curriculum, as advocated at Cornell.

> But we hold to the fundamental training in rhetoric in graduate work and for the present propose that thesis subjects have some relation to rhetorical study. . . . Its [rhetoric's] importance as a repository of training, theory, and experience in developing oral expression is being today reemphasized by such English scholars as Charles Sears Baldwin, and by the great and scholarly English Commission on The Teaching of English in England. Many English departments now sedulously keep the term rhetoric out of their announcements—this at a time when many English scholars and teachers are urging the importance of a return to oral expression, oral composition, and communication. Rhetoric is our traditional field, and at Cornell we consider it one of the best approaches to every phase of our subject. (1923, 145-146)

Drummond's remarks are interesting for more than one reason. Clearly, he articulated, perhaps in a fairly primitive form, the centrality of the study of rhetoric, which would distinguish the "Cornell Tradition" in the coming decades. In addition, he offered a brief insight into what was happening to English departments in the 1920s. In spite of the work of Baldwin (whose most important works, *Ancient Rhetoric* and *Poetic* and *Medieval Rhetoric and Poetic* were published after the appearance of the Drummond essay, (1924, 1928) and others rhetoric by 1923 had begun to be of lesser interest to scholars in English who were concentrating increasing interest in literary criticism, and bringing it to the central position in English studies. Although the new speech profession did not clearly recognize it at the time, the English discipline was no longer as interested in preserving the rhetorical tradition as it had been earlier. (See Chapter 2.)

An opportunity was now at hand for the speech discipline to pick up what English had abandoned. For some decades speech researchers played a central role in the study of rhetoric, although scholars in English, Philosophy and Classics continued to make the most important contributions to the understanding of rhetorical theory. In the 1990s Speech Communication's command of rhetorical studies is no longer so secure as a renaissance of the study of rhetoric in English departments has become increasingly more important.

Drummond's statement was also an indication that the profession remained dependent on and derivative from related disciplines. Drummond, in fact, clearly implied the perceived inferiority of the profession.

> ... *Most of the members of our profession now conducting graduate work do so under the guerdon [reward] of graduate work done and advanced degrees obtained in other departments; that work done in departments of older and more developed organization will be insurance of sound work and will be recognized as such , thus in many cases adding an academic prestige not everywhere granted to our own degrees. ... (1923, 137)*

It was interesting that Drummond, whose scholarly interests were primarily in theatre, chose a classical rhetorical text as the one he would most highly recommend to graduate students.

> *If I had one primary and practical suggestion for these scholars—and indeed for all of our profession—it might be this: that, along with a goodly number of the world's great books, there falls clearly within our field one of the great treatises on education; and I may add that it relates to a comprehensive scheme of education in our subject—and of education in general—all the important academic subjects I have heard discussed in the conventions of this association, and, I fancy, most that will ever be here discussed. This book might well be more thoroughly the basis of all our thinking. It is* Quintilian's Institutio Oratoria the Education of the Orator. *(1923, 138)*

Although Drummond's attachment to Quintilian was, in itself, laudable for its respect for a traditional rhetorical text, it did suggest a rather narrowed perspective. Drummond was willing to give to the Institutes an importance which should probably never be granted to a single text. If a single work was to be chosen, one is curious as to why he selected Quintilian rather than, say, Aristotle's Rhetorica. At this early stage of its development, the profession might well have been unaware of the choices of texts available to them. We, of course, cannot assume Drummond to be typical of the profession. Nevertheless, Drummond's remarks suggest that the field was seeking materials which might guide it to the establishment of genuine academic respectability, and Quintilian may have been as good a source as any.

Drummond provided an appendix to his essay titled, "Some Subjects for Graduate

Study Suggested by Members of the Department of Public Speaking at Cornell University." The appendix was a list of 129 items. A substantial number of the suggested subjects dealt with rhetorical theory, more than in any other category. Many of the subjects were remarkably sophisticated for their time, and many still merit investigation in our own time. Some of the more interesting topics dealing with rhetorical theory were the following:

1. *Formulation of a theory of public discourse as drawn from outstanding essays treatises, and speeches with examples.*

2. *Rhetoric as one of the seven liberal arts—its place in the liberal arts curriculum.*

3. *Contributions to the theory of rhetoric by Roman and Greek minor rhetoricians. . . .*

7. *Treatises on sermon making in the Middle Ages.*

8. *Comparative Study of Quintilian, Cicero and Seneca.*

9. *Rhetoric and logic.*

10. *Rhetoric and dialectic.*

11. *Rhetoric and Probability*

43. *Translation with introduction, comment, and critical notes of such work as: Navarre's* Essai sur la Rhetorique greque avant Aristotle; *Chaignet's* Le Rhetorique et son Histoire; Blass' Attische Beredsamskeit; *Volkman's* Die Rhetorik der Griechen und Romer; *Westerman's* Geschichte der Beredsamskeit in Griechenland und Rom.

96. *Invention in light of theories of psychoanalysis.*

99. *Aristotle and Modern Psychology of the Audience. (1923, 147-151)*

The Cornell faculty also suggested many thesis subjects in rhetorical criticism as well as rhetorical theory. The list is interesting in that a number of the proposed thesis subjects appeared as important contributions to our knowledge of rhetorical theory by Cornell students and faculty. Among the most significant works were William E. Utterback's "Aristotle's Contribution to the Psychology of Argument" (1925, 218-225) and the numerous bibliographies of tractates on preaching compiled by Harry Caplan and Henry King (1949, 243-252; 1950, 161-170; 1950, 296-325; 1954, 1-9; 1954, 235-247; 1955, 1-159 [special issue of *Speech Monographs*]; 1956 [special issue of *Speech Monographs*].

Viewed from the perspective of 70 years the list of proposed subjects appears remarkably prescient. The Cornell faculty appeared to have an understanding of what the field might become, especially of the possibilities of rhetorical studies. One can easily envision from the suggestions that Cornell would, for a number of years, represent the best in rhetorical scholarship. Many of the Cornell proposals are still worthwhile and might yet be undertaken as serious research projects. The Cornell compilation is of an entirely different order of sophistication from the more naive list proposed by the Research Committee in 1915. Perhaps the profession had matured somewhat in eight years.

The emergent importance of rhetoric was shown In an article titled "Speech", by James Winans in 1923. In the essay Winans argued that the term "speech" inadequately described the field. Winans sought to make the case that the time had come for "rhetoric" to be added to "speech." Not only was the title more descriptive than speech, it was also a name which was being abandoned by Departments of English.

> We should then have The National Association of Teachers of Speech and Rhetoric and The Quarterly Journal of Speech and Rhetoric. . . . The title page of The Quarterly would bear something like this: The Quarterly Journal Of Speech And Rhetoric Public Speaking Speech Correction Dramatic Art History of Oratory Voice Training Oral Reading Debate   Phonetics. The proposal is, then, that we add rhetoric to our names. (1923 230)

The Winans statement was, to be sure, important because of its advocacy of the inclusion of rhetoric in official titles. It was also significant because of Winans early recognition that what was formerly "public speaking" was now perceived, at least by one of the leading figures of the profession, as an umbrella discipline for all the oral arts. Oddly, the only specific inclusion of rhetoric in Winan's taxonomy was under the heading of the history of oratory.

Winans then went on to argue that rhetoric was no longer the property of English departments; they were no longer centrally concerned with rhetoric because their attention was now concentrated on literary criticism.

> It will be said of rhetoric that it is used still by some teachers of English. Well, most of them have given it up; chiefly, I am guessing, because they do not think it sufficiently emphasizes their favorite work, literature. They cannot object if we take the word up and restore its original meaning. No one can deny that, whoever else teaches rhetoric, we do teach it, in its ancient and honorable sense, fixed upon by Aristotle, the art of persuasion. Traditionally the word refers primarily to spoken discourse; and in connection with the word speech it should be clear that we are thinking of spoken discourse. (1923, 230)

Winans was concerned, as many rhetoricians are today, with the pejorative meaning sometime given to the term rhetoric, but he felt that the field had nothing for which to apologize.

> It will be said that rhetoric has some bad connotations. No doubt; but we have many other good words, and especially in our field, as elocution and oratory, and as speech will soon have, for it is being taken up by the very people who have made elocution a by-word. That is something we cannot prevent. On the other hand, rhetoric is a word with a long, and on the whole an honorable history. It is associated with such mighty names as Aristotle and Quintilian, to say nothing of notable modern scholars and philosophers. It is our word, a traditional family name. (1923, 230-231)

The Winans statement, which is almost forgotten in professional memory, was significant not only because of its advocacy of the name change; it was important also because it symbolized the increasing prominence of interest in rhetoric in the new profession. The perspective presented by Winans was also indicative of the increasing diversification of the discipline; rhetoric may not have an appropriate title at that time but speech, to Winans at least, did not adequately represent the diversity of the field. The suggested title page of *The Quarterly Journal* indicated how diverse the field had become only nine years after its establishment.

To be sure, the change proposed by Winans never took place. In spite of his professional prominence, the orientation he presented may have been more representative of Cornell, with its strong rhetorical emphasis than of the profession in general.

The problem of nomenclature has been persistent. Had Winans proposal been accepted, the name of the association would have undergone three changes in nine years—from Public Speaking to Speech to Speech and Rhetoric. In spite of further suggestions for change, the term Speech was continued in the titles of the association until 1970 when the Speech Association of America became the Speech Communication Association. Since 1970 numerous attempts have been made to remove Speech from the title in favor of Communication. Further evidence of the emergent importance of rhetorical theory as a field of study was supplied in 1923 by an article written by Herbert Wichelns, then of New York University, on behalf of the Research Committee. The bulk of the article consisted of a list titled "Some Research Papers In Process Or Lately Finished," as reported by members of the committee. Wichelns himself served as chairman of the committee as well as the reporter on "Rhetoric and General Bibliography." In the section titled "Speech Composition: Rhetoric" the following studies in rhetorical theory were reported.

Harry Caplan of Cornell: A Translation of the Rhetorica ad Herrenium.

Everett Hunt of Cornell: Rhetoric and Oratory in Classical Historiography. Dialectic: a Neglected Method of Argument.

Gordon R. Crecraft of Illinois: Three Scottish Rhetoricians of the Eighteenth Century: Kames, Campbell, and Blair.

Gertrude A. Sargent of Illinois: History of "Invention" in Literary Criticism.

Russell Wagner of Cornell: Rhetorical Theory of Isocrates.

Giles Wilkinson Gray of Illinois: Are We Wholly Dependent upon the Ancient Greeks and Romans?

The listing must have been encouraging to students and scholars contemplating studies in rhetorical theory, but they might also have noticed that all of the listed studies were carried out at only two universities—Cornell and Illinois. Perhaps the dominance of the two universities was not surprising since prominent persons were members of their departments—Winans and Hunt at Cornell and Woolbert at Illinois. Although Woolbert had earlier claimed not to be a friend of rhetoric, he directed Gray's work. As we shall see, however, Gray's study actually constituted an attack on classical rhetoric rather than an investigation of it. We, of course, will never know how influential Woolbert's direction might have been.

In fact, in the very same number of *The Quarterly Journal* Gray published his research under the title "How Much Are we Dependent upon the Ancient Greeks and Romans?. In his essay, Gray did not seek to praise the ancients or even to explicate their work. Rather his objective was to determine whether the rhetorical climates in ancient Greece and Rome were at all comparable to that of the United States in 1923. For the most part, Gray concluded, the historical and social settings of the ancients and of the present were so different from each other that we could learn relatively little from them. Although he professed to have begun his study out of admiration for the ancients, Gray quickly turned to an argument that the teachings and theories of the Greek and Roman rhetoricians were formulated for a time and an educational system completely unlike the America of the Post World War I era.

Although, as it was confessed, this inquiry was started with something of the feeling of the old Athenian . . . some study into the matter has led to the conclusion that there are a few things we can learn from the moderns as well, if not better than, from the ancients; that in certain circles too much attention is being paid to antiquity at the expense of the present; and that an attempt is being made to fasten upon us the tradition of yesterday, without granting the possibility that today may also bring forth its own achievements. (1923, 260)

In order to understand the reasons that ancient teaching might be applicable in the contemporary world, Gray found it necessary to delineate some of the characteristics of the Greek and Roman states.

In the first place, the purpose of speech education at the present time is not the same as it was in the days of Demosthenes and Cicero. Under the prevailing system of the day, success depended on the ability of the Greek and Roman citizen to enter into the politics of the state. . . . Leadership depended then, as much as it does now, though to a less degree, upon the ability to address an audience of men also versed in the technique of oratory. . . . (1923, 260)

In Greece and Rome, said Gray, speech was only oratory and its use was limited to those who were really proficient at it.

Thus it is that in the classical oratorical training we find the effort directed to enable man to take his place in the Forum or in the assembly as a political orator, or as a pleader in the courts of justice. . . . If a man gives promise of being a great orator encourage him. . . but if he promises to be only fair, let him go along as best he may and pay little attention to him; he will get discouraged some time and quit of his own accord. But if he gives no promise at all of being able to fit himself for the profession of orator, then by all means he should discontinue his efforts to better his speech. (1923, 262-263)

The Greeks and Romans were, from Gray's point-of-view, elitist societies and, in contrast to the American society of the 1920s, undemocratic. The need for speech training was much more narrow and specialized. By 1923 the communicative requirements of the nation were democratic and attention could no longer be restricted to oratorical training. Besides, the students of 1923 were not at all like those of Greece or Rome.

The theory of speech improvement as an educational force for the masses is a modern development. Contrast with the ancient ideals the purpose of today. We are not at present so much concerned with the development of orators. . . .The student in the schools of today has a thousand different possibilities open to him; he does not have to enter the Senate or the courts to be assured of a career. Most of the young men to graduate from our schools enter into professions and trades where oratory in the sense of a speech by Demosthenes would be sadly out of place. (1923, 263-264)

To illustrate his contention, Gray cited data from the "Alumni News Bulletin of a certain comparatively small Liberal Arts college in the Middle West" to demonstrate ". . . the diversity of vocations entered by the graduates of that school." He then cited the enrollments by colleges at Wisconsin, Illinois, Syracuse and Cornell. The distributions varied somewhat among the universities, but they all indicated how diverse were the student bodies of the 1920s. Perhaps Wisconsin's statistics were most representative.

> Liberal Arts..........................5258
> Commerce 1111
> Journalism 268
> Medicine 161
> Engineering 1284
> Law 253   *(1923, 264-265)*

What was one to make of the statistics which Gray quoted? They were intended to show that the very diversity of the students in modern colleges and universities called not for oratorical eloquence but for the ability to communicate in the modern world.

> *What is to be said of the large universities , with their different colleges, where the engineers, the agriculturists, the commerce students, and the "medics" form a far larger proportion of the enrollment, and for which students it is not the ability to make orations so much as the ability to speak plainly, eagerly, clearly, concisely , which is the demand? (1923, 264)*

Clinging to the tenets of the ancients, Gray said, results in the individual's subordination to the state. Instead the modern age is concerned with the development of the individual.

> *. . . The vast majority of the young men of today are finding their life work in other fields than the political arena or the law court; they are finding that the realization of their individuality is not in devotion to the state to the exclusion of personal interests. . . . (1923, 265)*

The statement concerning individual development was very much in keeping with the tenor of the times. The thoughts of social thinkers, especially John Dewey, and some early speech writers, had stressed the ideas of individual personality development.

The emphasis on individual development was occurring at the same time that the idea of education for the masses rather than for the privileged few was gaining strength, and that, said Gray, contained implications for how oral communication should be taught. The precepts of the Greeks and Romans were no longer applicable.

> *Besides the discarding of the notion that the individual is subordinate to the state has come the more advanced theory that education, instead of being for the select few, is for the masses. . . .Witness the establishment of the state universities upon the theory that all who will may come and partake from the fountains of wisdom. . . . With the changing and advancing theories and practices of education must come the changing theories of speech training. . . . The application of all the theories of the Attic orators to the present condition would be an utter impossibility, if, indeed, it were even desirable. With the extending of the horizon of the student body comes the necessity for extending the scope of speech training. . . . A glance at some of the catalogues of some of the leading colleges and universities will indicate the extent of the field as it is now presented. We find courses in oral expression, voice production, voice science, extempore speaking, oratory, argumentation, debate, dramatic production, interpretation, phonetics, correction of speech defects, psychology of speech, teaching of speech, forms of public address, history of oratory, story-telling, oral reading, parliamentary law, pageantry, and so on ad infinitum. . . . Search from one end of classical literature to the other, and we will not find anything to compare with recent writings on some of them. As for those that we have, the modern treatment is far better for the present day than is the ancient. (1923, 266)*

Gray then argued that we have no more reason to accept the word of the ancients on rhetoric than we have to accept their word on other subjects.

> *We do not consider that Plato and Aristotle are authorities in the field of economics and politics, outside of the economic and political practices of the ancient world. . . . Why, then, should we accept as final the dictum (sic) of the rhetoricians of that time, and argue that because they said certain things, they must ipso facto be right?. . . The agreement of ancient theory and practice with the modern argues not that we are right because we agree with them, but they are right because they agree with present day knowledge. (1923, 268)*

In the conclusion to his essay, Gray sought to give a modicum of credit to the rhetoricians of antiquity and, at the same time, to insist that we were now in a new era and that we had new lessons to learn.

> *In the foregoing there has been no thought of minimizing the real worth of classical speech. But the recent deluge of writings tending to indicate that all that we have or can hope ever to have comes from antiquity needs damming up. . . rather let it be said that we are just coming to realize for the first time in history that speech can be made the subject of a science. . . . Instead of continually looking backward and bewailing the decadence of past splendors, we need to be looking forward and anticipating the future achievements which will do more toward raising the general levels of speech. . . (1923, 279)*

We have devoted a significant amount of space to an article which was an attack on the classical foundations of rhetoric; and we have included it with articles which were genuinely concerned with the history of rhetorical theory. We have done so because of the importance of this all but forgotten article in depicting a conflict in the profession which continues to this day. Although many of us may think of the disagreements between the rhetoricians and the social scientists as a development of recent history, the Gray article, as well as earlier articles by Woolbert and others, indicate that the dispute really dates from the earliest days of the profession; the question of the proper orientation and direction of the discipline remains unanswered. Gray's article deserves our special attention because, in this case, in contrast to the Woolbert pronouncements, the target of attack was not the field in general; rather Gray focused on the rising field of rhetoric and he brought into question the validity of basing our study on the tenets of classical rhetorical theory. It is true that Woolbert had earlier written in disparagement of rhetoric and that he had proclaimed it to be "of the study if not the arm chair." Woolbert's attack, however, had been more general than Gray's and it was set in a much broader context. (See Chapter 3.) Gray's effort, to be sure, highlighted the differences between the scientists and the rhetoricians. At the same time he argued against an important development in research.

The early 1920s were an almost serendipitous time for the new profession. English was in the process of abandoning, at least partially, its previous interest in rhetoric and was turning its primary attention to Literary Criticism. Rhetoric was left almost unattended, waiting for the teachers of speech to pick it up. Previous work by scholars such as Winans, Wichelns, Hudson, Smith, Wagner and Hunt was by 1923 an indication of interest in rhetorical theory. Although Gray, "with faint praise" recognized the contributions of Classical theory, he actually questioned its value in the modern world in favor of a perspective which favored contemporary scientific knowledge over "the wisdom of the ancients." He, apparently, was engaged in a dispute about which scholarly tradition should dominate teaching and research in the new profession.

Should it be the study of traditional rhetorical theory, derived from Classics, Philosophy and Philology: or should it be the study of speech as a science, derived largely from Psychology?

Gray overstated his case somewhat in that he at least implied that a choice had to be made between the two approaches. He did not even suggest that the two traditions could exist side by side; that a choice had to be made. Further, as Gray certainly knew, the concerns about the focus of the field were more complex than he made them out to be. As he himself mentioned, the discipline by 1923 was quite diverse and its interests could not be subsumed under the bilateral labels of rhetoric and science. We may speculate that Gray, perhaps in collaboration with Woolbert, used the attack on rhetoric to carry on the argument between Woolbert and Hunt over whether the new profession should be rooted in the humanities or the sciences.

At least we must admit that Gray's arguments were not based in ignorance. The text of his essay, as well as the bibliography was clear evidence that he had read fairly widely in translations of Greek and Roman rhetoricians and orators. His interpretations of the writings were quite at variance with the readings given by other writers, however, but he did make his case against the ancients.

As was true in the earlier disputes, including the Hunt-Woolbert controversy, neither the statements by rhetoricians nor the argument by Gray were finally persuasive. The disagreement continued, in attenuated or exacerbated form, for the next 70 years. Gray's article, ironically was classified by Wichelns under the heading of "Speech Composition." Gray's essay was, of course, an attack on the theoretical foundations of rhetoric, and was one of the first direct anti-rhetorical assaults. Another article, "Speech From Another Angle" critical of Winan's proposal, if not of rhetoric itself, came in 1923 from E. C. Mabie of the University of Iowa. Mabie, whose chief interest was in theatre, resented Winans' arrogance in assuming the superiority of rhetoric over other divisions of the field. The name which Winans had suggested did not please Mabie at all.

> I do not wish to be read out of the party. I do not like being told that when members of the National Association of Teachers of Speech are classified in the order of importance, teachers of rhetoric are the aristocrats and the rest of us. . . are to be forever excluded from the aristocracy. . . . Just as certainly as the title "Teachers of Speech and Rhetoric" is proposed to the convention, I shall wish to propose a change to the title "Teachers of Speech and Acting" or "Teachers of Speech and Dramatic Production." And I hope some worker in another field will propose the title "Teachers of Speech and Interpretative Reading" or anything else that may emphasize his specialty. (331)

Mabie's position on the question of nomenclature was that the association could not find a title more suitable than "speech" because the term was fundamental and because it described human oral communication.

> The advantages of the title "Speech" do not lie in the fact that it covers everything. . . . Accept the term speech with the definition that it is "the faculty of articulate sounds or words; of expressing thoughts by words or language." Or accept another phrasing, "Speech is the communication of ideas through meaningful voice sounds and bodily actions." (332)

Speech, in fact, wrote Mabie, is the factor which binds together all the disparate elements of the discipline, and which gives it integrity. It is the one term to which all members of the profession, no matter their specialized interests, should adhere.

The advantage of the title Speech lies in the fact that it designates the particular ground which all those who are members of the Association must inevitably have in common. Professor Winans and Professor Hunt may do their special work in the field of rhetoric or the history of oratory: but they cannot escape the fact that they must give attention to speech in the sense in which I have defined it. . . . Professor Merry may specialize in voice science and applied phonetics, Professor Woolbert in behavior, Professor Blanton in the correction of speech defects; but in all their work not one of them can escape the necessity of giving attention to speech. It is in the study of speech in the sense of which I have defined it that all members of the National Association meet on common ground. . . . In the National Association are men who are interested in fields other than rhetoric. Unless there is a definite desire to exclude them, I would suggest that that we retain the term which designates a common basis of interest as both the title of both the National Association and The Quarterly Journal. *(332-333)*

Of course Mabie was right. It would have done a disservice to the new profession to regard itself exclusively as rhetoric. Although Winans did not, apparently, desire to change the entire focus of the profession, he appeared, to other members, to regard rhetoric as clearly the most important component of the discipline. Winans may have represented the views of Cornell; he certainly did not represent the views of the state universities of the Middle West, of whom Mabie was representative.

Mabie's reaction was of a different order than Gray's. His effort was not to repudiate rhetorical scholarship. Rather he sought to avoid rhetoric's domination of the profession. He did not raise, as Gray did, the questions of contemporary relevance or scientific accuracy. He did, however, recognize that rhetoric was one component of a highly diversified field. Mabie not only had a clear vision of the breadth of the field, he also described the field as it continued to exist until after World War II.

As a student at Iowa during E.C. Mabie's departmental administration in the 1950s, I recognize the roots of what Mabie came to designate as the "Speech Wheel," in which he displayed, in diagram form, the relation of all the branches of speech to each other.

Later in 1923 Wichelns and the Research Committee presented another summary of research in the profession under the title; "Research Papers In Progress Or Lately Finished." The listings under "Speech Composition: Rhetoric" was longer than the earlier list and it included work from institutions other than Cornell and Illinois. Cornell, however, dominated the entries and Wisconsin and Dartmouth replaced Illinois. We, of course, cannot vouch for the accuracy of the list. Because it was apparently compiled at Cornell, it may have included more work from Cornell because it was immediately available. It also included articles which had already been published in *The Quarterly Journal*. Articles on rhetorical theory included in the list were:

Marian L. Colcord (Cornell). "The Poetics of Aristotle and the Rhetoric Related."

Hoyt H. Hudson (Cornell). "Rhetorical Theory and Practice in England, 1500-1700."

Lee Hultzen (Cornell). "A Translation of Selected Parts of A.E. Chaignet's La Rhetorique et son Histoire."

Dora V. Ingraham (Wisconsin). "Translation of Such Parts as Have Particular Interest to Students and Teachers of Speech of Conseils Sur L'Art D'Ecrire by Gustave Lanson."

W.M. Parrish (Cornell). "Rhythm of Oratorical Prose."

Francis D. Wallace (Cornell). "Rhetorical Theories of British Orators of the Eighteenth Century."

William E. Utterback (Dartmouth). "Principles of Speech Construction." (1923, 365-368)

Wichelns, for whatever reason, also included the Bromley Smith articles on Protagoras, Gorgias, Prodicus and Corax which had been published in *The Quarterly Journal* between 1918 and 1921.

In a separate section titled "History Of Oratory," Wichelns included two studies from Wisconsin which, at least in part, were concerned with rhetorical theory. They were:

Hallie B. Ward Olander. A Tabular Survey of Orators and Rhetoricians, 600 A.D. to 1800.

Ruth N. Wentzelmann. A Tabular Survey of Orators and Rhetoricians, 1000 B.C to 600 A.D. (1923, 368)

Under the heading of "General Problems and Methods" Wichelns included a study, in progress at Cornell, titled "Theory of Speech Training in Quintilian and Its Modern Implications" (1923, 370).

The Wichelns listing is interesting not only because it indicated growth in graduate work and research in rhetorical theory; it is also interesting because it indicated something of the breadth of rhetorical concerns, and something about the preparation the scholars and graduate students brought to their work. The studies by Hultzen and Ingraham suggest that some of the students, at least, were competent in languages other than English, in these cases French. Both this list and the earlier one were significant because they included a number of persons who would be important scholarly contributors in the years to come. Hunt, Parrish and Hudson had, of course, already established their reputations. Among the future luminaries were Caplan, Wagner, Gray, Hultzen, and Utterback. It must be said, however, that by no means all of their contributions were in rhetorical theory, or for that matter, in rhetoric.

An editorial in *The Quarterly Journal* in 1923, apparently in response to the recent flurry of articles by Winans, Gray, Mabie and others, discussed the question of disciplinary fragmentation without specifically mentioning Winans' proposal, or rhetoric in particular. The editorial was a plea for good will and for tolerance of diversity. When we consider that the editorial and the one that follows were written by Woolbert, they are remarkably tolerant of dissent.

We are becoming denominational. Rather we are at the point of allowing denominations to be revealed. . . . Cults, coteries, and sects are at least concrete evidence of a lively interest. The problem is to keep them amiable, generous and wide-visioned. . . . It is natural that men of different tastes should make different choice of emphasis among the several branches. It is as natural also, that in so plastic a subject as speech, local pressures should shape the bent of any man's teaching. So the outcome is understandable when we find men of many minds, and many of them strong-minded indeed. It hardly seems conceivable that for a considerable time to come we shall or can have precisely the same aims or can employ the same emphasis. Nor is it at all apparent that unanimity is even desirable. . . . But by means of common meeting places and a common medium for exchange of ideas we can work out any problem and can effect any degree of unanimity of ambition. ("Holding Fast That Which Is Good," 1923, 372-373)

The good will expressed in the editorial was laudable as was the hope for unification and integration. Sadly, the diversity was not completely or permanently brought into being, and some of the elements of the discipline, cited by Winans, Gray and Mabie, left the shelter of "Speech" and ventured out on their own to become independent disciplines in the Post World War II years. Theatre and Speech Correction (now more commonly designated as Communication Disorders) were the most conspicuous fugitives. The dispute between the "scientists" and the "rhetoricians" has continued for more than 70 years, partly within the walls of speech communication. To an increasing degree, however, the two camps themselves have diversified. The descendents of Woolbert established the National Society for the Study of Communication, under the protection of the Speech Association of America, but that organization in time became the present-day International Communication Association (ICA). Many, if not most, of the workers with scientific bents retained their membership in the present-day Speech Communication Association as well as the ICA The study of rhetoric, which Winans correctly diagnosed as no longer of special interest to English departments also underwent change in the post war years as English came to have a renewed interest in rhetoric. In time a separate group of rhetorical scholars, largely from English, established the Rhetoric Society of America and the *Rhetoric Society Quarterly*. Scholars from a variety of disciplines and nations established the International Society for the History of Rhetoric and the journal *Rhetorica*. In some ways rhetoric came to resemble an inter-disciplinary field as much as it resembled an independent discipline. In the same issue of *The Quarterly Journal* another editorial addressed the same matter in a somewhat different tone. The hope of the editorial, written in anticipation of the annual convention in Cincinnati, was that the various components of the association would be able to talk out their disagreements at the convention. The editorial writer, while praising the field, recognized that speech has had varied relations with other disciplines.

> *The subject is the oldest in the category of scholastic learning; it has the longest and richest tradition; it is perennially vital and interesting. In one age it goes off on a tangent and merits at least death; and rises in another age with luster undimmed. It allows itself to be swallowed up in philosophy or theology or belles lettres or philology or politics or economics or law and then it comes back fully into its own. It cannot possibly be kept down or reduced to a hopeless absurdity, for it comes closest of all disciplines to the daily lives of every student, scholar, teacher, investigator, and administrator. The problem is to keep the subject vital and its teachers sane. One way is best; let those of common interests meet together and talk things over. As a profession we believe in talk, in its superior virtue as a solvent of misunderstanding and ignorance, and we can wisely agree that the sanest men in any profession will be who meet their colleagues in person and reason with them together.The Cincinnati Convention will be the best yet held by the Association if it is attended in large numbers by men and women anxious to cooperate, understand, and work for a common purpose ("Cooperation," 1923, 374-375). Although the editorials were not directly concerned with the question of the place of rhetoric in the profession, they, nonetheless, were indicative of the inner tension of the association and the attempts being made to hold together its various components. Certainly the claims made by the rhetoricians, as well as others, were instrumental in creating the problem perceived in the editorials.The program for the 1923 convention signified an increased interest in rhetoric. Among the papers presented were:*
>
> *Harry E. Caplan (Cornell), "Oratory and Rhetoric in the Roman Imperial Period."*

> A. Craig Baird (Bates), "The Rhetoric of Debate."
>
> Hoyt Hudson (Swarthmore), "Rhetoric and Poetry."
>
> Russell Wagner (Iowa State), "The Training of the Public Speaker in Rome in the Time of Cicero."

A further indication of the growing importance of rhetoric was Woolbert's willingness to dedicate seven pages of *The Quarterly Journal* to a review by Hunt of the Loeb Classical Library's editions of Thucydides, Livy, and Sallust, as well as Shotwell's *An Introduction to the History of History*. The review itself was unexceptional although it did reveal, through citations, Hunt's fairly extensive knowledge of classical sources in translation and his acquaintance with a variety of secondary sources. He concluded his review with a charge to teachers of public speaking to learn more about classical rhetoric through the Loeb Classical Library. Hunt hoped that such effort would be productive of scholarship.

> *The Loeb Classical Library will bring many delightful surprises to one whose Latin and Greek has been relegated to the limbo of forgotten things. And for public speaking teachers it will transform a study that was never quite convincing when presented in the light of formal discipline, into a practical professional pursuit. Investigations in the rhetorical elements of classical historiography need not be postponed until a leave of absence is at hand or a specialist is present to guide. The small college library, some work with the professors of Latin and Greek, a stiff resistance to deadening routine, a little of the diligence that we constantly recommend to our pupils, if combined with a modicum of intelligence, will produce studies of value to the individual and to the profession. (1923, 388-389)*

Laudable though Hunt's suggestions may have been, they, nonetheless, exposed some of the weaknesses of the position of rhetorical studies in the profession, as well as weaknesses of the discipline in general. Hunt was perfectly willing to have research in Greek and Roman rhetorical theory based on the translations of classical works and not on the works themselves. The reliance on translations and secondary sources was persistent in studies in rhetorical criticism for years to come. Hunt, at least, suggested that the potential scholars in classical rhetoric learn about rhetoric from "the professors of Latin and Greek." Nowhere did he suggest that teachers learn Latin or Greek or that they develop an indigenous rhetorical perspective. Hunt continued the dependence of the new profession on external sources. One must be impressed by Hunt's optimism that the procedures he described would allow the new scholars to "produce studies of value to the individual and the profession." Reading in the Loeb Classical Library and consulting with professors of Greek and Latin would not seem to be sufficient preparation for serious research in classical rhetorical theory.

In 1924 William E. Utterback of Dartmouth published the research which had been cited in Wicheln's 1923 summary. The article "A Psychological Approach to the Rhetoric of Speech Composition," had as its intent to create a modern psychological base for rhetorical theory and to overthrow the traditional rhetorical theory. Utterback's attack resembled that of Woolbert in some respects; in other respects it was quite different. Utterback was willing to affirm the existence and value of rhetoric and the psychological support was derived from William James, rather than from the behavioral psychology on which Woolbert based his view of communication. Utterback sought to clarify his position in summarizing his article.

> *The argument presented in this paper has, of course, been destructive. Its purpose*

has been to discredit the traditional ends of speech, which constitute the theoretical foundation or framework of modern rhetoric. But it does not follow that I would reduce rhetoric to an unorganized collection of rules of thumb unillumined by any set of general principles. Without a theoretical framework rhetoric is a mere bag of tricks. Only when its rules and devices are systematized and explained by a body of principles does it attain the dignity of a science. I believe that the time is ripe for modern students of rhetoric to formulate in terms of modern psychology a set of principles which will classify and explain that vast collection of rhetorical rules and devices which we have inherited from antiquity. The difference between Professor Woolbert's approach and the one I am suggesting is that he chooses Behavioristic psychology as his medium while I prefer the more conservative psychology of James and Pillsbury. This choice of psychology is a matter of first-rate importance. I have not time to justify my preference but must content myself with expressing a doubt that whether Behavioristic psychology is equal to to the task. . . . But that is another story. (1924, 22-23)

Utterback obviously avoided a direct confrontation with Woolbert by not precisely outlining their differences. Nevertheless, Utterback's contribution is interesting and insightful. In contrast to Gray, Utterback did not seek to discredit classical rhetorical theory in its entirety; rather he sought to use modern psychology to "classify and explain that vast collection of rhetorical rules and devices which we have inherited from antiquity." Not only did Utterback disagree with Woolbert concerning the psychological bases of the study of communication; he also sought to provide a psychological foundation for rhetoric—the body of knowledge that Woolbert had rejected.

As has often been the case, Utterback's message was not heard at the time of its utterance. Many years passed before rhetorical theorists became serious about investigating the psychological bases of rhetoric.

At the 1923 convention of the Association a number of the projects which Wichelns had reported were presented as papers, but they were the only presentations dealing with rhetorical theory.

Wicheln's research report for 1923 included one study in rhetorical criticism but none in rhetorical theory. Whether the change was due to omissions in reporting or to diminished interest is not clear.

In 1924 John Dolman of the University of Pennsylvania, whose primary interest was in theatre, succeeded Woolbert as editor of *The Quarterly Journal*. The number of articles dealing with rhetorical theory decreased abruptly in that year. The new editor offered at least a partial explanation for the decline. He was not so much neglecting rhetoric as encouraging more of what he termed "matters of research." Apparently Dolman did not consider work in rhetoric to be research. Rhetoric he classified as "humanities." Some "humanists" might have regarded his remarks as slightly patronizing.

In this number, according to promise, a little extra space is given to matters of research and the interests in general of graduate students and graduate schools. . . . Many of the leading articles are upon research topics; but lest the humanists should feel themselves slighted we have inserted Mr. Baird's article [Argumentation as a Humanistic Subject] and one or two others to furnish the proper measure of sweetness and light. (270)

It is of more than passing interest that Dolman, who was removed from the disputes between the rhetoricians and the scientists, imposed more restrictions on the rhetoricians than did Woolbert the declared antagonist of humanism. Dolman was open about his tilt toward science. His policy might also have reflected shifts in the orientation of the discipline.

It must be said of Dolman that he was at least slightly humorous about his position. He wrote, "So far, the Editor has received only favorable comments on the matter of shifting emphasis—but both of them came from particular friends (270). This Dolman was much more lighthearted than the Dolman who, more than a decade later, attacked Burgess Meredith and what Dolman saw as Communist influence in the theatre. (See Chapter 6.)

When Wichelns and the Research Committee reported on "Research Papers in Process or Lately Finished" only one paper in rhetorical theory was to be found. Helen Keane had undertaken a study at Cornell of "Theories of Rhetorical Delivery" (1924, 298).

Everett Hunt seems to have been assigned the task of reviewing books in classical rhetorical theory. In 1924 he reviewed *Rhetoric and Poetry in the Renaissance* by Donald Lemen Clark and Charles Sears Baldwin's *Ancient Rhetoric and Poetic*. Hunt provided a competent review of these works, which almost 70 years later are still regarded as classics in the history of rhetorical theory. In the conclusion of the review, Hunt recognized the deficiencies which the new profession faced in formulating its own approaches to rhetorical theory and criticism.

> *It may be remarked that in freeing literary criticism from the contamination of rhetoric, much has been accomplished; in constructing a pedagogy which recognizes the classical distinction between rhetoric and poetic, much less has been achieved; and in the creation of literary criticism of persuasive discourse based upon sound rhetoric, almost everything remains to be done. (1924, 401)*

Hunt's comments, and the review in general, tell us something about the state of rhetorical scholarship in 1924. Because of the youth of the profession, especially as contrasted to the venerable traditions of scholarship in Latin and Greek, it was necessary for scholars of rhetoric to depend on the work accomplished in older disciplines. Certainly, at that time, no one in the profession was prepared to undertake the kind of work done by Clark and Baldwin. The speech scholars simply did not have the knowledge or the linguistic skills to undertake this kind of serious scholarship. (Bromley Smith may have been an exception.) Regrettably the profession, for a number of years, continued its dependence on more respected disciplines in the study of rhetorical theory.

Hunt used a term, "literary criticism of persuasive discourse," which was similar to the title of his colleague Wichelns' landmark essay of the following year, "The Literary Criticism of Oratory." Perhaps Wichelns' labors partially satisfied the deficiency which Hunt perceived. It is significant that both Hunt and Wichelns seemed bound by a literary analogy. Judging from the nomenclature they used, they appeared to construe rhetoric as a subdivision of literature. (See Chapter 7.)

1925 saw a slight renaissance of rhetorical theory because of the publication of *Studies in Rhetoric and Public Speaking in Honor of James Albert Winans*, edited by Alexander Drummond. The book is best known for Wichelns' essay "The Literary Criticism of Oratory," but it contains a significant contributions to rhetorical theory as well. In fairness it must be said that some of the contributions were reworkings of previously published work.

The studies in honor of Winans have a curious history. The Wichelns essay has, of course, been widely reproduced, but the 1925 festschrift was issued in a very limited edition. The text from which I am working bears the inscription, "This edition is limited to four hundred copies of which this is No. 381."

The volume in honor of Winans was almost an in-house publication since in the words of the preface:

> *The papers in this volume of* Studies in Rhetoric and Public Speaking *have been contributed by several of Professor Winans' pupils, colleagues, and friends who prize their association with him in the work of the Department of Public Speaking in Cornell University. (1925)*

The terms public speaking in the title of the volume was, as was then common, interpreted broadly. Under that rubric were included essays on "Phonetics and Elocution" by Lee Hultzen, "Stuttering" by Smiley Blanton, and "Speech Defects Other than Stuttering" by Margaret Gray Blanton. Most of the Cornell authors of the collection became eminences in the discipline including, Hunt, Caplan, Hudson, Wichelns, Parrish, and Utterback in addition to those already mentioned.

Although the subjects of many the essays had been treated in earlier journal articles or convention programs, the Drummond volume gave Cornell scholars the opportunity to extend their analyses and to present more complete treatments.

The Wichelns essay on rhetorical criticism was not the lead essay; that honor was given to Hunt who extended his earlier work on Greek rhetorical theory into a 59 page monograph titled "Plato and Aristotle on Rhetoric and Rhetoricians." The scope of Hunt's work was broader than the title indicated. He dealt with almost the entire range of Greek rhetorical theory. In addition to Plato and Aristotle he treated the work of other figures including Prodicus, Protagoras, Gorgias, and Hippias. Hunt presented a highly competent summary of Greek rhetorical theory. It would, even today, be an acceptable work to orient undergraduates to Plato and Aristotle. Nothing in the lengthy treatment, however, was at all original. Hunt relied upon and his arguments were supported by judiciously selected citations from secondary sources. Hunt must be given credit for having read widely and for choosing his sources wisely. In fact, although Hunt's footnotes were plentiful, far more of them were references to secondary sources rather than to original works. When the Greek works were cited, the citations were always to translations.

To a generally naive audience, however, Hunt's essay, derivative though it was, probably provided members of the new profession with a valuable overview of Athenian rhetorical theory and practice. For example, to that time, none of the authors in the profession who had written on Greek rhetoric had offered a treatment of the Sophists. Hunt presented a journal article length discussion of the Sophists in which he was at pains to detach their true stature from the unfortunate reputation they had acquired. He was careful to point out that the Sophists were not devoid of merit. He attributed to Plato the major responsibility for defaming the Sophists.

> *The art of rhetoric offered to the Athenians of the fifth century B.C. a method of education and, beyond that a way of life. Plato attacked both. He gave rhetoric a conspicuous place in his dialogues because it represented in Athenian life that which he most disliked. . . . The sophists and rhetoricians of Athens have become symbolical of false pretense of knowledge, overweening conceit, fallacious argument, cultivation of style for its own sake, demagoguery, corruption of youth through a skepticism which professed complete indifference to truth, and, in general, a ready substitution of appearance for reality. (1925, 3)*

Hunt argued that the Sophists were concerned with the cultivation of virtue in their pupils, but, in the end, the Sophists could not be distinguished from rhetoricians; and that no single position on the connection of virtue and rhetoric was shared by all Sophists.

> *Ethics thus was often absorbed into rhetoric. . . . Some inclined to believe that if you teach a man to be virtuous, he will naturally be eloquent, and rhetorical instruction is unnecessary. Other sophists believed it quite impossible to teach virtue but by constant attention to becoming a persuasive speaker, virtue would be unconsciously acquired. The controversy over the relation of virtue to eloquence runs through the history of rhetoric. . . . The attitude of the sophists toward the teaching of virtue, then, cannot distinguish the sophists from rhetoricians, and for the purpose of our study the two terms may be used almost synonymously. . . . (1925, 7)*

Hunt buttressed his analyses with citations from a wide variety of scholars including Mill, Hegel and Grote. The bulk of Hunt's discussion of the Sophists consisted of summaries of the work of Prodicus, Protagoras, Hippias and Gorgias with most attention being given to Gorgias. The treatment of these four Sophists was quite conventional.

Hunt began his treatment of Plato with an explanation of Plato's opposition to rhetoric. His opposition was, first of all, to Athenian democracy and to rhetoric as the primary instrument of support for democracy. Hunt, however, did not exempt Plato himself from charges of having used or misused rhetoric.

> *We may say in the beginning, then, that Plato's condemnation of rhetoric and rhetoricians is merely a small part of his condemnation of all contemporary civilization. We may note in passing, that rhetoric has its uses even for those who attack it; and that Plato's contrast between the rhetorician's world of appearances and the philosophers world of reality is drawn with consummate rhetorical skill. (1925, 19)*

Hunt's knowledge of the rhetorical content in Plato's dialogues was shown in that he did not restrict himself to studying the most obvious choices—*Gorgias* and *Phaedrus*. He also examined *Protagoras, Hippias Major, Hippias Minor,* and *Euthydemus.* In his essay, Hunt presented very serviceable summaries of *Gorgias* and *Phaedrus.* Although few of Hunt's insights were startlingly original, his essay showed clear evidence that he read the texts of the dialogues carefully and intelligently. The conclusion to the section on Plato was exemplary of his balanced analysis.

> *To summarize briefly our whole discussion of Plato: we have shown that his treatment of rhetoric is based upon his feelings toward rhetoricians, and upon his dislike of the rhetorical tendency of all Athenian life. Plato never viewed rhetoric abstractly, as an art of composition, as an instrument that might be used or abused; he always considered it a false impulse in human thought. . . . At the conclusion of his earlier attacks. . . Plato offers the outline of a reconstructed rhetoric. Here too, he shows his inability to conceive of rhetoric as a tool; the ideal rhetoric sketched in the* Phaedrus *is as far from the possibilities of mankind as his Republic was from Athens. (1925, 41-42)*

Hunt stated that he did not intend to offer an explication of Aristotle's *Rhetoric.* Rather, he said, "In turning to Aristotle, we shall be chiefly interested in his relation to Plato. . . . It is not our purpose here to present an exposition of the *Rhetoric.*" (1925, 42). In his discussion of the *Rhetoric*, Hunt showed that he had read related works of

Aristotle, as well as numerous secondary sources. In his essay he cited *Sophisti Elenchi*, *Politics*, *Posterior Analytics*, *Ethics* and *Topics*. Hunt had read Jebb, Cope, Roberts, Baldwin, Grote and Gomperz among his secondary sources. Although Hunt professed not to offer "an exposition of the *Rhetoric*," his discussion was, in reality, a very adequate summary of the *Rhetoric*, although he kept the comparison with Plato clearly in mind throughout the essay. Hunt recognized that the perspectives of Plato and Aristotle originated from quite different assumptions.

> *While Aristotle agreed with Plato in his contempt for the unscientific nature given by other teachers of rhetoric. . . . his approach to rhetoric was affected by certain philosophical and personal divergences from Plato. . . . Plato sought to reform life, while Aristotle was more interested in reorganizing theory about life. For this reason Aristotle's* Rhetoric *is detached from both morality and pedagogy. It is neither a manual of rules nor a collection of injunctions. It is a unmoral and scientific analysis of the means of persuasion. (1925, 44)*

The comparisons between Plato and Aristotle which Hunt drew in the essay were, for the most part, apt and accurate. He contrasted the positions of the two philosophers on a number of issues including: the nature and function of rhetoric; rhetoric as an art; the content of rhetoric; the relationship of rhetoric probability and truth; the contingent nature of rhetoric; and the relationship of dialectic and rhetoric. Hunt in the summary of his essay offered a cogent explanation of the similarities and differences between the Athenian philosophers.

> *In comparing Aristotle with Plato, we have seen that the* Rhetoric *discusses most of the questions of rhetorical theory raised by Plato in the* Gorgias; *it agrees with the rhetoricians that rhetoric is an art, that the universality of its application does not mean that it has no subject matter of its own, that the evils of rhetoric arising from rhetoric are no greater than the evils that arise from the abuse of all good things, that truth and righteousness are, on the whole, more prevalent because of a general knowledge of rhetoric, and that the persuasion of multitudes of relatively ignorant people, instead of being a merely vulgar task fit only for demagogues is a necessary part of education and government in a stable society. A contrast of the* Rhetoric *with the* Phaedrus *makes it evident that even here Aristotle is closer to the rhetoricians than to Plato. Rhetoric is an art of appearance; and this fact neither prevents it from being an art, nor from serving the ends of righteousness. Rhetoric, instead of being a sham dialectic, is the counterpart of dialectic. . . (1925, 59)*

Hunt's essay in *Rhetoric and Public Speaking* must be regarded as a seriously neglected piece of scholarship. Although it presented material, much of which had been examined by scholars in other disciplines, the essay, for the first time in the brief history of the new profession, presented a comprehensive treatment of Platonic and Aristotelian perspectives on rhetoric, as well as an informed discussion of the rhetorical, political and social milieus of Athens. For a profession as naive about classical rhetorical theory as were the speech teachers, Hunt's essay offered them an intelligent introduction to Greek rhetorical theory; more perhaps than if the members had undertaken to read the translations and commentaries themselves, which they probably would not have done; the number of members with serious interests in the history of rhetorical theory was, undoubtedly quite small. We must remember, of course, that the essay was limited to 400 copies and may not have been widely read.

Harry Caplan's contribution to the festschrift was titled "A late Medieval Tractate on Preaching." The bulk of Caplan's work was devoted to a translation of a fifteenth century text found in the library of Cornell University, which Caplan claimed to be ". . . one of the first homiletical texts to appear in Germany" (1925, 68). Before the translation, however, Caplan, in eight pages, presented a summary of early Christian homiletic theory and practice. His summary was by no means comprehensive, but it allowed those who were interested to learn a little about a period in the history of rhetorical theory which had not yet been explored. Indeed, because of linguistic and historical limitations, the study of medieval rhetorical theory has never really flourished in the discipline.

Hoyt Hudson, in his essay, explored relatively recent rhetorical theory, in contrast to the work which had been carried on in classical theory. In "De Quincey on Rhetoric and Public Speaking" Hudson did not limit his examination to De Quincey's "Rhetoric"; he also included "Style" and "Brief Appraisal of the Greek Literature in its Foremost Pretensions."

Hudson's approach to the work of De Quincey is quite different from Hunt's. Where Hunt provided his readers with a carefully synthesized reading of secondary sources, Hudson embarked on quite a different course. His essay hardly drew on outside authorities. Instead, he presented an independent appraisal and analysis of De Quincey's rhetorical writings in which he relied, almost exclusively, on his own insights, analyses and judgments. Of course, Hudson had, in his brief career, displayed more knowledge of rhetoric than any of his contemporaries. He had also displayed his ability to think and write about rhetoric without necessarily being derivative from or subordinate to external authorities. Hudson's essay, although no longer of central interest, represented one of the first times that scholars in the new profession were able to free themselves from the influence of disciplines to whom they gave more respect than they did to themselves. Hudson might have become an even more significant contributor to research in rhetorical theory. Unfortunately for the profession, he soon left Public Speaking and spent the major portion of his career as Professor of English at Princeton.

Hudson's analysis of De Quincey's work was precise and discerning. His essay was essentially a fairly close textual study. Hudson was clear in his placement of De Quincey as a nineteenth century writer and very much a creature of his own time. Hudson's reading of the text is cogent in its revelation of De Quincey's internal inconsistencies. Perhaps the most important point which Hudson made concerning De Quincey's rhetorical theory was that invention and style are not distinct. They are, instead, two aspects of the same rhetorical process, but that rhetoric is fundamentally concerned with ideas.

> *Here is a fair synopsis of two branches of rhetoric, invention and style; and here, as elsewhere in De Quincey, we are made to see that invention and style are two phases—an inner and outer phase—of the same process. One heresy into which De Quincey never fell is that rhetoric has to do primarily with the disposition of words or the application of verbal embellishment. Even when he thought of it as fanciful play the objects played with. . . were ideas. He contrives to make clear that the process of rhetorical invention is a mode of thinking. (1925, 139)*

Hudson speculated that if De Quincey and other nineteenth century theorists, rather than eighteenth century writers had been used in the schools, rhetoric might have made a more substantial contribution to education than it had.

> *Rhetorical invention is a mode of thinking; and if the school rhetorics of the nineteenth century had followed De Quincey, Whately, and Newman, instead of*

Blair and Bain, we should not find rhetoric so far from the minds of educators when they are looking for "some way to make students think." (1925, 140-141)

Hudson's point is interesting and it is one that has seldom been made in the history of the profession. He was, of course, correct in his assumption that the "managerial rhetorics," in particular that of Blair, had been the staple fare of American school and college classes until late in the nineteenth century. Those rhetorics held a rather truncated view of invention. Writers such as Campbell and Blair held that rhetoric had no responsibility for the ideas of discourse; they must come from elsewhere—notably from the speaker's own resources. The skill of the rhetorician was brought into play in his ability to advise concerning the "management" or "conduct" of discourse. The rhetorician could offer assistance concerning structure, style, adaptation, and delivery, but the ideas of discourse did not come under his purview. Hudson may have over generalized, however, about the rhetoric texts of the late nineteenth century. A number of the writers of textbooks did acknowledge their indebtedness to theorists such as Whately. Many dealt specifically with invention, notably Genung. In fact, Fred Newton Scott, co-author of a prominent rhetoric-composition text in the early years of the twentieth century had written extensively on De Quincey. (See Chapter 2.)

Hudson, from his reading of De Quincey, proposed an area of study which might have been significant in a number of ways. He saw that rhetoric need not be limited to formal oral discourse and that it might deal with other forms of communication.

> *Here are the clues to a whole branch of rhetorical study, a branch dealing with the technique of publicity in its relation to the rhetorical and literary expression of a given period. Sporadic attempts at such investigations have been made by literary critics and sociologists, but there is much to be done. . . .The oration and the drama reached a high degree of perfection in Greece, says De Quincey, because the chief means of publication were oral. . . .To follow De Quincey's clue, one would have to take into account the size and architecture of auditoriums, stages, theatres, and pulpits. Or coming to recent phenomena, one might study the vogue of pamphleteering, the rise of the newspaper, and the significance of radio broadcasting as a means of publication. Is there a "Chautauqua style," and if so, is it determined largely by the audience, or are both audience and style controlled by the physical aspects of Chautauqua? Will the English of headlines and devices of billboards advertising invade poetry and uncommercial rhetoric? What of the appalling multiplication of pictures in recent publicity—will all this have it effect upon the speaker and writer? (1925, 147-148)*

> *Hudson concluded that if the spirit of De Quincey had been followed rhetoric would occupy the central position in all learning. . . . In reading De Quincey, fragmentary and desultory as he is, we catch a spirit which allowed to operate would transform all this; we hear echoes of a great past, and prophetic whispers of a return in education, to that rhetoric which can be and should be "the organon of all studies." (1925, 150-151)*

Hudson's essay, perhaps even more than Hunt's contribution to the volume, must be regarded as valuable study which has been overlooked, neglected or forgotten. The issues raised in the conclusion, based on Hudson's reading of De Quincey, were perfectly valid concerns which did were not addressed in the profession until many decades had passed. Hudson saw the importance of situating rhetorical studies historically, not simply in the chronology of the time, but with an understanding of the social, esthetic, cultural and technological aspects of places and times. Moreover,

Hudson perceived that, given the changes that had occurred, the study of rhetoric should encompass the range of human communication, broadly defined.

Hudson imposed no limitations of orality on his rhetorical perspective. Earlier, we have cited Hunt's admonition that such diverse rhetorical artifacts as radio, newspapers, billboards, and architecture should become proper objects of rhetorical study. Perhaps most importantly, Hudson at least suggested a path for rhetorical studies which would allow it to develop as an independent discipline. Instead of deriving its conceptions from other disciplines, Hudson proposed that rhetoric chart its own course and attend to issues which had been overlooked or neglected by other disciplines. We, of course, will never know what form rhetorical or speech studies might have taken had Hudson's essay been more widely read. We can speculate that it would have become a more broadly focused field which was fundamentally concerned with the ideas of discourse. The importance of the Hunt and Hudson essays argues for a re-issue of *Studies in Rhetoric and Public Speaking*, or at least the republication of the two essays; Wichelns' essay has, of course been widely reprinted. In Wicheln's 1925 report on research the only projects he included were the essays contained in *Studies in Rhetoric and Public Speaking*.

Under the heading of "Laboratory and Research," in the 1925 *Quarterly Journal*, was an article titled "Methods of Conducting Graduate Seminars." The article undertook a survey of the institutions offering graduate work. Much of the information was fragmentary, but the article was useful in indicating something of the status of rhetorical theory in graduate study. Cornell, for example, was described as "Starting with a year or two devoted to a common study of a fundamental subject (classical rhetoric as found in Aristotle, Cicero and Quintilian). . . ." ("Laboratory Research", 1925, 277.) Wisconsin reported a seminar in Rhetoric and Oratory taught by O'Neill, which was the only one described in any detail.

1. *Invention in ancient and modern rhetoric.*

2. *The differences between the rules of suggestion for a good style in speaking and for a good style in writing.*

3. *The relation of homiletics to a general rhetorical theory.*

4. *Imagery and imagination in public speaking—how they function in the speaker and the hearer.*

5. *Crowd psychology as factor in rhetoric and oratory.*

6. *Rhetoric and poetry—common ground and differences.*

7. *The relation of method and material to different speech ends.*

8. *Definition, classification, and exemplification of the most useful rhetorical devices. ("Laboratory Research", 1925, 279.)*

One is both impressed and bemused by the comprehensive content of the Wisconsin seminar. O'Neill deserved to be praised for his ambition in covering such a wide range of topics in one seminar. At the same time the modern reader is left with questions about how all the topics could have been addressed in a single seminar.

In a report on the 1925 meeting of the Eastern Public Speaking Conference it was noted that Hudson presented a version of his De Quincey essay. Two reviews were published in 1925 which brought hitherto neglected works to the attention of the readers of *The Quarterly Journal*. Harry Caplan reviewed the W. Rhys Roberts translation of Aristotle's *Rhetorica* and the translation of *De Rhetorica ad Alexandrum* by E.S.

Forster. Russell Wagner reviewed *Die Padagogik des Isocrates* by August Burk. Caplan's attention to the *Rhetorica* was almost perfunctory; most of the review was concerned with the *Ad Alexandrum*, of which Caplan did not have a high opinion, but a work, he thought, that should be read, both for historical and contemporary reasons.

> . . . *The author of the* Ad Alexandrumu *is so unscrupulous in his choice of methods to seduce an audience that he drives Cope to moral horror and prompts him to label the work the Art of Cheating. . . . Marked by a condemnable disregard for truth, pejurious recommendations, dedicated to plausibility and effect, this work is yet reminiscent even of American judicial and deliberative assemblies, as no one will deny. . . . Naturally, one should prefer Aristotle as champion of rhetoric against its traducers of every age and country, from Plato to Premier Baldwin. [Stanley Baldwin, the British Prime Minister] I deem the translation of minor ancient rhetorical works a useful service to students of public speaking, for doctrine and historical interest and for a point where the doctrine is of less universal quality. . . . Indeed the present reviewer hopes in the near future to attempt the same task with the Latin* Ad Herrenium. *(1925a, 300-301)*

Wagner's review of Burk's work on Isocrates indicated that at least some members of the new profession could read modern languages other than English. Wagner worked directly from Burk's German text. Wagner's review was different from Caplan's because Wagner responded to a commentary rather than to a new translation of an ancient figure. Other writers, such as Bromley Smith and Harry Caplan, had cited works in languages other than English, but Wagner's review, so far as we can determine, was the first review of a work in a modern European language. Wagner, as did Caplan in his review, saw the usefulness of Burk's work to American students and scholars of rhetoric.

> *Taking into consideration that Dr. Burk probably never imagined that teachers of public speaking would read this excellent brochure, it is astonishingly rich in the methods and theories of teaching public speaking, both in Ancient Greece and modern Germany and America. . . . But to the teacher of public speaking, the fresh, clear and thorough envisaging of the greatest problem of our field today—the relationship of public speaking to the grand scheme of education—should bring an added incentive to aid in the solution of that problem. It is to be hoped that a translation of this newest source-book in rhetorical education will not be long delayed. (1925a, 302-305)*

We have been unable to determine whether Burk's work was, in fact, translated; it is not listed in either the German or English holdings of the library at Penn State.

Hunt again introduced new editions of classical works in a 1925 review. This time, however, he handled his task with brevity, since he reviewed four books in two and a half pages. The first work which Hunt reviewed, *M. Fabii Quintiliani, Institutio Oratorio, Liber I*, edited by F.H. Colson, was not a translation, but Hunt restricted his comments to "the introduction of ninety-three pages" which was in English. The other works reviewed were the English translation of Lucian by A.H. Harmon; *A Study in Alcimadis and His Relation to to Contemporary Sophistic* by Marjorie J. Milne and *Augustine, the Orator* by Sister M. Inviolata Barry. Hunt took note that in the 1905 translation the Fowlers had translated Lucan's work as "The Rhetorician's Vade Mecum" and that Harmon gave it the title of "A Professor of Public Speaking." Hunt characterized Lucan's work as ". . . denunciation of a profession to which he once expected to belong" (1925a, 401).

In 1926 Bromley Smith, now at Johns Hopkins, continued his task of introducing classical rhetoricians to members of the new profession in his article "Hippias and a Lost Canon of Rhetoric." The canon to which Smith referred was memory although he was nine pages into his 17 page essay before he discussed memory specifically. In the first section of the article Smith placed Hippias in the historical scene; he discussed Hippias' polymathic accomplishments; and he explored the reasons for Plato's dislike of Hippias.

Smith credited Hippias with recognizing the relationship between rhetoric and other fields of knowledge.

> . . . *Hippias was doing in his day what many teachers of rhetoric have since attempted to do: feeling the connection of rhetoric with other branches of knowledge, the dependence of the orator upon history, economics, and philosophy for material upon which to apply the principles of public speaking; many of them have rebelled and have become perforce general-specialists. (1926, 136-137)*

"General-specialist" was the term Hunt had used to describe the speech teacher, and Smith acknowledged Hunt's use of the locution.

Smith, in his essay, undertook a brief history of the canon of memory. He attributed its introduction in rhetorical theory to the Romans; the Greeks had not treated memory as a component of rhetoric.

> . . . *It did not become embedded in the canons for sometime after Hippias had paved the way. Neither the* Rhetorica ad Alexandrum *nor the* Rhetoric of Aristotle *mentions it. . . Sometime before the Christian era it must have been adopted, for the* Auctor ad Herrenium *without question regards memory as one of the parts of oratory. A few years later Cicero in his* Oratorical Partitions *calls memory the guardian of invention, arrangement, voice and delivery. . . . Quintilian remarked that that most authorities agreed on the five parts of oratory; invention, arrangement, expression, memory, and delivery or action. Subsequent authorities continued the canon traditionally. (1926, 138-139)*

Memory remained as a canon, Smith said, until the eighteenth century.

> . . . *Wilson, [Thomas Wilson, author of* The Arte of Rhetorique *(1553)] writing in English still retained memory in the canonical list. Then came a change in treatment. By the middle of the 18th century, the important rhetorical works of Blair, Campbell and Kames had dropped memory. In the 19th century the texts of Whately, Hill, and Genung fail to notice the subject. Thus after two thousand years the principle taught by Hippias vanished from the art of public speaking. (1926, 139)*

Smith was historically accurate about the disappearance of memory as a canon in the eighteenth century. He did not, however, offer any explanation for its vanishing. The philosophical perspective of the new rhetoricians did not easily find a place for memory in their schemes. In a writer such as Blair traces of memoria are to be found in his treatment of what he termed "the conduct of discourse." Indeed, the eighteenth century writers did not adhere to the Ciceronian conceptions of "the five great arts." They integrated the canons with each other and they merged the proofs and the canons. To cite Blair once more, he treated pathos and logos as parts of dispositio, labeling them the "pathetic" and "argumentative" parts. His treatment of ethos was found in his lecture on "Means of Improving in Eloquence."

Not until the conclusion of his essay did Smith show an awareness that the invention of the printing press, and the resultant spread of literacy, made rote memory and mnemonic devices less essential than they had been in an earlier time. Smith takes his appraisal back to Plato's distrust of writing.

> Plainly Hippias, as a practical teacher of rhetoric, must have realized the importance of a good memory, especially in a day when texts were few and costly, when instruction was given by the lecture method, when orators carried their speeches in their minds. . . . With the passing of the years, however, the notion that the memory of orators can be trained by systematic devices has almost disappeared. . . . Long ago Plato foresaw this when he remarked that the invention of writing by the Egyptian god, Theuth, caused learners to trust external written characters rather than themselves. That he was right may be judged by the number of speakers who read their addresses. (1926, 139, 144)

Smith's significant contribution to rhetorical theory, in this essay, was not his explication of Hippias' and his teaching of memory. After all, Hippias remains a minor figure among the Sophists. Rather, the importance of the essay lies in the historical tracing of "the lost canon" of memory, and his provision of further knowledge of their rhetorical ancestry to neophyte rhetorical theorists.

It is significant that in spite of the frequent mention of such writers as Blair, Campbell, and Whately by authors in the discipline, no articles had been published about the most prominent eighteenth and nineteenth century theorists. Hudson, to be sure, had written about De Quincey; now Raymond F. Howes of the University of Pittsburgh followed Hudson's path by analyzing the rhetorical theory of another nineteenth century literary figure—in this case Samuel Taylor Coleridge, but Coleridge was a different case than De Quincey. De Quincey, after all, had written systematically about rhetoric where as Howes wrote:

> It seems strange somehow, that one whose influence was in so great part diffused through conversation, should have said so little about rhetoric. Almost never does Coleridge use the word, and his references to it are hardly direct. (Howes, 1926, 148)

Howes sought to make his case for Coleridge as a rhetorical theorist on the ground of his strong preference for oral over written discourse, based on information gleaned from letters, papers and memoirs. Much of the information about Coleridge's own views came from testimony from Coleridge's family, friends and correspondents. To support his case about Coleridge's preference for speech over writing, Howes cited an 1815 letter to Wordsworth.

> The most concise explanation of this idea is found in a letter to Wordsworth on May 30, 1815. "It is not in written words," says Coleridge, "but by the hundred modifications that looks make and tone, and denial of the full sense of the very words used, that one can reconcile the struggle between sincerity and diffidence." Oral discourse, to him, as to Plato, was a living, vital thing; written discourse a dead and far more cumbersome method of communication. (1926, 147-148)

Howes, in the continuation of his argument sought to portray Coleridge as a Platonist in his attitudes toward rhetoric, beginning with Coleridge's disapproval of the Sophists.

> . . . References in The Friend, the Biographia Literaria, and in his letters make it plain that Coleridge thought of rhetorical theory as a body of empty rules for making trivial ideas impressive and persuasive. As a result, he followed Plato in denouncing the sophists. . . . Coleridge followed Plato too in believing that the primary function is to find truth. Unless the rhetorician has one ultimate principle

on which to base his ideas, he accomplishes nothing worthy. His eloquence and logical skill render him only the more pernicious. . . . The true rhetorician then, is he who sees in everything basic principles or laws, and applies them to the particular problem under discussion. (1926, 148-149)

Howes was able to tease out a rough definition of rhetoric from Coleridge's conversations and correspondence. The definition is really a contrast between rhetoric (or oratory) and eloquence.

De Quincey tells us that Coleridge was "in the habit of drawing the line with much philosophical beauty between Rhetoric and Eloquence," but he adds, "on this topic we were never so fortunate as to hear him.". . . A hint to what he meant, may however, be gleaned from a letter to the Rev. Edward Coleridge, July 23, 1823: "I make and mean the same distinction between oratory and eloquence as between the mouth plus the windpipe and the heart plus the brain." (1926, 148)

Coleridge, apparently, held to an idea of rhetoric which gave primacy to thought and feelings over mere display. He deviated, however, from the standard practice of his time which regarded "rhetoric" and "eloquence" as synonyms. Campbell, Whately and Blair, together with numerous other writers used the terms interchangeably.

Howes gave Coleridge credit for recognizing the role of imagination both in rhetoric and literature.

Nowhere, however, does Coleridge go so far as to imply that good rhetoric should lack imagination. His passages dealing with the faculty are, on the contrary, perhaps his finest contribution to literary criticism. (1926, 153)

Howes interpreted Coleridge's position, that the will had the power to overcome the understanding, as "the traditional distinction between conviction and persuasion" (1926,154).

This theory that thought and images, acting by their own inherent power, may induce action, is important. If accepted, it means that the speaker, by rhetorical means can suspend, the judgment and understanding of his audience, and cause them to act contrary to their convictions. Images can overthrow belief. (1926, 154)

It is true that Coleridge differentiated between conviction and persuasion, but it was not quite "the traditional distinction" that Howes stipulated. Rather he seemed to emphasize the supremacy of persuasion over conviction and the dominance of emotional proof over logical proof. Howes did not regard Coleridge as a great rhetorical theorist although he did feel that Coleridge's contributions were worth noting.

To Coleridge, then, although he had a questionable understanding of the term rhetoric, and was often deficient himself in rhetorical practice, we can attribute a profound realization of the power of the spoken word, a statement of the value of the unity of thought and feeling, a sound conception of the relation of ideas to style and diction, a comprehensive definition of imagination, a psychological explanation of the distinction between persuasion and conviction, a note or two on rhetorical figures, and several practical suggestions for argumentation. His contribution, perhaps, is not great; certainly it is not unified; but it is nevertheless noteworthy from one who made no attempt to formulate a complete rhetorical theory. (1926, 155-156)

Howes was, of course, correct that Coleridge was not a major figure in rhetorical theory. His essay, however, was important because Howes was able to extract and synthesize a theory of rhetoric, rough though it may have been through the examination of a variety of sources. The Howe essay is also noteworthy as a very early demonstration that rhetorical theories were not limited to theories of oral communication; they could also be derived from literature and other forms.

Under the title "An Introduction to Classical Rhetoric", Everett Hunt provided a three page bibliography which he explained in the following words.

> *This reading list does not pretend to be exhaustive. It is selected with the purpose of presenting the most important references which are readily accessible in English, or English translations. As the substance of a college course, this material presents a body of literature which is worthy of study for its own sake; it supplements work which is very generally offered in ancient literature and philosophy, and it provides a background of ideas which greatly increase the significance of practical training in persuasive discourse. (Hunt, 1926, 201-202)*

Hunt arranged his bibliography chronologically. He listed 58 titles under the following headings.

1. *The Sophists*
2. *Plato*
3. *Aristotle*
4. *Isocrates*
5. *Demetrius*
6. *Dionysius*
7. *Longinus*
8. *Tacitus*
9. *Quintilian*
10. *St. Augustine*
11. *General Works (Hunt, 1926, 202-204)*

Somehow one doubts that Hunt was really serious when he described the book list "as the substance of a college course." To have expected students to master 58 works, mostly weighty tomes, in one course was unrealistic. The book list, without doubt, was valuable to rhetorical neophytes in the profession; and it must have been helpful in the preparation of courses in rhetorical theory. The materials in the bibliography were largely drawn from classical scholars; interestingly, articles in *The Quarterly Journal* by Smith, Wagner and Shorey were also included. Hunt recommended only the introductions to J.E. Sandys' *M. Tulli Ciceronis ad M. Brutum Orator*, and A.S. Wilkins' *M. Tulli Cicerones de Oratore Libre Tres* because the works themselves were in Latin and only the introductions were in English. These were the only non-English materials on Hunt's list.

The 1926 list of "Research Papers in Process or Lately Finished" included three works, all of them originating at Cornell. They were:

> W. E. Gilman: "Milton's Interest in Rhetoric"
> A. B. Hall: "Campbell's Philosophy of Rhetoric"
> A. L. Woehl: "Burke's Rhetorical Theory" (1926,235)

Howes' uncompleted M.A. thesis at Pittsburgh was also included on the list, but judging from its title, "Coleridge the Talker," it appeared more likely to be a rhetorical criticism. The brief list is interesting in that it shifted concentration away from classical theory. All of the papers cited dealt with the rhetorical theory of the Renaissance or later.

Bromley Smith continued to contribute knowledge about relatively obscure Greek rhetoricians, this time in his 1927 essay "Thrasymachus: A Pioneer Rhetorician," Smith argued that the contributions of Thrasymachus', who lived in the fifth century before Christ, had been neglected.

> *This man was accredited by the ancients with the discovery of periods, clauses, and tropes; with the invention of the middle style of speech; with the primary observation that good speech was rhythmical; and with the publication of the first text on Elocution. He was one of those early promoters mentioned by Aristotle, who gave a pedagogy to rhetoric:. . . (1927, 279)*

In his essay on Thrasymachus, Smith followed a pattern similar to that used in the Hippias article. Smith argued that Thrasymachus' most significant contribution to rhetorical theory was his treatment of the emotion of pity. We know from references in Plato and Aristotle of the existence of a work by Thrasymachus titled *Appeals to Pity*, but the book was no longer extant and Smith could not examine it directly. He had to rely on references to *Appeals to Pity* found in early Greek sources. Before he turned to his explication of Thrasymachus on pity, Smith undertook, as he had with Hippias on memory, a rapid historical survey of the rhetorical treatment of pity from Thrasymachus' time to Fulton and Trueblood and E. A. Phillips. Thrasymachus was concerned with the relation of the elicitation of pity and delivery; and much of Smith's attention was concentrated on that connection. Smith cited the mention of the relationship in Plato's *Republic*, the *Rhetorica* of Aristotle, the *Rhetorica ad Alexandrum*, Cicero's *Orator*, Quintilian's *Institutes*, Wilson's *Arte of Rhetorique*, Fulton and Trueblood's *Practical Elements of Elocution*, and A.E. Phillip's *Natural Drills in Expression*. (1927, 280-284). Smith was hampered, however, by the unavailability of *Appeals to Pity* and all his judgments had to be inferential, based on secondary testimony. As a result Smith told us more about the history of the treatment of pity and its relation to delivery than of Thrasymachus' teachings. Nevertheless, Smith offered a very useful quick survey of the treatment of pity, even including the ways in which the Elocutionists such as Benjamin Rush and Fulton and Trueblood associated particular vocal tones with the depiction and elicitation of pity. Such a compendium must have been useful to students of the history of rhetorical theory.

Also in 1927, Charles A. Fritz of Washington Square College New York University, in an article titled "Early American Works on Speech Training," wrote of his discovery of four books in the New York Public Library of which he claimed ". . . They are the earliest work on speech training published in America, of which the library has record" (152). The books discovered by Fritz were: *A System of Rhetoric* by John Sterling, *Lessons in Elocution*, by William Scott (1795), *The Art of Speaking* by James Burgh (1795), and *The Well Bred Scholar or Practical Essays on the Best Methods of Improving the Taste and Assisting the Emotions of Youth in Their Literary Pursuits* by William Milns (1797).

None of the books cited by Fritz were, strictly speaking, works of rhetorical theory. Nor, in fact were they "American works." All of them were American reprintings of British books and they did not represent indigenous work. Nevertheless, the books were worth Fritz's examination because they showed the influence of eighteenth century British rhetorical theory on early America. Most of the books promulgated versions of classical and neo-classical rhetorical theory. Sterling's book, which was originally published in Dublin in Latin, included an essay in English by John Holmes with the ponderous title "The Art of Rhetoric Made Easy, or the Elements of Oratory,

Briefly Stated and Fitted for the practice of the Studious Youth of Great Britain, Ireland and the United States of America." Since Fritz apparently did not read Latin, he quoted only from the appended Holmes essay. To show the classical character of the essay Fritz offered the following:

> All of the theory in the text is put in the form of questions and answers, as for example: Q. How many parts have Rhetorik? A. The parts it consists of are four; Invention, Disposition, Elocution and Pronunciation. . . . The discussion of the oration he begins as follows: Q. How many parts are there to an Oration? The parts of an Oration or Declamation are usually reckoned six: Exordium, Narration, Proposition, Confirmation, Refutation and Peroration. (152)

In Scott's *Lectures in Elocution* only Part III made any reference to traditional theory, and only to the standard eighteenth century classification of speeches.

> Part III he calls "Lessons in Speaking." There is a section each on the Eloquence of the Pulpit, the Eloquence of the Senate and the Eloquence of the Bar. . . . (153)

Burgh's *The Art of Speaking* was, in the late eighteenth century, a well known Elocution text which dealt hardly at all with any aspect of rhetorical theory. The edition which Fritz consulted was actually published twenty years after Burgh's death.

The Milns book seemed to be a synthesis of classical and eighteenth century theory, adapted to classroom use. Fritz reported in a paraphrase that Milns found the conventional rhetorical texts unsuitable for school audiences.

> The rhetorical and critical writings of Cicero, Quintilian and Longinus are far too refined and too sublime for the conception of schoolboys. Dr. Blair's Lectures on Rhetoric are excellent, but they are suited only to persons of riper understanding. . . .Then follows a summary of rhetorical observations taken chiefly from the writings of Cicero and Quintilian. Under the heading of "The Subject Matter of Oratory" the author quotes from Blair's Lectures on Rhetoric, then goes on to divide oratory into deliberative, demonstrative and judicial. The treatment of demonstrative oratory follows Quintilian closely. (159)

As Fritz himself acknowledged, none of these works were significant in rhetorical theory. His examination was useful, however, in that it gave the readers some historical understanding of the early influences of rhetorical theory in the schools of the United States.

Bromley Smith seemed determined to continue to explore ancient Greek theorists and to bring their work to the attention of the teachers of Speech. In 1928 his choice was "Theodorus of Byzantium: Wordsmith." Smith placed Theodorus in a distinguished group of immigrants who were unwelcome to Plato.

> The Byzantine was merely another of those roving teachers who came from the outside to annoy the great philosopher. Tisias and Gorgias had crossed from Sicily, Protagoras had ridden from Abdera, Prodicus had journeyed from Ceos, Hippias had walked from Elis on sandals made by his own hands, Thrasymachus had sailed from Chalcedon, and now Theodorus had been wafted down from the Bosphorus. Where were the native-born Athenian rhetoricians? Why should the outlying Greeks furnish all the teachers of rhetoric? (1928, 72)

Unfortunately, as was the case with Hippias, Smith had no extant texts from which to work. He was, therefore, constrained to present an inferential case, derived from statements not by but about Theodorus. He found references in the works of Plato,

Aristotle, Dionysius and Cicero. The conclusion he reached about Theodorus was that his contributions to Athenian rhetorical theory were substantial.

> *If we had the text issued by the Byzantine, we might follow him with greater confidence. Unfortunately, it is lost in the abyss along with his speeches and logographs. What little knowledge we have must be gleaned entirely from his critics. They assure us that the man from Byzantium invented terms for the subdivisions of the principal parts of an oration; that he showed how plaintiffs and defendants in their arguments might take advantage of the probabilities involved in mistakes; and that, scorning nakedness in style, he beat out, like an armorer upon his anvil, novel forms of expression. (1928, 81)*

Smith's conclusion pointed to one of the problems, not only with the work of Theodorus, but that of Hippias and Thrysamachus as well. For all his inferential diligence and skill, Smith was able to bring to his readers only a secondary and reconstructed version of the works of early theorists. Smith's essays were, undoubtedly, scholarly contributions. How they were to be used by the less informed members of the profession was another matter. In 1928 the Committee on Terminology, chaired by J.P. Ryan of Grinell College resented its report in *The Quarterly Journal*. Part of the report was a diagram titled "A Chart of a Department of Speech." The chart was divided into three categories: Articulate Speech (Science), Communicative Speech (Art), and Interpretative Speech (Art). Under the heading of Communicative Speech, courses in "Rhetoric and Oratory" were listed after the "First Course" and courses in "Public Speaking" and "Private Speaking", (presumably "conversation"). The description of Communicative Speech was indicative of the breadth of conception of the committee.

> *Communicative Speech, art, deals with the oral expression of one's own thought and feeling in private conversation or public gathering. Under communicative speech one studies the art of the beautiful and effective use of one's mother tongue in private or public speech situations. (146)*

The chart and the text of the report were quite vague about the content and direction of courses in rhetoric and oratory, or how rhetoric related to the other components of the discipline.

In 1928, Hunt, then editor of *The Quarterly Journal*, wrote an eight page editorial in response to a 1927 speech by Paul Shorey, Professor of Classics at the University of Chicago, presented at a convocation of the State University of New York and published in *School and Society*. Hunt titled his editorial "From Rhetoric Deliver Us." Shorey had spoken to the National Association in 1922, and Winans had published a report of his correspondence with Shorey concerning the meaning of the term "speech". (See Chapter 4.) Shorey had not been charitable towards rhetoric in his 1922 speech to the National Association, and Hunt regarded Shorey's 1927 speech as an attack on rhetoric which deserved refutation. At the same time he found merit in Shorey's proposals about the proper ways in which rhetoric might be taught.

> *. . . Professor Paul Shorey followed good classical precedents in characterizing our society as a tyranny of orators. The domination of ancient democracies by rhetoric is a commonplace of history, he said, but,. . . one of the most amazing illusions of modern optimism is the commonplace that science and critical scholarship have changed all this, and that our minds are no longer so easily swayed by rhetoric as were the minds of the ancients. . . [ellipse mine]. But man in the mass is still ever even more a rhetorical animal than he is a political, a logical, or a laughing animal.*

What deceives us is that tastes in rhetoric change, and certain forms of long-winded, sonorous, old fashioned bombast no longer appeal to the sophisticated among us. . . But if we take rhetoric in its truer and broader sense as a misuse of any kind of fallacy, irrelevance, ornament, emotion, suggestion, wit, epigram, to gain some advantage over sober reason and fact, then there has never been a time in the history of mankind when its power was so great. . . .The neglect of such study of rhetoric in our education is very surprising in view of the enormous and increasing part played by public speaking, directly, or in report or broadcast, in the formation of that public opinion which is the master of us all. . . [ellipse mine]. What I really mean is not that we don't study rhetoric in a fashion, but that we don't study it in the right way. The dominant aim in all university teaching of these subjects. . . should be the establishment of a resisting immunity. It is no legitimate function of public education to teach men how to overreach and persuade their fellows. Its proper task is to enlighten and harden the minds of those who make up the staple of audiences against such attempts. (1928, 261-262)

Shorey's 1927 address was not altogether different from the presentation he had made to the speech teachers five years earlier. In that speech he had advocated a similar approach to the problem and its solution.

. . . Our own teaching of rhetoric is too much concerned with the success of the speaker and too little with the edification of the audience. It is more interested in the "psychology" of "putting it over" and "getting it across" than in the training of the habits of logical analysis and suspense of judgement that would enable an audience to resist such hypnotization. Yet the greatest service which high school and college education could render to America today would be, not to multiply the number of fluent, plausible, and self-confident speakers, but to create in every audience a resisting minority that cannot be stampeded by plausible sophistry and emotional volubility. (116-117)

The teachers of speech had become somewhat more sophisticated about rhetoric in the ensuing five years. Hunt in his refutation, chose to make use of an argument which had been used since the time of Plato: that rhetoric is often used against rhetoric.

An examination of the arguments of even so well-trained a humanist as Professor Shorey suggests that when he is attacking the pseudo-sciences or other objects of his scorn, he does not regard his irrelevances and fallacies as misused; in such an occupation, apparently, any stick will do to beat a dog with; and as for ornament, emotion suggestion, wit epigram, his own pages are made sparkling by them; whether he thereby gains some undue advantage over sober reason and fact, who shall say? Rhetorical argument has always characterized the assailants of rhetoric. The profession of ignorance or distrust of the tricks of rhetoric is often itself a rhetorical trick. . . . Carlyle's long and repetitious diatribe against the stump orator bears a remarkable resemblance to a stump speech. . . . The early church fathers argued rhetorically against the use of rhetoric in sermons; and the most famous of all attacks on rhetoric, Plato's Gorgias, is full of sophistical argument and rhetorical ornament. (1928, 262-263)

Hunt's charges against the opponents of rhetoric hardly constituted an argument. His ad hominem attack was merely an accusation that the opponents were no better than the rhetoricians. Though historically accurate, his examples really did not address Shorey's concerns. Whether Shorey made use of rhetoric, or not, was there a problem with the use of rhetoric, especially with way in which it was taught? But, said Hunt, there is some value to the views articulated by Shorey.

> *There is much to be said for Professor Shorey's proposal, not so much as a substitute for present rhetorical instruction, as a complement to it. . . . But the rewards for resisting rhetoric and sophistry are likely to be social rather than individual. To this extent public educational institutions might well feel that greater public interest attaches to building up a resistance to self-seeking speakers—advertisers, salesmen, propagandists—than to creating them. (1928, 265)*

It was clear from Shorey's speech and Hunt's response that when they referred to instruction in rhetoric, they had in mind courses in public speaking more than courses in rhetorical theory or criticism. Hunt proposed to remedy the defects in rhetorical instruction by proposing a different kind of course.

> *It may well be, then, that teachers of rhetoric should have some course, or courses, in which they reverse the usual emphasis on performance. . . and aim specifically at the development of an intelligently critical attitude. . . . Of what would such a course consist? In the discussions of rhetoric by Plato and Isocrates we have a philosophical treatment of the function of rhetoric which raises practically all the questions one would desire to discuss today. The* Rhetoric of Aristotle *gives an admirably systematized view of the art, a penetrating analysis of human nature, and a philosophical notion of the relation of rhetoric to ethics, politics, logic, psychology and literary criticism. These three writers would furnish a comprehensive view of the field of rhetoric, and they would give the point of view from which the many modern methods of persuasion could be studied. (1928, 266)*

The course proposed by Hunt was quite consonant with his views, expressed earlier in his debate with Woolbert, that the public speaking course should be the central arena for general education. Indeed, in his response to Shorey, Hunt expanded his conception of rhetoric to include almost all human study. Hunt came close to saying that "everything is rhetoric."

> *A study of public opinion, which is often dignified with the title of political science, is properly a part of rhetoric; much of what passes for social psychology is rhetoric; the books on crowds and mob psychology are studies in rhetoric. Economic theory relating to the wants of men may profitably approached from the point of view of Aristotle's* Rhetoric. . . . *Professor Shorey deserves our gratitude for calling attention so forcibly to a neglected aspect of education; intelligent efforts should be made to develop the necessary materials and technique. (1928, 266, 268)*

Hunt actually went further in his proposal than Shorey's critique suggested. He took Shorey's admonitions so seriously that he proposed action which must have seemed audacious in its own day, and which might strike us even today as an improbable course of action. The proposal to study Plato, Isocrates and Aristotle was, of course, not remarkable, but the idea that rhetoric should invade the territory of other disciplines was daring. Hunt conceived of rhetoric as an an overarching discipline which spread its influence into almost all fields concerned with human behavior. To envision rhetoric as a component of disciplines as diverse as political science economics and psychology was a startling departure from the conventional view of rhetoric in 1928. In contrast to the common wisdom, Hunt advocated not a derivative conception of rhetoric; rather he espoused a view of rhetoric as a discipline which had made significant, although unrecognized, contributions to other disciplines. It was clear from

Hunt's editorial that rhetoric was not to be thought of as being entirely, or even largely, concerned with speechmaking, or even orality. Hunt saw rhetoric in action in any enterprise which involved human persuasive behavior.

The audacity of Hunt's editorial was apparently not recognized, or even noticed by the profession. Perhaps it was not read as a serious proposal. In any case, it seemed to sink without a ripple. Hunt's position was validated many years later when rhetoric turned to examine non-oral artifacts as objects of rhetorical study. Ironically, the central position of rhetoric in a number of disciplines came to be recognized, not by the rhetorical theorists of Speech Communication but by the scholars in disciplines such as Sociology, Economics and Law.

The discussion concerning the role and stature of rhetoric and rhetorical studies was continued in 1928 by V.E. Simrell of Dartmouth in his long and thoughtful essay "Mere Rhetoric." Early in the article Simrell placed the question in a historical context, going back to the dawn of Greek literature.

> *The rhetorician might be good or he might be evil, wise or foolish, but he was always to be feared by his enemies and admired by his friends. Homer gave the world one of its best picaresque novels, with a hero, Ulysses, whose greatest gift was the power of eloquence; but he thereby fastened upon Greek consciousness the notion that a man whose intellect would never have made him better than a dealer in used chariots was by power of eloquence made a hero. And Greek thought passed on the tradition by which the rogue-hero of many a later epic has been made. It was this that Socrates threatened to destroy. (1928, 359)*

But, said Simrell, rhetoric was never regarded by the Greeks as virtuous in itself. It was a necessary social instrument. Simrelll made the claim that, in spite of common wisdom, there was not much difference between the attitudes toward rhetoric of Socrates, Aristotle and the Sophists. They all sought the same end.

> *So that Socrates by making rhetorical heroes into cooks, Aristotle by justifying rhetoric as a necessary concession to human weakness, and the Sophists of the degenerate sort by their obvious effrontery and ignorance, were all actually working toward the same end, namely, the recognition that rhetoric was not heroic, but only necessary, not admirable in itself, but only an expedient method of controlling human thought. (1928, 360)*

Since the Greeks regarded rhetoric only as a means and not as end desirable in itself, the blame for the modern conception of rhetoric must be found elsewhere. Having exempted the Greeks from responsibility for the twentieth century view of rhetoric, Simrell found that the present condition was due to influences from unexpected times and places.

> *The conception of rhetoric which has dominated modern thought is inherited not from Socrates, not from Aristotle, not from the Sophists whom Lucan satirized, but from two largely independent but perfectly cooperative influences; the influence of Cicero and the influence of the Church. And that's where the trouble lies. Cicero and the Church Fathers were presumably moral, upright and intelligent men, but in order to make their uprightness and intelligence generally effective they recognized the necessity of flattering the weak judgment of their auditors with mere rhetoric. But Cicero and the Church Fathers perpetuated the notion that rhetoric was itself a good thing. . . . The effect of their influence has been the lasting belief that rhetoric is the proper method of civic and moral leadership and the best method of making civic and moral virtue prevail. (1928, 361)*

Simrell went on to make the case that rhetoric was essentially lacking in any moral purpose whatever and that its success was due to the moral and intellectual deficiencies of audiences, rather than to any inherent virtue of rhetoric. By drawing an analogy with war Simrell sought to expose the base nature of rhetoric, at least as it was then conceived and performed.

> *We know perfectly well that, however noble the purpose of a particular war may be, that war is, itself, as a method, wholly unreasonable, ineffective and wrong. We know also that mere rhetoric, i.e. all the devices of persuasion which are either substituted for or added to logical argument and veritable information, is likewise, as a method of enforcing justice and truth, unreasonable, ineffective and wrong. Either war or rhetoric may be justified, or at least necessitated, by circumstances and the weak judgments of men, but the recognition of the fact that they are not reasonable or in any way admirable as as method is quite essential to any relief of the circumstances which necessitate them. (1928, 361)*

How then shall we overcome the serious problems of a world, or at least a nation, dependent on rhetoric, with all its shortcomings, as a method for enforcing justice and truth? It will not come from Shorey's plan to create a "coercive public opinion" against rhetoric. Rather the solution, or amelioration, will come from a plan less coercive than Shorey's. Simrell's hope was that it would be possible to create a climate in which rhetoric was no longer necessary or effective.

> *The relief of the situation must come, not from righteous (i.e. rhetorical) indignation or Professor Shorey's plan of "establishing a coercive public opinion" against rhetoric, but from the perfection and general use of methods which will obviate the necessity for rhetoric, and will, instead of ministering to the weak judgment of audiences, minister to whatever good judgment audiences may have and at the same time seek to develop that good judgment by encouragement and responsibility. (1928, 361-362)*

But this statement was, after all, fairly general. How, exactly, did Simrell propose to bring into being a society in which rhetoric was no longer needed. After mentioning educating students in "rational certainty" and "a moral determination to be logical," Simrell turned to a Platonic scheme to save the world from rhetoric. He envisioned that the speech classroom might play an important role in the fostering of dialectic and the eventual elimination of rhetoric.

> *One of the best methods of protecting the rhetorician himself, and hence also his other victims, against the rhetorical habit is the constant practice of dialectic, in the sense of discussion by dialogue. . . . It would be very easy to for teachers of rhetoric to substitute dialectic for a large part of their speechmaking and debate. It would also be very easy to encourage class-room audiences to interrupt their speakers as freely and perhaps as intelligently as the hecklers of Hyde Park Interrupt theirs. (1928, 371)*

Dialectic, however, had its own disadvantages, said Simrell. It ". . . can easily become merely disorganized rhetoric."

In the end, Simrell called for nothing less than a profound social and intellectual change. We need to come to an entirely different mind set to avoid our own emotional biases; we must be determined to become more rational and, thus, to render rhetoric irrelevant. We will make of rhetoric nothing more than a pleasant pastime.

> *Finally we need a deliberate revision of our commonplaces of rhetorical judgment*

in order to overcome our emotional bias in favor of the orator, as against the well-informed man who merely tells the truth and lets it go at that. . . . We need to remember that the speaker or writer who, instead of proving his arguments, identifies them with our present beliefs is appealing to our common habits of rationalization and not to our reason. . . . These and similar revised standards of rhetorical criticism would give us greater accuracy in distinguishing. . . a vomit of words from a torrent of important knowledge, and the oracle. . . from the mere orator. Rhetoric has still a long and merry and even useful life before it. . . . Its users might still be honored as cooks, but not followed as heroes and leaders in affairs of state. . . . This expedient may serve us fairly well until such time as the human race generally develops a safe and scientific method of intellectual birth-control. (1928, 373-374)

Rhetoric had clearly taken several blows from external adversaries. At a time when many members of the Speech profession had begun to think of rhetoric as the field which would bring them the greatest academic respectability, distinguished scholars were questioning the very validity of rhetoric. If Shorey and Simrell were to be followed, rhetoric would be removed from the curriculum or so severely modified as to be unrecognizable. As construed by Storey and Simrell, rhetoric consisted of the knack of appealing to base emotions and of paying little attention to reason and intellect. Rhetoric was no more valid than Plato portrayed it in the *Gorgias* and actions must be taken severely to reduce its power, even if it were necessary to undertake the reeducation of the population.

Further, Storey and Simrell struck at one of the bases of the profession in general. They conceived, probably correctly, that the teaching of public speaking was equivalent to training in rhetoric. Thus the very foundation of the new field was brought into question. Simrell's and Storey's proposals may strike us now as unlikely Utopian solutions to what they perceived as fundamental social and political problems. The possibility that American thought could be realigned was, without question, unrealistic. Nevertheless, the speech profession had reason to be concerned if the presentations were indicative of the reputation of rhetoric in the academy. Ironically, the research path into Winans' "sheepfold" through rhetoric was not as open as it had seemed to be. As if attacks from the present were not enough, Hoyt Hudson presented to the readers of *The Quarterly Journal* a translation of John Jewel's mid-sixteenth century "Oration Against Rhetoric." Hudson's evaluation of the oration was not so different from Hunt's response to Shorey that rhetoric may very effectively be used against rhetoric.

As to the oration itself, the reader is at liberty to take it as seriously as he likes. The fundamental paradox of a man's using his best eloquence to denounce eloquence is amply exemplified in similar attacks elsewhere. (1928, 376)

Hudson was well aware that the attack on rhetoric in Jewel's oration was nothing new.

The principal topics of an anti-rhetoric may be traced back to Plato's Gorgias *and Lucan's* The Teacher of Rhetoric, *and had been drawn upon by many before Jewel took them up. (1928, 377)*

Interestingly, Simrell, in the issue immediately following his "Mere Rhetoric," undertook a review of Governor Alfred E. Smith's "Annual Message to the Legislature of New York State." Simrell found that Smith's address met his rhetorical criteria, at least when the Governor discussed Prohibition.

> *Even in his discussion of Prohibition, where he was most expected to indulge in campaign propaganda, the Governor limits himself to stating the business of the immediate audience. (1928a, 460)*

However praiseworthy were Smith's abilities, he was not able to defeat Herbert Hoover in the presidential campaign in that year. Smith's Catholicism and his stand against Prohibition were undoubtedly more decisive than his appeals to reason.

Simrell was taken to task in 1929 by Edwin H. Paget of Syracuse University in his article, "Woodrow Wilson: International Rhetorician." In "Mere Rhetoric" Simrell had referred to Wilson as a speaker who was both a victim of and a perpetrator of rhetoric. Simrell had written of Wilson that, "The habits of rhetorical thinking largely incapacitates him for disinterested impartial thought" (1928, 359). Although Paget's essay was essentially a rhetorical criticism, he directed a refutation at Simrell's general position before he turned to his own rhetorical criticism of Wilson.

> *But Mr. Simrell advances an even more serious objection, an objection to rhetoric itself. Men will never know the facts if public speakers use persuasive methods which appeal to the emotions and prejudices of their audiences. . . . Insufficient space prevents me at this time from pointing out the full implications of Mr. Simrell's attitude. Obviously, its adop[tion would completely change our methods of teaching public speaking and persuasion. (1929, 16-17)*

In the Forum section of the same issue of *The Quarterly Journal* Simrell was subjected to a more systematic and specific attack by Raymond Howes in an essay which he titled "In Defense of Rhetoric." Howes undertook to question Simrell's premise that our reason rather than our emotions must be appealed to.

> *. . . Mr. Simrell does not decry all rhetoric. He approves exposition and logic. What he dislikes is "mere rhetoric," which includes "all the devices of persuasion which are either substituted for or added to logical argument and veritable information." . . . But the majority of us are not that way, and never will be. . . Religion, for instance, is not based on reason. . . . Religion, faith, hope, charity, love, humanity, art may denote weakness but they supply much of the world's happiness. And since unreasonableness and emotion play so large a part in life, human decisions of all sorts are inevitably affected by them. (1929, 82)*

Howes rejected Simrell's contention that dialectic could replace rhetoric. It had, he said, problems as serious as rhetoric.

> *But Mr. Simrell offers another substitute for rhetoric—dialectic. . . . But even a cursory reading of Plato's Dialogues shows what any teacher can observe in the classroom, that in dialectic the person with the stronger mind reaches the conclusion he desires . . . . Dialectic, as a method, is as susceptible of misuse as rhetoric. . . . Dialectic is not a substitute for rhetoric, but as Aristotle says, its counterpart. (1929, 83-84)*

Rhetoric, said Howes, must continue the precedent set by Aristotle. We have a duty not to discourage the use of rhetoric, but to educate our students in its proper use.

> *Instead of being cynical, we should be thankful that intelligent leaders have at their command the power to persuade others. That the unintelligent and the corrupt have the same power is lamentable but not as dangerous as it might seem. Aristotle was not playing Pollyana when he said that in an even battle of rhetoric the better side will prevail. The duty of the American college is to see that the battle line of the*

intelligent is kept full. That can never be done if we teach our students that rhetoric is a dishonorable weapon. All we can say with justice is that it should not be used dishonorably. (1929, 85)

Although Richard Whately's *Elements of Rhetoric* had been referred to from time to time, the first examination of Whately's rhetorical theory did not appear until 1929 with the publication of "Whately and his Rhetoric" by Wayland Maxwell Parrish of the University of Pittsburgh. Parrish's essay was representative of its time; much more space was devoted to the details of Whately's life and the events surrounding the work than to the examination of the *Elements of Rhetoric*. Parrish divided his 22 page article into four sections.

> *A. Formative Influences.*
> *B. Probable Date of the Composition of the Rhetoric.*
> *C. Growth of the Rhetoric.*
> *D. Sources of the Rhetoric.*

Parrish told his readers more about Richard Whately than about his rhetorical theories. The readers learned about: the influence of Coppleston, the Oriel Common Room, Whately's independence of mind, his method of composition, and his interest in political economy. Only in the section captioned "Sources of the Rhetoric" did Parrish undertake an examination of Whately's work. He devoted a total of six pages to his analysis. The title of the section, "Sources of the Rhetoric," was accurate; Parrish chose to compare Whately's work with that of other rhetorical theorists, Aristotle in particular, rather than examine the work on its own merits. Parrish was apparently more interested in the influences brought to bear on Whately rather than the intrinsic character of the *Elements*. Parrish, sometimes, credited Whately with some originality, but he seemed puzzled or disturbed that he could find no source for some of Whately's ideas. This feature of Parrish's work was illustrated in his discussion of presumption and burden of proof.

> *Whately's ruminative habits are further evident in the long section on Presumption and burden of proof (112-132). There is no clue as to what caused him to insert this topic in the third edition, and to amplify it in subsequent editions. It owes no indebtedness to Aristotle or Campbell, but seems characteristically the product of Whately's own mind. (1929, 76)*

The idea of presumption and burden of proof was, of course, not "the product of Whately's own mind." As we have long known, the idea was taken from English Common Law, where it had been operative for centuries, as it had been in the United States.

Parrish actually kept count of the references to other authors in *The Elements of Rhetoric*, and in a division of the essay which he called "Sources of His Illustrations," he told his readers that "It may be well to tabulate the number of references to or quotations from his principal sources" (1929, 78). The most frequently cited sources were Aristotle's *Rhetoric* with 39 references, followed by Whately's *Elements of Logic* with 32.

Parrish undertook his examination of *The Elements* part by part, attributing sources of influences as he went. He made no attempt to offer a fully integrated evaluation. We must recognize that Parrish's work was the first serious examination of Whately, but, at the same time, we must acknowledge that Parrish's work was less sophisticated than earlier analyses of classical rhetoric.

Parrish's summary attributed influences on Whately to a number of writers and he credited Whately with only minimal contributions to rhetorical theory.

> *In summary, then, it may be said that Aristotle's* Rhetoric *furnished the bulk of the texts from which Whately developed his thoughts on rhetoric. The whole treatise bears evidence of his preoccupation with logic. He borrows frequently from Campbell and gets occasional thoughts from Cicero and Bacon. His thinking is colored throughout by his close familiarity with the writings of Butler, Paley, Adam Smith, and Copleston. . . . In conclusion, it may be said that inasmuch as the field of Rhetoric is somewhat limited and was completely surveyed by Aristotle, no new principles are to be expected in a modern work on this subject. Whatever claims to originality may be made for Whately, must consist in his novelty of arrangement and illustration. (1929, 77, 79)*

Parrish's analysis of the *Elements of Rhetoric* was a good example of how uninformed examination could lead to a wrong, even wrong-headed, examination. The citation count of sources told the readers almost nothing about the nature of Whatley's rhetorical theories. In addition, Parrish seemed to have no real understanding of the intellectual climate prevalent during Whately's career. Most serious, however, was Parrish's dismissal of the significance of Whately, who was regarded by Departments of English as a member of the Grand Triumvirate of British Rhetorical Theory—Blair, Campbell and Whately. Parrish was intellectually myopic in his assertion that nothing since Aristotle's *Rhetoric* was left to be learned. Parrish's essay, for all his eminence in 1928, could not have added to the prestige of a new discipline.

In 1929 Hunt assigned himself the task of reviewing four new books on propaganda and public opinion. In his review Hunt undertook to repeat, in a somewhat different setting, his response to Storey in which he asserted that much of what was studied in other disciplines was rhetoric. The range to which Hunt extended rhetoric was truly astounding for its time.

> *When Plato defined rhetoric as the art of persuading an ignorant multitude, without imparting any real instruction, he refused to allow it the dignity of a science, but a knack, a habit of a bold and ready wit. A systematic observation of rhetoricians and their ways in these days, however, contribute largely to that body of knowledge called political science. . . . Psychologists, many of whom claim to confine their interests to an explanation of the behavior of the human organism, find the phenomena of persuasion and public opinion increasingly significant in the interpretation of the individual. . . . When an economist studies persuasion "scientifically," he may join the "younger school" and discard most of his inheritance. . . . From the present-day observation of this despised knack of the persuader, then we get books on rhetoric, advertising, salesmanship, propaganda, publicity, psychology, political science, economics, history, sociology, sociological history,—and at times we have them all combined in philosophy. (1929, 111)*

Hunt's willingness to extend the boundaries of rhetoric to incorporate much of Social Science was as bold a move in 1929 as it had been in 1928. His position, however, received almost no response and did not become an issue among the membership.

Hunt found that some chapters in Frank R. Kent's *Political Behavior* would not pass muster in a rhetoric text, and Hunt could not resist yet another volley against Shorey.

> *The chapters on the art of seeming to say something without doing so, on giving the public a good show, on "hokum", on name and face stuff, on getting attention of the press, are specifically rhetorical instruction. If incorporated into texts on rhetoric*

> *they would probably shock even those who will admit that rhetoric is as unmoral as politics. Perhaps the best place for such information is in Professor Shorey's class in preventive rhetoric. (1929, 114)*

Hunt's willingness to spread the dimensions of rhetoric was a significant perception of the focus of the field. One can, of course, speculate as to what might have become of rhetorical theory if Hunt's thoughts had been put into action and what the response of the social sciences might have been. Hunt's description of the Kent book might also apply to politics in the 1990s. How, we wonder, would Hunt evaluate present day political rhetoric?

The Graduate Study and Research section of *The Quarterly Journal* printed the abstract of Russell Wagner's dissertation, Thomas Wilson's "Arte of Rhetorique," completed at Cornell (1929, 139-142).

Further knowledge of classical rhetoric was offered by J.P. Ryan of Grinnell College in the printing of his 1928 presidential address, "Quintilian's Message." Although Quintilian's work had been cited earlier, Ryan's was the first specific examination of the Institutes.

Ryan did not envision his task in writing the Quintilian essay as a work of true scholarship. He closely defined the limits of his study.

> *My purpose in this address is neither to deal with the history of this book, nor with the story of its influence. . . nor to give a summary of its contents. There is here no attempt at scholarship in exegesis and exposition. My modest purpose is to tell the story of his life and work in such a way as to make you feel its perennial freshness; and to comment upon some dicta about rhetoric so as to lead you to think there may be something of permanence in his message. (1929, 172)*

In fact the bulk of Ryan's address was dedicated to asserting the modernity and present-day application of Quintilian. In doing so, however, Ryan provided a brief, and very selective, introduction to the Institutes. He stressed the contemporaneous nature of Quintilian's educational philosophy by listing ten topics discussed by Quintilian which were of present interest.

> *Such a list might well be taken as the program of round-table discussions in a present day convention of teachers of education. Or it might suggest a series of topics set for graduate study. But to everyone it must demonstrate the surprising modernity of this man. (1929, 175)*

Ryan was quite unspecific in his description of Quintilian's theories. We must consider, however, that Ryan's essay was a presidential address of only a half hour's duration, delivered to a nighttime audience. His address was as much an epideictic as a scholarly event. Ryan concluded his speech by fantasizing what Quintilian's message would be to various members if he were to materialize on December 28, 1928 in Chicago.

> *To those plodding patiently in their graduate studies, cordial would be his greeting. . . . He knew what it costs to carry on research without the concomitant neglect of the students. Cordial too, would be his greeting to those whose primary interest is teaching. . . . No other subject in the curriculum can furnish more difficult teaching opportunities, or yield richer educational values. And very cordial and gracious would be his greeting to those who are interested in the relation of speech and personality. . . . He would go deeper and say that speaking is a virtue and*

> *hence all the rhetorical qualities: clearness, force, elegance, coherence, etc., are*
> *sourced in the spiritual side of man's personality. (1929,180)*

The dispute concerning Paul Shorey was briefly reignited by Hoyt Hudson who questioned Shorey's originality about defensive rhetoric. Hudson quoted from the preface of William Guthrie's 1755 translation of Cicero's *De Oratore*.

> *I shall only add while I am upon this Subject, that the following Pages are*
> *adapted not only for the use of a Speaker, but for that of a Hearer. They are fitted to*
> *enable one to judge as well as to speak. . . . (Guthrie as quoted by Hudson, 1929, 256)*

Whether Shorey claimed originality or not, Hudson's point was well taken. He could have easily pointed out that eighteenth century belletristic writers such as Blair and Rollin had also written their works to be of use for the critic as much as for the practitioner.

J. Fred McGrew of Western State College for Teachers at Kalamazoo, Michigan presented the readers of *The Quarterly Journal* with a 32 page annotated "Bibliography of the Works on Speech Composition in England during the 16th and 17th Centuries." Undoubtedly, McGrew rendered a valuable service to the profession since the sixteenth and seventeenth centuries had hardly been explored. Oddly, McGrew did not reveal the sources of his bibliography. He did acknowledge that:

> *This bibliography is a research paper begun in a Seminary (sic.) in the Speech*
> *department of the University of Michigan, during the summer session of 1928,*
> *under the guidance of Professor J. M. O'Neill. I have been materially aided by the*
> *helpful data and suggestions furnished by Professor Hoyt H. Hudson of Princeton*
> *University and Professor W.P. Sanford of the University of Illinois. (381)*

The length of McGrew's bibliography was misleading because he presented his information in two different forms. One list was arranged chronologically; the other was structured alphabetically. To his bibliography he appended two additional lists: "List of Catalogues and Books of Bibliographical Information Referred to in this Article" and "List of Books Containing Reprints of Early English Works, Specific Reference to Which Has Been Made in This Article" (409-412). William P. Sanford of the University of Illinois to whom McGrew had acknowledged his indebtedness, and who had been carrying on a dispute with Russell Wagner in *The Quarterly Journal* concerning the correct interpretation of Thomas Wilson, gave greater meaning to McGrew's bibliography. In his 1929 article, "English Rhetoric Reverts to Classicism, 1600-1650." Sanford, by focusing on a narrower time span than McGrew, and by devoting more than 20 pages to his study, was able to flesh out what McGrew had merely annotated.

The thesis of Sanford's argument was clearly stated at the very outset of his essay when he set out to demonstrate the difference between English rhetoric in the sixteenth and seventeenth centuries.

> *Sixteenth century Englishmen, typically, thought of rhetoric as the art of*
> *embellishing speech by means of elocutio—style, particularly figures and tropes and*
> *pronunciatio—oral delivery. By the middle of the seventeenth century, although the*
> *stylistic tradition was still influential, they thought of rhetoric as the faculty of*
> *planning speeches upon any subject with the end of persuasion. (1929, 503)*

After describing the English study of classicism and the continental rhetoricians, Sanford turned to a fairly brief analysis of the work of Francis Bacon. His view of Bacon was one which is not widely shared today. Sanford portrayed Bacon as returning rhetoric to classicism, whereas he is now considered to be more original than Sanford's description. Sanford, for example, said nothing about Bacon's reliance on faculty psychology and on induction. Sanford devoted more attention to Thomas Farnaby's *Index Rhetoricus* of 1625 and to Charles Butler's *Oratoriae Libri Duo* of 1629 than he did to the entire corpus of Bacon's work. Sanford attributed an exaggerated importance to Farnaby when he said of the *Index*:

> *In short, it must be accounted the most significant English rhetoric which has appeared since that of Wilson. Probably no work of equal influence appeared until 1776 when George Campbell wrote his* Philosophy of Rhetoric. *(1929, 518)*

Sanford summarized Butler's work by pointing out the classical elements to be found in it. In his final evaluation, Butler was to found at the pinnacle with Farnaby.

> *He has caught something of the richness and detail of classical lore, rather than the mere outlines. That his work was influential there is little doubt. . . . It deserves to rank with Farnaby, if not for influence, at least for thoroughness of classical treatment; and to rank above Farnaby for its details and its direct contact with ancient sources. (1929, 521)*

Thomas Hobbes *Whole Art of Rhetorick* of 1637 was disposed of in less than a page.

Although Sanford's essay was undoubtedly useful in 1929, it now seems naive and dated. The work of Farnaby and Butler is hardly known today, let alone written about. Sanford himself should not receive unnecessary criticism, however. We must remember how young the profession was and how little background many of the scholars had.

The article "Wilson and His Sources," which immediately followed Sanford's, was by his antagonist Russell Wagner. Wagner's essay, obviously based on his recently completed Cornell dissertation, was of the same genre as Parrish's Whately article, and Sanford's essay. Wagner's primary goal in his work was not to analyze, or even to describe Wilson's *The Arte of Rhetorique*. Rather, he saw as his task to trace the classical influences on Wilson. At least Wagner avoided Parrish's error of counting citations. Wagner realized the problems such a method would cause.

> *The mere listing of names of rhetoricians mentioned by Wilson scarcely permits the positive and categorical affirmation of their importance in the* Rhetoric. *At least one other test must be applied: what does a careful substantive examination of what he says reveal? (1929, 527)*

Having decided to undertake an examination rather than a counting, Wilson performed a careful textual analysis of Wilson's work and brought into question much of the common wisdom derived from earlier scholarship. Many authorities, including Jebb, Donald Lemen Clark, and Rhys Roberts had concluded that Wilson's *Rhetoric* was in total, or in large degree, influenced by Aristotle. Wagner's examination led him to a totally different conclusion.

> *It is safe to say that there is no instance of Wilson using Aristotle's* Rhetoric,. . . . *Every item of Wilson's theory, aside from his own homely advice, can be traced to indubitable sources, and they are all post-Aristotelian. (1929, 528)*

The most important source for Wilson's theories, Wagner argued, was Cicero.

> *If Wilson owes nothing to the first great name in the art of speaking, he is deeply indebted to the second. In the* Rule of Reason *he had defined rhetoric as the art of ornamentation, in the traditional English manner. But in the* Rhetoric *he defined*

*the subject as the art of artistic discourse, and his citation of Cicero as his authority
indicates that he had been reviewing the* De Oratore *and* De Inventione *since
writing his* Logic. *The three ends of rhetoric, to teach, to delight, and to persuade,
the methods by which one attains eloquence, the value of a written work on rhetoric
to the aspiring orator, are all broad, philosophical conceptions derived from the* De
Oratore. *(1929, 529-530)*

Wagner found only a little influence of Quintilian in Wilson's *Rhetoric*, but he did
detect possible influence from the *Ad Herrenium*. Wagner asserted that "The influence
of Erasmus on English rhetoric has thus far scarcely been suspected." Wagner also
speculated that Leonard Cox, an earlier rhetorical author of *The Arte or Craft of
Rhetorique*, "must be made a minor source." Wagner concluded that, with minor
exceptions, Wilson was dependent on classical sources.

> *The student who expects to find in Wilson traces of the evolution of rhetorical
> theory from classical to early modern times will be disappointed. . . . Wilson turned
> directly to the classics for his authority, with help now and then from such respected
> Renaissance interpreters of the ancients as Erasmus. (1929, 533)*

Certainly there were differences in quality among the articles of Parrish, Sanford
and Wagner. They all, however, had highly similar methods and objectives. All of the
articles sought to characterize the nature of the works of English rhetorical theorists
by comparing them with classical writers in an attempt to determine the influences on
the English theorists. In the young profession the early scholars, particularly in British
theory, seemed to searching for their roots through their explorations and finding their
identity in respected classical sources.

In a review contained in "Old Books" in *The Quarterly Journal*, Wagner presented an
appraisal of George Campbell's *Lectures on Pulpit Eloquence* in which he, again, sought
to assign classical derivations.

> *Here Campbell says all that is valuable in every modern "institute"on the
> rhetorical art is "serviley copied from Aristotle, Cicero and Quintilian, in whose
> writings, especially Quintilian's* Institutions, *and Cicero's* de inventione, *those
> called* ad Herennium *and his Dialogues de* Oratore, *every public speaker ought to
> be conversant." He adds to this list* Longinus on the Sublime *and Dionysius of
> Halicarnassus, "and some others." For the theory and practice of pulpit eloquence
> he recommends Rollin, Fenelon, Blair and a Mr. Farquhar. (1929a, 592)*

In spite of the prominence of such Eastern figures as Hudson, Hunt, Winans and
Wichelns, the program of the 1929 meeting of the Eastern Public Speaking Conference
did not contain a single paper on rhetoric ("New and Notes", 1929, 462-464).

Lester W. Thonssen of the University of Iowa undertook an analysis of Aristotle.
This time, however, Aristotle was approached from the perspective of modern psychology. Thonssen argued that Aristotle's rhetoric contains significant elements of
"functionalism."

> *Thus he implies that rhetoric enables human beings to adjust themselves more
> satisfactorily to the environmental settings in which they find themselves. In other
> words, it is able to perform a service, and to that end, is useful. This interpretation of
> the* Rhetoric *is highly suggestive of a modern school of psychological thought,
> functionalism, which has held a significant position in philosophical circles for more
> than a quarter of a century. (1930, 297)*

Thonssen thought that if Aristotle's *Rhetoric* could be thought of as a functionalist work its value might be enhanced.

> *. . . It will be interesting to raise the question of whether Aristotle, in writing the* Rhetoric, *presented the subject from a functional point of view. And it will be important to investigate this relationship because, if found to exist, it may be instrumental in vitalizing the place of the Rhetoric in modern speech theory. (1930, 297)*

Thonssen admitted that "Functionalism is difficult to define." After surveying the work of contemporary psychologists, including Tichener and Moore, Thonssen presented his not altogether clear definition which denied the mind-body distinction, and which conceived of mind and body as a unit.

> *. . . Functionalism is a school of thought in which the mind and body are regarded as a unit reacting to environment settings; the inherent make-up of the mind is not studied as a "content" but rather as a process which results in action and thereby effects a functional performance; and this activity is of the serviceable type. (1930, 300)*

Thonssen undertook to demonstrate, through references to passages in the *Rhetoric* and elsewhere, that Aristotle treated the human organism as a "psycho-biological unit," and that Aristotle's rhetorical theory was rooted in functionalism. Thonssen seemed to reduce serviceability to "practicality" so that any activity which performed a particular function might thus be classified as functional. Thonnsen, in quick order, surveyed the major contributions of Aristotle and found them to be reflective of functionalism, to the degree that they stressed serviceability and that they had a biological component. Thonssen felt that Aristotle's definition of rhetoric as "the faculty of observing in any case the available means of persuasion," placed the *Rhetoric* in a functional context.

> *. . . It is clear that the available means of persuasion perform a serviceable activity in that they effect a more satisfactory relationship between hearer and speaker and between hearer and environmental setting. Rhetoric, therefore, in effecting such adjustments, has as its function the performance of an activity which is serviceable. (1930, 304)*

Thonssen cited the modes of proof, the classification of the types of oratory, the example and the enthymeme, and arrangement as demonstrations of how functionalism operated in the *Rhetoric*. So far as can be determined, however, Thonnsen used functionalism to denote practical application, rather than "form" or theoretical knowledge. He illustrated this division in the summary of the section on arrangement and style. At the same time, he recognized that function and form might not be completely separable.

> *These functions have special reference to audience situations and, therefore, their forms have a multitude of possible applications. So the significant fact in the whole discussion of arrangement and style is the emphasis on the variations in form in order to meet particular situations, and thereby achieve particular ends. It is to be borne in mind, however, that a complete separation of function from form is quite impossible since the two are closely related features of rhetorical presentation. Elements of form, technically provided for, make possible satisfactory functional adaptations. (310)*

Thonssen's essay was very much of its time and represented fashionable intellectual currents. Functionalism had a certain popularity in the 20s and 30s, but it is heard of today only as a artifact of the times. Further, the distinction between function and form was pervasive in the arts as well as well as the social sciences. The call of the architects and designers of the period that "form follows function" illustrated the diffusion of the distinction. The influence, conscious or unconscious, of John Dewey and similar advocates of social adjustment was reflected in Thonssen's conclusions, although he did not seem completely confident about his findings.

> *The conclusions which may be drawn form such a brief study are tentative at*
> *their best. . . . When the work is taken as a whole, the prevailing tenor of the material*
> *is to the effect that all rhetorical forms are made to serve functional ends. Rhetoric is*
> *a practical art, designed to serve the ends of social adjustment. (1930, 310)*

Thonssen's was a valiant attempt to integrate the growing psychological influence in the profession with developing rhetorical scholarship. The mixture he might have hoped for was not produced, however. The effort to fit Aristotle into a functional frame seemed labored and the readers, when they read the essay, would be unlikely to know more about Aristotle than they had known before.

Apparently the article also had no great lasting influence on Thonssen himself; he did not venture into psychology after this effort and he went on to distinguish himself as a rhetorical scholar.

The "Graduate Study and Research" section of the 1930 *Quarterly Journal* abstracted the completed Ph.D. dissertations of 1929, and it listed the completed M.A. theses of the same year. Sanford's Ohio State dissertation, "English Theories of Public Address, 1530-1828," was abstracted. The scope of the study was formidable and today it seems much too broad for a single research project. The task of covering 300 years of the history of rhetorical theory in one dissertation would, today, seem impossible. In his dissertation Sanford examined ". . . about one hundred and fifty books on rhetoric, oratory and elocution written by Englishmen or used extensively in England" ("Graduate Study and Research," 1930, 387). The time span of the study was from Cox's *Art or Crafte of Rhetoryke* of 1530 to Whately's *Elements of Rhetoric* of 1828.

> *As was the case with his earlier cited article, Sanford's dissertation was a*
> *comparison and influence study. Their contents are compared with the five-fold*
> *theory of classical rhetoric, set forth by Aristotle, Cicero, Quintilian, and others. . . .*
> *("Graduate Study and Research," 1930, 387)*

In the same summary Parrish's Cornell dissertation on Whately was listed but not abstracted because his article on Whately, based on his dissertation, had already been published in *The Quarterly Journal*. Also listed was W.S. Howell's 1928 Cornell M.A. thesis "A Translation with Introduction and Notes of Alcuin's Disputatio de Rhetorica et Virtutibus." Howell, who spent his distinguished rhetorical career at Princeton, derived his book *The Rhetoric of Alcuin and Charlemagne* from his thesis.

Hoyt Hudson, at the 1930 meeting of the National Association, presented an address titled "The Tradition of Our Subject" which was published in *The Quarterly Journal* in 1931. In his speech/essay Hudson promised not to take his audience back to the very beginnings of the profession. Rather he chose to concentrate on later developments in rhetorical theory.

> *I do not intend to parade before your eyes the reverend figures of great and good*
> *men who in classical antiquity were teachers in some branch of the discipline we*
> *profess. In fact, disappointing as it may be to some, I hope to discuss the tradition of*

our subject without once mentioning the name of a certain Greek philosopher and scholar, the master of those who know. (I have always thought it would be interesting to attempt a performance of Hamlet with Hamlet left out.) Nor shall I mention a Roman orator who wrote treatises on speaking, or a Roman schoolmaster who did the same: there go Polonius and Horatio. (1931, 321)

For perhaps the first time in the history of the association, a serious scholar made a case not only that the discipline possessed an honorable tradition, but that it was of the utmost importance that the profession be aware of its history.

We have in keeping a discipline and a body of knowledge and an approach to education which have the interest and devoted labors of men in every one of these sixty-five generations. Surely we are in a rather graceless position if we act as a people without a history, as though wisdom was born with us, and hence would die with us. (1931, 327)

Sadly, Hudson's admonition was not taken seriously. Future generations were seemingly as ignorant of the history of the discipline as they were in 1931. This ignorance is particularly evident in the general lack of knowledge of the recent history of the profession. In 1985 I wrote of my own perception of the problem.

Speech communication is essentially a field without a history. . . . We are a field with no clear ideas of our sources and traditions. We really do not know what our roots are and. . . we reinvent our history from time to time, often creating different ones. . . . We are often not certain who we are. . . . Most of us are aware of the "state of the art," of the most recent research and thought, and what is being written in our field and in related disciplines. Few of us are, however, have a very coherent idea of how the art arrived at its present state. (Cohen in Benson, 1985, 283)

I had not yet read Hudson's essay when I wrote of the historical deficiencies. I felt, however, as if I had plagiarized Hudson when he wrote:

Every one of the sixty-five generations I spoke of was once the younger generation, intensely and very much modern, as now we are. And we, modern as we are, will be just as antiquated, just as dusty, just as quaint, just as funny—after a few years have come and gone. By studying thoroughly our tradition, by becoming acquainted with speech training as it was carried on in one or more of the centuries preceding ours, we can become acquainted with ourselves. . . We can see the pitfalls that lie about our path, the tangents upon which we are in danger of flying off, we can profit by the mistakes of our ancestors, who say to all of us too truly, "As I am now   so shall you be.". . . Keen as may be the thrill of the pioneer,. . . . However far we may have come, whatever new ground we have advanced upon, we shall go farther more surely, we shall hold that ground permanently, if we take care not to cut our lines of communication with the past. (Hudson, 1931, 328, 329)

Although said less gracefully, I made a similar point about the professional ig-norance about our recent history. Indeed the kind of argument made by Hudson impelled me to undertake this study.

We are not very aware of how questions came to be posed, of the various paths we have taken, which were detours, which were dead ends, and which led to bountiful fields. We are also not very cognizant of the paths not taken—those alternate paths available to us that we chose not to travel. (Cohen in Benson, 1985, 283)

Hudson offered his listeners and readers a brief reading list which would bring them

in touch with their own historical development. The list may strike us now as somewhat idiosyncratic, but almost any short list would strike most of us as eccentric.

> *I suggest it isn't too much to expect every one of us to know Thomas Wilson's*
> Arte of Rhetorique, *published in 1553, Thomas Sheridan's* Lectures on
> Elocution, *published in 1762, James Rush's* Philosophy of the Human Voice,
> *published in 1827, and Richard Whately's* Elements of Rhetoric *published in 1828.*
> *With these four, I would suggest an equal number of ancient works—eight books in*
> *all. Is it too much to expect? (1931, 328)*

Although Hudson had earlier sketched out the importance of some earlier contributions to theory, his recommendation might have seemed prescriptive to his readers
since he did not specifically state the reasons that this quartet was significant. The
"ancient works" were not specified; his audience apparently had to make educated
guesses. Obviously, two of the four books were not in rhetoric at all. They were,
however, an indication of the Hudson's breadth of interest. Hudson's essay, as with
his 1923 article "The Field of Rhetoric," is a much ignored contribution to the intellectual foundation of the profession. His articles delineate a clear and cogently thought
out conception of rhetoric, from both a historical and theoretical perspective.

Hudson himself is a largely unrecognized giant of our discipline. While his contemporaries, Winans, Wichelns and Woolbert, are widely recognized and are honored by
awards in their name by the Speech Communication Association, as well they should
as pioneers of the discipline, Hoyt Hudson's name, let alone his contributions, are all
but unknown to members of the profession. Hudson preceded Wichelns in delineating
the province of rhetoric and was a true pioneer in enunciating the need for the
discipline to be aware of its historical roots. Perhaps, if Hudson had not become a
Professor of English and Department Head at Princeton, he would be better known.

The first discussion of Thomas Hobbes as a rhetorical theorist was presented by
Lester Thonssen, by then at the College of the City of New York. Thonssen's, essay
"Thomas Hobbes' Philosophy of Speech" recognized Hobbes's summary of Aristole's
Rhetoric, a work known as *Whole Art of Rhetorik*. Principally, however, Thonssen sought
to find philosophical bases for Hobbes' rhetorical theory in other of his writings,
particularly *Human Nature* and *Of Man*.

In his brief treatment Thonssen was perceptive in identifying certain aspects of
Hobbes' thinking which were relevant to his conception of speech. He justified his
procedure by suggesting that all theories of human communication are based on
philosophical presuppositions.

> *. . . Even the most functional treatments of rhetoric and public speaking are*
> *heavily charged with the philosophical and what might be called the academic. Few*
> *would feel disposed to condemn the philosophical settlings and accompaniments of*
> *our rhetorical supports. (1932, 200)*

Because of its brevity, Thonssen's essay did not explicate Hobbes' assumptions in
depth. Rather the article identified the elements in Hobbes' philosophy which were
relevant to rhetoric. Thonssen discussed the way in which Hobbes connected mind-
body separation, imagination and voluntary motion to speech.

> *The human body, according to Hobbes, is composed of two principal parts, body*
> *and mind. . . . The powers of the mind are cognitive and imaginative while the*
> *powers of the body are nutritive, motive and generative. In Hobbes' thought world*
> *imagination plays a significant role. He speaks of two kinds of motion peculiar to all*
> *animals: the one is called vital motion and the other voluntary motion. Furthermore,*

imagination is fundamental to it. . . . Thus speech becomes an active principle. It is a
voluntary motion which has its roots deep in imagination. . . . Discourse has its
beginnings in the imagination. (1932, 201-203)

Thonssen integrated material from both *Human Nature* and *Of Man* to demonstrate
the importance of the passions in speech as manifestations of the "voluntary motions
which their nature requires." In delineating Hobbes' distinction between emotion and
thought, Thonssen saw the persistent distinction between conviction and persuasion.

> *Hobbes draws a distinction between speech which expresses emotional content*
> *and speech which expresses thought content. . . . It is to be recognized that there is a*
> *"feeling" attached to mere thought content inasmuch as thought involves motion.*
> *Nevertheless the division of speech forms for passion and speech forms for thought is*
> *highly suggestive of the dichotomous treatment of persuasion and conviction so*
> *prevalent in modern speech theory. (1932, 204)*

Thonssen perceived that Hobbes regarded speech to be distinct from thought.
Speech was a transmission agent.

> *Hobbes does not make speech and thought synonymous, it is to be observed, but*
> *instead, he makes speech the agency for transference of thought into verbal form.*
> *Mental discourse there could be without speech, but there could be no definite*
> *communication of thought sequences and so the social world would suffer. (1932,*
> *205)*

Hobbes, Thonssen wrote, was concerned with the persistent question of the
morality of rhetoric.

> *Although Hobbes observes that speech was man's most noble and profitable*
> *invention, he adds that it has brought about abuses as well as advantages. Speech*
> *enables men to register their thoughts wrongly, to use words metaphorically with*
> *consequent deception. . . and to cause grief to others. . . . In order to make truth*
> *prevail the person must make sure that. . . there must be no ambiguity.*
> *Understanding must result from speech. (1932, 205-206)*

Finally, of what value were the thoughts of Thomas Hobbes to rhetorical theorists
of 1932?

> *. . . His interest in rhetoric, his philosophical inquiry into the nature of speech*
> *and language, and his excellent brief of Aristotle's* Rhetoric *suggest the advisability*
> *of acknowledging him as a contributor of no mean distinction to a long and*
> *significant line of speech theory. (1932, 206)*

Thonssen's brief analysis of Hobbes was accurate and perceptive, but it seemed to
attract little interest in Hobbes as a rhetorical theorist. No really serious work on
Hobbes was done until 1986 with the publication of *The Rhetorics of Thomas Hobbes and
Bernard Lamy* by John T. Harwood (Harwood, 1986). Thonssen's important contribution was methodological. He demonstrated the possibility of bringing together
material from various sources to produce a synthesized understanding of one person's
rhetorical theory. A similar method would be used the next year in Donald Bryant's
examination of the works of Edmund Burke.

Donald C. Bryant (who was erroneously identified as Donald G.), then of the New
York State College for Teachers at Albany, began his distinguished career in *The
Quarterly Journal* with his 1933 essay, "Edmund Burke on Oratory." Bryant in time, of

course, would come to be recognized as a leading authority on Burke, within and outside the discipline.

Bryant set for himself the task of synthesizing a rhetorical theory for Burke since Burke had never written a work specifically dedicated to oratory or rhetoric. Bryant, therefore, found it necessary to consult almost the entire corpus of Edmund Burke's work and through his synthesis to bring forth an integrated portrait of Burke's remarks on rhetoric and oratory.

> But to discover Burke's opinions on oratory—his principles of rhetoric—recourse must be had to widely scattered fragments, inserted here and there through the whole library of his recorded utterances (sometimes, to be sure, virtually buried in volumes today almost never read). (1933, 1)

Bryant's task was quite different from that of Parrish, who concentrated on Whately's *Elements of Rhetoric*, and more nearly like Hudson's essay drawing out De Quincey's views on rhetoric from a number of his writings, and Thonssen's synthesis of Hobbes' contributions. Bryant, however, derived his synthesis by covering more works over a longer time span than did Hudson or Thonssen. Bryant consulted works ranging from Burke's *On the Sublime and the Beautiful* of 1756 to writing completed less than a year before Burke's death in 1797. Through his efforts Bryant was able to develop a framework of five rhetorical categories.

I.   *The Nature and Aim of Oratory*

II. *The Orator, his character, training and endowment*

III. *Some Practical Principles of Speech-making, including persuasion, argument, debate, consideration of the audience, and disposition or effective arrangement of the material*

IV. *Style, including the nature of oral and of written style*

V.   *Good Speech, a critical yard-stick (1933, 2)*

Bryant found in Burke's writings a relatively simple and thoroughly eighteenth century conception of rhetoric, yet one with clear resonances in classical rhetoric.

> The "end and purpose of oratory" is to be eloquent and convincing; its materials are the affairs of men in civil life. . . . (1933, 3)

Bryant's reconstruction of Burke's conception of the character of the orator was drawn from a number of Burke's writings, including: *Reflections on the Revolution in France, Letter to a Noble Lord*, and *Speech on Conciliation with the Colonies*. Bryant after examining Burke's writings on "character," concluded that Burke's ". . . conception of the orator was essentially that held by Cicero and Quintilian.

> . . . An orator ought to be acquainted with every great and important subject of art and nature—and we may add of politics, governments and economics. . . The orator is able, right fluent, convincing; he is also independent and fair, not imposing upon the understanding of the audience to gain its assent. He has respect as well for the persons and opinions of his opponents. . . . (1932, 3, 4, 5)

Bryant found in Burke a conception of persuasion which differed little from the standard eighteenth century position which held that persuasion was based on both reason and emotion. Although Bryant did not say so, Burke's position was similar to Campbell's.

> *Reason is the most important means of persuasion in political oratory, and should always be the foundation of persuasion. . . . Appeal to the emotions of an audience is, nevertheless, justifiable if it is done with fairness and decorum. . . He should know as much as possible about the operations of the emotions of men in general. (1933, 6)*

According to Bryant, Burke presented a conception of style, not unusual in the eighteenth century, which regarded style as the product of a particular mind. "Style grows out of the individual man and represents his peculiar way of thinking and of expressing his thoughts" (1933, 13). This description was much like Blair's definition of style as ". . . the peculiar manner in which a man expresses his conceptions by means of language." (101-102)

The description given by Bryant concerning Burke's standards for a good speech was much like that used by other rhetorical writers of the period.

> *A good speech being a work of art, has a single aim and purpose: and its limits are defined by that purpose. All the material contained in it supports that particular purpose and all else is excluded. (1933, 17)*

Bryant extracted his Burkean definition from *On the Sublime and the Beautiful* of 1756. It closely resembled the definitions of Campbell of 1776 and Blair of 1783. Campbell defined rhetoric as: "The word eloquence in its greatest latitude denotes 'that art or talent by which discourse is adapted to its end'" (23). Blair's conception was also similar. "For the best definition which, I think, can be given of eloquence, is the art of speaking in such a manner as to attain the end for which we speak" (261). Bryant's essay was as not important for the information it conveyed as it was for for evidence of skill in synthesizing a rhetorical theory from numerous sources. One could not imagine that Bryant was uninformed about the rhetorical theories of the late eighteenth century. In his essay, however, he does not mention any other rhetorical writer and, in fact, does not connect Burke to the intellectual and philosophical climates of his time. Bryant's later work revealed a much deeper understanding of eighteenth century thought.

Because of the research which had been done in early English Rhetoric by Hudson, Sanford and Wagner, among others, W. Norwood Brigance directed the attention of scholars to works to be found in the Henry Huntington Library. Brigance listed the works of Coxe, Wilson and Bacon as well as Gabriel Harvey's *Rhetor, Vel Duorum dierum Oratio De Natura, Arte et Exercitatione ad Suos Auditores* and Charles Butler's *Rhetoricae Libri Duo*. The dates of the various editions ranged from 1532 to 1640 (1933, 84-85).

A summary of the 1933 convention of the Eastern Public Speaking Conference noted that in the Public Speaking and Rhetoric sectional meeting a paper titled "An Early Seventeenth-Century View of Logic and Rhetoric" was presented by Wilbur S. Howell, then of Harvard. Lester Thonssen presented a paper titled "Some Notes on Criticism and the Tradition of our Subject" (1933, 458-459). Brigance, in his essay "Whither Research?" decried the lack of knowledge in the profession of their own rhetorical heritage.

> *Further, I think we ought to recognize that there is a great body of rhetorical or oratorical literature almost untouched by scholars in our field. Of it, I think we might safely say that this literature can do without our scholarship, but that our scholarship cannot do without that literature. (1933a, 556)*

The years in which Brigance wrote and succeeding years were actually the most fertile period for the exploration of historical rhetorical writings. In more recent times the study of the history of rhetorical theory has become increasingly less visible in the research of the discipline. At the same time, the rejuvenated interest in rhetoric in English departments has resulted in an enhanced historical interest in that discipline.

The summary of the 1933 convention of the association contained a report of the Committee on Bibliography. Brigance was the only rhetorician on the seventeen member committee. Nevertheless, the report did include a section on rhetoric and oratory.

II. *Rhetoric and Oratory*
1. *Rhetoric*
2. *Public Speaking*
3. *Preaching and Homiletics*
4. *Persuasion*
5. *Audience analysis and public opinion*
6. *History of rhetorical instruction   (We have in mind here such books as Baldwin's on ancient and medieval rhetoric and Roberts' on Greek rhetoric. If these can be covered by our first sub-heading, this may be omitted.)*
7. *History of oratory*
8. *Individual orators*
9. *Collections of speeches and oratory   (1934, 161.)*

Obviously, the terms "rhetoric" and "oratory" were given very broad definitions by the committee. The inclusion of sub-divisions as diverse as public speaking, homiletics, public opinion and persuasion made for an aggregative classification system which began with rhetoric undefined. The committee seemed uncertain whether the first category "rhetoric" also included the sixth category which dealt with the history of rhetorical pedagogy. Perhaps members of the committee had not read the essays of the past decade which sought to bring about a clearer understanding of rhetoric. Since the committee only recommended categories for the development of bibliographies, perhaps little harm was done.

Everett Hunt carried out an even more complex integrative study in his essay, "Matthew Arnold: The Critic as Rhetorician." Hunt undertook to examine the critical works of Arnold with the goal of extracting his attitude toward rhetoric. More specifically, Hunt isolated Arnold's objections to rhetoric, explained them and placed them in context. But Hunt set for himself a much grander goal. "This essay, then, is only a beginning of a more general study of the relations of criticism, rhetoric and scientific method" (1934, 485).

Hunt placed Arnold's criticism of rhetoric in a Platonic context and he included journalists and politicians under the rubric of "rhetorician."

> *The basis of Arnold's attack upon the rhetoricians, among whom he included most of the contemporary journalists and political leaders, was the Platonic conception of rhetoric as flattery. . . .This Arnold develops further as one of the reasons why journalistic comparisons of domestic and foreign institutions can rarely be trusted. The journalist is a confectioner intent on pleasing his own readers; all comparisons must and do flatter the home country and the truth is not in them.* (1934, 486)

Hunt's extension of his conception of rhetoric to include journalists and politicians certainly grew out of his reading of Arnold. Insight and perception, however, were required to translate Arnold's criticism into rhetorical criticism, especially at a time when the profession was largely oriented toward oral discourse. Hunt had the ability to recognize that all discourse which sought to influence was rhetorical. That point of view did not establish itself in the profession for a number of years.

Hunt described the ways in which Arnold maintained that rhetoricians had exploited human weakness.

> *But rhetoricians keep themselves in power by flattering the weaknesses of each of the classes. . . . Not only are the weaknesses of particular classes and organizations flattered by the rhetoricians, but those weaknesses which extend through all classes of society are made the common topics of patriotic oratory to the great increase of national complacency. Doctrines and pursuits entirely unworthy of a place as ends in themselves receive the blessings of rhetoricians. (1934, 487-488)*

As Arnold saw rhetorical exploitation in his day, Hunt applied the same standards to his own time. Similar standards of rhetorical judgment can be applied to the journalistic and political rhetoric of our time.

> *Hunt argued that the very act of criticism, no matter how it is designated, is a rhetorical act. Such a critic will be always and everywhere a rhetorician. If he is free from self seeking, refuses to become tied to organizations, and preserves his free play of ideas, he may be fortunate enough to be absolved from sophistry, but he belongs to the company of rhetoricians, weather (sic) he call himself philosopher or critic. Arnold's literary criticism, then, is as rhetorical as political and social writing. (1934, 505)*

Hunt's Matthew Arnold essay is another of the forgotten, or at least neglected, significant contributions to rhetorical theory. Hunt clearly was able to see that rhetoric need not be limited to oral discourse, or even to suasory discourse. Hunt's was perceptive in recognizing, through his study of Matthew Arnold, that criticism is in itself a rhetorical enterprise, no matter what the subject of the criticism may be. Hunt's essay was a bold departure from accepted rhetorical precepts. He was willing to extend the boundaries of rhetoric well beyond their contemporary limits. That Hunt extended his conception of rhetoric to cover Arnold was not as important as his understanding that the critical act is a rhetorical act. Unfortunately, Hunt's ideas were ignored, if they were understood, by the profession in general. Not for a quarter of a century would such an idea reemerge.

In 1934 William M. Lamers of Marquette University brought the members attention to a 1933 translation of the "Ratio Studiorum," in which he noted that St. Ignatius de Loyola and the Society of Jesus had encouraged rhetorical instruction and practice in the sixteenth century. Lamers specified the importance of classical sources.

> *A subdivision of the "Ratio Studiorum" is devoted to "Rules for the Professor of Rhetoric." Quintilian, Cicero, and particularly Aristotle are to supply the precepts, Cicero the model. (574)*

In 1934 the Association established a second journal, *Speech Monographs,* (now *Communication Monographs*). The new journal was designed as an outlet for longer and more research-oriented articles than had been published in *The Quarterly Journal.* Although articles on rhetoric were published in *Monographs,* the journal was also seen as an outlet for more "scientific "articles. Originally *Monographs* was published annually. Later it became the quarterly publication which it remains to this day. The first rhetorical theory essay to be published in *Monographs* was "Quintilian's Witnesses" by H.F. Harding of George Washington University. Harding's intention in his essay was not to offer a critical analysis of *The Institutes*. Rather, he chose to concentrate on the later day influence of Quintilian.

> *. . . There is evidence enough that Quintilian's book, the* Institutio Oratorio *or* The Education of the Orator, *has been studied and respected by English writers from the Renaissance to the present day. . . . In this paper I shall attempt to summon a few of the more important witnesses to the value of the Institutio. Their testimony will be found of two kinds: direct praise of the book, and secondly that more complimentary sign of preference—the appropriation of Quintilian's ideas, either knowingly or unknowingly. (1)*

Harding, as well as other writers on Classical Rhetoric, was limited to sources in English, presumably because of his lack of proficiency in other languages. Ironically, the authors cited by Harding had read the *Institutes* in Latin, not in English. All of his citations from Quintilian are drawn from the Watson translation.

Harding's work was largely a compendium of materials drawn from secondary sources in English. He cited the discovery of a complete manuscript by Poggio at St. Gall in 1416 as the point at which ". . . the treatise became one of the great books of the Renaissance."

> *It profoundly influenced writers on pedagogy, rhetoric and poetics; and a knowledge of its doctrine was essential to the scholarly equipment of every learned man. (2)*

Harding's sources told him that the work was not entirely unknown before Poggio's discovery but that its place in Renaissance and later literature dated from 1416. Harding chose to cite the influences of Quintilian century by century. In the sixteenth century the most significant influence was on Erasmus. In addition, Harding mentioned its influence on Roger Ascham, Francis Bacon's father Sir Nicholas Bacon, and the curricula of Oxford and Cambridge.

"In the seventeenth century, Quintilian's chief supporter was Ben Jonson." Bulwer's *Chironomia* and *Chirologia* were mentioned as works which drew on Quintilian. Indeed, said Harding, ". . . the *Chironomia* is indeed very largely a recast of the Roman professor's observations on actio." Harding, without any real evidence, other than the opinion of S.S. Laurie, in his *Studies in the History of Educational Opinion from the Renaissance*, asserted the influence of Quintilian on John Locke, in spite of Locke's dislike and distrust of rhetoric.

> *Despite his strictures on the study of rhetoric, however there is a strikingly sympathetic relationship between Locke's two essays* [Thoughts Concerning Education *and* Essay on Human Understanding] *and Quintilian's* Institutio. . . *In neither of these two works, apparently, does Locke name Quintilian. . . . As I have intimated, however, either knowingly or otherwise, "the English Rationalist" has several ideas, that historically viewed have proceeded from Quintilian. (11)*

Harding's attribution of Quintilian's influence on Locke was an example of some of the careless, if not shoddy, rhetorical research undertaken in the 1920s and 1930s. Harding's judgments were derived directly from secondary sources, or were speculations with little or no supporting argument. Harding himself should not be singled out for approbation; his limitations were the limitations of the profession in general, and of rhetorical scholarship in particular.

In his treatment of eighteenth century influences of Quintilian, Harding was on more solid ground. In that section he quoted more copiously and directly from rhetorical and literary works of the period. He cited passages from Lawson's *Lectures Concerning Oratory*, Ward's *A System of Oratory*, Blair's *Lectures on Rhetoric and Belles-Lettres*. Pope's *Essay on Criticism,* Samuel Johnson's *Rambler* and *Lives of the English Poets*, Gerard's *Essay on Taste*, Edward Gibbon, and Lord Chesterfield, among other writers.

Harding's discussion of the nineteenth century impact of the Institutes was more perfunctory than that of the eighteenth. He did cite passages from De Quincey's *Rhetoric* and John Stuart Mill's *Autobiography*. Harding mentioned Macauley and Disraeli's fondness for Quintilian, but he offered no citations.

In his discussion of "Recent Years," Harding gave one page of attention to Saintsbury and two other late nineteenth and early twentieth century literary critics.

Harding's essay contributed little, if any, new knowledge about Quintilian. The article bore some resemblance to an expanded citation index. Nevertheless, readers might have found it useful to learn of the persistent influence of Quintilian for more than 500 years.

Another article on rhetorical theory followed Harding's in the first issue of *Speech Monographs*. Wilbur Samuel Howell, then at Dartmouth, wrote on "Nathaniel Carpenter's Place in the Controversy Between Dialectic and Rhetoric." Carpenter was a philosopher at Exeter College, Oxford in the seventeenth century. "He was also a poet, a geographer, and a pulpit orator." The young Howell was on his path as an explicator of little known rhetorical theorists, as exemplified by his later work on Alcuin and Fenelon. Howell was among the few speech scholars proficient in languages other than English and he was, thus, able to provide a translation as well as a commentary on the essay on rhetoric and dialectic in Carpenter's *Philosophia Liberia* of 1622.

Howell's translation of the essay was hardly a page in length, yet he devoted more than 20 pages to his explication of Carpenter's essay. Howell's reading of the text was careful and scrupulous, but his commentary may have been more than Carpenter's essay could bear, by itself. Thus Howell's essay frequently diverted to other writers who dealt with matters raised but not amplified by Carpenter. In effect, Howell undertook a survey of the positions concerning rhetoric and dialectic held by theorists before Carpenter's time.

> . . . *Basically both arts work toward the same end and consider all common means which are pertinent to the accomplishment of that end. The difference between them arises from a difference in the audience which each addresses, and in other circumstances that surround their use. In the rest of our discussion, we shall attempt to trace the history of these two attitudes toward rhetoric and dialectic. (1934, 26)*

Howell traced the view that held rhetoric and dialectic to be different from Plato's time through the Renaissance. He examined the work of Plato in detail, with primary attention to the *Phaedrus*. He gave somewhat less attention to Cicero. John of Salisbury, Agricola, Ramus, Talon, Faunce, Sherry, Peacham, Butler and Fenner were treated rather perfunctorily.

Howell then undertook a survey of the theorists who held rhetoric and dialectic to be closely related disciplines. As one might expect, in this category Howell devoted more space to Aristotle's position than to any other writer. Howell provided a fairly detailed summary of Quintilian's attitude. Then barely mentioning the Middle Ages, he turned to Renaissance writers. Howell devoted respectable attention to Cox and Wilson, but the bulk of his treatment of Renaissance writers was given to Bacon. Howell returned to Carpenter only in the final paragraph of the essay.

Howell's essay seems to have been mistitled; he used Carpenter's work only as a point of departure for the presentation of an article tracing the historical relationship between rhetoric and dialectic from Plato through the Renaissance. Howell's purpose was revealed in his summary statement.

> *Carpenter's essay on rhetoric and dialectic, then, carries to an extreme a theory that originated in the brilliant inquiries of Plato, and influenced subsequent thinking at intervals throughout history. (1934, 41)*

Howell's essay was not startlingly original, but it provided the neophyte rhetoricians with a very useful synthesis and summary of the historical relationship between the two disciplines. In this respect, the works of Harding and Howell were similar in that they provided the readers of *The Quarterly Journal* with information, that although not new, provided a clearer understanding of the history of rhetorical theory.

William Norwood Brigance of Wabash College in 1935 published an interesting and important essay. In "Can We Redefine the James-Winans Theory of Persuasion," Brigance integrated traditional rhetorical theory with twentieth century psychology to reach a workable conception of persuasion. His aim was neither to advocate nor to destroy the conviction-persuasion dichotomy; rather he sought to bring Winans' 1915 statement on persuasion up to date with modern psychology (1915, 249-395). Brigance gave consideration to what in William James' work was still useful. He also related his conceptions to the writings of traditional theorists. Brigance began his essay by reminding his readers of the faculty centered definitions of persuasion offered by Whately and Blair. Those definitions, however, posed some problems.

> *Blair defined it [persuasion] as that which "affects. . . the will and practice." Whately defined it as the "art of influencing the Will." But these are mere descriptive words. They tell us what persuasion does, namely that it influences the "will," but they tell us nothing of the processes which induce it or the means of attaining it. (1935, 19-20)*

Winans, together with William James, deserved great credit for remedying some of the defects in the conception of persuasion. Yet some questions remained and Brigance hoped to address them.

> *Having reduced persuasion to this common denominator of attention, Winans proceeded to construct his whole concept of rhetoric upon it so that after finishing the book he could justifiably say in the preface, "The key word is Attention. . . . It seems to me that Professor Winans has made probably the greatest contribution to the field of rhetoric since Quintilian laid down his stylus. . . " (1935, 20)*

Modern psychology, wrote Brigance, has changed the idea of persuasion so that Winans' James derived conception was no longer as valid as it was earlier, and the notion of attention had all but disappeared.

> *. . . The psychological research of the past generation has wrought a fundamentally changed concept both of the nature of persuasion and of the nature of attention. . . James and Winans viewed it [persuasion] primarily as a mental process, colored of course by emotional influences. . . .The more generally accepted view today, however, is that persuasion takes place, not on an intellectual, but rather on a motor level. . . . At the same time that the concept of persuasion has been changing, that of attention has likewise been changing. Behaviorists and Gestaltists, of course, claim that attention is a term outworn and unneeded. Watson says we don't "need the term." (1935, 21)*

If the concept of attention was obsolete, what did Brigance find to replace it? Salvation came with the idea of desire. He cited Mary Follett's *Creative Experience* to establish his interpretation of desire. He went on, however, to demonstrate that the idea of desire has been present since Aristotle. Furthermore, it had become a standard conception in psychology.

> *As Mary Follett has said in her splendid book,* Creative Experience, *the nineteenth century talked of the will of the people, and the early twentieth century talked of the rights of man, but "now psychology has given us desire as the key word of life. . . ." We find indeed that Mary Follett is right. That astute old master Aristotle, 2300, years ago, wrote that, "Reason does not appear to produce movement independently of desire. . . . But desire prompts action in violation of reason.". . . Psychologists have studied both quantitatively and qualitatively the operation of desires of human conduct. F.H. Lund's studies are particularly impressive. . . . His results showed that the correlation between belief and desire was greater than that of any other force known to influence belief. (1935, 22-23)*

Understandably, Brigance formulated a two part definition of persuasion which was based on desire.

> 1. *Where the aim is to arouse indifference, to inspire, or to stimulate lagging enthusiasm and faiths—PERSUASION IS A PROCESS OF VITALIZING OLD DESIRES , PURPOSES OR IDEALS.*

> 2. *Where the aim is to secure the acceptance of new beliefs or courses of action—PERSUASION IS A PROCESS OF SUBSTITUTING NEW DESIRES, PURPOSES, OR IDEALS IN PLACE OF NEW ONES. Not until we explain the process in terms of changing wants, have we explained not merely what happened and how it happened, but also what made it happen. The true goal in the study of persuasion, it seems to me, is to explain this headspring of persuasion. (Brigance, 1935, 24, 26)*

Brigance's essay was, of course, a continuation of the discussion of persuasion and conviction, which began in the first year in the life of the association. Writers ranging from Woolbert to Wallace had addressed the matter from their own perspectives. Woolbert had framed the argument as one in which rhetoric had no role to play. The rhetorical theorists had examined works dating from Bacon's writings in which they discoursed on Faculty Psychology, but they, with the notable exception of Winans, did not relate persuasion or conviction to modern psychology. Brigance was able to accomplish that task and at the same he did not eliminate, but redefined Winans' ideas about persuasion and conviction. In the more than fifty years since Brigance wrote his essay, the idea of desire as the engine of persuasion has been as much modified as the attention centered theory. In 1935 *The Quarterly Journal* printed an address given at the 1934 meeting of the Eastern Public Speaking Conference by Lane Cooper, the distinguished classicist at Cornell, and the author and editor of the *The Rhetoric of Aristotle*. Much of Cooper's essay was given over to a discussion of the interrelationship between the *Rhetoric* and the *Poetics*. Interestingly, perhaps in deference to his audience, Cooper indicated his indebtedness to his Speech graduate students and the utility of his *Rhetoric* in Speech classes.

> *Then gradually my own pupils taught me better, Drummond at first and chiefly, and later Caplan among others. And finally, as some of the audience know, I was converted, and tried to do an English version of the* Rhetoric *that would help my*

students of poetics, and would meet the needs of public speakers, too. . . . I hoped the
book would find a use in larger classes than I think have used it, and believe that
anyone who tries it there will find not my translation, but Aristotle's Rhetoric, the
best book for written composition and as a practical guide to public speakers that
was ever set forth. (17-18)

It is enlightening to learn that Cooper had speech students in mind when he edited
and translated the *Rhetoric*, since his version was the most widely used and accepted
translation for almost half a century. Cooper intended that the *Rhetoric* not be used to
teach Aristotelian theory but as a text book for composition and public speaking
courses. That proposal certainly has been entertained by many speech teachers. I, in
fact, have used the *Rhetoric* (together with the *Gorgias* and the *Phaedrus*) as a text in
honors public speaking courses.

In preparation for the 1935 convention of the National Association the "Council
further decided that problems of curricular revision be a major consideration in the
drafting of this year's annual program." Wilbur Samuel Howell, therefore, made an
announcement in the "Forum" section of *The Quarterly Journal*.

> *In accordance with these suggestions, a program in Rhetoric and Public Speaking*
> *has been arranged to permit our members to review recent publications in the field.*
> *A critical examination of these publications cannot fail to suggest basic*
> *problems. . . . All interested members of The National Association are invited to*
> *discuss these books at the convention in December and to consider the basic problems*
> *which these books suggest.* History and Interpretation of Rhetorical Theory.
> *Discussion led by Karl Wallace, Iowa State College. Books and articles to be*
> *reviewed: Lionel Crocker.* The Rhetorical Theory of Henry Ward *Beecher,*
> *Chicago, 1933; W. P. Sanford.* English Rhetorical Theories of Public Address,
> *1530-1828, Columbus, 1931; Directions for Speech and Style. ed. by H. H.*
> *Hudson, Princeton, 1935; H. F. Harding. " Quintilian's Witnesses,"* Speech
> Monographs, *I (1934), 1-20; W. S. Howell. "Nathaniel Carpenter's Place in the*
> *Controversy between Dialectic and Rhetoric,"* Speech Monographs, *I (1934,*
> *20-41) (Howell, 1935, 575-576)*

In addition to the discussions in rhetorical theory others were scheduled in Oratori-
cal Criticism, Propaganda and Literature, Public Speaking, Propaganda and Public
Opinion. This classification was indicative of the breadth of definition still given to
"Rhetoric and Public Speaking."

The proposal to review the literature was undoubtedly a sign of the health of
rhetorical studies in 1935. The willingness of the association to review its own contributions to scholarship suggested both a critical and introspective attitude and an
opportunity to appraise the value of scholarship in rhetoric. How this task was to be
accomplished remains a question. If we understand Howell correctly, "a" program had
been arranged. If Howell intended that all the works in rhetorical theory, let alone those
in the other categories, were to be discussed in a single program, only the most
superficial discussion could take place. The classification is somewhat lacking in clarity
since "Propaganda" was included in two of the four divisions.

In 1935 C. K. Thomas of Cornell was the Book Review Editor of *The Quarterly Journal*.
We cannot say how the decision was made to review four works by his Cornell
colleague Harry Caplan. John P. Emporer of the University of Tennessee was the person
who undertook to review two books and two articles in a page and a half. Medieval
rhetorical theory was then, as it is now, an understudied field and Emporer indicated
that the profession was in debt to Caplan's for his work.

The serious student of speech owes a real debt to Professor Caplan for the light which his studies have thus far thrown upon an extensive and too much neglected portion of the history of rhetoric. (592)

At the 1935 meeting of the Eastern Public Speaking Conference a program titled "Rhetoric" was presented. The conception of that term was decidedly curious. Under the rhetoric heading were papers on "Public Speaking in the Colgate Plan," "What Listeners Like About Speakers," and "The Problem of Nervousness in Public Speaking." Only two of the papers were legitimately concerned with rhetoric: "Public Discussion in England under Elizabeth and the Early Stuarts" by Frederick George Marcham of Cornell, and "Rhetoric and Dialectic" by Lee S. Hultzen of Columbia University (1935, 631).

The discovery of rhetorical theorists was expanded in 1936 with the first article in the profession on St. Augustine. Floyd K. Riley of Baker University in his essay "St. Augustine, Public Speaker and Rhetorician in *The Quarterly Journal* undertook, in the space of six pages, to survey the contributions of Augustine, both as performer and a theorist. Obviously, his treatment was somewhat superficial. Since Riley cited both translations and original texts, we cannot be certain whether he was able to read Latin. About half the article was devoted to a brief sketch of Augustine's life and an exceedingly superficial critique of his public speaking. Thus St. Augustine's rhetorical theory was disposed of in three pages. Even in his cursory treatment of Augustine's theory, Riley seemed a bit confused, or at least uncertain.

It is sometimes difficult to follow St. Augustine's thinking, however, as he speaks of eloquence. One cannot but recall that his early training was in the sophistic rhetoric of the schools, where eloquence was symbolized by fluency in the standardized forms of the day. Yet at times he seems to base his ideas on the practices of his ideal orators, Cicero and Ambrose, both of whom developed a direct manner of speaking. At other times he appears to define eloquence in terms of exalted content. At all times he is influenced by the style of the Scriptures. (574-575)

Riley's statement suggests that he was reacting immediately to his reading of Augustine and that his confusion may have resulted from his failure to think through what he had read.

Riley devoted almost all of his brief treatment of St. Augustine to style, particularly the doctrines of Cicero. Riley's summary was indicative of the shallowness of much of the research in rhetorical theory of the time. He portrayed Augustine as no more than a later day Cicero and he relegated Augustine's place in rhetorical theory to a footnote citing various biographies.

This, then, was St. Augustine's contribution to the field of rhetoric: in an age of sophistic, he re-established Ciceronian concepts. He condemned the superficialities of the rhetorical usages of his day, not by attacking them but by redefining fundamentals.It has not been the purpose of this study to show the place of St. Augustine in later rhetorical theory, but references to this phase may be found in biographies . . . . (577)

The lack of curiosity or inquiry concerning Augustine's place in the history of rhetorical theory was an obvious oversight. To rely on biographers for an understanding of Augustinian theory is an indication of the unwillingness of some scholars to go beyond immediate descriptive exposition in their writings. At least Harding and

Howell traced the influence of Quintilian and the sources from which Carpenter drew his theory.

Karl Wallace's "Rhetorical Exercises in Tudor Education" was an entirely different kind of work than was Riley's. Although not strictly an essay in rhetorical theory, Wallace drew a cogent and detailed picture, not simply of the place rhetoric occupied in the schools of the Tudor era, but the place of rhetoric in that society. Wallace drew his descriptions from the examination of documents of the Tudor age as well as secondary sources. He thereby presented a well integrated historical essay. The purpose of the essay was clearly stated at its very outset.

> . . . I shall attempt in this paper to present a brief account of the rhetorical exercises in vogue in Tudor England, their nature, the extent to which they were employed, and the value that the men of the age placed upon them. (1936, 28)

Except for Richard Rainolde's *The Foundations of Rhetorike*, Wallace did not rely on "sixteenth century books on rhetoric." Rather he turned to the historical documents.

> For the most part, my observations are based on school statutes of the period, and on Tudor biography, history, books of manners, and letters and treatises on education. Except in one instance, I have not relied on sixteenth century books on rhetoric, because none of them appears to yield important information as to what actually happened in the grammar school. The exception is Richard Rainolde's Foundations of Rhetorike . . . . (1936, 29)

Wallace described a time in which instruction in rhetoric was central to the curricula in the grammar schools and the universities of sixteenth century England. His exposition provided a clear picture of rhetorical practices in the schools. It also is interesting as a comparison with later speech instruction. In his 24 page essay Wallace, painstakingly, explicated the range of rhetorical instruction given to students. He discussed the oration "whose core is a fable." (1936, 30); the narration, the chria, which he described as "a brief composition that elaborates a famous saying. . . " (1936, 31) the sentence "a short oration whose chief point is some godly precept of life" (1936, 31). He elaborated on the confutation, "the refutative composition. . . "; the eulogy; the oration of dispraise; description; and the thesis, "an oration that deals with abstract philosophical problems. . . " (1936, 32). In the legislation, a type of oration, the orator is required to attack or defend a law" (1936, 32). According to Wallace, "Of all the early rhetorical exercises, perhaps the commonplace oration receives most attention. It is a brief discourse dilating on the good and evil in mankind" (1936, 31).

> Two other school-boy exercises of the Tudor era are the theme and the declamation. . . . Both the theme and the declamation are intended to develop proficiency in composition, to afford training in delivery, at the same time supplying the youth with moral precepts that may influence his own character. . . The theme, as Tudor England conceived it, is any composition, oral or written, whose subject pertains to moral and political matters. . . . It is theremore [sic] an exercise that demands a higher type of intellectual activity than the elementary rhetorical exercise. (1936, 34)

After a lengthy explication of the theme, Wallace turned to the declamation, which he described as ". . . a species of the theme, from which it differs in only two respects: its subject matter is controversial, and its methods are similar to those of modern debate" (1936. 37). Wallace's discussion of the declamation was also fully developed as was his explanation of the disputation, ". . . the pedagogical instrument inherited from medieval scholasticism."

> *Despite the opinion of Erasmus, Ascham, Vives, and Bacon that the disputation was too difficult for boys of ten to fifteen years of age, it remains one of the cardinal methods of instruction throughout the century. . . . It is increasingly employed as a convenient method of teaching grammatical principles and of securing a graceful coherence in spoken discourse, which is gained chiefly by variety, copiousness and elegance in restatement, repetition, and other means of transition. The grammar school disputation therefore paid little attention to subject matter; the emphasis was on the ornament and trimmings of discourse. . . . (1936, 41)*

Wallace summarized the importance of rhetorical instruction in the grammar schools in shaping the English aristocracy of the sixteenth century.

> *Thus the rhetorical exercises of Tudor grammar schools . . . are of utmost significance to Tudor society, for they constitute the principal methods in the education of a governor, a courtier, or a gentleman who must write or speak well, whether in the vernacular or in Latin. (1936, 43)*

Wallace's discussion of the place of rhetoric in instruction at the universities was somewhat briefer than his treatment of the grammar schools. He mentioned the distinction of the position of university orator and the competition for that status. The place of rhetoric in the curriculum, however, in Wallace's view, was fairly limited.

> *It is true that at both universities [Oxford and Cambridge] throughout the century offer what their statutes refer to as rhetoric; but for the century as a whole, it is doubtful that this represents more than the reading and study of parts of the rhetorical books of Aristotle, Quintilian, Cicero, and Hermogenes, together with some criticism of the orations of Demosthenes, Cicero, Isocrates, and the church fathers. Exercises like those of the grammar school do not seem to be specified in the curriculum. (1936, 45.) Since Wallace was not very specific, we cannot know by what standards he judged the curricula. The offerings he described seem fairly generous. Perhaps his expectation of a course in rhetoric included presentations. We must remember, however that Wallace's objective was to discuss rhetorical exercises not rhetorical instruction. Later in the sixteenth century, Wallace wrote, ". . . the Reader in Humanities and Rhetoric required his students to carry on the rhetorical exercises of the schools." (1936, 46)*

Wallace devoted almost all of his treatment of rhetorical exercises at Oxford and Cambridge to the university disputation, of which he wrote: "Throughout our period, it is clearly the logical and rhetorical instrument par excellence (1936, 46). Proficiency in disputations was essential to the future lives of students. Therefore, exercise in disputation was a central factor at the universities.

> *Preachers, however, were not the only ones to receive the benefit of the disputation. Those interested in canon or in civil law, in medicine, in public life, also must be exercised in disputation, in the art of inventing arguments by applying the the machinery of the topics to composition. University practice seems to indicate quite definitely that he who would speak well, according to the classical model, be skilled in argument. The disputation, consequently, is more than a logical exercise and a form of university examination. So important is the disputation as an educational device that the candidate for the the degree of Bachelor of Arts probably argued, on the average, once a month during his four year course. . . . (1936, 46-47)*

Wallace outlined the rigorous plan by which the undergraduates were exposed to rhetorical exercises. Whether, and how much, they contributed to rhetorical excellence is open to question, however.

> *But so far as it may provide rhetorical training, its results are not always beneficial, even in Tudor eyes. It seems that so much time is given over to the machinery of topics and deductive inference that scant attention is paid to content. . . . But in spite of its weaknesses as a school and college exercise, the disputation remained a favorite pedagogical device well into the seventeenth century. (1936, 50)*

Wallace's essay was an excellent example, especially for its time, of rhetorical history. Rather than simply quoting from secondary sources, Wallace provided a complex cultural texture, and he clearly specified how rhetorical exercises were reflective of Tudor culture. This essay by the young Karl Wallace was a clear indication of the distinguished career which was to follow. Wallace's established himself early as a scholar of Renaissance rhetoric, in particular, and of the Renaissance in general. He published his first work on Francis Bacon the same year as his Tudor essay, in *Speech Monographs*. We will discuss that article shortly. His books on Bacon, *Francis Bacon On Communication and Rhetoric* (1943) and *Francis Bacon and the Nature of Man* (1967), met with general critical approbation. He attained eminent status as a thoughtful and wise contributor to rhetorical thought.

Wallace was the editor of the only comprehensive history of the field of speech with the publication of *A History of Speech Education in America* in 1954. He served as president of the Speech Association of America in 1954 and as editor of *The Quarterly Journal of Speech* from 1945 through 1947. Wallace was exemplary of the rhetoric program at Cornell. The faculty and graduates of the program were the leaders in rhetorical research from the 1920s into the 1950s. So dominant was the Cornell program that it has acquired the label of "The Cornell School." Winans, Hunt, Hudson, Wichelns, Bryant, Howell, Caplan and Wagner were among the prominent figures associated with the Cornell School.

Two essays of continuing significance were published in 1936 in *Speech Monographs*. They were Wallace's "Bacon's Conception of Rhetoric" and James H. McBurney's "The Place of the Enthymeme in Rhetorical Theory." Wallace brought to his Bacon essay all the attributes he displayed in the Tudor essay. In addition he demonstrated his understanding of seventeenth century philosophy and psychology. So far as I can determine, Wallace was the first scholar in the speech profession to comprehend and explicate the influence of Faculty Psychology on rhetorical theory. In time, of course, the understanding of Faculty Psychology became a significant analytical tool for the study of rhetorical theory in the seventeenth and eighteenth centuries.

Although the Bacon essay was apparently drawn from Wallace's Cornell dissertation, he recognized that a single essay could not do justice to Bacon's rhetorical theory and he anticipated the book which was to be published seven years later. His statement of the intent of the essay was clear and precise.

> *The purpose of this paper, accordingly, is to set forth in general Bacon's rhetorical theory, its special function and province, and some of the more important topics with which it must deal. To set out in detail Bacon's views on rhetorical address would require a volume; the present study aims to be merely an introductory chapter. . . .*
> *For such a study the most valuable of Bacon's writings are* The Advancement of Learning *and its expanded Latin translation,* De Augmentis Scientiarum. . . .
> *This investigation, accordingly, regards the rhetoric as presented in the*

Advancement *and the* De Augmentis *as the sine qua non of rhetorical discourse, takes the rhetorical allusions garnered from other rhetorical writings, and attempts to harmonize them with the rhetoric of the cyclopedia. [the* Advancement *and the* De Augmentis] *1936a, 21)*

From Bacon's definition *"The duty and office of Rhetoric is to apply Reason to Imagination for the better moving of the will,"* Wallace recognized how fundamental was the Renaissance conception of faculty psychology to an understanding of Bacon's rhetorical theory.

Such a definition suggests that the end of rhetorical endeavor is persuasion, that is the influencing of conduct; and to some extent the function of the faculties of the mind, as they appear in Baconian psychology, bears out this interpretation. Although, according to Bacon, we may know very little concerning the substance of the mind, with its faculties we are well acquainted: they comprise the "understanding, reason, imagination, memory, appetite, will; in short, all with which the logical and ethical sciences deal." (1936a, 22)

So important was Bacon's definition that Wallace characterized it as ". . . the core of his entire theory. . . They comprise 'the understanding, reason, imagination, memory, appetite, will; in short, all with which the logical and ethical sciences deal'." (1936a, 22.) The distinction between logic and ethics has implications for rhetoric, Wallace stated, and he quoted Bacon to make his point.

And logic, we perceive, "discourses of the Understanding and Reason; Ethics of the Will, Appetite and Affections: the one produces determinations, the other actions." In Bacon's view, then, the mind employs its faculties either as instruments of knowing or as means of action; and when he says that rhetoric operates to excite the appetite and the will. . . Bacon intends to say that rhetorical address is predominately the art which directly influences human behavior. Indeed, whenever Bacon alludes to a rhetorical situation he customarily describes it as persuasive. (1936a, 23). Wallace obviously understood the way in which Bacon and his contemporaries regarded the human faculties, and he, thereby, was able clearly to explicate the tenets of Faculty Psychology; more importantly, however, he saw how Faculty Psychology was fundamental to the New Rhetoric of the seventeenth and eighteenth centuries. Indeed the assumptions of Faculty Psychology guided the development of the Bacon essay. Wallace was the first theorist to make use of Faculty Psychology to provide a clear historical and philosophical comprehension of the intellectual climate in which Renaissance and Enlightenment rhetorical theory developed.

But, said Wallace, Bacon added an ethical element to his conception of rhetoric.

But to this statement of the function of rhetoric, Bacon adds a significant qualification. He believes that rhetoric lives up to its true function only by presenting pictures of conduct that is virtuous and good. He extends scant sympathy to Plato for condemning rhetoric merely because some men, by skillful application of its principles, make the worse appear the better reason, while others, through bungling attempts at artistry, manage only to destroy the natural force of reason. (1936a, 25)

As Wallace saw it, Imagination was a significant, but not a central faculty in the rhetorical enterprise, but Bacon was not writing about creative imagination, the kind of imagination which produces poetry. Rather imagination was, as Wallace put it, "a messenger."

> *Such a conception of the imagination is of extraordinary significance to rhetoric, for it means that the creative imagination. . . has no place in rhetorical address. The sole function of the imagination in speaking or writing is to render logical argument attractive and pleasing; the imagination merely translates logical inferences into pictures. Thus when Bacon writes that rhetoric applies reason to imagination, he means that rhetorical address must be, always and foremost logically sound; imaginative dress although highly desirable is not fundamental. (1936a, 27)*

Throughout his essay Wallace emphasized that Bacon's conception of rhetoric was one that was placed primary emphasis on logical proof. Although emotion is an important component of persuasive discourse, it must always remain subservient to reason. Wallace said Bacon went so far as to classify rhetoric as a part of logic.

> *In fact, Bacon is not content with merely asserting that rhetorical proof ought to be fundamentally logical; at one time he actually classifies rhetoric as part of logic. In the cyclopedia, logic is used to describe the four Intellectual Arts: The arts of Invention, of Judgement, of Memory, and of Transmission. According to this conception of logical activity, then, rhetoric as part of the Art of Transmission is also part of logic. (1936a, 32)*

Wallace made clear that when Bacon wrote of Invention as it applied to rhetoric that he distinguished between the Invention of the "Arts and Sciences" and "Speech and Argument." Properly speaking, rhetorical invention is not invention at all.

> *Somewhat loath to admit that this process may be properly called invention, Bacon clearly explains that the finding of arguments by a speaker or writer means essentially the recall and recovery of ideas. . . .The technique of of discovering arguments is accomplished in part by using the topics of conventional knowledge.(1936a, 38)*

Wallace, in the summary to his essay, offered a cogent description of Bacon's rhetorical theory.

> *Francis Bacon's theory of rhetorical address, then, by virtue of its reference to the imaginative faculty of man's mind and the peculiar function of the imagination in relation to the reason and the affections is essentially social. Conceived of as the most effective means of communicating knowledge for persuasive ends, rhetoric at the same time carries the social obligation of helping reason to prevail over passion, of establishing, on the level of popular knowledge, the just and good cause. (1936a, 47)*

Wallace's Bacon essay merits the space we have given it because for the first time we are able to see how a well educated and well prepared scholar was able to bring together analytical tools from such diverse fields as history, literature and philosophy in his analysis of Bacon's rhetorical theory. At the same time, Wallace maintained a steady focus on rhetoric and avoided the temptation to make his work an essay derived from other disciplines. Wallace's task was not an easy one since Bacon's theory is not conveniently isolated. Wallace mastered the task of synthesizing and integrating materials scattered throughout the *Advancement* and the *De Augmentis*. The result was a complete understanding of one theorist produced through the careful reading of texts based on the rich resources available to Wallace. His work differed markedly from earlier efforts which were more summaries than analyses. Wallace and McBurney, whose work we will treat next, were among the earliest scholars to recognize that traditional rhetorical theory was not limited to oral discourse; that rhetoric was equally applicable to written discourse.

Another landmark essay of in *Speech Monographs* of 1936, which is still useful today, is "The Place of the Enthymeme in Rhetorical Theory" by James H. McBurney of Northwestern. In an introductory footnote, he recognized James O'Neill's direction of the McBurney dissertation, and he characterized his 26 page essay as an "abstract" of his dissertation. The essay might, in fact, have been a condensation of a dissertation, but it was, by no means, an abstract.

The importance of McBurney's work was that he undertook to explore in depth a single element of rhetorical theory. His scholarly predecessors had examined the contribution of various theorists. McBurney, however, was the first to focus on a single aspect of rhetorical theory and to subject it to careful scrutiny.

McBurney began his essay by inviting his readers to what he termed "three propositions" which were really the presuppositions of the essay.

(1) Contemporary rhetorical theory is essentially Aristotelian;

(2) The enthymeme is the focal concept in the rhetoric of Aristotle; and

(3) The enthymeme is seriously misunderstood today. (1936, 50)

In an age when "Aristotelian" or "Neo Aristotelian" have become almost pejorative terms, it is interesting to recognize the status accorded to Aristotle's theories in those pre-war years. McBurney recognized, as early as 1936, that Aristotle's stature was not universally accepted.

> *For good or evil, depending on one's point of view, our ideas about reasoned discourse in speaking and writing remain essentially Aristotelian. Even those who complain against the Aristotelean influence in the field and seek new canons for these arts, will recognize the importance of this influence and should welcome interpretations. (1936, 50-51)*

It is not clear who it was that complained against Aristotle. Certainly in the pages of the association's journals there had been little or no complaint. Perhaps McBurney was referring to writers in related fields such as Classics, Philosophy and Philology. McBurney might also have been responding to the anti-rhetorical "scientists," among whom were those who honored the work of Woolbert, who had died in 1929.

As he had promised, McBurney began his essay with a discussion of "The Enthymeme in Aristotle." McBurney was not content to limit his examination of the enthymeme to Aristotle's *Rhetoric*. In addition, he also consulted *Categoriae, De Interpretatione, Analytica Priora, Analytica Posteriora, Topica,* and *De Sophisticis Elenchis* (McBurney, 1936).

Much of the material in the first section, viewed from the perspective of the 1990s, may seem obvious, or even dated. We must remember, however, that general knowledge in the profession about the work of Aristotle was still quite limited. Therefore, what may strike us today as the material of undergraduate classes was necessary to provide an orientation for McBurney's readers. A brief review of of artistic and non-artistic proofs and of the three rhetorical proofs was not really redundant and, indeed, might well have proved useful to many members of the profession.

McBurney's analysis was the product of close and scrupulous readings of Aristotelean texts. His apparent proficiency in languages other than English, as shown by citations from French, German sources and use of the Greek versions of Aristotle works, was undoubtedly helpful in his ability to explicate Aristotle. Drawing as much on the *Analytica Priora* as on the *Rhetoric*, McBurney examined the enthymeme from a number of perspectives. He first discussed "The Enthymeme and Probabilities and Signs." His conclusion demonstrated the relation of the enthymeme and probability.

> *An enthymeme, then, may be defined as a syllogism, drawn from probable causes, signs, (certain and fallible) and examples. As a syllogism drawn from these materials, it is important to add here, the enthymeme starts from the probable premises (probable in a material sense) and lacks formal validity in certain of the types explained. (1936, 58)*

McBurney then went on to discuss the enthymeme under several categories including:

2. *Example as a form of Enthymeme:*
3. *The Enthymeme and Topics:*
4. *The Enthymeme and Ethos and Pathos:*
5. *Demonstrative and Refutative Enthymemes. (1936, 58-66)*

In the sixth category, which he called "A Consideration of the Suppression of a Proposition in an Enthymeme," McBurney dealt with the question of whether the enthymeme, according to Aristotle, was simply a syllogism with one of the premises missing.

> *The only question raised here, therefore, is whether or not the omission of one or more of the propositions of a complete syllogism is necessary in the enthymeme. This question assumes considerable importance because of the almost universal tendency among recent writers to define the enthymeme as an elided syllogism and to make this differentiation the only difference between the syllogism and the enthymeme. . . . Most of those who object to the contemporary notion of the enthymeme merely as a truncated syllogism hold that the characteristic thing about the enthymeme is its identification with probable causes and signs, and that the omission of a proposition is purely accidental. . . . There appears to be no place in Aristotle's writings where he defined the enthymeme as an elided syllogism, nor is there any satisfactory evidence that he so understood it. . . . A syllogism drawn from probable causes and signs is an enthymeme without regard to the omission of a proposition. (1936, 61-62)*

More than fifty years have passed since McBurney wrote his essay and the notion of the enthymeme as a truncated syllogism still persists in certain quarters. McBurney was clear, however, that the enthymeme's distinguishing characteristic was as a rhetorical syllogism, relying on probability rather than certainty.

The major portion of McBurney's essay was devoted to the Aristotelian enthymeme; he did, however, include a section which he called "The Enthymeme after Aristotle." McBurney took his readers on a brief rhetorical journey in which he surveyed the status of the enthymeme among the Stoics, in the Roman Doctrine, in the Medieval Doctrine, and in contemporary rhetorical theory. McBurney's survey is exceedingly cursory and he, perhaps because of space limitations, did not make any significant contribution to our historical understanding of the enthymeme. In retrospect, the historical survey seems to be an almost useless appendage, which might well have been deleted. The importance of McBurney's essay lies its discerning analysis of Aristotle's texts and the consequent clarification of our understanding of the Aristotelian enthymeme.

McBurney combined his work on Greek rhetorical theory with his interest in group discussion in his 1937 essay "Some Contributions of Classical Dialectic and Rhetoric to a Philosophy of Discussion." We shall have additional comments to make about McBurney's essay in our chapter on group discussion. Although a separation will not be totally distinct, in this chapter, we will concentrate largely on McBurney's analysis of dialectic and rhetoric as they are applicable to discussion, and reserve the material dealing more specifically with discussion to a later chapter.

McBurney found the roots of discussion in Aristotle's distinction between probabilities and certainties and their assignment respectively to rhetoric and dialectic. Many supporters of discussion, however, regarded their specialty as being in opposition to classical rhetoric. McBurney disagreed.

> *Despite this interest in the discussion field, our knowledge about the philosophy and method of this type of speaking remains relatively scattered and underdeveloped. For this reason and because many protagonists of the discussion movement interpret it to be a reaction against classical influences as represented in contemporary theories of argumentation, debate and persuasion, I am proposing here certain conceptions in classical dialectic and rhetoric which appear to me capable of making significant contributions to a theory of discussion. (1937, 2)*

McBurney relied on the writings of John Dewey to establish a philosophical basis for his own position. Drawing particularly on Dewey's *Reconstruction in Philosophy*, (1920.) McBurney noted Dewey's description of "ordinary empirical, relatively real, phenomenal world of everyday experience," and he saw in Dewey's conception a likeness to Aristotle's world of probabilities and certainties.

> *. . . It will profit us in studying discussion to turn our attention to the realm in which the ancients conceived inquiry and deliberation to function. My point is that this "ordinary empirical, relatively real phenomenal world of every day experience," which for Aristotle was the realm of probabilities as distinguished from certainties and the province in which he placed his dialectic and rhetoric, is the field which has potentialities so far as discussion is concerned. (1937, 3)*

Part of the problem, McBurney declared, was a reaction, not to Aristotle's own work, but to the distorted versions of his work which were due to Scholasticism's reliance on partial texts ". . . secondary sources and reworkings of Aristotle which have been found to be misleading and inaccurate in many cases. . . . It should be emphasized that the revolt against Scholasticism was a revolt against the Aristotelian tradition as understood in that day" (1937, 4).

McBurney maintained that Aristotle's tainted reputation was continued well into the Enlightenment.

> *In Bacon, Locke, Campbell and others we find incipient attempts to apply empirical principles in the realm of public discussion, but these consisted largely of attacks on the scholastic logic and rhetoric and did not present anything approaching a fully developed theory. (1937, 5)*

McBurney was correct about seventeenth and eighteenth century opposition to Scholasticism. The revolt against Scholasticism was, of course characteristic of the Renaissance and the Enlightenment; indeed the intellectual revolution was, to a considerable extent an outcome of the rejection of Scholasticism. Although Locke, Bacon and Campbell, it is true, did not develop theories of public discussion, one should not infer that they were entirely opposed to rhetoric, or even to Aristotle. All three of the figures showed respect for Aristotle although they were opposed to syllogistic reasoning, especially as presented by Scholastics. Obviously, Bacon and

Campbell were themselves important contributors to rhetorical theory while Locke's attitude toward rhetoric was ambivalent, but generally disapproving.

When McBurney came to discuss the specific contributions of Aristotle, he devoted more attention to dialectic than to rhetoric, although he saw them as closely related modes of communication. It is important, said McBurney, to be aware that Aristotle's conception of dialectic recognized two kinds of discussion.

> *Throughout his treatment of dialectic in the Topics, Aristotle distinguishes between discussion in the spirit of competition, and to use his own words, "those who discuss things in the spirit of inquiry." (1937, 11)*

Perhaps the key to understanding the dialectical nature of group discussion is found in the function of the enthymeme and the dialectical syllogism, which are not subject to the rigid requirements of the logical syllogism.

> *. . . It must be realized that Aristotle introduces important modifications of the logical syllogism in his conceptions of the dialectical syllogism and the enthymeme, which meet many of the objections which are commonly raised against the applications of the syllogism in discussion. . . . The enthymene, if not the dialectical syllogism, not only employs probabilities understood in a propositional or material sense, but also waives the the necessity of formal validity in many cases. Here again it differs from the logical syllogism in a way that recommends its usefulness in discussion. (1937, 12)*

McBurney was modest about his accomplishments in the dialectic-discussion essay.

> *My only purposes have been to indicate the broad relationships of classical dialectic and rhetoric to the present discussion movement, and to point out some of the important respects in which the modifications of the logical syllogism found in the dialectical syllogism and the enthymeme adapt Aristotle's doctrine to discussion or constructive thinking (thought in process) in a way that does not appear commonly to be appreciated. (1937, 13)*

McBurney's article was perhaps not as thoroughgoing a work of scholarship as his enthymeme article, but it was important in that it connected two modes of communication which, until this time, had been viewed as unrelated, if not antagonistic to each other. In spite of McBurney's effort, little was done later to follow up on his perspectives concerning rhetoric and discussion. Indeed much of the writing about discussion, before and after World War II, emphasized the co-operative and conciliatory nature of discussion and gave little attention to discussion as a rhetorical enterprise. To be fair, McBurney himself did not advocate that discussion be modified to become more rhetorical; he wanted the profession to be aware that the probabilistic and conjectural natures of Aristotle's conceptions of the enthymeme made them useful in the discussion process.

In 1939 Kenneth G. Hance, then of Albion College, later McBurney's colleague and co-author at Northwestern, published "The Elements of the Rhetorical Theory of Phillip Brooks." As we have earlier pointed out, Brooks was one of the earliest subjects of rhetorical criticism. Hance's objective was different, however. He hoped to synthesize a rhetorical theory for "the greatest preacher in America."

> *Because Brooks was an outstanding Yale lecturer, because he has made contributions to our knowledge of rhetorical theory, he is worth our close attention. In fact a justification of a study of Brooks can be made on the grounds that his rhetorical theory has been little investigated, its parts have not been drawn together*

and systematically arranged, and its points of distinctiveness have been only
incidentally mentioned by biographers. Even though much of the material appertains
to preaching, it will be recognized as a body of rhetorical theory of concern to all
students of speaking. (1939, 17)

Hance brought together materials from "...*Lectures on Preaching, The Bohlen Lectures,*
the address on 'The Teaching of Religion,' the address on 'The Purposes of Scholarship,' the sermon entitled 'The Priesthood,' letters, notebooks, and other sources"
(1939, 17).

Hance intended nothing novel in his extraction of a rhetorical theory from Brooks'
writings. He planned to follow a strict Ciceronian plan, although Brooks himself had
proposed a different scheme.

In this paper I propose to survey the elements of Brooks' theory from the point of
view of the traditional constituents of rhetoric: Invention, Disposition, Style,
Memory, and Delivery. (1939, 17) Brooks' organization includes: Speaker, Speech,
Audience, and Delivery. However, I am using the organization of the ancients
because of its widespread use in rhetorical literature and its usefulness as a system of
classifying the rhetorical elements. (1939, 17n)

Hance's justification for his analytical scheme was so rooted in traditional rhetoric
that he neglected even to comment on the question of why Brooks had classified
rhetorical elements in a way which deviated from classical theory. As early as the time
of Bacon, writers on rhetorical theory no longer adhered to the "Five Great Arts" of
Cicero. They had found new classifications which more closely represented their
conceptions of rhetoric and which reflected the intellectual tone of the times. Hance
also failed to see that using Brooks' own organizational scheme might have given
greater insight into Brooks' thoughts about rhetoric.

Thus Hance proceeded category by category to examine what Phillip Brooks had to
say about rhetoric. Apparently Hance and the editor assumed that the readers of *Speech
Monographs* were naive about rhetoric since he found it necessary to define each of the
canons. Invention was defined as "that constituent of rhetoric concerned with finding
and analyzing the materials of the speech" (1939, 17). Under the heading of Invention,
Hance ranged a number of sub-topics, to many of which he gave not much more than
fleeting attention. They included Speech Purposes; Topics; Modes of Persuasion, under
which he listed Ethos, Pathos and Logical Argument; Speech Preparation and
Audience. Although Hance claimed that much of Brooks' theory would be equally
applicable to sermons and other forms of discourse, the extracts which Hance cited in
the discussion were almost exclusively concerned with the sermon. Since Hance tied
himself so closely to traditional rhetoric, most of his analysis identified those aspects
of Brooks theory which were also present in classical theory.

One of the few detailed treatments in the essay occurred in Hance's discussion of
Ethos. He devoted thirteen pages of his twenty-four page article to that topic alone. In
contrast, Pathos is allotted hardly half a page and Logical Argument fewer than two
pages. Hance offered an explanation for this disproportionate emphasis, and he
suggested that his analysis was reflective of Brooks' own emphasis.

Brooks places at the heart of all persuasion the presence of a moral character
which can stand the test of men's scrutiny: he says that Truth can prevail—— and
preaching is designed to make it prevail—only if there is moral goodness in the
speaker. But what elements comprise"character"? (1939, 21)

The answer to the question occupies many pages in which Hance lists almost every desirable attribute known to humanity. The speaker must possess "faithfulness," "honesty," "spirituality," "the proper degree of reserve," "courage," "humility," "breadth of character," "personal piety," "deep originality," "intelligence," and "mental aliveness." (1939, 21-23)

> *But to Brooks, "character" and "intelligence" are not enough. He presents a body of elements appertaining to the "desire to be of service," such as mental and spiritual usefulness, freedom from self-consciousness, gravity, hopefulness and enthusiasm, and a great joy from one's work. Considered as a group, these represent Brooks' stress upon communication, for he urges the speaker not to content himself with the possession of knowledge but to think of the "message" which he has to deliver, of the fact that he is a "witness" of the Truth and has the task of transmitting it. (1939, 23)*

But these were not only the attributes which the speaker must display. He was also expected to possess "good will," "good health," "value for the human soul" and "knowledge of the Spirit of the Lord." Nothing appears very remarkable about the list of character traits which Hance found in Brooks' writings. For example, the traits closely resemble those listed by Blair in his *Lectures*. Of course we must understand that by 1938 no systematic study of Blair had been undertaken, although he was mentioned here and there. Neither Brooks nor Hance told us whether these paragons were born or made. With all the emphasis on Truth, Hance did not tell us what it was or how it was to be found. He did not deal with the question in his treatment of logical proof. Perhaps there was a presumption that the preacher, by virtue of his position, possessed Truth.

The virtues we have enumerated are only part of the attributes of character which Hance discovered in Brooks' writings. Interestingly, Hance found that Brooks included speech preparation as a component of ethos. Hance offered a rather tenuous explanation for the inclusion of speech preparation and its connection with character.

> *Supplementing this thorough consideration of the qualities of the speaker is Brooks rather important contribution to Ethos, namely the preparation of the speaker. . . . He says that in the majority of cases failure in the ministry can be attributed to faulty preparation, also that the preacher's life must be one of large accumulation, not only from particular readings but also from wide contacts and extensive meditation. Implicitly, although not separately presented by Brooks, we find the the following four means of preparation: through reading and study; through knowledge of men; through association with the Infinite; and through careful discipline. (1939, 25)*

Hance devoted a fair amount of space to Brooks' writings on the audience. The material, however, was so specifically limited to church audiences that it did not have much applicability to a more general theory of audience adaptation. It is helpful to note, however, that Hance wrote that Brooks advocated ". . . the speaker's attention to both individual and group characteristics." The sections devoted to Disposition, Style, Memory and Delivery are very brief and they offer nothing which could not have been found in classical rhetoric.

> *Hance perhaps exaggerated a bit in his summary of Brooks' contributions to rhetorical theory. Brooks' body of rhetorical theory is of value to us today. It is a systematic, complete, and practical study; it is on a high ethical plane; it has a logical basis of cause and effect; and it contains much illustrative material which both supplements and reenforces the theory. (1939, 39)*

Hance was, of course, entitled to his judgment but his essay does not really demonstrate that Brooks had a systematically developed rhetorical theory. The material extracted seems to comprise informed instructions for the preparation of sermons. Phillips Brooks may still have a reputation as an orator. So far as I know, however, he is nowhere included among rhetorical theorists. A similar article, seeking to extract a rhetorical theory from a preacher's work was published in 1936 when Lionel Crocker published "The Rhetorical Theory of Harry Emerson Fosdick." (1936.)

In 1939 Ramon L. Irwin, of the University of Missouri published an article titled "The Classical Speech Divisions." The decision to publish Irwin's article might cause us to question the editorial judgment of Giles Gray. In a total of two pages Irwin sought to compare the organizational schemes of Aristotle, Cicero and Quintilian. The substance of the article can be summarized in its opening and its close.

> There is evidence, however, which indicated that although Cicero and Quintilian's divisions appear to be at variance with Aristotle they are actually in perfect accord. (212) Thus we may conclude that the famous "classical order" of a speech consists actually of only four divisions: exordium (opening, proem), narration (statement), proof (argument), and peroration (epilogue). (213)

Ordinarily we would pass by an article such as Irvin's. We comment on it because of wasted potential. If Irvin had really written a comparative analysis of classical ideas of disposition he might have done for structure what McBurney had done for the enthymeme. Instead the readers of *The Quarterly Journal* were presented a superficial, almost meaningless article.

Earlier articles in *The Quarterly Journal* had made mention of Charles Butler's seventeenth century work, *Oratoriae Libri Duo*. In 1939 Lee S. Hultzen of the University of California at Los Angeles published an article titled "Charles Butler on Memory." The principal contribution of the article was the presentation of a Hultzen's translation of Butler's chapter on memory. Only three pages were allotted to commentary on the chapter. We should be grateful to Hultzen for acquainting the profession with Butler's work but the article might have been more useful if Hultzen had devoted more attention to a more detailed treatment of Butler's conception of memory. His commentary is mostly concerned with a comparison of Butler and Thomas Wilson on memory. Butler specifically mentioned that Harry Caplan, ". . . kindly looked over all my translation of Butler" (1939, 47). The translation was supplemented by Hultzen's footnotes which were almost exclusively concerned with citing the influences of and derivation from classical rhetorical theorists. As might be expected, the principal influences were from Aristotle, Cicero and Quintilian. In fact Hultzen's notes gave the impression that Butler's work on memory was more derivative than original.

A work much more in the pattern of McBurney's work on the enthymeme was published in *Speech Monographs* in 1939 by Irving J. Lee, McBurney's colleague at Northwestern. In his essay "Some Conceptions of Emotional Appeal in Rhetorical Theory" Lee, whose reputation was to be made as a General Semanticist, saw a definitional and conceptual problem concerning pathos.

> It is a commonplace that a science advances only as its methodology is refined, and its concepts defined. For the student of rhetorical theory there is particular relevance in the latter effort. The available texts which are concerned with the techniques and precepts of public speaking from Aristotle to the turn of the twentieth century provide no uniform statement of the meaning and purposes of pathos. This study is an attempt to summarize some of these perspectives. (66)

Lee noted that the essay on emotional appeal had been extracted "From chapters I and V" of a his dissertation at Northwestern. Lee began his essay with a historical explication of a persistent problem in the history of rhetorical theory, "The Distinction Between Ethos and Pathos."Although the classical conceptions of proofs and appeals are no longer as commonly applied as they were in 1939, the question of whether we can differentiate among emotional, ethical and logical appeals remains as matter of concern in rhetorical theory and criticism.

Lee traced the ideas of ethos and pathos through the history of rhetorical theory from Aristotle, to Cicero to Quintilian, to John Quincy Adams. He also cited Volkmann's *Die Rhetorik der Griechen und Romer* and an article from the *American Sociological Review*. From his reading he concluded:

> *This is the larger sense in which the classical rhetorical definition of the ethos as a persuasive force is to be understood, thus differentiating it from pathos, the effect of which is the direct excitation of emotion. Ethos, then, is a matter of adaptation to existing attitudes, pathos a matter of arousing emotions. (70)*

Lee then devoted the balance of his essay to "The Varying Conceptions of Emotional Appeal." Lee's treatment was at the same time lucid and complex. He carefully traced the history of the idea of emotional proof, explicating the intellectual presuppositions which were at the foundations of the various conceptions. Lee began with Aristotle and ended his analysis in the twentieth century; he drew on major rhetorical figures and on those who were not so well known. An outline of Lee's development will be helpful.

> II. *The Varying Conceptions of Emotional Appeal.*
>   A. *Approaches to the Doctrine of Pathos:*
> B. *The Functions of Emotional Appeal:*
>   1. *Pathos and Perception:*
>   2. *Pathos as a Linear Adjunct:*
>   3. *The Conviction-Persuasion Duality:*
> C. *The Enlargement of the Doctrine of Pathos:*   *(70-86)*

Lee recognized at the outset that the idea of pathos changed over time because of differing perspectives of rhetorical theorists.

> *Any attempt to trace the development and changes in the many specific items and minutiae of the doctrine of pathos as it is discussed in invention, arrangement, and style must face an infinitely complex task. The problem is not made difficult because of additive changes but primarily because of shifts in treatment which result as the doctrine is enlarged or minimized in the schemes of the various treatises. (70)*

This passage was important not only because it illustrated the difficulty of undertaking a study in the history of rhetorical ideas. It was also significant because Lee perceived that the rhetorical proofs do not exist as independent entities; but, rather,that the generation of appeals, particularly emotional appeals, is dependent on the intimate connection with other rhetorical elements, namely "invention, arrangement, and style."

It was precisely in those kinds of connections that Lee saw the differences among theorists. In Aristotle, for example, ". . . pathos is treated separately and individually as a distinctive phase of the process of persuasion." In the work of the Roman rhetoricians, in contrast, said Lee, "the other tendency is to conceive of emotional appeal as a phase of the arrangement process. . . . primarily in the proem and perora-tion." The Roman approach is to be found in the *Rhetorica ad Alexandrum*, the *Rhetorica ad Herrenium*, *De Inventione*, and in Quintilian.

Lee cited nineteenth century theorists to provide a contrast with Aristotle's position that:

> . . . *pathos was considered as a mode of persuasion operative either with other modes of persuasion or separately. In Whately,* [Elements of Rhetoric,] *Day,* [The Art of Discourse,] *and Hepburn* [Manual of English Rhetoric] *this individual functioning disappears and pathos becomes but one phase in a connected persuasion process. (74)*

As can be seen from the outline of Lee's essay, he considered the role of emotional appeal in the traditional concern of the relationship between conviction and per-suasion. Lee saw the beginning of the concern with the conviction-persuasion duality in the rise of Faculty Psychology and he began his treatment with George Campbell.

> *The duality is an outgrowth of the analysis of the mind into a set of faculties in which the understanding and the will are conceived as the powers or actions of the mind. . . . If there is a different phase within the mental organization, limited to each of these elements, it then follows that it is possible to appeal to the understanding to produce conviction or to appeal to the will to produce persuasion. This separation is clearly made in Campbell. To produce conviction the arguments must merely be presented so that they may be understood, attended to and remembered by the hearer. Persuasion to some particular action or conduct can only be achieved when the hearer is interested and moved. Thus persuasion is the process of emotional appeal. (74-75)*

Lee then delineated the ways in which writers of the eighteenth, nineteenth and the early twentieth centuries had construed the conviction-persuasion dichotomy. He pointed out that the distinction was continued in the work of Blair (*Lectures on Rhetoric and Belles Lettres*), Coppee (*Elements of Rhetoric*), Hill (*The Principles of Rhetoric*), There-min (*Eloquence a Virtue*), Doyle (*An Introduction to the Study of Rhetoric*) and Baker (*The Principles of Argumentation*). Although he did not specifically attribute the dualism to the rise of Faculty Psychology, it is clear from Lee's context that the distinction arose from the conception of separate and identifiable faculties of the mind.

Lee pointed out that the dichotomy was not present in classical rhetorical theory and that it may have obscured rather than clarified the role of emotional proof.

> *This duality redefining the function of emotional appeals designed to effect a change in attitude and conduct does not appear in the classical conception. . . . Neither of these main functions alone is the task of the orator, but that the speaker's conviction should be persuasive and his persuasion convincing. If this line of argument is valid, it seems to make possible the evaluative conclusion that the dichotomy in terms of invention adds nothing more to a complete conception of what is involved in persuasion, and indeed, obscures the total picture of what is involved. (76)*

Lee's objection to the conviction-persuasion dichotomy was, of course, not original. Woolbert, at the very beginning of the profession, had argued against the distinction, as had numerous psychologists. Lee's contribution was to place the dichotomy in the history of rhetorical theory and to demonstrate its foundation in Faculty Psychology.

Lee's position did not allow emotional appeals to be limited to persuasion while conviction was characterized by logical appeals.

Lee undertook a comprehensive historical analysis to demonstrate how the conceptions of emotional proof had been changed and enlarged over time. He began by showing how Aristotle had connected pathos to the topoi of happiness, pleasure and emotion. He cited support for Aristotle's position in the *Rhetoric ad Alexandrum* and in Cox's *The Arte or Crafte of Rhetoryke*. With some alterations, the connection between pathos and topoi was continued by Melancthon, Wilson and Farnaby. A change occurred in the eighteenth century and Lee cited Lamy's *The Art of Speaking* and Lawson's *Lectures Concerning Oratory* as works that sought the origins of emotions in different sources.

> *This changed view of the origin of the emotions is to be found in the rhetoric of Lamy, for whom all emotions evolve from the basic emotions of admiration and contempt, whose objects are respectively present good and meanness and error. Similarly Lawson emphasizes the role of desire of happiness in the life of the individual. Everything which seems to contribute to the well-being of the individual is well liked, whereas those things which thwart that state are disliked. From these basic states are derived all the emotions. (81)*

The final enlargement of the doctrine of emotional appeal may be found in Campbell and Whately, as well as other eighteenth, nineteenth and even twentieth century rhetorical theorists, including Hepburn (*Manual of English Rhetoric*), Bain (*English Composition and Rhetoric*), Winans (*Speech Making*), Monroe (*Principles and Types of Speech*), Hayworth (*Public Speaking*), Sarett and Foster (*Basic Principles of Speech*), Brigance (*Speech Composition*) and Sanford and Yeager (*Practical Business Speaking*).

> *While recognizing the distinction between the virtues and the passions, Campbell has also asserted their their relation in terms of a common effect; each is able to affect the will: each is a motive to action. . . . With the theory of persuasion based upon achieving an influence on the will and exciting the individual to action, emotional appeal in the strict sense disappears. The basic emotions, including those analyzed by Aristotle, tend to disappear, the emphasis being placed on the constituents of happiness, pleasure and virtue. . . . This enlarged doctrine of emotional appeal is in essence the modern doctrine of persuasion. . . . It is pertinent to note that the contemporary texts continue what is essentially the tradition of Campbell, Whately, Bain, etc. Modern theory is thus substantially characterized by the absence of treatment of pathos in the classical sense. (84, 84n)*

The most significant of Lee's conclusions dealt with the changing conceptions of emotional proof.

> *Within the totality of rhetorical theory there have been three ways of looking at the function of pathos, i.e., as a means of affecting the perception, as a linear adjunct in a connected total persuasion process, and finally, as a phase of the conviction-persuasion duality, where its role is defined in connection with the will. (86)*

Lee's essay on pathos is one more of the significant essays to which little scholarly attention has been paid. He was able to examine a rhetorical concept in historical detail, an analysis which had not been undertaken earlier and is still relatively rare today. His work had both theoretical and pedagogical utility. The scholars in the field had a model of how longitudinal, historical research should be carried on, as well as a cogent statement concerning the development of ideas concerning pathos. Lee's later scholarship made important contributions to the discipline, but this essay was his last in rhetorical theory. His reputation today rests largely on the his writings in General Semantics.

In 1941, in the spirit of Lee's work, Fred J. Barton, of Abilene Christian College, undertook in *The Quarterly Journal* to explore "The Significations of 'Extempore Speech' in English and American Rhetorics." Barton's contribution, although useful, was not of the same quality as Lee's. Barton began with the statement of a difficulty which has been persistent through the history of rhetorical theory—the meaning of the term extempore. From this foundation Barton began his analysis and historical tracing. He, like Lee, was interested in the varying interpretations given to a rhetorical concept.

> *Therefore, since a thorough understanding of the theory of extempore speaking as it is today demands a knowledge of its relation to the rhetorical theory of the past; and since a change in its signification seems to be shrouded by a degree of mystery, it appeared to this writer that an attempt to trace that change would prove to be worthwhile and enjoyable. (237)*

In order to understand how the concept had been changed in English and American rhetorics, Barton felt that it was necessary briefly to examine how extempore had been understood in the classical period and to trace its evolution from Classicism to later British and American writers. He ignored Aristotle, and he limited his brief survey to Cicero's *de Oratore* and to Quintilian's *Institutes*. Barton concludes that both of the Roman theorists conceived of extempore speech as ". . . when it becomes necessary to speak at the call of the moment." Cicero and Quintilian recognized the importance of previous meditation and writing as preparation for the occasions when an extempore situation occurs.

According to Barton, early English writers, such as Thomas Wilson, paid little attention to extempore speech and ". . . presumed that the speech should be either read or recited. . . ." Wilson, said Barton, ". . . took it for granted that the speech was to be learned by heart." Hobbes ". . . recognizes that the pleadings of a court trial cannot be written . . . but he does not use the word 'extempore.'" The first mention, in British rhetorics of extempore speaking which Barton was able to find was in Thomas Blount's *Academy of Eloquence* of 1654 for whom ". . . extempore eloquence appears to depend on the inspiration of the moment. . . " By the time of David Hume's "Essay of Eloquence" of 1741, (who, despite the title of Barton's essay, was, together with Campbell and Blair, Scottish and not English) and John Lawson's *Lectures Concerning Eloquence* of 1752, the notion of extempore had been changed to include the suggestion that extempore speech might be construed as speech which is prepared but not memorized or read. Barton seemed unduly pedantic when he recognized that although Ward and Burgh advocated a means of preparation which was extemporaneous, they were disqualified because they did not use the magic word "extempore."

> *Though Ward speaks of reading and memoriter (sic) speaking, he does not apply a name to the type of discourse just described. We cannot say, therefore, whether or not he would call it extemporaneous speech." But though Burgh comes near to doing so, he does not label the whole process, preparation as well as delivery, "extemporaneous speech." (242)*

Barton treated Campbell and Blair in short order. He again found himself trapped in his own linguistic entanglement when he acknowledged that Blair spoke of something resembling extempore speech, but did not use the proper word.

*. . . The sermon may be fully written out and committed to memory; or there may
be study as to matter and thoughts, trusting the expression to the inspiration of the
moment. It should be emphasized, however, that it is not this premeditated type of
speech which Dr. Blair designates as "extemporaneous effort." (244)*

About Priestly Barton wrote that "Priestly in referring to his practice intended 'extempore' to refer to those parts of the discourse which were not read." For John Quincy Adams, ". . . extemporaneous speech was 'without preparation': the expression of 'unmeditated thought.'" Barton claimed that Henry Ware Jr. in his essay of 1824 "Hints on Extemporaneous Speech" was ". . . the first to use this title to signify premeditated speech." Barton then cited Lord Brougham and Richard Whately as later exponents of extempore speaking who perceived it to require preparation and premeditation. Most of the citations from the late nineteenth and early twentieth century were from homiletic texts which favored the extempore method.

Barton's conclusions to his essay were rather pedestrian. . .

*It is obvious that the signification of the term has changed. Up to a certain period
of time, extempore speech was unmeditated as to both thought and language. It has
lately come to include more or less elaborate preparation of thought and
arrangement, only the phrasing being left to the moment of delivery. . . This study
indicates the tendency to include premeditation in speech called extemporaneous
first became evident in rhetorical theory toward the end of the first quarter of the
nineteenth century. (250)*

Barton's essay offered him opportunities which he did not exploit. He simply charted the ways in which the term "extempore" had changed meaning over time. He made no attempt to set the variations in a historical or cultural context in order to explain and understand them. We have no way of knowing why the Enlightenment regarded "extempore" as having one meaning, and why it was assigned another meaning in the nineteenth century. Also, Barton's emphasis on homiletic texts in the late nineteenth and early twentieth century obscured the thought taking place in rhetoric texts.

Ironically, it appears that Barton recognized the deficiencies in his article; but he regarded them as outside the concern of the essay.

*It would be interesting to conjecture as to the possible forces entering into the
evolution of extempore speaking, and their reaction upon each other, but that is
beyond the limits of this paper. It has fulfilled its purposes in determining the
periods of that evolution. . . . (251)*

Elton Abernathy of Louisiana Polytechnic Institute followed Barton's concern with homiletics in his 1943 *Speech Monographs* essay "Trends in American Homiletic Theory Since 1860." An Abernathy footnote offered a partial explanation for Barton's emphasis on homiletic texts. He cited Barton's 1939 Iowa M.A. "The Contribution of Selected Works in American Homiletics from 1860 to 1880 to the Theory of Extempore Speaking" (69). Abernathy's article was based on his own Iowa Ph.D.

The essay was very limited in that it did not examine homiletic theory in the larger, more general context of rhetorical theory. Abernathy mentioned John Quincy Adams once and cited no other writers on rhetorical theory. Perhaps his point was to make clear that rhetorical theory and homiletic theory were entirely separate genres.

When George P. Rice of Pennsylvania State College published his 1943 *Quarterly Journal* article " Early Stuart Rhetorical Education," he frankly acknowledged that he was following a pattern set by an earlier essay. "The same general procedure employed by Karl Wallace in his paper on Tudor rhetoric is employed here" (433). Rice's analysis was considerably less thorough and less detailed than was Wallace's. Rice did, however, present a generally clear sketch of the rhetorical climate in the time of the Stuarts by examining rhetorical education in the schools and universities.

Rice described Stuart England by an analogy with ancient Rome.

> *Like Quintilian the Englishmen believed that oratory was the central subject of the curriculum from a pragmatic point of view, since "oratory needs the assistance of many arts," and because he knew that along the road of public speaking lay the easiest path for civil service preferment and especially to Parliament. (436)*

Much of Rice's essay was devoted to explication of the rhetorical exercises in the grammar schools, which had not changed much from the Tudor times described by Wallace. As Wallace had understood, so did Rice understand that rhetorical exercises were not limited to oral exercises.

> *As the seventeenth century moved on its way, written exercises were emphasized more and more. . . . The schools which followed his views [Roger Ascham] offered a course of study somewhat like this: "mastery of the eight parts of speech and of sentence structure in early forms;. . . for much wryting breedeth ready speaking," Those training for "eloquence and Civill lawe" read Demosthenes, Aeschines, Lysias, Antisthenes and Andocides. (435)*

As the students moved from the schools to the universities the rhetorical exercises were continued. Now, however, the students also studied the works of classical rhetoricians.

> *Every effort possible was made to teach the wisdom of the ancients, particularly Plato, Aristotle, Quintilian, Cicero, and Hermogenes. . . . their writings were utilized for study of content and for criticism of rhetoric and oratory. . . . In addition to the delivery of speeches, some attention was paid to rhetorical criticism. The works and speeches of such orators and rhetoricians as Demosthenes, Isocrates, and Cicero, together with those of the early church fathers were widely used. (436)*

Rice offered a succinct summary of rhetorical education in Stuart England.

> *. . . One may say that that the basic purpose of early Stuart educational philosophy was the adaptation of wisdom of classical times to contemporary needs; that to this end the grammar schools, the universities, and Inns of Court utilized rhetoric and oratory preeminently. (437)*

Rice's work did not have the depth of Wallace's, and although it was less analytical and less historically and culturally perceptive, it nonetheless presented a cogent portrait of rhetorical education at a particular point in history. He, thus, was able to contribute to the profession's understanding of the relation of rhetoric and society. Rice's essay added to our knowledge of the history of rhetoric.

During the war years the writings on rhetorical theory in the journals of the association diminished in quality and in number. Understandably, as we pointed out in another chapter, the mood of the country, as well as the profession, was directed to questions of patriotism and democracy, and not to theoretical rhetorical formulations. The essays published in rhetorical theory after 1941 were decidedly weaker than the landmark works of the 1930s. In 1942 Glenn E. Mills of Northwestern and in 1945 Lieutenant William A. Behl of Maxwell Field, Alabama published articles which sought to extract theories of rhetoric from the works of prominent American orators. Mills chose to synthesize "Daniel Webster's Principles of Rhetoric." Behl devoted his work to "Theodore Roosevelt's Principles of Speech Preparation and Delivery." Mills' article was based on his University of Michigan dissertation, "Daniel Webster's Theory and Practice of Public Speaking," which was representative of the "theory and practice" research in fashion at that time.

Since Webster had not written or spoken about rhetoric in a systematic way, Mills consulted writings by and about Webster, including Webster's *Private Correspondence*. The references to Webster's *Private Correspondence* and *The Writings and Speeches of Daniel Webster* are often identified only by page numbers, and it is, thus, sometimes difficult to place them in a context. Moreover, Mills attempted to accomplish his task of reconstructing a rhetorical theory for Webster in fewer than twenty pages.

As might be expected, Mills chose an Aristotelian-Ciceronian pattern for his analysis. The main headings of his article were:

> *His TrainingPrinciples of Rhetoric .*
> *Invention.*
> *Topics.*
> *Logical Proof.*
> *Ethical Proof .*
> *Pathetic Proof.*
> *General Preparation.*
> *Specific Preparation.*
> *Arrangement.*
> *Style.*
> *Delivery. (1942, 124-140)*

I cite Mills' organizational scheme to indicate how much rhetorical theorists of this period were limited by the Aristotelian-Ciceronian rhetorical perspective. (I take into consideration the fact that Mills was a brand new Ph.D.) In some ways, this kind of research told us more about the classical writers than about the subject of the research. More than half of Mills' essay was devoted to invention while only one paragraph was allotted to arrangement. Mills justified the emphasis on invention because "Invention, including topics, general and specific preparation, and ethical, logical, and emotional proofs, apparently was Webster's major interest in rhetoric" (1942, 127).

Because he was so restricted by his method, Mills synthesis of Webster made no important contribution to theoretical understanding. His slavish application of classical criteria allowed him only to show that one could extract a rhetorical theory for Webster based on the traditional canons and proofs. Mills' work stands in contrast to Wallace's synthesis of a fully developed theory for Bacon. Mills may have been handicapped because Daniel Webster never wrote specifically or systematically about rhetoric. Nevertheless, Mills gave a tolerably clear description of Webster's thoughts about rhetoric.

Behl's Roosevelt article was also the reworking of a dissertation, in this case at Northwestern. Behl was not as bound to the classical pattern as Mills. On the other hand, he said little of importance about rhetorical theory. The substance of the essay made it clear that Roosevelt was, in no way, a rhetorical theorist. Behl provided an picture of T.R.'s thoughts about public speaking drawn, in part, from anecdotal material and secondary sources, as well as Roosevelt's writings and letters and other documents contained in the Roosevelt House Papers. Behl also sought to extract a rhetorical theory for Roosevelt's own rhetorical practice—a dangerous procedure, at best. After a page and a half devoted to Roosevelt's speech training, Behl discussed "His Theory of Public Speaking" in another page and a half. He then went on to write about "Content," which was more concerned with the source of T.R.'s ideas for speeches than any ideas he had about invention. He treated delivery in very much the same way. Mills might have been criticized for his rigid treatment of Webster, but Behl's essay was marked by its vagueness and avoidance of the proofs and canons. Not a word was said about style or arrangement, and logical and emotional proof were hardly discussed. Behl did make one brief and superficial statement concerning Roosevelt on ethical proof.

> Roosevelt believed that character of the speaker was the most important source of his persuasive power. Among the important attributes of character was sincerity. . . . He believed, too, that that one should be friendly. But sincerity and friendliness should not be superficial; a speaker should use his persuasive powers to influence people to do good. (113)

To be fair to Behl, we must note that readers of Behl's article were given fair warning. Near the outset and in the conclusion of his essay Behl wrote:

> These scattered opinions concerning public speaking indicate that although Roosevelt was not a student of rhetoric, from his practical experience in public speaking he evolved fundamentally sound principles. (114)

From these bits of information it is clear that he was not a student of rhetoric. . . . Although he was not a student of classical rhetoric, the core of Roosevelt's theory on public speaking is that the orator must be a "good man" (121).

If Roosevelt was not "a student of rhetoric" and if he had no systematic rhetorical theory, why did a scholar of the eminence of Karl Wallace, then the editor of *The Quarterly Journal*, decide to publish Behl's article? The best explanation that comes to mind is that by 1945 many of the persons who might have contributed useful, or even valuable, research were, in the male dominated profession, engaged in military or other wartime service. Behl was one of a number of authors who contributed work while they were on military duty. The situation for editor Wallace was critical enough that he almost pleaded for articles.

> There's a war on and in one way or other it has practically engulfed those who in normal days would be sending in voluntary contributions to the Journal. This issue, for example, contains but one article we did not secure through solicitation. . . . But we can continue to produce a good journal, particularly if members of our association will do a little mind-searching and a little writing and keep material coming in to the editors' desks. Take a minute, lean back, and pin down the idea that you had not so long ago! What do you consider the soundest method of teaching your subject? Is there some phase of the history of your specialty that you had been meaning to work up. Is there another good article in your thesis or dissertation. After all, for those teaching speech now is the time to write. (1945, 93)

An obvious exception to this condition was Winans' essay "Whately on Elocution," published in 1945. At the age of 73, Winans was certainly exempt from military service and he had retired from Dartmouth. Winans' article was only eight pages in length and almost half of it did not concern itself with Whately. Apparently Winans felt it necessary to sketch the views on elocution of some of Whately's predecessors. He, thus, offered brief summaries of theories of delivery of Thomas Sheridan, John Walker and

Hugh Blair. Winans said that he discussed Sheridan and Walker because of their mechanical systems of delivery were so much in contrast to Whately's system of natural delivery. Walker's system was especially objectionable to Whately.

> *The methods of both are thoroughly mechanical and tend to take the speaker's mind off meaning and audience. My second reason for bringing in Walker is that his system is one of those, perhaps the chief one, that Whately objects to and ridicules. (1945, 3)*

Winans found that Blair contradicted himself. In one place he advocated copying "proper tones" and rehearsal "to search for the proper emphasis." In another place he wrote that speaker in his presentation ". . . should then not be employing his attention about his manner or thinking of his tones and his gestures." Winans was correct when he wrote that, "Plainly Blair had not thought out clearly a theory of delivery."

In rather rapid fashion, Winans uncritically explained Whately's theory of delivery. His own of appraisal of Whately he reserved for ". . . some comments of my own upon his doctrine." His comments also provided a useful summary for the essay.

1. *While Sheridan, Blair and, Whately all agree that thinking and feeling prompt adequate expression. . . Whately was the only one of these to state clearly and to make the statement an article of faith. . . . There should be no rules, no marks for emphasis, pause, inflection, tone or gesture.*
2. *Whately pays little attention to voice training and the like.*
3. *While the teachings of Sheridan and Blair would tend to produce conversational style and mode, through imitation of delivery in conversation, I doubt that Whately's teaching would do even that. . . He aimed at public delivery which sounds like conversation. But I fail to see how he could get that out of is teaching, for he puts all the stress on exclusive attention to matter. . . It is surprising that the keen Whately never came through to recognize the other necessary element in delivery, what I like to call "a sense of communication.". . . He never quite comes through to say that the feeling of contact with the audience has a definite effect upon delivery. (1945, 7-8)*

Winan's interest in delivery was not at all surprising. As far back as 1915, in the first edition of *Public Speaking*, he had given priority to delivery. The first chapter of the textbook was devoted to "The Problem of Delivery—Conversing with an Audience." Winans had promulgated his own theory of delivery which held that public speech was no more than "extended conversation." It, thus, was an adaptation of Whately's idea of "natural delivery."

> *I wish you to see that public speaking is a perfectly natural act, which calls for no strange artificial methods, but only for an extension and development of that most familiar act, conversation. (1915, 18)*

The "sense of communication" to which Winans alluded was also part of his 1915 conception of delivery. He illustrated it by using the example of a school boy speaking or reading about a horse.

> *The horse is to him a real and significant object at the instant he speaks the words. . . . He is "thinking on his feet;" He creates or re-creates the thought at the moment of delivery. . . . To throw that statement into a phrase we shall make much use of, Johnnie succeeds when he reads or speaks with a sense of communication. (1915, 27)*

Winans' *Quarterly Journal* article dealt with a much narrower aspect of Whately's rhetorical theory and it was, thus, more sharply focused than Parrish's earlier effort. From our present day perspective, the Winans essay may not seem remarkable. We must remember, however that his article was only one of two articles published on Whately in the history of the association—up to that time. In that context, it provided a knowledgeable discussion of Whately on delivery.

A full analysis of Whatley's theories was still some years in the future. The essay also indicated that, over a period of 30 years Winans' position on the theory of delivery did not essentially change.

Winans' essay was, in some ways, representative of the end of an era in rhetorical theory. After the end of World War II rhetorical theory began to draw on different sources than the works based on Aristotelianism and Faculty Psychology. A comment by Ray Ehrensberger of the University of Maryland argued that changes must take place.

> *Current rhetorical theory is based on the outmoded pluralistic psychology of mental faculties. . . Modern psychology is strongly monistic in nature. . . . (95)*

Ehrensberger cited work by three writers who had broken away from the restrictions and who had made attempts ". . . to restate rhetorical theory in terms of modern psychology." The authors who were the recipients of his praise were Woolbert (1917, 1918, 1919), Utterback (1924) and Brigance (1935).

I do not intend to suggest that work on classical and later rhetorical theory terminated at the end of the war. Indeed, the best work on such figures as Blair, Campbell and Whately was yet to come, as was much excellent scholarship on theorists of the classical and other periods. Nevertheless, the emphasis began to shift away from the traditional sources to contemporary sources who were, for the most part, literary critics. The post-war years were the years of discovery of such theorists as Kenneth Burke, Richard Weaver, Richard McKeon and Wayne Booth. It must be emphasized, however, that the shift was one of derivation rather than origination. Rhetorical theory continued to be dependent on outsiders to create theories. Those who called themselves rhetorical theorists continued to be students of the theories of others.

CONCLUSION

The complex history of research in rhetorical theory, in the early days of the profession, was largely a history of the search for roots. The profession came into being in 1914 with little knowledge of and little interest in rhetoric. The late years of the nineteenth century and the early years of the twentieth were years in which whatever scholarship took place was in the Departments of English. Since the early days of the discipline was a time in which the profession sought a means to enter Winans' "sheepfold"of research, rhetoric was an area to which it turned. The new profession took advantage of a serendipitous opportunity. During the second and third decades of the century English had turned away from its interest in rhetoric and toward its new concern with literary criticism. Rhetorical theory, as well as rhetorical criticism, was left on the ground for the speech people to pick up.

The earliest and dominant work in rhetorical theory was concerned with the explication of ancient Greek and Roman works on rhetoric. The work of Bromley Smith was especially prominent at this time; he possessed the rare attribute of being competent to deal with Greek texts in Greek. Most of the commentaries of Greek and Roman rhetoric following Smith were based on translations. The commentaries themselves were neither critical nor analytical. They were largely summaries of the works of ancient writers. But such essays were perhaps well suited to a discipline just beginning to learn about rhetoric.

Interest in rhetorical theorists, other than the traditional Greek and Roman writers, did not manifest itself until the middle of the 1920s when Hoyt Hudson examined the rhetorical theory of Thomas De Quincey. Hudson was also the the author of the first important essay to deal analytically with the work of a rhetorical theorist. Hudson examined De Quincey's texts in their own terms, instead of relying on secondary sources. Hudson was an early advocate of a rhetorical perspective which was not limited to oral discourse. He was also among the first to articulate the importance of understanding the history of the field of speech. Hudson, because of his formulative work in both theory and criticism, must be reckoned as one of the most distinguished figures in the early history of the profession. In contrast to Woolbert, Wichelns, Winans and Hunt, Hudson remains largely unrecognized.

The work of Everett Hunt must also be recognized. Hunt conceived of rhetoric as a field much broader than the study of speeches. Indeed, his formulation took rhetoric beyond the orality/literary dualism to a point where much of the study in the social sciences could be designated as rhetoric.

During this period the field of rhetoric had to withstand attacks both from within and from outside. Paul Shorey, a classicist at Chicago, and V.E. Simrell, a speech teacher at Dartmouth, launched serious attacks. Their attacks were different from Woolbert's criticism that rhetoric was not scientific. Shorey and Simrell saw rhetoric as an inherently corrupt craft.

Utterback, Thonssen, and later Brigance were the first scholars to connect rhetorical theory to contemporary psychology. Where Woolbert had disparaged rhetoric, these writers sought to provide a psychological foundation for rhetorical theory.

By the 1930s more modern rhetorical theorists were being studied. Thonssen examined the works of Thomas Hobbes, and Wallace analyzed the rhetorical theory of Francis Bacon. Donald Bryant also began his studies of Edmund Burke. Interestingly, except for the superficial study by Parrish and the specialized work of Winans on Whately, no specific attention had been paid to the British Rhetorical Renaissance. No serious articles on Blair, Campbell, Whately, Priestly and others were published until after World War II. Even later came work devoted to European theorists such as Vico, Rollin and Fenelon.

Careful studies of rhetorical concepts were exemplified by the work of James McBurney on the enthymeme, a valuable complement to Hudson's study of invention and to Irving Lee's work on emotional appeals.

The research in rhetorical theory in the first thirty years of the profession was more characterized by the study of historical figures in rhetorical theory than on theoretical formulations carried on by scholars in rhetorical theory. This situation was not altogether bad; the new profession was deficient in its historical knowledge of rhetoric, and it was very much to their advantage to become informed. Unfortunately, the acquisition of historical knowledge seemed to inhibit the motivation of rhetorical theorists to break their derivative bonds and to undertake independent work which did not rely so extensively on secondary sources. After 1945 the focus shifted from Aristotelianism to literary critics and social critics. Those figures were also used

derivatively and the creation of rhetorical theories in Speech Communication
remained inhibited.

■ 9
GROUP DISCUSSION

In spite of its early mention by the Research Committee, group discussion was a relatively late arrival in the research and writing of the speech profession. Alfred Dwight Sheffield, a member of the national association, apparently was the first member of the association to write a text on the subject. His book, *Joining in Public Discussion*, was not intended for a collegiate audience; it was published in 1922 as one of a number of volumes in the Workers' Bookshelf Series, issued under the auspices of the Workers Education Bureau of America. In the book Sheffield was variously identified as Associate Professor of Rhetoric, as Professor of English Literature at Wellesley College, and as Instructor in Public Discussion at the Boston Trade Union College. The books in the Bookshelf covered a range of topics including; Women and the Labor Movement, The Humanizing of Knowledge and The History of the American Labor Movement.

The title of Sheffield's first book was more than a little misleading. Although the title spoke of "public discussion," more than three quarters of the book was devoted to public speaking and parliamentary procedure. The working person who read the book might have been quite confused since the introduction was restricted to discussion, but in the book itself fewer than 40 pages out of more than 160 were given over to discussion. The most significant material on discussion was, in fact, contained in the introduction. There Sheffield laid out the premises about discussion, which came to be accepted for more than two decades.

> 1. Not "audience" but "discussion group" is the power plant for influence.
> 2. Group Thinking pools the ideas of all for the inspiration of each.
> 3. Not "majority win" nor compromise but "consensus" the ideal aim. (1922, v-xv)

Sheffield, not only was the first teacher of Public Speaking to write a discussion text, he also was the earliest author to write on discussion in the association's journal. In 1924 Sheffield and A. Craig Baird, then of Bates College, wrote articles dealing with discussion. Baird in "Argumentation as a Humanistic Subject" sought to retain the value of argumentation while not restricting it within the limits of formal debate. Baird's 1924 conception of discussion was a form of argument, and it was clearly intended to deal with public presentations.

> *Argumentation must continue to base its procedures on the sure foundation of logic and evidence. . . . Discussion will be substituted for formal debating; figures and citations of authority will not submerge vital thought; individual expression will have freer scope than is the usually the case in debate. (1924, 262)*

It is apparent that Baird conceived of discussion as a less restricted form of argumentation which, nonetheless, was still based on logic and reasoning.

In the two years between 1922 and 1924 Sheffield had narrowed his focus and in his *Quarterly Journal* article public speaking was ignored. In contrast to Baird, the perspective presented by Sheffield in "Training Speakers for Conference" was much closer to a later conception of group discussion. At the outset of his essay Sheffield was careful to differentiate between three modes of discourse.

> *Oratory is the voice of the mass meeting. It aims to focus and make articulate "the will of the people." Debate is the mode of the forum: it aims at a winning vote. Discussion is the the mode of group conference: it aims at collaborative action. (1924, 325)*

Sheffield did not forsee discussion replacing debate since the two forms were based on quite different communicative situations and had quite different objectives.

> *There hardly seems warrant to believe, as certain of its enthusiasts declare, that it will supplant debate. Some disputes, in the nature of the case, fall into two-sided line ups, and where the deliberating group is large and pressed by business, it is almost driven to take up issues, not where discussion takes them—farther up stream, with the disputants in a mood of experimenting with experience—but canalized into alternatives calling for a showdown of choice. (1924, 325)*

Sheffield, like Yost, Woolbert and Winans, was familiar with contemporary psychologists and he saw their work as being particularly applicable to discussion.

> *Still, in the field of social conflicts—the field now getting brought under the psychological scrutiny of Holt, Dewey, Krabbe, Follet, Lindeman and others —the future is with discussion. (1924, 325-326)*

Thus at the very outset of Speech Communication's interest in discussion, its future form was being specified by Sheffield. He saw discussion not as a substitute for public speaking and debate but a new form of communication concerned with group thinking and problem solving. He also understood that group discussion was involved with psychological questions. In our investigations we have not found an earlier reference to Dewey in connection with group discussion. Based on his experiences at three recent conferences Sheffield postulated the distinctive features of conferences as opposed to other forms of speech.

> *In these conferences the features that stood out were those that mark the essential nature of a conference as group-thinking. First of all, there was not an audience but an all-participant group. . . . Secondly the dispute was not two-sided but several-sided: There were as many sides as there were interests at stake. . . . Thirdly, the aim of the deliberations was the achieving not of a winning vote but of a solution, a plan of joint action that should enlist everybody concerned. . . . Finally, the speaking tended to deal not with arguments but with reasons. The distinction is important. A man's arguments are the reasons that recite well. They do his heart credit, and his logical head. They are objective and intellectualistic, and invite either assent or rebuttal. His reasons are things that lie deeper. They are the meaning to him of his own experience, and they invite first of all a real understanding. (1924, 327-328)*

Sheffield, in his article, specified a structure for discussion. Although he earlier had mentioned John Dewey, we have no way of knowing whether he had read *How We*

Think. In any case the what Sheffield called "thought-process" seemed to be a fragmentary version of Reflective Thinking. The author led the readers through a problem from identification to solution.

> *Conference does, in fact, move normally through three definite phases as a thought-process. The group must (1) face the situation ; (2) identify the problem; (3) test proposals for a solution. The first step assures the reality of the discussion as springing from the experience of the group; the second step discriminates the precise cross purposes that constitute the problem; the third step compares and appraises the constructive effects of alternative ways out. (1924, 328)*

Sheffield apparently viewed conference or discussion (he used the terms interchangeably) as being somewhat formal since he referred to the role of the chairman whom he described as ". . . a sort of psychological bandmaster exercising just so much direction as to make the group play up to its opportunities for mutual thought-enhancement" (1924, 328).

The perception of relations among group members was one of conciliation and good sportsmanship, a perception which continued for more than two decades. Sheffield sought to minimize conflict within the group, if not to eliminate it. The emphasis was on compromise and group thinking. He wrote, "Much of the finesse of conference turns on our ability to keep opponents talking without personal pique." To fortify his point he quoted from Herbert Kelly's *The Object & Method of Conference.*

> *We are free to state any difficulty or objection we think is involved, and we may put it as an argument, but we must be careful that neither form of statement nor tone of voice shall imply that the other man cannot answer. That, besides being bad manners, is bad policy since it provokes the man to invent an answer when otherwise he might have admitted the validity of the objection; and frank admissions are a great help. (Kelly in Sheffield, 1924, 330-331)*

In summarizing the advantages of conference Sheffield reflected the then prevalent view, presented by Dewey and others, that adjustment was a desirable social and individual goal.

> *Such a figure, however [an analogy with fencing] does little justice to conference as the agency of group-adjustments. Those who will carry on its development in a democratic technique will find their students roused by its possibilities, not as the cock-pit of smart egoistic rivalries but as the power plant of social influence. (1924, 331)*

In 1926 Sheffield published the first edition of *Creative Discussion: A Statement of Method for Leaders and Members of Discussion Groups and Conferences.* This brief work went through at least three editions. It was a practical work designed in the span of 68 pages to give discussion participants a step by step guide to participation and leadership in discussion. Sheffield distinguished between two types of discussion, a distinction which was not widely recognized for some time by most speech communication students of group discussion.

> *The desired outcome may be of an immediately practical sort, as where a board is deciding on a course of action to be carried out collectively, or where a joint committee is adjusting a conflict of interest between various parties to a situation. Again, the desired outcome may may be of an educational sort, as where the members of a study-circle thrash out the different aspects of an issue, and help each other to think their way through to socially sound convictions. Both kinds of group*

concern require a cooperative technique for group-thinking—a technique which in essentials is the same for both, but which develops certain tactical differences according as the immediate aim is group action or revised personal attitudes looking to future actions as personal or group occasions may arise.The present pamphlet is addressed to leaders and members of groups that meet with the second of these aims. (1933, 5)

The division made by Sheffield was one which did not appear in speech communication literature for a number of years. Sheffield, although he was a member of the new speech profession, apparently attracted little attention from his colleagues. His contemporaries continued to regard group discussion as an exclusively problem solving operation, and did not regard social change as desirable outcome. At the risk of over simplification, one might suggest that Sheffield was concerned with both behavioral and attitudinal change while the profession was concerned only with behavioral change.

Sheffield, under the heading "Discussing to Get Somewhere," devoted nine pages to laying out a case at Harvard which he regarded as a successful example of how discussion can lead to social change. In the present academic climate of diversity and affirmative action, the case must strike us as decidedly dated and reflective of a totally different social climate. The problem, as stipulated by Sheffield was:

Early in 1922 it became apparent that there was a growing feeling among among students, instructors, and alumni that the number of Jewish students in the college was becoming undesirably large. This feeling doubtlessly represented: (1) The natural dislike with which the predominating "Anglo-Saxon" clientele of the college found itself penetrated by a distinct ethnic group; (2) the special prejudice which "society" bears against Jews. The non-Jewish majority saw reason to fear that the social reputation of the college might become affected in a way to cause a falling-off of "Anglo-Saxon" students. (1933, 6)

In describing the attitude of participants Sheffield displayed a position which was reflective of the times and perhaps of his social class.

There were special difficulties, however, in points of attitude and feeling. The Jewish spokesman, taking the subject as something that touched their self-respect, were disposed to treat it not analytically, as a social force first of all to be accurately understood, but moralistically as an intolerance to be torn out of Gentile hearts. "The Jew," they said, "is a problem only to those who make him so. We are all Americans; Harvard is an American college. To discuss proposals here for special treatment of any special group is to repudiate our Americanism." This, of course, was an unconscious effort to short-cut the whole thought-process by a "slogan solution"—by an appeal, that is to emotionally charged ideas (intolerance, Americanism) which would simply dash the problem aside. (1933, 11-12)

We quote at length from the Harvard example not only because it displayed Sheffield's own biases, although it did, but also because throughout the book he returned to the example to illustrate effective discussion methodology.

Sheffield's explication of the tentative solution to the problem, recruiting a higher ratio of students from the West and South, suggested that the problem had been finessed rather than solved.

The effect of this measure was the building of a new group of students from rural schools and from regions West and South outside the normal Harvard recruiting grounds. Incidentally, these regions have but few Jews, so that this accession has raised the proportion of non-Jewish men in the college. (1933, 14)

Other examples of discussion problems used by Sheffield also indicated the social vantage of the times. Included were "What Associating Across Race Lines Do We Wish in Our Neighborhood?," and "Married Women in Business Jobs." (1933, 28, 30.)

The treatment Sheffield gave to group discussion in the little book differed from his earlier emphasis in several ways although the general emphasis was not markedly different. More than half the book concerned itself with the responsibilities of leaders. Although writers in the social sciences had dealt with the question of leadership, it had not yet been touched by the speech teachers. Sheffield touched on a topic which would not become current in speech communication for another generation. One section of the book was concerned with "The Group as a Clinic for 'Mind Sets'."In that section Sheffield dealt not with the logical progression in problem solving discussion but rather with the social and psychological conditions among the members of the group.

It is in the exchanges of thought about social values which people have at heart that discussion is most revealing. It shows how various attitudes and preconceptions gather into their emotional drive influences too deep in the subsoil of the mind for disputants to be aware of them. Where they inhibit or unconsciously weight people's responses to ideas the discussion can be focused, for a while, on these prejudices in ways that bring about a mutual self-scrutiny and release. (1933, 37)

Sheffield thus viewed group discussion as an arena where interpersonal elements played an important role and where the focus of the discussion would, at times, be concerned with the interpersonal dynamics of the group. Although his explanation was somewhat truncated, Sheffield's work was suggestive of Group Dynamics of a later period. Actually, his interest in the social and psychological aspects of the group was most clearly revealed in "Appendix B: Reading for Discussion Leaders." In the "Appendix" Sheffield included such topics as:

New values from conflict; Emotional complications of response; Personal and group bases of response; Attitude Group bond; Social differentiation; Types of complications to be reckoned with; Invasions of "self" feeling; Reactions to Prejudice? Clique reactions; Difficulties in expression; Blame-reactions; Platitudes and slogans; Fixed ideas (1933, 63-67)

Among other authorities cited by Sheffield in his reading list were John Dewey, Walter Lippman, Harry Overstreet, Horace Kallen, William H. Kilpatrick, and Floyd Allport. Sheffield's reliance on John Dewey was shown in the steps for discussion that he outlined, although he did not give credit to Dewey.

(1) Locating the Problem

(2) Examining Conflicting Interests

(3) Developing Possible Solutions

(4) What tests Should We Apply?

(5) Agreements and Disagreements

(6) Conflict Elements for Further Study (1933, 52-57)

Perhaps the first college text to carry the words "public discussion" in its title was A. Craig Baird's *Public Discussion and Debate of 1928.* In spite of its title, the book devoted only seven pages (out of 370) to discussion. It was really an argumentation and debate text. Baird's conception of public discussion was briefly stated, but he described its essential character, except that he certainly did not mean what we today would designate as group discussion. He correctly used the term "committee discussion" when he wrote about the difference between debate and discussion.

> *Whereas debate consists of competitive argumentation for the purpose of establishing a given proposition, committee discussion substitutes cooperative thinking for the purpose of uniting and crystallizing opinion. Discussion at its best means continual weighing of a proposition, modification of it, even substitution of a different proposal until the ideas of an assembly coalesce. The vote at the end represents a social judgment. The chairman of the group calls the meeting to order, states the problem, and calls for further interpretations and solutions. Each member rises in turn and states his opinion. (1928, 32, 34)*

Baird had a few, but only a few, words to say about the characteristics of discussion leaders and participants. As would be true in the profession for a number of years, he regarded discussion as a form of argument. Baird was considerably less detailed or insightful than Sheffield. In keeping with his background as a Dewey student, Baird placed emphasis on cognitive ability as expressed in "group thinking.

> *. . . A skilled chairman should be present to guide the thinking, summarize the progress, create and preserve the discussion atmosphere. Those who participate should have the mental alertness and open-mindedness necessary to a proper decision. Group discussion is a form of argument that will be more and more widely applied in fields where controversy may be controlled and group thinking developed. (1928, 37-38)*

To be sure, Baird's treatment of discussion was almost perfunctory and conceived of as committee meetings. Nevertheless, he should be credited with introducing discussion into speech textbooks and, thus to speech courses. A number of his assumptions, in the main derived from Dewey, became part of the standard perspective about group discussion in the pre-war years.

The first article in *The Quarterly Journal* dealing with group discussion was Sheffield's "Discussion. Lecture-Forum and Debate." Henrietta Prentiss in her preview of the 1932 convention recommended the Sheffield article to the convention program chairpersons.

> *May I call your attention to Professor Sheffield's article in this number. . . . I hope that a copy will be in the hands of every group chairman at the convention and that groups will be sufficiently familiar with the principles presented by Professor Sheffield to engage in constructive discussion for which the convention leaders are allowing time. (517)*

In spite of the title of Sheffield's article, it was mostly concerned with discussion. Lecture-forum and debate were given comparatively little attention. In the 1932 article Sheffield, devoted a considerable amount of space to a consideration of the skills and functions of the group leader. The most important characteristic of leaders, said Sheffield is that they know their groups, and Sheffield was precise and detailed about what it means to "know" a group.

> *A fruitful use of discussion therefore appears where the leader really knows his group—knows the type of gathering it is, and senses its present level of information and interest—and forms his discussion plan with due thought of its ultimate users.*

> *Leaders often think they know their groups when they merely feel at ease with them, having established a pleasant basis of congeniality in the meeting-place and personnel. Real knowledge of a group requires a scrutiny of its attitudes to the subject. . . . (1932, 517-518)*

Sheffield specified that the members of the discussion group ". . . must also take under view the different kinds of learning which will engage the members. . . " (1932, 518). Consensus was an important aspect of group discussion for Sheffield. It would be attained, he said said by ". . . modifying of the member points of view."

> *At the outset members see things differently because they feel the values differently, because their present attitudes and interests make them diversely sensitive and attentive to the whole situation. As a result they suggest courses of action which express the partialities of their vision—doing so with no lack of good intentions, and even unaware of their espousals of some interests at the cost of others. (1932, 522)*

How was this modification of attitudes to take place? It will be done, said Sheffield, by changing the objects of members' desires, a psychological perspective not unlike that adopted twelve years later by Brigance on persuasion. (See Chapter 8.)

> *This testing of the possibilities of action involves two kinds of effort which are simple enough to mention but which require time and skill to do; namely, (1) the applying of factual information, and (2) the reconsidering of partisan desires. It proceeds on the assumption that the people will modify what they now want either by finding better means for satisfying the desire, or by coming to recognize the essential trappings of it, or by shifting to a more enlightened desire. (1932, 522)*

Sheffield's faith in the rational and benevolent nature of humanity must be admired. He was confident that men and women who coldly looked at the facts and, further, who impartially examined their own desires, would choose a more enlightened desire. Later research in small groups, both inside and outside the profession, brought Sheffield's assumptions into question. At least, however, he wrote more insightfully than his speech contemporaries about the psychological and social settings for group discussion.

Sheffield was aware of the existence of conflict. He differentiated, however, between conflict and strife. Conflict could lead to cooperative decisions while strife inevitably resulted in discord and coercion. The goal was "a socially validated conclusion."

> *Here it gives way to a special way of looking at conflict; one that clearly differentiates between conflict and strife. Conflict it views as a natural phase of tension among people's interests—a phase inevitable where new interests arise and changed circumstances call for adjustments. Strife is conflict that has been embroiled by coercive handling. . . Hard feelings, suspicion, egoistic triumph and chagrin all come from treating as a battle what is essentially a problem. There are always two sides to a battle. There are two sides to an argument only when people are disposed to coerce rather than collaborate. . . . So conceived discussion is not a fight to be won. It is a process of cooperative testing of proposals for their maximum promise to all parties concerned. (1932, 523)*

The socially validated conclusion to a discussion, said Sheffield, does not necessarily lead to action or even to the solution of a problem. And it certainly is not simply a compromise.

> *In speaking of the "conclusion" here we must recognize that discussion may have either of two kinds of objective: it may seek a decision looking towards action, or it may simply seek the education of its participants. In a conference on disarmament government representatives hope to make their discussion reach real accord on mutually satisfactory things to do. In an educational discussion on the issue the group, of course, will not go that far. It will not go home with the armament situation solved. But it will have learned something of the solvability of such a problem where the modifying of people's claims and desires is managed not as a process of whittling them down to some compromise but of seeking for them new conditions and expressions on maturer levels of satisfaction. (1932, 523-524)*

Sheffield, in his examination of the kinds of questions facing discussion groups, and in his specification of outcomes, displayed the same kind of insight as in his earlier explanations of the group process. The fact that Sheffield's perspective may now seem a bit dated is irrelevant. He stipulated the characteristics and objectives of groups in ways which would not become prevalent in the profession until many years had passed. We must keep in mind that Sheffield wrote more than 60 years ago, when hardly anyone else in the association was in the least concerned about group communication. Yet he displayed a grasp of group decision-making and problem-solving consonant with the social science and philosophy of his day.

Sheffield understood that the discussion leader ". . . may at once recognize certain difficulties which would jeopardize the use of discussion in his present program." He included a long list of "difficulties." Some of the more salient and long lasting were the following.

> *The leaders who would be expected to handle a discussion meeting, if held, are accustomed to "chair" meetings according to parliamentary procedure.The leaders do not expect to make much preparation for the meeting. The members differ too much in maturity for satisfactory discussion. Members do not know how to participate in problem-solving approached in a cooperative manner rather than an argumentative manner. Members know each other so well that special skill would be required to present an issue in which they would not feel they could predict what each would say.   Where these difficulties appear in combination, the leader will make only a partial and tentative use of discussion, especially at first. A strong leader who is ready to take pains can minimize these handicaps, but he will move slowly and not overtax the willingness of his group. (1932, 525-526)*

Discussion was, for Sheffield, not free from limitations. ". . . There are difficulties which are felt in the nature of discussion itself." A skillful, leader, however, should be able to ameliorate the difficulties. Sheffield recognized before many later writers that a discussion leader must not allow the discussion to be governed by the mechanical structure of "discussion method."

(1) It is a slow process.

(2) It deals with the subject on a lower level of information and communication than a lecture."

(3) It stirs up antagonisms in the group."

All these possibilities of difficulty must be frankly faced by anyone desiring to lead his group into ways of discussion. They are not disabling difficulties, provided he has the good sense to use discussion flexibly, and not to overtax people's faith in it.

"Discussion method" should not be allowed to impose a patternized march of thought without checks and changes according to circumstances (1932, 526-527).

In the preceding citations it becomes clear that Sheffield was concerned with discussion leadership, as well as the discussion process. He understood how important was the guidance of a competent leader in carrying on an effective problem solving discussion. One can understand why Harriet Prentiss recommended that the chairpersons at the 1932 Association Convention read Sheffield's article. Sheffield wrote about the characteristics and duties of leaders well before the matter was noted in the professional literature.

Sheffield also showed insight into the natures of group members and the relationship between members and leaders. He required that the leader be perceptive about the maturity of the group as a whole, and of its individual members.

In contrast to some later works, particularly text books, Sheffield's view of "discussion method" was less rigid in its adherence to a particular structural pattern. He did not prescribe a method as specifically, for example, as did the advocates of Dewey's pattern of Reflective Thinking.

Sheffield concluded his essay with "the special considerations which invite the use of discussion."

1. *To maintain a balance of listening and of contributory activity for the members in an educational program.*
2. *To bring the information near to the members day-to-day concerns.*
3. *To increase the alertness of members toward information to be introduced.*
4. *To clarify the thinking of the group about material which has been presented.*
5. *To make problems carrying only academic interest more alive and personal.*
6. *To pool member experience around a common problem.*
7. *To induce the appreciation of differing points of view.*
8. *To help members face in a self-scrutinizing spirit the psychological difficulties in reaching agreement where emotions and prejudices are part of the problem.*
9. *To deal directly with opinions and assumptions which underlie the arguments used on controversial subjects.*
10. *To place the initiative toward better understanding between members on themselves.*
11. *To afford practice in cooperating with those who differ with one.*
12. *To increase confidence in the solvability of contentious problems. (1932, 528-529)*

The foregoing list is a cogent summary of Sheffield's perspective on group discussion. He was obviously strongly directed to educational and problem-solving discussion. At the same time he was aware of the importance of appreciating the emotional, psychological and social conditions which impeded or advanced the progress of discussion. In this respect, he was considerably in advance of his contemporaries who tended to see group discussion primarily as an application of logic to group communication.

Alfred Sheffield must be included in the list of unheralded pioneers in the young speech profession. He explored a new form of communication and dealt with its practical applications. Moreover, he examined group discussion with a remarkable degree of sophistication, especially for his time. He understood the roles of leaders and participants. He also perceived that groups were at different levels of maturity. Sheffield clearly pointed to the direction which the field would follow until the 1950s; yet his contributions were largely unrecognized and his name is hardly known today. Sheffield's work was included in the bibliography of McBurney and Hance's 1939 *The*

Principles and Methods of Discussion, but he was cited only once in a footnote in the text. By 1950 he had disappeared from their revision *Discussion in Human Affairs.* Baird listed Sheffield's *Creative Discussion* in one chapter reference in his *Public Discussion and Debate* of 1938. Ewbank and Auer, in their *Discussion and Debate* of 1941, cited Sheffield only in the reference at the ends of three chapters. In Sattler and Miller's *Discussion and Conference* of 1954 Sheffield was given a footnote; by the time of the second edition of 1968 Sheffield was nowhere to be found. McBurney mentioned Sheffield in the essay we are about to examine.

In an earlier chapter we discussed James McBurney's 1937 essay "Some Contributions of Classical Dialectic and Rhetoric to a Philosophy of Discussion" from the point of view of rhetorical theory. Since, however, it was a bridge between the two sub-fields, it is worthwhile to examine the essay from the perspective of group discussion.

McBurney relied on the writings of John Dewey to establish a rationale for the study of group discussion. McBurney and Dewey sought to find a methodology of problem solving similar to the natural sciences.

> *Professor John Dewey expresses the view of many social thinkers in his essay "Science and Society" when he makes the point that that civilization may hope to emerge from social and political confusion when there is developed and applied a methodology for dealing with social problems on the same level of experimental intelligence and reflective thought that has characterized our method of attacking problems in the natural sciences. Since any such social method must of necessity have its focus in those group situations in which social problems are being deliberated and determined, considerable attention has been given to to the development of a method of conference or discussion which will implement co-operative group thinking in a way that has been impossible under the older theories of competitive debate and persuasion. Professor Dewey has himself said that "the essential need is the improvement of the methods and conditions of debate, discussion and persuasion." "That," he concludes, "is the problem of the public." (1937, 1)*

Both McBurney and Sheffield regarded group discussion as more than simply an alternate mode of communication. They, together with Dewey, perceived discussion as the means whereby we improve our thinking in order to solve problems more effectively. Both of these writers were as much concerned with discussion as a cognitive modality as a communicative tool. The significance of discussion as a means of problem solving, McBurney noted, was exhibited by interest outside the field of speech.

> *. . . [It's use by] adult educational agencies; the widespread development of the forum and other types of discussion under the impetus of the forum program of the United States Office of Education; and the accumulation of a considerable body of literature in this field. (1937, 2)*

McBurney noted that in November of 1936 Lyman Judson had published a ten page bibliography on discussion in *The Gavel* of Delta Sigma Rho. The widespread interest in discussion which McBurney observed was, of course, a healthy sign for the profession. At the same time, however, it was an indication that discussion was not a scholarly interest that the discipline had initiated; nor had it taken an early position in research in discussion. For much of its history, until the present day, the field of discussion in Speech Communication has depended on other disciplines for its theoretical and conceptual base.

One of the reasons McBurney chose to explore the relationships among rhetoric, dialectic and discussion was that he sensed that the proponents of discussion were disdainful of the more traditional aspects of the discipline. Sadly, they were also not well informed about discussion.

> *Despite this interest in the discussion field, our knowledge about the philosophy and method of this type of speaking remains relatively scattered and undeveloped. For this reason and because of the protagonists of the discussion movement interpret it to be a reaction against classical influence as represented in contemporary theories of argumentation, debate and persuasion, I am proposing here certain concepts in classical dialectic and rhetoric which appear to me to be capable of making significant contributions to a theory of discussion. (1937, 2)*

After making his conceptual statement about discussion, McBurney devoted himself to the conjectural and probabilistic characters of dialectic and rhetoric, which we have already discussed. McBurney's essay, and its contribution to group discussion, should not be dismissed, however. It is a clear conceptual statement, and it almost anticipates another dispute between the rhetoricians and the social scientists. From the 1950s onward, scholars in discussion, increasingly, came to represent an empirical position which, if not disdainful of traditional rhetoric, was not altogether tolerant. Many of the rhetoricians, of course, were no more accepting of the social scientists than were the social scientists of the rhetoricians. In 1937 A. Craig Baird of the University of Iowa published a revision of *Public Discussion and Debate.* Although public discussion was listed first in the title, it definitely took second place in the book itself. Baird devoted only the last chapter to discussion per se and accomplished his task in thirteen pages (out of 390). Nevertheless, Baird's chapter was long enough to reveal a typical pedagogical perspective and to indicate the application of current theory in the classroom. The fact, however, that discussion was given only one chapter while debate, argumentation, and radio debating and discussion were assigned seventeen chapters may tell us about the relative importance of discussion in the 1930s.

When Baird specified the aims of group discussion for his students, he presented a point of view similar to that of Sheffield. He, however, specifically restricted the scope of group discussion to social rather than scientific problems.

> *The assumption of group and committee discussion is that social problems can be solved by cooperative thinking. A scientific problem in engineering or medicine can often be solved single-handed, but a social issue can be settled only by a meeting of a number of minds and by the agreement of those who are concerned. Force, law, debate, compromise, all fail frequently to settle a major issue; they merely suppress for the moment the intensity of the conflict. (1937, 357)*

Baird's removal of scientific problems from the domain of problem solving discussion is an indication of the clear line drawn in those times between subjective and objective knowledge. As research and study in small group communication became more sophisticated, it became clear that "scientific" problems were also amenable to group processes. It is also worth noting that Baird set as a goal for group discussion nothing less than unanimous agreement since he ruled out compromise as an aim, together with debate, law and force. He spoke of "only by a meeting of a number of minds and by the agreement of those who are concerned." "Cooperation" rather than "compromise" was the key word for Baird. Baird's distinction drew a clear procedural, and even cognitive, line between discussion and debate.

> *Whereas debate consists of competitive argument for the purpose of establishing a*

given proposition, committee discussion substitutes cooperative thinking for the purpose of uniting and crystallizing opinion. . . . The outcome is collective opinion. The vote at the end represents a social judgment. . . . Debate is an exercise for—one might say exhibition of—leaders. . . skilled in argument and enthusiastic in upholding their side. Group discussion is an informal session of a committee of the whole. . . Each member participates in the discussion and bears his share of responsibility for the discussion. (1937, 357-358)

Although Baird drew a clear distinction between discussion and debate, he apparently did not draw a precise line between discussion and committee meetings. Indeed his chapter was titled "Committee and Public Discussion." In spite of his advocacy of cooperative thinking, Baird spoke of "the vote at the end" as if his admonition against compromise had not been written.

Baird, in keeping with the spirit of the times, (see Chapter 6) connected discussion to democracy and citizenship, and the social adjustment of the participants.

Group discussion is an excellent exercise in training for social thinking . . . . The group discussion situation disarms the divisive spirit, substitutes the come-let-us reason-together atmosphere, and trains men and women in social self-control. It calls for emotional restraint and an absence of "crowd mindedness." It is a logical speaking technique to develop in a community. (1937, 358)

It is not too much to conclude that the protection and the growth of of American democracy depend on the practice of full and free public discussion. . . . His faith is that free and full discussion will enable our nation to adjust itself to the new demands and so will insure national stability and progress. (1937, 367-368)

Baird, in fact, devoted more space to public discussion, actually a forum presentation, than he did to problem solving group discussion, which he equated with "committee discussion." In addition to public discussion he also treated the lecture forum, the discussion contest and panel discussion (1937, 364-367). He apparently conceived of group discussion broadly and placed considerably greater emphasis on discussions observed by audiences as contrast to self-directed problem-solving discussion.

Under the heading "The Technique of Discussion," Baird offered suggestions concerning the behavior of group members. The suggestions were directed to remove as much conflict as possible and to develop an atmosphere of cooperation and tact. The question of interpersonal relations in the group was not merely minimized, it was completely avoided.

1. *Adopt a proper attitude toward the purpose of group discussion. If you succeed in the discussional situation, you will recognize that the end is not so much compromiseas consensus. . . . The result must be the triumph not of your individual point of view but that of the group. . .*

2. *Adopt a proper attitude toward your colleagues. You will have no opponents;. . . You will attempt as best you can to appreciate whatever angle is presented and to weigh fairly each idea.*

3. *Adopt a proper attitude toward yourself. Recognize your prejudices, your personality traits of optimism or pessimism, your idealism or materialism.*

4. *Analyze your group definitely. . . . Consider what interests the group may have in the issue, what is at stake in individual cases, what desires are most important, what unfortunate results will come to certain members if the problem is wrongly solved . . . .*

8. *In the discussion itself, inquire rather than dogmatize. Be persuasive, tactful and sincere in your speaking. . .*

9. *Above all cooperate in attempting to further the discussion so that time is conserved and so that ideas evolve. (1937, 359-361)*

Apparently Baird expected discussion participants to possess almost all the human virtues. They were to be tactful, open-minded, self analytical, perceptive about other group members, cooperative and tactful. Unfortunately, he gave the student no specific, or even general, instructions as to how these traits were to be acquired. One gets the impression that Baird expected discussion participants to be model ladies and gentlemen. They were not to be abrasive, aggressive, competitive or insensitive. Presumably persons who did not possess the desired characteristics could not participate in group discussion unless they could undergo significant personality change.

A simplified version of Dewey's Reflective Thinking pattern was used by Baird for his "Outline for a Group Discussion." His outline included three steps: analysis of the problem, weighing of the problem, and solution of the problem. Under analysis Baird included statement of the specific problem; history of the problem; definitions; limitations, qualifications and agreements affecting the analysis; and identification of issues. Weighing the problem was concerned with weighing solutions rather than consideration of the problem. The weighing for Baird was the comparison of arguments and evidence in support of solutions A, B, or C. The solution of the problem was phrased entirely in cognitive terms; Baird's concern was with the following questions; on what evidence and argument does the group agree or disagree, and what means can be found for executing a common solution (1937, 362-363).

Baird's perspective on group discussion was more logically centered and less psychologically centered than Sheffield's. His presumption about human nature seemed to be that college students could be trained to become highly rational thinking beings who were not likely to be distracted by emotional or interpersonal factors.

In 1938 William Utterback, by then at the College of the City of New York, wrote an essay, "Patterns of Public Discussion in School and Life," which put discussion in a historical context. In writing his historical essay, Utterback construed the meaning of "public discussion" in a broad sense. By "public discussion" he apparently meant something like "public communication." His opening paragraph illustrated the breadth of his definition.

> *Fourth of July oratory and senatorial debate passed with the horse and buggy. That their educational counterparts, the oratorical contest and the school debate, still form the staple training of students preparing for participation in public discussion is an anomalous fact. . . We are undoubtedly witnessing a revolution in our institutionalized forms of public discussion. . . In an attempt to understand the nature, cause and extent of that revolution, let us turn to recent political and economic history. (1938, 584)*

From a perspective of 50 or more years, Utterback's perspective seems decidedly myopic. Certainly, the debates concerning Vietnam, the Gulf War, Iran-Contra and other national concerns do not leave us with the impression that senatorial debates are extinct. I can't recall 1935 very well, but I have heard Fourth of July orations since then.

Utterback sketched a brief history of public discourse from the middle of the nineteenth century to his own time. He led his readers through the eras of epideictic oratory, the college oratorical contest and the formal debate. There has, however, been, said Utterback, a change in the nature of public discourse since the 1880s. The modifications were the consequences of political, social and demographic change.

> *Events of the last fifty years have created a new economic and political world. The passing of the western frontier, the rise of modern industrialism, the drift of population to urban centers, the development of mass production and the concentration of wealth have profoundly disturbed that balance of power among interest groups which was the basis of our political life during the twentieth century. . . Government is no longer a process of applying accepted principles to concrete situations. It has become in large measure a search for new principles. This new task of government and the political situation out of which it grows have profoundly influenced our institutional forms of public expression. Demonstrative oratory is declining. . . Public debate is also visibly on the decline. . . . As a method of adjusting conflicts and making collective decisions. . . debate has largely been supplanted by propaganda and conference. (1938, 586-587)*

We may think of the 1930s as a time far removed from our own; yet Utterback's description of the pre-war period bears some similarities to the present. Quite possibly he may have been reelecting the effects of changes brought about by Roosevelt's New Deal. Utterback had noted that "In the Senate important issues are decided in committee. . . . Most of our legislative assemblies transact serious business in the committee room and lobby, and use the chamber as a broadcasting studio" (1938, 586-587). He was not alone in sensing changes in legislative oratory. Well before 1938 Woodrow Wilson, for example, had written of the rise of committees in Congress and the consequent decline of deliberative oratory.

Utterback's linkage of propaganda and conference may strike us as unusual. He, however, saw them as two stages of the same process.

> *Conflicting interest groups preparing for the final stage of a controversy deluge their potential followers with propaganda in support of the group's demands, the primary object being not to influence judgment, but to mobilize force at the conference table. A conference is then called to negotiate a settlement. (1938, 587)*

It should be evident from this passage that Utterback's view of discussion, and conference discussion in particular, was quite different from Sheffield's or McBurney's. Utterback perceived a conference as an arena where contending parties met to achieve solutions satisfactory to both sides. One does not detect in this essay the ideas of reaching consensual solutions or of ameliorating personal disagreements. Nor did Utterback pay much attention to the characteristics of groups. Rather, his goal was a variety of compromise, of which Sheffield would have sharply disapproved. He used the example of the National Labor Relations Board to illustrate his perception.

> *. . . The problem to be solved grows out of a group conflict for the adjustment of which no principle is available in existing legislation or political tradition. . . .The purpose of the meeting is to devise a formula which expresses the balance of power between the groups with sufficient accuracy that all will accept the settlement rather than resort to force. (1938, 587)*

Utterback saw the historical change in public discussion as a rationale for modifying the pedagogy of the profession. Oddly, his emphasis was on forensic programs rather than classroom instruction. If he intended to prepare students for the new communicative order, ordinary speech classes would have seemed to be a more appropriate vehicle.

> *While teachers of speech have taken cognizance of this change in patterns of discussion, we have not yet fully appreciated its implications. We need to shift emphasis more decidedly from the oratorical contest and the formal debate to discussion of the conference type. . . . Only by the use of speech projects which realistically mirror the various contemporary forms of public discussion can the forensic program be made a vital part of the educational process. (1938, 588-589)*

The changes Utterback advocated were soon to come as more and more classes in group discussion were offered, although writers such as McBurney and Sheffield had cleared the path. In Utterback's particular area of concern, discussion came to be a standard event in forensic contests. The notion of introducing discussion, a co-operative mode of communication, into a competitive setting does, however, seem, at least, a bit contradictory.

Utterback's contribution to our understanding of the history of public discussion was not really significant. However, the view that he held of discussion as contention between opposing groups and as a mode of communication intended to reach solutions without force was one quite different from that perceived by other writers. His advocacy of compromise was unlike the position of the Dewey-influenced writers who argued for mutually arrived at solutions to which all group members agreed.

Twelve years later in 1950 when Utterback, then at Ohio State, published his textbook, *Group Thinking and Conference Leadership*, he had apparently abandoned his approach and he joined the bulk of the profession in championing the Dewey-based pattern of Reflective Thinking.

From 1939 on the number of articles and books devoted to group discussion increased dramatically. Indeed 1939 was a very good year for writers on group discussion. As many significant essays were published in that year alone as in the previous 25.

Lester Thonssen, in "The Social Value of Discussion and Debate," undertook, once more, a study of discussion and debate, partially on the grounds that ". . . A re-evaluation of of discussion and debate is periodically necessary," and partially to determine ". . . whether our work as at present conducted provides socially-significant experiences."

In contrast to some other writers, Utterback for example, Thonssen did not draw a firm line between discussion and debate. Rather he saw them as being closely connected. Debate was, for him, a continuation of discussion.

> *I link the words "discussion" and "debate" because I consider them a natural combination. During recent years we have often been led to believe that discussion and debate are somewhat different mediums of expression. . . I see no conflict between them. . . . As I see it discussion and debate are two aspects of one process. . . . Discussion and debate play complementary roles in the broader function of persuasion. Discussion precedes the formulation of definite convictions. . . . It represents as Professor Baird has indicated, "a stage immediately preceding argument proper.". . . Thus it follows, if this idea is correct, that debate is an inevitable outgrowth or result of discussion. (1939, 113-114)*

Obviously Thonssen's conception of discussion was quite different from that of other writers, such as Sheffield and McBurney. Where they believed discussion to be a mode of communication essentially different from oratory and debate, Thonssen thought of discussion as the prerequisite for debate. Other writers saw discussion as a means of reaching consensual, and in Utterback's case, compromise solutions for social, political and economic problems. Thonssen, however, thought of discussion as part of a debate-discussion continuum. Thonssen cited his graduate advisor, and later co-author, A. Craig Baird, to support his view. It is interesting to note that Baird's textbooks assumed such a continuity. Both his 1928 and 1937 texts were titled *Public Discussion and Debate*, and his 1950 text was called *Argumentation, Discussion and Debate*. I recall in my day as a Baird student that he also said that "debate is discussion that failed." In other words, if all the issues were not resolved in discussion they could then be resolved in the adverserial debate setting.

Thonssen turned to his original question of the social values of discussion-debate. He explored the question in some detail, but the summary of the essay contains a cogent statement of Thonssen's opinion of the social values of discussion and debate.

> *I have suggested, as many others before me have, that discussion and debate be considered a unit. The one naturally precedes and makes possible the other. As such they can become effective instruments for the development of intellectual integrity in the individual. Admittedly, they are not tools of magic power. They cannot remove all emotional barriers to rational conduct; neither can they unveil all ulterior designs and persuasive cunning in some men's reasoning. But they are responsible, in greater or lesser degree, for tempering the judgments of students. They tend to make students more tolerant and responsible members in the presence of conflicting ideas. This, it seems to me, is what discussion and debate, under proper supervision, can contribute to the development of the individual and of society. (1939, 117)*

This position about the social value of discussion and debate was very much of its time. The 1930s and early 1940s was a period, as we have pointed out elsewhere, (see chapter 5) which emphasized the importance of social adjustment and which also saw it as an objective of public education. Some members of the speech profession conceptualized a speech classroom whose central goal was to bring about beneficial changes in the personality of the students. Thonssen's views were not nearly as radical as those of Bryngelson, and other contemporaries. Nevertheless, the message emerged from his essay that changes in the students' values were as important as the mastery of the discussion process.

Thonssen said that ". . . The one value which I would mention particularly is open-mindedness." A strong case might have been made for discussion as a motivator of open-mindedness. The case for debate, however, was more dubious. Although we do not devote specific attention to debate in this volume, we should, in this context, mention the charges brought against debate in this period and later. The criticism of competitive debate did not arise from its propensity to encourage open-mindedness. Rather the attack on debate was based on the charge that the encouragement to debate both sides of questions produced not open-mindedness but glibness, irresponsibility, hypocrisy and lack of commitment.

As we have seen, the term "discussion" was subject to various interpretations. In 1939 Robert Allison of Teachers College at Columbia and Joseph F. O'Brien of Penn State sought to bring some clarity to the term. In his article, "Changing Concepts in the Meaning and Values of Group Discussion," Allison felt that group discussion was a ". . . a phase of speech work that has hitherto been rather overlooked." Because of adult education and other factors, Allison foresaw ". . . a greatly augmented demand for properly trained teachers in this specialized form of speech activity." In the spirit of the times, Allison portrayed discussion as "a poor relation of debate" and he stated his intent to ". . . deal with the meaning and spirit behind discussion, its relation to debate and its values both direct and implied." (118)

Allison's view of discussion, in the spirit of Thonssen and Baird, was still of a field related to debate. Nonetheless, he perceived the primary purpose of discussion to be educational; but the acquisition of information occurred in a social setting which required interaction and conflict.

> *For discussion is primarily a form of investigation decked out in the garb of controversy. It is a search for information concerning the thoughts of other people about things, but there must be present constantly conflicting elements in the various approaches made to any topic. Without difference of opinion discussion withers and agreement in discussion is only necessary when action is imperative. In all other instances a sharply drawn issue forms the basis for fertile discussion and controversy is more to be welcomed and sought after than discouraged. However, this controversial attitude and spirit ought never to descend to contentiousness or captiousness nor should it verge on the realm of debate. (1939, 118)*

Allison was the first writer to be explicit about the importance of controversy in group discussion and the necessity of conflict. He also was in disagreement with many of his contemporaries in his stance that agreement was not necessarily the desired outcome for discussion. Apparently, the sharing of opinions was sufficient ground for discussion, unless immediate action had to be taken.

Although both discussion and debate are concerned with differences of opinion, care must be taken, said Allison, that the attitudinal differences between them be recognized.

> *Where both debate and discussion start at a mutual base of difference of opinion and both are forms of investigation, there is a vast difference in the attitude of each toward the solution of the problem. Discussion is concerned with the thoughts of people in questions of subjective judgment and not primarily with questions of policy. That is to say that discussion is a search for information and thus seeks merely to investigate and probe into the opinions that people have on various issues rather than leading people to act in a specific way. (118-119)*

It appears that Allison did not conceive of group discussion as solely a problem-solving mode of communication. He, in contrast to many other writers, regarded the sharing of information and varying opinions as sufficient justification for carrying on group discussions.

Allison, after his departure from the generally accepted conception of group discussion, adopted a position which partook both of the Sheffield-McBurney idea of conciliation, and of the Thonssen-Baird view of discussion's relation to debate. He also reflected Dewey's posture that scientific thinking was essential for successful discussion to take place.

> *Yet, while discussion depends upon controversy for its life blood, it is ultimately dependent upon the scientific attitude for its continued state of well being. Discussion must be featured by an open-minded attitude on the part of the participants wherein each one endeavors to establish his particular point but not to the degree that he becomes argumentative or disputatious. Each person must be ready to see the wisdom of another opinion or admit the instability of his own position when it is pointed out to him. . . . One keen minded commentator succinctly stated the difference between discussion and debate when he termed it the difference in attitude between the scientist and the advocate. Discussion attempts to investigate, debate to demonstrate the solution to a problem. Discussion is thought in progress, debate is the outcome of thought. (119)*

One can detect a possible inconsistency in Allison's essay. Although he clearly recognized the importance of controversy, his description of the open-minded participant who was careful not to become argumentative sounded like a person who was avoiding controversy.

In the concluding section of his essay Allison connected group discussion with powerful ideas of the 1930s and 40s—discussion as mental hygiene, and the connection between discussion and democracy. He all but championed group discussion because of its cathartic power. (See Chapter 5.)

> *Furthermore, discussion has a hygienic value that is quite as important as many of its intellectual values. It often times serves as an emotional purgative that relieves tensions which grip people who are dealing with elements they cannot prove. Thus, a calm discussion in a friendly meeting while retaining the aesthetic value of mental competition and fencing of wits, also can serve as an emotional buffer. . . . Lastly, there remains one valuable adjunct that looms more and more important in light of the ever growing tendency toward dictatorship and minority rule. By this I mean the use of group thinking and discussion as the instrument of democracy. (1939, 120)*

Allison, like Thonssen, was involved in the 1930s ideology of social adjustment and mental hygiene, and his view of discussion was, in part, shaped by his value systems. At the same time, Allison perceived discussion as a communicative mode which bore a relationship to debate and which allowed, and even encouraged controversy.

Allison's essay was useful in offering a conceptual statement about discussion. He did, in keeping with his title, deal with the meanings and values of group discussion; but he did not really demonstrate how the concepts were changing.

O'Brien's work was more definitional than that of Allison in that he sought to develop a workable classification of discussion which would give clearer meaning to the term "discussion" and to the underlying conception. O'Brien began his essay "A Definition and Classification of the Forms of Discussion" with an statement that,

> *Discussion is here used as a generic term to include any private or public meeting in which two or more individuals express themselves concerning the nature of a problem at hand, its solution or both. The term discussion always implies an interchange of information and opinion. (1939, 236)*

Obviously O'Brien's definition was "generic" and in need of specification and clarification. In order to achieve those objectives, O'Brien proposed a taxonomic system which classified discussion from a number of perspectives. He began with "Classification on the Basis of the Size of the Group."

Form	Number Participating
Duo-Discussion	*Two*
Group Discussion	*Three to twenty*
Public Discussion	*Twenty to thousands. (1939, 236)*

O'Brien recognized, as we do now, that a classification based on size was not "a water-tight compartment." Furthermore, his classification was not very meaningful since the criterion of size does not deal with discussion conceptually. The range of O'Brien's classification was indicative of the fuzziness of the idea of discussion. The notion that discussion could take place with an audience of "thousands" must seem ludicrous today. In justice to O'Brien, we should note that he used the term "group discussion" to refer to groups of "three to twenty." In 1939 the idea of "small groups" had not entered the vocabulary of the profession, and would not be in widespread use until after 1945.

Acknowledging his debt to John Dewey, O'Brien sought to find additional criteria other than size. He claimed to classify discussions ". . . On the Basis of the Attitude of the Group." O'Brien devoted that section to what he called "The Progressive Attitudinal Stages of Discussion," accompanied by a full-page diagram. O'Brien traced the development of discussion through the early stages of Reflective Thinking (1) "A generally felt problem," (2) "Definition of the problem," (3) "Critical examination of various hypothetical solutions," and (4) "Further examination through gathering additional facts." From that point the diagram divided into two decision branches, which were representative of deliberation and debate. The deliberation branch included the following stages: (1) Recognition of possibility of unanimity, (2) Agreement by unanimous vote (consensus) and (3) Testing the adopted solution in action. The debate branch began with (1) Recognition of possibility of unanimity "The battle lines are drawn," and continued with (2) Debate "The battle," (3) Agreement by majority vote "The battle is won," and Testing the adopted solution in action (O'Brien, 1939, 239).

The classification advanced by O'Brien was not so a much a classification of forms as it was the stipulation of the widely accepted steps of Reflective Thinking, combined with a notion not unlike that of Thonssen and Baird concerning the relation of discussion and debate. The clear inference in O'Brien's diagram, and in his prose, was that discussions which could not arrive at consensual decisions were forced to settle their problems in the confrontational setting of debate. The nature of the adverserial encounter was reenforced by O'Brien's use of the "battle metaphor." The classification to be derived from the diagram was that some discussions were deliberative while others became debates. One form is characterized by cooperation; the other by confrontation. It was not clear, however that the two branches really were different forms of discussion.

O'Brien concluded his essay in a section titled "Classification on the Basis of the Organization of Presentation." In that section he did, in fact, classify various forms of communication. His division of the "symposium-forum" form into seven sub-forms was clear, but the division reflected varieties closer to public speaking than to the later standard conception of group discussion. Under this blanket form he included such varieties as the round table, the lecture, the debate and the parliamentary session.

The breadth of the prevailing conception probably prevented O'Brien from devising a really meaningful classification of discussion forms. Many members of the profession chose to regard almost any form of oral communication other than public speaking as discussion. In his essay O'Brien spent more time on what he called "public discussion" than on "group discussion."

The essay concluded, irrelevantly, with the listing of the characteristics of the group leader. That person, in O'Brien's eyes, was an absolute exemplar of virtue.

> *He it is who steers the bark of discussion—stimulates the desire to speak, encourages the timid, quiets the unduly loquacious, humorously dissolves acrimony, guides the discussion into profitable channels. He should be intelligent, informed, thoroughly versed in discussion techniques, be a good speaker, and have a sense of humor. (1939, 243)*

The question of the pedagogy of group discussion was raised when Alma Johnson, in an experiment conducted under McBurney's supervision, set out to explore whether the fundamentals of speech course could be taught through group discussion. One justification for Johnson's research was the recognition that the lives of students would be more involved with discussion than oratory.

> In most college classes in speech fundamentals an estimated ninety percent do not contemplate careers in which professional speech is the major factor. . . . Few of them will find themselves in the position of an orator swaying an audience with platform eloquence. But they will find themselves participating in group discussions—in their work, in their social lives, in their homes, in civic affairs. They will be obliged to talk with other people and to think with other people and their personal success and worth to society will depend greatly on their ability to think and talk effectively in the cooperative solving of group problems. (1939, 440)

Another justification for the teaching of group discussion was its often stated role in a democratic society. To be a participant in a democracy required that ordinary human beings become competent in discussion.

> Yet if discussion is the fundamental and essential factor in a democratic society which its exponents claim, then its techniques must be mastered by the average citizen and its philosophy must be inculcated in the habits and attitudes of all the people. Effective participation in discussion must become a commonplace achievement of the ordinary individual. (1939, 440)

Because of her commitment to group discussion, not exactly a recommendation for unbiased research, Johnson undertook an experiment to ". . . determine whether or not group discussion might an effective method of teaching the fundamentals of speech in a college course" (441). In her experiment Johnson matched two classes of freshmen enrolled in a fundamentals of speech course. The control group was taught ". . . by the usual platform speaking method." The experimental group ". . . by the use of group discussion as the main approach" (1939, 441). Each of the students made four voice recordings and motion pictures were made of the students in each section. Tests were administered to both groups: Noll's What Do You Think? test which determined ". . . the extent to which an individual has acquired the attitudes and habits of scientific thinking. . ." and the Poley Precis Tests which ". . . purport to indicate the student's ability to discriminate between the essential and the unimportant, the false and the simply inadequate" (Johnson, 1939, 441).

In spite of the title of her article, "Teaching the Fundamentals of Speech Through Group Discussion," Johnson's experimental and control groups did not perform comparable tasks. Her arrangement provided for a standard fundamentals course for the control group and a course in group discussion for the experimental group.

> . . . The teaching procedure in the control group was based on the traditional platform speaking approach with considerable drill in bodily action, voice and diction. . . . The important difference in the conduct of the experimental class was the use of group discussion instead of individual speaking from the platform. Preparation was made not only by the leader but by each participant—through investigation, study, deliberation, following the steps in reflective thinking as described by Dewey. . . . Even more than adequate preparation was stressed the necessity of approaching the problem and its discussion with tolerance and an eagerness to find the truth, rather than a dogged determination to justify personal opinion. (1939, 445)

Johnson's description of her methodology could hardly be considered to be impartial when she described the public speaking class' ". . . dogged determination to justify personal opinion." In her experimental class Johnson's subjects engaged in "informal group discussions," "panel discussions" and "symposium-forum." Apparently Johnson, together with other members of the profession, continued to regard discussion as a generic term covering a range of activities from small groups to symposia presented to large audiences.

It is interesting to note some of the topics discussed; they are markers of the tenor of the times and are reflective of our present-day concerns.

1. *What should be the foreign policy of the United States at the present time?*
2. *What is the divorce problem and how may it be met?*
3. *Is the United States tending toward Fascism?*
4. *Should the United States set up an economic boycott against Japan?*
5. *What is the solution to the Negro problem in the South? (1939, 939, 444)*

The myopic perspective to the late 1930s is shown by the perception that the problem was a Negro problem and only in the South. It was also possible, Johnson thought, to cover the entire foreign policy of the United States in one discussion.

The results of Johnson's experiment were dramatic, but not surprising, considering her assumptions. She found that on the tests of scientific thinking the experimental group made a gain of five points while the control group gained only two points. One should not be amazed that the experimental class did better on scientific thinking, in which they were specifically instructed, while the control group received no such instruction. Johnson did not disclose the significance of these differences although she reported that ". . . the gain of the experimental group was approximately seven times the average gain during a three month period, that of the control group somewhat more than three times the average" (1939, 445).

The tests to "indicate the student's ability to discriminate between the essential and the unimportant. . . " showed no differences between the two groups. Other test results showed some differences in favor of the experimental group, although their relevance to speech, or to group discussion were somewhat vague. The experimental class was 11% higher on the Contemporary Affairs Test and their participation in extra-curricular activities was ". . . almost 50% more for the control group. . . ."

The students in the discussion group scored 50% higher in voice and diction, but the platform speaking group was 30% higher "in the elimination of physical mannerisms . . . and in the general improvement of posture, manner of walking, gestures, etc. . . ." The vocal improvement, Johnson speculated, was due to the atmosphere in the discussion class.

> *The discussion class provides a greater incentive for improvement; and, secondly, the student himself is better able to judge directly and immediately the efforts to communicate his ideas and feelings. . . If he articulates poorly, he is made aware immediately of his failure to make himself understood by the group. (1939, 446)*

Johnson did not attempt to explain why the physical behaviors of the public speakers were superior. Instead she offered a speculative unvalidated, conclusion.

> *Observation prompts the writer to add, however, that the students in the discussion group appeared to gain physical poise and to lose self-consciousness more quickly than did the platform speakers; a fact, if accepted as such, to be explained by the greater stress on communicativeness and the total elimination of exhibitionism in the discussion approach. (1939, 446)*

The conclusions Johnson drew from her research went further than her data would allow. We must remember that in her study she compared classes with altogether different pedagogical approaches. In the conclusion to the essay, however, she wrote of "incorporating" units of discussion into the ordinary fundamentals course. We need not doubt that the results she found were valid, but they argued for a course in discussion rather a fundamentals course which included discussion. Since she wrote in 1939, it was almost to be expected that Johnson would justify the teaching of discussion because of its role in social adjustment and personality improvement.

> . . . It may be stated then that there seems to be important values in the use of discussion as a tool for teaching certain of the fundamentals of speech; the development of the habit of reflective thinking and of desirable social attitudes; the acquisition of necessary information; and training in the effective use of the vocal mechanism and of language. These values appear to justify the incorporation of units of discussion in the fundamentals course, as complementary to the usual projects and exercises in platform speaking and reading. . . . It seems to the writer that if the teacher of speech accepts speech as the principal means of achieving personal development and social adjustment, then we cannot ignore the values which are necessarily inherent in a method which actually creates the kind of situation in which speech as a tool is to be used most frequently throughout life. (446, 447)

In spite of its methodological flaws, Johnson deserves credit for undertaking her experiment in group discussion. At least someone possessed sufficient intellectual curiosity to test empirically some of the assumptions about group discussion. Alma Johnson continued in an active career as a researcher in group discussion. She was the author of The Rogers College Problem which was used extensively in the post-war years.

A somewhat better designed experiment in group discussion was presented by Ray H. Simpson of Barnard College in his article "The Effect of Discussion on Intra-Group Divergence of Judgment" Simpson's presentation clearly came from a quite different orientation than Johnson's, and from the speech profession in general. He drew his experimental method and his supporting authorities entirely from Psychology and Education. Not a single reference was made to any of the writers we have discussed, or to Dewey. The central question posed by Simpson was, "What is the effect of discussion on the divergencies of belief and judgment existing in a group prior to discussion?" Questions of this sort were not posed by experimenters in speech for at least a decade. It seems clear from the procedures used and the theoretical foundations of the essay that Simpson was outside the speech paradigm.

In his study Simpson administered the McAdroy Art Test to "132 college women, largely sophomores and juniors." The test contained sheets of pictures with four pictures on each sheet. The subjects were instructed to rank the pictures on each sheet from best to worst. His procedure was relatively simple and required that the students perform three tasks.

> (1) Take the McAdroy Art Test once before discussion.

> (2) Participate in a discussion of the test.

> (3) Retake the test after discussion. (547)

In his results Simpson found that 106 out of 108 subjects "moved closer to group means from pretest to retest (with discussion intervening.)" In his control group

Simpson found that the control group, which did not participate in a discussion, also decreased their divergence, but by a smaller amount.

> *Taking the test alone produced an average decreased divergency of 9 per cent (decrease in divergency of control subjects) while taking the test and discussion of one third of it for fifty minutes with three other individuals produced an average decrease in divergency amounting to 36 per cent. Apparently 9 percent of this latter decrease might be attributed to simply taking the test the first time which leaves 27 per cent decrease in divergency which which was apparently caused by discussion with peers or near peers. (549)*

Simpson's study can be criticized for its statistical naiveté: his control group was much smaller than the experimental group, his findings were communicated only in averages and percentages, the college student female population which he studied allowed for only narrow generalizations. Statistical sophistication, however, was well below the present level. Simpson did design an experiment which furnished useful, if restricted, information on one aspect of the discussion process.

As one might suspect, Simpson's future career was not in Speech Communication. His publications after 1939 were in Educational Psychology and teacher training. His last book was published in 1975. His *Quarterly Journal* article was apparently drawn from his 1938 Teachers College dissertation, *A Study of Those Who Influence and of Those Who Are Influenced in Discussion*, which was also published as a book by Teachers College, and which was cited in 1941 by Ewbank and Auer in their text *Discussion and Debate*. Simpson did publish an additional article on group discussion in *The Quarterly Journal* in 1960, as well as four other articles between 1944 and 1964. The case of Ray Simpson is indicative of how widespread was the interest in discussion. We, of course, do not know what prompted Simpson to submit his articles to *The Quarterly Journal*.

The discussion-debate continuum was dealt with again by J. Jefferey Auer of Oberlin College in an essay titled "Tools of Social Inquiry: Argumentation, Discussion and Debate." Auer's title was a bit misleading since his article was largely concerned with the teaching of discussion in argumentation courses.

Auer began from the same position as that stipulated by Utterback a year earlier; indeed Utterback's work was cited on the first page of Auer's essay. He too believed that formal public speaking and debate were being supplanted by propaganda and conference. Although Auer felt that most argumentation and public speaking curricula were taught in the traditional ways, he saw some hope in the fact that a few institutions and textbooks had shown increasing interest in discussion. He cited Monroe's *Principles and Types of Speech* (1935), Brigance's *Speech Composition* (1937), and Pellegrini and Sterling's *Argumentation and Discussion* (1936).

Based on his own experience with a combined discussion-argumentation course, Auer outlined the nine objectives of such a course.

1. *To recognize the importance and need of intelligent public discussion in a democratic society.*

2. *To know and understand the intellectual and emotional bases of our individual thinking processes.*

3. *To understand the general principles and techniques of valid reasoning, or argumentation, and to be able to use argumentation as a method of making sound reasoning acceptable and vital to audiences.*

4. *To be familiar with the various techniques and methods of determining collective*

action—the group discussion, the panel discussion or round table, the symposium or forum, and the formal debate, together with modifications of each technique.

5. *To be able to carry on efficient research on a given problem and to be able to present the ideas and information thus gained in a clear, forceful, and effective manner.*

6. *To study the principles of group leadership and organization and to become familiar with a simple code of parliamentary procedure.*

7. *To know and understand the intellectual and emotional bases of thinking in group situations.*

8. *To know and be able to analyze the characteristics and behavior of audiences.*

9. *To understand the principles of motivation and to become familiar with the techniques of persuasion. (1939, 536-539)*

The accomplishment of the objectives which Auer laid out would seem formidable, even for "a two semester three hour course." They are also indicative of the broad conception of discussion in general use by the profession. Auer, together with O'Brien and other writers, regarded discussion as encompassing a range of communicative activities from small group discussions to formal debates. He also conceived of discussion as a companion to debate and argumentation, certainly not as a distinct form of discourse. Not until the post-war years, under the influence of social science, did the idea of a small group discussion attain autonomy. During the 30s and 40s the standard textbook treated both argumentation and discussion. Indeed, Auer, in collaboration with Henry Ewbank of the University of Wisconsin, published two editions of *Discussion and Debate: Tools of a Democracy* in 1941 and 1951. They also wrote *Handbook for Discussion Leaders*, published in 1947. McBurney and Hance's discussion text, *Principles and Methods of Discussion*, also of 1939, which we will treat shortly, set a precedent by devoting an entire book to discussion alone.

The objectives specified by Auer could almost be guidelines for life, as well as guidelines for discussion; they have as much to do with the students' cognitive and psychological improvement as with their communicative improvement. Of course the profession's dependence on Dewey's conception of Reflective Thinking almost required that discussion be regarded as an intellectual as much as a communicative activity. *How We Think* was intended to be a descriptive work about thinking, and not a prescriptive work about communication. The profession in this time seemed to have a commitment to make better human beings of us as well as better communicators; public discussion was perhaps one of the most appropriate vehicles for attaining that objective. Auer's later scholarly career was not limited to discussion and debate. He was also a visible contributor to scholarship in rhetorical criticism.

In the outpouring of discussion publications in 1939 the most significant was a textbook, *The Principles and Methods of Discussion*, co-authored by James McBurney and Kenneth G. Hance of Albion College. The publication of McBurney and Hance was to discussion what Winan's Public Speaking was to the field of public speaking. In a text book for undergraduates the authors explored the entire range of discussion. They perceived discussion as a distinct mode of communication and did not seek to place it on a continuum with debate or to connect it with public speaking, although they did devote a chapter each to "The Panel, Dialogue, Symposium, Forum-Lecture" and "The Forum." They were even stronger adherents of Dewey than Baird, who had studied with Dewey at Columbia, and other writers. Besides McBurney and Hance had over 400 pages available to them to develop their ideas and were not restricted by the limitations of articles.

1939, as we have earlier written, was a time of admiration for American democracy, and the connection between speech and democracy seemed clear to writers of speech books and articles. McBurney and Hance asserted that connection in the "Preface" to their book. Furthermore, they also made clear, in the "Preface," the governing assumptions of Reflective Thinking.

> *This book is designed to present the working principles and the method of discussion in terms of a democratic philosophy. The basic concepts in every line and chapter are criticism, co-operation, and communication. The work is an attempt to implement the reflective deliberation of face-to-face and coacting groups. (1939, vii)*

From the very outset of the book, McBurney and Hance made clear their reliance on John Dewey and reflective thinking. Although *How We Think* had originally been published in 1910, a new edition had been published in 1933. The authors distinguished between intentional and constructive or reflective thought. They cited Rignano's *Psychology of Reasoning* to support their distinction.

> *In constructive reasoning it is the object of the reasoner to discover truths yet unknown. . . . In such reasoning, the reasoner has at the outset no desire to maintain certain points at the expense of certain others. He only wishes to discover the truth. The "intentional" reasoner, on the other hand, starts reasoning in order to try to demonstrate the accuracy of definite assertions in which he has a particular interest. (Rignano, 1927, 209-210)*

This distinction was valid, especially for its time. It was, however, a distinction in reasoning not a communicative distinction. Both Dewey and Rignano were fundamentally interested in thought. Communication, if it was a concern at all, was secondary. This classification was different, for example, from the conviction-persuasion dichotomy. Rignano and Dewey would have regarded both conviction and persuasion as "intentional." If this distinction was accepted, it meant that all suasory discourse was outside the realm of reflective thinking. Ironically, the acceptance of such a division suggested a rejection of those fields in which the new discipline claimed competence, and even a proprietary interest. Argument, persuasion and rhetoric, were, at least implicitly, outside the concern of discussion. The acceptance of the Dewey assumptions, as they were understood by speech teachers, argued for cooperation against persuasion, emotional detachment against emotional involvement, and the minimizing of personal considerations against the advancement of a personal position.

Dewey's definition of reflective thinking had to do almost entirely with internal cognitive states and not with how thought was to be communicated, and not with group thinking.

> *Active, persistent, and careful consideration of any belief or supposed form of knowledge in light of the grounds that support it, and the further conclusion to which it tends, . . . constitutes reflective thought. . . . Once begun it is a conscious and voluntary effort to establish belief upon a firm basis of reasons. (6)*

it is quite clear that Dewey was almost as opposed to persuasion and rhetoric as was Plato in the *Gorgias*. If action was to be effected, it would have to occur after the completion of reflective thinking since reflective thinking was concerned with belief and not with action. We must remember though that Plato placed no trust in belief; it was truth he pursued. Dewey did not accept the Platonic view of absolute, knowable truth. The acceptance of Dewey's premises meant that discussion participants would not, could not, engage in argument or persuasion. One is curious, in retrospect, to know why those interested in discussion did not, in their writings and research, see the application of their own tools of the trade—persuasion and argument—to the discussion process. Not only might Speech have contributed to investigations, it might well have been recognized for its contributions to the study of discussion. Sadly, this seems to be another time when the fledgling discipline missed a golden opportunity.

The emphasis on the logical process and the dimunition, if not the elimination, of interpersonal considerations gave a disjunctive sense to the study of groups. Even though Sheffield and others had earlier recognized that conflict would occur in groups, Dewey influenced writers were more interested in diminishing or eliminating conflict rather than understanding it.

On one side McBurney and Hance placed discussion, constructive reasoning and criticism; on the other side they placed persuasion, intentional reasoning and propaganda. This arrangement, with its sanction from Dewey, was undoubtedly a useful distinction between investigative and instrumental thought. It had the disadvantage, however, of placing persuasion together with propaganda, with the clear inference that those modes of thought and communication were the undesirable forms, while discussion and criticism were the forms to be desired. As we earlier indicated, this approach had as much to do with cognition as with communication. In some ways, the study of discussion was the study of oral reasoning and problem solving. Such a goal was by no means a bad thing. It provided a strong rational basis for group communication. At the same time, however, it ignored or minimized the persuasive, argumentative and interpersonal aspects of group communication.

The McBurney and Hance dichotomous perspective became the accepted point of view for more than a decade in the teaching and study of discussion. Not until the 1950s did the profession recognize, under the sway of the "small groups" scholars in the social sciences, that the group process involved more than the application of disciplined pure reasoning.

The definition of discussion offered by the authors grew out of this conception. Emphasis was placed on thinking, "conversing" and problem solving.

> *Discussion may be defined as the cooperative deliberation of a problem by persons thinking or conversing together in face-to-face or co-acting groups under the direction of a leader. (10)*

A cognitive structure evolved from the definition. The authors acknowledged that it came directly from Dewey's outline of reflective thinking in *How We Think*.

> *Upon each instance reveals, more or less clearly, five logically distinct steps: (i) a felt difficulty; (ii) its location and definition; (iii) suggestion of possible solution; (iv) development by reasoning of the bearings of the suggestion; (v) further observation and experiment leading to its acceptance or rejection; that is the conclusion of belief or disbelief. (12)*

McBurney and Hance adapted the Dewey pattern, "for purposes of analyzing and directing thought in discussion," into five only slightly different steps.

1. *Defining and Delimiting the Problem.*
2. *Analyzing the Problem.*
3. *The Suggestion of Solutions.*

    4. *Reasoned Development of the Proposed Solutions.*
    5. *Further Verification (1939, 11-13)*

Regardless of whether the Dewey model was appropriate for oral communication, problem solving models in the future were largely derived from or closely resembled the reflective thinking pattern.

In order for this scheme to work, however, the authors had to shift from Dewey's individualistic and descriptive view of reflective thinking to a position which would incorporate the basis of Dewey's thought and yet make reflective thinking suitable as a model of prescriptive group problem solving. They solved the difficulty by making an assumption, supported by the research of the social psychologist J.F. Dashiell that the individualistic problem solving was not so different from group decision making. Nevertheless, the assumption involved a considerable leap.

> *Dashiell, reporting a number of experimental studies in discussion and closely related fields, notes that "qualitatively group discussion seems to be adequately characterized by the traditional analyses of individual thinking as, e.g., stated by Dewey. . . ." In other words, we may say that that the reflective thinking of a group of individuals in its total, over-all pattern or form appears to correspond very closely to that of the solitary thought of a single individual. (1939, 10-11)*

McBurney returned to the material of his essay on rhetoric, dialectic and discussion to provide some historical background for discussion. He traced the origination of discussion to the dialectic of Athens. The primary impetus, though, for the development of discussion was to be found in the scientific method.

> *What the ancients called dialectic was probably the closest approximation of modern discussion. Developed and practiced by Plato, it was perhaps given its most complete and systematic treatment in Aristotle's* Topics. *. . . In the early part of the seventeenth century Francis Bacon and some of his contemporaries complained that the dialectical method was simply one of disputation actually adverse to discovery and the search for truth. . . . Out of this authoritarianism of the past came what we today know as the scientific method. . . . While the roots of the discussion method must be sought in ancient theory and practice, it is probably safe to say that it stems more directly from the conceptions of scientific method which have developed in the last few centuries. (1939, 15-18)*

One can understand that under the influence of the scientific orientation of the time and the power of the ideas of Dewey that the authors placed their theories of discussion in a scientific context. Whether the teaching of communication through the use of the scientific method was valid was another matter. Nonetheless, the attempt to apply a scientific perspective to this mode of communication continued for years.

When McBurney and Hance came to examine "Participating in Discussion" they still displayed some of the formalism about groups which had earlier been stated by Baird. The procedure of being recognized, for example, resembled a committee meeting or a parliamentary setting. The size of the groups advocated by McBurney and Hance might also have led to formalism and a loss of spontaneity.

> *As we have said, the typical situation for discussion is the small learning group, preferably eight to fifteen persons and not more than twenty or twenty-five.In groups of this kind it is good policy for the leader to reserve the privilege of asking members to address him before speaking. . . . Members who wish to speak may*

address the leader as "Mr. Chairman" or "Mr. Leader" or get his attention by
raising their hands or simply "getting his eye." (89-90)

As might be expected in a text book, the authors were specific, and sometimes
prescriptive, about the attitudes of participants. They assumed that discussion participants played an important role and they offered advice to group members about their
own attitudes. They also stressed that competition and individualistic behavior should
be discouraged.

> *The attitudes of the individuals composing the discussion group are as important,*
> *if not more important, than any other factor. No amount of attention to procedure*
> *can achieve cooperative group thinking if the attitudes of those doing the discussing*
> *are competitive, self-centered and individualistic. . .*
>
> *A. Consider the Common Good. If an individual is to be helpful in any*
> *cooperative undertaking, he must have concern for welfare of the group. If one's*
> *conduct in discussion stems wholly from selfish purposes it is almost inevitable that*
> *the group process will suffer. . .*
>
> *B. Assume Your Share of Group Responsibility. . . . Each member of the group*
> *should be concerned about the success of the discussion as he has a right to expect*
> *the leader to be.*
>
> *C. Think Before You Speak but Do Not Think Too Long. . . . Do not be afraid to*
> *express your ideas in discussion even if you are not perfectly sure of your ground.*
>
> *D. Contribute Objectively. In contributing ideas in discussion seek to avoid any*
> *personal identification with them which will make it difficult or impossible for you*
> *to treat these ideas objectively.*
>
> *E. Listen to Understand. . . . make an honest attempt to to understand the point*
> *he is trying to make. Deliberate misinterpretation is inexcusable. . . Another habit to*
> *be guarded against is that of listening solely from the standpoint of refuting what he*
> *has to say. (1939, 93-97)*

The emphasis which the authors placed on conciliation and impartiality was
equivalent to an ideological position which argued for the minimization of conflict and
personal points of view. The authors did include a separate chapter on "Resolving
Conflict in Discussion," which we will treat presently.

McBurney and Hance explained that although the responsibilities of the leader were
not as vital as those of group members, they were, nonetheless, important. They
assigned five "broad functions" to the group leader.

1. *To Secure the Process of Reflective Thinking.*
2. *To Secure the Most Cooperative Type of Participation.*
3. *To Provide for the Introduction of Information.*
4. *To Keep the Discussion Clear and Orderly.*
5. *To Handle Conflict Creatively. (1939, 117-118)*

The discussion leader, said McBurney and Hance, must possess qualities which the
authors classified as "intellectual equipment," "character and personality equipment"
and "communicative equipment." The categories included the following sub-
divisions.

A. Intellectual Equipment.

         1. Knowledge of Discussion.
         2. Alertness of Mind.
         3. Ability to Diagnose.
         4. Objectivity.
         5. Knowledge of People.
     B. Character and Personality Equipment.
         1. Patience and Self-restraint.
         2. Stimulating Personality.
         3. Sense of Humor.
     C. Communicative Equipment. (117-123)

The authors were aware that the traits they specified might have been beyond human attainment but that in discussion we must strive for the ideal.

> *We realize that the concept of the effective leader which we have presented may be too ideal or impossible of attainment. If this be true—and we hope it is not—we justify our point of view on the grounds that the ideal should be emphasized in order to make group discussion as effective as possible. (1939, 123)*

The connection with logic and reason in *The Principles and Methods of Discussion* became clear in four chapters of over 100 pages in length devoted to "The Role of Facts and Expert Opinions in Discussion," "The Logical Pattern of Discussion," "The Modes of Reasoning in Discussion" and "Obstacles to Reflective Thinking." Much of the material in the four chapters might just as easily have been included in a 1939 textbook in logic. This tendency to stress logic was also found in contemporary texts in argumentation, some of which might have been characterized as "oral logics."

The influence of the scientific method was apparent in the chapter on "The Logical Pattern of Discussion" where McBurney and Hance devoted a section to "The Suggestion of Hypothesis." They transformed the idea of the hypothesis somewhat by restricting its scope to the solution step of reflective thinking.

> *The third step in reflective thinking is the suggestion or calling up hypotheses or possible solutions to the problem which has been defined and analyzed in steps one and two. (1939, 175)*

It was in the chapter on "Obstacles to Reflective Thinking" that the influence of Dewey became obvious. Under the section titled "Some Causes of Obstacles to Reflective Thinking," the authors presented a classification of "Personal Causes" and "Social Causes." The personal causes were further sub-divided into "unintentional" and "intentional" causes. The explanation of unintentional cause seemed to sentence some people to permanent non -participation because of character flaws.

> *By the term "unintentional causes" we mean those factors which operate involuntarily without the operation of the will. To the extent that a person cannot overcome such deficiencies he is prevented from participating efficiently in individual thinking or group discussion. To the extent, however, that a person can overcome some of these deficiencies by self-discipline or training, these variables are subject almost entirely to his desire to think effectively. (1939, 205)*

McBurney and Hance provided a long list of the "cardinal sins" of discussants. Among them were the following defects.

     1. Inability to observe.

2. *Inability to remember.*
3. *Inability to organize*
4. *Inability to analyze.*
5. *Inability to make hypothesis.*
6. *Inability to appraise.*
7. *Mental inertia.*
8. *Lack of interest in "finding answers."*
9. *Gullibility*
10. *Stereotyped or tabloid thinking.*
11. *Excessive intellectuality.*
12. *Slowness in thinking.*
13. *Emotion, especially excessive emotion. (1939, 204-207)*

One wonders if the students of 1939 could have read the above list without it seriously affecting their self-esteem. Practically every one of them would have found in their own personalities some defect which might have disqualified them for participation in discussion. The list did indicate the emphasis placed on cognitive skills and the suppression of almost anything associated with emotion.

The social causes of obstacles to reflective thinking were largely the results of "group pressures."

> *Whether it is conscious or unconscious pressure from a church, political organization, the point is the same. The individual is thinking as the group dictates. (1939, 209)*

McBurney and Hance seemed to have envisioned a sterilized, utopian discussion environment where participants came to the discussion, to distort Wordsworth, trailing no "clouds of glory," or indeed any other clouds. Apparently members of groups were to make every effort not to be affected by their own family histories or their political and religious orientations. They were expected to come to the discussion table with a blank slate from which all social, religious and political biases or prejudices were to be excised.

The authors recognized that conflict needed to be discussed. In contrast to the treatment of reflective thinking, McBurney and Hance devoted only one chapter of twelve pages to "Resolving Conflict In Discussion." The chapter made clear that one could not ignore conflict, that it was an essential element in discussion.

> *. . . Conflict plays a necessary and important role in discussion. Conflict implies disagreement, and without disagreement there is usually little point in discussion. . . . The recognition that conflict has a place in discussion, however, should not blind us to the fact that there are kinds of conflict which impede the progress of discussion, and may even destroy it unless they are properly handled. (1939, 244) McBurney and Hance actually devoted more space to an analysis of the causes of conflict than they did to methods of resolving it. In their examination of "Factors Contributing to Conflict" McBurney and Hance spoke of "personal" and "social factors." Many of the social factors were identical to those which were cited earlier as personal impediments to discussion, including emotion, self-interest, self-esteem, prejudice and social pressures. The authors devoted a separate section of their chapter to "The Role of Emotion." They asserted that emotion might play a constructive role, so long as emotion meant enthusiasm, zest, and eagerness. They also recognized that a purely rational discussion could not exist.*

> *Certainly in the field of social and political problems the notion of a purely rational conflict is little more than a myth. The question, then, is not whether emotion should play a role in discussion, but rather what role should it play? So long as it does not result in prejudice and duplicity, emotion can act as a generative force in discussion. . . It is when emotion means blind allegiance to a cause that it becomes bad—whenever it tends to supersede reason or beg the question. (1939, 246)*

The authors seemed to distinguish between the cooperative emotional environment in a discussion and emotions which arose from the personal perspectives of the participants. They were apparently resolved that each member of the group enter the discussion with a completely open mind.

In order to talk about conflict resolution, the authors distinguished between "intrinsic conflict" and "extrinsic conflict." Intrinsic conflict they defined as ". . . one which is inherent in an adequate discussion of any given problem by any given group" (1939, 247). Extrinsic conflicts they defined as ". . . those disagreements which are foreign and unessential to the adequate discussion of any given problem by any given group" (1939, 250). Implicitly, they connected intrinsic conflict with rational discussion and extrinsic conflict with emotional discussion. Thus only intrinsic conflict was really legitimate. The resolution of intrinsic conflicts was to be found in the rational, orderly investigative form which McBurney and Hance had earlier advocated.

> *. . . It is ordinarily best to inquire into the facts and expert opinions first; if the cause does not lie here, then proceed to the interpretations and reasoning of the persons involved, and thence, if necessary to their standards of value. . . If the disagreement proves to have been caused by misunderstanding with respect to one or more of these factors we may assume that a recognition of that fact will resolve the conflict. . . All efforts to resolve intrinsic conflicts should be characterized by tolerance, willingness to listen to the other fellow, and patience. . . (1939, 248-249)*

One must applaud the faith of the authors that adherence to logic and orderly procedure was sufficient to resolve substantive conflict.

In the case of extrinsic conflict, resolution might come through the application of the same methods as with intrinsic conflict—"review of facts, interpretations, and values." When these remedies were not effective, the authors recommended conciliation and leadership skills.

> *. . . The keynote of the leader's approach to the problem should be patience and sympathy tactfully administered. Nothing but bad feeling, which disrupts the the entire discussion out of all proportion to the importance of the conflict can result from any other method. The best thing that can be done for all concerned is to move on to something else as swiftly and as deftly as possible. Certainly such conflict should not be allowed to waste the time of the group. . . . In all attempts to deal with such conflict methods should be used which make the offending members feel the pressure of group disapproval. (1939, 252-253)*

Of course McBurney and Hance's treatment of conflict seems naive and almost innocent from the perspective of the 1990s. We must remember, however, that no one before them had attempted to deal with the resolution of conflict. Of course they trusted to logic, science and reason to dispel antagonisms. Bound as they were to the Dewey model of reflective thinking, only this path was available to them.

We have given a good deal of space and attention to an undergraduate textbook, but with good reason. McBurney and Hance were the leaders in fully applying

Dewey's reflective thinking and group discussion. Others, notably Sheffield, had been aware of Dewey's *How We Think*, but their use of the work was much less thorough. We must also recognize that *Principles and Methods of Discussion* was the first college level book devoted to the subject. Sheffield's books were directed to a different non-academic audience; Baird's books were of the argumentation-debate-discussion variety. Although that textbook model persisted for a few years, the McBurney and Hance treatment of discussion provided a paradigm for teaching and research for more than a decade. James McBurney exhibited his professional discussion skill through his service for many years as the moderator of the Northwestern University Reviewing Stand, which was broadcast on CBS radio on Sunday mornings.

When Henry L. Ewbank of Wisconsin and J. Jefferey Auer, of Oberlin, published their text *Discussion and Debate: Tools of a Democracy* in 1941 they applied reflective thinking to both discussion and debate. Part II of their book was called "The Problem" and the chapters were arranged in the following order.

> V. *Locating and Defining the Problem*
> VI. *Exploring the Problem: Research*
> VII. *Exploring the Problem: Preliminary Analysis*
> VIII. *Exploring the Problem: Evidence*
> IX. *Exploring the Problem: Argument*
> X. *Exploring the Problem: Fallacies*
> XI. *Examining Suggested Solutions*
> XII. *Choosing the Best Solution (xi)*

Although the table of contents seemed to expand the Dewey pattern, in actuality, the authors, in the text proper, conformed closely to the accepted version of reflective thinking.

> *In this and succeeding chapters we will consider a methodology built upon four separate steps:*
>
> *(1) Locating and defining the problem (Chapter V);*
> *(2) Exploring the problem (Chapters VI-X);*
> *(3) Examining suggested solutions (Chapter XI);*
> *(4) Choosing the best solution (Chapter XII). (77)*

The Ewbank and Auer text began with an exploration of the relationship of discussion and debate to democracy. In 1941 the authors saw democracy under threat because of the abuse of freedom of speech, not only by Hitler, Mussolini, and Stalin, but by domestic, home grown orators.

> *Here in America, we have already seen freedom of speech abused by the unscrupulous when over five million people may be won to a "Share the Wealth" movement headed by a Louisiana politician, eight and half million people follow a Detroit radio priest into a "Union for Social Justice," and more than twice that number demand "Two Hundred Dollars a Month" under the gentle shepherding of a California doctor. . . If the educated and intelligent citizens do not intelligently use these great forces of discussion and debate the demagogues will. . . the Huey Longs, the Father Coughlins, and the Dr. Townsends of today. (1941, 8)*

The authors were consistent in their insistence on treating debate and discussion as closely related forms. In doing so, they placed the two modes of communication in historical and social contexts. They carefully explicated the connections between discussion and debate and democracy. They saw discussion and debate as characteristic of democratic societies, especially American society.

> *This freedom for discussion and debate is essentially the only type of freedom which differentiates a democracy from a dictatorship. . . . When that democratic force is destroyed, the other freedoms are also doomed. We share with peoples of Germany, Italy and Russia other forms of physical and intellectual force, but in a democracy alone do we find free and vigorous discussion and debate. This means, of course, that in a democracy the force of debate and discussion is available not only to the educated and intelligent citizens, but likewise to the educated and unintelligent. (1941, 8)*

This statement was very much in keeping with the ideological orientation of much of the profession in the years before the second World War. As we have pointed out elsewhere, the discipline saw a close connection between their enterprise and democratic societies. (See Chapter 6.) Not since the eighteenth century had that relationship been so clearly stated. Its application to discussion was hardly surprising; it was enunciated by McBurney and Hance, and Baird among others.

In a brief examination of the role of communication in American history, the authors pointed to changes over time which raised the question "Why does democracy need a special technique?" The trends which were threatening to democracy and which required ". . . essential tools of a democracy, discussion and debate. . . " were " (a) the expanding scope of government activity, (b) the growth of extremist groups, and (c) the gradual departure from representative government" (1941, 10-11) Although more than a half-century has passed since these words were written, they might well describe the threats to the communicative environment in present day America.

In the spirit of the times, and in agreement with McBurney and Hance, Ewbank and Auer based the techniques of discussion and debate on "the scientific method." Their listing of the factors of the scientific method, still based on Dewey's work, was more detailed than that of McBurney and Hance.

(1)   A recognized problem, properly located, defined and limited.

(2)   A body of facts concerning the problem derived from observation and inquiry.

(3)   A set a principles or laws, applicable to the problem at hand, which have been established by previous scientific investigation.

(4)   A knowledge of the basic laws of logic which may be used to verify claimed or acknowledged relationships.

(5)   A hypothesis or predicted solution set up on the basis of observation, analysis, and inference

(6)   Experimentation in which the hypothesis is applied to the problem for the purpose of determining its practicability or validity. . .

(7)   A conclusion reached as a result of the experimentation concerning the validity of the original hypothesis or predicted solution. (16)

Ewbank and Auer approached reflective thinking by contrasting it with "Random Thinking" and "Emotionalized Thinking." Random thought was perfunctorily dismissed but the authors devoted fourteen pages to emotionalized thought. The length to which the authors went in decrying emotionalized thinking was an indication of their reverence for scientific thought and of their motivation to remove emotion, as much as possible, from debate and discussion. Ewbank and Auer organized their statement of the problems of emotional thought under three headings.

    A. *Modes of Expressing Emotionalalized Thinking*
       1. We tend to rationalize.
       2. We tend to confuse desire and conviction.
    B. *Reasons for Emotionalized Thinking*
       1. We tend to be suggestible.
       2. We tend to succumb to personal appeals.
    C. *Results of Emotionalized Thinking*
       1. We tend to accept specious argument.
       2. We tend to ignore intellectual appeals. (53-66)

After they disposed of random thought as ". . . that which takes place when we daydream, when our thoughts wander idly from topic to topic. . . " and emotionalized thinking as ". . . that type of intellectual activity which is restricted or controlled by basic emotional reactions. . . ." Ewbank and Auer devoted their full attention, in seven chapters, to reflective thinking. Each of the steps prescribed by John Dewey was treated at length. The substance, of their treatment, however, was not much different from McBurney and Hance.

What was different about Ewbank and Auer's discussion of reflective thinking was their assumption that reflective thinking was not limited to discussion but that it was equally applicable to debate as well. The approach taken by the authors is reminiscent of the belletristic rhetoricians of the eighteenth century who wrote of such matters as style, taste, criticism and genius as generic topics which could be applied to many forms of discourse including public speaking, poetry, drama and history.

Ewbank and Auer devoted a chapter to "How Individuals in Groups Think." The title might, however, have been misleading. The individuals and groups which the authors had in mind were not members of discussion groups. Rather, the chapter dealt with the psychology and thought processes of audiences, particularly of crowds.

"The Nature and Purposes of Discussion" as they were laid out were quite broad and they encompassed more than those stipulated by McBurney and Hance. When the authors explained "The Purposes of Discussion," under the heading "Training the Individual," they seemed to have as their goal the remaking of the human being as much as improvement in discussion skills.

    A. *Training the Individual*
       1. To stimulate straight thinking and the desire for accurate information.
       2. To develop a concise, conversational manner of speaking.
       3. To develop the ability to listen accurately.
       4. To overcome timidity or stage fright.
       5. To learn to criticize and to take criticism without becoming emotionally upset.
       6. To learn the value of compromise.
       7. To train leaders of discussion. (290-291)

The perspective of Ewbank and Auer toward discussion was somewhat broader than that of their predecessors. In contrast to Sheffield, for example, they were willing to accept compromise, rather than consensual agreement as the outcome of discussion. Indeed they departed from the point of view of some of the other "Deweyites" by conceding that argument and persuasion were legitimate and proper activities in discussion. They, in fact gave a complete chapter to persuasion. Furthermore, in a sub-section of "The Purposes of Discussion," called "Forming Group Opinions," their conception of discussion was quite inclusive. They were less idealistic and more realistic about discussion than some earlier writers. They recognized that participants might come to a discussion with their own agendas.

> *The ideal discussion would take place if a group of intelligent people, without prejudices or preconceived ideas on the subject began at the beginning of the process of analyzing a problem and talked their way through to a conclusion. Actually this seldom happens. Some members of the group usually have solutions ready to propose; all members invariably come with some background of information and prejudice. The discussion method is sometimes used by those who are interested in presenting only one side of an issue. A survey of the various types of discussion meetings indicates that they are designed to serve one or more of the following purposes.*

> 1. *To exchange information.*
> 2. *To arrive at decisions.*
> 3. *To form attitudes.*
> 4. *To release tensions.*
> 5. *To "sell" accepted beliefs. (291-294)*

Although Ewbank and Auer's description of the role of the discussion leader was not much different from that described by McBurney and Hance, they were careful to distinguish between the discussion leader and the "presiding officer."

> *Quite different is the proper role of the discussion leader. He need not be president of the organization, nor should he be chosen just because of his prominence in the community. And, most certainly, he should not be a propagandist for one side of the problem. He should be chosen for his ability to help others think co-operatively. He should have faith in the ability of the average citizen to think his way through problems of general policy and arrive at basically sound decisions. (321)*

The authors stipulated six "Qualifications of the Discussion Leader."

> A. *Ability to Think and Act Quickly*
> B. *Ability to Get Along With Others*
> C. *Respect for the Opinion of Others*
> D. *Willingness to Remain in the Background*
> E. *Knowledge of the Objectives of Discussion*
> F. *Knowledge of the Reasoning Process*

The "General Rules for Participants in Discussion" were truly general, but they did not require the perfect human being as found in McBurney and Hance.

> A. *Understand the Purpose and Procedure*
> B. *Observe the Rule of Relevancy*
> C. *Avoid Personalities and Name Calling*
> D. *Question Glittering Generalities*
> E. *Remember, Discussion is "Thought in Process"*
> F. *Use the Language of the Group*

G. *Be Conversational (344-347)*

Admittedly, it may seem unusual to spend such a large amount of time on two discussion text books. As we look back more than a half century, however, we find that the only comprehensive and integrated treatment of group discussion took place in textbooks. From our perspective, most of the material in the journals was somewhat fragmented and lacking in the synthesis which McBurney and Hance and Ewbank and Auer were able to accomplish in the more numerous pages of their textbooks. In both instances, however, the authors relied very largely on outside sources for the development of the theoretical and conceptual bases of group discussion. The influence of John Dewey was, of course, pervasive, but ideas were also derived from a range of other disciplines, including philosophy, psychology and sociology.

After 1941 articles on discussion were continuous, but the contributions to theory were not very significant; and, in a field not yet fully developed, they tended to focus on the pedagogical aspects of discussion. This characteristic was addressed in 1941 by William M. Timmons of Ohio State in his essay "Discussion, Debating, and Research." At the outset Timmons sought to explain the paucity of research in debate and discussion.

> *There are at least four answers to this question: (1) Speech people have not been interested in experimental research, or generally speaking any kind of research, until recently. Every day practical problems held their interest. . . . (2) Appropriate tools of measurement did not exist. (3) Researchers in other fields for the most part worked on their own problems. (4) Research studies take time; the findings of experimentation accumulate slowly. Under the stimulation of workers in other fields, notably social psychology, pertinent findings have begun to accumulate. (1941, 416)*

Timmon's frank statement that the really significant research in discussion was not being done by speech people was, of course, correct. The derivative nature of the discipline's work in discussion was, by then, obvious, as it would continue to be. Indeed, Timmons himself when he asked ". . . What do the findings of research studies tell us of the values and deficiencies of discussion?" showed the dependence of the profession by his response.

> *With reference to this question we have the findings of several experimental studies upon which to base our answer, for researchers, particularly in social psychology, have been interested in the co-working group and incidentally in discussion as one form which such a group takes. (1941, 417)*

The experiments by Johnson and Simpson, which we discussed earlier, were cited by Timmons in his summary of research in discussion. The citations were certainly to the credit of the profession, as was his mention of his own 1939 dissertation, *Decisions and Attitudes as Outcomes of the Discussion of a Social Problem* at Teachers College, Columbia. Against these three citations Timmons mentioned fourteen books, monographs and articles in other fields. Among the journals most frequently cited were the *American Journal of Psychology*, the *Journal of Abnormal and Social Psychology* and *School and Society*.

After surveying the research literature in other disciplines, Timmons pointed to some yet unanswered questions and to some tentative conclusions.

> *Moreover, we still do not have experimental findings on whether discussion produces a superior product with all types of problems, or with all sorts of*

*populations, whether discussion produces better learning, recall, problem solving,
thinking, or decisions when these outcomes are considered with reference to varying
types of subject matter or varying populations. . . . In addition, we do not know
whether discussion has other educative outcomes, such as the acquisition of
information from the discussion and the development of tolerance toward those
holding different points of view. We have yet to learn whether discussion serves as
an emotional catharsis, whether it stimulates further thought, whether it provides
conciliation and adjustment to other people, to what extent the decision represents
pooled ignorance and compromise, whether it promotes co-operation or squabbling,
and whether it circulates ideas. Many more research studies need to be made. . . . We
have noted that discussion in a wide variety of tasks results in a product superior to
that occurring from individual work, that discussion produces certain outcomes in
the individual than do other activities. (1941, 421)*

Timmon's summary was not in agreement with the writers of textbooks and articles.
Most of the questions which he maintained required further empirical research had
already been answered by the writers based on their insight or received knowledge.
In fact speech people did not really begin to address the questions for a number of
years, well after the questions had been investigated by sociologists and psychologists.
Thus, Timmons' article described and validated just how derivative was the theoretical
and conceptual perspective of speech teachers toward discussion. The situation more
than fifty years later has improved somewhat; discussion researchers in speech communication are deeply involved in experimental research, yet they remain heavily
dependent on other fields to provide them with their theoretical tools.

In his 1941 article "Discussion in Difference Resolving" Joseph O'Brien of Penn State
made some assumptions about discussion, which were not common in the speech
literature. He conceded that conflict, even heated conflict, was almost inevitable in
discussion. Further, instead of using the standard "problem-solving" rubric, O'Brien
distinguished between policy making and difference resolving discussions.

*A policy making situation is "difficulty centered" in that the participants, at least
at the beginning, assume a mutual problem with the possibility of a mutually
satisfactory solution. . . . At times when bitter animosity develops, the actual issues
may be buried under an avalanche of personal attacks. But antagonism of this degree
is not common in a problem originally conceived as a mutual one. Debate may
become heated, it is true, but there is always a tendency to direct the primary attack
upon the difficulty, and only the secondary one upon the opponent. In contrast to the
original assumption of unity in policy making, a clash of inter-factional interests
characterize a difference resolving situation from the outset. Situations manifesting
such a pronounced bilateral, or multilateral, split in attitudes from the beginning
may well be termed "interest centered." There is no sense of "oneness," both sides
assume an irreconcilability of objective, take for granted the impossibility of a
solution fair to all, and hence set out to "adjust" the opposition rather than the
issue. . . . A significant characteristic of an interest centered dispute is the readiness
with which it tends to reach the debate stage. (1941, 422-423)*

Although he arrived at his distinction from a different direction, O'Brien seemed to
agree with some of the earlier writers that discussion was a prefatory step toward
debate, or that the unresolved questions of discussion were to be settled in debate.
More important, however, was his recognition of the prevalence of disagreement and
antagonism in discussions and his awareness that not all discussions were directed to
policy making. He thus brought to light a new genre of discussion for speech people,

one which did not have as its objective the arrival at mutual solutions to mutual problems. With this distinction in mind, O'Brien turned to an examination of difference resolving discussion. To advance his argument, he depended, to a great extent, on material drawn from the fields of labor negotiation and arbitration.

Some writers might have disputed whether O'Brien's industrial model really dealt with group discussion, since he was concerned, at least to some extent, with decisions which were influenced by outside forces, although some of the external influences might have been perceived of as discussion leaders. To explain his classification scheme, O'Brien depended on the example of collective bargaining.

> *In industrial disputes over both the making and interpretation of contracts three methods of reaching an agreement may be employed: (1) direct negotiation; (2) conciliation, or mediation; (3) arbitration. Direct negotiation, as the term implies is the process of reaching a settlement solely by the efforts of the two parties to the conflict. In conciliation or mediation (the terms are used synonymously) an impartial third party lends his assistance, but the agreement is still reached by the mutual agreement of the two factions. By arbitration is meant the adjudication, by consent of the participants, and after both sides have been heard, of a dispute, by an impartial umpire or tribunal. (1941, 424-425)*

O'Brien must be credited with the perception of seeing that not all problem solving discussions were governed by the paradigm which had been adopted from Dewey. He recognized how important were the vested interests of the parties involved. He also was aware that consensus was not attainable in all discussion settings; that sometimes problems must be solved through compromise, or even the intervention of outside parties. This perception was not original with O'Brien; he cited a number of authorities in other disciplines. He was, however, responsible for introducing an alternate point of view. As was often the case, there was little follow-up to O'Brien's essay. The profession remained loyal to the Dewey creed. O'Brien's essay, however, revealed the lack of clarity concerning the meaning of discussion.

The confusion about the meaning of discussion was illustrated in 1940 when the Committee on Nomenclature in Discussion presented its report to the association. The matter of definition had been of sufficient concern that the Section on Discussion passed a resolution at the 1937 convention asking the president ". . . to appoint a committee to study and report on nomenclature in the field of discussion." The committee, in good discussion style, specified a problem and solution.

> *The recent and very rapid development of Discussion as the type of public address best adapted to the democracy of today, has led to some confusion as to the exact terminology to be applied to the various forms which it may take. . . . The committee is of the opinion that teachers of speech can more effectively further the popularization of Discussion at the present time by developing and perfecting the basic types, and by more accurately employing the nomenclature as defined in this report. ("Forum," 1940, 311)*

It is doubtful that the committee's solution really solved the problem. Their answer to the problem did not reduce the complexity of nomenclature. Rather they presented several complicated charts which revealed the breadth of their conception of discussion. The charts included the following classification.

BASIC FORMS
   Informal Discussion
   Committee Discussion
   Group Discussion
   Round Table Discussion
   Formal Discussion
   Lecture-Forum Discussion
   Symposium
   Colloquy
   Dialogue

MODIFIED FORMS
   Court Techniques
   Discussion Contest ("Forum," 1940, 314)

Two experimental studies in group discussion were reported in 1941 by Karl F. Robinson of the State University of Iowa and William Timmons. Robinson's article was drawn from his Northwestern dissertation. In his study Robinson set out ". . . to determine the effects of discussion upon the attitudes of college students toward social problems." By present day standards Robinson's study might not have been a model of experimental design, but it was complex. (Perhaps the reduction of a dissertation to 24 pages made the article appear more complex than it really was.) We need not detail Robinson's procedure other than to say that he tested 336 sophomore Argumentation students and a control group of 225 sophomores in the College of Liberal Arts and the School of Speech. His subjects were tested under four experimental situations. The subjects for discussion were "(1) What Policies Should the United States Use in Keeping out of War; (2) Should the Several States Abolish Capital Punishment?"

The purpose of Robinson's study was guided by Thurstone's conception of attitude.

> The purpose of this study, as stated, is to determine the effects of discussion upon the attitudes of college students toward social problems. The term attitude, following Thurstone and others will be used here to denote the total sum of man's inclinations and feelings, prejudices or biases, preconceived notions, ideas, fears threats, and convictions about any specific topic. Opinion is the usual way in which we express our attitudes and will here mean a "verbal expression of attitude." (35)

After his complicated methodology and statistical analysis what did Robinson discover? He summarized his findings in no fewer than 17 points. Among the most significant were the following.

> Experimental subjects showed statistically significant shifts in attitude toward both questions, but so did the control group. Experimental Subjects shifted toward the Strongly Opposed position on the Capital Punishment question and toward the Extremely Pacifistic position on the War question. Men made a larger percentages of large shifts while the female subjects made a larger percentages of small attitudinal shifts.Both male and female subjects, in heterogeneous groups, shifted attitudes significantly greater than subjects in homogeneous groups. The subjects showing the largest shifts in attitude had ". . . components of temperament which marked them as being deficient in control and balance. . . and characterized by emotional thinking and fluctuations of activity."Ninety-three per cent of the experimental subjects showed gains in information. Approximately three-fourths of the groups reached a consensus. (55-57)

It is a pity that Robinson simply presented his conclusions without speculating about their implications. Granted that he observed attitudinal shifts under various conditions; but what were the readers to make of the findings? They were simply presented with a list of seventeen conclusions. The influence of social adjustment was shown in the attention Robinson gave to questions concerning the psychological conditions of group members.

No matter its shortcomings, Robinson's article was the first in the speech literature to make use of sophisticated statistical analysis in the conduct and the explanation of his research. Although his article may not have been a pattern setter, studies of this type would proliferate in years to come.

In the same issue of Speech Monographs, Timmons investigated ". . . whether as a result of discussion in mixed groups there are sex differences in the quality of individual decisions on social problems." (1941a, 69)

The problem Timmons set for his group was "What, if anything, should be done about Ohio's system of releasing convicts from prison?" The methodology of the experiment was, especially as contrasted with Robinson's, relatively simple. Timmons' population consisted of 78 "boys" and 78 "girls" who were high school juniors and seniors enrolled in courses in American History and Social Problems. "None had any special training in discussion techniques." Timmons did not make use of a control group.

The subjects were given the task of ranking five solutions to the parole problem. Timmons prepared a pamphlet which was given to the students.

> *It included factual information covering the systems involved in the alternative solutions. It was compiled from writings on the problem, from interviews with experts, and from correspondence with experts. Competent criminologists reviewed the pamphlet for accuracy and completeness. (1941a, 70)*

The subjects in Timmons' experiment were first placed in groups of four consisting of only males or only females. Next the subjects were assigned to groups of four made up of "two boys and two girls." Each time the groups discussed the problem for 38 minutes seeking to choose the best solution. After a month "the subjects ranked the solutions a third time." A possible problem with Timmons' study was that the students were not permitted to reason to their own solutions, since they were forced to choose from five pre-determined solutions. Besides, the quality of the solutions had already been decided by ". . . a consensus of the rankings made by experts."

After the completion of his research, Timmons was able to find only two significant results.

1. *Both boys and girls made reliable gains after discussion.*
2. *One month following the discussion, while both boys and girls had lost part of their gains, both still had scores significantly better than their pre-discussion scores. (1941a, 75)*

Timmons' found no significant differences between his male and female subjects. His other findings indicated that, in general, females showed greater gains than males, but the differences were not significant.

In spite of the meager findings, Timmons undertook to answer a question about discussion using experimental methodology. The dependence of the field, however, was shown by the fact that not a single writer in speech was cited in the study; all of Timmons' authorities were drawn from psychology and social psychology.

The last of the experimental studies which we will examine at length was that of Alma Johnson reported in *Speech Monographs* in 1943, titled "An Experimental Study in the Analysis and Measurement of Reflective Thinking." The study, based upon Johnson's dissertation and directed by McBurney, was the origin of the Rogers College Problems, which is in use to this day. Johnson stated that the purpose of her study was to determine whether a reliable measurement of reflective thinking could be devised and whether such a test might be used beyond the speech classroom.

> *There appears to be a need for a paper-and-pencil type of test which will facilitate the diagnosis and measurement of the process of reflective thinking. It is toward the construction of such a test that this study has been directed. That such an instrument may be of value to the teacher of discussion seems obvious; that it may also be of use to other teachers who believe that critical inquiry should precede "intentional reasoning" in support of a proposition, is no less desirable. (1943, 85-86)*

Johnson pre-tested the Rogers College, forms A and B, with 228 Northwestern students and with ". . . fifteen adults trained in scientific method and logic. . . psychologists, mathematicians, physicists, chemists, logicians, and public speaking instructors with backgrounds of graduate instruction also in economics, sociology, law, philosophy, or the physical sciences (1943, 87). After modifications, Form A was administered to a diverse group, the composition of which Johnson did not explain. Her population consisted of 322 undergraduates and seven graduate students at Northwestern, 23 students in the debate division of the National Institute for High School Students, 29 undergraduates at the University of Pittsburgh, and 48 under-graduates at Iowa State College. Form B was administered to another group of 100 undergraduates and three graduate students at Northwestern and 23 students in the National Institute (1943, 87).

As was true of the Timmons experiment, the subjects in the Rogers College Problems were to arrive only at the correct solution which had been predetermined by Johnson. The correctness was determined by the answers given by participants to multiple-choice options. The responses were classified as "critical," "uncritical," "hypercritical" or "dogmatic."

Johnson found that scores varied with class standing. The Freshmen mean score was lowest at 60.6; graduate students were highest with a mean score of 70.3—a significant difference. There were no significant differences between males and females.

The conclusions to Johnson's study were stated rather tentatively.

1. *Forms A and B of the test . . . are sufficiently valid and reliable to be used experimentally in diagnosing difficulties and measuring proficiency in reflective thinking.*
2. *Those habits and attitudes which are here assumed to constitute reflective thinking are learned behaviors and may thus be affected by training.*
3. *Although proficiency in reflective thinking, measured by this test, is dependent upon normal intelligence, it varies widely among individuals of the same general intelligence, thus indicating a dependence upon other variables.*
4. *The test is of some value as a teaching device and study outline. (1943, 96)*

Obviously the important finding of Johnson's study was different from the earlier experiments. Johnson was, to be sure, concerned with the discussion process, but her primary goal was to devise a test which would not only evaluate reflective thinking, but also, to construct an instrument which could be of help in teaching reflective thinking. Although Johnson stated her conclusions modestly and equivocally, she did, in fact, succeed in developing a test which served her purpose. Its popularity over the years was indicative of its usefulness.

The lack of a clear understanding of discussion was demonstrated by a brief study by Halbert Gully of Hannibal, Missouri High School. Gully sought to determine "Which activity, debate or discussion, is more effective in changing the opinions held by members of an audience?" It is obvious from the question posed by Gully and the procedure he used that he conceived of discussion as an externally directed mode of communication, and not an internally directed one, designed for mutual problem solving. Gully used ". . . college speakers of superior ability" who presented debates and discussions to three audiences for the debates and the same number for the discussions. Using The Woodward Shift of Opinion Ballot, Gully sought to determine which form was most persuasive. The idea of discussion as persuasion addressed to audiences outside the group ran contrary to the assumptions and purposes of group problem solving. Gully also assumed that "superior" speakers were also the best discussion participants, which certainly had not been validated since group discussion and debate are quite different modes of communication. Gully's position was certainly not aberrant for its time. "Public Discussion" was conceived so broadly that symposiums and forums designed to persuade were clearly within its sphere. For years after the Gully article forensic tournaments included discussion contests in which participants were competitively ranked on their conciliatory skills.

Gully arranged for the speakers to present debates and discussions on the topic of increasing the power of the federal government. We should not be surprised to learn that the debaters were more persuasive than the "discussers." Halbert Gully wrote this article early in his career. Later he joined the discussion scholars who were influenced by the social sciences and he gained a favorable reputation as a researcher and as a writer of textbooks.

William M. Sattler, of the University of Oklahoma, in his essay "Socratic Dialectic and Modern Group Discussion," returned to the ground earlier covered by McBurney. Sattler specified that the objective of his study was ". . . to identify the specific principles of the dialectical method of Socrates and to show in what respects these principles are a contribution to modern group discussion" (1943, 152). In order to proceed with his thesis, it was necessary for Sattler to specify what he meant by the term Socratic Dialectic."

> Socratic Dialectic is a cooperative search for valid judgments through the use of alternate question and answer. The discussion proceeds inductively by setting out large numbers of examples and analogies that serve as the basis for the acceptance or rejection of a proposed hypothesis. (1943, 153)

In his search for resemblances between dialectic and group discussion, Sattler consulted (in translation) a number of Platonic dialogues including: *Meno, Apology, Crito, Gorgias* and *Protagoras*. He asserted that, in important respects, there were similarities between Socrates and John Dewey.

> The Socratic method of testing hypotheses by a careful study of the particulars does not differ materially from John Dewey's interpretation of reflective thinking. . . . Socrates attaches great significance to the fact that several minds are simultaneously engaged in inquiry. All participants profit by a mutual exchange of ideas. . . The "sifting of particulars" is thus not only carried on co-operatively but also on a critical scientific basis. (1941, 156)

After his examination of the Socratic dialogues Sattler concluded that there were six "relationships of similarity" between the dialogues and group discussion.

> *(1) Both are representative of the scientific method as applied to social problems. . . .*
> *(2) Both exemplify cooperative inquiry as opposed to contentious debate.*
> *(3) Both insist upon conversational speaking rather than continuous discourse.*
> *(4) Both methods are deliberately designed to expose fallacies in reasoning.*
> *(5) Both have problem-solving or learning as their object. . . .*
> *(6) Socratic thinking seeks to promote the thinking of the respondent and in this
>   respect is related to the function performed by the discussion leader. (1943, 156)*

Although Sattler's insights into discussion and dialectic might not have been profound, his essay was useful in its understanding that what came to be called reflective thinking did not spring, without any history from the brain of Dewey. Rather it was a development in a long chain of ideas which could be traced back to Socrates. Of course, to have been complete Sattler would have been obliged to offer a history of epistemology. Sattler enjoyed a successful career as a researcher in discussion at the University of Michigan. Together with N. Edd Miller he wrote *Discussion and Conference* in 1954, one of the very earliest texts to be influenced by the emerging "small groups" movement (1954).

Another essay which probed the connection between discussion and philosophy was published by Douglas Ehninger, then at Western Reserve University, under the title "A Logic of Discussion Method." Ehninger justified his inquiry by his understanding concerning the role in discussion played by logic.

> *Any worth-while group discussion is in essence a process of controlled group
> thinking which attempts to arrive at sound judgments concerning a problem
> situation. (1943, 164)*

In contrast to a number of other writers, Ehninger denied that the logic of discussion was either Aristotelian or scientific. If not, what logical system was applicable?

> *On the one hand, it [logic of discussion] is clearly far removed from the system of
> "confirmation" that employs with little modification the formal principles of
> Aristotelian demonstration. On the other,. . . it deviates in a number of respects
> from the highly controlled method of experimental investigation that characterizes
> the sciences, and therefore cannot employ wholeheartedly the system of logic that
> governs them. In view of these facts, we are justified in asking what sort of logic
> controls the group thinking process. (164)*

It was, perhaps, not surprising that Ehninger chose as his logical model that of American Pragmatism, of which school Dewey was the leading proponent alive in 1943. Ehninger did offer criteria for his choice.

> *. . . It should be clear that the logic which governs it [the discussion process]
> cannot be dependent upon exact and categorizing definition. . . . It should be clear
> that inference in discussion cannot proceed according to hard and fast rules. . . .The
> logic that governs the discussion process must, therefore, be broad, flexible and
> general. It must be capable of securing some degree of pragmatic validity by
> progressing on the basis of probabilities and approximations rather than
> actualities. . . . Where is such a logic to be found?. . . . Now the logic that concerns
> itself with the study and analysis of the reflective thinking process is
> non-Aristotelian psycho-logic of the Pragmatist philosophers. (165)*

It was the informality and lack of rigid structure of Pragmatic thought, said Ehninger, that made it singularly appropriate for discussion.

> *In the stead of the formal laws of Aristotelian inference, they have promulgated new rules of implication that derive their validity only from the pragmatic value of the conclusions they bring forth. . . . Pragmatist logicians have. . . brought that much abused discipline into close contact with the realities of the reflective thinking process as it actually operates in the resolution of problem situations. . . . Now, since discussion is in essence a process of group reflection that attempts to put sound judgment at the service of intelligent belief and action, it is clear that the discussion method is much indebted to the general point of view of the Pragmatist logic and is greatly dependent upon its laws and principles. (166)*

Yet, Ehninger wrote, the adoption of Pragmatist logic for group discussion was not totally satisfactory since even Pragmatism was too controlled to adapt itself to the unpredictability of discussion. A much less structured and more flexible logic should govern discussion.

> *Upon reflection, however, it will become apparent that an unqualified acceptance of logic of Pragmatism as the logic of discussion method is not possible. It is not possible because of the fact that the logic of Pragmatism is necessarily the logic of a highly accurate and carefully controlled reflection such as can obtain only in relation to certain kinds of subject-matter and under what are essentially "laboratory" conditions. . . discussion method must be satisfied with a logic less stringent in its requirements concerning controls and verification. . . . Although the logic of discussion method can indeed learn much from the logic of Pragmatism,. . . it must in large measure evolve its own system and structure through extensive observation of the various thinking situations that arise in the course of actual discussions. (166-167)*

Ehninger, in his essay, perceived that discussion could not be as dependent as it was on the Pragmatic logic which produced reflective thinking. The almost blind adherence to Dewey's descriptive formulation obscured the fact that Dewey intended *How We Think* to apply to problem solving in general, and not to the flux and the give and take of discussion. Ehninger's contribution was valuable also because, for one of the first times, a speech researcher sought to find the epistemological basis for group discussion. Because of Dewey's own Pragmatic position, it was to be expected that a field so influenced by him would choose a Pragmatic logic. Ehninger too accepted much of Dewey's Pragmatism, but he also saw that a less formal system was required for discussion.

Douglas Ehninger over time became one of the most distinguished scholars in the discipline. His work in the history of rhetorical theory continues to have a strong reputation.

The last essay in group discussion which we will examine is "Discussion and Debate: a Re-Examination" by Wayne Thompson, then at Bowling Green State University. Thompson was disturbed that many members of the speech profession ". . . have become infatuated with certain secondary results to the degree that they no longer appreciate the distinctive contribution that discussion and debate can make to the education of young men and women." Out of this concern, grew Thompson's purpose in writing the essay.

> *This article, therefore, aims to expose secondary objectives and erroneous*

objectives for what they are, and to show the significance of the primary purposes.
(1944, 289)

Thompson presented the "secondary" and "erroneous" objectives as a listing of what discussion is not, followed by a brief statement of what discussion is.

> *Discussion is not glorified conversation.*
> *Discussion is not a method for propagating a preconceived opinion.*
> *Discussion is not a form of controversy.*
> *Discussion is not primarily an exercise in public speaking.*
> *Discussion is not primarily a method for social adjustment.*
> *Discussion is not primarily a therapeutic device for releasing tensions.*
> *Discussion is more than a means of generating thought and sharing information.*
> *Discussion is a technique for group action in studying and solving problems.*
>   *(289-290)*

Thompson's essay was an effort to return discussion to its pure form. The secondary objectives he listed had indeed been included in the work of earlier writers. Thompson saw those objectives as irrelevant, or even destructive, to the simple objective of all discussion ". . . a technique for group action in studying and solving problems." Anything else detracted from the true aim of discussion, with the result that many teachers, researchers and students were being led astray. Thompson, for example, disagreed with O'Brien, although he did not mention him by name, concerning conferences. Thompson did not consider them to be a legitimate form of group discussion. (See page 74.)

> *Although a group of business men, or politicians, or students, may seat*
> *themselves in a semi-circle, present facts, speak pleasantly, and even function under*
> *a leader, they are not engaging in discussion unless they are thinking cooperatively*
> *toward the solution of a common problem. If they are seeking to sell a product or an*
> *idea, to gain higher wages for the group they represent, or to maneuver themselves*
> *into favor, they are engaged in a process better labeled as conference. The reasoning*
> *is intentional rather than reflective; the purpose is self-centered; the desired and*
> *desirable solution, preconceived. (289)*

Thompson refused to go along with the prevalent notion that discussion could be helpful in social adjustment. There was nothing wrong with social adjustment except it had no place in discussion.

> *Other methods are available for promoting social adjustment and the by-product*
> *should not be confused with discussion itself. Those who wish to conduct a charm*
> *school should do so openly and not operate under the guise of teaching discussion,*
> *which is concerned with the forming and the testing of intellectual relationships.*
> *(290)*

Thompson also rejected the notion promulgated by Ewbank and Auer and others that discussion was useful, not only in social adjustment, but in the reduction of tension as well.

> *Certainly no one is going to object to the use of the discussion form in giving men*
> *in service a chance to "gripe." But the form is not the process, and a "gripe" session*
> *is not a discussion. Nor does it constitute a basis for teaching discussion. (290.)   For*

the class room teacher Thompson offered nine suggestions which would direct their efforts toward authentic discussion rather than some related or extraneous activity.

1. *Center attention upon the technique rather than upon the result.*
2. *Center attention upon the group rather than the individual.*
3. *Choose the topic so that the values of discussion are most likely to be achieved.*
4. *Teach the students the values of facts.*
5. *Make the classroom discussion situation as realistic as possible.*
6. *Center attention upon the fact that discussion aims to study and to solve problems.*
7. *Make the student aware of the more common shortcomings of discussion.*
8. *Give careful attention to the formation of habits.*
9. *Teach the students that the discussion technique is a practical one. (291-292)*

The habits mentioned by Thompson in the eighth point were really much like the components of reflective thinking mentioned often by earlier writers. They included stating and defining the problem, considering the problem thoroughly and finding all available solutions.

Although Thompson's essay was written for teachers, it is of interest because of its questioning of some of the received wisdom concerning discussion, and because he sought to return discussion to a pure problem solving mode growing out of Dewey's conception of reflective thinking.

Thompson's goal of restricting discussion to the narrow domain of "studying and solving problems" was not to be attained. Within a few years of the publication of his essay, the scope of discussion would expand rather than constrict. Pscyho-therapeutic groups, encounter groups, T groups, sensitivity groups, consciousness raising, and many other varieties of groups would proliferated and become the subject of serious study inside and outside the speech discipline.

CONCLUSION

Although something like group discussion had been mentioned by the Research Committee as early as 1915, it was not seriously written about until the early 1920s. Although his name is all but unknown now, much credit must be given to Alfred Sheffield for the introduction of discussion to the members of the new profession. He was the most prolific and insightful writer on discussion from the early 1920s to the mid 1930s.

From its very outset the writings on group discussion were heavily influenced by work done in other fields. In their own citations the speech people acknowledged their debt to workers in such disciplines as psychology, sociology and labor relations. The dominant influence of John Dewey, and particularly of his *How We Think* of 1910, became evident very early and continued throughout the 20s, 30s and 40s. No internal evidence tells us how Dewey came to the attention of speech teachers. It was clear, however, that in connection with his work with trade unions in Boston, Sheffield had read widely in other fields. We also know that A. Craig Baird had been a student in Dewey's classes at Columbia.

The first systematic and detailed treatment of reflective thinking did not occur until 1939, with the publication of a textbook, *The Principles and Methods of Discussion*. From that point on reflective thinking became almost an object of worship among writers on discussion. Dewey's work, however, posed some questions, if not problems for the field of speech. Dewey's interest was entirely with cognitive processes and not with communication. A large leap was needed to reach the assumption that reflective thinking was as applicable to externalized communication as it was for internalized thought. Hardly anyone questioned this assumption and it was treated as received wisdom. The same credulousness held for the assumption, that individual thought was not much different from group thinking and that the precepts of Dewey were as applicable to group decision making as to individual problem solving.

Another problem with the almost slavish adherence to *How We Think* was that the speech teachers sought to impose a prescriptive structure on what Dewey intended to be a descriptive work. The result was that much of the work in speech embodied a rigidity and adherence to a formula far beyond what Dewey advocated.

The willingness to accept Dewey's position without question meant that very little experimental research was carried on to validate or reject Dewey's assumptions. In the 1940s we saw a beginning of experimentation, but, even in those cases, the basic presuppositions were not brought into question. It was left to workers in the social sciences, social psychology in particular, to carry on significant research in group problem solving. The work of the social scientists was cited extensively in speech articles. A source of confusion among the writers on discussion was their insistence on connecting discussion to other speech modes. Thus, from Baird's 1928 work onward many writers of articles and textbooks dealt with a trio which they labelled as "Argumentation, Debate and Discussion." This arrangement caused a certain distortion in the understanding of what discussion was. Many writers insisted on connecting it with persuasive or argumentative discourse.

Some persons saw debate as an extension of discussion. Discussion, they said, set the ground for determining which issues were in contention and needed to be decided in the adverserial arena of debate. Debate was the outcome of unresolved discussion. Oddly, the methods of argumentative or persuasive discourse were to be rigorously excluded from discussion.

Throughout the period the profession was not able to reach consensus, or even agreement, about the focus of discussion. The strict Deweyites held to the position that discussion should be limited to the solving of problems of mutual interest. From Sheffield on, however, other writers included conference as a form of discussion. Discussion for the purpose of learning was also a common inclusion. Some writers went so far as to include therapeutic and cathartic discussions.

As we look back at the first twenty years or so of the study and research in group discussion, it seems, it many respects, a sterile form of communication. In their interpretation of Dewey, the profession in general, envisioned a form of communication in which the interpersonal elements of discussion were suppressed, if not eliminated. Apparently discussions leaders and participants were to be "logic machines" taking part in a setting where little emotion was to be shown and disputes would be settled by the application of pure reason. Because of their dependence on reflective thinking, the new speech profession missed the opportunity to put their own distinctive stamp on research in discussion. Other disciplines, to be sure, were interested in the study of groups. The speech profession, however, had declared its interest and competence in argument, persuasion and rhetoric; they could easily have examined how persuasion and argument work in discussion groups, and they could have offered advice as how best to integrate a rhetorical perspective into discussion.

In the post-war period group discussion came, even more strongly, under the influence of social science. Group Discussion metamorphized into "small groups" and its conceptions and methodologies underwent marked change.

■ Epilogue

The year 1945 provided a convenient stopping point for this study of the history of Speech Communication since the character of the profession underwent marked change in the post-war years. Many of the changes reflected those occurring in the academic world in general. Other changes were more indigenous and related to internal developments in the profession. In another work I described how the changing nature of social science research affected Speech Communication.

> *The tranquil, if obscure, life of speech communication was severely disturbed at the end of World War II. That period represented an intellectual revolution in the social sciences. They moved very rapidly from a descriptive methodological base to a quantitative, empirical, experimental and behavioral approach to the questions they asked. Many disciplines such as political science, sociology, economics, anthropology, and geography underwent radical and rapid change, and we saw considerable conflict and ferment between traditionalists and modernists in many disciplines. The lines between conventional fields became blurred and a general exchange of conceptualizations, and methodologies took place. Sociologists borrowed from political scientists, and geographers contributed to the work of anthropologists. Perhaps most important to us, the scope of the social scientists had broadened to include almost all aspects of human behavior, including communication. (294)*

The effects of the social scientific revolution were immediate, and almost inevitable. The fact that social scientists had begun to undertake experimental studies in communication meant that that speech communication would have to adapt, narrow its interests, or disappear. Speech communication had slumbered through the early days of the revolution and then awoke to find to find that social scientists had undertaken systematic studies of human communication. It was therefore necessary that we respond to the changing environment. A shift to a social science orientation was soon visible in the profession, especially among younger researchers.

The social science orientation in the post-war years brought about marked changes in the direction of the profession. At first our response was to cast a wide net to bring in material that might be useful to us. Our reaction was not so much that someone had invaded our territory as that someone was exploring territory that we should have discovered but had not. Under the influence of the burgeoning social sciences, speech communication scholars found themselves teaching and researching areas that were previously unknown to them, or that they had regarded as outside their jurisdiction.

Although some articles and textbooks had been written on "business speaking," the profession found itself involved in "organizational communication," which was only remotely related to the fairly simplistic "how to do it" courses of an earlier time. Organizational communication was not an area in which speech communication could claim sovereignty, since the original impetus had come from such areas as Business Administration, Industrial Psychology, Personnel Administration and Cultural Anthropology.

Before the emergence of an area known as Interpersonal Communication, a few writers such as Robert Oliver, Elwood Murray and Raymond Howes had written on "conversation" or "private speaking." Murray was the most explicit and detailed in his treatment. However, it took the work of social scientists, particularly social psychologists, to bring the area into clear focus. The increasing interest in interpersonal relations led to the study of the roles played by communication in interpersonal relations. The social scientists had certainly included communication in their studies.

The area previously designated as group or public discussion underwent a visible transformation. Research carried out by others, especially sociologists and social psychologists, brought about a new division which came to be called "small group research." Although the work of such workers as Bales, Homans, Hare and Shepherd was not specifically focused on communication, the study of group decision-making, for example, required that careful attention be paid to the talk in the group. Although reflective thinking, as a model of decision-making was retained in one form or another in much of the work in speech communication, the direct influence of John Dewey was significantly less in the post-war years. The narrow interest in problem-solving discussion was replaced by a much broader concern with such matters as the dynamics of the group, interpersonal factors in the group, emotional and task components in the group, group cohesiveness, conflict resolution, and leadership.

As the profession became more sophisticated about social sciences, some members began to be concerned with the theoretical foundations which underlay their work. The result was an overarching concept known as communication theory. Although work in communication theory had been carried on earlier, David Berlo's text *The Process of Communication* was an important synthesizing contribution which brought into focus much of what was known about the theories of communication (1960). In that sense, Berlo's work resembled that of earlier textbook writers such as Winans and Ewbank and Auer. It too provided a theoretical focus. Communication theory was, in fact, a broad interdisciplinary field. Contributions came from fields as diverse as Sociology, Political Science, Mass Communications and Linguistics.

Quantitative research was not entirely unknown to members of the profession in the pre-war years. We have noted some examples in the earlier chapters. In later years experimental studies proliferated and the profession, in general, became much more proficient in its use of statistical methodologies. This increasing emphasis on methodology was, in some ways, to be expected. In the earlier years of the post-war period, before we were well grounded in theory, we tended to borrow methodologies rather than conceptualizations.

Rhetorical studies also underwent dramatic changes. The dependence on classical rhetorical sources for the development of rhetorical theory weakened considerably, although *Speech Criticism* by Thonnsen and Baird, the most definitive statement of classical theory was published in 1948. In time, the term "Neo-Aristotelian" came to have a pejorative connotation. The work produced, in rhetorical criticism, in the later decades came to be increasingly less tied to the "three proofs and five canons" critical formulae. These rhetorical studies were decreasingly less centered on "effects" and more concerned with the intrinsic nature of the rhetorical efforts. Works such as Edwin Black's *Rhetorical Criticism* (1965) were helpful in moving rhetorical criticism away from the rigidity of its earlier classical orientation. The criticisms also became more specifically rhetorical. No longer were studies burdened by long disquisitions on biography, history and social settings. Those factors were not totally ignored however.

One must not be led to believe, however, that rhetorical criticism was no longer dependent on other fields. After all, replacements had to be found for Plato, Aristotle, Cicero and Quintilian. In their stead came influences from various aspects of literary studies, many of which would also be influential in research in rhetorical theory. The most significant development was the arrival of what came to be called "Burkean Criticism." Kenneth Burke had been a kind of wandering literary and social troubadour since the 1920s. Then the rhetorical critics discovered his *The Rhetoric of Motives* in the 1940s and 1950s. Since then Burke's contributions have become influential not only in literary and rhetorical criticism but in fields as diverse as sociology, economics and political science. Other divisions in the speech communication discipline, such as organizational communication, have also come to rely on Kenneth Burke's many books and essays.

Many critical approaches grew out of what was prevalent, or even fashionable, in contemporary literary criticism. New Criticism, Mythic Criticism, Psychoanalytic Criticism, Linguistic Analysis, Deconstruction and other modes of criticism all had their day. The names of literary figures such as Northrop Frye, Wayne Booth, Richard Weaver and Richard McKeon came to be familiar. Later European philosophers and social thinkers, including Foucalt, Habermas, Barthes, Toulmin and Perleman, were influential.

Another discernible shift in the emphasis of rhetorical criticism was the increase in work devoted to the nature of criticism and a corresponding decrease in the study of what E.C. Mabie once characterized as "dead old orators." Some scholars saw such efforts as meta-criticism rather than criticism. Also, in order that criticism be theory based, some scholarship centered more on the demonstration of the efficacy of a given theory and less on the criticism of a particular rhetorical effort.

The distinctions, earlier made by Wichelns and others, concerning the differences between literary and rhetorical criticism were no longer operable. For some time, particularly after the SCA rhetoric conference of 1970, the perception had been growing that rhetorical criticism need not limit itself to oral discourse or to "the literature of reality," as distinct from the "literature of the imagination." Rhetorical critics no longer felt constrained to avoid criticism of modes of discourse other than public speaking. In due course the field began to use its skills to make rhetorical criticisms not only of novels, but of films, plays, television commercials, architecture, graphic art, landscapes, newscasts, advertising campaigns and other communication forms. The previous emphasis on the rhetoric of a particular speaker gave way to much more broadly based studies. Rhetorical criticisms of movements and campaigns became more common. Before the post-war period the subjects of rhetorical criticism were overwhelmingly white males, with a disproportionate emphasis on clergymen. Slowly, some greater attention was paid to women and minorities, and feminist and minority perspectives began to function in criticism. With few exceptions, the work of the rhetorical critics was internalized and even hermetic. Much of it was written expressly for other critics, and it was not easily available to lay persons or to scholars outside the discipline.

The changes in rhetorical theory mirrored those in rhetorical criticism. There too, the sources of rhetorical theory were no longer drawn from the work of classical and eighteenth century writers. Theory was now derived from a variety of literary, philosophical and social sources. Little theory, however, was generated inside the discipline. Almost all of it was based on research and writing in other disciplines. The same writers we identified in the discussion of rhetorical criticism were also influential in theory. Instead of building our own theories, we continued rely on outside sources. Now, however, instead of Aristotle, we consulted the work of Burke, Cassirer, Adorno and others.

As time passed, speech communication found that it no longer occupied the dominant position in rhetoric it had inherited from English. English departments, after having been neglectful, or even disdainful, of rhetoric underwent a change of position which amounted to a movement approaching a Renaissance. Soon the research in English became strong and thriving. Doctoral programs in rhetoric were established in English departments. The Rhetoric Society of America, predominately populated by teachers of English came into being. Their journal *The Rhetoric Society Quarterly* achieved a solid reputation. English departments, at Penn State for example, began to offer conferences in rhetoric. English seemed to tie its interest in rhetoric to the teaching of English Composition more than speech communication did to its fundamental courses.

The increasing interest in rhetoric was by no means limited to English. Any number of disciplines had undertaken to study how rhetoric functioned in their specialties. This rhetoric of inquiry was found in a variety of disciplines including law, sociology and mathematics. These concerns with rhetoric led to collaboration between fields. In time rhetoric may assume the stature it has in Europe, where it is considered to be not a discipline, but an inter-disciplinary field. At the same time that speech communication became a more diverse discipline it also, in other ways, narrowed its focus as some of the divisions that had been welcomed under the protective umbrella of speech now emerged as distinct disciplines. The most prominent of these fields were Theater and Speech Correction (later called Communication Disorders.) Even the National Society for the study of Communication metamorphosed into the International Communication Association. The Speech Communication Association did, however, maintain traces of the departing fields in its divisional structure.

An indication of the diversification of the profession may be seen in the publications now available. From 1915 until 1934 *The Quarterly Journal* was the only national publication. *Speech Monographs* was first published in 1934, originally as an annual publication. *The Speech Teacher* (now *Communication Education*) was initiated in 1952. The *Journal of Applied Communication Research* appeared in 1973, followed by *Text and Performance Quarterly* in 1980, *Critical Studies in Mass Communication* in 1984 and *Speech Communication Teacher* in 1986. The S.C.A. issued books under its own auspices and was also the publisher of the *Free Speech Yearbook* and the *International and Intercultural Communication Annuals*. At the same time, the journals published by the regional speech communication associations improved markedly in the quality of articles, the diversity of their coverage and in the number of pages. Even some of the journals published by state associations achieved respectability.

The profession increased in its magnitude as well as its diversity. That increase was reflected by the fact that the printed program of the annual SCA meetings, as late as the late sixties, were small enough to fit in an inside coat pocket. The programs now are some 300 pages in length and they will fit in no pockets. The meetings are much less leisurely, and they are held from the very early hours until almost midnight.

The diversity of the profession may also be seen in the structure of the national association. In an early day the Association managed quite well with only a few committes. The 1992 edition of the *Speech Communication Association Directory* lists thirteen divisions, the same number of commissions, five sections, four boards, 28 committees, five task forces and five caucuses. These bodies deal with a range of professional concerns including Feminist and Women Studies, Communication and Aging, Communication Ethics, Freedom of Expression, Peace Communication, Black Caucus, Caucus on Gay and Lesbian Issues and Affirmative Action.

The disputes between the rhetoricians and the social scientists continues to the present day at varying stages of intensity. The disagreement really seems to resemble a family squabble rather than a fundamental argument. The differences seem to be more methodological than ideological. For more than two decades the dispute has taken the form of arguments concerning the name of the national association, and hence the discipline. The core of the disagreement is about whether "speech" should be retained in the name, or should the discipline be known simply as "communication." More than once a majority of the members have approved a change but the provision of the S.C.A. constitution requiring a two-thirds affirmative vote has not been met.

The historical situation for Speech Communication is not entirely salubrious, however. In the almost eighty years since the formal establishment of the discipline, it has not yet attained the central position in education, either in the schools or the colleges, that its founders had envisioned. Many institutions feel they can do very well without Speech Communication departments, and their reputations seem not to have suffered for their neglect. Indeed at the collegiate level most of the most prestigious colleges and universities offer no courses in speech communication. In the early days of the profession, especially in the Eastern Public Speaking Conference, Harvard, Yale, Princeton, Dartmouth and Swarthmore, among others were active. Today none of them are active. In more recent years, we have seen the elimination of departments in some of our leading universities such as Michigan, Stanford, U.C.L.A., Oregon and Vermont. The question may certainly be raised about whether the discipline has put a distinctive stamp on its research and teaching. I hope to deal with these kinds of questions in the succeeding volume.

■ REFERENCES
INTRODUCTION

Jeffrey, R. (Ed.). (1990). *The Past is Prologue.* Annandale, VA: Speech Communication Association.

Perengo, I. (1926). Analysis of a debate on evolution. *Quarterly Journal of Speech Education,* 12, 23-30.

Reid, L. (1990). *Speech Teacher: A Random Narrative.* Annandale, VA: Speech Communication Association.

Wallace, K.R. (Ed.). (1954). *A History of Speech Education in America.* New York: Appleton-Century-Crofts.

Wichelns, H. (1959). *A History of the Speech Association of the Eastern States.* Mineola, New York: Mineola Public Schools.

Windt, T.O. (1990). *Rhetoric as a Human Adventure: A Short Biography of Everett Lee Hunt.* Annandale, VA: Speech Communication Association.

Wise, C.M. (1933). Negro dialect. *Quarterly Journal of Speech,* 19, 522-528.

■ 1
THE ELOCUTIONISTS

Austin, G. (1806). *Chironomica: or A Treatise on Rhetorical Delivery.* M. M. Robb and L. Thonssen (Eds.). London: Printed for T. Cadell and W. Davies.

Bashford, J.W. (1893). "Appendix on Truth, Personality and Art in Oratory." in R.I. Fulton and T.C. Trueblood *Practical Elements of Elocution.* (3rd ed.). Boston: Ginn, 421-450.

Brown, M.T. (1886). *The Synthetic Philosophy of Expression.* New York: Houghton, Mifflin, and Co.

Bryan, W.J. (1906). *The World's Famous Orations.* New York: Funk and Wagnalls.

Burt, G.A. (1905). *The Art of Expression.* Boston: D.C. Heath and Co.

Delsarte, F.A. (1887). *Desarte System of Oratory.* (3rd ed.). New York: Werner.

Emerson, C.W. (1905). *Evolution of Expression.* (Vols 1-4). (rev. ed.). Boston: Emerson College of Oratory.

Fulton, R.I. and Trueblood, T.C. (1893). *Practical Elements of Elocution.* (3rd ed.). Boston: Ginn.

Haberman, F.W. (1954). "English Sources of American Elocution." in K.R. Wallace (Ed.). *History of Speech Education in America.* New York: Appleton-Century-Crofts, 105-128.

Hamill, S.S. (1882). *Science of Elocution.* New York: Phillips and Hunt.

Hillard, G.S. and Sprague, H.B. (1878). *The Webster-Franklin Sixth Reader and Speaker*. New York: Taintor Brothers, Merrill and Co.

Pertwee, E. (1914). *The Reciter's Treasury of Verse*. London: George Routledge and Sons, Limited.

Reed, T.B. (Ed.). (1900). *Modern Eloquence*. (Vols. 1-9). Philadelphia: J.D. Morris.

Sears, L. (1900). "Introduction." in T.B. Reed (Ed.). *Modern Eloquence* (Vols 1-9). Philadelphia: J.D. Morris.

Sheridan, T. (1762). *A Course of Lectures on Elocution*. London: Printed for W. Strahan for A. Millar (and others).

Southwick, F. T. (1900). *Steps to Oratory*. New York: American Books.

■ 2

THE TRADITION IS PRESERVED

Baker, G.P. and Huntington, H.B. (1905). *Principles of Argumentation*. (rev. ed.). Boston: Ginn.

Berlin, R.A. (1984). *Writing Instruction in Nineteenth Century American Colleges*. Carbondale: Southern Illinois University Press.

Blair, H. (1860). *Lectures on Rhetoric and Belle Lettres*. Philadelphia: T. Ellwood Zell.

Foster, W. T. (1908). *Argumentation and Debating*. Boston: Houghton and Mifflin.

Gardiner, H. H. (1912). *The Making of Arguments*. Boston: Ginn.

Genung, J.F. (1886). *Practical Elements of Rhetoric*. Boston: Ginn.

Hart, J.S. (1898). *Hart's Composition and Rhetoric*. (rev. ed. by J.M. Hart.). Philadelphia: Eldredge and Brother.

Hervey, G.W. (1873). *A System of Christian Rhetoric*. New York: Harper and Brothers.

Hill, A.S. (1878). *The Principle of Rhetoric*. New York: American Book.

Kames, H.H., (Boyd, J.R., Ed.) (1871). *Elements of Criticism*. New York: A.S. Barnes

MacEwan, E.J. (1899). *The Essentials of Argumentation*. Boston: D.C. Heath.

Mathews, W. (1879). *Oratory and Orators*. Chicago: C.S. Griggs & Co.

Phelps, A. (1883). *English Style in Public Discourse*. New York: Charles Scribner's Sons.

Ringwalt, R.C. (1898). *Modern American Oratory*. New York: Henry Holt.

Scott, F.N. and Denny, J.V. (1911). *The New Composition and Rhetoric*. Boston: Allyn and Bacon.

Whately, R. (1882). *Elements of Rhetoric*. London: Longmans, Green and Co.

■ 3

THE NEW PROFESSION

A master's degree in public speaking. (1916). *Quarterly Journal of Public Speaking*, 2, 95.

The Eastern Public Speaking Conference. (1916). *Quarterly Journal of Public Speaking*, 2, 301-303.

The first meeting of the national association. (1915). *Quarterly Journal of Public Speaking*, 1, 308-311.

Hunt, E.L. (1915). The scientific spirit in public speaking. *Quarterly Journal of Public Speaking*, 1, 185-193.

Hunt, E.L. (1916). General specialists. *Quarterly Journal of Public Speaking*, 2, 253-263.

Hunt, E.L. (1917). Academic public speaking. *Quarterly Journal of Public Speaking*, 3, 28-36.

Hunt, E.L. (1917a). An adventure in philosophy. *Quarterly Journal of Public Speaking*, 3, 297-303.

Improving the Quarterly. (1917). *Quarterly Journal of Public Speaking*, 3, 82-84.

Leff, M.C. and Procario, M.O. (1985). Rhetorical theory in speech communication. In T.W. Benson (Ed.). *Speech Communication in the 20th Century*. Carbondale, IL: Southern Illinois University Press.

Lyon, C.E. (1915). The English-public speaking situation. *Quarterly Journal of Public Speaking*, 1, 44-50.

Macleod, A.W. (Mrs.). (1916). Majors and credits in public speaking. *Quarterly Journal of Public Speaking*, 2, 149-152.

The National Speech League. (1917). *Quarterly Journal of Public Speaking*, 3, 84-85.

O'Neill, J.M. (1915). The national association. *Quarterly Journal of Public Speaking*, 1, 51-58.

O'Neill, J.M. (1916). The professional outlook. *Quarterly Journal of Public Speaking*, 2, 52-63.

O'Neill, J.M. (1928). After thirteen years. *Quarterly Journal of Speech*, 14, 242-253.

Phillips, A.E. (1908). *Effective Speaking*. Chicago: Newton.

The "Quarterly Journal" and research. (1915). *Quarterly Journal of Public Speaking*, 1, 84-85.

Research Committee. (1915). Research in public speaking. *Quarterly Journal of Public Speaking*, 1, 24-32.

Research Committee. (1915a). Making a start toward research work. *Quarterly Journal of Public Speaking*, 1, 194-196.

Reid, L. (1990). *Speech Teacher: A Random Narrative*. Annandale, VA: Speech Communication Association.

Smith, B. (1917). Public speaking in New England colleges. *Quarterly Journal of Public Speaking*, 3, 57-68.

The time and place for the annual convention. (1917). *Quarterly Journal of Public Speaking*, 3, 80-81.

Two important committees. (1915). *Quarterly Journal of Public Speaking*, 1, 74-75.

Wallace, K.R. (1954). *History of Speech Education in America*. New York: Appleton-Century-Crofts.

Wanted: An accurate title. (1916). *Quarterly Journal of Public Speaking*, 2, 294-295.

Weaver, A. (1959). Seventeen who made history. *Quarterly Journal of Speech*, 44, 195-199.

Wichlens, H. (1959). *A History of the Speech Association of the Eastern States*. Mineola, New York: Mineola Public Schools.

Winans, J.A. (1915). The need for research. *Quarterly Journal of Public Speaking*, 1, 17-23.

Winans, J.A. (1915a). Should we worry. *Quarterly Journal of Public Speaking*, 1, 197-201.

Winans, J.A. (1915b). *Public Speaking*. Ithaca: Sewell.

Winans, J.A. (1916). The second annual convention. *Quarterly Journal of Public Speaking*, 2, 293-294.

Winans, J.A. (1916a). The New York meeting. *Quarterly Journal of Public Speaking*, 2, 415-416.

Windt, T.O. (1990). *Rhetoric as a Human Adventure: A Short Biography of Everett Hunt*. Annandale, VA: Speech Communication Association.

Woolbert, C.H. (1916). The organization of departments of speech science in universities. *Quarterly Journal of Public Speaking, 2,* 64-67.

Woolbert, C.H. (1916a). A problem in pragmatism. *Quarterly Journal of Public Speaking,* 2, 264-274.

Woolbert, C.H. (1917). Suggestions as to methods in research. *Quarterly Journal of Public Speaking, 3,* 12-27.

Woolbert, C.H. (1917a). Conviction and persuasion: Some consequences of theory. *Quarterly Journal of Public Speaking, 3,* 249-264.

Woolbert, C.H. (1918). The place of logic in a system of persuasion. *Quarterly Journal of Public Speaking, 4,* 19-39.

Woolbert, C.H. (1920). *The Fundamentals of Speech.* New York: Harper and Brothers.

Yost, M. (1917). Argument from-the-point of view of sociology. *Quarterly Journal of Public Speaking, 3,* 109-124.

Yost, M. (1919). Training four minute men at Vassar. *Quarterly Journal of Speech Education, 5,* 246-253.

■ 4

THE PROFESSION DIVERSIFIES

Bauer, M.G. (1925). The influence of Lincoln's audience on his speeches. *Quarterly Journal of Speech Education, 11,* 225-229.

Brigance, W.N. (1953). *Speech Composition.* (2nd ed.). New York: Appleton-Century-Crofts.

Campbell, G. (1855). *The Philosophy of Rhetoric.* New York: Harper.

Dawson, C.A. (1916). Speech training in public high schools. *Quarterly Journal of Public Speaking, 2,* 1-8.

Dowd, M.H. (Mrs.). (1917). Oral English in the high school. *Quarterly Journal of Public Speaking, 3,* 1-12.

Doyle, J.H. (1916). The style of Wendell Phillips. *Quarterly Journal of Public Speaking, 2,* 331-339.

Duffy, W.R. (1917). The foundation course in public speaking at the University of Texas. *Quarterly Journal of Public Speaking, 3,* 163-171.

Flemming, E.G. (1918). A comparison of Cicero and Aristotle on style. *Quarterly Journal of Speech Education, 4,* 61-71.

Forncrook, E.M. (1918). A fundamental course in speech training. *Quarterly Journal of Speech Education, 4,* 271-289.

Forum. (1915). *Quarterly Journal of Public Speaking, 1,* 319-322.

French, J.C. (1916). Classroom use of the occasional speech. *Quarterly Journal of Public Speaking, 2,* 167-170.

Gaylord, J.S. (1916). Beginnings of expression. *Quarterly Journal of Public Speaking, 2,* 186-192.

Gislason, H.B. (1917). Elements of objectivity in Wendell Phillips. *Quarterly Journal of Public Speaking, 3,* 125-134.

Hannah, R. (1925). Burke's audience. *Quarterly Journal of Speech Education, 11,* 145-150.

Herring, B.F. (1917). A special course in oral expression for high schools. *Quarterly Journal of Public Speaking, 3,* 140-152.

Hollister, R.D.T. (1917). The beginning course in oratory at the University of Michigan. *Quarterly Journal of Public Speaking*, 3, 172-173.

Houghton, H.G. (1918). A beginning course in public speaking for colleges and universities. *Quarterly Journal of Speech Education*, 4, 150-159.

Hudson, H.H. (1923). The field of rhetoric. *Quarterly Journal of Speech Education*, 9, 167-180.

Hudson, H.H. (1924). Rhetoric and poetry. *Quarterly Journal of Speech Education*, 10, 143-154.

Hunt, E.L. (1917). Academic public speaking. *Quarterly Journal of Public Speaking*, 3, 27-36.

Jacobson, J.Z. (1951). *Scott of Northwestern, the Life of a Pioneer in Psychology and Education*. Chicago: L. Mariano.

Kay, W.J. (1917). Course I in public speaking at Washington and Jefferson College. *Quarterly Journal of Public Speaking*, 3, 242-248.

Kleiser, G. (1906). *How to Speak in Public*. New York: Funk and Wagnalls.

Lardner, J.L. (1917). A question of method. *Quarterly Journal of Public Speaking*, 3, 48-56.

Lyman, R.L. (1915). The forum as an educative agency. *Quarterly Journal of Public Speaking*, 1, 1-8.

Lyman, R.L. (1915a). Oral English in the high school. *Quarterly Journal of Public Speaking*, 1, 241-259.

Lynch, E.C. (1968). *Walter Dill Scott, Pioneer in Personnel Management*. Austin: Bureau of Business Research, University of Texas.

MacMurray, A. (1910). *Practical Lessons in Public Speaking*. Ames, Iowa.

Matthews, B. (1901). *Notes on Speech Making*. New York: Longmans, Green.

Newcomb, C.M. (1917). The educational value of expression. *Quarterly Journal of Public Speaking*, 3, 69-79.

O'Neill, J.M. (1916). The professional outlook. *Quarterly Journal of Public Speaking*, 2, 52-63.

Phillips, A.E. (1908). *Effective Speaking*. Chicago: Newton.

Rousseau, L.G. (1916). The rhetorical principles of Cicero and Adams. *Quarterly Journal of Public Speaking*, 2, 397-409.

Ryan, J.P. (1917). The department of speech at Grinnell. *Quarterly Journal of Public Speaking*, 3, 203-209.

Scott, W.D. (1907). *The Psychology of Public Speaking*. Philadelphia: Hinds.

Shurter, E.D. (1903). *Public Speaking: A Treatise on Delivery*. Boston: Allyn and Bacon.

Shurter, E.D. (1911). *The Rhetoric of Oratory*. New York: Macmillian.

Smith, B. (1917). Public Speaking in New England colleges. *Quarterly Journal of Public Speaking*, 3, 57-68.

Swift, W.B. (1919). How to begin speech correction in the public schools. *Quarterly Journal of Speech Education*, 5, 239-245.

Trueblood, T.C. (1915). College courses in public speaking. *Quarterly Journal of Public Speaking*, 1, 260-265.

Ward, C.C. 1915). *Oral Composition*. New York: Macmillian.

Wells, H.N. (1918). Coaching debates. *Quarterly Journal of Speech Education*, 4, 170-183.

Wichelns, H.A. (1925). The literary criticism of oratory. In A.M. Drummond (Ed.), *Studies in Rhetoric and Public Speaking, in honor of James Albert Winans*. New York: Century.

Williams, C.B. (1917). Spoken English 1-1 at Smith College. *Quarterly Journal of Public Speaking*, 3, 229-234.

Winans, J.A. (1915). *Public Speaking*. New York: Century.

Winans, J.A. (1915a). The need for research. *Quarterly Journal of Public Speaking*, 1, 17-23.

Winans, J.A. (1917). Public Speaking I at Cornell University. *Quarterly Journal of Public Speaking*, 3, 153-162.

Winter, I.L. (1917). *Public Speaking: Principles and Practices*. New York Macmillian.

■ 5

MENTAL HYGIENE, PSYCHOLOGY AND PERSONALITY

Baxter, E.D. (1937). A child guidance clinic through speech. *Quarterly Journal of Speech*, 23, 627-636.

Bryngelson, B. (1928). Personality changes. *Quarterly Journal of Speech*, 14, 207-218.

Bryngelson, B. (1933). The re-education of speech failures. *Quarterly Journal of Speech*, 19, 227-232.

Bryngelson, B. (1934). Clinical aids in the fundamental course. *Quarterly Journal of Speech*, 20, 535-539.

Bryngelson, B. (1936). Speech hygiene. *Quarterly Journal of Speech,* 22, 611-614.,

Bryngelson, B. (1943). Applying hygiene principles to speech problems. *Quarterly Journal of Speech*, 29, 351-354.

Cable, W.A. (1934). Speech education tomorrow. *Quarterly Journal of Speech*, 20, 383-402.

Dow, C.W. (1941). Intelligence and ability in public performance. *Quarterly Journal of Speech*, 27, 110-115.

Dow, C.W. (1941a). The personality traits of effective public speakers. *Quarterly Journal of Speech*, 27, 525-532.

Dressel, H.A. (1941). The platform interview as a device to secure dominance. *Quarterly Journal of Speech*, 27, 382-385.

Fay, P.J. and Middleton, W.C. (1942). Judgment of introversion from the transcribed voice. *Quarterly Journal of Speech*, 28, 226-228.

Fleischman, E.E. (1941). Speech and progressive education. *Quarterly Journal of Speech*, 27, 511-517.

Gilkinson, H. (1943). A questionnaire study of the causes of social fears among college speech students. *Speech Monographs*, 10, 74-83.

Gilkinson, H. and Knower, F.H. (1940). Individual differences among students of speech as revealed by psychological tests - I. *Quarterly Journal of Speech*, 25, 243-255.

Golden, A.L. (1940). Personality traits of drama school students. *Quarterly Journal of Speech*, 26, 564-575.

Gray, G.W. (1928). Gestalt, behavior, and speech. *Quarterly Journal of Speech*, 14, 334-359.

Hamilton, J.L. (1943). The psychodrama and its implications. *Quarterly Journal of Speech*, 29, 60-67.

Henrikson, E.H. (1940). The relation among knowing a person, liking a person, and judging him as a speaker. *Speech Monographs*, 7, 22-25.

Hunter, A.D. (1935). Personality studies in speech. *Speech Monographs*, 2, 50-53.

Knower, F.H. (1929). Psychological tests in public speaking. *Quarterly Journal of Speech*, 15, 216-222.

Knower, F.H. (1938). A study of speech adjustment and attitudes. *Speech Monographs*, 5, 130-203.

Mabie, E.C. (1933). Speech training and individual needs. *Quarterly Journal of Speech*, 19, 341-355.

MacGregor, V.C. (1934). Personal development in beginning speech training. *Quarterly Journal of Speech*, 20, 47-57.

Mayer, J.E. (1936). Personality development through debating. *Quarterly Journal of Speech*, 22, 607-611.

Moore, G.E. (1935). Personality changes resulting from training in speech fundamentals. *Speech Monographs*, 2, 56-59.

Morse, W.L. (1928). The mental-hygiene approach in a beginning speech course. *Quarterly Journal of Speech*, 14, 543-553.

Moses, P. (1941). Social adjustment and the voice. *Quarterly Journal of Speech*, 27, 532-537.

Murray, E. (1934). Speech training as a mental hygience method. *Quarterly Journal of Speech*, 20, 37-47.

Murray, E. (1934a). New books. *Quarterly Journal of Speech*, 20, 133-135.

Murray, E. (1935). Mental adjustment for the release of creative power in speech situations. *Quarterly Journal of Speech*, 21, 497-506.

Murray, E. (1937). *The Speech Personality*. Philadephia: J.B. Lippincott.

Murray, E. (1940). Speech standards and social integration. *Quarterly Journal of Speech*, 26, 73-80.

Murray, E. (Ed.). (1944). Studies in personal and social integration. *Speech Monographs*, 7, 9-27.

Nylen, D. (1938). Guidance and speech in the school program. *Quarterly Journal of Speech*, 24, 603-609.

Parrish, W.M. (1928). Implications of Gestalt psychology. *Quarterly Journal of Speech*, 14, 8-29.

Rahskopf, H.G. (1937). Principles of the speech curriculum. *Quarterly Journal of Speech*, 23, 452-456.

Rose, F.H. (1940). Training in speech and changes in personality. *Quarterly Journal of Speech*, 26, 193-196.

Rowell, E.Z. (1930). Public speaking in a new era. *Quarterly Journal of Speech*, 16, 62-69.

Tracy, J.A. (1935). A study of personality traits of mature actors and mature public speakers. *Speech Monographs*, 2, 53-56.

Utterback, W.E. (1937). An appraisal of psychological research in speech. *Quarterly Journal of Speech*, 23, 175-182.

West, R. (1936). Speech training as a preventive of neurosis. *Quarterly Journal of Speech*, 22, 614-617.

White, M.R. (1939). Psychological and physiological types in high school plays. *Quarterly Journal of Speech*, 25, 657-665.

■ 6

ETHICS, FREEDOM AND DEMOCRACY

Bagwell, P.D. (1945). A composite course in writing and speaking. *Quarterly Journal of Speech*, 31, 79-87.

Baird, A.C. (1938). The educational philosophy of the teacher of speech. *Quarterly Journal of Speech*, 24, 545-553.

Balduf, E.W. (1943). How departments of speech can cooperate with government in the war effort. *Quarterly Journal of Speech*, 29, 271-276.

Bartlett, K.G. (1943). Radio war programs. *Quarterly Journal of Speech*, 29, 101-103.

Bennett, W.D. (1938). College commencement addresses of 1937 and 1938. *Quarterly Journal of Speech*, 24, 538-541.

Brigance, W.N. (1942). The contribution of speech to national defense. *Quarterly Journal of Speech*, 28, 240-242.

Bryant, D.C. (1938). Speech for teachers. *Quarterly Journal of Speech*, 24, 244-247.

Butler, H. (Mrs.). (1944). Wanted: a speech salesman for the United States government. *Quarterly Journal of Speech*, 30, 269-272.

Cable, W.A. (1935). Speech, a basic training in the educational system. *Quarterly Journal of Speech*, 21, 510-524.

Carhart, R. (1943). War responsibilities of the speech correctionist. *Quarterly Journal of Speech*, 29, 137-140.

Cohen, H. (1976). 1975 presidential address. *Spectra*, 12, 34-,6,7.

Conner, W.R. (1921). Speech education for secondary schools. *Quarterly Journal of Speech Education*, 7, 109-115.

Davis, W.H. (1923). What is debating for? *Quarterly Journal of Speech Education*, 9, 195.

DeBoer, J.J. (1945). English in a "communications" program. *Quarterly Journal of Speech*, 31, 291-295.

Dolman, J., Jr., (1938). A reply to Mr. Burgess Meredith (president of the Actors' Equity Association). *Quarterly Journal of Speech*, 24, 324-328.

Grey, L. (1944). Toward better communication in 1944 and after. *Quarterly Journal of Speech*, 30, 131-136.

Hance, K.G. (1944). Public address in a democracy at war. *Quarterly Journal of Speech*, 30, 158-164.

Hansen, J.D. (1942). Speech in a nation at war. *Quarterly Journal of Speech*, 28, 271-274.

Held, M.W. and Held, C.C. (1943). Public speaking in the army training program. *Quarterly Journal of Speech*, 29, 143-146.

Holm, J.N. (1943). A war-time approach to public speaking. *Quarterly Journal of Speech*, 29, 101-13.

Hunt, E.L. (1922). Adding substance to form in public speaking. *Quarterly Journal of Speech Education*, 8, 256-265.

Hunt, E.L. (1923). Knowledge and skill. *Quarterly Journal of Speech Education*, 9, 67-76.

Hunt, E.L. (1930). "Pipe" courses. *Quarterly Journal of Speech*, 16, 353-354.

Hunt, E.L. (1943). The rhetorical mood of World War II. *Quarterly Journal of Speech*, 29, 1-5.

Huntsman, S. (1924). Public speaking as a means in education. *Quarterly Journal of Speech Education*, 10, 7-16.

Johnson, W. (1943). The status of speech defectives in the military service. *Quarterly Journal of Speech*, 29, 131-136.

Keiser, A. (1925). Intellectual parasites. *Quarterly Journal of Speech Education*, 11, 62-64.

Knower, F.H. (1943). Speech curricula and activities in wartime. *Quarterly Journal of Speech*, 29, 146-151.

Konigsberg, E., Douris, E.A., Edgecomb, C.F., Hoffmann, P.M., and Leahy, M.G. (1943). Teaching public discussion during the war. *Quarterly Journal of Speech*, 29, 13-18.

Lambertson, F.W. (1942). Hitler, the orator. *Quarterly Journal of Speech*, 28, 123-131.

Mallory, L.A. (1943). Speech training of army and navy officers. *Quarterly Journal of Speech*, 29, 140-143.

Monroe, A.H. (1941). Speech in the world today. *Quarterly Journal of Speech*, 27, 171-173.

Norvelle, L. (1942). The theatre in time of war. *Quarterly Journal of Speech*, 28, 267-271.

O'Neill, J.M. (1923). Speech content and course content in public speaking. *Quarterly Journal of Speech Education*, 9, 26-52.

O'Neill, J.M. (1941). Professional maturity. *Quarterly Journal of Speech*, 27, 173-182.

Pellegrini, A. (1934). Public speaking and social obligations. *Quarterly Journal of Speech*, 20, 345-351.

Pellegrini, A. (1986). *An Immigrant's Quest: American Dream*. San Francisco: North Point Press.

Robinson, K.F. and Keltner, J. (1946). Suggested units of discussion and debate for secondary schools. *Quarterly Journal of Speech*, 32, 385-390.

Roosevelt, F.D. (Mrs.). (1941). Speech training for the youth. *Quarterly Journal of Speech*, 27, 369-371.

Ryan, J.P. (1918). Terminology: The department of speech. *Quarterly Journal of Speech Education*, 4, 1-11.

Schrier, W. (1930). The ethics in persuasion. *Quarterly Journal of Speech*, 16, 476-486.

Shaw, W.C. (1922). The crime against public speaking. *Quarterly Journal of Speech Education*, 8, 138-144.

Smith, W.P. (1921). Americanization through speech in our high schools. *Quarterly Journal of Speech Education*, 7, 370-374.

Thomas, E.D. (1941). National defense. *Quarterly Journal of Speech*, 27, 292-294.

Utterback, W.E. (1940). The appeal to force in public discussion. *Quarterly Journal of Speech*, 26, 1-6.

Weaver, A.T. (1945). The challenge of the crisis. *Quarterly Journal of Speech*, 31, 128-134.

West, R. (1944). The prospect for speech education. *Quarterly Journal of Speech*, 30, 143-146.

Westfall, A. (1943). What speech teachers may do to help win the war. *Quarterly Journal of Speech*, 29, 5-9.

Wilchelns, H.A. (1935). Speech and the educational scene: Notes on the future. *Quarterly Journal of Speech*, 21, 557-560.

Wiley, E.B. (1943). The rhetoric of the American democracy. *Quarterly Journal of Speech*, 29, 157-163.

Williamson, A.B. (1939). Social standards in public speaking instruction. *Quarterly Journal of Speech*, 25, 371-377. Woolbert, C.H. (1923). The coach versus the professor. *Quarterly Journal of Speech Education*, 9, 284-285.

Yeager, W.H. (1942). Our contribution to the war. *Quarterly Journal of Speech*, 28, I.

■ 7

RHETORICAL CRITICISM

Aly, B. (1936). The scientist's debt to rhetoric. *Quarterly Journal of Speech*, 22, 584-590.

Aly, B. (1939). The history of American public address as a research field. *Quarterly Journal of Speech*, 29, 308-314.

Anderson, J. (1939). Man of the hour or man of the ages? The most honorable Stephen A. Douglas. *Quarterly Journal of Speech*, 25, 75-93.

Baird, A.C. (1943). Opportunities for research in state and sectional public speaking. *Quarterly Journal of Speech*, 29, 304-308.

Bauer, M.G. (1925). The influence of Lincoln's audience on his speeches. *Quarterly Journal of Speech Education*, 11, 225-229.

Bauer, M.G. (1927). Persuasive methods in the Lincoln-Douglas debates. *Quarterly Journal of Speech Education*, 13, 29-39.

Bohman, G.V. (1937). Political oratory in pre-revolutionary America. *Quarterly Journal of Speech*, 23, 243-251.

Booth, W. (1961). *The Rhetoric of Fiction*. Chicago: Univ of Chicago Press.

Brigance, W.N. (1933). Whither research? *Quarterly Journal of Speech*, 19, 552-561.

Brigance, W.N. (1938). The twenty eight foremost American orators. *Quarterly Journal of Speech*, 24, 376-380.

Brigance, W.N. (Ed.). (1943-1955). *A History and Criticism of American Public Address*. New York: McGraw-Hill.

Bryant, D.C. (1934). Edmund Burke's opinions of some orators of his day. *Quarterly Journal of Speech*, 20, 241-254.

Bryant, D.C. (1937). Some problems of scope and method in rhetorical scholarship. *Quarterly Journal of Speech*, 23, 182-189.

Buswell, L. E. (1935). Oratory of the Dakota Indians. *Quarterly Journal of Speech*, 21, 323-327.

Cooper, L. (1932). *The rhetoric of Aristotle, and Expanded Translation with Supplementary Examples for Students of Composition and Public Speaking*. New York: Appleton and Co.

Dale, E.E. (1941). The speech of the frontier. *Quarterly Journal of Speech*, 27, 353-363.

Dickey, D.C. (1943). What directions should future research in American public address take? *Quarterly Journal of Speech*, 29, 300-304.

Fitzpatrick, J.R. (1941). Congressional debating. *Quarterly Journal of Speech*, 27, 251-255.

Gisalson, H.B. (1917). Elements of objectivity in Wendell Phillips. *Quarterly Journal of Public Speaking*, 3, 125-134.

Graham, G.M. (1927). Concerning the speech power of Woodrow Wilson. *Quarterly Journal of Speech*, 13, 412-424.

Graham, G.M. (1930). The House of Lords debates the naval treaty. *Quarterly Journal of Speech*, 16, 414-420.

Hannah, R. (1925). Burke's audience. *Quarterly Journal of Speech Education*, 11, 145-150.

Hayworth, D. (1936). Samuel Gompers, orator. *Quarterly Journal of Speech*, 22, 578-584.

Hellman, H.E. (1938). The greatest American oratory. *Quarterly Journal of Speech*, 24, 36-39.

Hochmuth, M. (1941). Phillip Brooks. *Quarterly Journal of Speech*, 27, 227-236.

Hunt, E.L. (1935). Rhetoric and literary criticism. *Quarterly Journal of Speech*, 21, 564-568.

King, R.D. (1937). Franklin D. Roosevelt's second inaugural. *Quarterly Journal of Speech*, 23, 439-444.

Lindsley, C.F. (1919). George William Curtis. *Quarterly Journal of Speech Education*, 5, 79-100.

McKean, D.D. (1930). Notes on Woodrow Wilson's speeches. *Quarterly Journal of Speech*, 16, 176-184.

McKean, D.D. (1930a). Woodrow Wilson as a debate coach. *Quarterly Journal of Speech*, 16, 458-463.

Oliver, R.T. (1936). Studies in the political and social views of the slave-struggle orators. *Quarterly Journal of Speech*, 22, 413-429.

Oliver, R.T. (1937). Studies in the political and social views of the slave struggle orators: II. Webster. *Quarterly Journal of Speech*, 23, 13-32.

Oliver, R.T. (1937a). Behind the word: III. Clay. *Quarterly Journal of Speech*, 23, 409-426.

Paget, E. (1929). Woodrow Wilson: International rhetorician. *Quarterly Journal of Speech*, 15, 15-24.

Parrington, V.L. (1930). *Main Currents in American Thought*. New York: Harcourt, Brace and Co.

Powell, D. (1927). Bryon's oratory. *Quarterly Journal of Speech*, 13, 424-432.

Reid, L.D. (1938). Did Charles Fox prepare his speeches? *Quarterly Journal of Speech*, 24, 17-26.

Reid, L.D. (1944). The perils of rhetorical criticism. *Quarterly Journal of Speech*, 30, 416-422.

Scanlan, R. (1936). Rhetoric and the drama. *Quarterly Journal of Speech*, 22, 635-642.

Simrell, V.E. (1927). H.L. Mencken the rhetorician. *Quarterly Journal of Speech*, 13, 399-412.

Wichelns, H.A. (1925). The literary criticism of oratory. In A.M. Drummond (Ed.). *Studies in Rhetoric and Public Speaking in Honor of James Albert Winans*. New York: Century Co.

Wiley, E.W. (1932). A footnote on the Lincoln-Douglas debates. *Quarterly Journal of Speech*, 18, 216-224.

Wiley, E.W. (1934). Lincoln the speaker. *Quarterly Journal of Speech*, 20, 1-15.

Wiley, E.W. (1935). Lincoln the speaker. *Quarterly Journal of Speech*, 21, 305-322.

Wiley, E.W. (1938). Motivation as a factor in Lincoln's Rhetoric. *Quarterly Journal of Speech*, 24, 615-621.

Yoakam, D.G. (1937). Pioneer women orators of America. *Quarterly Journal of Speech*, 23, 251-259.

■ 8

RHETORICAL THEORY

Abernathy, E. (1943). *Trends in American homiletic theory since 1860*. Speech Monographs, 10, 68-74.

Baldwin, C.S. (1924). *Ancient Rhetoric and Poetic*. New York: Macmillian.

Baldwin, C.S. (1928). *Medieval Rhetoric and Poetic*. New York: Macmillian.

Barton, F.J. (1941). The signification of 'extempore speech' in English and American rhetorics. *Quarterly Journal of Speech*, 27, 237-251.

Behl, W.A. (1945). Theodore Roosevelt's principles of speech preparation and delivery. *Speech Monographs*, 12, 112-122.

Blair, H. (1860). *Lectures on Rhetoric and Belle Lettres*. Philadelphia: T. Ellwood Zell, Publisher.

Brigance, W.N. (1933). The Huntington library. *Quarterly Journal of Speech*, 19, 84-85.

Brigance, W.N. (1933a). Whither research? *Quarterly Journal of Speech*, 19, 552-561.

Brigance, W.N. (1935). Can we redefine the James-Winans theory of persuasion? *Quarterly Journal of Speech*, 21, 19-26.

Bryant, D.C. (1933). Edmund Burke on oratory. *Quarterly Journal of Speech*, 19, 1-18.

Campbell, G. (1855). *The Philosophy of Rhetoric*. New York: Harper and Brothers.

Caplan, H.A. (1925). A late medieval tractate on preaching. In A.M. Drummond (Ed.),

Studies in Rhetoric and Public Speaking in Honor of James Albert Winans. New York: Century Co.

Caplan, H.A. (1925a). New books. *Quarterly Journal of Speech Education*, 11, 299-301.

Cohen, H. (1985). The development of research in speech communication: A historical perspective. In T.W. Benson (Ed.). *Speech Communication in the 20th Century*. Carbondale, IL: Southern Illinois Univ Press.

Committee on Research. (1926). Research papers in process or lately finished. *Quarterly Journal of Speech Education*, 12, 234-236.

Convention report. (1934). *Quarterly Journal of Speech*, 20, 153-162.

Cooper, L. (1935). The rhetoric of Aristotle. *Quarterly Journal of Speech*, 21, 10-19.

Cooperation. (1923). *Quarterly Journal of Speech Education*, 9, 373-375.

Crocker, L. (1936). The rhetorical theory of Harry Emerson Fosdick. *Quarterly Journal of Speech*, 22, 207-213.

Dewey, J. (1920). *Reconstruction in Philosophy*. New York: H. Holt and Co.

Dolman, J., Jr. (1921). Minutes - Eastern Public Speaking Conference. *Quarterly Journal of Speech Education*, 7, 276-279.

Drummond, A.M. (1921). A list of topics for consideration and discussion. *Quarterly Journal of Speech Education*, 7, 389-393.

Drummond, A.M. (1923). Graduate work in public speaking. *Quarterly Journal of Speech Education*, 9, 136-146.

Drummond, A.M. (1923a). Some subjects from graduate study-department of public speaking, Cornell University. *Quarterly Journal of Speech Education*, 9, 147-153.

Drummond, A.M. (1925). Preface. *Studies in Rhetoric and Public Speaking in Honor of James Albert Winans*. A.M. Drummond, (Ed.). New York: Century Co.

Eastern public speaking contest. (1933). *Quarterly Journal of Speech*, 19, 457-460.

Ehrensberger, R. (1945). An experimental study of the relative effectiveness of certain forms of emphasis in public speaking. *Speech Monographs*, 12, 94-111.

Emporer, J.B. (1935). New books. *Quarterly Journal of Speech*, 21, 591-610.

Fritz, C.A. (1927). Early American works on speech training. *Quarterly Journal of Speech Education*, 13, 151-160.

Graduate study and research. (1929). *Quarterly Journal of Speech*, 15, 135-144.

Graduate study and research. (1930). *Quarterly Journal of Speech*, 16, 384-387.

Gray, G.W. (1923). How much are we dependent upon the ancient Greeks and Romans? *Quarterly Journal of Speech Education*, 9, 258-279.

Hance, K.G. (1938). The elements of the rhetorical theory of Phillips Brooks. *Speech Monographs*, 5, 16-39.

Harding, H.F. Quintillan's witnesses. *Speech Monographs*, 1, 1-20.

Harwood, J.T. (1986). *The Rhetorics of Thomas Hobbes and Bernard Lamy*. Carbondale, IL: Southern Illinois Univ Press.

Hitchcock, O.A. (1943). Jonathan Edwards. In W.N. Brigance (ed.), *A History and Criticism of American Public Address*. v.I. New York: McGraw-Hill.

Holding fast that which is good. (1923). *Quarterly Journal of Speech*, 9, 372-373.

Howell, W.S. (1934). Nathaniel Carpenter's place in the controversy between dialectic and rhetoric. *Speech Monographs*, 1, 20-41.

Howell, W.S. (1935). Rhetoric and public speaking. *Quarterly Journal of Speech*, 21, 575-576.

Howes, R.F. (1926). Coleridge and rhetoric. *Quarterly Journal of Speech Education*, 12, 145-156.

Howes, R.F. (1929). In defense of rhetoric. *Quarterly Journal of Speech*, 15, 80-85.

Hudson, H.H. (1921). Can we modernize the study of invention? *Quarterly Journal of Speech Education*, 7, 325-334.

Hudson, H.H. (1925). De Quincey on rhetoric and public speaking. In A.M. Drummond (Ed.), *Studies in Rhetoric and Public Speaking in Honor of James Albert Winans*. New York: Century Co.

Hudson, H.H. (1928). Jewel's oration against rhetoric: A translation. *Quarterly Journal of Speech*, 14, 374-392.

Hudson, H.H. (1929). The forum. *Quarterly Journal of Speech*, 15, 256.

Hudson, H.H. (1931). The tradition of our subject. *Quarterly Journal of Speech*, 17, 320-329.

Hultzen, L.S. (1939). Charles Butler on memory. *Speech Monographs*, 6, 44-65.

Hunt, E.L. (1920). Plato on rhetoric and rhetoricians. *Quarterly Journal of Speech Education*, 6 (3), 35-56.

Hunt, E.L. (1921). New books. *Quarterly Journal of Speech Education*, 7, 181-185.

Hunt, E.L. (1923). Rhetoric and oratory in classical historiography. *Quarterly Journal of Speech Education*, 9, 383-389.

Hunt, E.L. (1924). New books. *Quarterly Journal of Speech Education*, 10, 400-401.

Hunt, E.L. (1925). Plato and Aristotle on rhetoric and rhetoricians. In A.M. Drummond (Ed.), *Studies in Rhetoric and Public Address in Honor of James Albert Winans*. New York: Century Co.

Hunt, E.L. (1925a). New books. *Quarterly Journal of Speech Education*, 11, 400-402.

Hunt, E.L. (1926). An introducation to classical rhetoric. *Quarterly Journal of Speech Education*, 12, 201-204.

Hunt, E.L. (1928). From rhetoric deliver us. *Quarterly Journal of Speech*, 14, 261-268.

Irwin, R.L. (1939). The classical speech divisions. *Quarterly Journal of Speech*, 15, 212-213.

Lamers, W.M. (1934). New books. *Quarterly Journal of Speech*, 20, 573-574.

Lee, I. J. (1939). Some conceptions of emotional appeal in rhetorical theory. *Speech Monographs*, 6, 66-86.

Mabie, E.C. (1923). 'Speech' from another angle. *Quarterly Journal of Speech Education*, 9, 330-333.

The matter of emphasis. (1924). *Quarterly Journal of Speech Education*, 10, 270.

McBurney, J.H. (1936). The place of the enthymeme in rhetorical theory. *Speech Monographs*, 3, 49-74.

McBurney, J.H. (1937). Some contributions of classical dialectic and rhetoric to a philosophy of discussion. *Quarterly Journal of Speech*, 23, 1-13.

McGrew, J.F. (1929). A biliography of the works on rhetoric and related subjects in England during the 16th and 17th centuries. *Quarterly Journal of Speech*, 15, 380-412.

Merry, G.N. (1921). Research in speech education. *Quarterly Journal of Speech Education*, 7, 97-108.

Methods of conducting graduate seminars. (1925). *Quarterly Journal of Speech Education*, 11, 277-280.

Mills, G.E. (1942). Daniel Webster's principles of rhetoric. *Speech Monographs*, 9, 124-140.

Minutes of the seventh annual convention of the National Association of Teachers of Speech. (1923). *Quarterly Journal of Speech Education*, 9, 96-102.

News and notes. (1929). *Quarterly Journal of Speech*, 15, 462-464. News and notes. (1935). *Quarterly Journal of Speech*, 21, 629-639.

Paget, E. (1929). Woodrow Wilson: International rhetorician. *Quarterly Journal of Speech*, 15, 15-24.

Parrish, W.M. (1929). Whately and his rhetoric. *Quarterly Journal of Speech*, 15, 58-79.

The research committee. (1921). *Quarterly Journal of Education*, 7, 78-89.

Rice, G.P., Jr. (1943). Early Stuart rhetorical education. *Quarterly Journal of Speech*, 29, 433-437.

Riley, F.K. (1936). St Augustine, public speaker and rhetorician. *Quarterly Journal of Speech*, 22, 572-578.

Ryan, J.P. (1928). Syllabus of the report of the committee on terminology. *Quarterly Journal of Speech*, 14, 142-146.

Ryan, J.P. (1929). Quintilian's message. *Quarterly Journal of Speech*, 15, 171-180.

Sanford, W.P. (1929). English rhetoric reverts to classicism. *Quarterly Journal of Speech*, 15, 503-525.

Shorey, P. (1922). What teachers of speech may learn from the theory and practice of the Greeks. *Quarterly Journal of Speech Education*, 8, 105-131.

Simrell, V.E. (1928). Mere rhetoric. *Quarterly Journal of Speech*, 14, 359-374.

Simrell, V.E. (1928a). Contemporary speeches. *Quarterly Journal of Speech*, 14, 459-461.

Smith, B. (1918). The father of debate: Protagoras of Abdera. *Quarterly Journal of Speech Education* , 4, 196-215.

Smith, B. (1920). Prodicus of Ceos: The sire of synonomy. *Quarterly Journal of Speech Education*, 6 (2), 51-68.

Smith, B. (1921). Corax and probability. *Quarterly Journal of Speech Education*, 6, 13-42.

Smith, B. (1921a). Gorgias: A study of oratorical style. *Quarterly Journal of Speech Education*, 6, 335-359.

Smith, B. (1926). Hippias and a lost canon of rhetoric. *Quarterly Journal of Speech Education*, 12, 129-145.

Smith, B. (1927). Thrasymachus: A pioneer rhetorician. *Quarterly Journal of Speech Education*, 13, 278-291.

Smith, B. (1928). Theodorus of Byzantium: Word-smith. *Quarterly Journal of Speech*, 14, 71-81.

Thonssen, L.W. (1930). A functional interpretation of Aristotle's rhetoric. *Quarterly Journal of Speech*, 16, 297-310.

Thonssen, L.W. (1932). Thomas Hobbes' philosophy of speech. *Quarterly Journal of Speech*, 18, 200-206.

Utterback, W.E. (1924). Psychological approach to the rhetoric of speech communication. *Quarterly Journal of Speech Education*, 10, 17-23.

Wagner, R.H. (1922). The rhetorical theory of Isocrates. *Quarterly Journal of Speech Education*, 8, 322-337.

Wagner, R.H. (1925). A rhetorician's son: His advice to public speakers. *Quarterly Journal of Speech Education*, 11, 207-218.

Wagner, R.H. (1925a). New books. *Quarterly Journal of Speech Education*, 11, 301-305.

Wagner, R.H. (1929). Wilson and his sources. *Quarterly Journal of Speech*, 15, 525-537.

Wagner, R.H. (1929a). Old books. *Quarterly Journal of Speech*, 15, 592-594.

Wallace, K. (1936). Rhetorical exercises in Tudor education. *Quarterly Journal of Speech*, 22, 28-51.

Wallace, K. (1936a). Bacon's conception of rhetoric. *Speech Monographs*, 3, 21-48.

Wallace, K. (1943). *Francis Bacon on Communication and Rhetoric*. Chapel Hill: Univ of North Carolina Press.

Wallace, K. (1945). New men at work. *Quarterly Journal of Speech*, 31, 93.

Wallace, K. (1954). *A History of Speech Education in America*. New York: Appleton-Century-Crofts.

Wallace, K. (1967). *Francis Bacon on the nature of man*. Urbana, IL: Univ of Illinois Press.

Winans, J.A. (1915). *Public Speaking*. Ithaca: Sewell Publishing Co.

Winans, J.A. (1923). Speech. *Quarterly Journal of Speech Education*, 9, 223-231.

Winans, J.A. (1945). Whately on elocution. *Quarterly Journal of Speech*, 31, 1-8.

Wichelns, H.A. (1923). Research papers in process or lately finished-compiled by the Committee on Research. *Quarterly Journal of Speech Education*, 9, 363-370.

Wichelns, H.A. (1924). Research papers in process or lately finished. *Quarterly Journal of Speech Education*, 10, 297-298.

■ 9

GROUP DISCUSSION

Allison, R. (1939). Changing concepts in the meaning and values of group discussion. *Quarterly Journal of Speech*, 25, 117-120.

Auer, J.J. (1939). Tools of social inquiry: Argumentation, discussion and debate. *Quarterly Journal of Speech*, 25, 533-539.

Baird, A.C. (1928). *Public Discussion and Debate*. Boston: Ginn.

Baird, A.C. (1937). *Public Discussion and Debate*. (rev. ed.). Boston: Ginn.

Dewey, J. (1910). *How We Think*. New York: D.C. Heath and Co.

Ehninger, D. (1943). A logic of discussion method. *Quarterly Journal of Speech*, 29, 163-167.

Ewbank, H.L. and Auer, J.J. (1941). *Discussion and Debate: Tools of a Democracy*. New York: F.S. Crofts and Co.

Gulley, H. (1942). Debate versus discussion. *Quarterly Journal of Speech*. 28, 305-307.

Johnson, A. (1939). Teaching the fundamentals of speech through group discussion. *Quarterly Journal of Speech*, 25, 440-447.

Johnson, A. (1943). An experimental study in the analysis and measurement of reflective thinking. *Speech Monographs*, 10, 83-96.

Kelly, H. (1924). The Object: Method of Conference. In A.D. Sheffield. *Quarterly Journal of Speech Education*, 10, 325-331.

McBurney, J.H. (1937). Some contributions of classical dialectic and rhetoric to a philosophy of discussion. *Quarterly Journal of Speech*, 18, 1-13.

McBurney, J.H. and Hance, K.G. (1939). *The Principles and Methods of Discussion*. New York: Harper and Brothers.

O'Brien, J.F. (1939). A definition and classification of the forms of discussion. *Quarterly Journal of Speech*, 25, 236-243.

O'Brien, J.F. (1941). Discussion in difference resolving. *Quarterly Journal of Speech*, 27, 422-429.

Prentiss, H. (1932). A message from the president. *Quarterly Journal of Speech*, 18, 515-517.

Rignano, E. (1927). *The Psychology of Reasoning* (W.A. Holt, Trans.). New York: Harcourt, Brace and Co.

Robinson, K.F. (1941). An experimental study of the effects of group discussion upon the social attitudes of college students. *Speech Monographs*, 8, 34-57.

Ross, H.T., Garland, J.V., and Sattler, J.W. (1940). Report of the committee on nomenclature in the field of discussion. *Quarterly Journal of Speech*, 26, 311-316.

Sattler, W.M. (1943). Socratic dialectic and modern group discussion. *Quarterly Journal of Speech*, 29, 152-157.

Sattler, W.M. and Miller, N.E. (1954). *Discussion and Conference.* New York: Prentice-Hall.

Sheffield, A.D. (1922). *Joining in Public Discussion.* New York: George H. Doran, Co.

Sheffield, A.D. (1924). Training speakers for conference. *Quarterly Journal of Speech Education*, 10, 325-331.

Sheffield, A.D. (1932). Discussion, lecture-forum and debate. *Quarterly Journal of Speech*, 18, 517-531.

Sheffield, A.D. (1933). (3rd ed.). *Creative Discussion: A Statement of Method for Leaders: Members of Discussion Groups and Conferences.* New York: The Inquiry, Association Press.

Simpson, R.H. (1939). The effect of discussion on intra-group divergences of judgment. *Quarterly Journal of Speech*, 25, 546-552.

Thompson, W.N. (1944). Discussion and debate: a re-examination. *Quarterly Journal of Speech*, 30, 288-299.

Thonssen, L. (1939). The social values of discussion and debate. *Quarterly Journal of Speech*, 25, 113-117.

Timmons, W.M. (1941). Discussion, debating, and research. *Quarterly Journal of Speech*, 27, 415-421. Timmons, W.M. (1941a). Sex differences in discussion. *Speech Monographs*, 8, 68-75.

Utterback, W.E. (1938). Patterns of public discussion in school and life. *Quarterly Journal of Speech*, 24, 584-589.

Utterback, W.E. (1950). *Group Thinking and Conference Leadership.* New York: Holt, Rinehart and Winston.

EPILOGUE

Berlo, D. (1960). *The Process of Communication.* New York: Holt, Rinehart and Winston.

Black, E. (1965). *Rhetorical Criticism.* New York: Macmillian.

Cohen, H. (1985). The development of research in speech communication: A historical perspective. In T.W. Benson (Ed.). *Speech Communication in the 20th Century.* Carbondale, IL: Southern Illinois University Press.

Thonnsen, L. and Baird, A.C. (1948). *Speech Criticism.* New York: Rowland Press.

AUTHOR INDEX

SUBJECT INDEX